By
PANEL OF AUTHORS

EDITION : 2022

ISBN : 978-93-92563-14-0

PRICE : ₹ 269.00

PUBLISHED BY

OSWAL PUBLISHERS

Head Office : 1/12, Sahitya Kunj, M.G. Road, Agra - 282 002

Phone : (0562) 2527771-4

Whatsapp : +91 74550 77222

E-mail : info@oswalpublishers.in

Website : www.oswalpublishers.com

The cover of this book has been designed using resources from Freepik.com

PREFACE

Board exams are a crucial milestone for every student. For students to perform well in this exam, we have introduced CBSE Chapterwise Objective and Subjective book for the TERM II Examinations for class XII. We have designed this book, keeping in mind all the changing scenarios and exam patterns. The content of the book is strictly based on the latest circular (Acad- 51 and 53) issued by the board in July, 2021 for TERM II examinations. This book will help the learners achieve the learning objectives in an easy to grasp manner.

This book contains matter compiled by highly proficient teachers and subject matter experts from across the country. Questions are segregated as per their respective chapters to facilitate easy navigation between them. Every attempt has been made to keep the language of the book crisp and accessible.

We hope you will find this book helpful in your preparations for Std. XII board examinations. We would advise you to stay calm and manage your time wisely. Don't be overwhelmed with the amount of resources and study guides available; be selective and efficient in your preparation.

—Publisher

Note : Questions marked with :
* are board exam questions from previous years.

CONTENTS

SYLLABUS

Mathematics
One Paper

90 minutes   **Max. Marks : 40**

S. No.	Units	Marks
III	Calculus	18
IV	Vectors and Three-Dimensional Geometry	14
VI	Probability	8
	Total	40
	Internal Assessment	10
Total		**50**

Unit-III: Calculus

1. Integrals

Integration as inverse process of differentiation. Integration of a variety of functions by substitution, by partial fractions and by parts, Evaluation of simple integrals of the following types and problems based on them.

$$\int \frac{dx}{x^2 \pm a^2}, \int \frac{dx}{\sqrt{x^2 \pm a^2}}, \int \frac{dx}{\sqrt{a^2 - a^2}}, \int \frac{dx}{ax^2 + bx + c}, \int \frac{dx}{\sqrt{ax^2 + bx + c}}$$

$$\int \frac{px + q}{ax^2 + bx + c}\,dx, \int \frac{px + q}{\sqrt{ax^2 + bx + c}}\,dx, \int \sqrt{a^2 \pm x^2}\,dx, \int \sqrt{a^2 - x^2}\,dx,$$

Fundamental Theorem of Calculus (without proof).Basic properties of definite integrals and evaluation of definite integrals.

2. Applications of the Integrals

Applications in finding the area under simple curves, especially lines, parabolas; area of circles /ellipses (in standard form only) (the region should be clearly identifiable).

3. Differential Equations

Definition, order and degree, general and particular solutions of a differential equation. Solution of differential equations by method of separation of variables, solutions of homogeneous differential equations of first order and first degree of the type: $\frac{dy}{dx} = f(y / x)$. Solutions of linear differential equation of the type: $\frac{dy}{dx} + py = q$, where p and q are functions of x or constant.

Unit-IV: Vectors and Three-Dimensional Geometry

1. Vectors

Vectors and scalars, magnitude and direction of a vector. Direction cosines and direction ratios of a vector. Types of vectors (equal, unit, zero, parallel and collinear vectors), position vector of a point, negative of a vector, components of a vector, addition of vectors, multiplication of a vector by a scalar, position vector of a point dividing a line segment in a given ratio. Definition, Geometrical Interpretation, properties and application of scalar (dot) product of vectors, vector (cross) product of vectors.

2. Three - dimensional Geometry

Direction cosines and direction ratios of a line joining two points. Cartesian equation and vector equation of a line, coplanar and skew lines, shortest distance between two lines. Cartesian and vector equation of a plane. Distance of a point from a plane.

Unit-VI: Probability

1. Probability

Conditional probability, multiplication theorem on probability, independent events, total probability, Bayes' theorem, Random variable and its probability distribution.

INTERNAL ASSESSMENT	10 MARKS
Periodic Test	5 Marks
Mathematics Activities: Activity file record +Term end assessment of one activity & Viva	5 Marks

Note: For activities NCERT Lab Manual may be referred

Integrals

Chapter 7

Basic Concepts

1. Integration is the inverse process of differentiation. If we are given the derivative of a function and asked to find the original function, such a process is called **Integration.**

2. Some important formulae of Integration :

(i) $\int [f(x) + g(x)]\, dx = \int f(x)\, dx + \int g(x)\, dx$

(ii) $\int Af(x)dx = A\int f(x)dx$, where A is any real number

(iii) $\int x^n\, dx = \dfrac{x^{n+1}}{n+1} + c$ is valid only for those algebraic expressions in which $n \neq -1$ and base is always linear

Where c is the constant of integration

(iv) $\int 1\, dx = x + c$

(v) $\int e^x dx = e^x + c$

(vi) $\int \dfrac{1}{x} dx = \log x + c$

(vii) $\int a^x dx = \dfrac{a^x}{\log a} + c$

(viii) $\int \cos x\, dx = \sin x + c$

(ix) $\int \sin x\, dx = -\cos x + c$

(x) $\int \tan x\, dx = \log |\sec x| + c$

$\qquad\qquad = -\log |\cos x| + c$

(xi) $\int \cot x\, dx = \log |\sin x| + c$

$\qquad\qquad = -\log |\csc x| + c$

(xii) $\int \sec x\, dx = \log |\sec x + \tan x| + c$

(xiii) $\int \csc x\, dx = \log |\csc x - \cot x| + c$

(xiv) $\int \sec x \tan x\, dx = \sec x + c$

(xv) $\int \csc x \cot x\, dx = -\csc x + c$

(xvi) $\int \sec^2 x\, dx = \tan x + c$

(xvii) $\int \csc^2 x\, dx = -\cot x + c$

(xviii) $\int \dfrac{1}{\sqrt{x^2 - a^2}}\, dx = \log |x + \sqrt{x^2 - a^2}| + c$

(xix) $\int \dfrac{1}{\sqrt{a^2 - x^2}}\, dx = \sin^{-1} \dfrac{x}{a} + c$

(xx) $\int \dfrac{1}{\sqrt{x^2 + a^2}}\, dx = \log |x + \sqrt{x^2 + a^2}| + c$

(xxi) $\int \dfrac{1}{x^2 + a^2}\, dx = \dfrac{1}{a} \tan^{-1} \dfrac{x}{a} + c$

(xxii) $\int \dfrac{1}{x\sqrt{x^2 - a^2}}\, dx = \dfrac{1}{a} \sec^{-1} \dfrac{x}{a} + c$

(xxiii) $\int \dfrac{1}{x^2 - a^2}\, dx = \dfrac{1}{2a} \log \left| \dfrac{x-a}{x+a} \right| + c$

(xxiv) $\int \dfrac{1}{a^2 - x^2}\, dx = \dfrac{1}{2a} \log \left| \dfrac{a+x}{a-x} \right| + c$

Note: While using formulae from (xviii) to (xxiv), coefficient of x^2 must be unity.

3. **Some important methods of integration :**

(i) Integration by decomposition :

(a) $\int (ax^2 + bx + c)\, dx$

$$= \int ax^2\, dx + \int bx\, dx + \int c\, dx$$

$$= a\int x^2\, dx + b\int x\, dx + c\int 1\, dx$$

$$= \dfrac{ax^3}{3} + \dfrac{bx^2}{2} + cx + d$$

(b) $\int \dfrac{1}{\sin^2 x \cos^2 x}\, dx$

$$= \int \dfrac{\sin^2 x + \cos^2 x}{\sin^2 x \cos^2 x}\, dx$$

$$= \int \dfrac{\sin^2 x}{\sin^2 x \cos^2 x}\, dx + \int \dfrac{\cos^2 x}{\sin^2 x \cos^2 x}\, dx$$

$$= \int \dfrac{1}{\cos^2 x}\, dx + \int \dfrac{1}{\sin^2 x}\, dx$$

$$= \int \sec^2 x \, dx + \int \cosec^2 x \, dx$$

$$= \tan x - \cot x + c$$

(ii) Integration by substitution : In this method we change the variable by substituting in place of the given variable.

Example:

$$\int \tan x \, dx = \int \frac{\sin x}{\cos x} \, dx$$

Put $\qquad \cos x = t$

Differentiating w.r.t. x

$$- \sin x = \frac{dt}{dx}$$

$$\sin x \, dx = - \, dt$$

$$\therefore \quad \int \tan x \, dx = -\int \frac{dt}{t}$$

$$= - \log |t| + c$$

$$= - \log |\cos x| + c$$

$$= - \log \left| \frac{1}{\sec x} \right| + c$$

$$= - \{\log 1 - \log \cdot | \sec x |\} + c$$

$$\int \tan x \, dx = \log |\sec x| + c$$

(iii) Integration by parts: This method is used when the given function is the product of two different functions as follows:

$$\int \underset{I}{f(x)} \cdot \underset{II}{g(x)} \, dx$$

$$= f(x) \left[\int g(x) \, dx \right] - \int \left[\frac{d}{dx} \{f(x)\} \cdot \int g(x) \, dx \right] dx$$

where I and II functions are taken according to

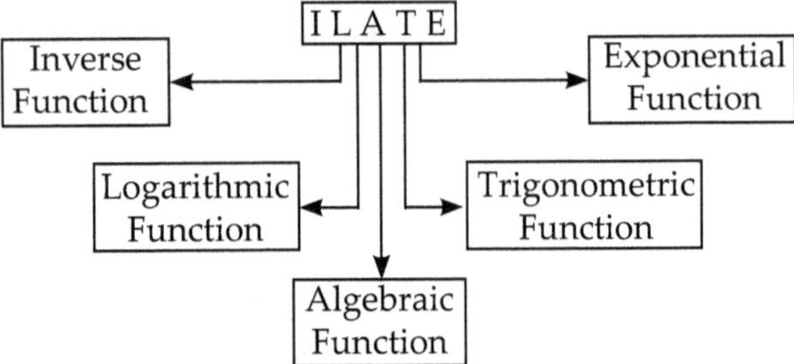

(iv) Integration by partial fraction : In this method the proper fraction can be expressed as the sum of partial functions. If the degree of numerator is greater than the degree of denominator then using long division method the given fraction can be expressed as proper fraction.

Example:

$$\frac{3x+1}{(x-2)^2 \, (x+2)} \, dx = \frac{A}{x-2} + \frac{B}{(x-2)^2} + \frac{C}{x+2}$$

then by equating the coefficients find the value of A, B and C.

(v) Some important properties of definite integral:

(a) $\int_a^b f(x) \, dx = - \int_b^a f(x) \, dx$ or $\int_a^b f(t) \, dt$

(b) $\int_a^a f(x) \, dx = 0$

(c) $\int_a^b f(x) \, dx$

$$= \int_a^c f(x) \, dx + \int_c^b f(x) \, dx \ \text{ for } a < c < b$$

(d) $\int_a^b f(x) \, dx = \int_a^b f(a+b-x) \, dx$

(e) $\int_0^{2a} f(x) \, dx$

$$= \int_0^a f(x) \, dx + \int_0^a f(2a-x) \, dx$$

(f) $\int_0^{2a} f(x) \, dx$

$$= \begin{cases} 2\int_0^a f(x) \, dx & \text{if } f(x) \text{ is even} \\ 0 & \text{if } f(x) \text{ is odd} \end{cases}$$

$$f(x) \text{ is even if } f(-x) = f(x)$$
$$\text{and} \quad f(x) \text{ is odd if } f(-x) = -f(x)$$

(g) $\int_{-a}^a f(x) \, dx$

$$= \begin{cases} 0 & \text{if } f(x) \text{ is an odd function} \\ 2\int_0^a f(x) \, dx & \text{if } f(x) \text{ is an even function} \end{cases}$$

4. Some important forms of integration:

(i) $\int \frac{f'(x)}{f(x)} \, dx = \log |f(x)| + c$

(ii) $\int [f(x)]^n \times f'(x) \, dx = \dfrac{[f(x)]^{n+1}}{n+1} + c$

(iii) $\int e^x [f(x) + f'(x)] \, dx = e^x \, f(x) + c$

(iv) $\int \sqrt{a^2 - x^2} \, dx = \dfrac{x}{2} \sqrt{a^2 - x^2} + \dfrac{a^2}{2} \sin^{-1} \dfrac{x}{a} + c$

(v) $\int \sqrt{x^2 + a^2} \, dx = \dfrac{x}{2} \sqrt{x^2 + a^2}$

$$+ \dfrac{a^2}{2} \log |x + \sqrt{x^2 + a^2}| + c$$

(vi) $\int \sqrt{x^2 - a^2} \, dx = \dfrac{x}{2} \sqrt{x^2 - a^2}$

$$- \dfrac{a^2}{2} \log |x + \sqrt{x^2 - a^2}| + c$$

Multiple Choice Questions

1. $\int \dfrac{\cos 2x - \cos 2\theta}{\cos x - \cos \theta} \, dx$ is equal to:

[NCERT Exemplar]

(a) $2(\sin x + x \cos \theta) + C$
(b) $2(\sin x - x \cos \theta) + C$
(c) $2(\sin x + 2x \cos \theta) + C$
(d) $2(\sin x - 2x \cos \theta) + C$

Sol. (a) $2(\sin x + x \cos \theta) + C$

Explanation :

Let $I = \int \dfrac{\cos 2x - \cos 2\theta}{\cos x - \cos \theta} \, dx$

$= \int \dfrac{(2\cos^2 x - 1) - (2\cos^2 \theta - 1)}{\cos x - \cos \theta} \, dx$

$= 2\int \dfrac{(\cos x - \cos \theta) \times (\cos x + \cos \theta)}{(\cos x - \cos \theta)} \, dx$

$= 2\int (\cos x + \cos \theta) \, dx$

$= 2(\sin x + x \cos \theta) + C.$

2. $\int \dfrac{dx}{\sin (x-a) \sin (x-b)}$ is equal to:

[NCERT Exemplar]

(a) $\sin (b-a) \log \left| \dfrac{\sin (x-b)}{\sin (x-a)} \right| + C$

(b) $\operatorname{cosec} (b-a) \log \left| \dfrac{\sin (x-a)}{\sin (x-b)} \right| + C$

(c) $\operatorname{cosec} (b-a) \log \left| \dfrac{\sin (x-b)}{\sin (x-a)} \right| + C$

(d) $\sin (b-a) \log \left| \dfrac{\sin (x-a)}{\sin (x-b)} \right| + C$

Sol. (c) $\operatorname{cosec} (b-a) \log \left| \dfrac{\sin (x-b)}{\sin (x-a)} \right| + C$

Explanation :

Let $I = \int \dfrac{dx}{\sin (x-a) \sin (x-b)}$

$= \dfrac{1}{\sin (b-a)} \int \dfrac{\sin (b-a)}{\sin (x-a) \sin (x-b)} \, dx$

$= \dfrac{1}{\sin (b-a)} \int \dfrac{\sin (x-a-x+b)}{\sin (x-a) \sin (x-b)} \, dx$

$= \dfrac{1}{\sin (b-a)} \int \dfrac{\sin \{(x-a)-(x-b)\}}{\sin (x-a) \sin(x-b)} \, dx$

$= \dfrac{1}{\sin (b-a)}$

$\times \int \dfrac{\sin (x-a) \cos (x-b) - \cos (x-a) \sin (x-b)}{\sin (x-a) \sin (x-b)} \, dx$

$= \dfrac{1}{\sin (b-a)} \int [\cot (x-b) - \cot (x-a)] \, dx$

$= \dfrac{1}{\sin (b-a)} [\log | \sin (x-b) |$

$\qquad\qquad\qquad - \log | \sin (x-a) |] + C$

$= \operatorname{cosec} (b-a) \log \left| \dfrac{\sin (x-b)}{\sin (x-a)} \right| + C.$

3. $\int \dfrac{x^3}{x+1} \, dx$ is equal to: **[NCERT Exemplar]**

(a) $x + \dfrac{x^2}{2} + \dfrac{x^3}{3} - \log |1 - x| + C$

(b) $x + \dfrac{x^2}{2} - \dfrac{x^3}{3} - \log |1 - x| + C$

(c) $x - \dfrac{x^2}{2} - \dfrac{x^3}{3} - \log |1 + x| + C$

(d) $x - \dfrac{x^2}{2} + \dfrac{x^3}{3} - \log |1 + x| + C$

Sol. (d) $x - \dfrac{x^2}{2} + \dfrac{x^3}{3} - \log |1 + x| + C$

Explanation :

Let $I = \int \dfrac{x^3}{x+1} \, dx$

$= \int \dfrac{x^3 + 1 - 1}{x+1} \, dx$

$= \int \left(\dfrac{(x+1)(x^2 - x + 1)}{x+1} - \dfrac{1}{x+1} \right) dx$

$= \int \left((x^2 - x + 1) - \dfrac{1}{(x+1)} \right) dx$

$= \dfrac{x^3}{3} - \dfrac{x^2}{2} + x - \log |x+1| + C.$

4. $\int 7e^{7x+5} \, dx =$

(a) $7(7e^{7x+5}) + C$ 　　(b) $\dfrac{7e^{7+5}}{5} + C$

(c) $e^{7x+5} + C$ 　　(d) $\dfrac{7e^{7+5}}{7x+5} + C$

Sol. (c) $e^{7x+5} + C$

Explanation :

$$\int 7e^{7x+5}\,dx = 7\cdot\frac{e^{7x+5}}{7} + C = e^{7x+5} + C.$$

5. $\displaystyle\int \frac{(1+x)^2}{x(1+x^2)}\,dx$

(a) $\log x + C$
(b) $(\log x)(\tan^{-1} x) + C$
(c) $2\log x + \tan^{-1} x + C$
(d) $\log x + 2\tan^{-1} x + C$

Sol. (d) $\log x + 2\tan^{-1} x + C$

Explanation :

$$\int \frac{(1+x)^2}{x(1+x^2)}\,dx = \int \left(\frac{(1+x^2)+2x}{x(1+x^2)}\right) dx$$

$$= \int \left(\frac{1}{x} + 2\cdot\frac{1}{1+x^2}\right) dx$$

$$= \int \frac{1}{x}\,dx + \int \frac{2}{(1+x^2)}\,dx$$

$$= \log x + 2\tan^{-1} x + C.$$

6. If $f'(x) = \dfrac{1}{x} + x$ and $f(1) = \dfrac{5}{2}$, then $f(x) =$

(a) $\log x + \dfrac{x^2}{2} + 2$ (b) $\log x + \dfrac{x^2}{2} + 1$

(c) $\log x - \dfrac{x^2}{2} + 2$ (d) $\log x - \dfrac{x^2}{2} + 1$

Sol. (a) $\log x + \dfrac{x^2}{2} + 2$

Explanation :

$$f(x) = \int f'(x)\,dx = \int \left(\frac{1}{x} + x\right) dx$$

$$= \log x + \frac{x^2}{2} + C$$

$$f(1) = \log 1 + \frac{1^2}{2} + C$$

$$\Rightarrow \qquad \frac{5}{2} = 0 + \frac{1}{2} + C$$

$$\Rightarrow \qquad C = 2$$

$$\therefore \qquad f(x) = \log x + \frac{x^2}{2} + 2.$$

7. $\displaystyle\int 2^x \cdot 3^{x+1} \cdot 4^{x+2}\,dx =$

(a) $\dfrac{(48)^x}{\log 48} + C$

(b) $\dfrac{2^x\,3^{x+1}\,4^{x+2}}{\log 2 + \log 4 + \log 3} + C$

(c) $\dfrac{(24)^{x+2}}{\log 24} + C$

(d) $\dfrac{2^{x+1}\,3^{x+2}\,4^{x+3}}{\log 2 + \log 4 + \log 3} + C$

Sol. (b) $\dfrac{2^x\,3^{x+1}\,4^{x+2}}{\log 2 + \log 4 + \log 3} + C$

Explanation :

$$\int 2^x\,3^{x+1}\,4^{x+2}\,dx = 16\times 3\int 2^x\,3^x\,4^x\,dx$$

$$= 48\int (24)^x\,dx = \frac{48(24)^x}{\log 24} + C$$

$$= \frac{2^x\,3^{x+1}\,4^{x+2}}{\log 2 + \log 4 + \log 3} + C.$$

8. $\displaystyle\int \frac{dx}{\cos 2x + \sin^2 x}$

(a) $\sin x + C$ (b) $\cos x + C$
(c) $\tan x + C$ (d) 0

Sol. (c) $\tan x + C$

Explanation :

$$\int\frac{dx}{\cos 2x + \sin^2 x} = \int\frac{dx}{\cos^2 x - \sin^2 x + \sin^2 x}$$

$$= \int\frac{dx}{\cos^2 x} = \int \sec^2 x\,dx$$

$$= \tan x + C.$$

9. $\displaystyle\int x^{51}\,(\tan^{-1} x + \cot^{-1} x)\,dx =$

(a) $\dfrac{x^{52}}{52}\,(\tan^{-1} x + \cot^{-1} x) + C$

(b) $\dfrac{x^{52}}{52}\,(\tan^{-1} x - \cot^{-1} x) + C$

(c) $\dfrac{\pi x^{52}}{104} + \dfrac{\pi}{2} + C$

(d) $\dfrac{x^{52}}{52} + \dfrac{\pi}{2} + C$

Sol. (a) $\dfrac{x^{52}}{52}\,(\tan^{-1} x + \cot^{-1} x) + C$

Explanation :

$$\int x^{51}\,(\tan^{-1} x + \cot^{-1} x)\,dx$$

$$= \int x^{51}\cdot\frac{\pi}{2}\,dx \quad \left\{\because \tan^{-1} x + \cot^{-1} x = \frac{\pi}{2}\right\}$$

$$= \frac{\pi x^{52}}{104} + C = \frac{x^{52}}{52}\,(\tan^{-1} x + \cot^{-1} x) + C.$$

10. The value of $\int \dfrac{1}{1+\cos\ 8x}\ dx$ is:

(a) $\dfrac{\tan 2x}{8}+C$ (b) $\dfrac{\tan 8x}{8}+C$

(c) $\dfrac{\tan 4x}{4}+C$ (d) $\dfrac{\tan 4x}{8}+C$

Sol. (d) $\dfrac{\tan 4x}{8}+C$

Explanation :

$$\int \frac{1}{1+\cos\ 8x}\ dx = \int \frac{1}{2\cos^2 4x}\ dx$$

$$= \frac{1}{2}\int \sec^2 4x\ dx$$

$$= \frac{\tan 4x}{8}+C.$$

11. By the inspection method, evaluate:

$$\int (au^2 +bu +c)\,du$$

(a) $a\left(\dfrac{u^3}{3}\right)+b\left(\dfrac{u^2}{2}\right)+cu+C$

(b) $-a\left(\dfrac{u^3}{3}\right)+b\left(\dfrac{u^2}{2}\right)-cu+C$

(c) $a\left(\dfrac{u^3}{3}\right)+b\left(\dfrac{u^2}{2}\right)-cu+C$

(d) $a\left(\dfrac{u^3}{3}\right)-b\left(\dfrac{u^2}{2}\right)-cu+C$

Sol. (a) $a\left(\dfrac{u^3}{3}\right)+b\left(\dfrac{u^2}{2}\right)+cu+C$

Explanation :

The given integral is $\int (au^2 +bu +c)\ du$.

$$\int (au^2 +bu +c)\ du = \int au^2 du +\int budu +\int cdu$$

$$= a\int u^2 du +b\int udu +c\int du$$

$$= a\left(\frac{u^3}{3}\right)+b\left(\frac{u^2}{2}\right)+cu+C$$

So the correct option is (a).

12. Find the integral of $\sqrt{u}+\dfrac{1}{\sqrt{u}}$.

(a) $\dfrac{2}{3}u^{3/2}+2u^{1/2}+C$ (b) $\dfrac{2}{3}u^{3/2}-2u^{1/2}+C$

(c) $-\dfrac{2}{3}u^{3/2}-2u^{1/2}+C$ (d) $-\dfrac{2}{3}u^{3/2}+2u^{1/2}+C$

Sol. (a) $\dfrac{2}{3}u^{3/2}+2u^{1/2}+C$

Explanation :

$$\int\left(\sqrt{u}+\frac{1}{\sqrt{u}}\right)du = \int(\sqrt{u})du +\int\left(\frac{1}{\sqrt{u}}\right)du$$

$$= \int(u^{1/2})du +\int\left(\frac{1}{u^{1/2}}\right)du$$

$$= \frac{u^{3/2}}{\frac{3}{2}}+\frac{u^{1/2}}{\frac{1}{2}}+C$$

$$= \frac{2}{3}u^{3/2}+2u^{1/2}+C$$

So the correct option is (a).

13. Find the integral of $\sin u \sin 2u \sin 3u$.

(a) $\dfrac{1}{4}[\cos 6u -\cos 4u -\cos 2u\}+C$

(b) $\dfrac{1}{4}[\cos 4 -\cos 4u -\cos 2u]+C$

(c) $\dfrac{1}{8}\left[\dfrac{\cos 6u}{3}-\dfrac{\cos 4u}{2}-\cos 2u\right]+C$

(d) $\dfrac{1}{8}\left[\dfrac{\cos 6u}{3}-\dfrac{\cos 4u}{2}+\cos 2u\right]+C$

Sol. (c) $\dfrac{1}{8}\left[\dfrac{\cos 6u}{3}-\dfrac{\cos 4u}{2}-\cos 2u\right]+C$

Explanation :

The given integral is,

$$\int \sin u \sin 2u \sin 3u\ du.$$

We know that,

$$\sin A \sin B = \frac{1}{2}\big[\cos(A-B)-\cos(A+B)\big]$$

Using the above formula for $\sin 2u \sin 3u$ in the given integral, we get

$$\int \sin u \sin 2u \sin 3u\ du$$

$$= \int \sin u\cdot\frac{1}{2}\big[\cos(2u-3u)-\cos(2u+3u)\big]du$$

$$= \frac{1}{2}\int\big[\sin u \cos (-u)-\sin u \cos 5u\big]du$$

$$= \frac{1}{2}\int(\sin u \cos u -\sin u \cos 5u)du$$

We know that,

$$2 \sin A \cos A = \sin 2A \text{ and } \sin A \cos B$$

$$= \frac{1}{2}\big[\sin (A+B)+\sin (A-B)\big]$$

Using the above two formulas in the integral, we get

$$\frac{1}{2}\int (\sin u \cos u - \sin u \cos 5u)\,du$$

$$= \frac{1}{2}\int \frac{2\sin u \cos u}{2}\,du$$

$$-\frac{1}{2}\int \frac{1}{2}\left[\sin(u+5u) + \sin(u-5u)\right]du$$

$$= \frac{1}{4}\int \sin 2u\,du - \frac{1}{4}\int \left[\sin 6u + \sin(-4u)\right]du$$

$$= \frac{1}{4}\left[\int \sin 2u\,du - \left\{\int \sin 6u\,du - \int \sin 4u\,du\right\}\right]$$

$$= \frac{1}{4}\left[\frac{-\cos 2u}{2} - \left(\frac{-\cos 6u}{6} + \frac{\cos 4u}{4}\right)\right]+C$$

$$= \frac{1}{4}\times\frac{1}{2}\left[-\cos 2u + \frac{\cos 6u}{3} - \frac{\cos 4u}{2}\right]+C$$

$$= \frac{1}{8}\left[\frac{\cos 6u}{3} - \frac{\cos 4u}{2} - \cos 2u\right]+C$$

So the correct option is (c).

14. $\int 4^x 3^x\,dx$ equals :*

(a) $\dfrac{12^x}{\log 12}+C$ 　　(b) $\dfrac{4^x}{\log 4}+C$

(c) $\left(\dfrac{4^x \cdot 3^x}{\log 4.\log 3}\right)+C$ 　(d) $\dfrac{3^x}{\log 3}+C$

Sol. (a) $\dfrac{12^x}{\log 12}+C$

Explanation :

Let 　　　　　$I = \int 4^x 3^x\,dx$

$\Rightarrow$ 　　　　$I = \int 12^x\,dx$

$\Rightarrow$ 　　　　$I = \dfrac{12^x}{\log 12}+C$

So the correct option is (a).

15. $\int \tan^{-1}\sqrt{x}\,dx$ is equal to: **[NCERT Exemplar]**

(a) $(x+1)\tan^{-1}\sqrt{x} - \sqrt{x}+C$

(b) $x\tan^{-1}x - \sqrt{x}+C$

(c) $\sqrt{x} - x\tan^{-1}\sqrt{x}+C$

(d) $\sqrt{x} - (x+1)\tan^{-1}\sqrt{x}+C$

Sol. (a) $(x+1)\tan^{-1}\sqrt{x} - \sqrt{x}+C$

*are board exam questions from previous years

Explanation :

Let 　　$I = \int 1\cdot \tan^{-1}\sqrt{x}\,dx$

$$= \tan^{-1}\sqrt{x}\cdot x - \int \frac{1}{1+(\sqrt{x})^2}\cdot\frac{1}{2\sqrt{x}}\cdot x\,dx$$

$$= x\tan^{-1}\sqrt{x} - \frac{1}{2}\int \frac{\sqrt{x}}{1+x}\,dx$$

Put $x = t^2 \Rightarrow dx = 2t\,dt$

$\therefore$ 　　$I = x\tan^{-1}\sqrt{x} - \dfrac{1}{2}\int \dfrac{t\cdot 2t}{(1+t^2)}\,dt$

$$= x\tan^{-1}\sqrt{x} - \int \frac{t^2}{1+t^2}\,dt$$

$$= x\tan^{-1}\sqrt{x} - \int \left(1 - \frac{1}{1+t^2}\right)dt$$

$$= x\tan^{-1}\sqrt{x} - t + \tan^{-1}t + C$$

$$= x\tan^{-1}\sqrt{x} - \sqrt{x} + \tan^{-1}\sqrt{x} + C$$

$$\left(\begin{array}{c}\because x = t^2 \\ \therefore t = \sqrt{x}\end{array}\right)$$

$$= (x+1)\tan^{-1}\sqrt{x} - \sqrt{x}+C.$$

16. $\int \dfrac{x^9}{(4x^2+1)^6}\,dx$ is equal to: **[NCERT Exemplar]**

(a) $\dfrac{1}{5x}\left(4+\dfrac{1}{x^2}\right)^{-5}+C$ 　(b) $\dfrac{1}{5}\left(4+\dfrac{1}{x^2}\right)^{-5}+C$

(c) $\dfrac{1}{10x}(1+4)^{-5}+C$ 　(d) $\dfrac{1}{10}\left(4+\dfrac{1}{x^2}\right)^{-5}+C$

Sol. (d) $\dfrac{1}{10}\left(4+\dfrac{1}{x^2}\right)^{-5}+C$

Explanation :

Let 　　　　$I = \int \dfrac{x^9}{(4x^2+1)^6}\,dx$

$$= \int \frac{x^9}{x^{12}\left(4+\dfrac{1}{x^2}\right)^6}\,dx$$

$$= \int \frac{dx}{x^3\left(4+\dfrac{1}{x^2}\right)^6}$$

Put 　　$4+\dfrac{1}{x^2} = t$

$\Rightarrow$ 　　$\dfrac{-2}{x^3}\,dx = dt$

$\Rightarrow$ 　　$\dfrac{1}{x^3}\,dx = -\dfrac{1}{2}\,dt$

$$\therefore \quad I = -\frac{1}{2}\int \frac{dt}{t^6} = -\frac{1}{2}\left[\frac{t^{-6+1}}{-6+1}\right] + C$$

$$= \frac{1}{10}\left[\frac{1}{t^5}\right] + C = \frac{1}{10}\left(4+\frac{1}{x^2}\right)^{-5} + C.$$

17. If $\int \dfrac{x^3}{\sqrt{1+x^2}}\, dx = a(1+x^2)^{3/2} + b\sqrt{1+x^2} + C$, then:

[NCERT Exemplar]

(a) $a = \dfrac{1}{3},\ b = 1$ (b) $a = \dfrac{-1}{3},\ b = 1$

(c) $a = \dfrac{-1}{3},\ b = -1$ (d) $a = \dfrac{1}{3},\ b = -1$

Sol. (d) $a = \dfrac{1}{3},\ b = -1$

Explanation :

Let $\quad I = \int \dfrac{x^3}{\sqrt{1+x^2}}\, dx$

$$= a(1+x^2)^{3/2} + b\sqrt{1+x^2} + C$$

$\because \quad I = \int \dfrac{x^3}{\sqrt{1+x^2}}\, dx$

$$= \int \dfrac{x^2 \cdot x}{\sqrt{1+x^2}}\, dx$$

Put $\quad 1 + x^2 = t^2$

$\Rightarrow \quad 2x\, dx = 2t\, dt$

$$I = \int \dfrac{t(t^2-1)}{t}\, dt$$

$$= \int (t^2-1)\, dt = \frac{t^3}{3} - t + C$$

$$= \frac{1}{3}(1+x^2)^{3/2} - \sqrt{1+x^2} + C$$

By comparison $a = \dfrac{1}{3}$ and $b = -1$.

18. $\int \dfrac{1}{\log a}(a^x \cos a^x)\, dx =$

(a) $\sin a^x + C$ (b) $a^x \sin a^x + C$

(c) $\dfrac{1}{(\log a)^2} \sin a^x + C$ (d) $\log (\sin a^x) + C$

Sol. (c) $\dfrac{1}{(\log a)^2} \sin a^x + C$

Explanation :

Put $\quad a^x = t$

$$a^x \log a\, dx = dt$$

$\Rightarrow \quad a^x\, dx = \dfrac{dt}{\log a}$

$$\therefore \quad \int \frac{1}{\log a}(a^x \cos a^x)\, dx = \int \frac{1}{(\log a)^2}\cos t\, dt$$

$$= \frac{1}{(\log a)^2} \sin t + C$$

$$= \frac{1}{(\log a)^2} \sin a^x + C.$$

19. Find the integral of $\dfrac{5x^4}{\sqrt{x^5+9}}$

(a) $\sqrt{x^5+9} + C$ (b) $2\sqrt{x^5-9} + C$

(c) $2(x^5+9) + C$ (d) $2\sqrt{x^5+9} + C$

Sol. (d) $2\sqrt{x^5+9} + C$

Explanation :

Let $\quad x^5 + 9 = t$

Differentiating w.r.t. x, we get

$$5x^4\, dx = dt$$

$$\int \frac{5x^4}{\sqrt{x^5+9}}\, dx = \int \frac{dt}{\sqrt{t}}$$

$$= \frac{t^{-\frac{1}{2}+1}}{-\frac{1}{2}+1} + C = 2\sqrt{t} + C$$

Replacing t with $x^5 + 9$, we get

$$\int \frac{5x^4}{\sqrt{x^5+9}}\, dx = 2\sqrt{x^5+9} + C.$$

20. $\int \dfrac{\sec x\, dx}{\sqrt{\cos 2x}} =$

(a) $\sin^{-1}(\tan x)$ (b) $\tan x$

(c) $\cos^{-1}(\tan x)$ (d) $\dfrac{\sin x}{\sqrt{\cos x}}$

Sol. (a) $\sin^{-1}(\tan x)$

Explanation :

$$\int \frac{\sec x\, dx}{\sqrt{\cos 2x}} = \int \frac{\sec x}{\sqrt{\cos^2 x - \sin^2 x}}\, dx$$

$$= \int \frac{\sec^2 x\, dx}{\sqrt{1 - \tan^2 x}}$$

{Multiplying N'r and D'r by sec x}

Now putting $\tan x = t$

$\Rightarrow \quad \sec^2 x\, dx = dt,$

$$= \int \frac{dt}{\sqrt{1-t^2}} = \sin^{-1} t$$

$$= \sin^{-1}(\tan x).$$

21. If $\int x^6 \sin(5x^7)\,dx = \dfrac{k}{5}\cos(5x^7) + C,\ x \neq 0,$

then:

(a) $k = 7$ (b) $k = -7$

(c) $k = \dfrac{1}{7}$ (d) $k = -\dfrac{1}{7}$

Sol. (d) $k = -\dfrac{1}{7}$

Explanation :

Put
$$5x^7 = t$$
$$\Rightarrow \quad 35x^6\,dx = dt$$
$$\Rightarrow \quad x^6\,dx = \frac{dt}{35}$$

$$\therefore \quad \int x^6 \sin(5x^7)\,dx = \int \sin t \cdot \frac{dt}{35}$$
$$= -\frac{\cos t}{35} + C$$
$$= \frac{-\cos(5x^7)}{35} + C$$

$$\therefore \quad k = -\frac{1}{7}.$$

22. $\displaystyle \int \frac{1}{(e^x + e^{-x})}\,dx =$

(a) $-\dfrac{1}{2(e^{2x}+1)} + C$ (b) $\dfrac{1}{2(e^{2x}+1)} + C$

(c) $-\dfrac{1}{e^{2x}+1} + C$ (d) None of these

Sol. (a) $-\dfrac{1}{2(e^{2x}+1)} + C$

Explanation :

$$\int \frac{1}{(e^x + e^{-x})^2}\,dx = \int \frac{e^{2x}}{(e^{2x}+1)^2}\,dx$$

Put $e^{2x} + 1 = t \Rightarrow 2e^{2x}\,dx = dt$, then it reduces to

$$\frac{1}{2}\int \frac{1}{t^2}\,dt = -\frac{1}{2}\cdot\frac{1}{t} + C = -\frac{1}{2(e^{2x}+1)} + C.$$

23. $\displaystyle \int \left(\frac{(x^2+2)\,a^{(x+\tan^{-1}x)}}{x^2+1} \right)\,dx =$

(a) $\log a \cdot a^{x\,\tan^{-1}x} + C$

(b) $\dfrac{(x+\tan^{-1}x)}{\log a} + C$

(c) $\dfrac{a^{x+\tan^{-1}x}}{\log a} + C$

(d) $\log a \cdot (x + \tan^{-1}x) + C$

Sol. (c) $\dfrac{a^{x+\tan^{-1}x}}{\log a} + C$

Explanation :

Put
$$x + \tan^{-1}x = t$$
$$\Rightarrow \quad \left(1 + \frac{1}{1+x^2}\right)dx = dt$$
$$\Rightarrow \quad \frac{2+x^2}{1+x^2}\,dx = dt$$

$$\int \left[\frac{(x^2+2)a^{(x+\tan^{-1}x)}}{x^2+1}\right]dx = \int a^t\,dt$$
$$= \frac{a^t}{\log a} + C$$
$$= \frac{a^{x+\tan^{-1}x}}{\log a} + C.$$

24. $\displaystyle \int \frac{1}{1+\cos^2 x}\,dx =$

(a) $\dfrac{1}{\sqrt{2}}\tan^{-1}(\tan x) + C$

(b) $\dfrac{1}{\sqrt{2}}\tan^{-1}\left(\dfrac{1}{2}\tan x\right) + C$

(c) $\dfrac{1}{\sqrt{2}}\tan^{-1}\left(\dfrac{1}{\sqrt{2}}\tan x\right) + C$

(d) None of the above

Sol. (c) $\dfrac{1}{\sqrt{2}}\tan^{-1}\left(\dfrac{1}{\sqrt{2}}\tan x\right) + C$

Explanation :

$$\int \frac{dx}{1+\cos^2 x} = \int \frac{\sec^2 x\,dx}{\sec^2 x+1}\,dx = \int \frac{\sec^2 x}{\tan^2 x+2}\,dx$$
$$= \int \frac{dt}{t^2+2} = \frac{1}{\sqrt{2}}\tan^{-1}\left(\frac{t}{\sqrt{2}}\right) + C$$

$$\{\text{Putting } \tan x = t$$
$$\sec^2 x\,dx = dt\}$$

$$= \frac{1}{\sqrt{2}}\tan^{-1}\left(\frac{1}{\sqrt{2}}\tan x\right) + C.$$

25. Evaluate : $\displaystyle \int \frac{10u^9 + 10^u \log_e 10}{u^{10} + 10^u}\,du.$

(a) $\log(10^u + u^{10}) + C$ (b) $(10^u - u^{10}) + C$

(c) $10^u + u^{10} + C$ (d) $-10^u + u^{10} + C$

Sol. (a) $\log(10^u + u^{10}) + C$

Explanation :

The given integral is $\displaystyle \int \frac{10u^9 + 10^u \log_e 10}{u^{10} + 10^u}\,du$

Let $\qquad u^{10} + 10^u = v$

Differentiating both sides, we get

$$\frac{d}{du}(u^{10} + 10^u) = \frac{dv}{du}$$

$$10u^9 + 10^u \log_e 10 = \frac{dv}{du}$$

$(10u^9 + 10^u \log_e 10)\, du = dv$

Substitue v for $u^{10} + 10^n$ and dv for $(10u^9 + 10^u \log_e 10)\, du$ in the given integral.

$$\int \frac{10u^9 + 10^u \log_e 10}{u^{10} + 10^u}\, du = \int \frac{dv}{v}$$

$$= \int \frac{1}{v}\, dv$$

$$= \log v + C$$

$$= \log (u^{10} + 10^u) + C$$

$$(\because v = u^{10} + 10^u)$$

So the correct option is (a).

26. Integrate : $\dfrac{u^2}{1 - u^6}$

(a) $\dfrac{1}{6} \log \left|\dfrac{1+u^3}{1-u^3}\right| + C$ $\quad$ (b) $\log \left|\dfrac{1+u^3}{1-u^3}\right| + C$

(c) $\log \left|\dfrac{1+u}{1-u}\right| + C$ $\quad$ (d) $\log |\, 1 + u^3\,| + C$

Sol. (a) $\dfrac{1}{6} \log \left|\dfrac{1+u^3}{1-u^3}\right| + C$

Explanation :

The given integral is $\displaystyle\int \frac{u^2}{1 - u^6}\, du$

$$\int \frac{u^2}{1 - u^6}\, du = \int \frac{u^2}{1 - (u^3)^2}\, du$$

Substitute z for u^3 and differentiate w.r.t. x,

$$u^3 = z$$

$$\frac{d}{du} u^3 = \frac{dz}{du}$$

$$3u^2 = \frac{dz}{du}$$

$$3u^2\, du = dz$$

$$\int \frac{u^2}{1 - (u^3)^2}\, du = \frac{1}{3} \int \frac{dz}{1 - z^2}$$

$$= \frac{1}{3}\left[\frac{1}{2} \log \left|\frac{1+z}{1-z}\right|\right] + C$$

$$= \frac{1}{3}\left[\frac{1}{2} \log \left|\frac{1+u^3}{1-u^3}\right|\right] + C \; (\because z = u^3)$$

$$= \frac{1}{6} \log \left|\frac{1+u^3}{1-u^3}\right| + C$$

So the correct option is (a).

27. $\displaystyle\int x^2 e^{x^3}\, dx$ equals :*

(a) $\dfrac{1}{3} e^{x^3} + C$ $\qquad$ (b) $\dfrac{1}{3} e^{x^4} + C$

(c) $\dfrac{1}{2} e^{x^3} + C$ $\qquad$ (d) $\dfrac{1}{2} e^{x^2} + C$

Sol. (a) $\dfrac{1}{3} e^{x^3} + C$

Explanation :

Let $\qquad I = \displaystyle\int x^2 e^{x^3}\, dx$

Put $\qquad x^3 = t$

$\Rightarrow \qquad 3x^2 dx = dt$

$\Rightarrow \qquad x^2 dx = \dfrac{1}{3} dt$

$\therefore \qquad I = \dfrac{1}{3} \displaystyle\int e^t dt$

$$I = \frac{1}{3} e^t + C$$

$$I = \frac{1}{3} e^{x^3} + C$$

So the correct option is (a).

28. If $\displaystyle\int \frac{dx}{(x+2)(x^2+1)} = a \log |1 + x^2| + b \tan^{-1} x$

$+ \dfrac{1}{5} \log |\, x + 2\,| + C$, then: **[NCERT Exemplar]**

(a) $a = \dfrac{-1}{10}, b = \dfrac{-2}{5}$ $\quad$ (b) $a = \dfrac{1}{10}, b = -\dfrac{2}{5}$

(c) $a = \dfrac{-1}{10}, b = \dfrac{2}{5}$ $\quad$ (d) $a = \dfrac{1}{10}, b = \dfrac{2}{5}$

Sol. (c) $a = \dfrac{-1}{10}, b = \dfrac{2}{5}$

Explanation :

Given that,

$$\int \frac{dx}{(x+2)(x^2+1)} = a \log |1 + x^2| + b \tan^{-1} x$$

$$+ \frac{1}{5} \log |x + 2| + C$$

Now, $\qquad I = \displaystyle\int \frac{dx}{(x+2)(x^2+1)}$

$$\frac{1}{(x+2)(x^2+1)} = \frac{A}{x+2} + \frac{Bx + C}{x^2+1}$$

$\Rightarrow \qquad 1 = A(x^2 + 1) + (Bx + C)(x + 2)$

$\Rightarrow \qquad 1 = Ax^2 + A + Bx^2 + 2Bx + Cx + 2C$

$\Rightarrow \qquad 1 = (A + B)x^2 + (2B + C)x + A + 2C$

$\Rightarrow \qquad A + B = 0,\ A + 2C = 1,\ 2B + C = 0$

We have, $A = \dfrac{1}{5},\ B = -\dfrac{1}{5}$ and $C = \dfrac{2}{5}$

$$\therefore \int \frac{dx}{(x+2)(x^2+1)} = \frac{1}{5}\int \frac{1}{x+2}\,dx + \int \frac{-\frac{1}{5}x + \frac{2}{5}}{x^2+1}\,dx$$

$$= \frac{1}{5}\int \frac{1}{x+2}\,dx - \frac{1}{5}\int \frac{x}{1+x^2}\,dx + \frac{1}{5}\int \frac{2}{1+x^2}\,dx$$

$$= \frac{1}{5}\int \frac{1}{x+2}\,dx - \frac{1}{5\times 2}\int \frac{2x}{1+x^2}\,dx + \frac{2}{5}\int \frac{1}{1+x^2}\,dx$$

$$= \frac{1}{5}\log|x+2| - \frac{1}{10}\log|1+x^2| + \frac{2}{5}\tan^{-1}x + C$$

$$\therefore \qquad b = \frac{2}{5}\ \text{and}\ a = \frac{-1}{10}.$$

29. $\displaystyle \int \frac{x+3}{(x+4)^2}\,e^x\,dx$ is equal to: **[NCERT Exemplar]**

(a) $e^x\left(\dfrac{1}{x+4}\right) + C$ \qquad (b) $e^{-x}\left(\dfrac{1}{x+4}\right) + C$

(c) $e^{-x}\left(\dfrac{1}{x-4}\right) + C$ \qquad (d) $e^{2x}\left(\dfrac{1}{x-4}\right) + C$

Sol. (a) $e^x\left(\dfrac{1}{x+4}\right) + C$

Explanation :

Let $\qquad I = \displaystyle\int \frac{x+3}{(x+4)^2}\,e^x\,dx$

$$\frac{x+3}{(x+4)^2} = \frac{A}{x+4} + \frac{B}{(x+4)^2}$$

$\Rightarrow \qquad x + 3 = A(x+4) + B$

$\Rightarrow \qquad x + 3 = Ax + (4A + B)$

$\Rightarrow \qquad A = 1,\ 4A + B = 3$

We have, $\quad A = 1,\ B = -1$

$$\therefore \qquad I = \int\left(\frac{1}{x+4} - \frac{1}{(x+4)^2}\right)e^x\,dx$$

$$= \int \frac{e^x}{(x+4)} - \int \frac{e^x}{(x+4)^2}\,dx$$

$$= \int e^x\left(\frac{1}{(x+4)} - \frac{1}{(x+4)^2}\right)dx$$

$$= e^x\left(\frac{1}{x+4}\right) + C$$

$$\left[\because \int e^x\{f(x) + f'(x)\}\,dx = e^x\,f(x) + C\right]$$

30. $\displaystyle \int \frac{1}{x^2 - x^3}\,dx =$

(a) $\log\left|\dfrac{1-x}{x}\right| - \dfrac{1}{x} + C$ \quad (b) $\log\left|\dfrac{1-x}{x}\right| + \dfrac{1}{x} + C$

(c) $\log\left|\dfrac{x}{1-x}\right| + \dfrac{1}{x} + C$ \quad (d) $\log\left|\dfrac{x}{1-x}\right| - \dfrac{1}{x} + C$

Sol. (d) $\log\left|\dfrac{x}{1-x}\right| - \dfrac{1}{x} + C$

Explanation :

$$\int \frac{dx}{x^2 - x^3} = \int \frac{1 - x + x}{x^2(1-x)}\,dx$$

$$= \int \frac{(1-x)\,dx}{x^2(1-x)} + \int \frac{x\,dx}{x^2(1-x)}$$

$$= \int \frac{1}{x^2}\,dx + \int \frac{dx}{x(1-x)}$$

$$= -\frac{1}{x} + \int \frac{dx}{x} + \int \frac{dx}{1-x}$$

$$= -\frac{1}{x} + \log|x| - \log|1-x| + C$$

$$\forall\ -1 < x < 1$$

$$= \log\left|\frac{x}{1-x}\right| - \frac{1}{x} + C.$$

31. $\displaystyle \int \frac{dx}{(x - x^2)} =$

(a) $\log x - \log(1 - x) + C$

(b) $\log(1 - x^2) + C$

(c) $-\log x + \log(1 - x) + C)$

(d) $\log(x - x^2) + C$

Sol. (a) $\log x - \log(1 - x) + C$

Explanation :

$$\int \frac{dx}{(x - x^2)} = \int\left(\frac{1}{x} + \frac{1}{1-x}\right)dx$$

$$= \log x - \log(1 - x) + C.$$

32. $\displaystyle \int \frac{dx}{(x^2+1)(x^2+4)} =$

(a) $\dfrac{1}{3}\tan^{-1}x - \dfrac{1}{3}\tan^{-1}\dfrac{x}{2} + C$

(b) $\dfrac{1}{3}\tan^{-1}x + \dfrac{1}{3}\tan^{-1}\dfrac{x}{2} + C$

(c) $\dfrac{1}{3}\tan^{-1}x - \dfrac{1}{3}\tan^{-1}\dfrac{x}{2} + C$

(d) $\tan^{-1}x - 2\tan^{-1}\dfrac{x}{2} + C$

Sol. (c) $\dfrac{1}{3}\tan^{-1}x - \dfrac{1}{6}\tan^{-1}\dfrac{x}{2} + C$

Explanation :

$$\int \frac{dx}{(x^2+1)(x^2+4)} = \frac{1}{3}\left[\int \frac{dx}{x^2+1} - \int \frac{dx}{x^2+4}\right]$$

$$= \frac{1}{3}\left[\tan^{-1} x - \frac{1}{2}\tan^{-1}\frac{x}{2}\right] + C$$

$$= \frac{1}{3}\tan^{-1} x - \frac{1}{6}\tan^{-1}\frac{x}{2} + C.$$

33. $\int \dfrac{x+\sin x}{1+\cos x}\, dx$ is equal to: **[NCERT Exemplar]**

(a) $\log |1-\cos x| + C$

(b) $\log |x+\sin x| + C$

(c) $x - \tan \dfrac{x}{2} + C$

(d) $x \cdot \tan \dfrac{x}{2} + C$

Sol. (d) $x \cdot \tan \dfrac{x}{2} + C$

Explanation :

$$I = \int \frac{x+\sin x}{1+\cos x}\, dx$$

$$= \int \frac{x}{1+\cos x}\, dx + \int \frac{\sin x}{1+\cos x}\, dx$$

$$= \int \frac{x}{2\cos^2 \frac{x}{2}}\, dx + \int \frac{2\sin \frac{x}{2}\cos \frac{x}{2}}{2\cos^2 \frac{x}{2}}\, dx$$

$$= \frac{1}{2}\int x \sec^2 \frac{x}{2}\, dx + \int \tan \frac{x}{2}\, dx$$

$$= \frac{1}{2}\left[x\cdot\tan \frac{x}{2}\cdot 2 - \int \tan \frac{x}{2}\cdot 2\, dx\right] + \int \tan \frac{x}{2}\, dx$$

$$= x\cdot\tan \frac{x}{2} + C.$$

[By cancelling the last two integral]

34. $\int e^x (1-\cot x + \cot^2 x)\, dx =$

(a) $e^x \cot x + C$ (b) $e^x \operatorname{cosec} x + C$

(c) $-e^x \operatorname{cosec} x + C$ (d) $-e^x \cot x + C$

Sol. (d) $-e^x \cot x + C$

Explanation :

$$\int e^x (1-\cot x + \cot^2 x)\, dx$$

$$= \int e^x (-\cot x + \operatorname{cosec}^2 x)\, dx$$

$$= e^x (-\cot x) + C$$

$$\left[\because \int e^x \{f(x)+f'(x)\}\, dx = e^x f(x)+C\right]$$

$$= -e^x \cot x + C.$$

35. $\int \dfrac{1}{\log_x e}\, dx =$

(a) $\log \log_x e + C$ (b) $\dfrac{1}{(\log_x e)^2} + C$

(c) $x \log \left(\dfrac{x}{e}\right) + C$ (d) None of these

Sol. (c) $x \log_e \left(\dfrac{x}{e}\right) + C$

Explanation :

$$\int \frac{1}{\log_x e}\, dx = \int \log_e x\, dx$$

$$= \int 1\cdot\log_e x\, dx = \log_e x\cdot x - \int \frac{1}{x}\cdot x\, dx$$

$$= x \log_e x - x + C$$

$$= x(\log_e x - \log_e e) + C$$

$$= x \log_e \left(\frac{x}{e}\right) + C.$$

36. $\int e^x \sin x(\sin x + 2\cos x)\, dx =$

(a) $e^x \sin^2 x + C$ (b) $e^x \sin x + C$

(c) $e^x \sin 2x + C$ (d) None of these

Sol. (a) $e^x \sin^2 x + C$

Explanation :

$$\int e^x \sin x(\sin x + 2\cos x)\, dx$$

$$= \int e^x \sin^2 x\, dx + \int e^x\, 2\sin x \cos x\, dx$$

$$= \int e^x \sin^2 x\, dx + \int e^x \sin 2x\, dx$$

$$= e^x \sin^2 x - \int e^x\, 2\sin x \cos x\, dx$$

$$+ \int e^x \sin 2x\, dx + C$$

$$= e^x \sin^2 x - \int e^x \sin 2x\, dx + \int e^x \sin 2x\, dx + C$$

$$= e^x \sin^2 x + C.$$

37. Evaluate $\int 1.\sin^{-1} x\, dx.$

(a) $x\sin^{-1} x - (1-x^2)^{-\frac{1}{2}} + C$

(b) $\sin^{-1} x - (1-x^2)^{-\frac{1}{2}} + C$

(c) $x \sin^{-1} x + (1-x^2)^{-\frac{1}{2}} + C$

(d) $x \sin^{-1} x + (1-x^2)^{\frac{1}{2}} + C$

Sol. (d) $x \sin^{-1} x + (1-x^2)^{\frac{1}{2}} + C$

Explanation :

Let, the given integral be

$$I = \int 1.\sin^{-1} x \, dx$$

Integrating by parts,

$$I = \sin^{-1} x \int 1.dx - \int \left\{ \left(\frac{d}{dx} \sin^{-1} x \right) \int 1.dx \right\} dx$$

$$= \sin^{-1} x.x - \int \frac{1}{\sqrt{1-x^2}}.x \, dx$$

Substitute $1 - x^2 = t$ in the given integral and differentiate it.

$$\frac{d}{dx}(1-x^2) = \frac{dt}{dx}$$

$$-2x = \frac{dt}{dx}$$

$$x \, dx = -\frac{1}{2} dt$$

$$= x \sin^{-1} x - \int -\frac{1}{2} \frac{dt}{\sqrt{t}}$$

$$= x \sin^{-1} x + \frac{1}{2} t^{\frac{1}{2}} \times (2) + C$$

$$= x \sin^{-1} x + (1-x^2)^{\frac{1}{2}} + C$$

$$(\because t = 1 - x^2)$$

So the correct option is (d).

38. Find the integral of $x^2 . \sin^{-1} x \, dx$

(a) $\frac{1}{3} x^3 \sin^{-1} x - \frac{1}{3} \sqrt{1-x^2} - \frac{1}{9}(1-x^2)^{3/2} + C$

(b) $\frac{1}{3} x^3 \sin^{-1} x + \frac{1}{3} \sqrt{1-x^2} - \frac{1}{9}(1-x^2)^{3/2} + C$

(c) $\frac{1}{3} x^3 \sin^{-1} x + \frac{1}{3} \sqrt{1+x^2} + \frac{1}{9}(1-x^2)^{-3/2} + C$

(d) $\frac{1}{3} x^3 \sin^{-1} x - \frac{1}{3} \sqrt{1-x^2} + \frac{1}{9}(1-x^2)^{3/2} + C$

Sol. (b) $\frac{1}{3} x^3 \sin^{-1} x + \frac{1}{3} \sqrt{1-x^2} - \frac{1}{9}(1-x^2)^{3/2} + C$

Explanation :

The given integral is

$$I = \int x^2 . \sin^{-1} x \, dx$$

Integrating by parts, taking $\sin^{-1} x$ as the first function, we get

$$I = \int x^2 . \sin^{-1} x \, dx$$

$$= \sin^{-1} x . \frac{x^3}{3} - \int \frac{1}{\sqrt{1-x^2}} . \frac{x^3}{3} \, dx$$

$$= \sin^{-1} x . \frac{x^3}{3} - \frac{1}{3} \int \frac{x^3}{\sqrt{1-x^2}} \, dx$$

$$= \frac{x^3}{3} . \sin^{-1} x - \frac{1}{3} \int \frac{x \cdot x^2}{\sqrt{1-x^2}} \, dx$$

Substituting t^2 for $1 - x^2$ and differentiate w.r.t. x.

$$\frac{d}{dx}(1-x^2) = \frac{d}{dx}(t^2)$$

$$\Rightarrow \qquad -2x = 2t \frac{dt}{dx}$$

$$\Rightarrow \qquad x \, dx = -t \, dt$$

Substitute the values, $1 - x^2 = t^2$ and $x \, dx = -t \, dt$ in the integral.

$$\therefore \quad I = \frac{x^3}{3} \sin^{-1} x - \frac{1}{3} \int \frac{(-t).(1-t^2)}{t} \, dt$$

$$= \frac{x^3}{3} \sin^{-1} x + \frac{1}{3} \int 1 \, dt - \frac{1}{3} \int t^2 \, dt$$

$$= \frac{x^3}{3} \sin^{-1} x + \frac{1}{3} t - \frac{1}{9} t^3 + C$$

$$= \frac{1}{3} x^3 \sin^{-1} x + \frac{1}{3} \sqrt{1-x^2} - \frac{1}{9}(1-x^2)^{3/2} + C$$

So, the correct option is (b).

39. Evaluate the integral :

$$\int e^x (\cos x - \sin x) \, dx$$

(a) $e^x \sin x + C$ (b) $\cos x + C$

(c) $e^x \cos x + C$ (d) $e^{-x} \cos x + C$

Sol. (c) $e^x \cos x + C$

Explanation :

The given integral is,

$$I = \int e^x (\cos x - \sin x) \, dx$$

Let, $\qquad f(x) = \cos x$

Differentiating $f(x)$,

$$f'(x) = -\sin x$$

Substitute $f(x)$ for $\cos x$ and $f'(x)$ for $-\sin x$ in the given integral.

$$I = \int e^x (\cos x - \sin x) \, dx$$

$$= \int e^x \{f(x) + f'(x)\} \, dx$$

We know that $\int e^x \{f(x) + f'(x)\} \, dx$

$$= e^x f(x) + C$$

$$\therefore \qquad I = e^x \cos x + C$$

So the correct option is (c).

40. Find the value of:

$$\int e^x \left(\frac{1}{x^4} - \frac{1}{3x^3} \right) dx.$$

(a) $e^x \dfrac{1}{x^4} + C$ (b) $e^x x^2 + C$

(c) $e^x x + C$ (d) $e^x + C$

Sol. (a) $e^x \dfrac{1}{x^4} + C$

Explanation :

The given integral is,

$$I = \int e^x \left(\frac{1}{x^4} - \frac{1}{3x^3} \right) dx$$

Let, $\quad f(x) = \dfrac{1}{x^4}$

Differentiating $f(x)$,

$$f'(x) = -\frac{1}{3x^3}$$

Substituting $f(x)$ for $\dfrac{1}{x^4}$ and $f'(x)$ for $-\dfrac{1}{3x^3}$ in the given integral, we get

$$I = \int e^x \left(\frac{1}{x^4} - \frac{1}{3x^3} \right) dx$$

$$= \int e^x \{ f(x) + f'(x) \} dx$$

We know that

$$\int e^x \{ f(x) + f'(x) \} dx = e^x f(x) + C$$

$$\therefore \qquad I = e^x \frac{1}{x^4} + C$$

So the correct option is (a).

41. $\displaystyle\int_{-\pi/4}^{\pi/4} \frac{dx}{1+\cos 2x}$ is equal to:

[NCERT Exemplar]

(a) 1 (b) 2

(c) 3 (d) 4

Sol. (a) 1

Explanation :

Let $\quad I = \displaystyle\int_{-\pi/4}^{\pi/4} \frac{dx}{1+\cos 2x}$

$$= \int_{-\pi/4}^{\pi/4} \frac{dx}{2\cos^2 x}$$

$$= \frac{1}{2} \int_{-\pi/4}^{\pi/4} \sec^2 x \, dx = \int_0^{\pi/4} \sec^2 x \, dx$$

$$= [\tan x]_0^{\pi/4} = \tan \frac{\pi}{4} - \tan 0$$

$$= 1 - 0 = 1.$$

42. $\displaystyle\int_0^{\pi/2} \sqrt{1 - \sin 2x} \; dx$ is equal to:

[NCERT Exemplar]

(a) $2\sqrt{2}$ (b) $2(\sqrt{2}+1)$

(c) 2 (d) $2(\sqrt{2}-1)$

Sol. (d) $2(\sqrt{2}-1)$

Explanation :

Let $\quad I = \displaystyle\int_0^{\pi/2} \sqrt{1 - \sin 2x} \; dx$

$$= \int_0^{\pi/2} \sqrt{\cos^2 x + \sin^2 x - 2 \sin x \cos x} \; dx$$

$$= \int_0^{\pi/4} \sqrt{(\cos x - \sin x)^2} \; dx$$

$$= \int_0^{\pi/4} \sqrt{(\cos x - \sin x)^2} \; dx$$

$$\left[\because \cos x > \sin x \text{ for } x \in \left(0, \frac{\pi}{4} \right) \right]$$

$$+ \int_{\pi/4}^{\pi/2} \sqrt{(\sin x - \cos x)^2} \; dx$$

$$\left[\because \sin x > \cos x \text{ for } x \in \left(\frac{\pi}{4}, \frac{\pi}{2} \right) \right]$$

$$= [\sin x + \cos x]_0^{\pi/4} + [-\cos x - \sin x]_{\pi/4}^{\pi/2}$$

$$= \left[\sin \frac{\pi}{4} + \cos \frac{\pi}{4} - \sin 0 - \cos 0 \right]$$

$$+ \left[-\cos \frac{\pi}{2} - \sin \frac{\pi}{2} + \cos \frac{\pi}{4} + \sin \frac{\pi}{4} \right]$$

$$= \frac{1}{\sqrt{2}} + \frac{1}{\sqrt{2}} - 0 - 1 + \left(-0 - 1 + \frac{1}{\sqrt{2}} + \frac{1}{\sqrt{2}} \right)$$

$$= 2\sqrt{2} - 2 = 2(\sqrt{2}-1).$$

43. $\displaystyle\int_0^{\pi/2} \cos x e^{\sin x} \; dx$ is equal to:

[NCERT Exemplar]

(a) $e + 1$ (b) $e - 1$

(c) e (d) $-e$

Sol. (b) $e - 1$

Explanation :

Let $\quad I = \displaystyle\int_0^{\pi/2} \cos x e^{\sin x} \; dx$

Put $\qquad \sin x = t$

$\Rightarrow \qquad \cos x \, dx = dt$

As $x \to 0$, then $t \to 0$

and $x \to \pi/2$, then $t \to 1$

$$\therefore \qquad I = \int_0^1 e^t \, dt = [e^t]_0^1$$

$$= e^1 - e^0$$

$$= e - 1.$$

44. $\int_1^2 e^x \left(\dfrac{1}{x} - \dfrac{1}{x^2} \right) dx =$

(a) $\dfrac{e^2}{2} + e$

(b) $e - \dfrac{e^2}{2}$

(c) $\dfrac{e^2}{2} - e$

(d) None of these

Sol. (c) $\dfrac{e^2}{2} - e$

Explanation :

$$\int_1^2 e^x \left(\dfrac{1}{x} - \dfrac{1}{x^2} \right) dx = \left[\dfrac{1}{x} e^x \right]_1^2$$

$$\left[\because \int e^x \left[f(x) + f'(x) \right] dx = e^x \, f(x) + C \right]$$

$$= \dfrac{e^2}{2} - e.$$

45. $\int_0^{\pi/2} \dfrac{\cos x}{(1+\sin x)(2+\sin x)} \, dx =$

(a) $\log \dfrac{4}{3}$

(b) $\log \dfrac{3}{4}$

(c) $\log \dfrac{1}{3}$

(d) None of these

Sol. (a) $\log \dfrac{4}{3}$

Explanation :

Put $\sin x = t \Rightarrow \cos x \, dx = dt$, at $x = 0$, $t = 0$; at $x = \pi/2$, $t = 1$

so that reduced integral is

$$\int_0^1 \dfrac{dt}{(1+t)(2+t)} = \int_0^1 \left(\dfrac{1}{1+t} - \dfrac{1}{2+t} \right) dt$$

$$= [\log (1+t) - \log (2+t)]_0^1$$

$$= [\log 2 - \log 3] - [\log 1 - \log 2]$$

$$= \log \dfrac{2}{3} - \log \dfrac{1}{2} = \log \dfrac{4}{3}.$$

46. $\int_0^2 \sqrt{\dfrac{2+x}{2-x}} \, dx =$

(a) $\pi + 2$

(b) $\pi + \dfrac{3}{2}$

(c) $\pi + 1$

(d) None of these

Sol. (a) $\pi + 2$

Explanation :

Put $x = 2 \cos \theta \Rightarrow dx = -2 \sin \theta \, d\theta$,

At $x = 0 \Rightarrow 0 = 2 \cos \theta \Rightarrow \cos \theta = \cos \dfrac{\pi}{2} \Rightarrow \theta = \dfrac{\pi}{2}$

and $x = 2 \Rightarrow 2 = 2 \cos \theta \Rightarrow \cos \theta = \cos 0° \Rightarrow \theta = 0$.

then $\int_0^2 \sqrt{\dfrac{2+x}{2-x}} \, dx$

$$= \int_{\pi/2}^0 \sqrt{\dfrac{2+2\cos\theta}{2-2\cos\theta}} (-2 \sin \theta) \, d\theta$$

$$= -\int_0^{\pi/2} \sqrt{\dfrac{1+\cos\theta}{1-\cos\theta}} (-2 \sin \theta) \, d\theta$$

$$= 2\int_0^{\pi/2} \sqrt{\dfrac{1+2\cos^2 \dfrac{\theta}{2} - 1}{1-\left(1-2\sin^2 \dfrac{\theta}{2}\right)}} \cdot 2 \sin \dfrac{\theta}{2} \cos \dfrac{\theta}{2} \, d\theta$$

$$= 2\int_0^{\pi/2} \dfrac{\cos \dfrac{\theta}{2}}{\sin \dfrac{\theta}{2}} \, 2 \sin \dfrac{\theta}{2} \cos \dfrac{\theta}{2} \, d\theta$$

$$= 2\int_0^{\pi/2} 2 \cos^2 \dfrac{\theta}{2} \, d\theta$$

$$= 2\int_0^{\pi/2} (1+\cos \theta) \, d\theta$$

$$= 2[\theta + \sin \theta]_0^{\pi/2} = 2\left[\dfrac{\pi}{2} + 1 \right]$$

$$= \pi + 2.$$

47. $\int_{-4}^4 |x+2| \, dx =$

(a) 50

(b) 24

(c) 20

(d) None of these

Sol. (c) 20

Explanation :

$$\int_{-4}^4 |x+2| \, dx = \int_{-4}^{-2} -(x+2) \, dx + \int_{-2}^4 (x+2) \, dx$$

$$= \left[\dfrac{-x^2}{2} - 2x \right]_{-4}^{-2} + \left[\dfrac{x^2}{2} + 2x \right]_{-2}^4$$

$$= \left[\dfrac{-4}{2} + 4 + \dfrac{16}{2} - 8 \right] + \left[\dfrac{16}{2} + 8 - \dfrac{4}{2} + 4 \right]$$

$$= 2 + 18$$

$$= 20.$$

48. $\int_0^{\pi/2} \dfrac{\cos x - \sin x}{1 + \sin x \cos x} \, dx =$

(a) 2

(b) -2

(c) 0

(d) None of these

Sol. (c) 0

Explanation :

$$\int_0^{\pi/2} \dfrac{\cos x - \sin x}{1 + \sin x \cos x} \, dx = I \qquad \ldots(i)$$

Now $I = \int_0^{\pi/2} \dfrac{\cos\left(\dfrac{\pi}{2}-x\right)-\sin\left(\dfrac{\pi}{2}-x\right)}{1+\sin\left(\dfrac{\pi}{2}-x\right)\cos\left(\dfrac{\pi}{2}-x\right)}\, dx$

$$\left[\because \int_0^a f(x)\, dx = \int_0^a f(a-x)\, dx\right]$$

$$= \int_0^{\pi/2} \frac{\sin x - \cos x}{1+\sin x \cos x}\, dx \qquad \ldots(ii)$$

On adding (i + ii),
$$2I = 0 \Rightarrow I = 0.$$

49. $\int_{-1/2}^{1/2} (\cos x)\left[\log\left(\dfrac{1-x}{1+x}\right)\right]dx =$

(a)　0　　　　　　　　(b)　1
(c)　$e^{1/2}$　　　　　　(d)　$2e^{1/2}$

Sol. (a)　0

Explanation :

$$I = \int_{-1/2}^{1/2} (\cos x)\left[\log\left(\frac{1-x}{1+x}\right)\right]dx \qquad \ldots(i)$$

$$\Rightarrow \quad I = \int_{-1/2}^{1/2} \cos(-x)\left[\log\left(\frac{1+x}{1-x}\right)\right]dx$$

$$\left[\because \int_0^a f(x)dx = \int_0^c f(ax-x)\, dx\right]$$

$$\Rightarrow \quad I = -\int_{-1/2}^{1/2} \cos x\left[\log\left(\frac{1-x}{1+x}\right)\right]dx \qquad \ldots(ii)$$

Adding (i) and (ii), we get

$$2I = \int_{-1/2}^{1/2} \cos x\left[\log\left(\frac{1-x}{1+x}\right)\right]dx$$

$$-\int_{-1/2}^{1/2} \cos x\left[\log\left(\frac{1-x}{1+x}\right)\right]dx$$

or　　$2I = 0$ or $I = 0.$　　　　$[\because \log(1) = 0]$

50. $\int_0^{1.5} [x^2]\, dx,$ where $[\,.\,]$ denotes the greatest integer function, equals:*

(a)　$2+\sqrt{2}$　　　　　(b)　$2-\sqrt{2}$

(c)　$-2+\sqrt{2}$　　　　(d)　$-2-\sqrt{2}$

Sol. (b)　$2-\sqrt{2}$

Explanation :

$$\int_0^{1.5} [x^2]\, dx = \int_0^1 [x^2]\, dx + \int_1^{\sqrt{2}} [x^2]\, dx + \int_{\sqrt{2}}^{1.5} [x^2]\, dx$$

$$= 0 + \int_1^{\sqrt{2}} 1\, dx + \int_{\sqrt{2}}^{1.5} 2\, dx$$

$$= \sqrt{2} - 1 + 3 - 2\sqrt{2}$$

$$= 2 - \sqrt{2}.$$

---

51. $\int_0^{\pi/2} \sin 2x \log \tan x \, dx$ is equal to:

(a)　π　　　　　　　　(b)　$\pi/2$
(c)　0　　　　　　　　(d)　2π

Sol. (c)　0

Explanation :

$$I = \int_0^{\pi/2} \sin 2x \log \tan x \, dx \qquad \ldots(1)$$

$$\Rightarrow \quad I = \int_0^{\pi/2} \sin 2\left(\frac{\pi}{2}-x\right)\log \tan\left(\frac{\pi}{2}-x\right) dx$$

$$\left[\because \int_0^a f(x)\, dx = \int_0^a f(a-x)\, dx\right]$$

$$= \int_0^{\pi/2} \sin 2x \log \cot x \, dx \qquad \ldots(2)$$

Adding (1) and (2), we get

$$\Rightarrow \quad 2I = \int_0^{\pi/2} \sin 2x \, [\log \tan x + \log \cot x]\, dx$$

$$= \int_0^{\pi/2} \sin 2x.\log\, [\tan x.\cot x]\, dx$$

$$= \int_0^{\pi/2} \sin 2x.\log 1 \, dx \quad \left[\because \tan x = \frac{1}{\cot x}\right]$$

$$2I = 0 \qquad\qquad [\because \log 1 = 0]$$

$$\Rightarrow \quad I = 0.$$

52. $\int_0^{\pi/8} \tan^2 (2x)\, dx$ is equal to*

(a)　$\dfrac{4-\pi}{8}$　　　　　　(b)　$\dfrac{4+\pi}{8}$

(c)　$\dfrac{4-\pi}{4}$　　　　　　(d)　$\dfrac{4-\pi}{2}$

Sol. (a)　$\dfrac{4-\pi}{8}$

Explanation :

$$\int_0^{\pi/8} \tan^2(2x)\, dx = \int_0^{\pi/8} \left(\sec^2(2x)-1\right) dx$$

$$= \left[\frac{\tan(2x)}{2} - x\right]_0^{\pi/8}$$

$$= \frac{1}{2} - \frac{\pi}{8} + 0 - 0$$

$$= \frac{4-\pi}{8}$$

So the correct option is (a).

Assertion and Reason Based Questions

(a) Both (A) and (R) are individually true and (R) is the correct explanation of (A).

(b) Both (A) and (R) are individually true but (R) is not the correct explanation of (A).

(c) (A) is true but (R) is false.

(d) (A) is false but (R) is true.

53. Assertion (A) : $\int \tan 5x \, \tan 3x \, \tan 2x \, dx =$

$$= \frac{\log|\sec 5x|}{5} - \frac{\log|\sec 3x|}{3} - \frac{\log|\sec 2x|}{2} + C$$

Reason (R) :

$$\tan 5x - \tan 3x - \tan 2x = \tan 5x \, \tan 3x \, \tan 2x$$

Sol. (a) Both (A) and (R) are individually true and (R) is the correct explanation of (A).

Explanation :

$$\because \qquad 5x = 3x + 2x$$

$$\therefore \qquad \tan 5x = \frac{\tan 3x + \tan 2x}{1 - \tan 3x \tan 2x}$$

$$\therefore \ \tan 5x - \tan 3x - \tan 2x = \tan 5x \, \tan 3x \, \tan 2x$$

54. Assertion (A) : If $y(x-y)^2 = x$, then

$$\int \frac{dx}{(x-3y)} = \frac{1}{2} \ln \{(x-y)^2 - 1\}$$

Reason (R) : $\displaystyle \int \frac{dx}{(x-3y)} = \ln(x-3y) + C$

Sol. (c) (A) is true but (R) is false.

Explanation :

Let $\qquad P = \displaystyle\int \frac{dx}{(x-3y)} = \frac{1}{2} \log \{(x-y)^2 - 1\}$

$\therefore \qquad P = \displaystyle\int \frac{dx}{(x-3y)}$

$\Rightarrow \qquad \dfrac{dP}{dx} = \dfrac{1}{(x-3y)} \qquad \qquad \text{...(i)}$

Also, $\qquad P = \dfrac{1}{2} \log \{(x-y)^2 - 1\}$

$\therefore \qquad \dfrac{dP}{dx} = \dfrac{2(x-y)\left(1 - \dfrac{dy}{dx}\right)}{2\{(x-y)^2 - 1\}}$

$$= \frac{(x-y)\left(1 - \dfrac{dy}{dx}\right)}{(x-y)^2 - 1} \qquad \text{...(ii)}$$

Given, $\qquad \qquad y(x-y)^2 = x$

$$\log y + 2 \log(x-y) = \log x$$

$\Rightarrow \quad \dfrac{1}{y}\dfrac{dy}{dx} + \dfrac{2}{(x-y)}\left(1 - \dfrac{dy}{dx}\right) = \dfrac{1}{x}$

$\Rightarrow \quad \dfrac{dy}{dx}\left(\dfrac{1}{y} - \dfrac{2}{x-y}\right) = \dfrac{1}{x} - \dfrac{2}{x-y} = \dfrac{x-y-2x}{x(x-y)}$

$\Rightarrow \quad \dfrac{dy}{dx}\left(\dfrac{x-3y}{y(x-y)}\right) = -\dfrac{(x+y)}{x(x-y)}$

or $\qquad \dfrac{dy}{dx} = -\dfrac{y(x+y)}{x(x-3y)}$

Now, from equation (ii),

$$\frac{dP}{dx} = \frac{(x-y)\left\{1 + \dfrac{y(x+y)}{x(x-3y)}\right\}}{(x-y)^2 - 1}$$

$$= \frac{(x-y)\left\{\dfrac{x^2 - 2xy + y^2}{x(x-3y)}\right\}}{\left(\dfrac{x}{y} - 1\right)} \quad [\because y(x-y)^2 = x]$$

$$= \frac{y(x-y)^2}{x(x-3y)} = \frac{1}{x-3y} \ [\because y(x-y)^2 = x] \ \text{...(iii)}$$

$\therefore$ It is true from (i),

Hence, $\displaystyle\int \frac{dx}{x-3y} = \frac{1}{2} \log \{(x-y)^2 - 1\}$

$\because y$ is variable

$\therefore \qquad \displaystyle\int \frac{dx}{x-3y} \neq \log(x-3y) + C$

55. Assertion (A) : $\displaystyle\int e^{x^2} dx = e^{x^2} + C$

Reason (R) : $\displaystyle\int e^x dx = e^x + C$

Sol. (d) (A) is false but (R) is true.

Explanation :

$\because \displaystyle\int e^{x^2} dx$ cannot expressed in terms of elementary function, then integral is known as inexpressible or that is "cannot be found".

56. Assertion (A) : If $\displaystyle\int \frac{1}{f(x)} dx = 2 \log |f(x)| + C$,

then $f(x) = \dfrac{x}{2}$

Reason (R) : When $f(x) = \dfrac{x}{2}$ then

$$\int \frac{1}{f(x)} dx = \int \frac{2}{x} dx = 2 \log |x| + C$$

Sol. (a) Both (A) and (R) are individually true and (R) is the correct explanation of (A).

Explanation :

$$\because \quad \int \frac{1}{f(x)}\, dx = 2 \log \mid f(x) \mid + C$$

Differentiating both sides w.r.t. x, then

$$\because \quad \frac{1}{f(x)} = \frac{2}{f(x)} f'(x)$$

or $\qquad f'(x) = \dfrac{1}{2}$

$$\therefore \qquad f(x) = \frac{x}{2} + C$$

If $\qquad f(0) = 0, \therefore f(x) = \dfrac{x}{2}\cdot$

then $\qquad C = 0.$

57. Assertion (A) : The function $F(x) = \int \sin^2 x\, dx$

satisfies $F(x + \pi) = F(x)\ \forall\ x \in R$

Reason (R) : $\sin^2 (x + \pi) = \sin^2 x$

Sol. (a) Both (A) and (R) are individually true and (R) is the correct explanation of (A).

Explanation :

$$\because \quad F(x + \pi) = \int \sin^2 (x + \pi)\, dx$$

$$= \int \sin^2 x\, dx \quad [\because \sin^2 (x + \pi) = \sin^2 x]$$

$$= F(x).$$

58. Assertion (A) : If $I_n = \int \cot^n x\, dx$, then

$$5(I_6 + I_4) = - \cot^5 x$$

Reason (R) : If $I_n = \int \cot^n x\, dx$

then $I_n = - \dfrac{\cot^{n-1} x}{n} - I_{n-2}$, where $n \geq 2$

Sol. (c) (A) is true but (R) is false.

Explanation :

$$\because \quad I_n = \int \cot^n x\, dx$$

$$= \int \cot^{n-2} x \cdot (\operatorname{cosec}^2 x - 1)\, dx$$

$$= \int \cot^{n-2} x\, \operatorname{cosec}^2 x\, dx - I_{n-2}$$

$$= - \frac{\cot^{n-1} x}{(n-1)} - I_{n-2}$$

For $n = 6$

$$5(I_6 + I_4) = - \cot^5 x.$$

59. Assertion (A) : $\int e^x (\tan x + \sec^2 x)\, dx = e^x \cdot \tan x + C$

Reason (R) : $\int e^x \{f(x) + f'(x)\}\, dx = e^x f(x) + C$

Sol. (a) Both (A) and (R) are individually true and (R) is the correct explanation of (A).

Explanation :

$$\because \quad \int e^x \{f(x) + f'(x)\}\, dx$$

$$= \int e^x f(x)\, dx + \int e^x f'(x)\, dx$$

$$= f(x) \cdot e^x - \int f'(x)\, e^x dx + \int e^x f'(x)\, dx$$

$$= e^x f(x)$$

For $\quad f(x) = \tan x$

$$\int e^x (\tan x + \sec^2 x)\, dx = e^x \cdot \tan x + C.$$

60. Assertion (A) : $\int \dfrac{dx}{\sqrt{1 - (x^2)^2}} = \sin^{-1} x^2 + C$

Reason (R) : $\int \dfrac{dx}{\sqrt{1 - x^2}} = \sin^{-1} x + C$

Sol. (d) (A) is false but (R) is true.

Explanation :

The formula $\int \dfrac{dx}{\sqrt{1 - x^{2n}}} = \sin^{-1} x^n$

is valid only for $n = 1$.

61. Assertion (A) :

$$\int \frac{(3 - 2x)}{\sqrt{(4 + 2x - x^2)}}\, dx$$

$$= 2\sqrt{(4 + 2x - x^2)} + \sin^{-1} \left(\frac{x - 1}{\sqrt{5}} \right) + C$$

Reason (R) :

$$\int \frac{dx}{\sqrt{(a^2 - x^2)}} = \frac{x}{2} \sqrt{a^2 - x^2} + \frac{a^2}{2} \sin^{-1} \left(\frac{x}{a} \right) + C$$

Sol. (c) (A) is true but (R) is false.

Explanation :

Let $\qquad I = \int \dfrac{(3 - 2x)}{\sqrt{(4 + 2x - x^2)}}\, dx$

$$= \int \frac{(2 - 2x)}{\sqrt{(4 + 2x - x^2)}}\, dx + \int \frac{dx}{\sqrt{(4 + 2x - x^2)}}$$

$$= 2\sqrt{(4 + 2x - x^2)} + \int \frac{dx}{\sqrt{5 - (x - 1)^2}}$$

$$= 2\sqrt{(4 + 2x - x^2)} + \sin^{-1} \left(\frac{x - 1}{\sqrt{5}} \right) + C$$

and $\int \sqrt{(a^2 - x^2)}\, dx$

$$= \frac{x}{2} \sqrt{(a^2 - x^2)} + \frac{a^2}{2} \sin^{-1} \left(\frac{x}{a} \right) + C$$

62. Assertion (A) : $\int_{-1}^{1} |x|\, dx$ can be found while $\int |x|\, dx$ can not be found.

Reason (R) : $|x|$ is non-differentiable at $x = 0$.

Sol. (b) Both (A) and (R) are individually true but (R) is not the corect explanation of (A).

Explanation :

$$\because \quad \int_{-1}^{1} |x|\, dx = \int_{-1}^{0} |x|\, dx + \int_{0}^{1} |x|\, dx$$

$$= \int_{-1}^{0} (-x)\, dx + \int_{0}^{1} (x)\, dx$$

$$= -\left\{\frac{x^2}{2}\right\}_{-1}^{0} + \left\{\frac{x^2}{2}\right\}_{0}^{1}$$

$$= -\left(0 - \frac{1}{2}\right) + \left(\frac{1}{2} - 0\right) = 1$$

and $\int |x|\, dx$ cannot be found, since condition on x is not given.

Also, $|x|$ is non-differentiable at $x = 0$.

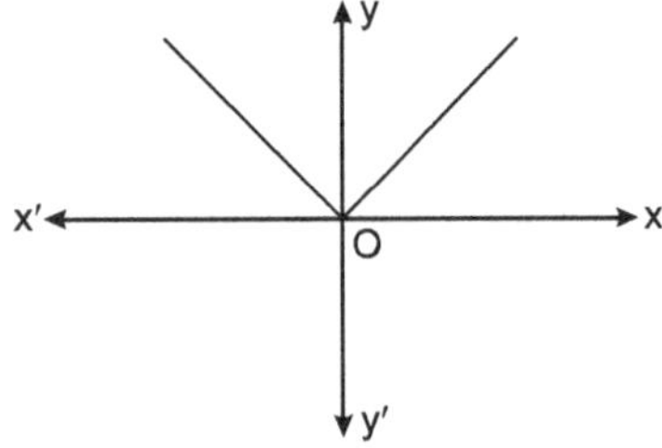

63. Assertion (A) : $F(x) = \int_{0}^{x} \log\left(\dfrac{1-t}{1+t}\right) dt$ is an even function.

Reason (R) : $\log\left(\dfrac{1-t}{1+t}\right)$ is an odd function.

Sol. (a) Both (A) and (R) are individually true and (R) is the correct explanation of (A).

Explanation :

$$\because \qquad F(x) = \int_{0}^{x} \log\left(\frac{1-t}{1+t}\right) dt$$

$$\therefore \qquad F'(x) = \log\left(\frac{1-x}{1+x}\right)$$

$$\Rightarrow \qquad F'(-x) = \log\left(\frac{1+x}{1-x}\right) = -\log\left(\frac{1-x}{1+x}\right)$$

$$= -F'(x)$$

$\Rightarrow$ F$'(x)$ is an odd function.

Hence, F$'(x)$ is an odd function.

64. Assertion (A) : $\int_{0}^{1} e^{-x} \cos^2 x\, dx < \int_{0}^{1} e^{-x^2} \cos^2 x\, dx$

Reason (R) : $\int_{a}^{b} f(x)\, dx < \int_{a}^{b} g(x)\, dx \ \forall\ f(x) \geq g(x)$

Sol. (c) (A) is true but (R) is false.

Explanation :

$$\because \qquad\qquad 0 < x < 1$$

$$\text{Then} \qquad\qquad x > x^2$$

$$\Rightarrow \qquad\qquad -x < -x^2$$

$$\Rightarrow \qquad\qquad e^{-x} < e^{-x^2}$$

$$\Rightarrow \qquad e^{-x} \cos^2 x < e^{-x^2} \cos^2 x$$

$$\text{Then,} \quad \int_{0}^{1} e^{-x} \cos^2 x\, dx < \int_{0}^{1} e^{-x^2} \cos^2 x\, dx$$

$$\text{and if} \qquad\qquad f(x) \geq g(x)$$

$$\text{Then,} \qquad \int_{a}^{b} f(x)\, dx \geq \int_{a}^{b} g(x)\, dx$$

65. Assertion (A) : $\int_{0}^{\pi/2} \dfrac{\sin x}{x}\, dx < \dfrac{\pi}{2}$

Reason (R) : $\lim\limits_{x \to 0} \dfrac{\sin x}{x} = 1$

Sol. (b) Both (A) and (R) are individually true but (R) is not the correct explanation of (A).

Explanation :

$$\text{For} \qquad\qquad x > 0$$

$$\sin x < x$$

$$\Rightarrow \qquad\qquad \frac{\sin x}{x} < 1$$

$$\Rightarrow \quad \int_{0}^{\pi/2} \frac{\sin x}{x}\, dx < \int_{0}^{\pi/2} 1 \cdot dx$$

$$\Rightarrow \quad \int_{0}^{\pi/2} \frac{\sin x}{x}\, dx < \frac{\pi}{2}$$

$$\text{and} \qquad \lim_{x \to 0} \frac{\sin x}{x} = 1.$$

66. Assertion (A) : $\int_{\pi/6}^{\pi/3} \dfrac{(\sin x)^{\sqrt{2}}}{(\sin x)^{\sqrt{2}} + (\cos x)^{\sqrt{2}}}\, dx = \dfrac{\pi}{12}$

Reason (R) : $\int_{\pi/6}^{\pi/3} \dfrac{f(x)\, dx}{f(x) + f\left(\dfrac{\pi}{2} - x\right)}\, dx = \dfrac{\pi}{12}$

Sol. (a) Both (A) and (R) are individually true and (R) is the correct explanation of (A).

Explanation :

$$\text{Let I} = \int_{\pi/6}^{\pi/3} \frac{f(x)}{f(x) + f\left(\dfrac{\pi}{2} - x\right)}\, dx \qquad \text{...(i)}$$

$$= \int_{\pi/6}^{\pi/3} \frac{f\left(\dfrac{\pi}{3} + \dfrac{\pi}{6} - x\right)}{f\left(\dfrac{\pi}{3} + \dfrac{\pi}{6} - x\right) + f\left[\dfrac{\pi}{2} - \left(\dfrac{\pi}{3} + \dfrac{\pi}{6} - x\right)\right]}\, dx$$

(by property)

$$= \int_{\pi/6}^{\pi/3} \frac{f\left(\frac{\pi}{2}-x\right)}{f\left(\frac{\pi}{2}-x\right)+f(x)}\, dx \qquad \text{...(ii)}$$

Adding equations (i) and (ii), then

$$2I = \int_{\pi/6}^{\pi/3} 1.\, dx = \frac{\pi}{3} - \frac{\pi}{6} = \frac{\pi}{6}$$

$$\therefore \qquad I = \frac{\pi}{12}$$

Also for $f(x) = (\sin x)^{\sqrt{2}}$, $I = \dfrac{\pi}{12}$.

67. Assertion (A) : If

$$\int_0^1 e^{\sin x} dx = \lambda, \text{ then } \int_0^{200} e^{\sin x} dx = 200\lambda$$

Reason (R) : $\int_0^{na} f(x)\, dx = n\int_0^a f(x)\, dx$, $n \in I$ and

$f(a + x) = f(x)$

Sol. (d) (A) is false but (R) is true.

Explanation :

∵ Period of $e^{\sin x}$ is 2π

$$\therefore \qquad \int_0^{200} e^{\sin x} dx \ne 200.$$

68. Assertion (A) : $\int_1^6 \{x+5\}^2 dx = 41,$

where { } denotes the fractional part function.

Reason (R) : $\{x + 5\}$ is a periodic function.

Sol. (d) (A) is false but (R) is true.

Explanation :

$$\therefore \quad \int_1^6 \{x+5\}^2 dx = \int_0^5 \{x+6\}^2 dx \quad \text{(by property)}$$

$$= \int_0^5 \{x\}^2\, dx = 5\int_0^1 \{x\}^2 dx$$

$$[\because \{\ \} \text{ is periodic with period 1}]$$

$$= 5\int_0^1 x^2 dx$$

$$= \frac{5}{3}.$$

69. Assertion (A) : $\int_0^{2\pi} \sin^3 x\, dx = 0$

Reason (R) : $\sin^3 x$ is an odd function.

Sol. (a) Both (A) and (R) are individually true and (R) is the correct explanation of (A).

Explanation :

Now $\qquad f(x) = \sin^3 x$

and $\qquad f(-x) = -\sin^3 x$

Clearly $\qquad f(-x) = -f(x)$

$\therefore f(x)$ is odd – (R) is correct.

Also $\quad \int_0^{2a} f(x)\, dx = \begin{cases} 2\int_0^a f(x)\, dx & \text{if } f(x) \text{ is even} \\ 0 & \text{if } f(x) \text{ is odd.} \end{cases}$

$$\therefore \quad \int_0^{2\pi} \sin^3 x\, dx = 0 - \text{(A) is correct}$$

Evidently (A) is correct and (R) is the correct explanation of (A).

So answer is (a).

70. Assertion (A) : $\int_{-\pi/2}^{\pi/2} |\sin x|\, dx = 2$

Reason (R) : $\int_a^b f(x)\, dx = \int_a^c f(x)\, dx + \int_c^b f(x)\, dx$,

where $c \in (a, b)$

Sol. (b) Both (A) and (R) are individually true but (R) is not the correct explanation of (A).

Explanation :

∵ $|\sin x|$ is an even function

$$\therefore \quad \int_{-\pi/2}^{\pi/2} |\sin x|\, dx = 2\int_0^{\pi/2} |\sin x|\, dx$$

$$= 2\int_0^{\pi/2} \sin x\, dx$$

$$= -2(\cos x)_0^{\pi/2}$$

$$= -2\,(0-1) = 2.$$

71. Assertion (A) : $\int_{\pi/2}^{3\pi/2} [2\sin x]\, dx = 0,$

where [ ] denotes the greatest integer function.

Reason (R) : $2\sin x$ decreasing function in $\left(\dfrac{\pi}{2}, \dfrac{3\pi}{2}\right)$

Sol. (d) (A) is false but (R) is true.

Explanation :

$$\therefore \quad \int_{\pi/2}^{3\pi/2} [2\sin x]\, dx$$

$$= \int_{\pi/2}^{5\pi/6} [2\sin x]\, dx + \int_{5\pi/6}^{\pi} [2\sin x]\, dx$$

$$+ \int_{\pi}^{7\pi/6} [2\sin x]\, dx + \int_{7\pi/6}^{3\pi/2} [2\sin x]\, dx$$

$$= \int_{\pi/2}^{5\pi/6} 1.\, dx + 0 - \int_{\pi}^{7\pi/6} 1.\, dx - 2\int_{7\pi/6}^{3\pi/2} 1.\, dx$$

$$= \frac{\pi}{3} - \frac{\pi}{6} - \frac{2\pi}{3}$$

$$= -\frac{\pi}{2}$$

$$\left[\because 2\sin x \text{ is decreasing function is } \left(\frac{\pi}{2}, \frac{3\pi}{2}\right)\right]$$

72. Assertion (A) : $\int_0^t \cos x \, dx = \sin t$

Reason (R) : $\cos x$ is continuous in any closed interval $[0, t]$.

Sol. (a) Both (A) and (R) are individually true and (R) is the correct explanation of (A).

Explanation :

$\because \cos x$ is continuous in $[0, t]$

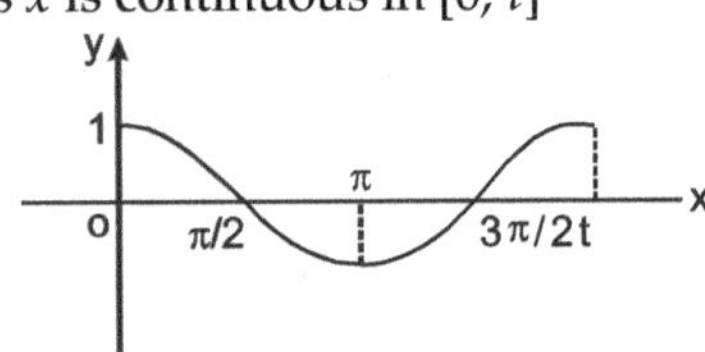

$\therefore \int_0^t \cos x \, dx = [\sin x]_0^t = \sin t - \sin 0 = \sin t$

73. Assertion (A) : $\int_0^{1/4} \dfrac{dx}{1 + (\cot 2\pi x)^{\sqrt{2}}} = \dfrac{1}{4}$

Reason (R) : If $a + b = \pi/2$, then
$$\int_a^b \frac{f(\sin x)}{f(\sin x) + f(\cos x)} \, dx = \frac{(b-a)}{2}$$

Sol. (d) (A) is false but (R) is true.

Explanation :

Let $\quad I = \int_0^{1/4} \dfrac{dx}{1 + (\cot 2\pi x)^{\sqrt{2}}}$

Put $\quad 2\pi x = t$

$\Rightarrow \quad 2\pi \, dx = dt \Rightarrow dx = \dfrac{1}{2\pi} \, dt$

also, at $x = 0$, $t = 0$

at $x = \dfrac{1}{4}$, $t = \dfrac{\pi}{2}$

and we know that
$$\int f(t) \, dt = \int f(x) \, dt$$

$\therefore \quad I = \dfrac{1}{2\pi} \int_0^{\pi/2} \dfrac{dx}{1 + (\cot x)^{\sqrt{2}}}$

$\quad = \dfrac{1}{2\pi} \int_0^{\pi/2} \dfrac{(\sin x)^{\sqrt{2}}}{(\sin x)^{\sqrt{2}} + (\cos x)^{\sqrt{2}}} \, dx$

$\quad = \dfrac{1}{2\pi} \left(\dfrac{\frac{\pi}{2} - 0}{2} \right) = \dfrac{1}{8}$

and $\quad$ let $I_1 = \int_a^b \dfrac{f(\sin x)}{f(\sin x) + f(\cos x)} \, dx \quad \text{...(i)}$

$I_1 = \int_a^b \dfrac{f(\sin(a+b-x))}{f(\sin(a+b-x)) + f(\cos(a+b-x))} \, dx$

$\quad = \int_a^b \dfrac{f(\cos x)}{f(\cos x) + f(\sin x)} \, dx \quad \text{...(ii)}$

Adding equations (i) and (ii), then
$$2I_1 = \int_a^b dx = b - a$$

$\therefore \quad I_1 = \dfrac{(b-a)}{2}$.

74. Assertion (A) : $\int_{-1}^1 \dfrac{|x|}{x} \, dx = 2$

Reason (R) : $\dfrac{|x|}{x}$ is undefined at $x = 0$

Sol. (d) (A) is false but (R) is true.

Explanation :

The function $\dfrac{|x|}{x}$ is undefined at $x = 0$

$\therefore \quad \int_{-1}^1 \dfrac{|x|}{x} \, dx = \int_{-1}^0 \dfrac{|x|}{x} \, dx + \int_0^1 \dfrac{|x|}{x} \, dx$

$\quad = \int_{-1}^0 \dfrac{-x}{x} \, dx + \int_0^1 \dfrac{x}{x} \, dx$

$\quad = -\int_{-1}^0 dx + \int_0^1 dx = -[x]_{-1}^0 + [x]_0^1$

$\quad = -(0 - (-1)) + (1 - 0)$

$\quad = 0.$

75. Assertion (A) : $\int_0^2 f(x) \, dx = \dfrac{4(\sqrt{2}-1)}{3}$,

where $f(x) = \begin{cases} x^2, & \text{for} \quad 0 \le x < 1 \\ \sqrt{x}, & \text{for} \quad 1 \le x \le 2 \end{cases}$

Reason (R) : $f(x)$ is continuous in $[0, 2]$

Sol. (d) (A) is false but (R) is true.

Explanation :

$\because f(x)$ is continuous in $[0, 2]$

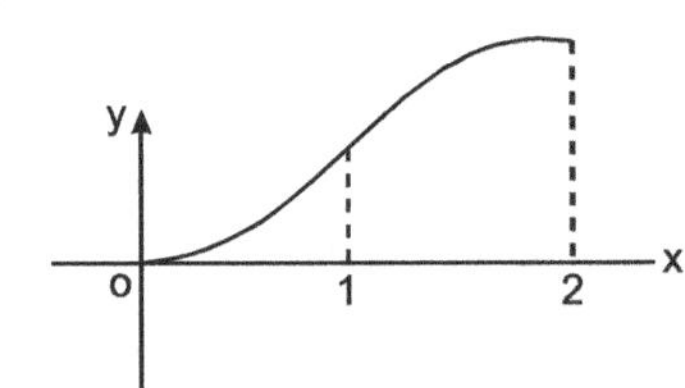

$\therefore \quad \int_0^2 f(x) \, dx = \int_0^1 f(x) \, dx + \int_1^2 f(x) \, dx$

$\quad = \int_0^1 x^2 dx + \int_1^2 \sqrt{x} \, dx$

$\quad = \left[\dfrac{x^3}{3} \right]_0^1 + \left[\dfrac{x^{3/2}}{3/2} \right]_1^2$

$\quad = \dfrac{1}{3} + \dfrac{2}{3}(2^{3/2} - 1) = \dfrac{1}{3} + \dfrac{4\sqrt{2}}{3} - \dfrac{2}{3}$

$\quad = \left(\dfrac{4\sqrt{2}-1}{3} \right).$

76. Assertion (A) : $\int_0^{\pi/2}(\sin^6 x+\cos^6 x)\,dx$ lies in the interval $\left(\dfrac{\pi}{8},\dfrac{\pi}{2}\right)$

Reason (R) : $\sin^6 x+\cos^6 x$ is periodic with period $\pi/2$.

Sol. (b) Both (A) and (R) are individually true but (R) is not the correct explanation of (A).

Explanation :

$\because \sin^6 x + \cos^6 x$

$= (\sin^2 x)^3 + (\cos^2 x)^3$

$= (\sin^2 x + \cos^2 x)^3 - 3\sin^2 x \cos^2 x\,(\sin^2 x + \cos^2 x)$

$= 1 - 3\,\sin^2 x \cos^2 x$

$= 1 - \dfrac{3}{4}\sin^2 2x \quad \left[\because \text{period } \dfrac{\pi}{2}\right]$

$\therefore$ Least and greatest value of $\sin^6 x + \cos^6 x$ are $\dfrac{1}{4}$ and 1

Hence,

$\left(\dfrac{\pi}{2}-0\right)\times\dfrac{1}{4} < \int_0^{\pi/2}(\sin^6 x+\cos^6 x)dx$

$< \left(\dfrac{\pi}{2}-0\right) \times 1$

$\Rightarrow \dfrac{\pi}{8} < \int_0^{\pi/2}(\sin^6 x+\cos^6 x)\,dx < \dfrac{\pi}{2}.$

77. Assertion (A) : If $f(x) = x - x^2 + 1$ and $g(x) = \max \{f(t) : 0 \le t \le x\}$,

then $\int_0^1 g(x)\,dx = \dfrac{29}{24}$

Reason (R) : $f(x)$ is increasing in $\left(0,\dfrac{1}{2}\right)$ and decreasing in $\left(\dfrac{1}{2},1\right)$

Sol. (A) Both (A) and (R) are individually true and (R) is the correct explanation of (A).

Explanation :

$\because \qquad f(x) = x - x^2 + 1$

$\therefore \qquad f'(x) = 1 - 2x$

$f'(x) > 0 \Rightarrow 1 - 2x > 0 \Rightarrow x < \dfrac{1}{2}$

and $\quad f'(x) < 0 \Rightarrow 1 - 2x < 0 \Rightarrow x > \dfrac{1}{2}$

$\Rightarrow f(x)$ is increasing in $\left(0,\dfrac{1}{2}\right)$ and decreasing in $\left(\dfrac{1}{2},1\right)$

Now, $\qquad g(x) = \max \{f(t); 0 \le t \le x\}$

$= \begin{cases} x - x^2 + 1, & 0 \le x \le \dfrac{1}{2} \\[2mm] \dfrac{1}{2} - \dfrac{1}{4} + 1, & \dfrac{1}{2} \le x \le 1 \end{cases}$

$= \begin{cases} x - x^2 + 1, & 0 \le x \le \dfrac{1}{2} \\[2mm] \dfrac{5}{4}, & \dfrac{1}{2} \le x \le 1 \end{cases}$

$\therefore \quad \int_0^1 g(x)\,dx = \int_0^{1/2}(x - x^2 + 1)\,dx + \int_{1/2}^1 \dfrac{5}{4}\,dx$

$= \left[\dfrac{x^2}{2} - \dfrac{x^3}{3} + x\right]_0^{1/2} + \dfrac{5}{4}[x]_{1/2}^1$

$= \left(\dfrac{1}{8} - \dfrac{1}{24} + \dfrac{1}{2}\right) + \dfrac{5}{4}\left(1 - \dfrac{1}{2}\right)$

$= \dfrac{1}{8} - \dfrac{1}{24} + \dfrac{1}{2} + \dfrac{5}{8}$

$= \dfrac{3 - 1 + 12 + 15}{24} = \dfrac{29}{24}.$

Case Based Questions

78. Consider the following equations of curve $x^2 = y$ and $y = x$. On the basis of above informations, answer the following questions :

(i) The point of intersection of both the curve is :

(a) $(0, 0), (2, 2)$ (b) $(0, 0), (1, 1)$

(c) $(0, 0), (-1, -1)$ (d) $(0, 0), (-2, -2)$

Sol. (b) $(0, 0), (1, 1)$

Explanation :

$x^2 = y \ \& \ y = x$

$x^2 = x$

$x^2 - x = 0$

$x(x - 1) = 0$

$x = 0, x = 1$

$y = 0, y = 1$

Intersecting points are $(0, 0), (1, 1)$.

(ii) The graph of the above given curve :

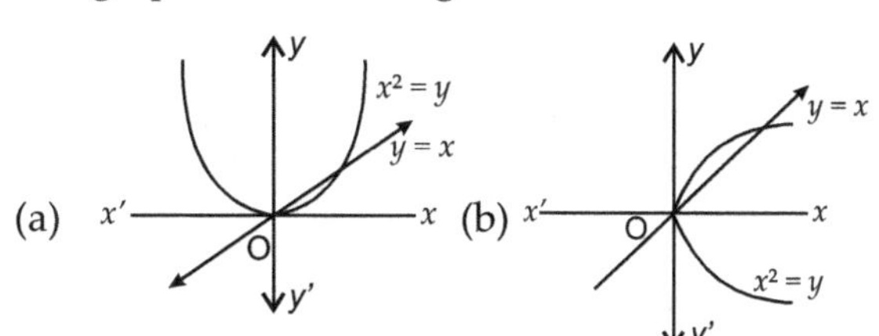

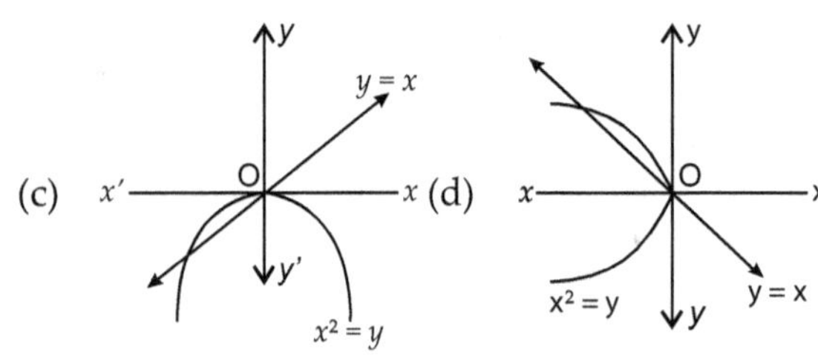

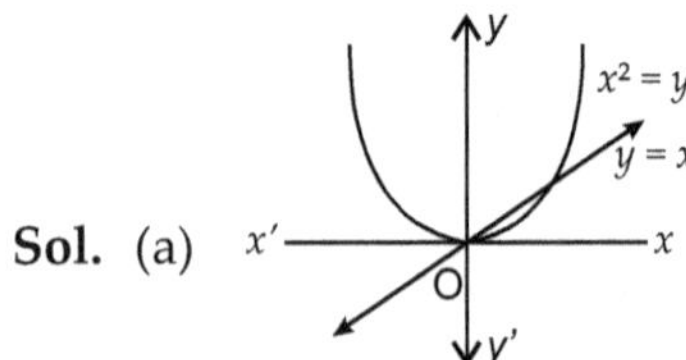

(c) x' ... x (d) ... (graphs of $y = x$, $x^2 = y$)

Sol. (a)

(iii) The value of integral $\int\limits_0^1 x\, dx$ is:

(a) $\dfrac{1}{4}$
(b) $\dfrac{1}{3}$

(c) $\dfrac{1}{2}$
(d) 1

Sol. (c) $\dfrac{1}{2}$

Explanation :

$$\int\limits_0^1 x\,dx = \left.\frac{x^2}{2}\right|_0^1 = \frac{1}{2} - 0$$

$$= \frac{1}{2}$$

(iv) The value of integral $\int\limits_0^1 x^2\, dx$ is :

(a) $\dfrac{1}{4}$
(b) $\dfrac{1}{3}$

(c) $\dfrac{1}{2}$
(d) 1

Sol. (b) $\dfrac{1}{3}$

Explanation :

$$\int\limits_0^1 x^2\,dx = \left.\frac{x^3}{3}\right|_0^1 = \frac{1}{3} - 0 = \frac{1}{3}$$

(v) The value of area bounded by the curves $x^2 = y$ & $y = x$ is :

(a) $\dfrac{1}{8}$
(b) $\dfrac{1}{4}$

(c) $\dfrac{1}{3}$
(d) $\dfrac{1}{2}$

Sol. (a) $\dfrac{1}{8}$

Explanation :

$$\int\limits_0^1 x\,dx - \int\limits_0^1 x^2\,dx$$

$$\frac{1}{2} - \frac{1}{3} = \frac{1}{6}$$

Very Short Answer Type Questions

79. Evaluate : $\int \sin^2 (2x + 5)\, dx.$ **[NCERT]**

Sol. $\int \sin^2 (2x + 5)\, dx$

$$= \int \frac{1 - \cos(4x + 10)}{2}\, dx$$

$$\left[\because \sin^2 x = \frac{1 - \cos 2x}{2} \right]$$

$$= \frac{1}{2}\int 1\, dx - \frac{1}{2}\int \cos(4x + 10)\, dx$$

$$= \frac{x}{2} - \frac{\sin(4x + 10)}{8} + C.$$

80. Find $\int \dfrac{x^3 - x^2 + x - 1}{x - 1}\, dx$

Sol. We have, $\int \dfrac{x^3 - x^2 + x - 1}{x - 1}\, dx$

$$= \int \frac{x^2(x - 1) + 1(x - 1)}{x - 1}\, dx$$

$$= \int \frac{(x^2 + 1)\,(x - 1)}{x - 1}\, dx$$

$$= \frac{x^3}{3} + x + C.$$

81. Find $\int (ax + b)^3\, dx.$ *

Sol. $\int (ax + b)^3\, dx = \dfrac{(ax + b)^{3+1}}{3 + 1} \times \dfrac{1}{a} + C$

$$= \frac{(ax + b)^4}{4a} + C$$

82. Find $\int \sec x\,(\sec x + \tan x)\, dx$

Sol. Let $I = \int \sec x\,(\sec x + \tan x)\, dx$

$$= \int (\sec^2 x + \sec x\,\tan x)\, dx$$

$$I = \tan x + \sec x + C.$$

83. Find $\displaystyle\int \frac{2-3\sin x}{\cos^2 x}\,dx.$ *

Sol. Let $\quad I = \displaystyle\int \frac{2-3\sin x}{\cos^2 x}\,dx$

$$= \int \left(\frac{2}{\cos^2 x} - \frac{3\sin x}{\cos x} \cdot \frac{1}{\cos x} \right) dx$$

$$= \int (2\sec^2 x - 3\tan x\sec x)\,dx$$

$$= 2\tan x - 3\sec x + C.$$

84. The value of $\displaystyle\int \frac{\sin^2 x - \cos^2 x}{\sin x \cos x}\,dx$ is ....

Sol. $-\log |\sin 2x| + C$

We have, $\displaystyle\int \frac{\sin^2 x - \cos^2 x}{\sin x \cos x}\,dx$

$$= -2\int \frac{\cos^2 x - \sin^2 x}{2\sin x \cos x}\,dx$$

$$= -2\int \frac{\cos 2x}{\sin 2x}\,dx$$

$$= -2\int \cot 2x\,dx$$

$$= \frac{-2\log|\sin 2x|}{2} + C$$

$$= -\log |\sin 2x| + C.$$

85. Find $\displaystyle\int \frac{x+\cos 6x}{3x^2 + \sin 6x}\,dx$

Sol. Let $\quad I = \displaystyle\int \frac{x+\cos 6x}{3x^2 + \sin 6x}\,dx$

Multiply and divide by 6

$$\Rightarrow \quad I = \frac{1}{6}\int \frac{6x+6\cos 6x}{3x^2 + \sin 6x}\,dx$$

$$= \frac{1}{6}\log |3x^2 + \sin 6x| + C$$

$$\left[\because \int \frac{f'(x)}{f(x)}\,dx = \log|f(x)| + C \right]$$

86. Find $\displaystyle\int \frac{2x}{1+x^2}\,dx$

Sol. $\because \quad \displaystyle\int \frac{f'(x)}{f(x)}\,dx = \log|f(x)| + C$

$$\therefore \quad \int \frac{2x}{1+x^2}\,dx = \log|1+x^2| + C.$$

87. Find $\displaystyle\int \frac{x-1}{\sqrt{x^2-1}}\,dx.$

Sol. We have, $\displaystyle\int \frac{x-1}{\sqrt{x^2-1}}\,dx$

$$= \int \frac{x}{\sqrt{x^2-1}}\,dx - \int \frac{1}{\sqrt{x^2-1}}\,dx$$

$$= \frac{1}{2}\int \frac{2x}{\sqrt{x^2-1}}\,dx - \int \frac{1}{\sqrt{x^2-1}}\,dx$$

$$= \frac{1}{2}\int (x^2-1)^{-1/2}\cdot 2x\,dx - \int \frac{1}{\sqrt{x^2-1}}\,dx$$

Let $x^2 - 1 = t \Rightarrow 2x\,dx = dt$

$$= \frac{1}{2}\int t^{-1/2}\,dt - \int \frac{1}{\sqrt{x^2-1}}\,dx$$

$$= \frac{1}{2}\cdot \frac{\sqrt{t}}{1/2}\,dt - \int \frac{1}{\sqrt{x^2-1}}\,dx$$

$$= \frac{1}{2}\frac{(x^2-1)^{1/2}}{1/2} - \log|x+\sqrt{x^2-1}| + C$$

$$= \sqrt{x^2-1} - \log|x+\sqrt{x^2-1}| + C$$

88. $\displaystyle\int \frac{\log(\sin x)}{\tan x}\,dx.$

Sol. Let $\quad I = \displaystyle\int \frac{\log(\sin x)}{\tan x}\,dx$

$$= \int \log(\sin x)\cot x\,dx$$

Put $\log(\sin x) = t$

Differentiate w.r.t. x

$$\frac{1}{\sin x}\cos x = \frac{dt}{dx}$$

$$\cot x\,dx = dt$$

$$\therefore \quad I = \int t\,dt$$

$$= \frac{t^2}{2} + C$$

$$= \frac{(\log|\sin x|)^2}{2} + C.$$

89. The value of $\displaystyle\int \frac{3x^2}{x^6+1}\,dx$ is ....

Sol. $\tan^{-1}|x^3| + C$

$$\int \frac{3x^2}{x^6+1}\,dx = \int \frac{3x^2}{(x^3)^2+1}\,dx$$

Put $\quad x^3 = t$

Differentiate both sides w.r.t. x

$$3x^2 = \frac{dt}{dx}$$

$$3x^2\,dx = dt$$

$$\therefore \quad \int \frac{3x^2}{x^6+1}\,dx = \int \frac{dt}{t^2+1} = \tan^{-1}|t| + C$$

$$= \tan^{-1}|x^3| + C.$$

---

* are board exam questions from previous years

90. The value of $\int \dfrac{2 \cos x}{3 \sin^2 x}\, dx$ is ....

Sol. $\dfrac{-2}{3 \sin x} + C$

Let $\qquad I = \int \dfrac{2 \cos x}{3 \sin^2 x}\, dx = \dfrac{2}{3}\int \dfrac{\cos x}{\sin^2 x}\, dx$

Put $\qquad \sin x = t$

$\qquad\qquad \cos x\, dx = dt$

$$I = \dfrac{2}{3}\int \dfrac{dt}{t^2} = \dfrac{2}{3}\int t^{-2}\, dt$$

$$= \dfrac{2}{3}\left[\dfrac{t^{-1}}{-1}\right] + C$$

$$= -\dfrac{2}{3t} + C = -\dfrac{2}{3 \sin x} + C$$

91. The value of $\int \dfrac{(\log x)^2}{x}\, dx$ is ....

Sol. $\dfrac{(\log x)^3}{3} + C$

Let $\qquad I = \int \dfrac{(\log x)^2}{x}\, dx$

Put $\qquad \log x = t$

$\qquad\qquad \dfrac{1}{x}\, dx = dt$

$\therefore \qquad\qquad I = \int t^2\, dt$

$$= \dfrac{t^3}{3} + C$$

$$I = \dfrac{(\log x)^3}{3} + C.$$

92. If $\int e^x (\tan x + 1) \sec x\, dx = e^x f(x) + C$, then the value of $f(x)$ satisfying the above is ....

Sol. $\sec x$

$$\int e^x (\sec x \tan x + \sec x)\, dx = e^x f(x) + C$$

$\because \qquad\qquad \int e^x [g(x) + g'(x)]\, dx = e^x g(x) + C$

$\therefore \qquad \int e^x (\sec x + \sec x \tan x)\, dx = e^x \sec x + C$

$\Rightarrow \qquad\qquad e^x \sec x + c = e^x f(x) + C$

$\therefore$ By comparing $\qquad f(x) = \sec x.$

93. Evaluate $\int \dfrac{dx}{\sqrt{1 - x^2}}$ *

Sol. $\int \dfrac{dx}{\sqrt{1 - x^2}} = \sin^{-1} x + C$

$$\left[\because \int \dfrac{dx}{\sqrt{a^2 - x^2}} = \sin^{-1}\dfrac{x}{a} + C\right]$$

94. Evaluate : $\int_0^2 \sqrt{4 - x^2}\, dx.$ *

Sol. Given, $\int_0^2 \sqrt{2^2 - x^2}\, dx$

$\because \int \sqrt{a^2 - x^2}\, dx = \dfrac{x}{2}\sqrt{a^2 - x^2} + \dfrac{a^2}{2}\sin^{-1}\dfrac{x}{a} + C$

$\therefore \int_0^2 \sqrt{2^2 - x^2}\, dx = \left[\dfrac{x}{2}\sqrt{4 - x^2} + \dfrac{4}{2}\sin^{-1}\dfrac{x}{2}\right]_0^2$

$$= \left(\dfrac{2}{2}\sqrt{4 - 4} + 2 \sin^{-1}\dfrac{2}{2}\right) - (0 + 2 \sin^{-1} 0)$$

$$= 0 + 2 \sin^{-1} 1 - 0$$

$$= 2 \times \dfrac{\pi}{2} = \pi$$

95. The value of $\int_{-\pi/4}^{\pi/4} \sin^3 x\, dx$ is ....

Sol. 0

$$\int_{-\pi/4}^{\pi/4} \sin^3 x\, dx$$

As $\sin^3 x$ is odd function

$\because \qquad \sin^3 (-x) = (-\sin x)^3$

$$= -\sin^3 x$$

$\therefore \quad \int_{-\pi/4}^{\pi/4} \sin^3 x\, dx = 0 \quad \left[\begin{array}{l}\because \int_{-a}^{a} f(x)\, dx = 0 \\ \text{if } f(x) \text{ is odd function}\end{array}\right]$

Short Answer Type Questions

96. Find $\int \cos 2x \cos 4x \cos 6x\, dx$ **[NCERT]**

Sol. Let $\qquad I = \dfrac{1}{2}\int (2 \cos 2x \cos 4x) \cos 6x\, dx$

$\Rightarrow \qquad I = \dfrac{1}{2}\int (\cos 6x + \cos 2x)\cos 6x\, dx$

$[\because 2 \cos A \cos B = \cos (A + B) + \cos (A - B)]$

$$= \dfrac{1}{2}\int \cos 6x \cos 6x\, dx + \dfrac{1}{2}\int \cos 2x \cos 6x\, dx$$

$$= \dfrac{1}{4}\int 2 \cos 6x \cos 6x\, dx + \dfrac{1}{4}\int 2 \cos 2x \cos 6x\, dx$$

$$= \dfrac{1}{4}\int (\cos 12x + \cos 0)\, dx + \dfrac{1}{4}\int \cos 8x + \cos 4x\, dx$$

$$= \frac{1}{4}\left[\int (\cos 12x + 1 + \cos 8x + \cos 4x)\,dx \right]$$

$$= \frac{1}{4}\left[\frac{\sin 12x}{12} + \frac{\sin 8x}{8} + \frac{\sin 4x}{4} + x \right] + C$$

97. Evaluate $\int \dfrac{1}{\cos(x-a)\cos(x-b)}\,dx$ **[NCERT]**

Sol. Let $I = \int \dfrac{1}{\cos(x-a)\cos(x-b)}\,dx$

Divide and multiply by $\sin(b-a)$

$$I = \frac{1}{\sin(b-a)} \int \frac{\sin(b-a)}{\cos(x-a)\cos(x-b)}\,dx$$

$$= \frac{1}{\sin(b-a)} \int \frac{\sin\left[(x-a)-(x-b)\right]}{\cos(x-a)\cos(x-b)}\,dx$$

(By adding and subtracting x)

$$= \frac{1}{\sin(b-a)}$$

$$\int \frac{\sin(x-a)\cos(x-b) - \cos(x-a)\sin(x-b)}{\cos(x-a)\cos(x-b)}\,dx$$

$$= \frac{1}{\sin(b-a)} \int \frac{\sin(x-a)\cos(x-b)}{\cos(x-a)\cos(x-b)}\,dx$$

$$- \frac{1}{\sin(b-a)} \int \frac{\cos(x-a)\sin(x-b)}{\cos(x-a)\cos(x-b)}\,dx$$

$$= \frac{1}{\sin(b-a)} \int \tan(x-a)\,dx - \frac{1}{\sin(b-a)} \int \tan(x-b)\,dx$$

$$= \frac{1}{\sin(b-a)} \{ -\log |\cos(x-a)| + \log |\cos(x-b)| \}$$

$$\left[\because \int \tan x\,dx = -\log|\cos x| + C \right]$$

$$I = \frac{1}{\sin(b-a)} \log \left| \frac{\cos(x-b)}{\cos(x-a)} \right| + C.$$

98. Find $\int \dfrac{1}{\sec x + \operatorname{cosec} x}\,dx$ **[NCERT]**

Sol. Given, $\int \dfrac{1}{\sec x + \operatorname{cosec} x}\,dx$

$$= \int \frac{1}{\dfrac{1}{\cos x} + \dfrac{1}{\sin x}}\,dx$$

$$= \int \frac{1}{\dfrac{\sin x + \cos x}{\sin x \cos x}}\,dx$$

$$= \int \frac{\sin x \cos x}{\sin x + \cos x}\,dx$$

$$= \frac{1}{2} \int \frac{2\sin x \cos x}{\sin x + \cos x}\,dx \;[\because \text{Divide and multiple by 2}]$$

$$= \frac{1}{2} \int \frac{\sin 2x}{\sin x + \cos x}\,dx \qquad [\because \sin 2A = 2\sin A \cos A]$$

$$= \frac{1}{2} \int \frac{(1 + \sin 2x) - 1}{\sin x + \cos x}\,dx \qquad [\text{add and subtract 1}]$$

$$= \frac{1}{2} \int \frac{(\sin^2 x + \cos^2 x + 2\sin x \cos x) - 1}{\sin x + \cos x}\,dx$$

$$[\because \sin^2 x + \cos^2 x = 1]$$

$$= \frac{1}{2} \int \frac{(\sin x + \cos x)^2 - 1}{\sin x + \cos x}\,dx$$

$$= \frac{1}{2} \int \frac{(\sin x + \cos x)^2}{\sin x + \cos x}\,dx - \frac{1}{2} \int \frac{1}{\sin x + \cos x}\,dx$$

$$= \frac{1}{2} \int (\sin x + \cos x)\,dx$$

$$- \frac{1}{2} \int \frac{1}{\sqrt{2}\left(\dfrac{1}{\sqrt{2}} \sin x + \dfrac{1}{\sqrt{2}} \cos x \right)}\,dx$$

Multiple & divide by $\sqrt{2}$

$$= \frac{1}{2} \int (\sin x + \cos x)\,dx$$

$$- \frac{1}{2\sqrt{2}} \int \frac{dx}{\sin x \cos \dfrac{\pi}{4} + \cos x \sin \dfrac{\pi}{4}}$$

$$= \frac{1}{2}[-\cos x + \sin x] - \frac{1}{2\sqrt{2}} \int \operatorname{cosec}\left(x + \frac{\pi}{4} \right)$$

$$= \frac{-1}{2}\cos x + \frac{1}{2}\sin x$$

$$- \frac{1}{2\sqrt{2}} \log \left| \operatorname{cosec}\left(x + \frac{\pi}{4} \right) - \cot\left(x + \frac{\pi}{4} \right) \right| + C.$$

99. Evaluate $\int \dfrac{e^x}{\sqrt{5 - 4e^x - e^{2x}}}\,dx$

Sol. We have, $\int \dfrac{e^x}{\sqrt{5 - 4e^x - e^{2x}}}\,dx$

put $\qquad e^x = t$

Differentiate both sides w.r.t. x

$$e^x\,dx = dt$$

$$\int \frac{dt}{\sqrt{5 - 4t - t^2}} = \int \frac{dt}{\sqrt{4 + 5 - (t^2 + 4t + 4)}}$$

[Add and subtract 4]

$$= \int \frac{dt}{\sqrt{(3)^2 - (t+2)^2}}$$

$$\left[\because \int \frac{dt}{\sqrt{a^2 - x^2}} = \sin^{-1}\frac{x}{a} + C \right]$$

$$= \sin^{-1}\left(\frac{t+2}{3}\right) + C$$

$$= \sin^{-1}\left(\frac{e^x+2}{3}\right) + C$$

100. Find $\int \dfrac{x+2}{\sqrt{(x-2)(x-3)}}\,dx$

Sol. Let $\quad I = \int \dfrac{x+2}{\sqrt{(x-2)(x-3)}}\,dx$

$$I = \int \frac{x+2}{\sqrt{x^2-5x+6}}\,dx$$

$$= \frac{1}{2}\int \frac{2x+4}{\sqrt{x^2-5x+6}}\,dx = \frac{1}{2}\int \frac{2x+4-5+5}{\sqrt{x^2-5x+6}}\,dx$$

$$= \frac{1}{2}\int \frac{2x-5}{\sqrt{x^2-5x+6}}\,dx + \frac{9}{2}\int \frac{dx}{\sqrt{x^2-5x+\frac{25}{4}+6-\frac{25}{4}}}$$

$$= \frac{1}{2}\int (x^2-5x+6)^{-1/2}\cdot(2x-5)\,dx + \frac{9}{2}\int \frac{dx}{\sqrt{\left(x-\frac{5}{2}\right)^2-\frac{1}{4}}}$$

$$= \frac{1}{2}\left[\frac{(x^2-5x+6)^{-1/2+1}}{-\frac{1}{2}+1}\right] + \frac{9}{2}\int \frac{dx}{\sqrt{\left(x-\frac{5}{2}\right)^2-\left(\frac{1}{2}\right)^2}}$$

$$\left[\because \int [f(x)]^n \times f'(x)\,dx = \frac{f(x)^{n+1}}{n+1} + C\right]$$

$$I = \sqrt{x^2-5x+6} + \frac{9}{2}\log\left|\left(x-\frac{5}{2}\right)+\sqrt{x^2-5x+6}\right| + C.$$

101. Evaluate $\int (\sqrt{\tan x}+\sqrt{\cot x})\,dx$

Sol. Let $I = \int (\sqrt{\tan x}+\sqrt{\cot x})\,dx$

$$= \int \left(\sqrt{\tan x}+\frac{1}{\sqrt{\tan x}}\right)dx$$

$$= \int \frac{\tan x+1}{\sqrt{\tan x}}\,dx$$

Put $\quad \sqrt{\tan x} = t$

then $\quad \tan x = t^2$

Differentiate both side w.r.t. x

$$\sec^2 x\,dx = 2t\,dt$$

$$dx = \frac{2t}{\sec^2 x}\,dt = \frac{2t}{1+\tan^2 x}\,dt$$

$$dx = \frac{2t}{1+t^4}\,dt$$

$\therefore \qquad I = \int \dfrac{t^2+1}{t}\cdot\dfrac{2t}{1+t^4}\,dt$

$$I = 2\int \frac{t^2+1}{t^4+1}\,dt$$

$$I = 2\int \frac{t^2\left(1+\frac{1}{t^2}\right)}{t^2\left(t^2+\frac{1}{t^2}\right)}\,dt$$

Let $\quad t - \dfrac{1}{t} = y$

Squaring both side and then differentiating both sides

$$t^2 + \frac{1}{t^2} - 2 = y^2,$$

$$t^2 + \frac{1}{t^2} = y^2+2, \quad 1+\frac{1}{t^2} = \frac{dy}{dt}$$

On differentiation, we get

$$1+\frac{1}{t^2} = \frac{dy}{dt} \Rightarrow \left(1+\frac{1}{t^2}\right)dt = dy$$

$\therefore \qquad I = 2\int \dfrac{dy}{y^2+2} = 2\int \dfrac{dy}{y^2+(\sqrt{2})^2}$

$\therefore \qquad I = 2\cdot\dfrac{1}{\sqrt{2}}\tan^{-1}\dfrac{y}{\sqrt{2}} + C$

$$= \frac{2}{\sqrt{2}}\tan^{-1}\frac{t-\frac{1}{t}}{\sqrt{2}} + C$$

$$= \sqrt{2}\tan^{-1}\frac{t^2-1}{\sqrt{2}t} + C$$

$\Rightarrow \qquad I = \sqrt{2}\tan^{-1}\left(\dfrac{\tan x-1}{\sqrt{2}\sqrt{\tan x}}\right) + C$

$\Rightarrow \qquad I = \sqrt{2}\tan^{-1}\left(\dfrac{\tan x-1}{\sqrt{2}\tan x}\right) + C$

102. Find $\int \dfrac{e^{2x}-e^{-2x}}{e^{2x}+e^{-2x}}\,dx$ **[NCERT]**

Sol. Let $\quad I = \int \dfrac{e^{2x}-e^{-2x}}{e^{2x}+e^{-2x}}\,dx$

Multiply and divide by 2

$$I = \frac{1}{2}\int \frac{2e^{2x}-2e^{-2x}}{e^{2x}+e^{-2x}}\,dx$$

$$= \frac{1}{2}\log|e^{2x}+e^{-2x}| + C$$

$$\left[\because \int \frac{f'(x)}{f(x)}\,dx = \log|f(x)| + C\right]$$

103. Evaluate $\int \dfrac{x^3 \sin(\tan^{-1} x^4)}{1+x^8}\,dx$ **[NCERT]**

Sol. Let $I = \int \dfrac{x^3 \sin(\tan^{-1} x^4)}{1+x^8}\,dx$

Put $\tan^{-1} x^4 = t$

Differentiate w.r.t. x

$\Rightarrow \quad \dfrac{1}{1+x^8} \cdot 4x^3 = \dfrac{dt}{dx}$

$\dfrac{x^3}{1+x^8}\,dx = \dfrac{dt}{4}$

$I = \dfrac{1}{4}\int \sin t\,dt$

$= \dfrac{1}{4}(-\cos t) + C$

$\Rightarrow \quad I = -\dfrac{1}{4}\cos(\tan^{-1} x^4) + C$

104. Find $\int \tan^3 2x \sec 2x\,dx$ **[NCERT]**

Sol. Let $I = \int \tan^2 2x \tan 2x \sec 2x\,dx$

$= \int (\sec^2 2x - 1)\tan 2x \sec 2x\,dx$

Put $\sec 2x = t$

Differentiate both sides w.r.t. x

$2\sec 2x \tan 2x = \dfrac{dt}{dx}$

$\therefore \quad \sec 2x \tan 2x\,dx = \dfrac{dt}{2}$

$I = \dfrac{1}{2}\int (t^2 - 1)dt$

$\Rightarrow \quad I = \dfrac{1}{2}\left[\dfrac{t^3}{3} - t\right] + C$

$\Rightarrow \quad I = \dfrac{1}{2}\left[\dfrac{\sec^3 2x}{3} - \sec 2x\right] + C$

$\Rightarrow \quad I = \dfrac{\sec^3 2x}{6} - \dfrac{\sec 2x}{2} + C$

105. Evaluate : $\int \dfrac{\sin^6 x + \cos^6 x}{\sin^2 x . \cos^2 x}\,dx.$ *

Sol. Let $I = \int \dfrac{\sin^6 x + \cos^6 x}{\sin^2 x . \cos^2 x}\,dx$

Here, Numerator $= \sin^6 x + \cos^6 x$

$= (\sin^2 x)^3 + (\cos^2 x)^3$

$= (\sin^2 x + \cos^2 x)(\sin^4 x + \cos^4 x - \sin^2 x \cos^2 x)$

$[\because a^3 + b^3 = (a+b)(a^2 + b^2 - ab)]$

$= 1.[(\sin^2 x + \cos^2 x)^2 - 2\sin^2 x \cos^2 x - \sin^2 x \cos^2 x]$

$= 1 - 3\sin^2 x \cos^2 x$

$\therefore \quad I = \int \dfrac{1 - 3\sin^2 x \cdot \cos^2 x}{\sin^2 x \cos^2 x}\,dx$

$= \int \dfrac{1}{\sin^2 x \cos^2 x}\,dx - 3\int 1\,dx + C$

Multiplying and dividing denominator by $\cos^2 x$ in first Integral

$= \int \dfrac{\sec^4 x}{\tan^2 x}\,dx - 3x + C$

$= \int \dfrac{\sec^2 x . \sec^2 x}{\tan^2 x}\,dx - 3x + C$

$= \int \dfrac{(1 + \tan^2 x)\sec^2 x}{\tan^2 x}\,dx - 3x + C$

Put $\tan x = t$

$\Rightarrow \quad \sec^2 x\,dx = dt$

$\Rightarrow \quad I = \int \dfrac{(t^2 + 1)}{t^2}\,dt - 3x + C$

$= \int \left[1 + \dfrac{1}{t^2}\right]dt - 3x + C$

$= t - \dfrac{1}{t} - 3x + C$

$= \tan x - \cot x - 3x + C.$

106. Find : $\int \dfrac{\sqrt{x}}{\sqrt{a^3 - x^3}}\,dx.$ *

Sol. Let $I = \int \dfrac{\sqrt{x}}{\sqrt{a^3 - x^3}}\,dx$

$= \int \dfrac{\sqrt{x}}{\sqrt{(a^{3/2})^2 - (x^{3/2})^2}}\,dx \quad …(i)$

then put $x^{3/2} = t$

$\dfrac{3}{2}\sqrt{x}.dx = dt$

$\Rightarrow \quad \sqrt{x}.dx = \dfrac{2}{3}.dt$

Putting the values in (i), we get

$I = \dfrac{2}{3}\int \dfrac{1}{\sqrt{(a^{3/2})^2 - t^2}}\,dt$

$\Rightarrow \quad I = \dfrac{2}{3}\sin^{-1}\left(\dfrac{t}{a^{3/2}}\right) + C$

or $\quad I = \dfrac{2}{3}\sin^{-1}\left(\dfrac{x}{a}\right)^{3/2} + C$

____

* are board exam questions from previous years

107. Find $\int \dfrac{1-x^2}{x(1-2x)}\,dx$

Sol. Let

$$I = \int \dfrac{1-x^2}{x(1-2x)}\,dx$$

$$= \int \dfrac{1-x^2}{x-2x^2}\,dx$$

$\because$ deg (num) = deg (den)

$\therefore$

$$-2x^2 + x \overline{\smash{\big)}\, -x^2 + 1}\ \ \frac{1/2}{}$$
$$\underline{-x^2 + \tfrac{1}{2}\,x}$$
$${+}\qquad{-}$$
$$\overline{\qquad\qquad}$$
$$-\tfrac{1}{2}\,x + 1$$

$$I = \int \left(\dfrac{1}{2} + \dfrac{-\dfrac{1}{2}x + 1}{x(1-2x)} \right) dx$$

$$I = \dfrac{1}{2}x + \int \dfrac{-\dfrac{1}{2}x + 1}{x(1-2x)}\,dx \qquad \text{...(i)}$$

Let

$$I_1 = \int \dfrac{-\dfrac{1}{2}x + 1}{x(1-2x)}\,dx$$

Let

$$\dfrac{-\dfrac{1}{2}x + 1}{x(1-2x)} = \dfrac{A}{x} + \dfrac{B}{1-2x}$$

$$-\dfrac{1}{2}x + 1 = A(1-2x) + Bx \qquad \text{...(ii)}$$

If $x = 0$

then from equation (ii),

$$1 = A$$

If $x = \dfrac{1}{2}$

them from equation (ii),

$$-\dfrac{1}{4} + 1 = \dfrac{B}{2}$$

$$\dfrac{-1+4}{4} = \dfrac{B}{2}$$

$$\dfrac{3}{4} = \dfrac{B}{2}$$

$\therefore$ $B = \dfrac{3}{2}$

$\therefore$ $I_1 = \int \dfrac{1}{x}\,dx + \dfrac{3}{2}\int \dfrac{dx}{1-2x}$

$$= \log |x| + \dfrac{3}{2(-2)}\int \dfrac{-2}{1-2x}\,dx$$

$$= \log |x| - \dfrac{3}{4}\log |1-2x|$$

$$\left[\because \int \dfrac{f'(x)}{f(x)}\,dx = \log|f(x)| + C \right]$$

$\therefore$ $I = \dfrac{1}{2}x + \log |x| - \dfrac{3}{4}\log |1-2x| + C.$

108. Find $\int \dfrac{2x}{(x^2+1)(x^2+3)}\,dx$ **[NCERT]**

Sol. We have, $\int \dfrac{2x}{(x^2+1)(x^2+3)}\,dx$

Put $x^2 = t$

Differentiate both side w.r.t. x

$$2x\,dx = dt$$

$\therefore$ $I = \int \dfrac{dt}{(t+1)(t+3)}$

$$\dfrac{1}{(t+1)(t+3)} = \dfrac{A}{t+1} + \dfrac{B}{t+3}$$

Multiplication both side by $(t+1)\,(t+3)$

$$I = A(t+3) + B(t+1) \qquad \text{...(1)}$$

Put $t = -1$ in equation (1)

then $1 = A(-1+3)$

$\Rightarrow$ $1 = 2A$

$\Rightarrow$ $A = \dfrac{1}{2}$

If $t = -3$

Put the value in equation (1)

then $1 = B(-3+1)$

$$1 = -2B$$

$$B = -\dfrac{1}{2}$$

$\therefore$ $I = \int \dfrac{\dfrac{1}{2}}{t+1}\,dt + \int \dfrac{-\dfrac{1}{2}}{t+3}\,dt$

$\Rightarrow$ $I = \dfrac{1}{2}\log |t+1| - \dfrac{1}{2}\log |t+3| + C$

$$= \dfrac{1}{2}\left[\log \left| \dfrac{t+1}{t+3} \right| \right] + C$$

$\Rightarrow$ $I = \dfrac{1}{2}\log \left| \dfrac{x^2+1}{x^2+3} \right| + C$

109. Evaluate : $\int \dfrac{2}{(1-x)(1+x^2)}\,dx$

Sol. Let $\dfrac{2}{(1-x)(1+x^2)} = \dfrac{A}{1-x} + \dfrac{Bx+C}{1+x^2}$

$$2 = A(1+x^2) + (Bx+C)(1-x)$$

Put $\quad x = 1$

$\Rightarrow \quad 2 = 2A$

$\Rightarrow \quad A = 1$

Put $\quad x = 0$

$\Rightarrow \quad 2 = A + C$

$\Rightarrow \quad 2 = 1 + C$

$\Rightarrow \quad C = 1$

Put $\quad x = 2$

$\Rightarrow \quad 2 = 5A + (2B+C)(1-2)$

$\Rightarrow \quad 2 = 5A - 2B - C$

$\Rightarrow \quad 2 = 5 - 2B - 1$

$\Rightarrow \quad 2 = 4 - 2B$

$\Rightarrow \quad B = \dfrac{4-2}{2}$

$\Rightarrow \quad B = 1$

$\therefore \quad I = \int \dfrac{2\,dx}{(1-x)(1+x^2)}$

$$= \int \dfrac{dx}{1-x} + \int \dfrac{x}{1+x^2}\,dx + \int \dfrac{dx}{1+x^2}$$

$$= -\int \dfrac{dx}{x-1} + \dfrac{1}{2}\int \dfrac{2x}{1+x^2} + \int \dfrac{dx}{1+x^2}$$

$$I = -\log|1-x| + \dfrac{1}{2}\log|1+x^2| + \tan^{-1}x + C.$$

110. Evaluation : $\int \dfrac{dx}{x(x^5+3)}$

Sol. Let $\quad I = \int \dfrac{dx}{x(x^5+3)}$

Multiplying num. & deno. by x^4

$$= \int \dfrac{x^4}{x^5(x^5+3)}\,dx$$

Put $\quad x^5 = t$

Differentiate both sides w.r.t. x

$$5x^4 = \dfrac{dt}{dx} \Rightarrow dx = \dfrac{dt}{5x^4}$$

$\therefore \quad I = \dfrac{1}{5}\int \dfrac{dt}{x^5(t+3)} = \dfrac{1}{5}\int \dfrac{dt}{t(t+3)}$

$$\dfrac{1}{t(t+3)} = \dfrac{A}{t} + \dfrac{B}{t+3}$$

$\Rightarrow \quad 1 = A(t+3) + Bt$

If $t = 0$, $\qquad 1 = 3A$

$\Rightarrow \qquad A = \dfrac{1}{3},$

If $t = -3$

$\qquad 1 = -3B$

$\Rightarrow \qquad B = -\dfrac{1}{3}$

$\therefore \quad I = \dfrac{1}{5}\left[\int \dfrac{\frac{1}{3}}{t}\,dt + \int \dfrac{-\frac{1}{3}}{t+3}\,dt\right]$

$$= \dfrac{1}{15}\log|t| - \dfrac{1}{15}\log|t+3| + C$$

$$= \dfrac{1}{15}\log\left|\dfrac{t}{t+3}\right| + C$$

$\therefore \quad I = \dfrac{1}{15}\log\left|\dfrac{x^5}{x^5+3}\right| + C.$

111. Find $\int \dfrac{2x}{(x^2+1)(x^2+2)^2}\,dx.$ *

Sol. Let $\quad I = \int \dfrac{2x}{(x^2+1)(x^2+2)^2}\,dx$

Put $\quad x^2 = t$

$\Rightarrow \quad 2x\,dx = dt$

$$I = \int \dfrac{dt}{(t+1)(t+2)^2}$$

Let $\dfrac{1}{(t+1)(t+2)^2} = \dfrac{A}{t+1} + \dfrac{B}{t+2} + \dfrac{C}{(t+2)^2}$ ...(A)

$$\dfrac{1}{(t+1)(t+2)^2} = \dfrac{A(t+2)^2 + B(t+1)(t+2) + C(t+1)}{(t+1)(t+2)^2}$$

$$1 = A(t+2)^2 + B(t+1)(t+2) + C(t+1)$$

Equating coefficients, t^2, t and constant terms on both sides, we get

$\qquad A + B = 0 \hspace{3cm}$ ...(i)

$\qquad 4A + 3B + C = 0 \hspace{2.5cm}$ ...(ii)

$\qquad 4A + 2B + C = 1 \hspace{2.5cm}$ ...(iii)

Subtracting equation (iii) from (ii), we get

$\qquad B = -1$

Substitute in equation (i)

$\Rightarrow \qquad A = 1$

Substitute the value of A and B in (ii), we get

$\qquad 4 - 3 + C = 0$

$\qquad C = -1$

From equation (A)

$$\dfrac{1}{(t+1)(t+2)^2} = \dfrac{1}{t+1} + \left(\dfrac{-1}{t+2}\right) + \left(\dfrac{-1}{(t+2)^2}\right)$$

$$\int \frac{1}{(t+1)(t+2)^2} \, dt = \int \frac{1}{t+1} \, dt - \int \frac{1}{t+2} \, dt$$

$$- \int \frac{1}{(t+2)^2} \, dt$$

$$= \log(t+1) - \log(t+2) + \frac{1}{t+2} + C$$

Where C is constant of integration.

$$\therefore \int \frac{2x}{(x^2+1)(x^2+2)^2} \, dx = \log \left| \frac{x^2+1}{x^2+2} \right| + \frac{1}{x^2+2} + C$$

112. Evaluate : $\displaystyle\int \frac{3x-1}{(x-1)(x-2)(x-3)} \, dx$ **[NCERT]**

Sol. $\dfrac{3x-1}{(x-1)(x-2)(x-3)} = \dfrac{A}{x-1} + \dfrac{B}{x-2} + \dfrac{C}{x-3}$

$3x - 1 = A(x-2)(x-3) + B(x-1)(x-3)$
$$+ C(x-1)(x-2)$$

If $x = 1$, then
$$2 = A(-1)(-2)$$
$$\Rightarrow \qquad 2A = 2$$
$$\Rightarrow \qquad A = 1$$
If $x = 2$, then
$$5 = B(1)(-1)$$
$$\Rightarrow \qquad B = -5$$
If $x = 3$, then
$$8 = C(2)(1)$$
$$\Rightarrow \qquad C = 4$$

$$\therefore \int \frac{3x-1}{(x-1)(x-2)(x-3)} \, dx$$

$$= \int \frac{dx}{x-1} + \int \frac{-5}{x-2} \, dx + \int \frac{4}{x-3} \, dx$$

$$\Rightarrow \int \frac{3x-1}{(x-1)(x-2)(x-3)} \, dx$$

$$= \log |x-1| - 5 \log |x-2| + 4 \log |x-3| + C.$$

113. Find : $\displaystyle\int \frac{(3\sin\theta - 2)\cos\theta}{5 - \cos^2\theta - 4\sin\theta} \, d\theta.$ *

Sol. $I = \displaystyle\int \frac{(3\sin\theta - 2)\cos\theta}{5 - \cos^2\theta - 4\sin\theta} \, d\theta$

$$\Rightarrow \quad I = \int \frac{(3\sin\theta - 2)\cos\theta}{4 + 1 - \cos^2\theta - 4\sin\theta} \, d\theta$$

$$I = \int \frac{(3\sin\theta - 2)\cos\theta}{4 + \sin^2\theta - 4\sin\theta} \, d\theta$$

$$[\because 1 - \cos^2\theta = \sin^2\theta]$$

$$I = \int \frac{(3\sin\theta - 2)\cos\theta}{(\sin\theta - 2)^2} \, d\theta$$

Put $\sin\theta = t$
$$\Rightarrow \qquad \cos\theta \, . \, d\theta = dt$$

$$\therefore \qquad I = \int \frac{(3t-2)}{(t-2)^2} \, . \, dt$$

Consider,
$$\frac{3t-2}{(t-2)^2} = \frac{A}{(t-2)} + \frac{B}{(t-2)^2}$$

$$\Rightarrow \qquad A(t-2) + B = 3t - 2$$

On comparing, we get
$$A = 3 \text{ and } B = 4$$

$$\therefore \qquad I = \int \left(\frac{3}{t-2} + \frac{4}{(t-2)^2} \right) dt$$

$$\Rightarrow \quad I = 3 \log |t-2| - \frac{4}{(t-2)} + C$$

$$\Rightarrow \quad I = 3 \log |\sin\theta - 2| - \frac{4}{(\sin\theta - 2)} + C$$

$$\text{or} \quad I = 3 \log |2 - \sin\theta| + \frac{4}{(2 - \sin\theta)} + C$$

114. Find : $\displaystyle\int \frac{e^x}{(e^x - 1)^2 (e^x + 2)} \, dx.$ *

Sol. Let $I = \displaystyle\int \frac{e^x}{(e^x - 1)^2 (e^x + 2)} \, dx$

Puting $e^x = t$ and $e^x \, dx = dt$, we get

$$I = \int \frac{dt}{(t-1)^2 (t+2)}$$

Let, $\dfrac{1}{(t-1)^2 (t+2)} = \dfrac{A}{t-1} + \dfrac{B}{(t-1)^2} + \dfrac{C}{t+2}$

$$\Rightarrow 1 = A(t-1)(t+2) + B(t+2) + C(t-1)^2$$

Putting, $t = 1$
$$\Rightarrow \qquad 1 = 38 \Rightarrow B = 1/3$$
Putting, $t = -2$
$$\Rightarrow \qquad 1 = 9C \Rightarrow C = 1/9$$
Putting, $t = 0$
$$\Rightarrow \qquad 1 = -2A + 2B + C$$
$$\Rightarrow \qquad 1 = -2A + \frac{2}{3} + \frac{1}{9}$$
$$\Rightarrow \qquad A = -1/9$$

$$\therefore I = \frac{-1}{9} \int \frac{1}{(t-1)} \, dt + \frac{1}{3} \int \frac{1}{(t-1)^2} \, dt + \frac{1}{9} \int \frac{1}{(t+2)} \, dt$$

$$I = \frac{-1}{9} \log |t-1| - \frac{1}{3 \cdot (t-1)} + \frac{1}{9} \log |t+2| + C$$

$$\therefore I = \frac{1}{9} \log \left| \frac{e^x + 2}{e^x - 1} \right| - \frac{1}{3(e^x - 1)} + C.$$

*** are board exam questions from previous years**

115. Find : $\int \dfrac{(3\sin x - 2)\cos x}{13 - \cos^2 x - 7\sin x}\, dx.$ *

Sol. Let, $\quad I = \int \dfrac{(3\sin x - 2)\cos x}{13 - \cos^2 x - 7\sin x}\, dx$

$$= \int \dfrac{(3\sin x - 2)\cos x}{\sin^2 x - 7\sin x + 12}\, dx$$

$$[\because \cos^2 x = 1 - \sin^2 x]$$

Put $\sin x = t \Rightarrow \cos x\, dx = dt$

$$I = \int \dfrac{(3t - 2)}{t^2 - 7t + 12}\, dt = \int \dfrac{3t - 2}{(t-3)(t-4)}\, dt$$

Let, $\quad \dfrac{3t - 2}{(t-3)(t-4)} = \dfrac{A}{t-3} + \dfrac{B}{t-4} \qquad …(A)$

$$\dfrac{3t - 2}{(t-3)(t-4)} = \dfrac{A(t-4) + B(t-3)}{(t-3)(t-4)}$$

$$3t - 2 = A(t-4) + B(t-3)$$

Equating coefficient of t and constant term on both sides, we get

$$A + B = 3 \qquad …(i)$$
$$-4A - 3B = -2 \qquad …(ii)$$

Solving the above two equations, we get

$$A = -7,\ B = 10$$

From equation A

$$\dfrac{3t - 2}{(t-3)(t-4)} = \dfrac{-7}{t-3} + \dfrac{10}{t-4}$$

$$\int \dfrac{3t - 2}{(t-3)(t-4)}\, dt = -7\int \dfrac{1}{t-3}\, dt + 10\int \dfrac{1}{t-4}\, dt$$

$$I = -7 \log |t-3| + 10 \log |t-4| + C$$

Where c is constant of integration.

$$\therefore \quad I = 10 \log|\sin x - 4| - 7 \log|\sin x - 3| + C.$$

116. Find $\int \dfrac{2\cos x}{(1-\sin x)(1+\sin^2 x)}\, dx.$ *

Sol. Let $\quad I = \int \dfrac{2\cos x}{(1-\sin x)(1+\sin^2 x)}\, dx$

Put $\quad \sin x = t$

$\Rightarrow \quad \cos x\, dx = dt$

$\therefore \quad I = \int \dfrac{2}{(1-t)(1+t^2)}\, dt$

Let $\dfrac{2}{(1-t)(1+t^2)}\, dt = \dfrac{A}{1-t} + \dfrac{Bt+C}{1+t^2}$

$$2 = A(1 + t^2) + (Bt + C)(1 - t)$$

$\Rightarrow \qquad 2 = (A - B)t^2 + (B - C)t + A + C$

Put $t = 1$,

We get, $\qquad 2 = 2A$

$\Rightarrow \qquad A = 1$

Comparing coefficients of t^2 and t on both sides.

$$A - B = 0$$
$\Rightarrow \qquad B = A$
$\Rightarrow \qquad B = 1$

Also, $\qquad B - C = 0$
$\Rightarrow \qquad B = C = 1$

$\therefore\ I = \int \left(\dfrac{1}{1-t} + \dfrac{t+1}{t^2+1} \right) dt$

$$= \dfrac{\log(1-t)}{-1} + \dfrac{1}{2}\int \dfrac{2t}{t^2+1}\, dt + \int \dfrac{1}{t^2+1}\, dt$$

$$= -\log(1-t) + \dfrac{1}{2}\log(t^2+1) + \tan^{-1} t + C$$

$$= -\log(1-\sin x) + \dfrac{1}{2}\log(\sin^2 x + 1)$$

$$+ \tan^{-1}(\sin x) + C$$

117. Evaluate $\int x\sin^{-1} x\, dx$

Sol. Let $\qquad I = \int x\sin^{-1} x\, dx$

$$= \int \underset{\text{I}}{\sin^{-1} x} . \underset{\text{II}}{x}\ dx$$

$$= \sin^{-1} x \int x\, dx - \int \left[\dfrac{d}{dx}(\sin^{-1} x).\int x\, dx \right] dx$$

$$= \sin^{-1} x.\dfrac{x^2}{2} - \int \dfrac{1}{\sqrt{1-x^2}} . \dfrac{x^2}{2}\, dx$$

$$= \dfrac{x^2 \sin^{-1} x}{2} + \dfrac{1}{2}\int \dfrac{-x^2}{\sqrt{1-x^2}}\, dx$$

$$= \dfrac{x^2 \sin^{-1} x}{2} + \dfrac{1}{2}\int \dfrac{1-x^2-1}{\sqrt{1-x^2}}\, dx$$

[Add and subtract 1]

$$= \dfrac{x^2 \sin^{-1} x}{2} + \dfrac{1}{2}\int \dfrac{1-x^2}{\sqrt{1-x^2}}\, dx - \dfrac{1}{2}\int \dfrac{dx}{\sqrt{1-x^2}}$$

$$= \dfrac{x^2 \sin^{-1} x}{2} + \dfrac{1}{2}\int \sqrt{1-x^2}\, dx - \dfrac{1}{2}\int \dfrac{dx}{\sqrt{1-x^2}}$$

We know that

$$\int \sqrt{a^2 - x^2}\, dx = \dfrac{x}{2}\sqrt{a^2 - x^2} + \dfrac{a^2}{2}\sin^{-1}\dfrac{x}{a} + C$$

and $\int \dfrac{dx}{\sqrt{a^2 - x^2}} = \sin^{-1}\dfrac{x}{a} + C$

*** are board exam questions from previous years**

$$\therefore I = \frac{x^2 \sin^{-1} x}{2} + \frac{1}{2}\left(\frac{x}{2}\sqrt{1-x^2} + \frac{1}{2}\sin^{-1}\frac{x}{1}\right)$$

$$-\frac{1}{2}\sin^{-1}\frac{x}{1} + C$$

$$= \frac{x^2 \sin^{-1} x}{2} + \frac{x\sqrt{1-x^2}}{4} + \frac{1}{4}\sin^{-1} x - \frac{1}{2}\sin^{-1} x + C$$

$$= \frac{x^2 \sin^{-1} x}{2} + \frac{x\sqrt{1-x^2}}{4} + \frac{\sin^{-1} x - 2\sin^{-1} x}{4} + C$$

$$= \frac{x^2 \sin^{-1} x}{2} + \frac{x\sqrt{1-x^2}}{4} - \frac{1}{4}\sin^{-1} x + C$$

$$= \sin^{-1} x \left(\frac{x^2}{2} - \frac{1}{4}\right) + \frac{x\sqrt{1-x^2}}{4} + C$$

$$= \frac{2x^2 - 1}{4}\sin^{-1} x + \frac{x\sqrt{1-x^2}}{4} + C$$

$$= \frac{(2x^2 - 1)\sin^{-1} x}{4} + \frac{x\sqrt{1-x^2}}{4} + C$$

118. Evaluation : $\int \dfrac{x+2}{\sqrt{x^2 + 5x + 6}}\, dx.$ *

Sol. Let $\quad x + 2 = A\dfrac{d}{dx}(x^2 + 5x + 6) + B$

$$\Rightarrow \quad x + 2 = A(2x + 5) + B \qquad \qquad ...(i)$$
$$\Rightarrow \quad x + 2 = 2Ax + 5A + B$$

On equating the coefficients of x and constant term on both sides, we get

$$2A = 1$$
$$\Rightarrow \qquad \qquad A = \frac{1}{2}$$

and $\qquad 5A + B = 2$

$$\Rightarrow \qquad \frac{5}{2} + B = 2$$

$$\Rightarrow \qquad B = 2 - \frac{5}{2} = -\frac{1}{2}$$

$\therefore$ Equation (i) becomes,

$$x + 2 = \frac{1}{2}(2x + 5) - \frac{1}{2}$$

$$\therefore \int \frac{x+2}{\sqrt{x^2 + 5x + 6}}\, dx = \int \frac{\frac{1}{2}(2x+5) - \frac{1}{2}}{\sqrt{x^2 + 5x + 6}}\, dx$$

$$= \frac{1}{2}\int \frac{2x+5}{\sqrt{x^2 + 5x + 6}}\, dx - \frac{1}{2}\int \frac{dx}{\sqrt{x^2 + 5x + 6}}$$

Puting $x^2 + 5x + 6 = t$

$$\Rightarrow \qquad (2x + 5)\, dx = dt$$

$$= \frac{1}{2}\int \frac{dt}{\sqrt{t}} - \frac{1}{2}\int \frac{dx}{\sqrt{\left(x + \frac{5}{2}\right)^2 - \left(\frac{1}{2}\right)^2}} + C$$

$$= \frac{1}{2}\frac{t^{1/2}}{1/2} \cdot \frac{1}{2}\frac{2t^{1/2}}{1}$$

$$-\frac{1}{2}\log\left| \left(x + \frac{5}{2}\right) + \sqrt{\left(x + \frac{5}{2}\right)^2 - \left(\frac{1}{2}\right)^2}\right| + C$$

$$\left[\because \int \frac{dx}{\sqrt{x^2 - a^2}} = \log|x + \sqrt{x^2 - a^2}|\right]$$

$$= \sqrt{x^2 + 5x + 6} - \frac{1}{2}\log\left| \left(x + \frac{5}{2}\right) + \sqrt{x^2 + 5x + 6}\right| + C$$

119. Find $\displaystyle\int_0^\pi \frac{x \tan x}{\sec x \csc x}\, dx$

Sol. Let $I = \displaystyle\int_0^\pi \frac{x \tan x}{\sec x \csc x}\, dx \qquad ...(i)$

$$I = \int_0^\pi \frac{(\pi - x)\tan(\pi - x)}{\sec(\pi - x)\csc(\pi - x)}\, dx$$

$$\left[\because \int_0^a f(x)dx = \int_0^a f(a - x)dx\right]$$

$$I = \int_0^\pi \frac{\pi(-\tan x)}{(-\sec x)\csc x}\, dx - \int_0^\pi \frac{x(-\tan x)}{(-\sec x)\csc x}\, dx$$

$$I = \int_0^\pi \frac{\pi \tan x}{\sec x \csc x}\, dx - \int_0^\pi \frac{x \tan x}{\sec x \csc x}\, dx \qquad ...(ii)$$

Add equations (i) and (ii), we get

$$2I = \int_0^\pi \frac{x \tan x}{\sec x \csc x}\, dx + \pi\int_0^\pi \frac{\tan x}{\sec x \csc x}\, dx$$

$$-\int_0^\pi \frac{x \tan x}{\sec x \csc x}\, dx$$

$$2I = \pi\int_0^\pi \frac{\frac{\sin x}{\cos x}}{\frac{1}{\cos x}\cdot\frac{1}{\sin x}}\, dx = \pi\int_0^\pi \sin^2 x\, dx$$

$$= \pi\int_0^\pi \frac{(1 - \cos 2x)}{2}\, dx = \frac{\pi}{2}\int_0^\pi (1 - \cos 2x)dx$$

$$= \frac{\pi}{2}\left(x - \frac{\sin 2x}{2}\right)_0^\pi$$

$$= \frac{\pi}{2}\left[\left(\pi - \frac{\sin 2\pi}{2}\right) - \left(0 - \frac{\sin 0}{2}\right)\right]$$

$$= \frac{\pi}{2}[(\pi - 0) - (0 - 0)]$$

$$2I = \frac{\pi}{2}(\pi)$$

$$I = \frac{\pi^2}{4}.$$

120. Evaluate $\int_0^\pi \dfrac{x}{1+\sin x}\,dx$

Sol. Let $\quad I = \int_0^\pi \dfrac{x}{1+\sin x}\,dx$

$$I = \int_0^\pi \dfrac{(\pi - x)}{1+\sin(\pi - x)}\,dx$$

$$\left[\because \int_0^a f(x)\,dx = \int_0^a f(a-x)\,dx\right]$$

$$= \int_0^\pi \dfrac{\pi}{1+\sin x}\,dx - \int_0^\pi \dfrac{x}{1+\sin x}\,dx$$

$$I = \int_0^\pi \dfrac{\pi\,dx}{1+\sin x} - I$$

$$2I = \pi\int_0^\pi \dfrac{1}{1+\sin x} \times \dfrac{1-\sin x}{1-\sin x}\,dx$$

[By rationalising the denominator]

$$= \pi\int_0^\pi \dfrac{1-\sin x}{1-\sin^2 x}\,dx$$

$$= \pi\int_0^\pi \dfrac{1-\sin x}{\cos^2 x}\,dx$$

$$= \pi\left[\int_0^\pi \dfrac{1}{\cos^2 x}\,dx - \int_0^\pi \dfrac{\sin x}{\cos^2 x}\,dx\right]$$

$$= \pi\left[\int_0^\pi (\sec^2 x)\,dx - \int_0^\pi (\sec x \tan x)\,dx\right]$$

$$= \pi\left[(\tan x)_0^\pi - (\sec x)_0^\pi\right]$$

$$= \pi[(\tan \pi - \tan 0) - (\sec \pi - \sec 0)]$$

$$I = \dfrac{\pi}{2}[(0-0) - (-1-1)]$$

$$\therefore \quad I = \dfrac{\pi}{2}\,[0 - (-2)]$$

$$I = \dfrac{\pi}{2} \times 2$$

$$\therefore \quad I = \pi$$

121. Using properties of integration evaluate :

$$\int_0^{\pi/4} \log(1+\tan x)\,dx$$

Sol. $I = \int_0^{\pi/4} \log(1+\tan x)\,dx$

Put the value of $x = \left(\dfrac{\pi}{4} - x\right)$

$$= \int_0^{\pi/4} \log\left[1 + \tan\left(\dfrac{\pi}{4} - x\right)\right]\,dx$$

$$\left[\because \int_0^a f(x)\,dx = \int_0^a f(a-x)\,dx\right]$$

$$\Rightarrow I = \int_0^{\pi/4} \log\left[1 + \dfrac{\tan\dfrac{\pi}{4} - \tan x}{1 + \tan\dfrac{\pi}{4}\tan x}\right]\,dx$$

$$= \int_0^{\pi/4} \log\left(1 + \dfrac{1-\tan x}{1+\tan x}\right)\,dx$$

$$= \int_0^{\pi/4} \log\left(\dfrac{1+\tan x + 1 - \tan x}{1+\tan x}\right)\,dx$$

$$= \int_0^{\pi/4} \log\left(\dfrac{2}{1+\tan x}\right)\,dx$$

$$= \int_0^{\pi/4} \log 2\,dx - \int_0^{\pi/4} \log(1+\tan x)\,dx$$

$$= \log 2\,[x]_0^{\pi/4} - I$$

$$\Rightarrow I = \log 2\left[\dfrac{\pi}{4} - 0\right] - I$$

$$\Rightarrow 2I = \dfrac{\pi}{4}\log 2$$

$$\Rightarrow I = \dfrac{\pi}{8}\log 2.$$

122. Evaluate : $\int_0^{\pi/4} \dfrac{\sin x + \cos x}{9 + 16\sin 2x}\,dx$

Sol. Let $I = \int_0^{\pi/4} \dfrac{\sin x + \cos x}{9 + 16\sin 2x}\,dx$

$$= \int_0^{\pi/4} \dfrac{\sin x + \cos x}{9 + 16 - 16 + 16\sin 2x}\,dx$$

$$= \int_0^{\pi/4} \dfrac{\sin x + \cos x}{25 - 16(1 - \sin 2x)}\,dx$$

$$= \int_0^{\pi/4} \dfrac{\sin x + \cos x}{25 - 16(\sin^2 x + \cos^2 x - 2\sin x \cos x)}\,dx$$

$$\Rightarrow I = \int_0^{\pi/4} \dfrac{\sin x + \cos x}{25 - 16(\sin x - \cos x)^2}\,dx$$

Put $\quad \sin x - \cos x = t$

Differentiate both sides w.r.t.x

$$\cos x + \sin x = \dfrac{dt}{dx}$$

$$(\cos x + \sin x)\,dx = dt$$

If $x = 0$, $t = \sin 0 - \cos 0$

$$t = 0 - 1 = -1$$

If $\quad\quad x = \dfrac{\pi}{4}, \ t = \sin\dfrac{\pi}{4} - \cos\dfrac{\pi}{4}$

$$= \dfrac{1}{\sqrt{2}} - \dfrac{1}{\sqrt{2}}$$

$$t = 0$$

$\therefore \qquad I = \int_{-1}^{0} \dfrac{dt}{25 - 16t^2} = \dfrac{1}{16}\int_{-1}^{0} \dfrac{dt}{\dfrac{25}{16} - t^2}$

$\qquad = \dfrac{1}{16}\int_{-1}^{0} \dfrac{dt}{\left(\dfrac{5}{4}\right) - t^2}$

$\qquad = \dfrac{1}{16} \times \dfrac{1}{2 \times \dfrac{5}{4}} \log \left| \dfrac{\dfrac{5}{4} + t}{\dfrac{5}{4} - t} \right|_{-1}^{0}$

$\qquad \left[\because \int \dfrac{dx}{a^2 - x^2} = \dfrac{1}{2a} \log \left| \dfrac{a+x}{a-x} \right| + C \right]$

$\Rightarrow \qquad I = \dfrac{1}{40} \left\{ \log \left| \dfrac{\dfrac{5}{4} + 0}{\dfrac{5}{4} - 0} \right| - \log \left| \dfrac{\dfrac{5}{4} - 1}{\dfrac{5}{4} + 1} \right| \right\}$

$\qquad = \dfrac{1}{40} \left\{ \log \dfrac{5}{4} \times \dfrac{4}{5} - \log \dfrac{\dfrac{1}{4}}{\dfrac{9}{4}} \right\}$

$\qquad = \dfrac{1}{40} \left[\log 1 - \log \dfrac{1}{4} \times \dfrac{4}{9} \right]$

$\qquad = \dfrac{1}{40} (\log 1 + \log 9)$

$\qquad = \dfrac{1}{40} (\log 9) = \dfrac{1}{40} \log 3^2$

$\qquad = \dfrac{1}{40} \cdot 2 \log 3$

$\Rightarrow \qquad I = \dfrac{1}{20} \log 3$

123. Evaluate : $\int_{-1}^{2} |x^3 - x|\, dx$

Sol. Clearly, $f(x) = x^3 - x = x\,(x-1)\,(x+1)$

The sign of $f(x)$ for different values of x are given in figure

$$\xleftarrow{\qquad}\underset{-\infty}{\quad}\ \overset{-}{\quad}\ \underset{-1}{|}\ \overset{+}{\quad}\ \underset{0}{|}\ \overset{-}{\quad}\ \underset{1}{|}\ \overset{+}{\quad}\ \underset{+\infty}{\quad}\xrightarrow{\qquad}$$

We observe that

$f(x) > 0$ for all $x \in (-1, 0) \cup (1, 2)$

$f(x) < 0$ for all $x \in (0, 1)$

$\therefore \int_{-1}^{2} |x^3 - x|\, dx$

$= \int_{-1}^{0} (x^3 - x)dx + \int_{0}^{1} -(x^3 - x)dx + \int_{1}^{2} (x^3 - x)dx$

$= \left[\dfrac{x^4}{4} - \dfrac{x^2}{2} \right]_{-1}^{0} + \left[-\dfrac{x^4}{4} + \dfrac{x^2}{2} \right]_{0}^{1} + \left[\dfrac{x^4}{4} - \dfrac{x^2}{2} \right]_{1}^{2}$

$\qquad = \left\{ (0 - 0) - \left(\dfrac{1}{4} - \dfrac{1}{2} \right) \right\} + \left\{ \left(-\dfrac{1}{4} + \dfrac{1}{2} \right) - 0 \right\}$

$\qquad \qquad + \left\{ \left(\dfrac{16}{4} - \dfrac{4}{2} \right) - \left(\dfrac{1}{4} - \dfrac{1}{2} \right) \right\}$

$\qquad = -\dfrac{1}{4} + \dfrac{1}{2} - \dfrac{1}{4} + \dfrac{1}{2} + 4 - 2 - \dfrac{1}{4} + \dfrac{1}{2}$

$\qquad = -\dfrac{1}{4} + \dfrac{1}{2} - \dfrac{1}{4} + \dfrac{1}{2} + 2 - \dfrac{1}{4} + \dfrac{1}{2}$

$\qquad = \dfrac{-1 + 2 - 1 + 2 + 8 - 1 + 2}{4} = \dfrac{11}{4}.$

124. Evaluate : $\int_{0}^{\pi} \dfrac{4x \sin x}{1 + \cos^2 x}\, dx.$ *

Sol. $\qquad I = \int_{0}^{\pi} \dfrac{4x \sin x}{1 + \cos^2 x}\, dx \qquad \ldots(i)$

$\Rightarrow \qquad I = \int_{0}^{\pi} \dfrac{4(\pi - x)\sin(\pi - x)}{1 + \cos^2(\pi - x)}\, dx$

$\qquad \left[\because \int_{0}^{a} f(x)dx = \int_{0}^{a} f(a - x)dx \right]$

$\therefore \qquad I = \int_{0}^{\pi} \dfrac{4(\pi - x)\sin x}{1 + \cos^2 x}\, dx \qquad \ldots(ii)$

Adding equations (i) and (ii), we get

$$2I = 4\pi \int_{0}^{\pi} \dfrac{\sin x}{1 + \cos^2 x}\, dx$$

$\Rightarrow \qquad I = 2\pi \int_{0}^{\pi} \dfrac{\sin x}{1 + \cos^2 x}\, dx$

Put $\qquad \cos x = t$

$\Rightarrow \qquad \sin x\, dx = -dt$

If $\qquad x = 0$

$\Rightarrow \qquad t = 1$

If $\qquad x = \pi$

$\Rightarrow \qquad t = -1$

$\therefore \qquad I = 2\pi \int_{1}^{-1} \dfrac{-dt}{1 + t^2}$

$\qquad = 2\pi \int_{-1}^{1} \dfrac{dt}{t^2 + 1}$

$\qquad \left[\because \int_{a}^{b} f(x)dx = -\int_{b}^{a} f(x)dx \right]$

$\qquad = 2\pi \left[\tan^{-1} t \right]_{-1}^{1}$

$\qquad = 2\pi [\tan^{-1} 1 - \tan^{-1} (-1)]$

$\qquad = 2\pi \left[\dfrac{\pi}{4} - \left(-\dfrac{\pi}{4} \right) \right]$

$\qquad = 2\pi \left[\dfrac{2\pi}{4} \right] = \pi^2.$

125. Find: $\int_0^{\pi/4} \dfrac{dx}{\cos^3 x\sqrt{2\sin 2x}}$ *

Sol. Let $\quad I = \int_0^{\pi/4} \dfrac{dx}{\cos^3 x\sqrt{2\sin 2x}}$

Multiplying and dividing denominator by $\cos x$

$$\int_0^{\pi/4} \dfrac{dx}{\cos^4 x \cdot \dfrac{\sqrt{2\sin 2x}}{\cos x}} = \int_0^{\pi/4} \dfrac{\sec^4 x}{\sqrt{\dfrac{2\sin 2x}{\cos^2 x}}}\, dx$$

$$I = \int_0^{\pi/4} \dfrac{(1+\tan^2 x)\sec^2 x}{2\sqrt{\dfrac{\sin x\cos x}{\cos^2 x}}}\, dx$$

$$[\because \sin 2x = 2\sin x\cos x]$$

$$\Rightarrow \quad I = \int_0^{\pi/4} \dfrac{(1+\tan^2 x)\sec^2 x}{2\sqrt{\tan x}}\, dx$$

Put $\quad \tan x = t$

$\Rightarrow \quad \sec^2 x\, dx = dt$, we get

$$\therefore \qquad I = \int_0^1 \dfrac{(1+t^2)\, dt}{2\sqrt{t}}$$

$$\Rightarrow \quad I = \dfrac{1}{2}\int_0^1 \left(\dfrac{1}{\sqrt{t}} + t^{3/2}\right) dt \quad \begin{pmatrix} \because \text{ when } x = 0, t = 0 \\ \text{and } x = \dfrac{\pi}{4}, t = 1 \end{pmatrix}$$

$$\Rightarrow \quad I = \dfrac{1}{2}\left[2\sqrt{t} + \dfrac{2}{5}t^{5/2}\right]_0^1$$

$$\Rightarrow \quad I = \left[\sqrt{t} + \dfrac{1}{5}t^{5/2}\right]_0^1$$

$$\Rightarrow \quad I = \left[\sqrt{1} + \dfrac{1}{5}1^{5/2}\right] - (0)$$

$$\therefore \quad I = \dfrac{6}{5}$$

126. Evaluate : $\int_0^{3/2} |x\cos\pi x|\, dx.$ *

Sol. We have,

$$0 < x < \dfrac{3}{2} \Rightarrow 0 < \pi x < \dfrac{3\pi}{2}$$

Now, $\qquad 0 < x < \dfrac{1}{2}$

$$0 < \pi x < \dfrac{\pi}{2}$$

$\Rightarrow \qquad \cos\pi x > 0$

$\Rightarrow \qquad x\cos\pi x > 0$

$\Rightarrow \qquad |x\cos\pi x| = x\cos\pi x$ for $0 < \pi x < \dfrac{\pi}{2}$

and $\qquad \dfrac{1}{2} < x < \dfrac{3}{2}$

$\Rightarrow \qquad \dfrac{\pi}{2} < \pi x < \dfrac{3\pi}{2}$

$\Rightarrow \qquad \cos\pi x < 0$

$\Rightarrow \qquad x\cos\pi x < 0$

$\Rightarrow \qquad |x\cos\pi x| = -x\cos\pi x$ for $\pi < \pi x < \dfrac{3\pi}{2}$

$$\therefore \int_0^{3/2} |x\cos\pi x|\, dx$$

$$= \int_0^{1/2} |x\cos\pi x|\, dx + \int_{1\backslash 2}^{3\backslash 2} |x\cos\pi x|\, dx$$

$$= \int_0^{1/2} (x\cos\pi x)dx + \int_{1/2}^{3/2} (-x\cos\pi x)dx$$

$$= \int_0^{1/2} (x\cos\pi x)dx - \int_{1/2}^{3/2} (x\cos\pi x)dx$$

$$= \left[\left(\left[\dfrac{x\sin\pi x}{\pi}\right]_0^{1/2} - \int_0^{1/2} \dfrac{\sin\pi x}{\pi}dx\right)\right.$$

$$\left. -\left(\left[\dfrac{x\sin\pi x}{\pi}\right]_{1/2}^{3/2} - \int_{1/2}^{3/2} \dfrac{\sin\pi x}{\pi}dx\right)\right]$$

$$= \left[\left\{\dfrac{1}{\pi}\left(\dfrac{1}{2}\sin\dfrac{\pi}{2} - 0\right) + \dfrac{\cos\pi x}{\pi^2}\Big|_0^{1/2}\right\}\right.$$

$$\left. -\left\{\dfrac{1}{\pi}\left(\dfrac{3}{2}\sin\dfrac{3\pi}{2} - \dfrac{1}{2}\sin\dfrac{\pi}{2}\right) + \dfrac{\cos\pi x}{\pi^2}\Big|_{1/2}^{3/2}\right\}\right]$$

$$= \left\{\dfrac{1}{2\pi} + \dfrac{1}{\pi^2}\left(\cos\dfrac{\pi}{2} - \cos 0\right)\right\} - \left\{\dfrac{1}{\pi}\left(\dfrac{3}{2}(-1) - \dfrac{1}{2}(1)\right)\right.$$

$$\left. + \dfrac{1}{\pi^2}\left(\cos\dfrac{3\pi}{2} - \cos\dfrac{\pi}{2}\right)\right\}$$

$$= \dfrac{1}{2\pi} + \dfrac{1}{\pi^2}(0-1) - \dfrac{1}{\pi}\left(-\dfrac{3}{2} - \dfrac{1}{2}\right) - \dfrac{1}{\pi^2}(0-0)$$

$$= \dfrac{1}{2\pi} - \dfrac{1}{\pi^2} + \dfrac{2}{\pi}$$

$$= \dfrac{\pi - 2 + 4\pi}{2\pi^2}$$

$$= \dfrac{5\pi - 2}{2\pi^2}.$$

127. Evaluate $\int_0^{\pi/2} \sqrt{\sin\phi}\cos^5\phi\, d\phi$ **[NCERT]**

Sol. Let $\quad I = \int_0^{\pi/2} \sqrt{\sin\phi}\cos^5\phi\, d\phi$

$$= \int_0^{\pi/2} \sqrt{\sin\phi}\cos^4\phi\cos\phi\, d\phi$$

$$= \int_0^{\pi/2} \sqrt{\sin\phi}(\cos^2\phi)^2\cos\phi\, d\phi$$

$\Rightarrow \qquad I = \int_0^{\pi/2} \sqrt{\sin\phi}(1-\sin^2\phi)^2 \cos\phi \, d\phi$

Put $\sin\phi = t$

$\Rightarrow \cos\phi \, d\phi = dt$

When $\phi = 0$, $t = \sin 0 = 0$

when $\phi = \dfrac{\pi}{2}$, $t = \sin\dfrac{\pi}{2} \Rightarrow t = 1$

$\therefore \qquad I = \int_0^1 \sqrt{t}(1-t^2)^2 \, dt$

$\qquad = \int_0^1 \sqrt{t}(1+t^4 - 2t^2) dt$

$\qquad = \int_0^1 (t^{1/2} + t^{9/2} - 2t^{5/2}) dt$

$\qquad = \left[\dfrac{t^{3/2}}{3/2} + \dfrac{t^{11/2}}{11/2} - 2\dfrac{t^{7/2}}{7/2} \right]_0^1$

$\qquad = \left[\dfrac{2}{3} t^{3/2} + \dfrac{2}{11} t^{11/2} - 2\times\dfrac{2}{7} t^{7/2} \right]_0^1$

$\qquad = \left(\dfrac{2}{3} + \dfrac{2}{11} - \dfrac{4}{7} \right) - 0$

$\qquad = \dfrac{154 + 42 - 132}{231}$

$\qquad = \dfrac{196 - 132}{231} = \dfrac{64}{231}$

128. Find $\int_0^1 \sin^{-1}\left(\dfrac{2x}{1+x^2} \right) dx$ $\qquad$ **[NCERT]**

Sol. Put $\qquad x = \tan\theta$

$\Rightarrow \qquad dx = \sec^2\theta \, d\theta$

and $\qquad \theta = \tan^{-1} x$

When $x = 1$, $\theta = \tan^{-1} 1 = \dfrac{\pi}{4}$

When $x = 0$, $\theta = \tan^{-1} 0 = 0$

$\therefore \qquad I = \int_0^{\pi/4} \sin^{-1}\left(\dfrac{2\tan\theta}{1+\tan^2\theta} \right).\sec^2\theta \, d\theta$

$\qquad \left[\because \sin 2A = \dfrac{2\tan A}{1+\tan^2 A} \right]$

$\qquad = \int_0^{\pi/4} \sin^{-1}(\sin 2\theta)\sec^2\theta \, d\theta$

$\qquad = \int_0^{\pi/4} 2\theta\sec^2\theta \, d\theta = 2\int_0^{\pi/4} \underset{\text{I}}{\theta} \ \underset{\text{II}}{\sec^2\theta} \, d\theta$

$\qquad = 2\left[\theta\int_0^{\pi/4}\sec^2\theta \, d\theta - \int_0^{\pi/4} 1.\tan\theta \, d\theta \right]$

$\qquad = 2\left[\theta\tan\theta + \log|\cos\theta| \right]_0^{\pi/4}$

$\qquad = 2\left\{ \dfrac{\pi}{4}\tan\dfrac{\pi}{4} + \log\left|\cos\dfrac{\pi}{4}\right| \right\} - \{0 + \log 1\}$

$\qquad = 2\left[\dfrac{\pi}{4} + \log\dfrac{1}{\sqrt{2}} \right]$

$\qquad = \dfrac{\pi}{2} + 2\log 2^{-1/2} = \dfrac{\pi}{2} - 2\times\dfrac{1}{2}\log 2$

$\qquad = \dfrac{\pi}{2} - \log 2.$

129. Evaluate : $\int_0^{\pi/2} \dfrac{\sin^{3/2} x}{\sin^{3/2} x + \cos^{3/2}} dx$ $\qquad$ **[NCERT]**

Sol. $\qquad I = \int_0^{\pi/2} \dfrac{\sin^{3/2} x}{\sin^{3/2} x + \cos^{3/2} x} dx$ $\qquad$ ...(i)

We know that

$\int_0^a f(x) \, dx = \int_0^a f(a-x) dx$

$\therefore \quad I = \int_0^{\pi/2} \dfrac{\sin^{3/2}\left(\dfrac{\pi}{2} - x \right)}{\sin^{3/2}\left(\dfrac{\pi}{2} - x \right) + \cos^{3/2}\left(\dfrac{\pi}{2} - x \right)} dx$

$I = \int_0^{\pi/2} \dfrac{\cos^{3/2} x}{\cos^{3/2} x + \sin^{3/2} x} dx$ $\qquad$ ...(ii)

Adding equations (i) and (ii),

$2I = \int_0^{\pi/2} \dfrac{\sin^{3/2} x + \cos^{3/2} x}{\sin^{3/2} x + \cos^{3/2} x} dx$

$\Rightarrow \qquad 2I = \int_0^{\pi/2} 1 dx$

$\qquad = \left[x \right]_0^{\pi/2}$

$\Rightarrow \qquad 2I = \dfrac{\pi}{2}$

$\Rightarrow \qquad I = \dfrac{\pi}{4}.$

130. Evaluate $\int_{-5}^{5} |x+2| \, dx$ $\qquad$ **[NCERT]**

Sol. We know that

$\qquad x + 2 = 0$

$\qquad x = -2$

$\int_{-5}^{5} f(x) dx = \int_a^c f(x) dx + \int_c^b f(x) dx$

$\therefore \qquad I = \int_{-5}^{-2} -(x+2) dx + \int_{-2}^{5} (x+2) dx$

$\qquad = -\left[\dfrac{x^2}{2} + 2x \right]_{-5}^{-2} + \left[\dfrac{x^2}{2} + 2x \right]_{-2}^{5}$

$\qquad = -\left\{ \left(\dfrac{4}{2} - 4 \right) - \left(\dfrac{25}{2} - 10 \right) \right\} + \left\{ \left(\dfrac{25}{2} + 10 \right) - \left(\dfrac{4}{2} - 4 \right) \right\}$

$\qquad = \dfrac{4}{2} + \dfrac{5}{2} + \dfrac{45}{2} + \dfrac{4}{2} = \dfrac{58}{2}$

$\therefore \qquad I = 29.$

131. Find $\int_{-\pi/2}^{\pi/2} \sin^7 x \, dx$.   **[NCERT]**

Sol. We know that

$$\int_{-a}^{a} f(x)dx = \begin{cases} 0, \text{if } f(x) \text{ is odd} \\ 2\int_{0}^{a} f(x)dx, \text{if } f(x) \text{ is even} \end{cases}$$

Here $f(x) = \sin^7 x$

$$f(-x) = \sin^7(-x)$$
$$= -\sin^7 x$$

$\therefore f(x)$ is odd function.

$$\therefore \quad \int_{-\pi/2}^{\pi/2} \sin^7 x \, dx = 0.$$

132. Find $\int_{0}^{2\pi} \cos^5 x \, dx$ **[NCERT]**

Sol. Since,

$$\int_{0}^{2a} f(x)dx = \begin{cases} 0, \text{if } f(x) \text{ is odd} \\ 2\int_{0}^{a} f(x)dx, \text{if } f(x) \text{ is even} \end{cases}$$

We have, $\int_{0}^{2\pi} \cos^5 x \, dx$

Here $f(x) = \cos^5 x$

Then, $f(2\pi - x) = \cos^5(2\pi - x)$
$$= \cos^5 x$$

$\therefore f(x)$ is an even function.

$$\therefore \quad \int_{0}^{2\pi} \cos^5 x \, dx = 2\int_{0}^{\pi} \cos^5 x \, dx$$

Now, $f(\pi - x) = \cos^5(\pi - x)$
$$= -\cos^5 x$$
$$= -f(x)$$

$\because \cos^5 x$ is odd

$$\therefore \quad \int_{0}^{2\pi} \cos^5 x \, dx = 2 \times 0 = 0.$$

133. Evaluate : $\int_{0}^{\pi} \dfrac{x \tan x}{\sec x + \tan x} dx.$ *

Sol. Let $I = \int_{0}^{\pi} \dfrac{x \tan x}{\sec x + \tan x} dx.$ ...(i)

Now $I = \int_{0}^{\pi} \dfrac{(\pi - x) \tan(\pi - x)}{\sec(\pi - x) + \tan(\pi - x)} dx$

$$= \int_{0}^{\pi} \dfrac{(\pi - x)(-\tan x)}{-\sec x - \tan x} dx$$

$$\Rightarrow I = \int_{0}^{\pi} \dfrac{(\pi - x) \tan x}{\sec x + \tan x} dx \quad \text{...(ii)}$$

Adding (i) and (ii), we get

$$\Rightarrow 2I = \int_{0}^{\pi} \dfrac{x \tan x}{\sec x + \tan x} dx + \int_{0}^{\pi} \dfrac{(\pi - x) \tan x}{\sec x + \tan x} dx$$

$$\Rightarrow 2I = \int_{0}^{\pi} \dfrac{\tan x}{\sec x + \tan x} dx$$

$$\Rightarrow I = \dfrac{\pi}{2} \int_{0}^{\pi} \dfrac{\tan x}{\sec x + \tan x} \times \dfrac{\sec x - \tan x}{\sec x - \tan x} dx$$

$$\Rightarrow I = \dfrac{\pi}{2} \int_{0}^{\pi} \dfrac{(\sec x \tan x - \tan^2 x)}{\sec^2 x - \tan^2 x} dx$$

$$\Rightarrow I = \dfrac{\pi}{2} \int_{0}^{\pi} (\sec x \tan x - \sec^2 x + 1) dx$$

$$\Rightarrow I = \dfrac{\pi}{2} \left[\sec x - \tan x + x\right]_{0}^{\pi}$$

$$\Rightarrow I = \dfrac{\pi}{2} \left[(\sec \pi - \tan \pi + \pi) - (\sec 0 - \tan 0 + 0)\right]$$

$$\Rightarrow I = \dfrac{\pi}{2} \left[(-1 - 0 + \pi) - (1 - 0)\right] = \dfrac{\pi}{2} [\pi - 1 - 1]$$

$$\therefore \quad I = \dfrac{\pi(\pi - 2)}{2}.$$

Long Answer Type Questions

134. Evaluate: $\int \dfrac{1}{\sin^4 x + \sin^2 x \cos^2 x + \cos^4 x} dx.$ *

Sol. Let $I = \int \dfrac{1}{\sin^4 x + \sin^2 x \cos^2 x + \cos^4 x} dx$

Dividing by $\cos^4 x$ in Nr. and Dr., we get

$$= \int \dfrac{\sec^4 x \, dx}{\tan^4 x + \tan^2 x + 1}$$

$$= \int \dfrac{\sec^2 x . \sec^2 x}{\tan^4 x + \tan^2 x + 1} dx$$

$$= \int \dfrac{(1 + \tan^2 x) \sec^2 x}{\tan^4 x + \tan^2 x + 1} dx$$

$$[\because \sec^2 x = 1 + \tan^2 x]$$

Put $\tan x = t$
$$\Rightarrow \sec^2 x \, dx = dt$$

$\therefore$ $I = \int \dfrac{1 + t^2}{t^4 + t^2 + 1} dt$

$$= \int \dfrac{1 + \dfrac{1}{t^2}}{t^2 + 1 + \dfrac{1}{t^2}} dt = \int \dfrac{1 + \dfrac{1}{t^2}}{\left(t - \dfrac{1}{t}\right)^2 + 3} dt$$

Again put

$$t - \dfrac{1}{t} = y$$

$$\Rightarrow \left(1 + \dfrac{1}{t^2}\right) dt = dy$$

____

Thus,
$$I = \int \frac{dy}{y^2 + (\sqrt{3})^2}$$

$$= \frac{1}{\sqrt{3}} \tan^{-1}\left(\frac{y}{\sqrt{3}}\right) + C$$

$$\left(\because \int \frac{dx}{x^2 + a^2} = \frac{1}{a}\tan^{-1}\frac{x}{a} + C\right)$$

$$= \frac{1}{\sqrt{3}} \tan^{-1}\left(t - \frac{1}{t}\right)/\sqrt{3} + C$$

$$= \frac{1}{\sqrt{3}} \tan^{-1}\left(\frac{\tan x - \cot x}{\sqrt{3}}\right) + C$$

135. Find: $\int \dfrac{1}{x - x^3}\, dx$ **[NCERT]**

Sol.
$$\int \frac{1}{x - x^3}\, dx = \int \frac{dx}{x(1 - x^2)}$$

$$= \int \frac{dx}{x(1-x)(1+x)}$$

$$\frac{1}{x(1-x)(1+x)} = \frac{A}{x} + \frac{B}{1-x} + \frac{C}{1+x}$$

$$1 = A(1 - x^2) + B(x)(1 + x) + C(x)(1 - x)$$

Put $x = 1$, then
$$1 = 2B$$
$$\Rightarrow \quad B = \frac{1}{2}$$

Put $x = 0$, then
$$1 = A(1)$$
$$\Rightarrow \quad A = 1$$

Put $x = -1$, then
$$1 = C(-1)(1 + 1)$$
$$\Rightarrow \quad -2C = 1$$
$$\Rightarrow \quad C = -\frac{1}{2}$$

$$I = \int \frac{dx}{x} + \frac{1}{2}\int \frac{dx}{1-x} - \frac{1}{2}\int \frac{dx}{1+x}$$

$$= \log x + \frac{1}{2}\frac{\log|1-x|}{-1} - \frac{1}{2}\log(1+x) + C$$

$$= \log x - \frac{1}{2}\{\log(1-x) + \log(1+x)\} + C$$

$$= \log x - \frac{1}{2}\log\{(1-x)(1+x)\} + C$$

$$I = \log x - \frac{1}{2}\log(1 - x^2) + C$$

136. Evaluate: $\displaystyle\int_{\pi/6}^{\pi/3} \dfrac{dx}{1 + \sqrt{\cot x}}$ *

Sol. Let $I = \displaystyle\int_{\pi/6}^{\pi/3} \dfrac{dx}{1 + \sqrt{\cot x}}$

$$= \int_{\pi/6}^{\pi/3} \frac{dx}{1 + \dfrac{\sqrt{\cos x}}{\sqrt{\sin x}}}$$

$$= \int_{\pi/6}^{\pi/3} \frac{\sqrt{\sin x}}{\sqrt{\sin x} + \sqrt{\cos x}}\, dx \qquad \ldots(i)$$

$$\Rightarrow \quad I = \int_{\pi/6}^{\pi/3} \frac{\sqrt{\sin(\pi/2 - x)}}{\sqrt{\sin(\pi/2 - x)} + \cos(\pi/2 - x)}\, dx$$

$$\left[\because \int_a^b f(x)\, dx = \int_a^b (a + b - x)\, dx \text{ and } a + b = \frac{\pi}{6} + \frac{\pi}{3} = \frac{\pi}{2}\right]$$

$$\Rightarrow \quad I = \int_{\pi/6}^{\pi/3} \frac{\sqrt{\cos x}}{\sqrt{\cos x} + \sqrt{\sin x}}\, dx \qquad \ldots(ii)$$

Adding (i) and (i), we get

$$\therefore \quad I + I = \int_{\pi/6}^{\pi/3}\left[\frac{\sqrt{\sin x} + \sqrt{\cos x}}{\sqrt{\sin x} + \sqrt{\cos x}}\right] dx$$

$$\Rightarrow \quad 2I = \int_{\pi/6}^{\pi/3} 1.dx$$

$$\Rightarrow \quad 2I = [x]_{\pi/6}^{\pi/3} = \frac{\pi}{3} - \frac{\pi}{6} = \frac{\pi}{6}$$

$$\therefore \quad I = \frac{\pi}{12}.$$

137. Evaluate: $\displaystyle\int_0^{\pi/2} \dfrac{x \sin x \cos x}{\sin^4 x + \cos^4 x}\, dx$ *

Sol. Let $I = \displaystyle\int_0^{\pi/2} \dfrac{x \sin x \cos x}{\sin^4 x + \cos^4 x}\, dx \qquad \ldots(i)$

$$\therefore \quad I = \int_0^{\pi/2} \frac{\left(\dfrac{\pi}{2} - x\right)\sin\left(\dfrac{\pi}{2} - x\right)\cos\left(\dfrac{\pi}{2} - x\right)}{\sin^4\left(\dfrac{\pi}{2} - x\right) + \cos^4\left(\dfrac{\pi}{2} - x\right)}\, dx$$

$$\left[\because \int_0^a f(x)\, dx = \int_0^a f(a - x)\, dx\right]$$

$$= \int_0^{\pi/2} \frac{\left(\dfrac{\pi}{2} - x\right)\cos x \sin x}{\cos^4 x + \sin^4 x}\, dx$$

$$\left[\because \sin\left(\frac{\pi}{2} - x\right) = \cos x \text{ and } \cos\left(\frac{\pi}{2} - x\right) = \sin x\right]$$

$$\therefore \quad I = \int_0^{\pi/2} \frac{\left(\dfrac{\pi}{2} - x\right)\sin x \cos x}{\sin^4 x + \cos^4 x}\, dx \qquad \ldots(ii)$$

Adding (i) and (ii), we get

$$2I = \int_0^{\pi/2} \frac{\dfrac{\pi}{2}\sin x \cos x}{\sin^4 x + \cos^4 x}\, dx$$

Dividing Nr. and Dr. by $\cos^4 x$, we get

$$I = \frac{\pi}{4}\int_0^{\pi/2} \frac{\tan x \, \sec^2 x}{\tan^4 x + 1}\, dx$$

Put $\tan^2 x = t$

$\Rightarrow$ $2 \tan x \sec^2 x \, dx = dt$

Also, $x = 0$

$\Rightarrow$ $t = 0$

and $x = \dfrac{\pi}{2}$

$\Rightarrow$ $t = \infty$

$\therefore$
$$I = \frac{\pi}{8}\int_0^{\infty} \frac{dt}{t^2 + 1} = \frac{\pi}{8}\Big[\tan^{-1} t\Big]_0^{\infty}$$

$$= \frac{\pi}{8}\,[\tan^{-1}\infty - \tan^{-1} 0]$$

$$= \frac{\pi}{8}\left(\frac{\pi}{2} - 0\right) = \frac{\pi^2}{16}.$$

138. Evaluate: $\displaystyle\int_0^{\pi/4} \frac{\sin x + \cos x}{16 + 9\sin 2x}\cdot dx^*$

Sol. Let $\displaystyle I = \int_0^{\pi/4} \frac{\sin x + \cos x}{16 + 9\sin 2x}\cdot dx$

$$= \int_0^{\pi/4} \frac{\sin x + \cos x}{16 + 9[1 - (\sin x - \cos x)^2]}\cdot dx$$

$$= \int_0^{\pi/4} \frac{\sin x + \cos x}{25 - 9(\sin x - \cos x)^2]}\cdot dx$$

Put $\sin x - \cos x = t$

$\Rightarrow$ $(\cos x + \sin x)\, dx = dt$

When $x = 0$, $t = -1$

When $x = \dfrac{\pi}{4}$, $t = 0$

$$I = \int_{-1}^{0} \frac{dt}{25 - 9t^2} = \frac{1}{9}\int_{-1}^{0} \frac{dt}{\dfrac{25}{9} - t^2}$$

$$= \frac{1}{9}\int_{-1}^{0} \frac{dt}{\left(\dfrac{5}{3}\right)^2 - t^2}$$

$$= \frac{1}{9}\left[\frac{1}{2 \times \dfrac{5}{3}}\log\left|\frac{\dfrac{5}{3} + t}{\dfrac{5}{3} - t}\right|\right]_{-1}^{0}$$

$$= \frac{1}{9}\left[\frac{3}{10}\left(\log\left|\frac{\dfrac{5}{3}}{\dfrac{5}{3}}\right| - \log\left|\frac{\dfrac{2}{3}}{\dfrac{8}{3}}\right|\right)\right]$$

$$= \frac{1}{30}\left[\log 1 - \log\frac{1}{4}\right]$$

$$= \frac{1}{30}\,[\log 1 - (\log 1 - \log 4)]$$

$$= \frac{1}{30}\log 4 = \frac{1}{30}\log (2)^2 = \frac{2}{30}\log 2$$

$$= \frac{1}{15}\log 2.$$

139. Evaluate: $\displaystyle\int_0^{1} \frac{dx}{\sqrt{1+x} - \sqrt{x}}.$ **[NCERT]**

Sol. Rationalising the denominator

$$I = \int_0^{1} \frac{\sqrt{1+x} + \sqrt{x}}{(\sqrt{1+x} - \sqrt{x})(\sqrt{1+x} + \sqrt{x})}\, dx$$

$$= \int_0^{1} \frac{\sqrt{1+x} + \sqrt{x}}{(\sqrt{1+x})^2 - (\sqrt{x})^2}\, dx$$

$$= \int_0^{1} \frac{\sqrt{1+x} + \sqrt{x}}{1 + x - x}\, dx$$

$$= \int_0^{1} (\sqrt{1+x} + \sqrt{x})\, dx$$

$$= \left[\frac{(1+x)^{1/2 + 1}}{1/2 + 1}\right]_0^1 + \left[\frac{x^{1/2+1}}{1/2+1}\right]_0^1$$

$$= \frac{2}{3}\left[(1+x)^{3/2} + (x)^{3/2}\right]_0^1$$

$$= \frac{2}{3}[(1+1)^{3/2} + (1)^{3/2}] - \frac{2}{3}[1 + 0]$$

$$= \frac{2}{3}(2^{3/2} - 1) + \frac{2}{3}$$

$$= \frac{2}{3}\cdot 2^{3/2} - \frac{2}{3} + \frac{2}{3}$$

$$= \frac{2}{3}(8)^{1/2} = \frac{2}{3}\cdot 2\sqrt{2}$$

$$I = \frac{4\sqrt{2}}{3}.$$

140. Evaluate: $\displaystyle\int_{\pi/4}^{\pi/2} \cos 2x \, \log \sin x \, dx$

Sol. $\displaystyle I = \int_{\pi/4}^{\pi/2} \underset{\text{II}}{\cos 2x} \, \underset{\text{I}}{(\log \sin x)}\, dx$

$$= \left[\frac{\log \sin x \cdot \sin 2x}{2}\right]_{\pi/4}^{\pi/2}$$

$$\qquad - \int_{\pi/4}^{\pi/2} \frac{1}{\sin x}\cdot \cos x \cdot \frac{\sin 2x}{2}\, dx$$

$$= \left[\frac{1}{2}\log \sin \frac{\pi}{2}\sin \pi - \frac{1}{2}\log \sin \frac{\pi}{4}\sin \frac{\pi}{2}\right]$$

$$\qquad - \int_{\pi/4}^{\pi/2} \frac{1}{2}\frac{\cos x}{\sin x}\cdot 2 \sin x \cos x \, dx$$

$$= 0 - \frac{1}{2}\log \sin \frac{\pi}{4}\cdot \sin \frac{\pi}{2} - \int_{\pi/4}^{\pi/2} \cos^2 x \, dx$$

$$= -\frac{1}{2} \log \frac{1}{\sqrt{2}} - \int_{\pi/4}^{\pi/2} \frac{1+\cos 2x}{2} \, dx$$

$$= -\frac{1}{2} \log 2^{-1/2} - \frac{1}{2}\left[x + \frac{\sin 2x}{2}\right]_{\pi/4}^{\pi/2}$$

$$= \frac{1}{4} \log 2 - \frac{1}{2}\left[\frac{\pi}{2} + \frac{1}{2}\sin \pi - \frac{\pi}{4} - \frac{1}{2}\sin \frac{\pi}{2}\right]$$

$$= \frac{1}{4} \log 2 - \frac{1}{2}\left[\frac{\pi}{2} + 0 - \frac{\pi}{4} - \frac{1}{2}\right]$$

$$= \frac{1}{4} \log 2 - \frac{\pi}{4} + \frac{\pi}{8} + \frac{1}{4}$$

$$= \frac{1}{4} \log 2 + \frac{\pi - 2\pi}{8} + \frac{1}{4}$$

$$= \frac{1}{4} \log 2 - \frac{\pi}{8} + \frac{1}{4}.$$

141. Evaluate: $\int_0^{\pi/2} 2 \sin x \cos x \tan^{-1} (\sin x) \, dx$

Sol. Let $\quad I = \int_0^{\pi/2} 2\sin x \cos x \tan^{-1}(\sin x) \, dx$

Put $\quad \sin x = t$
$\quad\quad \cos x \, dx = dt$
if $x = 0, \quad t = 0$

if $x = \dfrac{\pi}{2}, \quad t = 1$

$\therefore \quad\quad I = 2\int_0^1 \underset{\text{II}}{t} \ \underset{\text{I}}{\tan^{-1} t} \ dt$

$$= 2\left[\tan^{-1} t \int_0^1 t \, dt - \int_0^1 \frac{1}{1+t^2} \cdot \frac{t^2}{2} \, dt\right]$$

$$= 2\left[\frac{t^2 \tan^{-1} t}{2}\right]_0^1 - \frac{2}{2}\int_0^1 \frac{t^2}{1+t^2} \, dt$$

$$= 2\left\{\frac{1 \cdot \tan^{-1} 1}{2} - 0\right\} - \int_0^1 \frac{1+t^2-1}{1+t^2} \, dt$$

$$= 2 \times \frac{\pi}{8} - \int_0^1 \frac{1+t^2}{1+t^2} \, dt + \int_0^1 \frac{dt}{1+t^2}$$

$$= \frac{\pi}{4} - \int_0^1 1 \, dt + \int_0^1 \frac{dt}{1+t^2}$$

$$= \frac{\pi}{4} - [t]_0^1 + [\tan^{-1} t]_0^1$$

$$= \frac{\pi}{4} - (1 - 0) + (\tan^{-1} 1 - \tan^{-1} 0)$$

$$= \frac{\pi}{4} - 1 + \frac{\pi}{4} = \frac{2\pi}{4} - 1 = \frac{\pi}{2} - 1.$$

Self - Assessment

142. $\int x^2 e^x \, dx$

Sol. $x^2 e^x - 2xe^x + 2e^x + c$

143. $\int \tan^{-1} x \, dx$

Sol. $x \tan^{-1} x - \dfrac{1}{2} \log |1 + x| + C$

144. $\int \dfrac{dx}{x^2 - 9}$

Sol. $\dfrac{1}{6} \log \left|\dfrac{x-3}{x+3}\right| + c$

145. $\int \dfrac{3x}{1+2x^4} \, dx$

Sol. $\dfrac{3}{2\sqrt{2}} \tan^{-1} (\sqrt{2}x^2) + C$

146. $\int \dfrac{1-\cos x}{1+\cos x} \, dx$

Sol. $2 \tan \dfrac{x}{2} - x + c$

147. $\int x\sqrt{x+2} \, dx$

Sol. $\dfrac{2}{5}(x+2)^{5/2} - \dfrac{4}{3}(x+2)^{3/2} + C$

148. $\int \dfrac{e^{\tan^{-1} x}}{1+x^2} \, dx$

Sol. $e^{\tan^{-1} x} + C$

149. $\int_0^{\pi/2} \dfrac{\sin x}{1 + \cos^2 x} \, dx$

Sol. $\dfrac{\pi}{4}$

150. $\int \dfrac{dx}{\sin (x-a) \sin (x-b)}$

Sol. $\dfrac{1}{\sin (b-a)} \log \left|\dfrac{\sin (x-b)}{\sin (x-a)}\right| + C$

151. $\int e^{\sin^2 x} \sin 2x \, dx$

Sol. $e^{\sin^2 x} + C$

152. $\int_0^{\pi/2} \dfrac{\cos^2 x}{\cos^2 x + 4 \sin^2 x} \, dx$

Sol. $\dfrac{\pi}{6}$

153. $\int \dfrac{1}{x^3 + 1} \, dx$

Sol. $\dfrac{1}{3} \log |x+1| - \dfrac{1}{6} \log (x^2 - x + 1)$

$$+ \frac{1}{\sqrt{3}} \tan^{-1}\left(\frac{2x-1}{\sqrt{3}}\right) + C$$

154. $\displaystyle \int \frac{\cos\theta}{(2+\sin\theta)\,(3+4\sin\theta)}\,d\theta$

Sol. $\dfrac{1}{5}\{\log|3+4\sin\theta|-\log|2+\sin\theta|\}+C$

155. $\displaystyle \int \frac{x}{1+x+x^2+x^3}\,dx$

Sol. $-\dfrac{1}{2}\log|x+1|+\dfrac{1}{4}\log|x^2+1|+\dfrac{1}{2}\tan^{-1}x+c$

156. $\displaystyle \int \frac{dx}{5+4\cos x}$

Sol. $\dfrac{2}{3}\tan^{-1}\left(\dfrac{\tan x/2}{3}\right)+C$

157. $\displaystyle \int \frac{\cos\sqrt{x}}{\sqrt{x}}\,dx$

Sol. $2\sin\sqrt{x}+C$

158. $\displaystyle \int \sin x\,\sin 2x\,\sin 3x\,dx$

Sol. $-\dfrac{\cos 4x}{16}+\dfrac{\cos 6x}{24}-\dfrac{\cos 2x}{8}+C$

159. $\displaystyle \int \sin^3(2x+1)\,dx$

Sol. $-\dfrac{3}{8}\cos(2x+1)+\dfrac{1}{24}\cos(6x+3)+C$

160. $\displaystyle \int \frac{1}{\sqrt{9-25x^2}}$

Sol. $\dfrac{1}{5}\sin^{-1}\left(\dfrac{5x}{3}\right)+C$

161. $\displaystyle \int \frac{4x+1}{\sqrt{2x^2+x-3}}\,dx$

Sol. $2\sqrt{2x^2+x-3}+C$

162. $\displaystyle \int \frac{dx}{x(x^4-1)}\,dx$

Sol. $\dfrac{1}{4}\log\left|\dfrac{x^4-1}{x^4}\right|+C$

163. $\displaystyle \int_0^1 \cos^{-1}x\,dx$

Sol. 1

164. $\displaystyle \int_0^1 x\log(1+2x)\,dx$

Sol. $\dfrac{3}{8}\log 3$

165. $\displaystyle \int_2^e \left(\frac{1}{\log x}-\frac{1}{(\log x)^2}\right)dx$

Sol. $e-\dfrac{2}{\log 2}$

166. $\displaystyle \int_0^\pi \frac{x\sin x}{1+\cos^2 x}\,dx$

Sol. $\dfrac{\pi^2}{4}$

167. $\displaystyle \int_0^{\pi/2} \sin^6 x\,dx$

Sol. $\dfrac{5\pi}{32}$

168. $\displaystyle \int_0^{\pi/2} \log|\sin x|\,dx$

Sol. $-\dfrac{\pi}{2}\log 2$

169. $\displaystyle \int_0^{\pi/2} \frac{\sin^3 x}{\sin^3 x+\cos^3 x}\,dx$

Sol. $\dfrac{\pi}{4}$

170. $\displaystyle \int_1^2 \frac{5x^2}{x^2+4x+3}\,dx$

Sol. $5-10\log\left(\dfrac{15}{8}\right)+\dfrac{25}{2}\log\left(\dfrac{6}{5}\right)$

171. $\displaystyle \int (\sin^{-1}x)^2\,dx$

Sol. $x(\sin^{-1}x)^2+2\sqrt{1-x^2}\,\sin^{-1}x-2x+C$

172. $\displaystyle \int_0^{\pi/2} 2\tan^3 x\,dx$

Sol. $1-\log 2$

173. $\displaystyle \int_0^{\pi/4} \frac{\sin x+\cos x}{9+16\sin 2x}\,dx$

Sol. $\dfrac{1}{40}\log 9$

174. $\displaystyle \int \frac{e^x}{(1+e^x)\,(2+e^x)}\,dx$

Sol. $\log\left(\dfrac{1+e^x}{2+e^x}\right)+C$

175. $\displaystyle \int_0^2 x\sqrt{2-x}\,dx$

Sol. $\dfrac{16\sqrt{2}}{15}$

176. $\displaystyle \int_0^a \frac{\sqrt{x}}{\sqrt{x}+\sqrt{a-x}}\,dx$

Sol. $\dfrac{1}{2}a$

177. $\displaystyle \int_0^\pi \log(1+\cos x)\,dx$

Sol. $-\pi\log 2$

178. $\displaystyle \int_{-\pi/4}^{\pi/4} \log(\sin x+\cos x)\,dx$

Sol. $\dfrac{-\pi}{4}\log 2$

∞

Applications of the Integrals

Basic Concepts

1. By using the concepts of integration we will find the area bounded by curves.

   Area under simple curves:

   (i) The area enclosed by the curve $y = f(x)$ and the ordinates $x = a$, $x = b$ and X-axis is given by

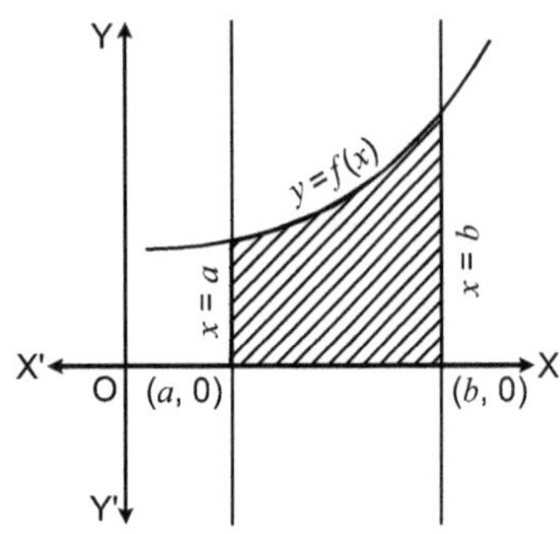

$$\text{Area} = \int_a^b y\, dx$$

$$= \int_a^b f(x)\, dx$$

   (ii) The area enclosed by the curve $x = f(y)$, y-axis and abscissas $y = a$ and $y = b$ is given by

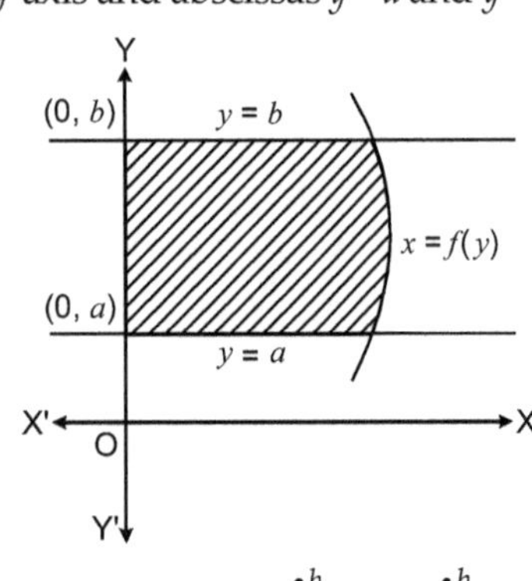

$$A = \int_a^b x\, dy = \int_a^b f(y)\, dy$$

   (iii) When the curve $y = f(x)$ lies below the X-axis, then $y = f(x)$ is negative so the area under the curve is also negative so we take the modulus of the area *i.e.*, area will be given by

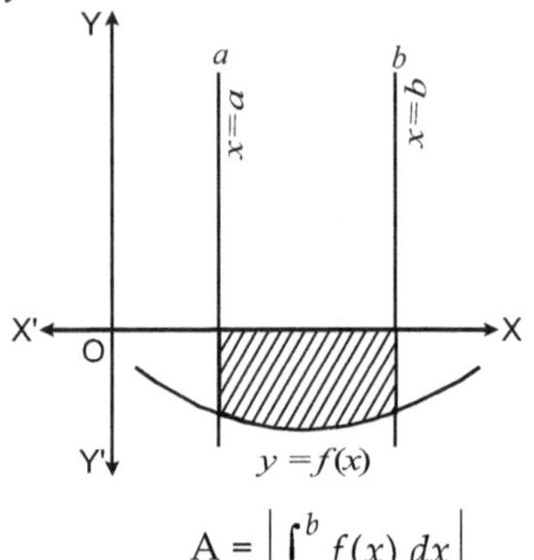

$$A = \left| \int_a^b f(x)\, dx \right|$$

   (iv) To find the area of a circle $x^2 + y^2 = a^2$

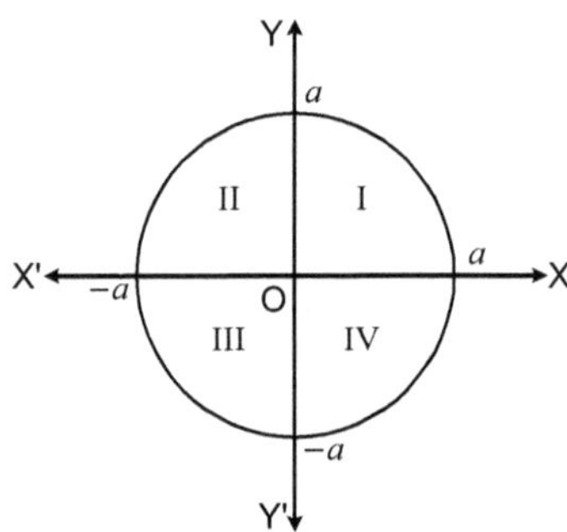

   Area of the circle is divided into four equal parts I, II, III and IV

$$A = \int_a^b y\, dx$$

$$= \int_a^b \sqrt{a^2 - x^2}\, dx$$

Multiple Choice Questions

1. The area of the region bounded by the curve $x = 2y + 3$ and the lines $y = 1$, $y = -1$ is:

   [NCERT Exemplar]

   (a) 4 sq. units

   (b) $\dfrac{3}{2}$ sq. units

   (c) 6 sq. units

   (d) 8 sq. units

   Sol. (c) 6 sq. units

   Explanation :

   Required area, $A = \int_{-1}^{1} (2y + 3)\, dy$

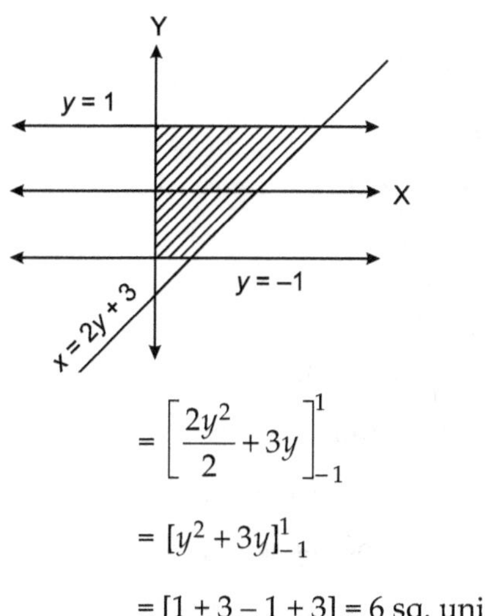

$$= \left[\frac{2y^2}{2} + 3y \right]_{-1}^{1}$$

$$= [y^2 + 3y]_{-1}^{1}$$

$$= [1 + 3 - 1 + 3] = 6 \text{ sq. units.}$$

2. The area of the region bounded by the curves $y = |\,x - 2\,|$, $x = 1$, $x = 3$ and the x-axis is:

(a)   4 sq. units (b)   2 sq. units
(c)   3 sq. units (d)   1 sq. unit

Sol. (d) 1 sq. unit

Explanation :

$$\text{Required area} = \int_1^3 |\,x - 2\,|\, dx$$

$$= \int_1^2 (2 - x)\, dx + \int_2^3 (x - 2)\, dx$$

$$= \left[2x - \frac{x^2}{2} \right]_1^2 + \left[\frac{x^2}{2} - 2x \right]_2^3$$

$$= \frac{1}{2} + \frac{1}{2} = 1 \text{ sq unit.}$$

3. The area bounded by the curve $y = x$, x-axis and ordinates $x = -1$ to $x = 2$ is:

(a)   0 (b) $\frac{1}{2}$ sq. unit

(c) $\frac{3}{2}$ sq. units (d) $\frac{5}{2}$ sq. units

Sol. (d) $\frac{5}{2}$ sq. units

Explanation :

$$\text{Bounded area} = \left| \int_{-1}^0 x\, dx \right| + \left| \int_0^2 x\, dx \right|$$

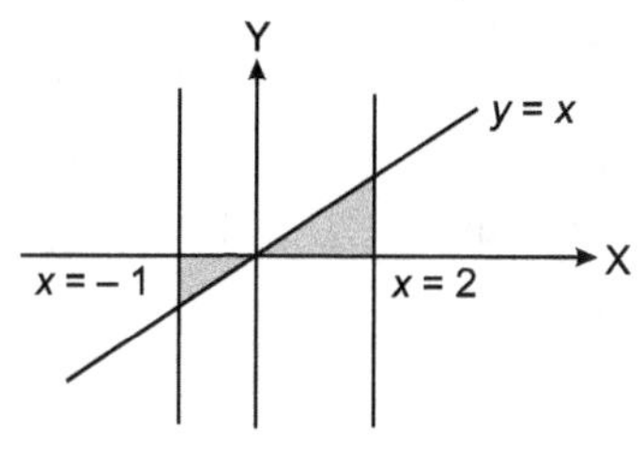

$$= \left| -\frac{1}{2} \right| + |\,2\,| = 2 + \frac{1}{2} = \frac{5}{2} \text{ sq. units.}$$

4. The area of the region bounded by the line $2y + x = 8$, X-axis and the lines $x = 2$ and $x = 4$.

(a)   5 sq. units (b)   7 sq. units
(c)   9 sq. units (d)   10 sq. units

Sol. (a) 5 sq. units

Explanation :

Required area = Area of the shaded region

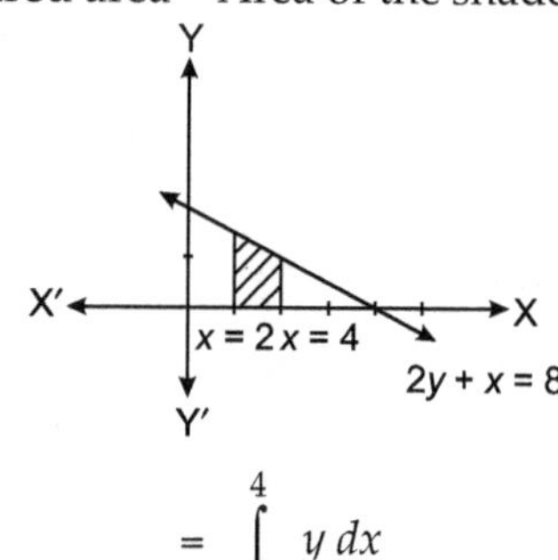

$$= \int_{x=2}^{4} y\, dx$$

$$= \int_2^4 \frac{1}{2} (8 - x)\, dx$$

$$= \frac{1}{2} \left[8x - \frac{x^2}{2} \right]_2^4$$

$$= \frac{1}{2} \left[\left(8 \cdot (4) - \frac{4^2}{2} \right) - \left(8 \cdot (2) - \frac{2^2}{2} \right) \right]$$

$$= 5 \text{ sq. unit.}$$

5. The area of the region bounded by the curve $y = x + 1$ and the lines $x = 2$, $x = 3$ is:

[NCERT Exemplar]

(a) $\frac{7}{2}$ sq. units (b) $\frac{9}{2}$ sq. units

(c) $\frac{11}{2}$ sq. units (d) $\frac{13}{2}$ sq. units

Sol. (a) $\frac{7}{2}$ sq. units

Explanation :

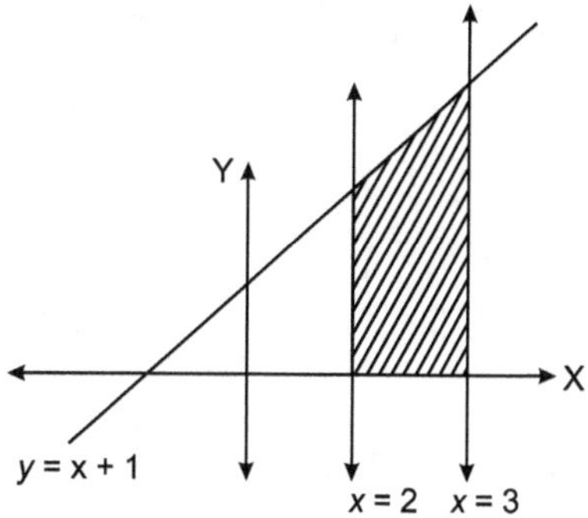

$$\text{Required area, A} = \int_2^3 (x + 1)\, dx = \left[\frac{x^2}{2} + x \right]_2^3$$

$$= \left[\frac{9}{2} + 3 - \frac{4}{2} - 2\right]$$

$$= \left[\frac{5}{2} + 1\right] = \frac{7}{2} \text{ sq. units}$$

6. Area of the region in the first quadrant enclosed by the X-axis, the line $y = x$ and the circle $x^2 + y^2 = 32$ is: **[NCERT Exemplar]**

(a) 16π sq. units   (b) 4π sq. units

(c) 32π sq. units   (d) 24π sq. units

Sol. (b) 4π sq. units

Explanation :

We have, area enclosed by X-axis *i.e.*, $y = 0$, $y = x$ and the circle $x^2 + y^2 = 32$ in first quadrant.

Since, $\qquad x^2 + (x)^2 = 32 \qquad [\because y = x]$

$\Rightarrow \qquad\qquad 2x^2 = 32$

$\Rightarrow \qquad\qquad x = \pm 4$

So, the intersection point of circle $x^2 + y^2 = 32$ and line $y = x$ are $(4, 4)$ or $(-4, 4)$.

and $\qquad x^2 + y^2 = (4\sqrt{2})^2$

Since, $\qquad\qquad y = 0$

$\therefore \qquad\qquad x^2 + (0)^2 = 32$

$\Rightarrow \qquad\qquad x = \pm 4\sqrt{2}$

So, the circle intersects the X-axis at $(\pm 4\sqrt{2}, 0)$.

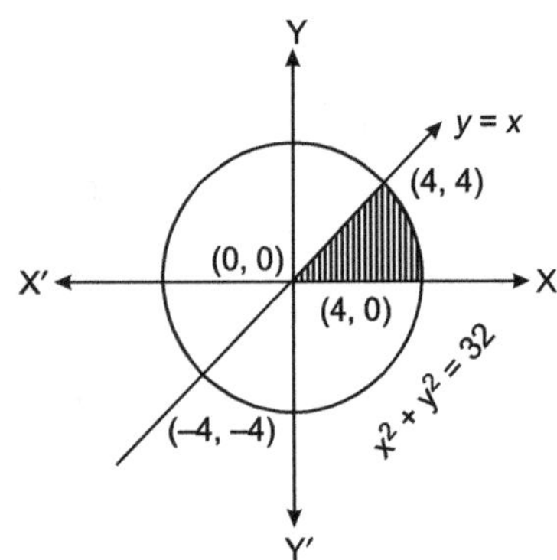

Area of shaded region

$$= \int_0^4 x\, dx + \int_4^{4\sqrt{2}} \sqrt{(4\sqrt{2})^2 - x^2}\, dx$$

$$= \left| \frac{x^2}{2} \right|_0^4 + \left[\frac{x}{2}\sqrt{(4\sqrt{2})^2 - x^2}\right.$$

$$\left. + \frac{(4\sqrt{2})^2}{2}\sin^{-1}\frac{x}{4\sqrt{2}} \right]_4^{4\sqrt{2}}$$

$$= \frac{16}{2} + \left[\frac{4\sqrt{2}}{2}\cdot 0 + 16\sin^{-1}\frac{(4\sqrt{2})}{(4\sqrt{2})}\right.$$

$$\left. - \frac{4}{2}\sqrt{(4\sqrt{2})^2 - 16} - 16\sin^{-1}\frac{4}{4\sqrt{2}}\right]$$

$$= 8 + \left[16\cdot\frac{\pi}{2} - 2\cdot\sqrt{16} - 16\cdot\frac{\pi}{4}\right]$$

$$= 8 + [8\pi - 8 - 4\pi] = 4\pi \text{ sq units.}$$

7. The area of the region bounded by the curve $y = \sqrt{16 - x^2}$ and X-axis is: **[NCERT Exemplar]**

(a) 8π sq. units   (b) 20π sq. units

(c) 16π sq. units   (d) 256π sq. units

Sol. (a) 8π sq. units

Explanation :

Given equation of curve is $y = \sqrt{16 - x^2}$ and the equation of line is X-axis *i.e.*, $y = 0$.

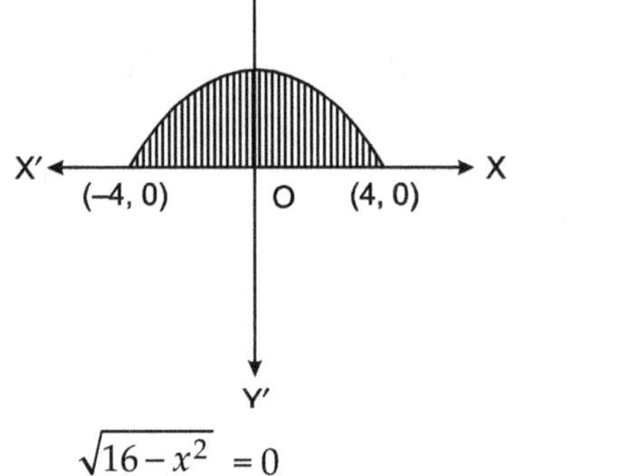

$\therefore \qquad \sqrt{16 - x^2} = 0 \qquad\qquad ...(i)$

$\Rightarrow \qquad 16 - x^2 = 0$

$\Rightarrow \qquad x^2 = 16 \Rightarrow x = \pm 4$

So, the intersection points of $(4, 0)$ and $(-4, 0)$.

$\therefore$ Area of curve,

$$A = \int_{-4}^{4} (16 - x^2)^{1/2}\, dx$$

$$= \int_{-4}^{4} \sqrt{(4^2 - x^2)}\, dx$$

$$= \left[\frac{x}{2}\sqrt{4^2 - x^2} + \frac{4^2}{2}\sin^{-1}\frac{x}{4} \right]_{-4}^{4}$$

$$= \left[\frac{4}{2}\sqrt{4^2 - 4^2} + 8\sin^{-1}\frac{4}{4}\right]$$

$$- \left[-\frac{4}{2}\sqrt{4^2 - (-4)^2} + 8\sin^{-1}\left(-\frac{4}{4}\right)\right]$$

$$= \left[2\cdot 0 + 8\cdot\frac{\pi}{2} - 0 + 8\cdot\frac{\pi}{2}\right] = 8\pi \text{ sq. units.}$$

8. The area of the region bounded by the circle $x^2 + y^2 = 1$ is: **[NCERT Exemplar]**

(a) 2π sq. units   (b) π sq. units

(c) 3π sq. units   (d) 4π sq. units

Sol. (b) π sq. units

Explanation :

We have, $\qquad x^2 + y^2 = 1^2 \qquad [\because r = \pm 1]$

$\Rightarrow \qquad\qquad y^2 = 1 - x^2$

$$\Rightarrow \qquad y = \sqrt{1-x^2}$$

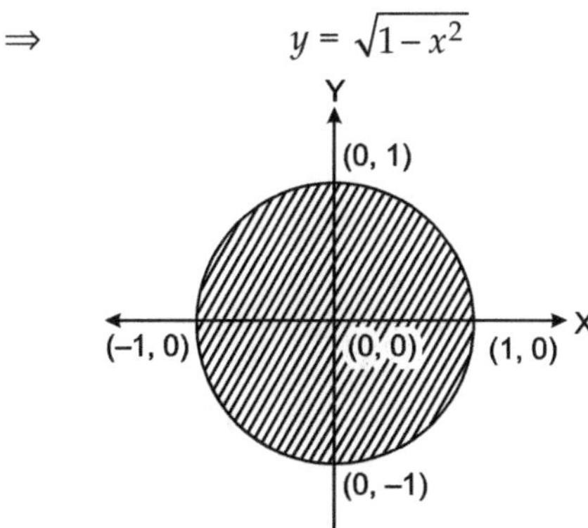

$\therefore$ Area enclosed by circle

$$= 2\int_{-1}^{1} \sqrt{1^2 - x^2}\, dx$$

$$\left[\because \int_{-a}^{a} f(x)\, dx = 2\int_{0}^{a} f(x)\, dx\right]$$

$$= 2\cdot 2\int_{0}^{1} \sqrt{1^2 - x^2}\, dx$$

$$= 2\cdot 2\left[\frac{x}{2}\sqrt{1^2 - x^2} + \frac{1^2}{2}\sin^{-1}\frac{x}{1}\right]_0^1$$

$$= 4\left[\frac{1}{2}\cdot 0 + \frac{1}{2}\cdot\frac{\pi}{2} - 0 - \frac{1}{2}\cdot 0\right]$$

$$= 4\cdot\frac{\pi}{4} = \pi \text{ sq. units.}$$

9. Area lying in the first quadrant and bounded by the circle $x^2 + y^2 = 4$ and the lines $x = 0$ and $x = 2$ is:

(a) π sq. units
(b) $\dfrac{\pi}{2}$ sq. units

(c) $\dfrac{\pi}{3}$ sq. units
(d) $\dfrac{\pi}{4}$ sq. units

Sol. (a) π sq. units

Explanation :

The area bounded by the circle and the lines, $x = 0$ and $x = 2$, in the first quadrant is represented as shaded region.

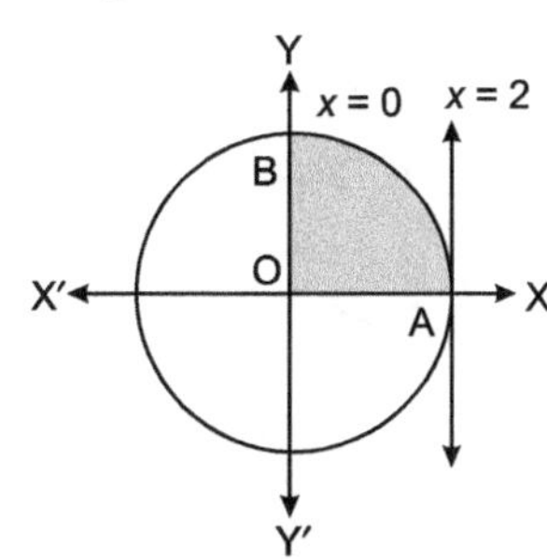

$$\text{Area OAB} = \int_{0}^{2} y\, dx$$

$$= \int_{0}^{2} \sqrt{4 - x^2}\, dx$$

$$= \left[\frac{x}{2}\sqrt{4-x^2} + \frac{4}{2}\sin^{-1}\frac{x}{2}\right]_0^2$$

$$= 2\left(\frac{\pi}{2}\right) = \pi.$$

10. The area of smaller part between the circle $x^2 + y^2 = 4$ and the line $x = 1$ is:

(a) $\dfrac{4\pi}{3} - \sqrt{3}$ sq. units
(b) $\dfrac{8\pi}{3} - \sqrt{3}$ sq. units

(c) $\dfrac{4\pi}{3} + \sqrt{3}$ sq. units
(d) $\dfrac{5\pi}{3} + \sqrt{3}$ sq. units

Sol. (a) $\dfrac{4\pi}{3} - \sqrt{3}$ sq. units

Explanation :

Area of smaller part

$$= 2\int_{1}^{2} \sqrt{4 - x^2}\, dx$$

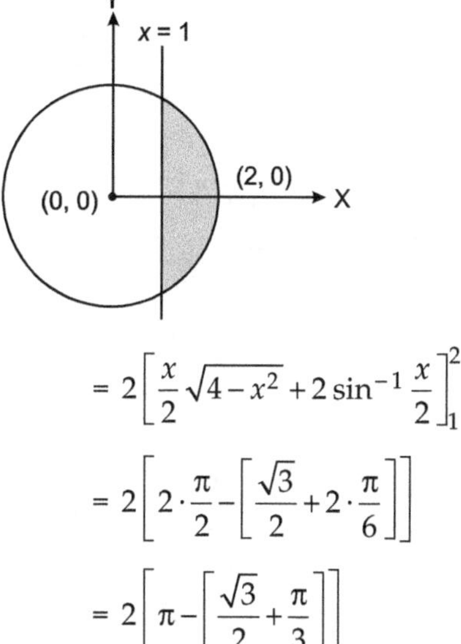

$$= 2\left[\frac{x}{2}\sqrt{4-x^2} + 2\sin^{-1}\frac{x}{2}\right]_1^2$$

$$= 2\left[2\cdot\frac{\pi}{2} - \left[\frac{\sqrt{3}}{2} + 2\cdot\frac{\pi}{6}\right]\right]$$

$$= 2\left[\pi - \left[\frac{\sqrt{3}}{2} + \frac{\pi}{3}\right]\right]$$

$$= \frac{4\pi}{3} - \sqrt{3} \text{ sq. units.}$$

11. The area enclosed by the circle $x^2 + y^2 = 2$ is equal to:

(a) 4π sq. units
(b) $2\sqrt{2}\,\pi$ sq. units
(c) $4\pi^2$ sq. units
(d) 2π sq. units

Sol. (d) 2π sq. units

Explanation :

$$\because \qquad \text{Area} = 4\int_{0}^{\sqrt{2}} \sqrt{2 - x^2}\, dx$$

$$= 4\left(\frac{x}{2}\sqrt{2-x^2} + \sin^{-1}\frac{x}{\sqrt{2}}\right)_0^{\sqrt{2}}$$

$$= 2\pi \text{ sq. units}$$

So the correct option is (d).

12. The area of the region bounded by parabola $y^2 = x$ and the straight line $2y = x$ is:

[NCERT Exemplar]

(a) $\dfrac{4}{3}$ sq. units

(b) 1 sq. unit

(c) $\dfrac{2}{3}$ sq. unit

(d) $\dfrac{1}{3}$ sq. unit

Sol. (a) $\dfrac{4}{3}$ sq. units

Explanation :

We have to find the area enclosed by parabola $y^2 = x$ and the straight line $2y = x$.

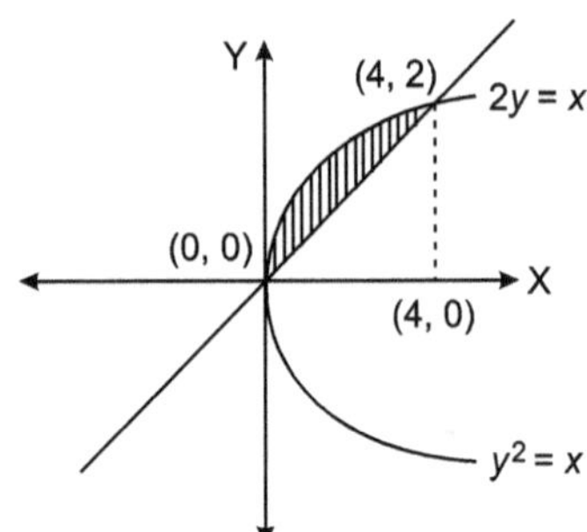

$\therefore$ $\left(\dfrac{x}{2}\right)^2 = x$

$\Rightarrow$ $x^2 = 4x$

$\Rightarrow$ $x(x-4) = 0$

$\Rightarrow$ $x = 4$

$\Rightarrow$ $y = 2$

and $x = 0$

$\Rightarrow$ $y = 0$

So, the intersection points are $(0, 0)$ and $(4, 2)$.

Area enclosed by shaded region,

$$A = \int_0^4 \left[\sqrt{x} - \dfrac{x}{2}\right] dx$$

$$= \left[\dfrac{x^{\frac{1}{2}+1}}{\frac{1}{2}+1} - \dfrac{1}{2}\cdot\dfrac{x^2}{2}\right]_0^4 = \left[2\cdot\dfrac{x^{3/2}}{3} - \dfrac{x^2}{4}\right]_0^4$$

$$= \dfrac{2}{3} 4^{3/2} - \dfrac{16}{4} - \dfrac{2}{3}\cdot 0 + \dfrac{1}{4}\cdot 0$$

$$= \dfrac{16}{3} - \dfrac{16}{4} = \dfrac{64-48}{12} = \dfrac{16}{12} = \dfrac{4}{3} \text{ sq. units.}$$

13. Area bounded by the parabola $y = 4x^2$, y-axis and the lines $y = 1$, $y = 4$ is:

(a) 3 sq. units

(b) $\dfrac{7}{5}$ sq. units

(c) $\dfrac{7}{3}$ sq. units

(d) None of these

Sol. (c) $\dfrac{7}{3}$ sq. units

Explanation :

Given, $y = 4x^2$

Area to be found between y-axis $y = 1$ & $y = 4$.

The figure is as follows:

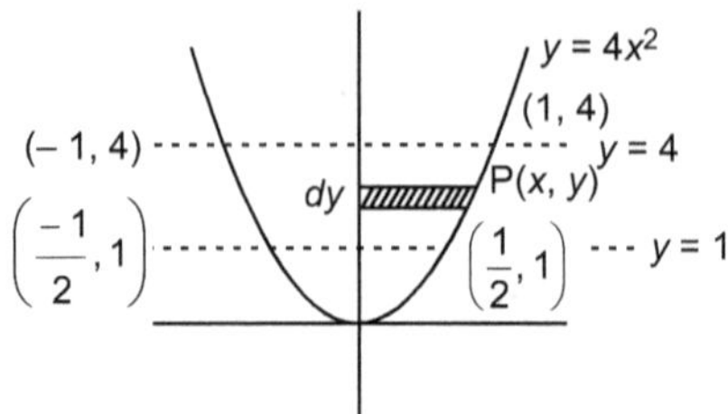

at $y = 1 \rightarrow y = 4x^2$ gives $x = \dfrac{1}{2}$ & $-\dfrac{1}{2}$

at $y = 4 \rightarrow y = 4x^2$ gives $4 = 4x^2$ or $x = 1, -1$

Here $\text{Area} = \int_1^4 x\,dy = \int_1^4 \dfrac{\sqrt{y}}{2}\,dy$

$$= \dfrac{1}{2}\int_1^4 y^{1/2}\,dy$$

$$= \dfrac{1}{2}\left[\dfrac{2}{3} y^{3/2}\right]_1^4 = \dfrac{1}{3}\left[y^{3/2}\right]_1^4$$

$$= \dfrac{1}{3}[4^{3/2} - 1^{3/2}] = \dfrac{1}{3}[8-1]$$

$$= \dfrac{7}{3} \text{ sq. units.}$$

14. The area bounded by the parabola $y^2 = 4ax$, its axis and two ordinates $x = 4$, $x = 9$ is:

(a) $4a^2$ sq. units

(b) $4a^2.4$ sq. units

(c) $4a^2 (9-4)$ sq. units

(d) $\dfrac{152\sqrt{a}}{3}$ sq. units

Sol. (d) $\dfrac{152\sqrt{a}}{3}$ sq. units

Explanation :

Shaded area $A = 2\int_4^9 \sqrt{4ax}\,dx$

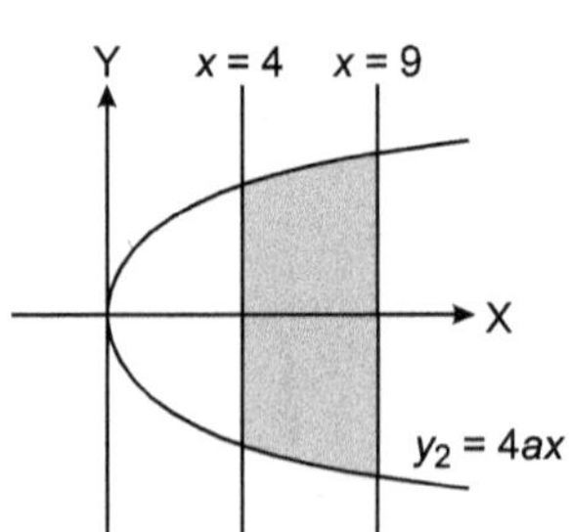

$$A = 4\sqrt{a}\times\dfrac{2}{3}[x^{3/2}]_4^9 = \dfrac{152\sqrt{a}}{3} \text{ sq. units.}$$

15. Area bounded by the parabola $y^2 = 4ax$ and its latus rectum is:

(a) $\dfrac{2}{3} a^2$ sq. unit

(b) $\dfrac{4}{3} a^2$ sq. unit

(c) $\dfrac{8}{3} a^2$ sq. unit

(d) $\dfrac{3}{8} a^2$ sq. unit

Sol. (c) $\dfrac{8}{3} a^2$ sq. unit

Explanation :

$$\text{Area} = 2\int_0^a y\, dx = 2\int_0^a \sqrt{4ax}\, dx$$

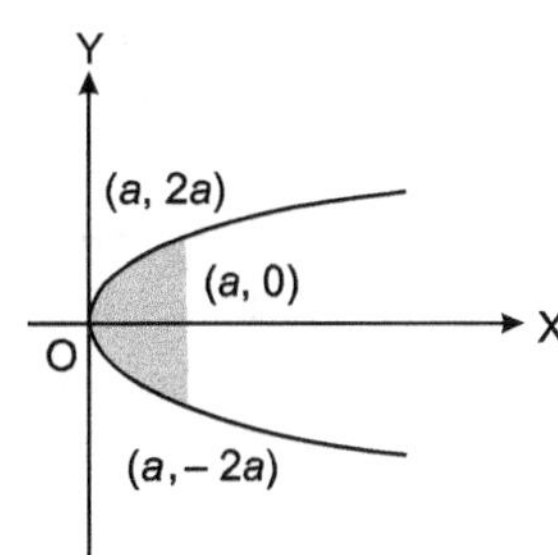

$$= 2 \times 2\sqrt{a} \times \frac{2}{3}\, |\, x^{3/2}\, |_0^a = \frac{8}{3} a^2 \text{ sq. units.}$$

16. The area between the curve $y^2 = 4ax$, x-axis and the lines $x = 0$ and $x = a$ is:

(a) $\dfrac{4}{3} a^2$ sq. units

(b) $\dfrac{8}{3} a^2$ sq. units

(c) $\dfrac{2}{3} a^2$ sq. units

(d) $\dfrac{5}{3} a^2$ sq. units

Sol. (b) $\dfrac{8}{3} a^2$ sq. units

Explanation :

$$\text{Required area} = 2\int_0^a y\, dx$$

$$= 2\int_0^a \sqrt{4ax}\, dx$$

$$= 4\sqrt{a} \times \frac{2}{3}[x^{3/2}]_0^a$$

$$= \frac{8\sqrt{a}}{3} \cdot a\sqrt{a}$$

$$= \frac{8}{3} a^2 \text{ sq. units.}$$

17. The area bounded by the curve $y = x^2$, the Y-axis and the X-axis and $x = 3$ is:

(a) 5 sq. units

(b) 7 sq. units

(c) 9 sq. units

(d) 10 sq. units

Sol. (b) 7 sq. units

Explanation :

$$\text{The required area A} = \int_{x=0}^{3} y \cdot dx$$

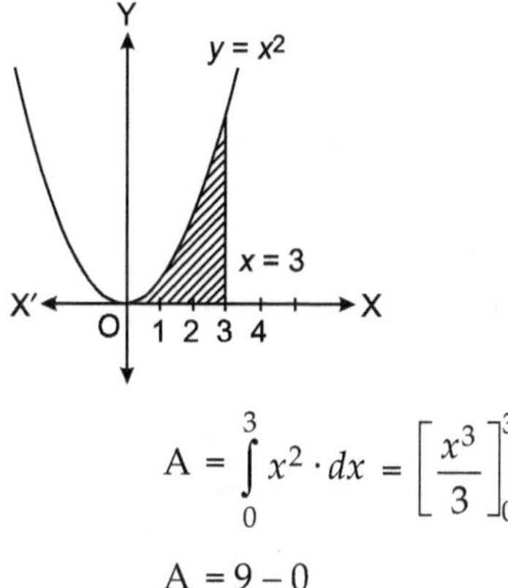

$$A = \int_0^3 x^2 \cdot dx = \left[\frac{x^3}{3}\right]_0^3$$

$$A = 9 - 0$$

$$= 9 \text{ sq. units.}$$

18. The area of the regions bounded by the curve $y = x^2$, the X-axis and the lines $x = 1$ and $x = 2$:

(a) $\dfrac{26}{3}$ sq. units

(b) $\dfrac{14}{5}$ sq. units

(c) $\dfrac{26}{5}$ sq. units

(d) $\dfrac{14}{3}$ sq. units

Sol. (a) $\dfrac{26}{3}$ sq. units

Explanation :

Let A be the required area

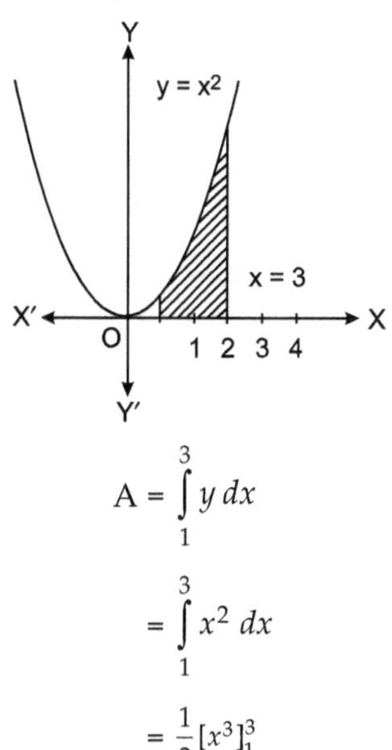

$$A = \int_1^3 y\, dx$$

$$= \int_1^3 x^2\, dx$$

$$= \frac{1}{3}[x^3]_1^3$$

$$= \frac{1}{3}[27-1]$$

$$A = \frac{26}{3} \text{ sq. units.}$$

19. The area of the regions bounded by the curve $y^2 = 4x$, the X-axis and the lines $x = 1$, $x = 4$ $y \geq 0$:

(a) $\dfrac{26}{3}$ sq. units (b) $\dfrac{14}{5}$ sq. units

(c) $\dfrac{28}{3}$ sq. units (d) $\dfrac{14}{3}$ sq. units

Sol. (c) $\dfrac{28}{3}$ sq. units

Explanation :

Let A be the required area

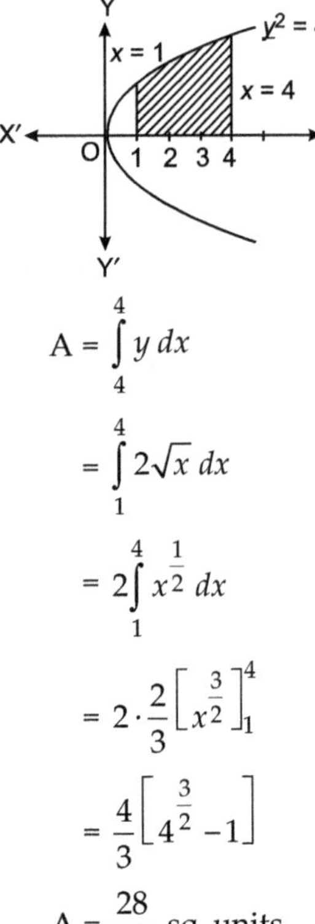

$$A = \int_4^4 y \, dx$$

$$= \int_1^4 2\sqrt{x} \, dx$$

$$= 2\int_1^4 x^{\frac{1}{2}} \, dx$$

$$= 2 \cdot \frac{2}{3}\left[x^{\frac{3}{2}}\right]_1^4$$

$$= \frac{4}{3}\left[4^{\frac{3}{2}} - 1\right]$$

$$A = \frac{28}{3} \text{ sq. units.}$$

20. The area of the given bounded by the curves $x^2 = 16y$, $y = 1$, $y = 4$ and the Y-axis, lying in the first quadrant:

(a) $\dfrac{26}{3}$ sq. units (b) $\dfrac{28}{3}$ sq. units

(c) $\dfrac{56}{3}$ sq. units (d) $\dfrac{14}{3}$ sq. units

Sol. (c) $\dfrac{56}{3}$ sq. units

Explanation :

Let A be the required area

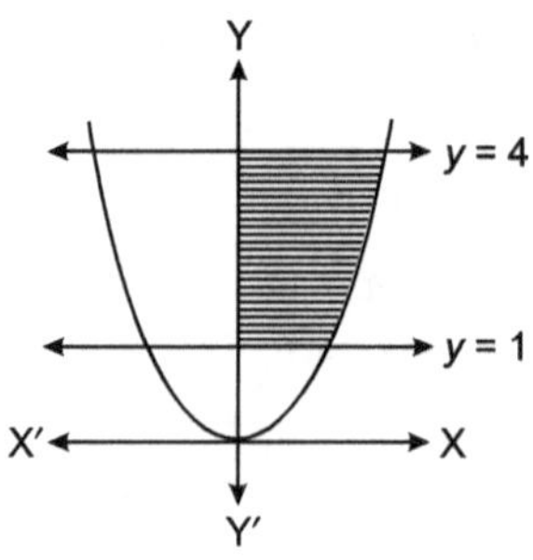

$$\text{Required area} = \int_1^4 x \, dy$$

$$A = \int_1^4 \sqrt{16y} \, dy$$

$$= 4\int_1^4 \sqrt{y} \cdot dy$$

$$= 4\left[\frac{2}{3}y^{3/2}\right]_1^4$$

$$= \frac{8}{3} \times [8-1] = \frac{8}{3} \times 7$$

$$A = \frac{56}{3} \text{ sq. units.}$$

21. The area of the region bounded by the curve $x^2 = 4y$ and the straight line $x = 4y - 2$ is:

[NCERT Exemplar]

(a) $\dfrac{3}{8}$ sq. unit (b) $\dfrac{5}{8}$ sq. unit

(c) $\dfrac{7}{8}$ sq. unit (d) $\dfrac{9}{8}$ sq. units

Sol. (d) $\dfrac{9}{8}$ sq. units

Explanation :

Given equation of curve is $x^2 = 4y$ and the straight line $x = 4y - 2$.

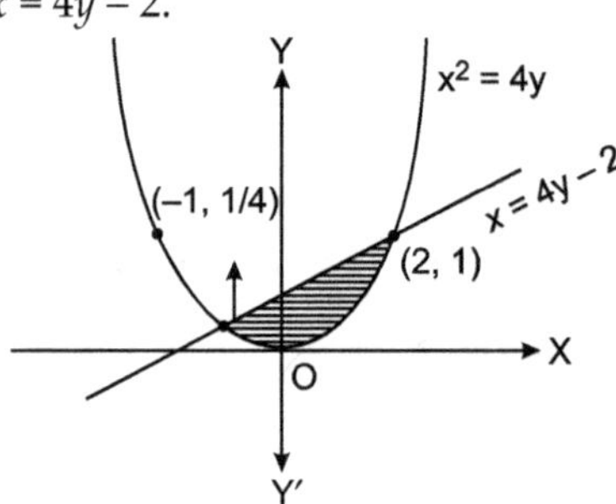

For intersection point, put $x = 4y - 2$ in equation of curve, we get

$$(4y - 2)^2 = 4y$$

$$\Rightarrow \quad 16y^2 + 4 - 16y = 4y$$

$$\Rightarrow \quad 16y^2 - 20y + 4 = 0$$

$$\Rightarrow \quad 4y^2 - 5y + 1 = 0$$

$\Rightarrow \qquad 4y^2 - 4y - y + 1 = 0$

$\Rightarrow \qquad 4y(y - 1) - 1(y - 1) = 0$

$\Rightarrow \qquad (4y - 1)(y - 1) = 0$

$\therefore \qquad\qquad y = 1, \dfrac{1}{4}$

For $y = 1$, $x = \sqrt{4 \cdot 1} = 2$ [since, negative value

does not satisfy the equation of line]

For $y = \dfrac{1}{4}$, $x = \sqrt{4 \cdot \dfrac{1}{4}} = -1$ [positive value does

not satisfy the equation of line]

So, the intersection points are $(2, 1)$ and $\left(-1, \dfrac{1}{4}\right)$.

$\therefore$ Area of shaded region

$$= \int_{-1}^{2}\left(\dfrac{x+2}{4}\right) dx - \int_{-1}^{2}\dfrac{x^2}{4}\, dx$$

$$= \dfrac{1}{4}\left[\dfrac{x^2}{2} + 2x\right]_{-1}^{2} - \dfrac{1}{4}\left|\dfrac{x^3}{3}\right|_{-1}^{2}$$

$$= -\dfrac{1}{4}\left[\dfrac{4}{2} + 4 - \dfrac{1}{2} + 2\right] - \dfrac{1}{4}\left[\dfrac{8}{3} + \dfrac{1}{3}\right]$$

$$= \dfrac{1}{4} \cdot \dfrac{15}{2} - \dfrac{1}{4} \cdot \dfrac{9}{3} = \dfrac{45 - 18}{24}$$

$$= \dfrac{27}{24} = \dfrac{9}{8} \text{ sq. units.}$$

22. If area bounded by the curve $y^2 = 4ax$ and $y = mx$ is $\dfrac{a^2}{3}$, then the value of m is:

(a)   2   (b) -2

(c) $\dfrac{1}{2}$ (d)   None of these

Sol. (a)   2

Explanation :

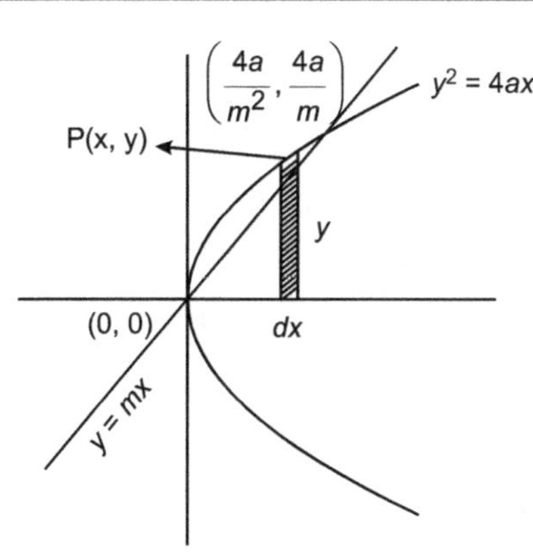

Given, $\qquad y^2 = 4ax \qquad\qquad$ ...(i)

$\qquad\qquad\qquad y = mx \qquad\qquad$ ...(ii)

Substitutes (ii) in (i)

$$(mx)^2 = 4ax$$

which gives $m^2x^2 - 4ax = 0$

$$x[m^2x - 4a] = 0$$

i.e., $\qquad\qquad x = 0, x = \dfrac{4a}{m^2}$

From (ii) equation $x = 0$, $y = 0$

and $\qquad\qquad x = \dfrac{4a}{m^2}$

$\Rightarrow \qquad\qquad y = m \times \dfrac{4a}{m^2}$

$$y = \dfrac{4a}{m}$$

$\therefore$ Area $= \displaystyle\int_0^{4a/m^2} y\, dx - \int_0^{4a/m^2} y\, dx$

$$= \int_0^{4a/m^2} (\sqrt{4ax} - mx)\, dx$$

$$\text{Area} = 2\sqrt{a}\left[\dfrac{x^{3/2}}{3/2}\right]_0^{4a/m^2} - m\left[\dfrac{x^2}{2}\right]_0^{4a/m^2}$$

$$\text{Area} = \dfrac{2\sqrt{a} \times 2}{3}\left[\left(\dfrac{4a}{m^2}\right)^{3/2}\right] - \dfrac{m}{2}\left[\dfrac{4a}{m^2}\right]^2 - (0) - (0)$$

$$= \dfrac{4\sqrt{a}}{3}\left[\dfrac{8a^{3/2}}{m^3}\right] - \dfrac{16a^2}{2m^3}$$

$$= \dfrac{32a^2}{3m^3} - \dfrac{16a^2}{2m^3}$$

Now it is given

$$\dfrac{32a^2}{3m^3} - \dfrac{16a^2}{2m^3} = \dfrac{a^3}{3}$$

$\Rightarrow \qquad \dfrac{64a^2 - 48a^2}{6m^3} = \dfrac{a^3}{3}$

$\Rightarrow \qquad\qquad \dfrac{16a^2}{6m^3} = \dfrac{a^2}{3}$

$\Rightarrow \qquad\qquad \dfrac{16}{6} \times 3 = m^3$

$\Rightarrow \qquad\qquad m^3 = 8$

$\therefore \qquad\qquad m = 2.$ **Ans.**

23. The area of the region bounded by the ellipse $\dfrac{x^2}{25} + \dfrac{y^2}{16} = 1$ is: **[NCERT Exemplar]**

(a) 20π sq. units   (b) $20\pi^2$ sq. units

(c) $16\pi^2$ sq. units   (d) 25π sq. units

Sol. (a) 20π sq. units

Explanation :

We have

$$\dfrac{x^2}{5^2} + \dfrac{y^2}{4^2} = 1$$

Here, $a = \pm 5$ and $b = \pm 4$

and $\dfrac{y^2}{4^2} = 1 - \dfrac{x^2}{5^2}$

$\Rightarrow \qquad y^2 = 16\left(1 - \dfrac{x^2}{25}\right)$

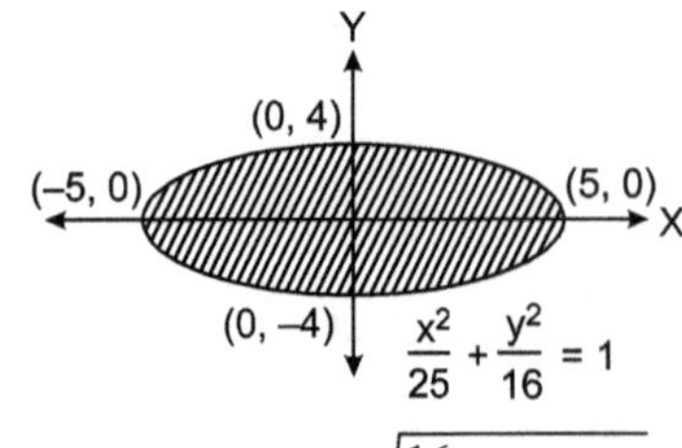

$\Rightarrow \qquad y = \sqrt{\dfrac{16}{25}(25 - x^2)}$

$\Rightarrow \qquad y = \dfrac{4}{5}\sqrt{(5^2 - x^2)}$

$\therefore$ Area enclosed by ellipse,

$A = 2 \cdot \dfrac{4}{5} \int_{-5}^{5} \sqrt{5^2 - x^2}\, dx$

$= 2 \cdot \dfrac{8}{5} \int_{0}^{5} \sqrt{5^2 - x^2}\, dx$

$= 2 \cdot \dfrac{8}{5}\left[\dfrac{x}{2}\sqrt{5^2 - x^2} + \dfrac{5^2}{2}\sin^{-1}\dfrac{x}{5}\right]_0^5$

$= 2 \cdot \dfrac{8}{5}\left[\dfrac{5}{2}\sqrt{5^2 - 5^2} + \dfrac{5^2}{2}\sin^{-1}\dfrac{5}{5} - 0 - \dfrac{25}{2}\cdot 0\right]$

$= 2 \cdot \dfrac{8}{5}\left[\dfrac{25}{2}\cdot\dfrac{\pi}{2}\right]$

$= \dfrac{16}{5}\cdot\dfrac{25\pi}{4}$

$= 20\pi$ sq. units.

24. Area of the ellipse $\dfrac{x^2}{a^2} + \dfrac{y^2}{b^2} = 1$ is:

(a) πab sq. units
(b) $\dfrac{1}{2}\pi ab$ sq. units

(c) $\dfrac{1}{4}\pi ab$ sq. units
(d) None of these

Sol. (a) πab sq. units

Explanation :

Since the given equation contains only even powers of x and only even powers of y, the curve is symmetrical about y-axis as well as x-axis.

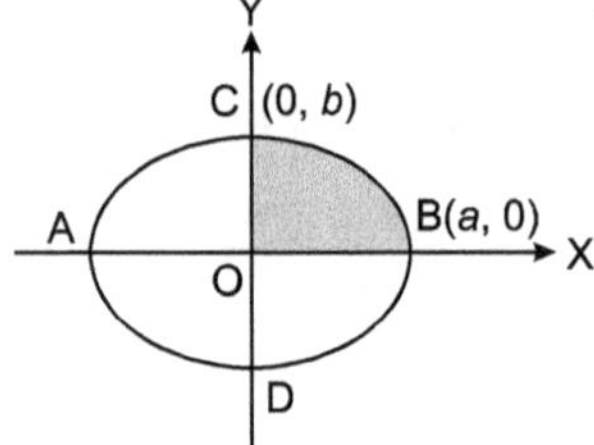

$\therefore$ Whole area of given ellipse

$= 4(\text{area of BCO}) = 4\times\int_0^a y\, dx = 4\int_0^a \dfrac{b}{a}\sqrt{a^2 - x^2}\, dx$

$= 4ab\int_0^{\pi/2}\left(\dfrac{1 + \cos 2\theta}{2}\right)d\theta,$ {Putting $x = a\sin\theta$}

$= 2ab\left(\int_0^{\pi/2} d\theta + \int_0^{\pi/2}\cos 2\theta\, d\theta\right)$

$= 2ab\left[[\theta]_0^{\pi/2} - \left[\dfrac{\sin 2\theta}{2}\right]_0^{\pi/2}\right]$

$= 2ab\left[\dfrac{\pi}{2} - 0 - (0 - 0)\right]$

$= \pi ab$ sq. unit.

Case Based Questions

25. A school is to be constructed for the rural area children on the wasted land which is lying under the area covered by the lines $3x - 2y + 1 = 0$, $2x + 3y - 21 = 0$ and $x - 5y + 9 = 0$.

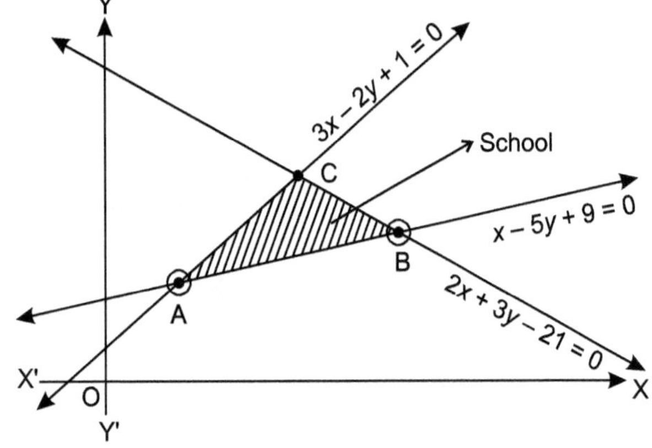

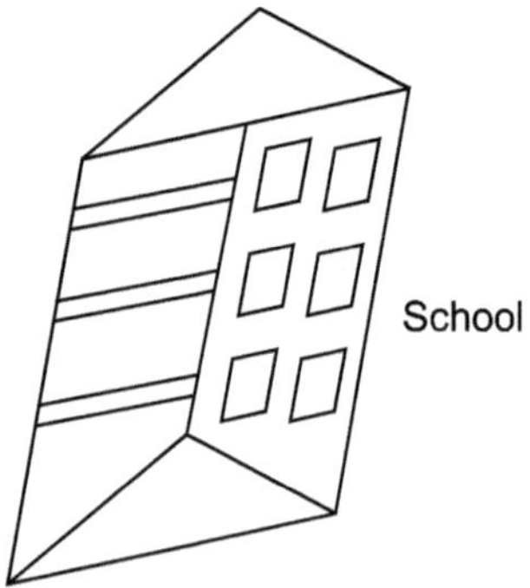

Answer the following questions based on above case study :

(i) What is coordinates of point A ?

(a) (1, 2)
(b) (2, 1)
(c) (2, 2)
(d) (1, 1)

Sol. (a) (1, 2)

Explanation :

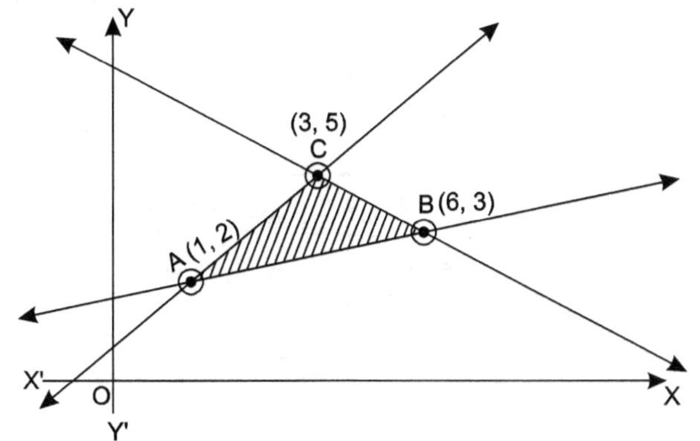

Equation of AB :

$$x - 5y + 9 = 0 \qquad \text{...(i)}$$

$$5y = x + 9$$

$$y = \frac{x+9}{5}$$

Equation of CB :

$$2x + 3y - 21 = 0 \qquad \text{...(ii)}$$

$$3y = 21 - 2x$$

$$y = 7 - \frac{2}{3}x$$

Equation of AC :

$$3x - 2y + 1 = 0 \qquad \text{...(iii)}$$

$$2y = 3x + 1$$

$$y = \frac{3}{2}x + \frac{1}{2}$$

Solving (i) and (iii) we get co-ordinates of A

$$A = (1, 2).$$

(ii) Find the coordinates of B :

(a) (6, 3) (b) (1, 6)

(c) (1, 3) (d) (2, 5)

Sol. (a) (6, 3)

Explanation :

On solving (i) and (ii), we get coordinates of B.

So, B = (6, 3).

(iii) Write the coordinates of point C :

(a) (6, 3) (b) (3, 5)

(c) (1, 2) (d) (0, 1)

Sol. (b) (3, 5)

Explanation :

On solving (ii) and (iii), we get coordinates of C.

So, C = (3, 5).

(iv) Write the limits of equation of AC which is to be integrated :

(a) $\displaystyle\int_{1}^{6} f(x)\,dx$ (b) $\displaystyle\int_{0}^{3} f(x)\,dx$

(c) $\displaystyle\int_{3}^{6} f(x)\,dx$ (d) $\displaystyle\int_{1}^{3} f(x)\,dx$

Sol. (d) $\displaystyle\int_{1}^{3} f(x)\,dx$

Explanation :

Equation of AC is in terms of x is

$$y = \frac{3}{2}x + \frac{1}{2}$$

It will be integrated from 1 to 3 $\displaystyle\int_{1}^{3} f(x)\,dx$.

(v) What is the total area coverd by the school ?

(a) $\dfrac{2}{15}$ sq. units (b) $\dfrac{13}{2}$ sq. units

(c) 15 sq. units (d) 10 sq. units

Sol. (b) $\dfrac{13}{2}$ sq. units

Explanation :

Area will be:

$$\int_{1}^{3} eq^{n} \text{ of AC}\,dx + \int_{3}^{6} eq^{n} \text{ of CB}\,dx - \int_{1}^{6} eq^{n} \text{ of AB}\,dx$$

$$= \int_{1}^{3}\left(\frac{3}{2}x + \frac{1}{2}\right)dx + \int_{3}^{6}\left(7 - \frac{2}{3}x\right)dx - \int_{1}^{6}\frac{x+9}{5}\,dx$$

$$= \left[\frac{3}{2}\cdot\frac{x^2}{2} + \frac{1}{2}x\right]_{1}^{3} + \left[7x - \frac{2}{3}\frac{x^2}{2}\right]_{3}^{6} - \left[\frac{1}{5}\left(\frac{x^2}{2} + 9x\right)\right]_{1}^{6}$$

$$= \frac{3}{4}(3)^2 + \frac{1}{2}(3) - \frac{3}{4}(1)^2 - \frac{1}{2}\right] + \left[\left(42 - \frac{36}{3}\right) - (21 - 3)\right]$$

$$- \frac{1}{5}\left[\left(\frac{36}{2} + 54\right) - \left(\frac{1}{2} + 9\right)\right]$$

$$= \frac{13}{2} \text{ sq. units.}$$

Very Short Answer Type Questions

26. The area bounded by the axes and the line $y = x + 1$ is ....

Sol. Here $y = x + 1$

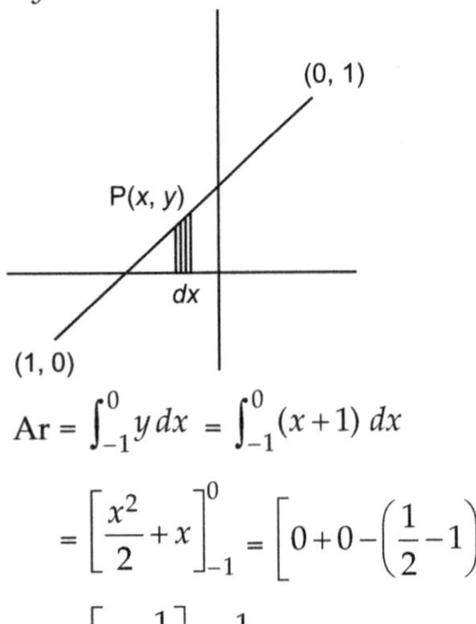

$$\text{Ar} = \int_{-1}^{0} y\,dx = \int_{-1}^{0} (x+1)\,dx$$

$$= \left[\frac{x^2}{2} + x\right]_{-1}^{0} = \left[0 + 0 - \left(\frac{1}{2} - 1\right)\right]$$

$$= \left[0 + \frac{1}{2}\right] = \frac{1}{2} \text{ sq. units.}$$

27. Area bounded by the lines $x = 0$, $y = 0$ and $x + y = 1$ is ....

Sol. Here $x + y = 1$

or $y = 1 - x$

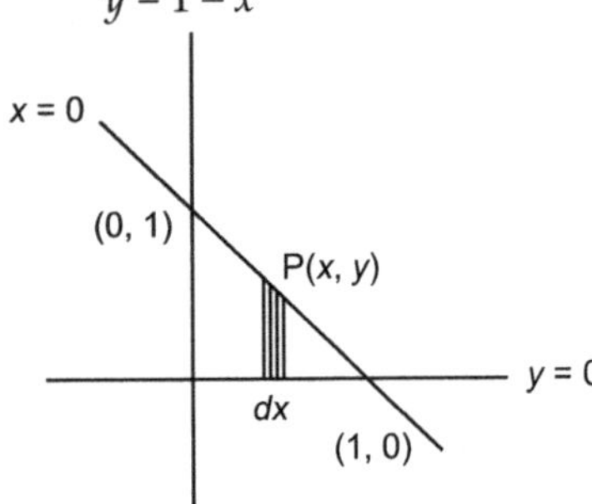

$$\therefore \qquad \text{Ar} = \int_{0}^{1} y\,dx$$

$$A = \int_{0}^{1} (1-x)\,dx = \left[x - \frac{x^2}{2}\right]_{0}^{1}$$

$$A = \left[\left(1 - \frac{1}{2}\right) - (0 - 0)\right]$$

$$A = \frac{1}{2} \text{ sq units.}$$

28. The area of the region bounded by the curve $x = y^2$, Y-axis and the lines $y = 3$ and $y = 4$ is ....

Sol. Here $x = y^2$

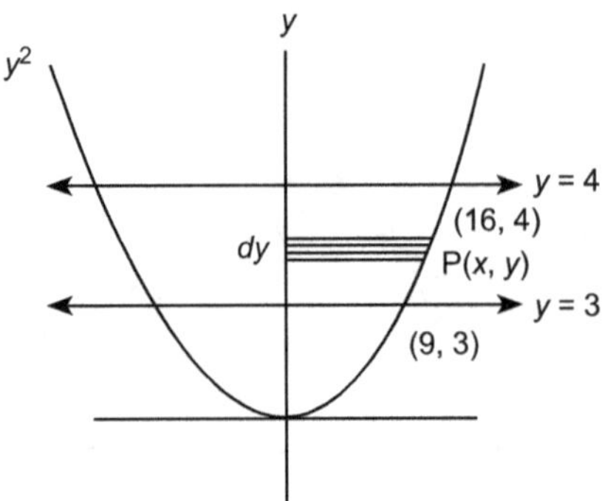

$$A = \int_{3}^{4} x\,dy$$

$$= \int_{3}^{4} y^2\,dy = \left[\frac{y^3}{3}\right]_{3}^{4}$$

$$\text{Ar} = \left[\frac{64}{3} - \frac{27}{3}\right]$$

$$= \left[\frac{37}{3}\right]$$

$$A = \frac{37}{3} \text{ sq. units.}$$

29. The area of the region bounded by the curve $y = x^2 + x$, X-axis and the lines $x = 2$ and $x = 5$ is equal to ....

Sol. Here $y = x^2 + x$

$$\therefore \qquad A = \int_{2}^{5} y\,dx = \int_{2}^{5} (x^2 + x)\,dx$$

$$A = \left[\frac{x^3}{3} + \frac{x^2}{2}\right]_{2}^{5}$$

$$A = \left[\left(\frac{125}{3} + \frac{25}{2}\right) - \left(\frac{8}{3} + \frac{4}{2}\right)\right]$$

$$A = \left[\left(\frac{250 + 75}{6}\right) - \left(\frac{28}{6}\right)\right]$$

$$A = \left[\frac{325}{6} - \frac{28}{6}\right]$$

$$A = \frac{297}{6} \text{ sq. units.}$$

Short Answer Type Questions

30. Using integration, find the area of the region bounded by the line $2y = 5x + 7$, X-axis and the lines $x = 2$ and $x = 8$. **[NCERT Exemplar]**

Sol. We have, $2y = 5x + 7$

$$\Rightarrow \qquad y = \frac{5x}{2} + \frac{7}{2}$$

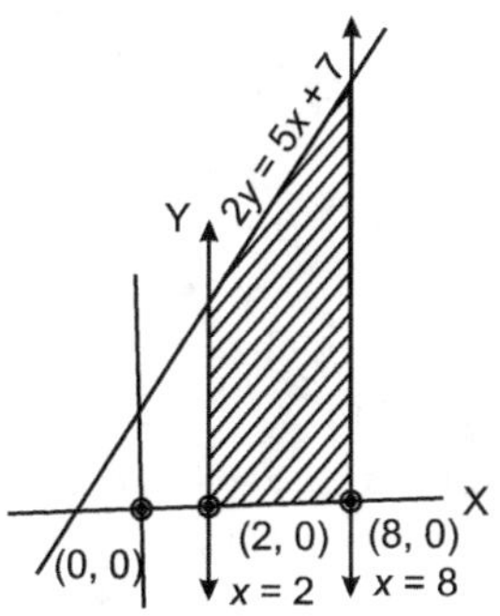

$\therefore$ Area of shaded region

$$A = \int_2^8 y\,dx$$

$$= \frac{1}{2}\int_2^8 (5x+7)\,dx = \frac{1}{2}\left[5\cdot\frac{x^2}{2}+7x\right]_2^8$$

$$= \frac{1}{2}[5\cdot32+7\cdot8-10-14]$$

$$= \frac{1}{2}[160+56-24]$$

$$= \frac{192}{2} = 96 \text{ sq. units.}$$

31. Find the area of the region included between $y^2 = 9x$ and $y = x$. **[NCERT Exemplar]**

Sol. We have, $\qquad y^2 = 9x$ and $y = x$

$$\Rightarrow \qquad x^2 = 9x$$
$$\Rightarrow \qquad x^2 - 9x = 0$$
$$\Rightarrow \qquad x(x-9) = 0$$
$$\Rightarrow \qquad x = 0, 9$$

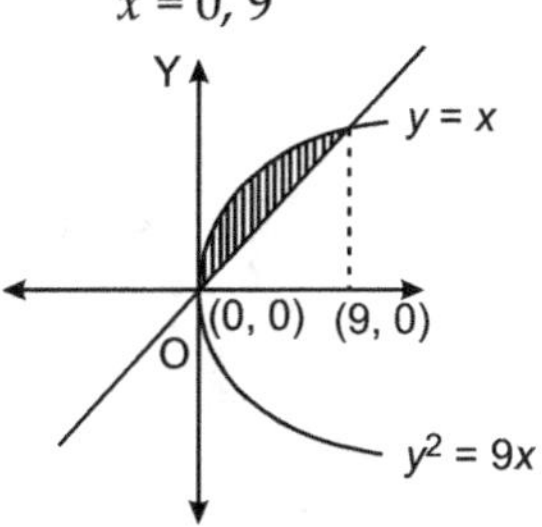

$\therefore$ Area of shaded region

$$= \int_0^9 \sqrt{9x}\,dx - \int_0^9 x\,dx$$

$$= \int_0^9 (\sqrt{9x}-x)\,dx = \int_0^9 3x^{1/2}\,dx - \int_0^9 x\,dx$$

$$= \left[3\cdot\frac{x^{3/2}}{3}\cdot2\right]_0^9 - \left[\frac{x^2}{2}\right]_0^9$$

$$= \left[\frac{3\cdot3^{\frac{3}{2}\times2}}{3}\cdot2-0\right] - \left[\frac{81}{2}-0\right]$$

$$= 54 - \frac{81}{2} = \frac{108-81}{2} = \frac{27}{2} \text{ sq units.}$$

32. Calculate the area under the curve $y = 2\sqrt{x}$ included between the lines $x = 0$ and $x = 1$.

Sol. We have, $\qquad y = 2\sqrt{x},\ x = 0$ and $x = 1$

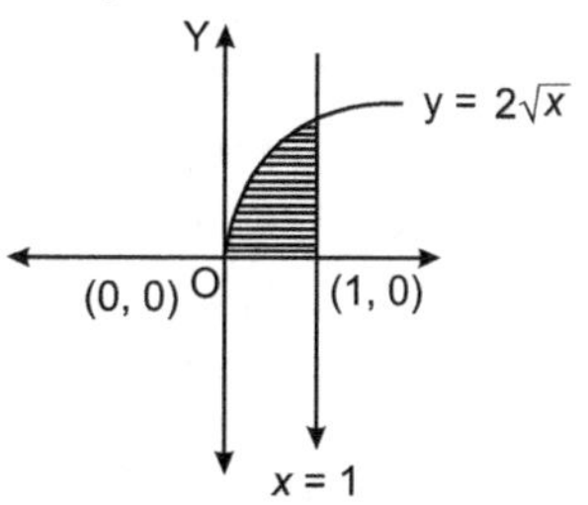

$\Rightarrow$ Area of shaded region,

$$A = \int_0^1 y\,dx$$

$$= \int_0^1 (2\sqrt{x})\,dx = 2\cdot\left[\frac{x^{3/2}}{3}\cdot2\right]_0^1$$

$$= 2\left(\frac{2}{3}\cdot1-0\right) = \frac{4}{3} \text{ sq. units.}$$

33. Find the area of the region bounded by the curves $y^2 = 9x$ and $y = 3x$. **[NCERT Exemplar]**

Sol. We have $\qquad y^2 = 9x$ and $y = 3x$

$$\Rightarrow \qquad (3x)^2 = 9x \Rightarrow 9x^2 - 9x = 0$$
$$\Rightarrow \qquad 9x(x-1) = 0 \Rightarrow x = 1, 0$$

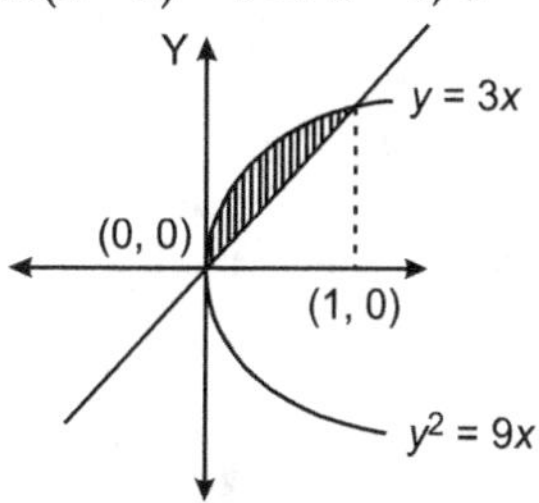

$\therefore$ Required area, $A = \int_0^1 \sqrt{9x}\,dx - \int_0^1 3x\,dx$

$$= 3\int_0^1 x^{1/2}\,dx - 3\int_0^1 x\,dx$$

$$= 3\left[\frac{x^{3/2}}{3/2}\right] - 3\left[\frac{x^2}{2}\right]_0^1$$

$$= 3\left(\frac{2}{3}-0\right) - 3\left(\frac{1}{2}-0\right)$$

$$= 2 - \frac{3}{2} = \frac{1}{2} \text{ sq. unit.}$$

34. Find the area of the region enclosed by the parabola $x^2 = y$ and the line $y = x + 2$.

Sol. We have, $x^2 = y$ and $y = x + 2$

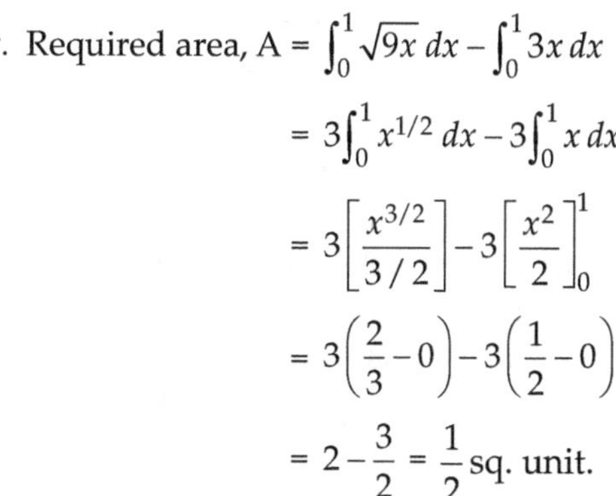

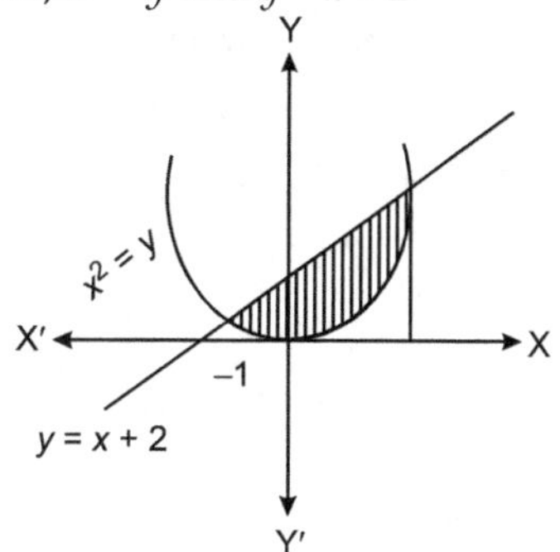

$$\Rightarrow \qquad x^2 = x + 2$$
$$\Rightarrow \qquad x^2 - x - 2 = 0$$
$$\Rightarrow \qquad x^2 - 2x + x - 2 = 0$$
$$\Rightarrow \qquad x(x - 2) + 1(x - 2) = 0$$
$$\Rightarrow \qquad (x + 1)(x - 2) = 0$$
$$x = -1, 2$$

∴ Required area of shaded region

$$= \int_{-1}^{2} (x + 2 - x^2)\, dx = \left[\frac{x^2}{2} + 2x - \frac{x^3}{3}\right]_{-1}^{2}$$

$$= \left[\frac{4}{2} + 4 - \frac{8}{3} - \frac{1}{2} + 2 - \frac{1}{3}\right]$$

$$= 6 + \frac{3}{2} - \frac{9}{3} = \frac{36 + 9 - 18}{6} = \frac{27}{6}$$

$$= \frac{9}{2} \text{ sq. units.}$$

35. Draw a rough sketch of the curve $y = \sqrt{x-1}$ in the interval [1, 5. Find the area under the curve and between the lines $x = 1$ and $s = 5$.

Sol. Given equation of the curve is

$$y = \sqrt{x - 1}$$
$$\Rightarrow \qquad y^2 = x - 1$$

∴ Area of shaded region,

$$A = \int_{1}^{5} (x-1)^{1/2}\, dx = \left[\frac{2 \cdot (x-1)^{3/2}}{3}\right]_{1}^{5}$$

$$= \left[\frac{2}{3} \cdot (5-1)^{3/2} - 0\right]$$

$$= \frac{16}{3} \text{ sq. units.}$$

36. Find the area enclosed by the curve $y = -x^2$ and the straight line $x + y + 2 = 0$.

Sol. We have, $y = x^2$ and $x + y + 2 = 0$

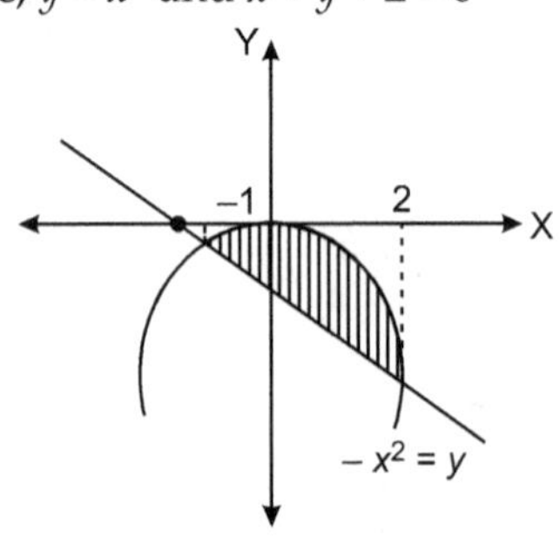

$$\Rightarrow \qquad -x - 2 = -x^2$$
$$\Rightarrow \qquad x^2 - x - 2 = 0$$
$$\Rightarrow \qquad x^2 + x - 2x - 2 = 0$$
$$\Rightarrow \qquad x(x + 1) - 2(x + 1) = 0$$
$$\Rightarrow \qquad (x - 2)(x + 1) = 0$$
$$\Rightarrow \qquad x = 2, -1$$

∴ Area of shaded region,

$$A = \left|\int_{-1}^{2} (-x - 2 + x^2)\, dx\right|$$

$$= \left|\int_{-1}^{2} (x^2 - x - 2)\, dx\right|$$

$$= \left|\left[\frac{x^3}{3} - \frac{x^2}{2} - 2x\right]_{-1}^{2}\right|$$

$$= \left|\left[\frac{8}{3} - \frac{4}{2} - 4 + \frac{1}{3} + \frac{1}{2} - 2\right]\right|$$

$$= \left|\frac{16 - 12 - 24 + 2 + 3 - 12}{6}\right|$$

$$= \left|-\frac{27}{6}\right| = \frac{9}{2} \text{ sq. units.}$$

Long Answer Type Questions

37. Using the method of integration, find the area of the region bounded by the lines

$$2x + y = 4,\ 3x - 2y = 6 \text{ and } x - 3y + 5 = 0$$

Sol. The given lines are :

$$2x + y = 4 \qquad \qquad \text{...(i)}$$
$$\Rightarrow \qquad y = 4 - 2x$$

x	0	2
y	4	0

and $\qquad 3x - 2y = 6 \qquad \qquad \text{...(ii)}$

$$\Rightarrow \qquad 2y = 3x - 6$$
$$\Rightarrow \qquad y = \frac{3x - 6}{2}$$

x	0	2
y	-3	0

and $\qquad x - 3y + 5 = 0 \qquad \qquad \text{...(iii)}$

$$3y = x + 5$$
$$y = \frac{x + 5}{3}$$

x	1	-2
y	2	1

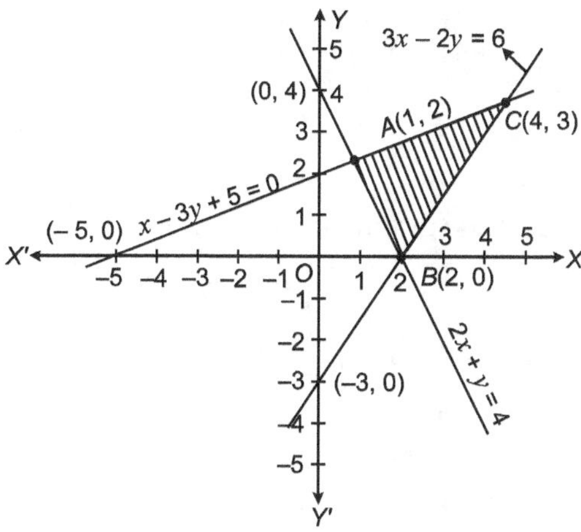

Coordinates of C :

Multiplying equation (iii) by 3 and then subtracting equation (ii) from it, we get

$$3x - 9y = -15$$
$$3x - 2y = 6$$
$$\underline{\quad - \quad + \qquad - \quad}$$
$$-7y = -21$$
$$y = 3$$

Put in equation (iii),

$$x - 9 + 5 = 0$$
$$x = 4$$

$\Rightarrow$ Coordinates of C are (4, 3).

Coordinates of A :

Multiplying equation (iii) by 2 and then subtracting equation (i) from it we get,

$$2x - 6y + 10 = 0$$
$$2x + y - 4 = 0$$
$$\underline{\quad - \quad - \quad + \quad}$$
$$-7y + 14 = 0$$
$$y = 2$$

Put $y = 2$ in equation (iii),

$$x - 6 + 5 = 0$$
$$x = 1$$

$\Rightarrow$ Coordinates of A are (1, 2)

Coordinates of B are (2, 0)

Required area

$$= \int_1^4 (\text{Under line iii}) \, dx - \int_1^2 (\text{Under line i}) \, dx$$

$$- \int_2^4 (\text{Under line ii}) \, dx$$

$$= \int_1^4 \frac{x+5}{3} \, dx - \int_1^2 (4 - 2x) \, dx - \int_2^4 \left(\frac{3x-6}{2} \right) dx$$

____

*** are board exam questions from previous years**

$$= \frac{1}{3} \left(\frac{x^2}{2} + 5x \right)_1^4 - \left(4x - \frac{2x^2}{2} \right)_1^2 - \frac{1}{2} \left(\frac{3x^2}{2} - 6x \right)_2^4$$

$$= \frac{1}{3} \left[\left(\frac{16}{2} + 20 \right) - \left(\frac{1}{2} + 5 \right) \right] - \left[\left(8 - \frac{8}{2} \right) - \left(4 - \frac{2}{2} \right) \right]$$

$$- \frac{1}{2} \left[\left(\frac{48}{2} - 24 \right) - \left(\frac{12}{2} - 12 \right) \right]$$

$$= \frac{1}{3} \left[28 - \frac{11}{2} \right] - [4 - 3] - \frac{1}{2} (0 + 6)$$

$$= \frac{1}{3} \times \frac{45}{2} - 1 - 3$$

$$= \frac{15}{2} - \frac{4}{1} = \frac{7}{2} \text{ sq. units.}$$

38. Using integration, find the area of the region bounded by the triangle whose vertices are $(-1, 2)$, $(1, 5)$ and $(3, 4)$.*

Sol. Let A$(-1, 2)$; B$(1, 5)$ and C$(3, 4)$.

Equation of AB is

$$\left[\because y - y_1 = \frac{y_2 - y_1}{x_2 - x_1} (x - x_1) \right]$$

$$y - 5 = \frac{5-2}{1+1} (x - 1)$$

$$\Rightarrow \qquad y = \frac{3}{2} x + \frac{7}{2} \qquad \qquad ...(i)$$

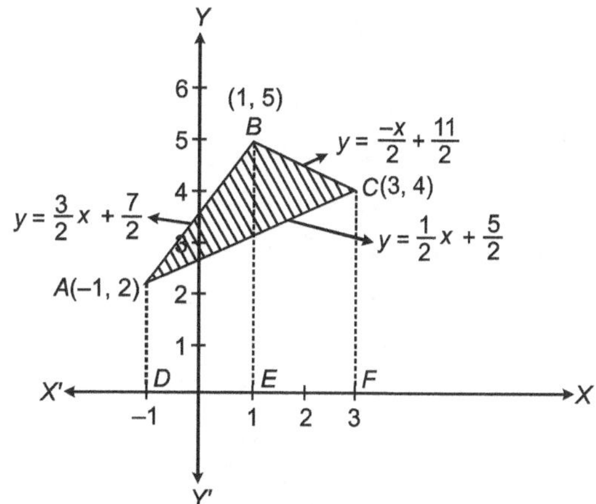

Equation of BC is

$$y - 4 = \frac{4-5}{3-1} (x - 3)$$

$$\Rightarrow \qquad y = -\frac{1}{2} x + \frac{11}{2} \qquad \qquad ...(ii)$$

Equation of AC is

$$y - 2 = \frac{4-2}{3+1} (x + 1)$$

$$\Rightarrow \qquad y = \frac{1}{2}x + \frac{5}{2} \qquad \qquad ...(iii)$$

Area of the required triangular region, ABC

= Area of trapezium ADEB

$$+ \text{ Area of trapezium BEFC}$$
$$- \text{ Area of the trapezium ADFC}$$

$$= \int_{-1}^{1} y_{AB}\, dx + \int_{1}^{3} y_{BC}\, dx - \int_{-1}^{3} y_{AC}\, dx$$

$$= \int_{-1}^{1}\left(\frac{3}{2}x + \frac{7}{2}\right)dx + \int_{1}^{3}\left(\frac{-1}{2}x + \frac{11}{2}\right)dx$$

$$- \int_{-1}^{3}\left(\frac{1}{2}x + \frac{5}{2}\right)dx$$

$$= \left[\frac{3}{4}x^2 + \frac{7}{2}x\right]_{-1}^{1} + \left[-\frac{x^2}{4} + \frac{11}{2}x\right]_{1}^{3} - \left[\frac{x^2}{4} + \frac{5}{2}x\right]_{-1}^{3}$$

$$= \left(\frac{3}{4} + \frac{7}{2}\right) - \left(\frac{3}{4} - \frac{7}{2}\right) + \left(-\frac{9}{4} + \frac{33}{2}\right) - \left(\frac{-1}{4} + \frac{11}{2}\right)$$

$$- \left(\frac{9}{4} + \frac{15}{2}\right) + \left(\frac{1}{4} - \frac{5}{2}\right)$$

$$= \frac{3}{4} + \frac{7}{2} - \frac{3}{4} + \frac{7}{2} - \frac{9}{4} + \frac{33}{2} + \frac{1}{4} - \frac{11}{2} - \frac{9}{4} - \frac{15}{2} + \frac{1}{4} - \frac{5}{2}$$

$$= 7 - 4 + 1 = 4 \text{ sq. units.}$$

39. Using integration, find the area of the triangular region whose sides have the equations

$$y = 2x + 1,\ y = 3x + 1 \text{ and } x = 4.$$

Sol. Given
$$y = 2x + 1 \qquad ...(i)$$
$$y = 3x + 1 \qquad ...(ii)$$
and
$$x = 4 \qquad ...(iii)$$

From equations (i) and (ii),
$$3x + 1 = 2x + 1$$
$$x = 0$$

When $x = 0$, $\quad y = 1$

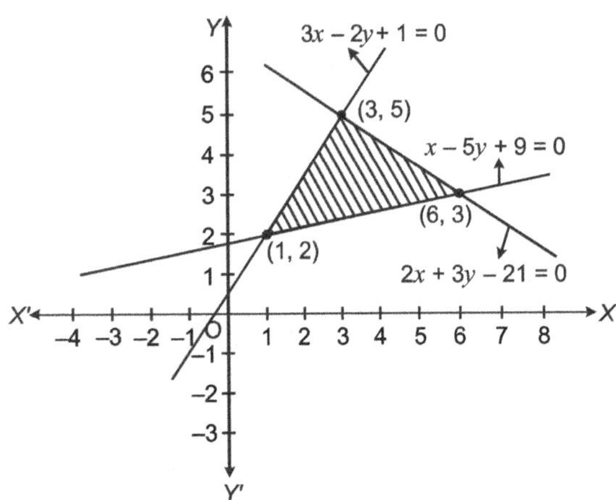

Required area

$$= \int_{0}^{4}(3x+1)dx - \int_{0}^{4}(2x+1)\, dx$$

$$= \left[\frac{3x^2}{2} + x\right]_{0}^{4} - \left[\frac{2x^2}{2} + x\right]_{0}^{4}$$

$$= \left[\left\{\frac{48}{2} + 4\right\} - \{0\}\right] - \left[\{16 + 4\} - \{0\}\right]$$

$$= 28 - 20$$

$$= 8 \text{ sq. units.}$$

40. Sketch the graph of $y = |\,x + 3\,|$ and evaluate :

$$\int_{-6}^{0} |\,x+3\,|\, dx.$$

Sol. Given $\qquad y = |\,x + 3\,|$

Required area

$$= \int_{-6}^{0} |\,x+3\,|\, dx$$

$$= \int_{-6}^{-3} -(x+3)\, dx + \int_{-3}^{0}(x+3)\, dx$$

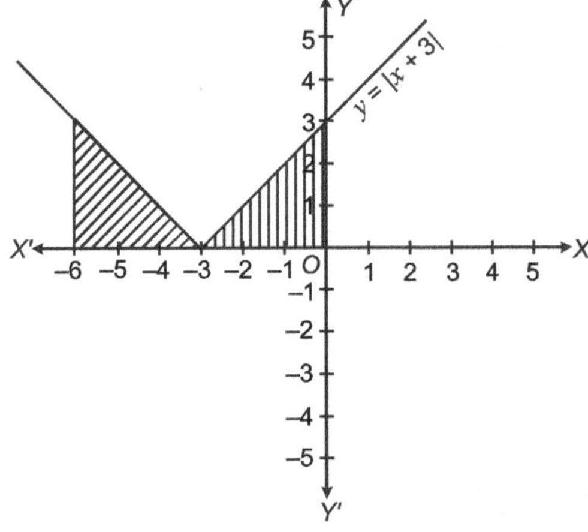

$$= -\left[\frac{x^2}{2} + 3x\right]_{-6}^{-3} + \left[\frac{x^2}{2} + 3x\right]_{-3}^{0} \times 1$$

$$= -\left[\left\{\frac{9}{2} - 9\right\} - \left\{\frac{36}{2} - 18\right\}\right] + \left[\{0+0\} - \left\{\frac{9}{2} - 9\right\}\right]$$

$$= -\left\{\frac{-9}{2} - 0\right\} + \left\{0 - \left(\frac{-9}{2}\right)\right\}$$

$$= \frac{9}{2} + \frac{9}{2}$$

$$= \frac{18}{2} = 9 \text{ sq. units.}$$

41. Using the method of integration, find the area of the region bounded by the lines :

$$3x - 2y + 1 = 0,\ 2x + 3y - 21 = 0 \text{ and } x - 5y + 9 = 0.$$

Sol. Given equations are
$$3x - 2y + 1 = 0 \qquad ...(i)$$
$$2x + 3y - 21 = 0 \qquad ...(ii)$$
$$x - 5y + 9 = 0 \qquad ...(iii)$$

From equations (i) and (ii),

Multiplying equation (i) by 2 and equation (ii) by 3 and then subtracting we get

$$6x - 4y + 2 = 0$$
$$6x + 9y - 63 = 0$$
$$\underline{-\quad -\quad +}$$
$$-13y + 65 = 0$$
$$y = 5$$

Put value of y in equation (i), we get

$$3x - 2(5) + 1 = 0$$
$$3x - 10 + 1 = 0$$
$$3x - 9 = 0$$
$$x = 3$$

So, equations (i) and (ii) intersect at (3, 5)

Multiplying equation (iii) by 2, we get

$$2x - 10y + 18 = 0 \qquad \ldots \text{(iv)}$$

From equations (ii) and (iv),

$$2x + 3y - 21 = 0$$
$$2x - 10y + 18 = 0$$
$$\underline{-\quad +\quad -} \qquad [\text{ By subtracting}]$$
$$13y - 39 = 0$$
$$y = 3$$

Put value of y in equation (iii),

$$x - 15 + 9 = 0$$
$$x - 6 = 0$$
$$x = 6$$

So equations (ii) and (iii) intersect at (6, 3).

Multiplying equation (iii) by 3, we get

$$3x - 15y + 27 = 0 \qquad \ldots \text{(v)}$$

From equation (i) and (v), we get

$$3x - 2y + 1 = 0$$
$$3x - 15y + 27 = 0$$
$$\underline{-\quad +\quad -} \qquad [\text{By subtracting}]$$
$$13y - 26 = 0$$
$$y = 2$$

Put $y = 2$ in equation (iii),

$$x - 10 + 9 = 0$$
$$x - 1 = 0$$
$$x = 1$$

So equations (i) and (iii) intersect at (1, 2)

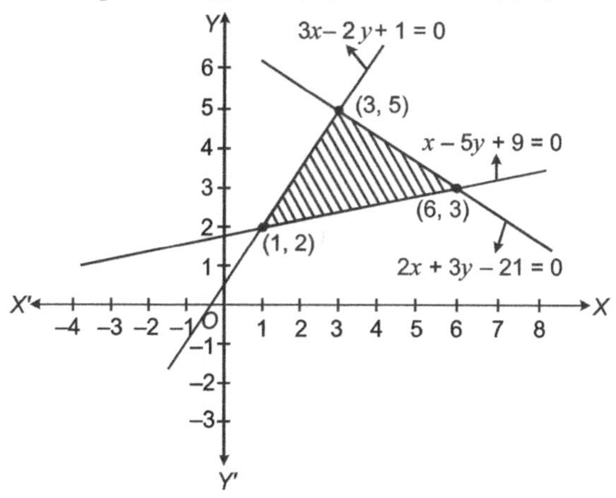

From equation (i), $y = \dfrac{1}{2}(3x + 1)$

From equation (ii), $y = \dfrac{1}{3}(-2x + 21)$

From equation (iii), $y = \dfrac{1}{5}(x + 9)$

Required area

$$= \int_1^3 \frac{1}{2}(3x + 1)\,dx + \int_3^6 \frac{1}{3}(-2x + 21)\,dx - \int_1^6 \frac{1}{5}(x + 9)\,dx$$

$$= \frac{1}{2}\left[\frac{3x^2}{2} + x\right]_1^3 + \frac{1}{3}\left[\frac{-2x^2}{2} + 21x\right]_3^6 - \frac{1}{5}\left[\frac{x^2}{2} + 9x\right]_1^6$$

$$= \frac{1}{2}\left[\left\{\frac{27}{2} + 3\right\} - \left\{\frac{3}{2} + 1\right\}\right] + \frac{1}{3}\left[\left\{\frac{-72}{2} + 126\right\} - \left\{\frac{-18}{2} + 63\right\}\right]$$

$$\qquad - \frac{1}{5}\left[\left\{\frac{36}{2} + 54\right\} - \left\{\frac{1}{2} + 9\right\}\right]$$

$$= \frac{1}{2}\left[\frac{33}{2} - \frac{5}{2}\right] + \frac{1}{3}[90 - 54] - \frac{1}{5}\left[72 - \frac{19}{2}\right]$$

$$= \frac{1}{2} \times \frac{28}{2} + \frac{1}{3} \times 36 - \frac{1}{5}\left(\frac{125}{2}\right)$$

$$= 7 + 12 - \frac{25}{2}$$

$$= \frac{19}{1} - \frac{25}{2} = \frac{38 - 25}{2}$$

$$= \frac{13}{2}$$

$$= 6.5 \text{ sq. units.}$$

42. Using integration, find the area of region bounded by the triangle whose vertices are (−2, 1), (0, 4) and (2, 3).*

Sol. The vertices of the $\triangle ABC$ are A(−2, 1), B(0, 4) and C(2, 3)

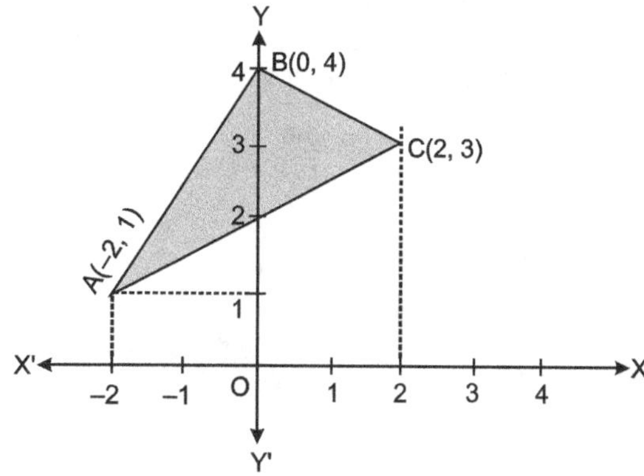

Equation of the side AB is

$$y - y_1 = \frac{y_2 - y_1}{x_2 - x_1}(x_1 - x_1)$$

$$y - 1 = \frac{4-1}{0-(-2)}\,(x-(-2))$$

$$= \frac{3}{2}\,(x+2)$$

$$y = \frac{3}{2}x + 4$$

Equation of the side BC is

$$y - 4 = \frac{3-4}{2-0}\,(x-0) = \frac{-1}{2}x$$

$$y = \frac{-1}{2}x + 4$$

Equation of the side AC is

$$y - 1 = \frac{3-1}{2-(-2)}\,(x-(-2))$$

$$= \frac{1}{2}\,(x+2)$$

$$y = \frac{x}{2} + 2$$

Required area = Shaded area

$$= \int_{-2}^{0}\left(\frac{3}{2}x+4\right)dx + \int_{0}^{2}\left(\frac{-1}{2}x+4\right)dx$$

$$- \int_{-2}^{2}\left(\frac{1}{2}x+2\right)dx$$

$$= \left[\frac{3}{2}\frac{x^2}{2}+4x\right]_{-2}^{0} + \left[\frac{-1}{2}\frac{x^2}{2}+4x\right]_{0}^{2} - \left[\frac{1}{2}\frac{x^2}{2}+2x\right]_{-2}^{2}$$

$$= (0+0)-\left(\frac{3}{2}\times\frac{4}{2}-8\right)+\left(\frac{-1}{2}\times\frac{4}{2}+8\right)-(0+0)$$

$$-\left(\frac{1}{2}\times\frac{4}{2}+4\right)-\left(\frac{1}{2}\times\frac{4}{2}-4\right)$$

$$= -3 + 8 - 1 + 8 - 0 - 8 = 4 \text{ sq. units.}$$

43. Using the method of integration find the area of the triangle ABC, coordinates of whose vertices are A(4, 1), B(6, 6) and C(8, 4).*

Sol. We have, A(4, 1), B(6, 6) and (8,4)

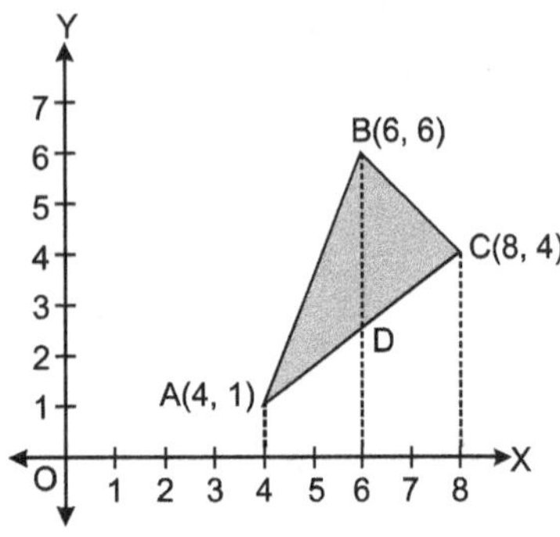

Then, equation of AB is

$$\left[\because y - y_1 = \frac{y_2 - y_1}{x_2 - x_1}\,(x - x_1)\right]$$

$$\frac{x-4}{6-4} = \frac{y-1}{6-1}$$

$$\frac{x-4}{2} = \frac{y-1}{5}$$

$$5x - 20 = 2y - 2$$

$$5x - 2y - 18 = 0 \qquad \qquad \text{...(i)}$$

Equation of BC is

$$\frac{x-6}{8-6} = \frac{y-6}{4-6}$$

$$\frac{x-6}{2} = \frac{y-6}{-2}$$

$$-2x + 12 = 2y - 12$$

$$-2x - 2y + 24 = 0$$

$$x + y - 12 = 0 \qquad \qquad \text{...(ii)}$$

and equation of CA is

$$\frac{x-8}{4-8} = \frac{y-4}{1-4}$$

$$\frac{x-8}{-4} = \frac{y-4}{-3}$$

$$-3x + 24 = -4y + 16$$

$$-3x + 4y + 8 = 0 \qquad \qquad \text{...(iii)}$$

Clearly, Area of ΔABC = Area of ADB + Area of BDC

$$\therefore \text{ Area of } \Delta ADB = \int_{4}^{6}(y_2 - y_1)\,dx$$

$$= \int_{4}^{6}\left\{\frac{5x-18}{2}-\left(\frac{3x-8}{4}\right)\right\}dx$$

Similarly, we have

$$\text{Area of } \Delta BDC = \int_{6}^{8}(y_4 - y_3)\,dx$$

$$= \int_{6}^{8}\left\{12-x-\left(\frac{3x-8}{4}\right)\right\}dx$$

$$\therefore \text{ Area of } \Delta ABC = \int_{4}^{6}\left\{\frac{5x-18}{2}-\left(\frac{3x-8}{4}\right)\right\}dx$$

$$+ \int_{6}^{8}\left\{12-x-\left(\frac{3x-8}{4}\right)\right\}dx$$

$$= \frac{1}{4}\int_{4}^{6}(7x-28)\,dx + \frac{1}{4}\int_{6}^{8}(56-7x)\,dx$$

$$= \frac{1}{4}\left[\left\{\frac{7x^2}{2} - 28x\right\}_4^6 + \left\{56x - \frac{7x^2}{2}\right\}_6^8\right]$$

Area of $\triangle$ABC $= \frac{1}{4}\left[\left(\frac{252}{2} - 168 - \frac{112}{2} + 112\right)\right.$

$$\left. + \left(448 - \frac{448}{2} - 336 + \frac{252}{2}\right)\right]$$

$$= \frac{1}{4}[70 - 56 - 98 + 112]$$

$$= \frac{28}{4}$$

$$= 7 \text{ sq. units.}$$

44. Using integration find the area of the region bounded by the triangle whose vertices are (1, 3), (2, 5) and (3, 4).

Sol. Let A(1, 3), B(2, 5) and C(3, 4) are vertices of $\triangle$ABC.

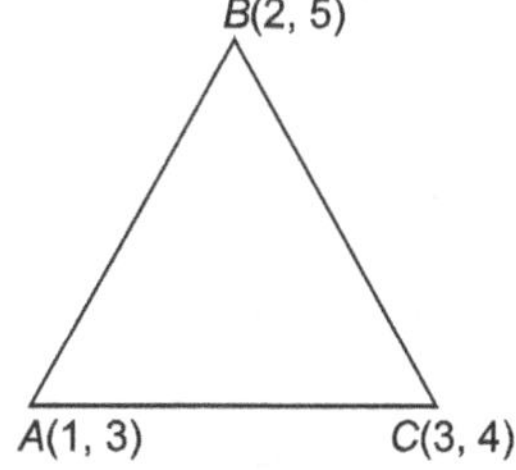

Equation of line AB :

$$y - 3 = \frac{5-3}{2-1}(x-1)$$

$$y - 3 = 2(x - 1)$$
$$2x - 2 = y - 3$$
$$2x - y = -1$$
$$y = 2x + 1 \qquad \text{...(i)}$$

Equation of line BC :

$$y - 5 = \frac{4-5}{3-2}(x-2)$$

$$y - 5 = -1(x - 2)$$
$$y - 5 = -x + 2$$
$$x + y = 7$$
$$y = -x + 7 \qquad \text{...(ii)}$$

Equation of line CA :

$$y - 4 = \frac{3-4}{1-3}(x-3)$$

$$y - 4 = \frac{-1}{-2}(x-3)$$

$$2y - 8 = x - 3$$
$$2y = x - 3 + 8$$
$$2y = x + 5$$

$$y = \frac{x+5}{2} \qquad \text{...(iii)}$$

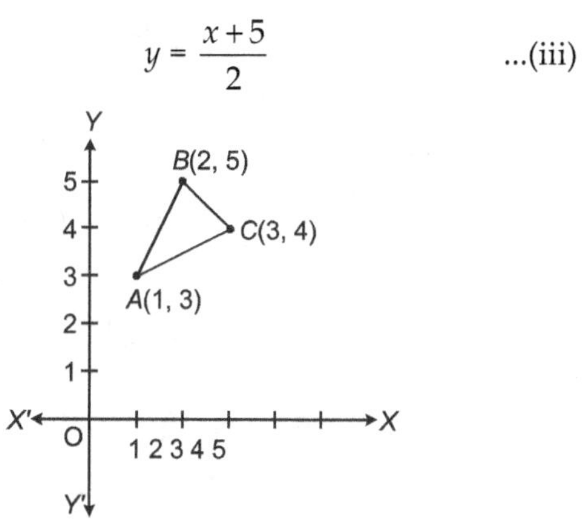

Required area :

$$= \int_1^2 (\text{eq. of AB})\,dx + \int_2^3 (\text{eq. of BC})\,dx$$

$$- \int_1^3 (\text{eq. of AC})\,dx$$

$$= \int_1^2 (2x+1)\,dx + \int_2^3 (-x+7)\,dx - \int_1^3 \left(\frac{x+5}{2}\right)dx$$

$$= \left(\frac{2x^2}{2} + x\right)_1^2 + \left(-\frac{x^2}{2} + 7x\right)_2^3 - \frac{1}{2}\left(\frac{x^2}{2} + 5x\right)_1^3$$

$$= [(4+2)-(1+1)] + \left[\left(-\frac{9}{2}+21\right) - \left(-\frac{4}{2}+14\right)\right]$$

$$- \frac{1}{2}\left[\left(\frac{9}{2}+15\right) - \left(\frac{1}{2}+5\right)\right]$$

$$= 6 - 2 + \left(-\frac{9}{2}+21+2-14\right) - \frac{1}{2}\left(\frac{9}{2}+15-\frac{1}{2}-5\right)$$

$$= 4 + \left[\frac{-9+18}{2}\right] - \frac{1}{2}\left[\frac{9+20-1}{2}\right]$$

$$= 4 + \frac{9}{2} - \frac{1}{2}\times\frac{28}{2}$$

$$= \frac{8+9-14}{2} = \frac{3}{2} \text{ sq. units.}$$

45. Draw a rough sketch of the given curve $y = 1 + |\,x+1\,|$, $x = -3$, $x = 3$ and find the area of the region bounded by them, using integration.

Sol. We have, $y = 1 + |x+1|$, $x = -3$, $x = 3$

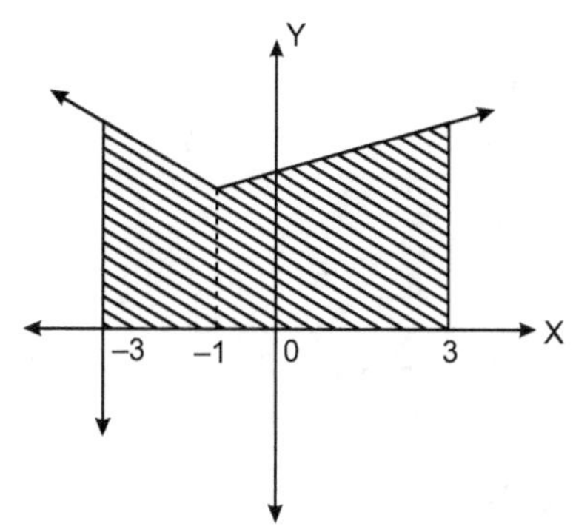

$\because \qquad y = \begin{cases} -x, & \text{if } x < -1 \\ x+2, & \text{if } x \geq -1 \end{cases}$

$\therefore$ Area of shaded region,

$$A = \int_{-3}^{-1} -x \, dx + \int_{-1}^{3} (x+2) \, dx$$

$$= -\left[\frac{x^2}{2}\right]_{-3}^{-1} + \left[\frac{x^2}{2} + 2x\right]_{-1}^{3}$$

$$= -\left[\frac{1}{2} - \frac{9}{2}\right] + \left[\frac{9}{2} + 6 - \frac{1}{2} + 2\right]$$

$$= -[-4] + [8+4]$$

$$= 12 + 4 = 15 \text{ sq. units.}$$

46. Find the area of the region bounded by the parabola $y = x^2$ and $y = |x|$.* **[NCERT]**

Sol. Given curves are

$$y = x^2 \qquad \qquad \text{...(i)}$$

and $\qquad \qquad y = |x| \qquad \qquad \text{...(ii)}$

$\Rightarrow \qquad x^2 - |x| = 0$

$\qquad |x| \{|x| - 1\} = 0$

$\qquad |x| = 0 \qquad$ or $\qquad |x| = 1$

$\qquad x = 0 \qquad \qquad \qquad x = -1 \text{ or } +1$

If $x = 0$, $\qquad \qquad \qquad y = 0$

If $x = \pm 1$, $\qquad \qquad \quad y = 1$

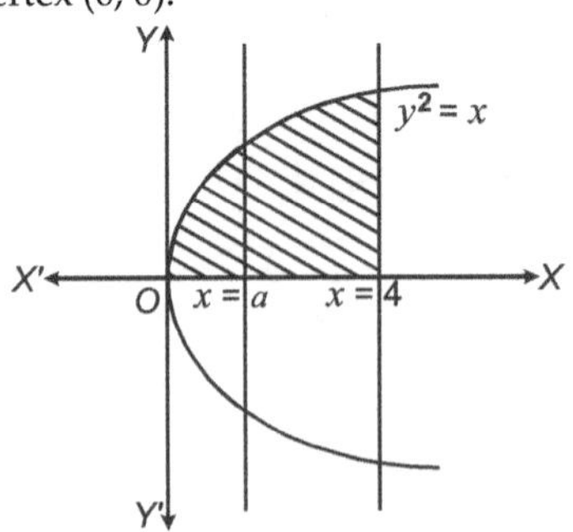

$\therefore y = x^2$ is upward parabola with vertex $(0, 0)$

$$\text{Required area} = 2 \int_0^1 (|x| - x^2) \, dx$$

$$= 2\left[\frac{x^2}{2} - \frac{x^3}{3}\right]_0^1$$

$$= 2\left[\left(\frac{1}{2} - \frac{1}{3}\right) - (0)\right]$$

$$= 2\left(\frac{3-2}{6}\right)$$

$$= \frac{1}{3} \text{ sq. units.}$$

47. The area between $x = y^2$ and $x = 4$ is divided into two equal parts by the line $x = a$, find the value of a. **[NCERT]**

___

Sol. Given $x = y^2$ is a parabola symmetric to positive X-axis with vertex $(0, 0)$.

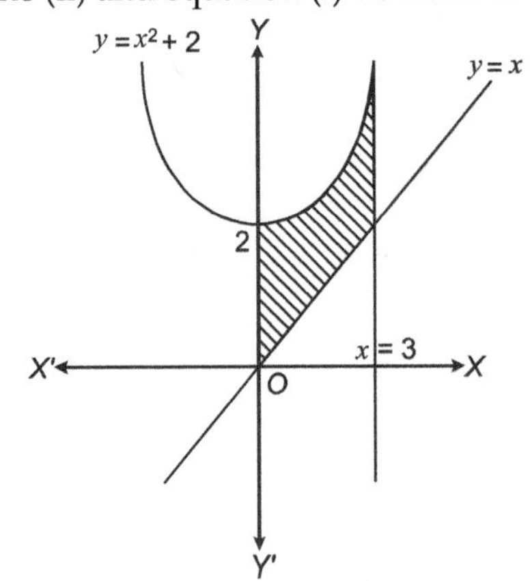

We have given that

$$\int_0^a \sqrt{x} \, dx = \int_a^4 \sqrt{x} \, dx$$

$$\left[\frac{x^{3/2}}{3/2}\right]_0^a = \left[\frac{x^{3/2}}{3/2}\right]_a^4$$

$$\frac{2}{3}(a)^{3/2} = \frac{2}{3}(4^{3/2} - a^{3/2})$$

$$\frac{2}{3}a^{3/2} + \frac{2}{3}a^{3/2} = \frac{2}{3} \times 8$$

$$\frac{4}{3}a^{3/2} = \frac{8 \times 2}{3}$$

$$a\sqrt{a} = \frac{16}{3} \times \frac{3}{4}$$

$$a\sqrt{a} = 4$$

$$a^{3/2} = 4$$

$$a = 4^{2/3} = (2^2)^{2/3}$$

$$a = 2^{4/3}.$$

48. Find the area of the region bounded by the curves $y = x^2 + 2$, $y = x$, $x = 0$ and $x = 3$.

Sol. Given, $\qquad \qquad y = x^2 + 2 \qquad \qquad \text{...(i)}$

and $\qquad \qquad \qquad y = x \qquad \qquad \text{...(ii)}$

From equations (i) and (ii),

$$x = x^2 + 2$$

$$x^2 - x + 2 = 0$$

which shows the value of x do not exist.

$\therefore$ line (ii) and equation (i) do not intersect.

Required area $= \int_0^3 (x^2 + 2)\, dx - \int_0^3 x\, dx$

$$= \left[\frac{x^3}{3} + 2x\right]_0^3 - \left(\frac{x^2}{2}\right)_0^3$$

$$= \left(\frac{27}{3} + 6\right) - 0 - \left(\frac{9}{2} - 0\right)$$

$$= 15 - \frac{9}{2} = \frac{30 - 9}{2}$$

$$= \frac{21}{2} \text{ sq. units.}$$

49. Find the area of the smaller part of the circle $x^2 + y^2 = a^2$ cut off by the line $x = \dfrac{a}{\sqrt{2}}$. * **[NCERT]**

Sol. Given, $x^2 + y^2 = a^2$ is a circle with centre $(0, 0)$ and radius a units and $x = \dfrac{a}{\sqrt{2}}$ is a line parallel to Y-axis.

$$x^2 + y^2 = a^2 \qquad \text{...(i)}$$

Put $\qquad x = \dfrac{a}{\sqrt{2}}$ in equation (i)

$$\left(\frac{a}{\sqrt{2}}\right)^2 + y^2 = a^2$$

$$\frac{a^2}{2} + y^2 = a^2$$

$$y^2 = a^2 - \frac{a^2}{2}$$

$$y^2 = \frac{a^2}{2}$$

$$y = \frac{a}{\sqrt{2}}$$

Required area $= 2\int_{a/\sqrt{2}}^{a}$ Area under circle dx

$$= 2\int_{a/\sqrt{2}}^{a} \sqrt{a^2 - x^2}\, dx$$

$$= 2\left[\frac{x}{2}\sqrt{a^2 - x^2} + \frac{a^2}{2}\sin^{-1}\frac{x}{a}\right]_{a/\sqrt{2}}^{a}$$

$$= 2\left\{\frac{a}{2}\times 0 + \frac{a^2}{2}\sin^{-1}\left(\frac{a}{a}\right)\right\}$$

$$\qquad - \left\{\frac{a/\sqrt{2}}{2}\sqrt{a^2 - \frac{a^2}{2}} + \frac{a^2}{2}\sin^{-1}\left(\frac{a}{\sqrt{2}a}\right)\right\}$$

$$= 2\left[0 + \frac{a^2}{2}\sin^{-1}(1) - \frac{a}{2\sqrt{2}}\sqrt{\frac{a^2}{2} - \frac{a^2}{2}}\sin^{-1}\frac{1}{\sqrt{2}}\right]$$

$$= 2\left[\frac{a^2}{2}\times\frac{\pi}{2} - \frac{a}{2\sqrt{2}}\times\frac{a}{\sqrt{2}} - \frac{a^2}{2}\times\frac{\pi}{4}\right]$$

$$= 2\left[\frac{a^2\pi}{4} - \frac{a^2}{4} - \frac{a^2\pi}{8}\right]$$

$$= 2\left[\frac{2a^2\pi - a^2\pi}{8} - \frac{a^2}{4}\right]$$

$$= 2\times\frac{a^2\pi}{8} - \frac{a^2}{4}\times 2 = \left(\frac{a^2\pi}{4} - \frac{a^2}{2}\right) \text{ sq. units.}$$

50. Using integration, find the area of the triangle formed by positive X-axis and tangent and normal to the circle $x^2 + y^2 = 4$ at $(1, \sqrt{3})$. *

Sol. The equation of the given circle is $x^2 + y^2 = 4$.

The equation of the normal to the circle at $(1, \sqrt{3})$ is same as the line joining the points $(1, \sqrt{3})$ and $(0, 0)$ which is given by

$$y - 0 = \frac{\sqrt{3} - 0}{1 - 0}(x - 0)$$

$$\left[\because y - y_1 = \frac{y_2 - y_1}{x_2 - x_1}(x - x_1)\right]$$

$$y = \sqrt{3}x \qquad \text{...(i)}$$

So, the slope of the normal is $\sqrt{3}$.

We know that,

Slope of normal $\times$ Slope of tangent $= -1$.

$\therefore\qquad$ The slope of tangent $= \dfrac{-1}{\sqrt{3}}$

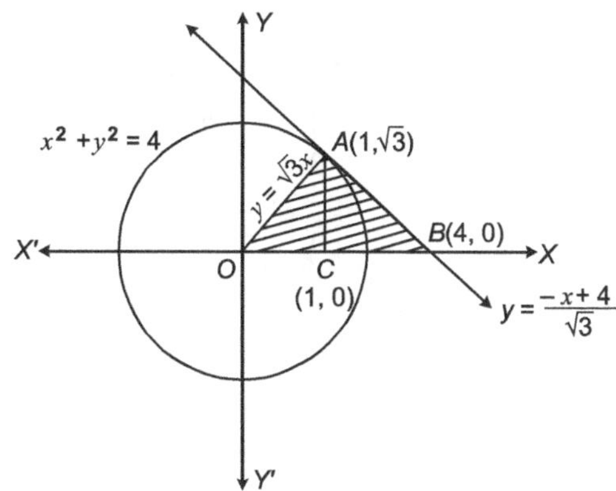

Now, the equation of the tangent to the circle at is $(1, \sqrt{3})$ given by

$$y - \sqrt{3} = \frac{-1}{\sqrt{3}}(x-1)$$

$$[\because y - y_1 = m(x - x_1)]$$

$$\sqrt{3}y - 3 = -x + 1$$

$$y = \frac{-x+4}{\sqrt{3}} \qquad \text{...(ii)}$$

Putting $y = 0$ in (ii), we get $x = 4$.

Thus, AOB is triangle formed by the tangent, normal and the positive X-axis.

Now, Area of $\triangle$AOB

$$= \text{Area of } \triangle\text{AOC} + \text{Area of } \triangle\text{ACB}$$

$$= \int_0^1 y \, dx + \int_1^4 y \, dx$$

$$= \int_0^1 \sqrt{3}x \, dx + \int_1^4 \left(\frac{-x+4}{\sqrt{3}} \right) dx$$

$$= \sqrt{3}\int_0^1 x \, dx - \frac{1}{\sqrt{3}}\int_1^4 x \, dx + \frac{4}{\sqrt{3}}\int_1^4 1 \cdot dx$$

$$= \sqrt{3}\left[\frac{x^2}{2} \right]_0^1 - \frac{1}{\sqrt{3}}\left[\frac{x^2}{2} \right]_1^4 + \frac{4}{\sqrt{3}}[x]_1^4$$

$$= \sqrt{3}\left(\frac{1}{2} - 0 \right) - \frac{1}{\sqrt{3}}\left(\frac{16}{2} - \frac{1}{2} \right) + \frac{4}{\sqrt{3}}(4-1)$$

$$= \frac{\sqrt{3}}{2} - \frac{15}{2\sqrt{3}} + \frac{12}{\sqrt{3}}$$

$$= \frac{\sqrt{3}}{2} + \frac{9}{2\sqrt{3}} = \frac{\sqrt{3}}{2} + \frac{3\sqrt{3}}{2}$$

$$= 2\sqrt{3} \text{ sq. units}$$

Hence, the area of the triangle so formed $2\sqrt{3}$ is sq. units.

51. Find the area bounded by the circle $x^2 + y^2 = 16$ and the line $\sqrt{3}y = x$ in the first quadrant, using integration.*

Sol.

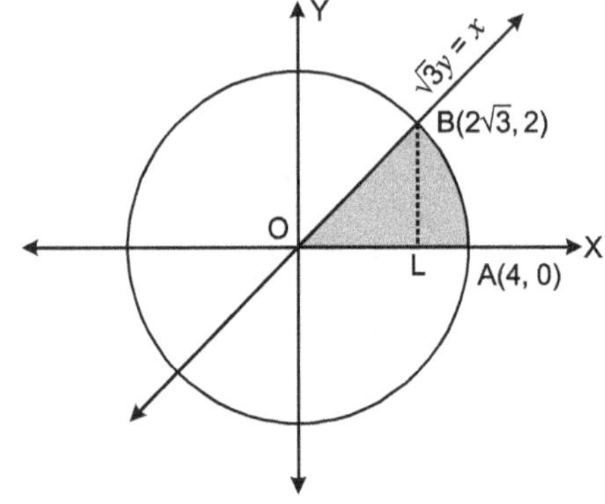

Given, $\qquad x = \sqrt{3}y$

and $\qquad x^2 + y^2 = 16$

$$\Rightarrow \quad (\sqrt{3}y)^2 + y^2 = 16$$

$$4y^2 = 16$$

$$y^2 = 4$$

$$\Rightarrow \qquad y = 2$$

$$\therefore \qquad x = \sqrt{3}y = 2\sqrt{3}$$

$\therefore$ B($2\sqrt{3}$, 2) is the point of intersection in first quadrant.

Required area = area under OBL + area under LBA

$$= \int_0^{2\sqrt{3}} \frac{x}{\sqrt{3}} \, dx + \int_{2\sqrt{3}}^4 \sqrt{16 - x^2} \, dx$$

$$= \frac{1}{\sqrt{3}}\left(\frac{x^2}{2} \right)_0^{2\sqrt{3}} + \left[\frac{x}{2}\sqrt{16 - x^2} + \frac{16}{2}\sin^{-1}\frac{x}{4} \right]_{2\sqrt{3}}^4$$

$$= \frac{1}{2\sqrt{3}}(12 - 0) + (0 + 8\sin^{-1}1)$$

$$\qquad - \left(\frac{2\sqrt{3}}{2}\sqrt{16 - 12} + 8\sin^{-1}\frac{2\sqrt{3}}{4} \right)$$

$$= \frac{6}{\sqrt{3}} + 8 \times \frac{\pi}{2} - 2\sqrt{3} - 8\sin^{-1}\frac{\sqrt{3}}{2}$$

$$= \frac{6\sqrt{3}}{3} + 4\pi - 2\sqrt{3} - 8 \times \frac{\pi}{3}$$

$$= 2\sqrt{3} + \frac{4\pi}{3} - 2\sqrt{3} = \frac{4\pi}{3} \text{ sq. units.}$$

52. Using integration, find the area of the following region :

$$\left\{ (x, y) : \frac{x^2}{9} + \frac{y^2}{4} \le 1 \le \frac{x}{3} + \frac{y}{2} \right\}$$

Sol. Given equations are

$$\frac{x^2}{9} + \frac{y^2}{4} = 1 \qquad \text{...(i)}$$

$$\frac{x}{3} + \frac{y}{2} = 1 \qquad \text{...(ii)}$$

Equation (i) represents an ellipse whose major axis is along X-axis and minor axis is along Y-axis and equation (ii) represents a straight line.

From equation (ii), we have

$$\frac{y}{2} = 1 - \frac{x}{3}$$

Put this value of y in equation (i)

$$\frac{x^2}{9} + \left(1 - \frac{x}{3} \right)^2 = 1$$

$$\frac{x^2}{9} + 1 + \frac{x^2}{9} - \frac{2x}{3} = 1$$

$$\frac{2x^2}{9} - \frac{2x}{3} = 0$$

$$\frac{2x^2 - 6x}{9} = 0$$

$$2x(x - 3) = 0$$

$$x = 0, 3$$

When $x = 0$ $\quad \dfrac{y}{2} = 1$

$$y = 2$$

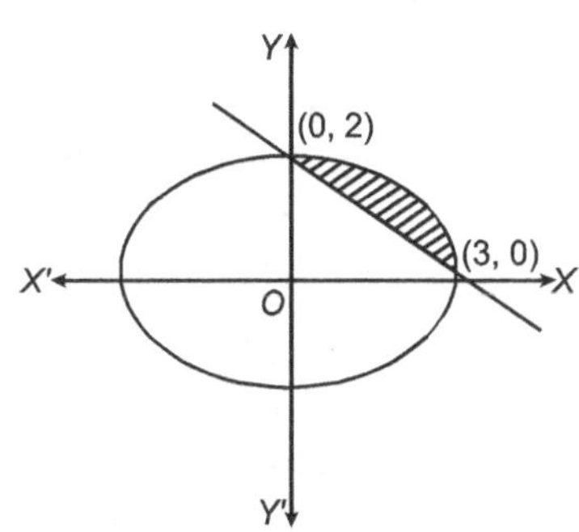

When $x = 3$ $\quad \dfrac{y}{2} = 1 - \dfrac{3}{3}$

$$\frac{y}{2} = 0$$

$$y = 0$$

Required area

$$= \int_0^3 \text{Area under ellipse } dx - \int_0^3 \text{Area under line } dx$$

$$= \int_0^3 \frac{2}{3}\sqrt{9 - x^2}\, dx - \int_0^3 \frac{2}{3}(3 - x)\, dx$$

$$= \frac{2}{3}\left[\frac{x}{2}\sqrt{9 - x^2} + \frac{9}{2}\sin^{-1}\frac{x}{3}\right]_0^3 - \frac{2}{3}\left[3x - \frac{x^2}{2}\right]_0^3$$

$$= \frac{2}{3}\left[\left\{\frac{3}{2}\times 0 + \frac{9}{2}\sin^{-1}(1)\right\} - \left\{0 + \frac{9}{2}\sin^{-1}(0)\right\}\right]$$

$$\qquad - \frac{2}{3}\left[\left\{9 - \frac{9}{2}\right\} - \{0\}\right]$$

$$= \frac{2}{3}\left(\frac{9}{2}\times\frac{\pi}{2} - 0\right) - \frac{2}{3}\left(\frac{9}{2} - 0\right) = \frac{2}{3}\times\frac{9}{4}\pi - 3$$

$$= \frac{3\pi}{2} - \frac{3}{1} = \frac{3\pi - 6}{2} = \frac{3}{2}(\pi - 2) \text{ sq. units.}$$

Self - Assessment

53. Find the area of region bounded by the curve $x^2 = 4y$ and the straight line $x = 4y - 2$.

Sol. $\dfrac{9}{8}$ sq. units

54. Draw the rough sketch of the curves $y = (x - 1)^2$ and $y = |\,x - 1\,|$. Hence, find the area of the region bounded by these curves.

Sol. $\dfrac{1}{3}$ sq. units

55. Find the area of the region bounded by the parabola $y^2 = 4ax$ and the chord $y = mx$.

[NCERT]

Sol. $\dfrac{8a^2}{3m^3}$ sq. units

56. Sketch the graph of $y = |\,x + 3\,|$ and evaluate :

$$\int_{-6}^{0} |\,x + 3\,|\, dx.$$

[NCERT]

Sol. 9 sq. units

57. Using integration, find the area of the region bounded by the lines $x + 2y = 2$, $y - x = 1$ and $2x + y = 7$.

Sol. 6 sq. units

58. Using integration, find the area of the triangle whose vertices are $A(0, 5)$, $B(-1, 1)$ and $C(3, 2)$.

Sol. 7.5 sq. units

59. Find the area of the region given by

$$\{(x, y) : x^2 \le y \le |\,x\,|\}.$$

Sol. $\dfrac{1}{3}$ sq. units

60. Find the area of the region bounded by the curves $y^2 = 4x$, $x = 1$, $x = 4$ and X-axis in the first quadrant.

Sol. $\dfrac{28}{3}$ sq. units

61. Sketch the region of the ellipse and find its area, using integration $\dfrac{x^2}{a^2} + \dfrac{y^2}{b^2} = 1, a > b$.　**[NCERT]**

Sol. πab sq. units

62. Find the area bounded by lines $x + 2y = 2$, $y - x = 1$ and $2x + y = 7$.

Sol. 6 sq. units

63. Using integration find the area of the region bounded by the parabola $y = x^2$ and line $y = x$.

Sol. $\dfrac{1}{6}$ sq. units

○○

Differential Equations

Chapter 9

Basic Concepts

1. **Differential equation** is an equation which involves unknown functions and their derivatives with respect to one or more independent variables.

2. **Ordinary differential equation** is an equation which involves only one independent variable and its derivatives with respect to that independent variable.

3. The **order** of the differential equation is the order of the highest order derivative, which occurs in the differential equation.

4. The **degree** of a differential equation is the index of the highest power of the highest order derivative when it has been made free from negative and fractional numbers, so as derivatives are concerned and it does not contain logarithmic, exponential and trigonometric functions of derivatives.

   For example :

   $$\frac{d^2y}{dx^2} = x^2 \sin^2 x + x^3 + y$$

   is ordinary differential equation whose order is 2 and degree is 1.

5. **Solution of differential equation:** Solution of differential equation is a relation between the variables which satisfy the given differential equation.

6. The most general solution of an ordinary differential equation of first order contains one arbitrary constant, of second order contains two arbitrary constants and so on.

7. Particular solution of differential equation satisfies the differential equation but contains no arbitrary constant.

8. **Solving a differential equation with variable separable :** Equation whose variables are separable can be put into the given form :

   $$f(x)\,dx + f(y)\,dy = 0$$

   The general solution of this equation is obtained by integrating above equation.

   $$\int f(x)\,dx + \int f(y)\,dy = c$$

   where c is an arbitrary constant.

9. **Homogeneous equation** is the differential equation of the form

   $$\frac{dy}{dx} = \frac{f(x,\,y)}{g(x,\,y)}$$

   Where $f(x,\,y)$ and $g(x,\,y)$ are homogeneous functions of same degree in x and y, i.e., equation of the form $\frac{dy}{dx} = f\left(\frac{y}{x}\right)$, is called homogeneous differential equation.

10. Let $\frac{dy}{dx} = f\left(\frac{y}{x}\right)$ be the given homogeneous differential equation, to solve this we substitute

    $$y = vx \Rightarrow \frac{dy}{dx} = v + x\,\frac{dv}{dx}$$

    and proceed by substitution for $\frac{dy}{dx}$ and y in given equation.

11. **Linear differential equation** is the differential equation of the form

    $$\frac{dy}{dx} + Py = Q$$

    To solve linear differential equation we multiply both sides of the given differential equation by integrating factor of the given differential equation.

    where $e^{\int P dx}$ is the integrating factor of equation $\frac{dy}{dx} + Py = Q.$

Multiple Choice Questions

1. The degree of the differential equation

   $$\left(\frac{d^2y}{dx^2}\right)^2 + \left(\frac{dy}{dx}\right)^2 = x \sin\left(\frac{dy}{dx}\right) \text{ is:}$$

   [NCERT Exemplar]

   (a) 1
   (b) 2
   (c) 3
   (d) not defined

Sol. (d) not defined

Explanation :

The degree of above differential equation is not defined because when we expand $\sin\left(\dfrac{dy}{dx}\right)$ we get an infinite series in the increasing powers of $\dfrac{dy}{dx}$. Therefore, its degree is not defined.

2. The degree of the differential equation
$$\left[1+\left(\dfrac{dy}{dx}\right)^2\right]^{3/2} = \dfrac{d^2y}{dx^2} \text{ is:} \quad \textbf{[NCERT Exemplar]}$$

(a) 4
(b) $\dfrac{3}{2}$
(c) not defined
(d) 2

Sol. (d) 2

Explanation :

Given that,
$$\left[1+\left(\dfrac{dy}{dx}\right)^2\right]^{3/2} = \dfrac{d^2y}{dx^2}$$

On squaring both sides, we get
$$\left[1+\left(\dfrac{dy}{dx}\right)^2\right]^{3} = \left(\dfrac{d^2y}{dx^2}\right)^2$$

So, the degree of differential equation is 2.

3. The order and degree of the differential equation
$$\dfrac{d^2y}{dx^2}+\left(\dfrac{dy}{dx}\right)^{1/4} + x^{1/5} = 0 \text{ respectively, are:}$$

$$\textbf{[NCERT Exemplar]}$$

(a) 2 and 4
(b) 2 and 2
(c) 2 and 3
(d) 3 and 3

Sol. (a) 2 and 4

Explanation :

Given that,
$$\dfrac{d^2y}{dx^2}+\left(\dfrac{dy}{dx}\right)^{1/4} + x^{1/5} = 0$$

$$\Rightarrow \quad \dfrac{d^2y}{dx^2}+\left(\dfrac{dy}{dx}\right)^{1/4} = -x^{1/5}$$

$$\Rightarrow \quad \left(\dfrac{dy}{dx}\right)^{1/4} = -\left(x^{1/5}+\dfrac{d^2y}{dx^2}\right)$$

On squaring both sides, we get
$$\left(\dfrac{dy}{dx}\right)^{1/2} = \left(x^{1/5}+\dfrac{d^2y}{dx^2}\right)^2$$

Again, on squaring both sides, we have
$$\dfrac{dy}{dx} = \left(x^{1/5}+\dfrac{d^2y}{dx^2}\right)^4$$

order = 2, degree = 4.

4. Which of the following is a second order differential equation? **[NCERT Exemplar]**

(a) $(y')^2 + x = y^2$
(b) $y'y'' + y = \sin x$
(c) $y''' + (y'')^2 + y = 0$
(d) $y' = y^2$

Sol. (b) $y'y'' + y = \sin x$

Explanation :

The second order differential equation is $y'y'' + y = \sin x$.

5. The degree of differential equation
$$\dfrac{d^2y}{dx^2}+\left(\dfrac{dy}{dx}\right)^3 + 6y^5 = 0 \text{ is:} \quad \textbf{[NCERT Exemplar]}$$

(a) 1
(b) 2
(c) 3
(d) 5

Sol. (a) 1

Explanation :

$$\dfrac{d^2y}{dx^2}+\left(\dfrac{dy}{dx}\right)^3 + 6y^5 = 0$$

We know that, the degree of a differential equation is exponent highest of order derivative.

$\therefore$ Degree = 1.

6. The order and degree of differential equation
$$\left(\dfrac{d^3y}{dx^3}\right)^2 - 3\dfrac{d^2y}{dx^2} + 2\left(\dfrac{dy}{dx}\right)^4 = y^4 \text{ are:}$$

$$\textbf{[NCERT Exemplar]}$$

(a) 1, 4
(b) 3, 4
(c) 2, 4
(d) 3, 2

Sol. (d) 3, 2

Explanation :

Given that, $\left(\dfrac{d^3y}{dx^3}\right)^2 - 3\dfrac{d^2y}{dx^2} + 2\left(\dfrac{dy}{dx}\right)^4 = y^4$

$\therefore$ Order = 3
and Degree = 2.

7. The order and degree of differential equation
$$\left[1+\left(\dfrac{dy}{dx}\right)^2\right] = \dfrac{d^2y}{dx^2} \text{ are:} \quad \textbf{[NCERT Exemplar]}$$

(a) $2, \dfrac{3}{2}$
(b) 2, 3
(c) 2, 1
(d) 3, 4

Sol. (c) 2, 1

Explanation :

Given that,
$$\left[1+\left(\dfrac{dy}{dx}\right)^2\right] = \dfrac{d^2y}{dx^2}$$

$\therefore$ Order = 2 and degree = 1.

8. Order and degree of the differential equation $r\dfrac{dr}{d\theta} + \cos\theta = 5$.

(a) order 2, degree 1
(b) order 2, degree 2
(c) order 1 and degree 1
(d) order 2, degree not define

Sol. (c) order 1 and degree 1

Explanation :

In $r\dfrac{dr}{d\theta} + \cos\theta = 5$, order 1 and degree = 1.

9. Order and degree of the differential equation $\dfrac{dy}{dx} + \dfrac{3xy}{\left(\dfrac{dy}{dx}\right)} = \cos x$:

(a) order 2, degree 1
(b) order 2, degree 2
(c) order 1, degree 2
(d) order 2, degree not define

Sol. (c) order 1, degree 2

Explanation :

This equation can be expressed as $\left(\dfrac{dy}{dx}\right)^2 + 3xy = \cos x\left(\dfrac{dy}{dx}\right)$.

So, its order is 1 and degree is 2.

10. Order and degree of the differential equation $e^{\frac{dy}{dx}} + \dfrac{dy}{dx} = x$:

(a) order 2, degree 1
(b) order 2, degree 2
(c) order 1, degre 2
(d) order 1, degree not defined

Sol. (d) order 1, degree not defined

Explanation :

It's order is 1, but equation cannot be expressed as a polynomial differential equation.
$\therefore$ The degree is not defined.

11. Order and degree of the differential equation
$$\begin{vmatrix} x^3 & y^3 & 3 \\ 2x^2 & 3y\dfrac{dy}{dx} & 0 \\ 5x & 2\left[y\dfrac{d^2y}{dx^2} + \left(\dfrac{dy}{dx}\right)^2\right] & 0 \end{vmatrix} = 0:$$

(a) order 2, degree 1
(b) order 2, degree 2
(c) order 1, degree 2
(d) order 1, degree not defined

Sol. (a) order 2, degree 1

Explanation :
$$x^3\,[0-0] - y^2\,[0-0]$$
$$+3\left\{4x^2\left[y\dfrac{d^2y}{dx^2} + \left(\dfrac{dy}{dx}\right)^2\right] - 15xy\dfrac{dy}{dx}\right\} = 0$$
$$4x^2y\dfrac{d^2y}{dx^2} + 4x^2\left(\dfrac{dy}{dx}\right)^2 - 15xy\dfrac{dy}{dx} = 0$$

$\therefore$ Its order is 2 and degree is 1.

12. The order and the degree of differential equation $\dfrac{d^4y}{dx^4} - 4\dfrac{d^3y}{dx^3} + 8\dfrac{d^2y}{dx^2} - 8\dfrac{dy}{dx} + 4y = 0$ are respectively.

(a) order 4, degree 1 (b) order 1, degree 4
(c) order 1, degree 1 (d) none of these

Sol. (a) order 4, degree 1

Explanation :

In the given equation, highest differential power is 4 and degree is one.

13. Which of the following differential equation has the same order and degree:

(a) $\dfrac{d^4y}{dx^4} + 8\left(\dfrac{dy}{dx}\right)^6 + 5y = e^x$

(b) $5\left(\dfrac{d^3y}{dx^3}\right)^4 + 8\left(1+\dfrac{dy}{dx}\right)^2 + 5y = x^8$

(c) $\left[1+\left(\dfrac{dy}{dx}\right)^3\right]^{2/3} = 4\dfrac{d^3y}{dx^3}$

(d) $y = x^2\dfrac{dy}{dx} + \sqrt{1+\left(\dfrac{dy}{dx}\right)^2}$

Sol. (c) $\left[1+\left(\dfrac{dy}{dx}\right)^3\right]^{2/3} = 4\dfrac{d^3y}{dx^3}$

Explanation :

Option (a) has order = 4, degree 1
Option (b) has order = 3, degree = 4
Option (c) has order = 3, degree = 3 (taking cube)
Option (d) has order = 1, degree = 2 (squaring)

14. If m and n are the order and degree of the differential equation $\left(\dfrac{d^2y}{dx^2}\right)^5 + 4\dfrac{\left(\dfrac{d^2y}{dx^2}\right)^3}{\left(\dfrac{d^3y}{dx^3}\right)} + \dfrac{d^3y}{dx^3} = x^2 - 1$, then:

(a) $m = 3$ and $n = 5$ (b) $m = 3$ and $n = 1$
(c) $m = 3$ and $n = 3$ (d) $m = 3$ and $n = 2$

Sol. (d) $m = 3$ and $n = 2$

Explanation :

The highest order (m) of the given equation is $\dfrac{d^3y}{dx^3} = 3$ and degree (n) of the given equation is $\left(\dfrac{d^3y}{dx^3}\right)^2 = 2$. Therefore $m = 3$ and $n = 2$.

15. The sum of the order and degree of the differential equation $\dfrac{d}{dx}\left\{\left(\dfrac{dy}{dx}\right)^3\right\} = 0$:

(a) 3   (b) 4

(c) 2   (d) 8

Sol. (a) 3

Explanation :

We have, $\dfrac{d}{dx}\left\{\left(\dfrac{dy}{dx}\right)^3\right\} = 0$

$\Rightarrow \quad 3\left(\dfrac{dy}{dx}\right)^2 \times \left(\dfrac{d^2y}{dx^2}\right) = 0$

So order is 2 and degree is 1 so their sum is $2 + 1 = 3$.

16. The degree of the differential equation $\left(1+\dfrac{dy}{dx}\right)^3 = \left(\dfrac{d^2y}{dx^2}\right)^2$ is:

(a) 1   (b) 2

(c) 3   (d) 4

Sol. (b) 2

17. The degree of the differential equation $\dfrac{d^2y}{dx^2} + 3\left(\dfrac{dy}{dx}\right)^2 = x^2 \log\left(\dfrac{d^2y}{dx^2}\right)$ is:

(a) 1   (b) 2

(c) 3   (d) Not defined

Sol. (d) Not defined

Explanation :

The given differential equation is not a polynomial equation in terms of its derivatives, so its degree is not defined.

So, the correct option is (d).

18. The order and degree of the differential equation $\left[1+\left(\dfrac{dy}{dx}\right)^2\right]^2 = \dfrac{d^2y}{dx^2}$ respectively, are:

(a) 1, 2   (b) 2, 2

(c) 2, 1   (d) 4, 2

Sol. (c) 2, 1

19. The order of the differential equation of all circles of given radius a is:

(a) 1   (b) 2

(c) 3   (d) 4

Sol. (b) 2

Explanation :

Let the equation of given family be $(x - h)^2 + (y - k)^2 = a^2$. It has two arbitrary constants h and k. Therefore, the order of the given differential equation will be 2.

So, the correct option is (b).

20. Number of arbitrary constants in general solution of differential equation of fourth order is:

(a) 0   (b) 2

(c) 4   (d) 3

Sol. (c) 4

Explanation :

Number of arbitrary constants in the general solution of differential equation is equal to the order of differential equation.

21. Number of arbitrary constants in particular solution of differential equation of second order is:

(a) 0   (b) 2

(c) 4   (d) 3

Sol. (a) 0

Explanation :

Number of arbitrary constants in particular solution of differential equation is 0.

22. The solution of differential equation $xdy - ydx = 0$ represents: **[NCERT Exemplar]**

(a) a rectangular hyperbola

(b) parabola whose vertex is at origin

(c) straight line passing through origin

(d) a circle whose centre is at origin

Sol. (c) straight line passing through origin

Explanation :

Given that,

$$xdy - ydx = 0$$

$\Rightarrow \quad xdy = ydx$

$\Rightarrow \quad \dfrac{dy}{y} = \dfrac{dx}{x}$

On integrating both sides, we get

$$\log y = \log x + \log C$$

$\Rightarrow \quad \log y = \log Cx$

$\Rightarrow \quad y = Cx$

which is a straight line passing through origin.

23. The solution of differential equation $\tan y \sec^2 x\, dx + \tan x \sec^2 y\, dy = 0$ is: **[NCERT Exemplar]**

(a) $\tan x + \tan y = k$ (b) $\tan x - \tan y = k$

(c) $\dfrac{\tan x}{\tan y} = k$ (d) $\tan x \cdot \tan y = k$

Sol. (d) $\tan x \cdot \tan y = k$

Explanation :

Given that, $\tan y \sec^2 x\, dx + \tan x \sec^2 y\, dy = 0$

$\Rightarrow \qquad \tan y \sec^2 x\, dx = -\tan x \sec^2 y\, dy$

$\Rightarrow \qquad \dfrac{\sec^2 x}{\tan x}\, dx = \dfrac{-\sec^2 y}{\tan y}\, dy \qquad \dots(i)$

On integrating both sides, we get

$$\int \dfrac{\sec^2 x}{\tan x}\, dx = -\int \dfrac{\sec^2 y}{\tan y}\, dy$$

Put $\tan x = t$ in LHS integral, we get

$\Rightarrow \qquad \sec^2 x\, dx = dt$

and $\tan y = u$ in RHS integral, we get

$$\sec^2 y\, dy = du$$

On substituting these values in equation (i), we get

$$\int \dfrac{dt}{t} = -\int \dfrac{du}{u}$$

$$\log t = -\log u + \log k$$

(where k is an integration constant)

$\Rightarrow \qquad \log (t \cdot u) = \log k$

$\Rightarrow \qquad \log (\tan x \tan y) = \log k$

$\Rightarrow \qquad \tan x \tan y = k.$

24. The solution of $\dfrac{dy}{dx} - y = 1$, $y(0) = 1$ is given by:

[NCERT Exemplar]

(a) $xy = -e^x$ (b) $xy = -e^{-x}$

(c) $xy = -1$ (d) $y = 2e^x - 1$

Sol. (d) $y = 2e^x - 1$

Explanation :

Given that,

$$\dfrac{dy}{dx} - y = 1$$

$\Rightarrow \qquad \dfrac{dy}{dx} = 1 + y$

$\Rightarrow \qquad \dfrac{dy}{1+y} = dx$

On integrating both sides, we get

$$\log (1 + y) = x + C \qquad \dots(i)$$

When $x = 0$ and $y = 1$, then

$$\log 2 = 0 + C$$

$\Rightarrow \qquad C = \log 2$

The required solution is

$$\log (1 + y) = x + \log 2$$

$\Rightarrow \qquad \log \left(\dfrac{1+y}{2}\right) = x$

$\Rightarrow \qquad \dfrac{1+y}{2} = e^x$

$\Rightarrow \qquad 1 + y = 2e^x$

$\Rightarrow \qquad y = 2e^x - 1.$

25. The number of solutions of $\dfrac{dy}{dx} = \dfrac{y+1}{x-1}$, when $y(1) = 2$ is: **[NCERT Exemplar]**

(a) none   (b) one

(c) two   (d) infinite

Sol. (b) one

Explanation :

Given that, $\qquad \dfrac{dy}{dx} = \dfrac{y+1}{x-1}$

$\Rightarrow \qquad \dfrac{dy}{y+1} = \dfrac{dx}{x-1}$

On integrating both sides, we get

$$\log (y + 1) = \log (x - 1) - \log C$$

$\Rightarrow \qquad C(y + 1) = (x - 1)$

$\Rightarrow \qquad C = \dfrac{x-1}{y+1}$

When $x = 1$ and $y = 2$, then $C = 0$

So, the required solution is $x - 1 = 0$.

Hence, only one solution exist.

26. The differential equation $y\dfrac{dy}{dx} + x = C$ represents:

[NCERT Exemplar]

(a) family of hyperbolas

(b) family of parabolas

(c) family of ellipses

(d) family of circles

Sol. (d) family of circles

Explanation :

Given that,

$$y\dfrac{dy}{dx} + x = C$$

$\Rightarrow \qquad y\dfrac{dy}{dx} = C - x$

$\Rightarrow \qquad y\, dy = (C - x)\, dx$

On integrating both sides, we get

$$\dfrac{y^2}{2} = Cx - \dfrac{x^2}{2} + K$$

(where K is an integration constant)

$\Rightarrow \qquad \dfrac{x^2}{2} + \dfrac{y^2}{2} = Cx + K$

$\Rightarrow \qquad \dfrac{x^2}{2} + \dfrac{y^2}{2} - Cx = K$

which represent family of circles.

27. The general solution of $e^x \cos ydx - e^x \sin ydy = 0$ is: **[NCERT Exemplar]**

(a) $e^x \cos y = k$ (b) $e^x \sin y = k$

(c) $e^x = k \cos y$ (d) $e^x = k \sin y$

Sol. (a) $e^x \cos y = k$

Explanation :

Given that,

$$e^x \cos ydx - e^x \sin ydy = 0$$

$$\Rightarrow \qquad e^x \cos ydx = e^x \sin ydy$$

$$\Rightarrow \qquad \frac{dx}{dy} = \tan y$$

$$\Rightarrow \qquad dx = \tan ydy$$

On integrating both sides, we get

$$x = \log \sec y + C$$

$$\Rightarrow \qquad x - C = \log \sec y$$

$$\Rightarrow \qquad \sec y = e^{x-C}$$

$$\Rightarrow \qquad \sec y = e^x e^{-C}$$

$$\Rightarrow \qquad \frac{1}{\cos y} = \frac{e^x}{e^C}$$

$$\Rightarrow \qquad e^x \cos y = e^C$$

$$\Rightarrow \qquad e^x \cos y = k. \qquad [\text{where } k = e^C]$$

28. The solution of differential equation $\dfrac{dy}{dx} = \dfrac{1+y^2}{1+x^2}$ is: **[NCERT Exemplar]**

(a) $y = \tan^{-1} x$ (b) $y - x = k(1 + xy)$

(c) $x = \tan^{-1} y$ (d) $\tan (xy) = k$

Sol. (b) $y - x = k(1 + xy)$

Explanation :

Given that, $\qquad \dfrac{dy}{dx} = \dfrac{1+y^2}{1+x^2}$

$$\Rightarrow \qquad \frac{dy}{1+y^2} = \frac{dx}{1+x^2}$$

On integrating both sides, we get

$$\tan^{-1} y = \tan^{-1} x + C$$

$$\Rightarrow \quad \tan^{-1} y - \tan^{-1} x = C$$

$$\Rightarrow \quad \tan^{-1}\left(\frac{y-x}{1+xy}\right) = C$$

$$\Rightarrow \quad \frac{y-x}{1+xy} = \tan C$$

$$\Rightarrow \quad y - x = \tan C(1 + xy)$$

$$\Rightarrow \quad y - x = k(1 + xy)$$

where, $k = \tan C$.

29. The solution of differential equation $\cos x \sin ydx + \sin x \cos ydy = 0$ is: **[NCERT Exemplar]**

(a) $\dfrac{\sin x}{\sin y} = C$ (b) $\sin x \sin y = C$

(c) $\sin x + \sin y = C$ (d) $\cos x \cos y = C$

Sol. (b) $\sin x \sin y = C$

Explanation :

Given differential equation is

$$\cos x \sin ydx + \sin x \cos ydy = 0$$

$$\Rightarrow \qquad \cos x \sin ydx = -\sin x \cos ydy$$

$$\Rightarrow \qquad \frac{\cos x}{\sin x} dx = -\frac{\cos y}{\sin y} dy$$

$$\Rightarrow \qquad \cot x \, dx = -\cot ydy$$

On integrating both sides, we get

$$\log \sin x = -\log \sin y + \log C$$

$$\Rightarrow \quad \log \sin x \sin y = \log C$$

$$\Rightarrow \quad \sin x \cdot \sin y = C.$$

30. The general solution of $\dfrac{dy}{dx} = 2xe^{x^2 - y}$ is: **[NCERT Exemplar]**

(a) $e^{x^2 - y} = C$ (b) $e^{-y} + e^{x^2} = C$

(c) $e^y = e^{x^2} + C$ (d) $e^{x^2 + y} = C$

Sol. (c) $e^y = e^{x^2} + C$

Explanation :

Given that,

$$\frac{dy}{dx} = 2xe^{x^2 - y} = 2xe^{x^2} \cdot e^{-y}$$

$$\Rightarrow \qquad e^y \frac{dy}{dx} = 2xe^{x^2}$$

$$\Rightarrow \qquad e^y dy = 2xe^{x^2} dx$$

On integrating both sides, we get

$$\int e^y \, dy = 2\int xe^{x^2} \, dx$$

Put $x^2 = t$ in RHS integral, we get

$$2x \, dx = dt$$

$$\therefore \qquad \int e^y \, dy = \int e^t \, dt$$

$$\Rightarrow \qquad e^y = e^t + C$$

$$\Rightarrow \qquad e^y = e^{x^2} + C.$$

31. The curve for which the slope of the tangent at any point is equal to the ratio of the abscissa to the ordinate of the point is: **[NCERT Exemplar]**

(a) an ellipse

(b) parabola

(c) circle

(d) rectangular hyperbola

Sol. (d) rectangular hyperbola

Explanation :

Slope of tangent of the curve $= \dfrac{dy}{dx}$

and ratio of abscissa to the ordinate $= \dfrac{x}{y}$

According to the question,

$$\frac{dy}{dx} = \frac{x}{y}$$

$$ydy = xdx$$

On integrating both sides, we get

$$\frac{y^2}{2} = \frac{x^2}{2} + C$$

$$\Rightarrow \quad \frac{y^2}{2} - \frac{x^2}{2} = C$$

$$\Rightarrow \quad y^2 - x^2 = 2C$$

which is an equation of rectangular hyperbola.

32. The solution of equation $(2y - 1)\,dx - (2x + 3)\,dy = 0$ is: **[NCERT Exemplar]**

(a) $\dfrac{2x-1}{2y+3} = k$ 　　(b) $\dfrac{2y+1}{2x-3} = k$

(c) $\dfrac{2x+3}{2y-1} = k$ 　　(d) $\dfrac{2x-1}{2y-1} = k$

Sol. (c) $\dfrac{2x+3}{2y-1} = k$

Explanation :

Given that, $(2y - 1)\,dx - (2x + 3)\,dy = 0$

$$\Rightarrow \quad (2y - 1)\,dx = (2x + 3)\,dy$$

$$\Rightarrow \quad \frac{dx}{2x+3} = \frac{dy}{2y-1}$$

On integrating both sides, we get

$$\frac{1}{2}\log(2x+3) = \frac{1}{2}\log(2y-1) + \log C$$

$$\Rightarrow \quad \frac{1}{2}[\log \cdot (2x+3) - \log(2y-1)] = \log C$$

$$\Rightarrow \quad \frac{1}{2}\log\left(\frac{2x+3}{2y-1}\right) = \log C$$

$$\Rightarrow \quad \left(\frac{2x+3}{2y-1}\right)^{1/2} = C$$

$$\Rightarrow \quad \frac{2x+3}{2y-1} = C^2$$

$$\Rightarrow \quad \frac{2x+3}{2y-1} = k, \text{ where } k = C^2.$$

33. The general solution of differential equation $(e^x + 1)\,ydy = (y + 1)\,e^x\,dx$ is: **[NCERT Exemplar]**

(a) $(y + 1) = k(e^x + 1)$

(b) $y + 1 = e^x + 1 + k$

(c) $y = \log\{k(y + 1)(e^x + 1)\}$

(d) $y = \log\left\{\dfrac{e^x + 1}{y + 1}\right\} + k$

Sol. (c) $y = \log\{k(y + 1)(e^x + 1)\}$

Explanation :

Given differential equation,

$$(e^x + 1)\,ydy = (y + 1)e^x\,dx$$

$$\Rightarrow \quad \left(\frac{y}{1+y}\right)dy = \left(\frac{e^x}{e^x+1}\right)dx$$

On integrating both sides, we get

$$\int \frac{y}{1+y}\,dy = \int \frac{e^x}{1+e^x}\,dx$$

$$\Rightarrow \quad \int \frac{1+y-1}{1+y}\,dy = \int \frac{e^x}{1+e^x}\,dx$$

$$\Rightarrow \quad \int 1\,dy - \int \frac{1}{1+y}\,dy = \int \frac{e^x}{1+e^x}\,dx$$

$$\Rightarrow \quad y - \log(1 + y) = \log(1 + e^x) + \log k$$

$$\Rightarrow \quad y = \log(1 + y) + \log(1 + e^x) + \log(k)$$

$$\Rightarrow \quad y = \log\{k(1 + y)(1 + e^x)\}.$$

34. The solution of differential equation $\dfrac{dy}{dx} = e^{x-y} + x^2 e^{-y}$ is : **[NCERT Exemplar]**

(a) $y = e^{x-y} - x^2 e^{-y} + C$ 　(b) $e^y - e^x = \dfrac{x^3}{3} + C$

(c) $e^x + e^y = \dfrac{x^3}{3} + C$ 　(d) $e^x - e^y = \dfrac{x^3}{3} + C$

Sol. (b) $e^y - e^x = \dfrac{x^3}{3} + C$

Explanation :

Given that, $\quad \dfrac{dy}{dx} = e^{x-y} + x^2 e^{-y}$

$$\Rightarrow \quad \frac{dy}{dx} = e^x e^{-y} + x^2 e^{-y}$$

$$\Rightarrow \quad \frac{dy}{dx} = \frac{e^x + x^2}{e^y}$$

$$\Rightarrow \quad e^y\,dy = (e^x + x^2)\,dx$$

On integrating both sides, we get

$$\int e^y\,dy = \int (e^x + x^2)\,dx$$

$$\Rightarrow \quad e^y = e^x + \frac{x^3}{3} + C$$

$$\Rightarrow \quad e^y - e^x = \frac{x^3}{3} + C.$$

35. The solution of the differential equation $\dfrac{dy}{dx} = e^x + \cos x + x + \tan x$ is:

(a) $y = e^x + \sin x + \dfrac{x^2}{2} + \log\cos x + C$

(b) $y = e^x + \sin x + \dfrac{x^2}{2} + \log\sec x + C$

(c) $y = e^x - \sin x + \dfrac{x^2}{2} + \log \cos x + C$

(d) $y = e^x - \sin x + \dfrac{x^2}{2} + \log \sec x + C$

Sol. (b) $y = e^x + \sin x + \dfrac{x^2}{2} + \log \sec x + C$

Explanation :

$$\frac{dy}{dx} = e^x + \cos x + x + \tan x$$

On integrating both sides, we get

$$y = e^x + \sin x + \frac{x^2}{2} + \log \sec x + C.$$

36. The solution of the equation $(1 + x^2)\dfrac{dy}{dx} = 1$ is:

(a) $y = \log(1 + x^2) + C$
(b) $y + \log(1 + x^2) + C = 0$
(c) $y - \log(1 + x) + C$
(d) $y = \tan^{-1} x + C$

Sol. (d) $y = \tan^{-1} x + C$

Explanation :

$$(1 + x^2)\frac{dy}{dx} = 1$$

$$\Rightarrow \qquad \frac{dy}{dx} = \frac{1}{1 + x^2}$$

On integrating, $y = \tan^{-1} x + C$.

37. The solution of the differential equation $\dfrac{dy}{dx} + \dfrac{1 + \cos 2y}{1 - \cos 2x} = 0$:

(a) $\tan y + \cot x + C$ (b) $\tan y \cot x = C$
(c) $\tan y - \cot x = C$ (d) None of these

Sol. (c) $\tan y - \cot x = C$

Explanation :

$$\frac{dy}{dx} = -\frac{1 + \cos 2y}{1 - \cos 2x}$$

$$\Rightarrow \qquad \frac{dy}{dx} = -\frac{2\cos^2 y}{2\sin^2 x}$$

$$\Rightarrow \qquad \sec^2 y\, dy = -\cosec^2 x\, dx$$

On integrating both sides, we get

$$\tan y = \cot x + C$$

$$\Rightarrow \qquad \tan y - \cot x = C.$$

38. The general solution of differential equation $\dfrac{dy}{dx} = e^{x+y}$ is:

(a) $e^x + e^{-y} = C$ (b) $e^{-x} + e^y = C$
(c) $e^x + e^y = C$ (d) $e^{-x} + e^{-y} = C$

Sol. (a) $e^x + e^{-y} = C$

Explanation :

$$\frac{dy}{dx} = e^x \times e^y$$

$$\Rightarrow \qquad e^{-y}\, dy = e^x\, dx$$

Integrating both side

$$\Rightarrow \qquad \int e^{-y}\, dy = \int e^x\, dx$$

$$\Rightarrow \qquad -e^{-y} = e^x + A$$

$$\Rightarrow \qquad -e^{-y} - e^x = A$$

$$\Rightarrow \qquad e^{-y} + e^x = -A$$

$$e^{-y} + e^x = C \text{ where } C = -A.$$

39. The solution of the differential equation $\dfrac{dx}{x} + \dfrac{dy}{y} = 0$ is:

(a) $\dfrac{1}{x} + \dfrac{1}{y} = C$ (b) $\log x \log y = C$

(c) $xy = C$ (d) $x + y = C$

Sol. (c) $xy = C$

Explanation :

We have, $\dfrac{dx}{x} + \dfrac{dy}{y} = 0$

$$\int \frac{dx}{x} + \int \frac{dy}{y} = 0$$

$$\log_e x + \log_e y = \log_e C$$

$$\Rightarrow \qquad \log_e(xy) = \log_e(C)$$

$$\Rightarrow \qquad xy = C.$$

40. The general solution of the differential equation $\dfrac{dy}{dx} = \cot x \cot y$ is:

(a) $\cos x = C \cosec y$ (b) $\sin x = C \sec y$
(c) $\sin x = C \cos y$ (d) $\cos x = C \sin y$

Sol. (b) $\sin x = C \sec y$

Explanation :

$$\frac{dy}{dx} = \cot x \cot y$$

$$\Rightarrow \qquad \cot x\, dx - \tan y\, dy = 0$$

Integrating on both sides, we get

$$\Rightarrow \int \cot x\, dx - \int \tan y\, dy = 0$$

$$\log \sin x - \log \sec y = \log C$$

$$\Rightarrow \qquad \log\left(\frac{\sin x}{\sec y}\right) = \log C$$

$$\Rightarrow \qquad \sin x = C \sec y.$$

41. Which of the following is not a homogeneous function of x and y.

(a) $x^2 + 2xy$ (b) $2x - y$

(c) $\cos^2\left(\dfrac{y}{x}\right) + \dfrac{y}{x}$ (d) $\sin x - \sin y$

Sol. (d) $\sin x - \sin y$

Explanation :

By law of homogeneous function, the right option is (d).

42. Which of the following is a homogeneous differential equation?

(a) $(4x + 6y + 5)\,dy - (3y + 2x + 4)\,dx = 0$

(b) $xy\,dx - (x^3 + y^3)\,dx = 0$

(c) $(x^3 + 2y^2)\,dx + 2xy\,dy = 0$

(d) $y^2\,dx + (x^2 - xy - y^2)\,dy = 0$

Sol. (d) $y^2\,dx + (x^2 - xy - y^2)\,dy = 0$

Explanation :

By equation $y^2\,dx + (x^2 - xy - y^2)\,dy = 0$

$$\therefore \qquad \frac{dy}{dx} = \frac{-y^2}{x^2 - xy - y^2}$$

Power of numerator and denominator are of same order. Hence, it is a homogeneous differential equation.

43. The solution of the differential equation $xdy - ydx = \sqrt{x^2 + y^2}\ dx$ is:

(a) $x + \sqrt{x^2 + y^2} = Cx^2$ (b) $y - \sqrt{x^2 + y^2} = Cx$

(c) $x - \sqrt{x^2 + y^2} = Cx$ (d) $y + \sqrt{x^2 + y^2} = Cx^2$

Sol. (d) $y + \sqrt{x^2 + y^2} = Cx^2$

Explanation :

$$xdy - ydx = \sqrt{x^2 + y^2}\ dx$$

$$\Rightarrow \qquad xdy = \sqrt{x^2 + y^2}\ dx + ydx$$

$$\Rightarrow \qquad \frac{dy}{dx} = \frac{\sqrt{x^2 + y^2} + y}{x} \qquad \ldots(i)$$

Put $\qquad y = vx \qquad \ldots(ii)$

$$\Rightarrow \qquad \frac{dy}{dx} = v + x\frac{dv}{dx} \qquad \ldots(iii)$$

Substituting (ii) and (iii) in (i), we get

$$\Rightarrow \qquad v + x\frac{dv}{dx} = \frac{\sqrt{x^2 + v^2 x^2} + vx}{x}$$

$$\Rightarrow \qquad v + x\frac{dv}{dx} = \sqrt{1 + v^2} + v$$

$$\Rightarrow \qquad x\frac{dv}{dx} = \sqrt{1 + v^2}$$

Integrating on both sides, we get

$$\int \frac{dv}{\sqrt{1 + v^2}} = \int \frac{dx}{x}$$

$$\Rightarrow \quad \log(v + \sqrt{1 + v^2}) = \log x + \log C$$

$$\Rightarrow \qquad v + \sqrt{1 + v^2} = xC$$

$$\Rightarrow \qquad \frac{y}{x} + \sqrt{1 + \frac{y^2}{x^2}} = xC$$

$$\Rightarrow \qquad y + \sqrt{x^2 + y^2} = Cx^2.$$

44. The integrating factor of differential equation $\cos x\,\dfrac{dy}{dx} + y \sin x = 1$ is: **[NCERT Exemplar]**

(a) $\cos x$ (b) $\tan x$

(c) $\sec x$ (d) $\sin x$

Sol. (c) $\sec x$

Explanation :

Given that,

$$\cos x\,\frac{dy}{dx} + y \sin x = 1$$

$$\Rightarrow \qquad \frac{dy}{dx} + y \tan x = \sec x$$

Here, $P = \tan x$ and $Q = \sec x$

$$\text{IF} = e^{\int P\,dx} = e^{\int \tan x\,dx} = e^{\log \sec x}$$

$$\Rightarrow \qquad = \sec x.$$

45. The integrating factor of $\dfrac{xdy}{dx} - y = x^4 - 3x$ is:

[NCERT Exemplar]

(a) x (b) $\log x$

(c) $\dfrac{1}{x}$ (d) $-x$

Sol. (c) $\dfrac{1}{x}$

Explanation :

Given that,

$$x\frac{dy}{dx} - y = x^4 - 3x$$

$$\Rightarrow \qquad \frac{dy}{dx} - \frac{y}{x} = x^3 - 3$$

Here, $P = -\dfrac{1}{x}$, $Q = x^3 - 3$

$$\text{IF} = e^{\int P\,dx} = e^{-\int \frac{1}{x}\,dx} = e^{-\log x}$$

$$= e^{\log x^{-1}} = x^{-1} = \frac{1}{x}.$$

46. The integrating factor of differential equation $(1 - x^2)\dfrac{dy}{dx} - xy = 1$ is: **[NCERT Exemplar]**

(a) $-x$ (b) $\dfrac{x}{1 + x^2}$

(c) $\sqrt{1 - x^2}$ (d) $\dfrac{1}{2}\log(1 - x^2)$

Sol. (c) $\sqrt{1-x^2}$

Explanation :

Given that,

$$(1-x^2)\frac{dy}{dx} - xy = 1$$

$$\Rightarrow \quad \frac{dy}{dx} - \frac{x}{1-x^2}\,y = \frac{1}{1-x^2}$$

which is a linear differential equation.

$$\therefore \quad IF = e^{-\int \frac{x}{1-x^2}\,dx}$$

Put $\quad 1-x^2 = t$

$$\Rightarrow \quad -2x\,dx = dt$$

$$\Rightarrow \quad x\,dx = -\frac{dt}{2}$$

Now, $\quad IF = e^{\frac{1}{2}\int \frac{dt}{t}} = e^{\frac{1}{2}\log t}$

$$= e^{\frac{1}{2}\log(1-x^2)}$$

$$= \sqrt{1-x^2}$$

47. The solution of $\dfrac{dy}{dx} + y = e^{-x}$, $y(0) = 0$ is:

[NCERT Exemplar]

(a) $y = e^x(x-1)$ (b) $y = xe^{-x}$
(c) $y = xe^{-x} + 1$ (d) $y = (x+1)e^{-x}$

Sol. (b) $y = xe^{-x}$

Explanation :

Given, that

$$\frac{dy}{dx} + y = e^{-x}$$

Here, $P = 1$, $Q = e^{-x}$

$$IF = e^{\int P\,dx} = e^{\int 1\,dx} = e^x$$

The general solution is

$$y \cdot e^x = \int e^{-x}\,e^x\,dx + C$$

$$\Rightarrow \quad y \cdot e^x = \int 1\,dx + C$$

$$\Rightarrow \quad y \cdot e^x = x + C \qquad \ldots(i)$$

When $x = 0$ and $y = 0$, then

$$0 = 0 + C \Rightarrow C = 0$$

Equation (i) becomes

$$y \cdot e^x = x$$

$$\Rightarrow \quad y = xe^{-x}.$$

48. The integrating factor of differential equation $\dfrac{dy}{dx} + y \tan x - \sec x = 0$ is: **[NCERT Exemplar]**

(a) $\cos x$ (b) $\sec x$
(c) $e^{\cos x}$ (d) $e^{\sec x}$

Sol. (b) $\sec x$

Explanation :

Given that, $\dfrac{dy}{dx} + y \tan x - \sec x = 0$

Here, $P = \tan x$, $Q = \sec x$

$$IF = e^{\int P\,dx} = e^{\int \tan x\,dx}$$
$$= e^{(\log \sec x)}$$
$$= \sec x.$$

49. The integrating factor of differential equation $\dfrac{dy}{dx} + y = \dfrac{1+y}{x}$ is: **[NCERT Exemplar]**

(a) $\dfrac{x}{e^x}$ (b) $\dfrac{e^x}{x}$

(c) xe^x (d) e^x

Sol. (b) $\dfrac{e^x}{x}$

Explanation :

Given that,

$$\frac{dy}{dx} + y = \frac{1+y}{x}$$

$$\Rightarrow \quad \frac{dy}{dx} = \frac{1+y}{x} - y$$

$$\Rightarrow \quad \frac{dy}{dx} = \frac{1+y-xy}{x}$$

$$\Rightarrow \quad \frac{dy}{dx} = \frac{1}{x} + \frac{y(1-x)}{x}$$

$$\Rightarrow \quad \frac{dy}{dx} - \left(\frac{1-x}{x}\right)y = \frac{1}{x}$$

Here, $\quad P = \dfrac{-(1-x)}{x}$, $Q = \dfrac{1}{x}$

$$IF = e^{\int P\,dx} = e^{-\int \frac{1-x}{x}\,dx} = e^{\int \frac{x-1}{x}\,dx}$$

$$= e^{\int \left(1-\frac{1}{x}\right)dx}$$

$$= e^{x-\log x}$$

$$= e^x \cdot e^{\log\left(\frac{1}{x}\right)}$$

$$= \frac{e^x}{x}.$$

50. The solution of $x\dfrac{dy}{dx} + y = e^x$ is:

[NCERT Exemplar]

(a) $y = \dfrac{e^x}{x} + \dfrac{k}{x}$ (b) $y = xe^x + Cx$

(c) $y = xe^x + k$ (d) $x = \dfrac{e^y}{y} + \dfrac{k}{y}$

Sol. (a) $\quad y = \dfrac{e^x}{x} + \dfrac{k}{x}$

Explanation :

Given that,

$$x\dfrac{dy}{dx} + y = e^x$$

$$\Rightarrow \qquad \dfrac{dy}{dx} + \dfrac{y}{x} = \dfrac{e^x}{x}$$

which is a linear differential equation.

$$\therefore \qquad IF = e^{\int \frac{1}{x}\,dx} = e^{(\log x)} = x$$

The general solution is

$$\Rightarrow \qquad y \cdot x = \int\left(\dfrac{e^x}{x} \cdot x\right) dx$$

$$\Rightarrow \qquad y \cdot x = \int e^x \, dx$$

$$\Rightarrow \qquad y \cdot x = e^x + k$$

$$\Rightarrow \qquad y = \dfrac{e^x}{x} + \dfrac{k}{x}\cdot$$

51. The general solution of differential equation $\dfrac{dy}{dx} = e^{x^2/2} + xy$ is: **[NCERT Exemplar]**

(a) $\quad y = Ce^{-x^2/2}$ (b) $\quad y = Ce^{x^2/2}$

(c) $\quad y = (x+C)e^{x^2/2}$ (d) $\quad y = (C-x)e^{x^2/2}$

Sol. (c) $\quad y = (x+C)e^{x^2/2}$

Explanation :

Given that, $\quad \dfrac{dy}{dx} = e^{x^2/2} + xy$

$$\Rightarrow \qquad \dfrac{dy}{dx} - xy = e^{x^2/2}$$

Here, $P = -x, Q = e^{x^2/2}$

$$\therefore \qquad IF = e^{\int -x\,dx} = e^{-x^2/2}$$

The general solution is

$$y \cdot e^{-x^2/2} = \int e^{-x^2/2} \cdot e^{x^2/2}\, dx + C$$

$$\Rightarrow \qquad y \cdot e^{-x^2/2} = \int 1\, dx + C$$

$$\Rightarrow \qquad y \cdot e^{-x^2/2} = x + C$$

$$\Rightarrow \qquad y = xe^{x^2/2} + Ce^{x^2/2}$$

$$\Rightarrow \qquad y = (x+C)e^{x^2/2}.$$

52. The general solution of $\dfrac{dy}{dx} + y \tan x = \sec x$ is:

[NCERT Exemplar]

(a) $\quad y \sec x = \tan x + C$ (b) $\quad y \tan x = \sec x + C$

(c) $\quad \tan x = y \tan x + C$ (d) $\quad x \sec x = \tan y + C$

Sol. (a) $\quad y \sec x = \tan x + C$

Explanation :

Given differential equation is

$$\dfrac{dy}{dx} + y \tan x = \sec x$$

which is a linear differential equation.

Here, $P = \tan x, Q = \sec x$

$$\therefore \qquad IF = e^{\int \tan x\,dx} = e^{\log\,|\sec x|}$$

$$= \sec x$$

The general solution is

$$y \cdot \sec x = \int \sec x \cdot \sec x + C$$

$$\Rightarrow \qquad y \cdot \sec x = \int \sec^2 x\, dx + C$$

$$\Rightarrow \qquad y \cdot \sec x = \tan x + C.$$

53. The solution of differential equation $\dfrac{dy}{dx} + \dfrac{y}{x} = \sin x$

is: **[NCERT Exemplar]**

(a) $\quad x(y + \cos x) = \sin x + C$

(b) $\quad x(y - \cos x) = \sin x + C$

(c) $\quad xy \cos x = \sin x + C$

(d) $\quad x(y + \cos x) = \cos x + C$

Sol. (a) $\quad x(y + \cos x) = \sin x + C$

Explanation :

Given differential equation is

$$\dfrac{dy}{dx} + y\dfrac{1}{x} = \sin x$$

which is linear differential equation.

Here, $P = \dfrac{1}{x}$ and $Q = \sin x$

$$\therefore \qquad IF = e^{\int \frac{1}{x}dx} = e^{\log x} = x$$

The general solution is,

$$y \cdot x = \int x \cdot \sin x\, dx + C \qquad \text{...(i)}$$

Take $\qquad I = \int x \sin x\, dx$

$$= -x \cos x - \int -\cos x\, dx$$

$$= -x \cos x + \sin x$$

Put the value of I in equation (i), we get

$$xy = -x \cos x + \sin x + C$$

$$\Rightarrow \qquad x(y + \cos x) = \sin x + C.$$

54. The solution of differential equation $\dfrac{dy}{dx} + \dfrac{2xy}{1+x^2}$

$$= \dfrac{1}{(1+x^2)^2} \text{ is:} \qquad \text{[NCERT Exemplar]}$$

(a) $\quad y(1 + x^2) = C + \tan^{-1} x$

(b) $\quad \dfrac{y}{1+x^2} = C + \tan^{-1} x$

(c) $y \log (1 + x^2) = C + \tan^{-1} x$

(d) $y(1 + x^2) = C + \sin^{-1} x$

Sol. (a) $y(1 + x^2) = C + \tan^{-1} x$

Explanation :

Given that,

$$\frac{dy}{dx} + \frac{2xy}{1+x^2} = \frac{1}{(1+x^2)^2}$$

Here, $P = \dfrac{2x}{1+x^2}$ and $Q = \dfrac{1}{(1+x^2)^2}$

which is a linear differential equation.

$\therefore \qquad IF = e^{\int \frac{2x}{1+x^2} dx}$

Put $\quad 1 + x^2 = t \Rightarrow 2x \, dx = dt$

$\therefore \qquad IF = e^{\int \frac{dt}{t}} = e^{\log t} = e^{\log (1+x^2)} = 1 + x^2$

The general solution is

$$y \cdot (1 + x^2) = \int (1+x^2) \frac{1}{(1+x^2)^2} + C$$

$$\Rightarrow \quad y(1 + x^2) = \int \frac{1}{1+x^2} \, dx + C$$

$$\Rightarrow \quad y(1 + x^2) = \tan^{-1} x + C.$$

55. The general solution of a differential equation of the type is $\dfrac{dy}{dx} + P_1 y = Q_1$ is:

(a) $ye^{\int P_1 \, dx} = \int \left\{ Q_1 e^{\int P_1 \, dx} \right\} dy + C$

(b) $ye^{\int P_1 \, dx} = \int \left\{ Q_1 e^{\int P_1 \, dx} \right\} dx + C$

(c) $xe^{\int P_1 \, dy} = \int \left\{ Q_1 e^{\int P_1 \, dy} \right\} dy + C$

(d) $xe^{\int P_1 \, dy} = \int \left\{ Q_1 e^{\int P_1 \, dy} \right\} dx + C$

Sol. (b) $ye^{\int P_1 \, dx} = \int \left\{ Q_1 e^{\int P_1 \, dx} \right\} dx + C$

Explanation :

By using definition of differential equation.

56. Which of the following equation is linear?

(a) $\dfrac{dy}{dx} + xy^2 = 1$ (b) $x^2 \dfrac{dy}{dx} + y = e^x$

(c) $\dfrac{dy}{dx} + 3y = xy^2$ (d) $x \dfrac{dy}{dx} + y^2 = \sin x$

Sol. (b) $x^2 \dfrac{dy}{dx} + y = e^x$

Explanation :

$x^2 \dfrac{dy}{dx} + y = e^x$ can be written as

$\dfrac{dy}{dx} + \dfrac{y}{x^2} = \dfrac{e^x}{x^2}$, which is a linear equation.

57. Which of the following equation is non-linear?

(a) $\dfrac{dy}{dx} + \dfrac{y}{x} = \log x$ (b) $y \dfrac{dy}{dx} + 4x = 0$

(c) $dx + dy = 0$ (d) $\dfrac{dy}{dx} = \cos x$

Sol. (b) $y \dfrac{dy}{dx} + 4x = 0$

Explanation :

A differential equation in which the dependent (y) and its differential coefficient occur only in the first degree and are not multiplied together is called a linear differential equation.

Hence $y \dfrac{dy}{dx} + 4x = 0$ is a non-linear differential equation.

58. Integrating factor of the equation $(x^2 + 1) \dfrac{dy}{dx} + 2xy = x^2 - 1$ is:

(a) $x^2 + 1$ (b) $\dfrac{2x}{x^2+1}$

(c) $\dfrac{x^2 - 1}{x^2 + 1}$ (d) $\dfrac{x^2 + 1}{x^2 - 1}$

Sol. (a) $x^2 + 1$

Explanation :

$$\Rightarrow \frac{dy}{dx} + \frac{2x}{1+x^2} y = \frac{x^2 - 1}{x^2 + 1}$$

$$\text{I.F.} = e^{\int \frac{2x}{1+x^2} dx} = e^{\log (1+x^2)} = 1 + x^2.$$

59. If $\sin x$ is the integrating factor of the linear differential equation $\dfrac{dy}{dx} + Py = Q$, then P is:

(a) $\log \sin x$ (b) $\cos x$

(c) $\tan x$ (d) $\cot x$

Sol. (d) $\cot x$

Explanation :

$\Rightarrow \qquad \text{I.F.} = \sin x$

$\therefore \qquad e^{\int P \, dx} = \sin x$

$\Rightarrow \qquad e^{\int P \, dx} = e^{\log (\sin x)}$

$\Rightarrow \qquad P = \dfrac{d}{dx} [\log (\sin x)]$

$\Rightarrow \qquad P = \dfrac{1}{\sin x} \times \cos x = \cot x.$

60. The solution of $\dfrac{dy}{dx} + P(x)y = 0$ is:

(a) $y = Ce^{\int P \, dx}$ (b) $x = Ce^{-\int P \, dy}$

(c) $y = Ce^{-\int P \, dx}$ (d) $x = Ce^{\int P \, dy}$

Sol. (c) $\quad y = Ce^{-\int P\,dx}$

Explanation :

$$\frac{dy}{dx} + P(x).y = 0$$

Here, $\qquad Q = 0$

$\therefore \qquad\qquad$ I.F. $= e^{\int P\,dx}$

$\therefore$ solution of the given equation is

$$y(\text{I.F.}) = \int Q(\text{I.F.})\,dx + C$$

$$\Rightarrow \qquad y.e^{\int P\,dx} = 0 + C$$

$$\Rightarrow \qquad\qquad y = C.e^{-\int P\,dx}$$

61. The integrating factor of the differential equatio

$$\frac{dy}{dx}(x\log x) + y = 2\log x \text{ is:}$$

(a) e^x $\qquad\qquad$ (b) $\log x$

(c) $\log(\log x)$ $\qquad$ (d) x

Sol. (b) $\log x$

Explanation :

Given equation can be written as

$$\frac{dy}{dx} + \frac{y}{x\log x} = \frac{2}{x}.$$

$$\therefore \quad \text{I.F.} = e^{\int \frac{1}{x\log x}dx} = e^{\log(\log x)} = \log x.$$

So the correct option is (b).

62. The solution of the differential equation

$$x\frac{dy}{dx} + 2y = x^2 \text{ is:}$$

(a) $\quad y = \dfrac{x^2 + C}{4x^2}$ $\qquad$ (b) $\quad y = \dfrac{x^2}{4} + C$

(c) $\quad y = \dfrac{x^4 + C}{x^2}$ $\qquad$ (d) $\quad y = \dfrac{x^4 + C}{4x^2}$

Sol. (d) $\quad y = \dfrac{x^4 + C}{4x^2}$

Explanation :

$$\text{I.F.} = e^{\int \frac{2}{x}dx} = e^{2\log x} = e^{\log x^2} = x^2.$$

$\therefore$ The solution is

$$y.x^2 = \int x^2.x\,dx = \frac{x^4}{4} + k$$

$i.e., \qquad\qquad y = \dfrac{x^4 + C}{4x^2}.$

So the correct option is (d).

Assertion and Reason Based Questions

(a) Both (A) and (R) are individually true and (R) is the correct explanation of (A).

(b) Both (A) and (R) are individually true but (R) is not the correct explanation of (A).

(c) (A) is true but (R) is false.

(d) (A) is false but (R) is true.

63. Assertion (A) : Order of the differential equation whose solution is $y = c_1 e^{x + c_2} + c_3 e^{x + c_4}$ is 4.

Reason (R) : Order of the differential equation is equal to the number of independent arbitrary constant mentioned in the solution of differential equation.

Sol. (d) (A) is false but (R) is true.

Explanation :

$\because \qquad\qquad y = (c_1 e^{c_2} + c_3 e^{c_4})\,e^x = ce^x \text{ (say)}$

$\therefore \qquad\qquad \dfrac{dy}{dx} = ce^x = y$

$\therefore$ Order is 1.

64. Assertion (A) : The degree of the differential equation $\dfrac{d^2y}{dx^2} + \dfrac{dy}{dx} = \log\left(\dfrac{d^2y}{dx^2}\right)$ is 2.

Reason (R) : The degree of a differential equation which can be written as polynomial in the derivatives is the degree of the derivative of the higher order occuring in it.

Sol. (d) (A) is false but (R) is true.

Explanation :

$\because$ The given equation cannot be written as a polynomial in all the differentials.

$\therefore$ Degree of the equation is not defined.

65. Assertion (A) : The differential equation of the form $y\,f(xy)\,dx + x\,\phi(xy)\,dy = 0$ can be converted to homogeneous forms by substitution $xy = v$.

Reason (R) : All differential equation of first order and first degree become homogeneous, if we put $y = vx$.

Sol. (d) (A) is false but (R) is true.

Explanation :

$$xy = v$$

$\therefore \qquad\qquad x\dfrac{dy}{dx} + y = \dfrac{dv}{dx}$

Then, the given equation reduces to

$$\frac{v}{x}f(v) + x\phi(v)\left[\frac{1}{x}\left(\frac{dv}{dx} - y\right)\right] = 0$$

$$\Rightarrow \quad \frac{v}{x}f(v) + \phi(v)\frac{dv}{dy} - y\phi(v) = 0$$

$$\Rightarrow \quad \left\{\frac{v(f(v) - \phi(v))}{x}\right\} + \phi(v)\frac{dv}{dx} = 0$$

$$\Rightarrow \quad \frac{dx}{x} + \frac{\phi(v)dv}{v(f(v) - \phi(v))} = 0$$

which is variable separable form.

Case Based Questions

66. Consider the given equation $\dfrac{dy}{dx} + py = Q$.

The above equation is known as linear differential equation

Here, IF $= e^{\int pdx}$ and solution is given by

y. IF $= \int Q.IF\, dx + C$

Consider the given equation

$(1 + \sin x)\dfrac{dy}{dx} + y\cos x + x = 0$

On the above information, answer the following questions:

(i) The value of P and Q are:

(a) $\dfrac{\cos x}{1 + \sin x}, \dfrac{-x}{1 + \sin x}$ (b) $\dfrac{-x}{1 + \sin x}, \dfrac{\cos x}{1 + \sin x}$

(c) $\dfrac{-\cos x}{1 + \sin x}, \dfrac{x}{1 + \sin x}$ (d) $\dfrac{x}{1 + \sin x}, \dfrac{-\cos x}{1 + \sin x}$

Sol. (a) $\dfrac{\cos x}{1 + \sin x}, \dfrac{-x}{1 + \sin x}$

Explanation :

$(1 + \sin x)\dfrac{dy}{dx} + \cos x\, y = -x$

$\dfrac{dy}{dx} + \dfrac{\cos x}{1 + \sin x}y = \dfrac{-x}{1 + \sin x}$

$p = \dfrac{\cos x}{1 + \sin x}, Q = \dfrac{-x}{1 + \sin x}.$

(ii) The value of integrating factor (I.F.) is:

(a) $\cos x$ (b) $1 + \sin x$

(c) $\dfrac{1}{1 + \sin x}$ (d) $1 - \sin x$

Sol. (b) $1 + \sin x$

Explanation :

$If = e^{\int Pdx} = e^{\int \frac{\cos x}{1 + \sin x}dx}$

$\Rightarrow e^{\int \log(1 + \sin x)} = 1 + \sin x.$

(iii) Solution of given equation is:

(a) $y(1 + \sin x) = \dfrac{x^2}{2} + C$

(b) $y(1 + \sin x) = x^2 + C$

(c) $y(1 + \sin x) = \dfrac{-x^2}{2} + C$

(d) None of these

Sol. (c) $y(1 + \sin x) = \dfrac{-x^2}{2} + C$

Explanation :

Solution of given equation is

$$y.\,IF = \int Q.IF\, dx + C$$

$$y(1 + \sin x) = \int \frac{-x}{1 + \sin x}(1 + \sin x)dx$$

$$y(1 + \sin x) = \frac{-x^2}{2} + C$$

(iv) If $y(0) = 1$ then $y =$

(a) $\dfrac{2 - x^2}{2(1 + \sin x)}$ (b) $\dfrac{1 + x^2}{2(1 + \sin x)}$

(c) $\dfrac{1 - x^2}{4(1 + \sin x)}$ (d) $\dfrac{1 + x^2}{4(1 + \sin x)}$

Sol. (a) $\dfrac{2 - x^2}{2(1 + \sin x)}$

Explanation :

Put $x = 0, y = 1$

$$1(1 + \sin 0) = \frac{0}{2} + C$$

$$\Rightarrow \quad 1 = C$$

$$\therefore \quad y(1 + \sin x) = \frac{-x^2}{2} + 1$$

$$\Rightarrow \quad y = \frac{2 - x^2}{2(1 + \sin x)}.$$

(v) Value of $y\left(\dfrac{\pi}{2}\right) =$

(a) $\dfrac{4 + \pi^2}{4}$ (b) $\dfrac{8 - \pi^2}{16}$

(c) $\dfrac{4 + \pi^2}{2}$ (d) $\dfrac{4 + \pi^2}{16}$

Sol. (b) $\dfrac{8-\pi^2}{16}$

$$y = \dfrac{2-\dfrac{\pi^2}{4}}{2\left(1+\sin\dfrac{\pi}{2}\right)} = \dfrac{8-\pi^2}{2(1+1)4}$$

Explanation :

Put $x = \dfrac{\pi}{2}$ in (iv)

$\therefore \qquad y = \dfrac{8-\pi^2}{16}.$

Very Short Answer Type Questions

67. What is the degree and order of the following differential equation ?

(i) $\quad 5x\left(\dfrac{dy}{dx}\right)^2 - \dfrac{d^2y}{dx^2} - 6y = \log x$

(ii) $\quad \dfrac{d^4y}{dx^4} + \sin\left(\dfrac{dy}{dx}\right) = 0$

(iii) $\quad y' + 5y = 0$

(iv) $\quad \left(\dfrac{ds}{dt}\right)^4 + 3s\dfrac{d^2s}{dt^2} = 0$

(v) $\quad (y''')^2 + (y'')^3 + (y)^4 + y^5 = 0$

(vi) $\quad y''' + 2y'' + y' = 0$

(vii) $\quad y' + y = e^x$

(viii) $\quad y'' + (y')^2 + 2y = 0$

(ix) $\quad y'' + 2y' + \sin y = 0$

(x) $\quad \left(\dfrac{d^2y}{dx^2}\right)^3 + \left(\dfrac{dy}{dx}\right)^2 + \sin\left(\dfrac{dy}{dx}\right) + 1 = 0$

(xi) $\quad x\dfrac{dy}{dx} + y = 2$

(xii) $\quad \dfrac{dy}{dx} + y\sin x = \sqrt{x\dfrac{dy}{dx} + 3}$

Sol. (i) Degree = 1, Order = 2

(ii) $\because$ It is not a polynomial in $\dfrac{dy}{dx}$

$\therefore$ degree is not defined, order = 4

(iii) Order = 1, Degree = 1

(iv) Order = 2, Degree = 1

(v) Order = 3, Degree = 2

(vi) Order = 3, Degree = 1

(vii) Order = 1, Degree = 1

(viii) Order = 2, Degree = 1

(ix) Order = 2, degree = 1

(x) Order = 2, Degree is not defined as it is not a polynomial in differential coefficients.

(xi) Order = 1, Degree = 1

(xii) Squaring both sides

$$\left(\dfrac{dy}{dx}\right)^2 + y^2\sin^2 x + 2y\sin x\,\dfrac{dy}{dx} = x\dfrac{dy}{dx} + 3$$

$\therefore$ Order = 1, Degree = 2.

68. The order of differential equation

$$\left(\dfrac{d^2y}{dx^2}\right)^2 + \cos\left(\dfrac{dy}{dx}\right) = 0 \text{ is } \ldots\ldots\ldots .$$

Sol. 2

69. The order and degree of differential equation $2x^2\dfrac{d^2y}{dx^2} - 3\dfrac{dy}{dx} + y = 0$ are $\ldots\ldots\ldots$ and $\ldots\ldots\ldots$ respectively.

Sol. 2 and 1.

70. The degree of the differential equation $1+\left(\dfrac{dy}{dx}\right)^2 = x$ is $\ldots\ldots\ldots .$

Sol. 2.

71. The solution of the differential equation $(e^x + e^{-x})\,dy = (e^x - e^{-x})\,dx$ is $\ldots\ldots\ldots .$

Sol. $\qquad y = \log |e^x + e^{-x}| + C$

Given differential equation is

$$(e^x + e^{-x})\,dy = (e^x - e^{-x})\,dx$$

$\Rightarrow \qquad dy = \dfrac{(e^x - e^{-x})}{(e^x + e^{-x})}\,dx$

On integrating both sides, we get

$$y = \int \dfrac{(e^x - e^{-x})}{(e^x + e^{-x})}\,dx$$

$$= \log |e^x + e^{-x}| + C.$$

72. The solution of differential equation $\dfrac{dy}{dx} = x^3 + e^x + x^e$ is $\ldots\ldots\ldots .$

Sol. $\qquad y = \dfrac{x^4}{4} + e^x + \dfrac{x^{e+1}}{e+1} + C$

Given differential equation is

$$\frac{dy}{dx} = x^3 + e^x + x^e$$

On integrating both sides, we get

$$y = \int x^3\, dx + \int e^x\, dx + \int x^e\, dx + C$$

$$= \frac{x^4}{4} + e^x + \frac{x^{e+1}}{e+1} + C.$$

73. Write integrating factor of the following differential equations :

(i) $\dfrac{dy}{dx} + \dfrac{1}{1+x^2}\, y = \sin x$

(ii) $x\dfrac{dy}{dx} + y \log x = x + y$

Sol. (i) Given differential equation is,

$$\frac{dy}{dx} + \frac{1}{1+x^2}\, y = \sin x$$

Integrating factor of above equation is given by

$$e^{\int \frac{1}{1+x^2}\, dx} = e^{\tan^{-1} x}$$

(ii) Given differential equation is,

$$x\frac{dy}{dx} + y \log x = x + y$$

$$\Rightarrow \quad \frac{dy}{dx} + \frac{\log x}{x}\, y = \frac{x+y}{x}$$

Integrating factor of above equation is given by

$$e^{\int \frac{\log x}{x}\, dx} = e^{\frac{(\log x)^2}{2}}$$

74. Find the integrating factor of the differential equation $\left(\dfrac{e^{-2\sqrt{x}}}{\sqrt{x}} - \dfrac{y}{\sqrt{x}}\right)\dfrac{dx}{dy} = 1.$

Sol. We have,

$$\left(\frac{e^{-2\sqrt{x}}}{\sqrt{x}} - \frac{y}{\sqrt{x}}\right)\frac{dx}{dy} = 1$$

$$\frac{dy}{dx} = \frac{e^{-2\sqrt{x}}}{\sqrt{x}} - \frac{y}{\sqrt{x}}$$

$$\frac{dy}{dx} + \frac{y}{\sqrt{x}} = \frac{e^{-2\sqrt{x}}}{\sqrt{x}}$$

Which is a linear differential equation of the form

$$\frac{dy}{dx} + Py = Q$$

where $\qquad P = \dfrac{1}{\sqrt{x}}$

and $\qquad Q = \dfrac{e^{-2\sqrt{x}}}{\sqrt{x}}$

$\therefore \qquad$ I.F. $= e^{\int P\, dx}$

$$= e^{\int \frac{1}{\sqrt{x}}\, dx} = e^{2\sqrt{x}}$$

75. The integrating factor of $x\dfrac{dy}{dx} - 3y = x^3$ is ....

Sol. $\dfrac{1}{x^3}$

$\because \qquad \dfrac{dy}{dx} - \dfrac{3}{x}\, y = x^2$

Here $\qquad P = \dfrac{-3}{x},\ Q = x^2$

$\therefore \qquad$ I.F. $= e^{\int P\, dx}$

$$= e^{\int \frac{-3}{x}\, dx} = e^{-3 \log x}$$

$$= e^{\log x^{-3}} = x^{-3} = \frac{1}{x^3}.$$

76. The integrating factor of $\dfrac{dy}{dx} + y \sec^2 x = \sec x + \tan x$ is ....

Sol. $e^{\tan x}$

$\because \qquad \dfrac{dy}{dx} + \sec^2 x.y = \sec x + \tan x$

Here, $\qquad P = \sec^2 x,$

$$Q = \sec x + \tan x$$

$\therefore \qquad$ I.F. $= e^{\int P\, dx}$

$$= e^{\int \sec^2 x\, dx}$$

$$= e^{\tan x}.$$

77. The integrating factor of the differential equation $x\dfrac{dy}{dx} + 2y = x^2$ is ....

Sol. x^2

$\because \qquad x\dfrac{dy}{dx} + 2y = x^2$

$\Rightarrow \qquad \dfrac{dy}{dx} + \dfrac{2y}{x} = x$

Here, $\qquad P = \dfrac{2}{x},\ Q = x$

$\therefore \qquad$ I.F. $= e^{\int P\, dx} = e^{\int \frac{2}{x}\, dx}$

$$= e^{2 \log x}$$

$$= e^{\log x^2}$$

$$= x^2.$$

Short Answer Type Questions

78. Find the particular solution of the differential equation satisfying the given condition.*

$$\frac{dy}{dx} = y \tan x, \text{ given that } y = 1 \text{ when } x = 0.$$

Sol. Given differential equation is

$$\frac{dy}{dx} = y \tan x \qquad \text{...(i)}$$

$$\Rightarrow \qquad \frac{dy}{y} = \tan x \, dx$$

On integrating both sides, we get,

$$\log y = \log |\sec x| + \log C$$
$$\Rightarrow \qquad \log y = \log |C \sec x|$$
$$\Rightarrow \qquad y = C \sec x \qquad \text{...(ii)}$$

When $y = 1$ and $x = 0$

Equation (ii) becomes

$$1 = C \sec 0$$
$$C = 1$$

Put it in equation (ii)

$$y = \sec x \text{ is required solution.}$$

79. Solve the following differential equation:*

$$(x^3 + x^2 + x + 1)\frac{dy}{dx} = 2x^2 + x$$

Sol. Given differential equation is,

$$(x^3 + x^2 + x + 1)\frac{dy}{dx} = 2x^2 + x$$

$$dy = \frac{(2x^2 + x)}{x^3 + x^2 + x + 1} dx$$

On integrating both sides, we get

$$y = \int \frac{2x^2 + x}{x^3 + x^2 + x + 1} dx \qquad \text{...(i)}$$

Also $\dfrac{2x^2 + x}{x^3 + x^2 + x + 1} = \dfrac{2x^2 + x}{x^2(x+1) + 1(x+1)}$

$$= \frac{2x^2 + x}{(x+1)(x^2 + 1)}$$

$$= \frac{A}{x+1} + \frac{Bx + C}{x^2 + 1}$$

$$\Rightarrow \qquad 2x^2 + x = A(x^2 + 1) + (Bx + C)(x+1)$$
$$\Rightarrow \qquad 2x^2 + x = Ax^2 + A + Bx^2 + Bx + Cx + C$$
$$= x^2(A + B) + x(B + C) + A + C$$

When $x = -1$

$$2 - 1 = 2A$$

$$\Rightarrow \qquad A = \frac{1}{2}$$

When $x = 0$

$$0 = A + C$$
$$\Rightarrow \qquad 0 = \frac{1}{2} + C$$
$$\Rightarrow \qquad C = \frac{-1}{2}$$

When $x = 1$

$$3 = 2A + 2B + 2C$$
$$\Rightarrow \qquad 3 = 2 \times \frac{1}{2} + 2B + 2\left(-\frac{1}{2}\right)$$
$$\Rightarrow \qquad 3 = 1 + 2B - 1$$
$$\Rightarrow \qquad 2B = 3$$
$$\Rightarrow \qquad B = \frac{3}{2}$$

From equation (i),

$$y = \frac{1}{2}\int \frac{dx}{x+1} + \int \frac{\frac{3}{2}x - \frac{1}{2}}{x^2 + 1} dx + C$$

$$= \frac{1}{2}\log |x + 1| + \frac{3}{2}\int \frac{x}{x^2 + 1}dx - \frac{1}{2}\int \frac{dx}{x^2 + 1} + C$$

$$= \frac{1}{2}\log |x + 1| + \frac{3}{2} \times \frac{1}{2}\int \frac{2x}{x^2 + 1}dx - \frac{1}{2}\tan^{-1} x + C$$

$$\Rightarrow y = \frac{1}{2}\log |x + 1| + \frac{3}{4}\log |x^2 + 1| - \frac{1}{2}\tan^{-1} x + C.$$

is the required solution.

80. Solve the following differential equation:*

$$(1 + y^2)(1 + \log x) dx + x \, dy = 0$$

Sol. Given differential equation is

$$(1 + y^2)(1 + \log x) dx + x \, dy = 0$$
$$(1 + y^2)(1 + \log x) dx = -x \, dy$$
$$\frac{(1 + \log x)}{x} dx = \frac{-dy}{1 + y^2}$$

On integrating both sides

$$\int (1 + \log x)\frac{1}{x} dx = -\int \frac{dy}{1 + y^2} + C$$

$$\frac{(1 + \log x)^2}{2} = -\tan^{-1} y + C$$

$$\left[\because \int [f(x)]^n \cdot f'(x) \, dx = \frac{[f(x)]^{n+1}}{n+1}\right]$$

$$\frac{1}{2}(1 + \log x)^2 + \tan^{-1} y = C$$

which is required solution.

81. Solve the following differential equation:*

$$e^x \tan y \, dx + (1 - e^x) \sec^2 y \, dy = 0$$

Sol. Given differential equation is,

$$e^x \tan y \, dx + (1 - e^x) \sec^2 y \, dy = 0$$

$$\Rightarrow \qquad (1 - e^x) \sec^2 y \, dy = - e^x \tan y \, dx$$

$$\Rightarrow \qquad \frac{\sec^2 y}{\tan y} dy = - \frac{e^x}{1 - e^x} dx$$

Integrating both sides

$$\log |\tan y| = \log |1 - e^x| + C$$

$$\left[\because \int \frac{f'(x)}{f(x)} dx = \log |f(x)| + c \right]$$

$$\Rightarrow \qquad \log |\tan y| - \log |1 - e^x| = C$$

$$\Rightarrow \qquad \log \left| \frac{\tan y}{1 - e^x} \right| = C$$

$$\Rightarrow \qquad \frac{\tan y}{1 - e^x} = e^C$$

$$\Rightarrow \qquad \tan y = e^C (1 - e^x).$$

which is the required solution.

82. Find the particular solution of the following differential equation:*

$$xy \frac{dy}{dx} = (x + 2)(y + 2) : y = -1 \text{ when } x = 1$$

Sol. Given differential equation is

$$xy \frac{dy}{dx} = (x + 2)(y + 2)$$

$$\Rightarrow \qquad \frac{y}{y + 2} dy = \frac{(x + 2)}{x} dx$$

On integrating both sides, we have

$$\int \frac{y}{y + 2} dy = \int \frac{x + 2}{x} dx \qquad \qquad ...(i)$$

Put $y + 2 = t \Rightarrow y = t - 2$

Differentiate w.r.t. x

$$1 = \frac{dt}{dy}$$

$$\therefore \qquad dy = dt$$

Equation (i) becomes:

$$\int \frac{t - 2}{t} dt = \int 1 dx + 2 \int \frac{dx}{x}$$

$$\Rightarrow \qquad \int \left(1 - \frac{2}{t}\right) dt = x + 2 \log x + C$$

$$\Rightarrow \qquad t - 2 \log t = x + 2 \log x + C$$

$$\Rightarrow \qquad y + 2 - 2 \log (y + 2) = x + 2 \log x + C \qquad ...(ii)$$

When $x = 1$ and $y = -1$

$$-1 + 2 - 2 \log 1 = 1 + 2 \log 1 + C$$

$$\Rightarrow \qquad \qquad 1 = 1 + C$$

$$\therefore \qquad \qquad C = 0$$

Equation (ii) becomes:

$$y + 2 - 2 \log (y + 2) = x + 2 \log x$$

which is the particular solution of the given differential equation.

83. Find the general solution of the differential equation $\dfrac{dy}{dx} = \dfrac{1 - \cos x}{1 + \cos x}$. **[NCERT]**

Sol. Given differential equation is

$$\frac{dy}{dx} = \frac{1 - \cos x}{1 + \cos x}$$

$$dy = \left(\frac{1 - \cos x}{1 + \cos x}\right) dx$$

$$dy = \left(\frac{2 \sin^2 \frac{x}{2}}{2 \cos^2 \frac{x}{2}}\right) dx$$

$$dy = \tan^2 \frac{x}{2} \, dx$$

$$dy = \left(\sec^2 \frac{x}{2} - 1\right) dx$$

Integrating both sides:

$$y = \int \left(\sec^2 \frac{x}{2} - 1\right) dx + C$$

$$y = \frac{\tan \frac{x}{2}}{\frac{1}{2}} - x + C$$

$$y = 2 \tan \frac{x}{2} - x + C$$

which is the required general solution.

84. Find the general solution of the differential equation $\dfrac{dy}{dx} + y = 1, (y \neq 1)$. **[NCERT]**

Sol. Given differential equation is,

$$\frac{dy}{dx} + y = 1$$

$$\Rightarrow \qquad \frac{dy}{dx} = 1 - y$$

$$\Rightarrow \qquad \frac{dy}{1 - y} = dx$$

Integrating both sides

$$-\log(1-y) = x + C$$
$$\Rightarrow \quad \log(1-y) = -x - C$$
$$\Rightarrow \quad 1-y = e^{-x-C} = e^{-x}.\,e^{-C}$$
$$\Rightarrow \quad 1-y = Ae^{-x}, \quad \text{where } A = e^{-C}$$
$$\Rightarrow \quad y = 1 - Ae^{-x}$$

which is the required general solution.

85. Find the particular solution of the following differential equation:*

$$\frac{dy}{dx} = 1 + x^2 + y^2 + x^2y^2.$$

given that $y = 1$ when $x = 0$.

Sol. Given differential equation is

$$\frac{dy}{dx} = 1 + x^2 + y^2 + x^2y^2$$

$$= (1 + x^2) + y^2(1 + x^2)$$

$$\Rightarrow \quad \frac{dy}{dx} = (1 + x^2)(1 + y^2)$$

$$\Rightarrow \quad \frac{dy}{1+y^2} = (1 + x^2)\,dx$$

On integrating both sides, we have

$$\int \frac{dy}{1+y^2} = \int (1+x^2)\,dx$$

$$\tan^{-1} y = x + \frac{x^3}{3} + C \qquad \text{...(i)}$$

put $y = 1$ and $x = 0$ in equation (i),

$$\tan^{-1} 1 = 0 + 0 + C$$

$$C = \frac{\pi}{4}$$

Equation (i) becomes:

$$\tan^{-1} y = x + \frac{x^3}{3} + \frac{\pi}{4}$$

$$\Rightarrow \quad y = \tan\left(x + \frac{x^3}{3} + \frac{\pi}{4}\right)$$

is the required particular solution of given equation.

86. Find the particular solution of the differential equation $(1 - y^2)(1 + \log x)\,dx + 2xy\,dy = 0$, given that $y = 0$ when $x = 1$.*

Sol. The given differential equation is

$$(1 - y^2)(1 + \log x)\,dx + 2xy\,dy = 0$$

$$\frac{(1+\log x)}{x}\,dx = \frac{-2y}{(1-y^2)}\,dy$$

On integrating both sides, we have

$$\int \frac{1+\log x}{x}\,dx = \int \frac{-2y}{(1-y^2)}\,dy$$

In first integral,

put $1 + \log x = t$

$$\Rightarrow \quad \frac{1}{x}\,dx = dt$$

Also in second integral,

put $1 - y^2 = u$

$$\Rightarrow \quad -2y\,dy = du$$

$$\therefore \quad \int t.dt = \int \frac{1}{u}\,du$$

$$\Rightarrow \quad \frac{t^2}{2} - \log|u| = C$$

or $\dfrac{1}{2}(1 + \log x)^2 - \log|1 - y^2| = C$

It is given that $y = 0$ when $x = 1$

So, $\dfrac{1}{2}(1 + \log 1)^2 - \log|1 - 0^2| = C$

$$\Rightarrow \quad C = \frac{1}{2}$$

$$\therefore \quad \frac{(1+\log x)^2}{2} - \log|1 - y^2| = \frac{1}{2}$$

or $(1 + \log x)^2 - 2\log|1 - y^2| = 1$

It is the required particular solution.

87. Find the particular solution, satisfying given condition, for the following differential equation:

$$\frac{dy}{dx} - \frac{y}{x} + \cosec\,\frac{y}{x} = 0;\ y = 0 \text{ when } x = 1.$$

Sol. Given differential equation is

$$\frac{dy}{dx} - \frac{y}{x} + \cosec\,\frac{y}{x} = 0 \qquad \text{...(i)}$$

Put $\dfrac{y}{x} = t \Rightarrow y = xt$

Differentiate both side w.r.t.x

$$\frac{dy}{dx} = x\frac{dt}{dx} + t$$

Put in equation (i),

$$x\frac{dt}{dx} + t - t + \cosec\,t = 0$$

$$\Rightarrow \quad x\frac{dt}{dx} = -\cosec\,t$$

$$\Rightarrow \quad x\frac{dt}{dx} = -\frac{1}{\sin t}$$

$$\Rightarrow \quad \sin t\,dt = -\frac{dx}{x}$$

On integrating both sides, we get

$$-\cos t = -\log x + C$$

$\Rightarrow \qquad \log x - \cos t = C$

$\Rightarrow \log x - \cos\left(\dfrac{y}{x}\right) = C, \qquad \qquad ...(ii)\left[\because t = \dfrac{y}{x}\right]$

When $y = 0$ and $x = 1$

$\qquad \log 1 - \cos 0 = C$

$\therefore \qquad\qquad\qquad C = -1$

Put the value of C in equation (ii),

$\qquad \log x - \cos\left(\dfrac{y}{x}\right) = -1$

$\Rightarrow \qquad \log x + 1 = \cos\left(\dfrac{y}{x}\right)$

$\Rightarrow \qquad \log x + \log e = \cos\left(\dfrac{y}{x}\right)$

$\Rightarrow \qquad \log|xe| = \cos\left(\dfrac{y}{x}\right)$

88. Find the particular solution of the differential equation satisfying the given condition:

$x^2 dy + (xy + y^2)\, dx = 0;\ y = 1$ when $x = 1$

Sol. Given differential equation is

$x^2 dy + (xy + y^2)\, dx = 0 \qquad\qquad ...(i)$

$\Rightarrow \qquad x^2 dy = -(xy + y^2)dx$

$\Rightarrow \qquad x^2 \dfrac{dy}{dx} = -(xy + y^2)$

$\Rightarrow \qquad \dfrac{dy}{dx} = -\dfrac{xy}{x^2} - \dfrac{y^2}{x^2}$

$\Rightarrow \qquad \dfrac{dy}{dx} = -\dfrac{y}{x} - \left(\dfrac{y}{x}\right)^2 \qquad\qquad ...(ii)$

Put $\qquad \dfrac{y}{x} = t \qquad\qquad\qquad ...(iii)$

$\Rightarrow \qquad y = xt$

Differentiate w.r.t. x

$\qquad \dfrac{dy}{dx} = x\dfrac{dt}{dx} + t \qquad\qquad ...(iv)$

From equations (ii), (iii) and (iv)

$\qquad x\dfrac{dt}{dx} + t = -t - t^2$

$\Rightarrow \qquad x\dfrac{dt}{dx} = -t - t^2 - t$

$\Rightarrow \qquad x\dfrac{dt}{dx} = -2t - t^2$

$\Rightarrow \qquad x\dfrac{dt}{dx} = -t(2 + t)$

$\Rightarrow \qquad \dfrac{dt}{t(2 + t)} = -\dfrac{dx}{x}$

On integrating both sides, we get

$\qquad \displaystyle\int \dfrac{dt}{t(2 + t)} = \int -\dfrac{dx}{x} \qquad\qquad ...(v)$

Now, $\qquad \dfrac{dt}{t(2 + t)} = \dfrac{A}{t} + \dfrac{B}{2 + t}$

$\Rightarrow \qquad\qquad 1 = A(2 + t) + Bt$

If $\qquad\qquad t = -2$

$\Rightarrow \qquad\qquad 1 = -2B + 0$

$\Rightarrow \qquad\qquad B = \dfrac{-1}{2}$

If $\qquad\qquad t = 0$

$\Rightarrow \qquad\qquad 1 = 2A$

$\Rightarrow \qquad\qquad A = \dfrac{1}{2}$

$\therefore \quad \displaystyle\int \dfrac{dt}{t(2 + t)} = \dfrac{1}{2}\int\dfrac{dt}{t} - \dfrac{1}{2}\int\dfrac{dt}{2 + t}$

$\qquad\qquad = \dfrac{1}{2}\log t - \dfrac{1}{2}\log|2 + t| + C \quad ...(vi)$

Equation (v) becomes

$\dfrac{1}{2}\log t - \dfrac{1}{2}\log|2 + t| = -\log x + C$

$\Rightarrow \quad [\log t - \log|2 + t|] = -2\log x + 2C$

$\Rightarrow \quad \log t - \log|2 + t| = -\log x^2 + 2C$

$\Rightarrow \quad \log\left|\dfrac{t}{2 + t}\right| + \log x^2 = 2C$

$\Rightarrow \quad \log\left|\dfrac{t}{2 + t} \times x^2\right| = 2C$

$\Rightarrow \quad \log\left|\dfrac{\dfrac{y}{x}}{2 + \dfrac{y}{x}} \times x^2\right| = 2C \qquad \left[\because t = \dfrac{y}{x}\right]$

$\Rightarrow \quad \log\left|\dfrac{yx^2}{2x + y}\right| = 2C$

$\Rightarrow \quad \dfrac{yx^2}{2x + y} = e^{2C}$

$\Rightarrow \quad \dfrac{yx^2}{2x + y} = A,\ \text{where } A = e^{2C}$

When $x = 1,\ y = 1$

$\qquad\qquad \dfrac{1}{3} = A$

Hence $\qquad \dfrac{x^2 y}{2x + y} = \dfrac{1}{3}$

$\Rightarrow \qquad 3x^2 y = 2x + y$

is required particular solution.

89. Show that the following differential equation is homogeneous and then solve it:

$$y\,dx + x\log\left(\frac{y}{x}\right)dy - 2x\,dy = 0$$

Sol. Given equation is

$$y\,dx + x\log\left(\frac{y}{x}\right)dy - 2x\,dy = 0$$

Divide by x:

$$\Rightarrow \frac{y}{x}\,dx + \log\left(\frac{y}{x}\right)dy - 2dy = 0$$

$$\Rightarrow \frac{y}{x} + \log\left(\frac{y}{x}\right)\frac{dy}{dx} - 2\frac{dy}{dx} = 0$$

$$\Rightarrow \left(\log\frac{y}{x} - 2\right)\frac{dy}{dx} = -\frac{y}{x}$$

$$\Rightarrow \left(2 - \log\frac{y}{x}\right)\frac{dy}{dx} = \frac{y}{x}$$

$$\Rightarrow \frac{dy}{dx} = \frac{y/x}{2 - \log y/x} \qquad \text{...(i)}$$

$\therefore$ It is a homogeneous differential equation of the from $f\left(\dfrac{y}{x}\right)$

To solve it put $\dfrac{y}{x} = t$

$$\Rightarrow y = xt$$

Differentiate both sides w.r.t. x, we get

$$\frac{dy}{dx} = x\frac{dt}{dx} + t$$

Put in equation (i),

$$\Rightarrow x\frac{dt}{dx} + t = \frac{t}{2 - \log t}$$

$$\Rightarrow x\frac{dt}{dx} = \frac{t}{2 - \log t} - \frac{t}{1}$$

$$\Rightarrow x\frac{dt}{dx} = \frac{t - 2t + t\log t}{2 - \log t}$$

$$\Rightarrow x\frac{dt}{dx} = \frac{t\log t - t}{2 - \log t}$$

$$\Rightarrow \frac{2 - \log t}{t(\log t - 1)}dt = \frac{dx}{x}$$

$$\Rightarrow \frac{1 - (\log t - 1)}{t(\log t - 1)}dt = \frac{dx}{x}$$

$$\Rightarrow \left(\frac{1}{t(\log t - 1)} - \frac{1}{t}\right)dt = \frac{dx}{x}$$

$$\Rightarrow \left(\frac{1/t}{(\log t - 1)} - \frac{1}{t}\right)dt = \frac{dx}{x}$$

On integrating both sides, we get

$$\int\frac{1/t}{\log t - 1}dt - \int\frac{1}{t}dt = \int\frac{dx}{x} + C$$

$$\Rightarrow \log|\log t - 1| - \log|t| = \log|x| + C$$

$$\Rightarrow \log|\log t - 1| - \log|t| - \log|x| = C$$

$$\Rightarrow \log\left|\frac{\log t - 1}{tx}\right| = C$$

$$\Rightarrow \left|\frac{\log t - 1}{tx}\right| = e^C$$

$$\Rightarrow \frac{\log t - 1}{tx} = \pm e^C = A$$

$$\Rightarrow \frac{\log\dfrac{y}{x} - 1}{\dfrac{y}{x}\times x} = A \qquad \left[\because t = \frac{y}{x}\right]$$

$$\Rightarrow \log\left(\frac{y}{x}\right) - 1 = Ay$$

which is the required general solution.

90. Solve the differential equation:*

$$y + x\frac{dy}{dx} = x - y\frac{dy}{dx}$$

Sol. We have,

$$y + x\frac{dy}{dx} = x - y\frac{dy}{dx}$$

$$\Rightarrow x\frac{dy}{dx} + y\frac{dy}{dx} = x - y$$

$$\Rightarrow \frac{dy}{dx} = \frac{x - y}{x + y} \qquad \text{...(i)}$$

Which is a homogeneous differential equation.

Putting $y = Vx \Rightarrow \dfrac{dy}{dx} = V + x\dfrac{dV}{dx}$ in (i), we get

$$V + x\frac{dV}{dx} = \frac{x - Vx}{x + Vx}$$

$$\Rightarrow V + x\frac{dV}{dx} = \frac{1 - V}{1 + V}$$

$$\Rightarrow x\frac{dV}{dx} = \frac{1 - V}{1 + V} - V$$

$$\Rightarrow x\frac{dV}{dx} = \frac{1 - V - V - V^2}{1 + V}$$

$$\Rightarrow x\frac{dV}{dx} = \frac{1 - 2V - V^2}{1 + V}$$

$$\Rightarrow \quad \frac{1+V}{1-2V-V^2}\,dV = \frac{dx}{x}, \quad x \neq 0 \qquad \text{...(ii)}$$

Putting $t = 1 - 2V - V^2$

$$\Rightarrow \qquad dt = (-2 - 2V)\,dV$$

$$\Rightarrow \qquad -\frac{1}{2}\,dt = (1 + V)\,dV$$

Now, equation (ii) becomes,

$$-\frac{1}{2t}\,dt = \frac{dx}{x}$$

On integrating above equation, we get

$$-\frac{1}{2}\int \frac{1}{t}\,dt = \int \frac{1}{x}\,dx$$

$$-\frac{1}{2}\,\log|t| = \log|x| + \log C$$

$$-\frac{1}{2}\,\log|1 - 2V - V^2| = \log\{C|x|\}$$

$$\log\{C|x|\} + \log|1 - 2V - V^2|^{1/2} = 0$$

$$C|x|\left(1 - \frac{2y}{x} - \frac{y^2}{x^2}\right)^{1/2} = 0$$

$$C(x^2 - 2xy - y^2)^{1/2} = 0.$$

91. Solve the following differential equation:*

$$(1 + x^2)\,\frac{dy}{dx} + y = \tan^{-1} x.$$

Sol. Given differential equation is,

$$(1 + x^2)\,\frac{dy}{dx} + y = \tan^{-1} x$$

Divide by $(1 + x^2)$ in above equation, we get

$$\frac{dy}{dx} + \frac{1}{1+x^2}\,y = \frac{\tan^{-1} x}{1+x^2} \qquad \text{...(i)}$$

The above equation is of the form $\dfrac{dy}{dx} + Py = Q$

Where, $P = \dfrac{1}{1+x^2}$ and $Q = \dfrac{\tan^{-1} x}{1+x^2}$

$$\therefore \qquad \text{I.F.} = e^{\int P\,dx}$$

$$= e^{\int \frac{1}{1+x^2}\,dx}$$

$$= e^{\tan^{-1} x}$$

Solution of the equation is given by

$$y.\text{I.F} = \int Q \times \text{I.F.}\,dx + C$$

$$ye^{\tan^{-1} x} = \int \frac{e^{\tan^{-1} x}\,\tan^{-1} x}{1+x^2}\,dx + C \quad \text{...(ii)}$$

Put $\qquad \tan^{-1} x = t$

_____

Differentiate both side w.r.t x

$$\frac{1}{1+x^2}\,dx = dt$$

$\therefore$ Equation (ii) becomes

$$ye^{\tan^{-1} x} = \int e^t.\,t\,dt + C$$

$$ye^{\tan^{-1} x} = t\,e^t - \int e^t.\,dt + C$$

$$= t\,e^t - e^t + C$$

$$= \tan^{-1} x\,e^{\tan^{-1} x} - e^{\tan^{-1} x} + C$$

$$\Rightarrow \quad ye^{\tan^{-1} x} = e^{\tan^{-1} x}(\tan^{-1} x - 1) + C$$

$$\Rightarrow \quad y = \tan^{-1} x - 1 + Ce^{-\tan^{-1} x}$$

92. Solve the following differential equation :*

$$\cos^2 x\,\frac{dy}{dx} + y = \tan x$$

Sol. Given differential equation is

$$\cos^2 x\,\frac{dy}{dx} + y = \tan x$$

$$\Rightarrow \quad \frac{dy}{dx} + \frac{1}{\cos^2 x}\,y = \frac{\tan x}{\cos^2 x}$$

divided by $(\cos^2 x)$ in above equation, we get

$$\frac{dy}{dx} + (\sec^2 x)y = \tan x \sec^2 x \qquad \text{...(i)}$$

Here, $P = \sec^2 x$, $Q = \tan x \sec^2 x$

$\text{I.F.} = e^{\int P\,dx} = e^{\int \sec^2 x\,dx} = e^{\tan x}$

Solution of above equation will be given by

$$y.\text{I.F.} = \int Q\,\text{I.F.}\,dx + C$$

$$y.e^{\tan x} = \int \tan x \sec^2 x\,e^{\tan x}\,dx + C \quad \text{...(ii)}$$

Let $I = \int e^{\tan x} \tan x \sec^2 x\,dx$

Put $\tan x = t$

Differentiate both side w.r.t x

$$\sec^2 x = \frac{dt}{dx}$$

$$\Rightarrow \quad \sec^2 x\,dx = dt$$

$$\therefore \quad \int e^t.\,t\,dt = t\int e^t\,dt - \int\left(\frac{d}{dt}(t).\int e^t dt\right)dt + C$$

$$= t\,e^t - \int e^t\,dt + C$$

$$= t\,e^t - e^t + C$$

$$= \tan x\,e^{\tan x} - e^{\tan x} + C$$

From equation (ii)

$$ye^{\tan x} = e^{\tan x}(\tan x - 1) + C$$

$$y = \tan x - 1 + Ce^{-\tan x}.$$

93. Solve the differential equation is,

$$x \log x\,\frac{dy}{dx} + y = 2 \log x$$

Sol. Given differential equation is,

$$x \log x\,\frac{dy}{dx} + y = 2 \log x$$

$$\Rightarrow \quad \frac{dy}{dx} + \frac{1}{x\log x} y = \frac{2}{x} \qquad \qquad ...(i)$$

Here $P = \dfrac{1}{x\log x}$, $Q = \dfrac{2}{x}$.

$$\text{I.F.} = e^{\int P\,dx} = e^{\int \frac{1}{x\log x}dx}$$

$$= e^{\int \frac{1/x}{\log x}dx}$$

$$= e^{\log(\log x)} = \log x$$

Solution of given equation will be given by,

$$y.\text{I.F.} = \int Q\,\text{I.F.}\,dx + C$$

$$\Rightarrow \quad y\log x = 2\int \log x \cdot \frac{1}{x}\,dx + C$$

$$\Rightarrow \quad y\log x = \frac{2(\log x)^2}{2} + C$$

$$\left[\because \int [f(x)]^n \cdot f'(x)dx = \frac{[f(x)]^{n+1}}{n+1} + C\right]$$

$$\Rightarrow \quad y = \log x + \frac{C}{\log x}.$$

94. Find the general solution of the differential equation.*

$$x\log x.\frac{dy}{dx} + y = \frac{2}{x}\log x$$

Sol. Given differential equation is

$$x\log x.\frac{dy}{dx} + y = \frac{2}{x}\log x \qquad ...(i)$$

Divide by $x\log x$ on both sides

$$\frac{dy}{dx} + \frac{1}{x\log x} y = \frac{2}{x^2} \qquad ...(ii)$$

Here, $P = \dfrac{1}{x\log x}$, $Q = \dfrac{2}{x^2}$,

$$\text{I.F.} = e^{\int P\,dx}$$

$$\Rightarrow \quad \text{I.F.} = e^{\int \frac{1}{x\log x}dx}$$

Put the value of P

$$= e^{\log(\log x)}$$

$$\text{I.F.} = \log x$$

Multiply equation (ii) by I.F.

$$\log x \frac{dy}{dx} + \log x.\frac{1}{x\log x} y = \frac{2}{x^2}\log x$$

$$\log x \frac{dy}{dx} + \frac{1}{x} y = \frac{2}{x^2}\log x$$

$$\frac{d}{dx}(y\log x) = \frac{2}{x^2}\log x$$

Integrating both sides

$$\therefore \quad y\log x = \int \frac{2}{x^2}\log x\,dx + C$$

$$= \int 2\log x.\,x^{-2}\,dx + C$$

$$= 2\left[\log x.\frac{x^{-1}}{-1} - \int \frac{1}{x}.\frac{x^{-1}}{-1}\,dx\right] + C$$

$$= 2\left[-\frac{\log x}{x} + \int x^{-2}dx\right] + C$$

$$\Rightarrow \quad y\log x = 2\left[-\frac{\log x}{x} + \frac{x^{-1}}{-1}\right] + C$$

$$\Rightarrow \quad y\log x = 2\left[-\frac{\log x}{x} - \frac{1}{x}\right] + C$$

$$\Rightarrow \quad y\log x = \frac{2}{x}[-\log x - 1] + C$$

$$\Rightarrow \quad y\log x = \frac{-2}{x}(\log x + 1) + C$$

is the required equation.

95. Solve the following differential equation:*

$$(x^2 + 1)\frac{dy}{dx} + 2xy = \sqrt{x^2 + 4}$$

Sol. Solve differential equation is

$$(x^2 + 1)\frac{dy}{dx} + 2xy = \sqrt{x^2 + 4} \qquad ...(i)$$

Divide by $(x^2 + 1)$

$$\frac{dy}{dx} + \frac{2x}{x^2 + 1} y = \frac{\sqrt{x^2 + 4}}{x^2 + 1} \qquad ...(ii)$$

Here, $P = \dfrac{2x}{x^2 + 1}$, $Q = \dfrac{\sqrt{x^2 + 4}}{x^2 + 1}$

$$\text{I.F.} = e^{\int P\,dx} = e^{\int \frac{2x}{x^2+1}dx}$$

$$\text{I.F.} = e^{\log|x^2 + 1|}$$

$$\therefore \quad \text{I.F.} = (x^2 + 1)$$

Multiply equation (ii) by I.F.

$$(x^2 + 1)\frac{dy}{dx} + 2xy = \sqrt{x^2 + 4}$$

$$\frac{d}{dx}[y(x^2 + 1)] = \sqrt{x^2 + 2^2}$$

Integrating both sides, we get

$$y(x^2 + 1) = \frac{1}{2}x\sqrt{x^2 + 4} + \frac{1}{2}(2)^2\log|x + \sqrt{x^2 + 4}| + C$$

$$y(x^2 + 1) = \frac{x}{2}\sqrt{x^2 + 4} + 2 \log |x + \sqrt{x^2 + 4}| + C$$

is the required solution of given differential equation.

96. Solve the following differential equation:*

$$(x^2 - 1)\frac{dy}{dx} + 2xy = \frac{1}{x^2 - 1} : |x| \neq 1$$

Sol. Given differential equation is

$$(x^2 - 1)\frac{dy}{dx} + 2xy = \frac{1}{x^2 - 1}$$

Divide by $(x^2 - 1)$

$$\frac{dy}{dx} + \frac{2x}{x^2 - 1}y = \frac{1}{(x^2 - 1)^2} \qquad \text{...(i)}$$

Here, $P = \dfrac{2x}{x^2 - 1}$, $Q = \dfrac{1}{(x^2 - 1)^2}$

$$\text{I.F.} = e^{\int P\, dx}$$
$$= e^{\int \frac{2x}{x^2 - 1}dx} = e^{\log (x^2 - 1)}$$
$$= x^2 - 1$$

Multiply equation (i) by I.F.

$$(x^2 - 1)\frac{dy}{dx} + 2xy = \frac{1}{(x^2 - 1)}$$

$$\frac{d}{dx}[y(x^2 - 1)] = \frac{1}{x^2 - 1}$$

Integrating both sides

$$y(x^2 - 1) = \int \frac{1}{x^2 - 1}\, dx + C$$

$$y(x^2 - 1) = \frac{1}{2} \log \left|\frac{x - 1}{x + 1}\right| + C$$

$$y = \frac{1}{2(x^2 - 1)} \log \left|\frac{x - 1}{x - 1}\right| + \frac{C}{x^2 - 1}$$

which is the required solution.

97. Solve the following differential equation:*
$$x\, dy - (y + 2x^2)\, dx = 0.$$

Sol. Given differential equation

$$x\, dy - (y + 2x^2)\, dx = 0$$
$$\Rightarrow \qquad x\, dy = (y + 2x^2)\, dx$$
$$\Rightarrow \qquad \frac{dy}{dx} = \frac{(y + 2x^2)}{x}$$
$$\Rightarrow \qquad \frac{dy}{dx} = \frac{y}{x} + 2x \qquad \text{...(i)}$$
$$\Rightarrow \qquad \frac{dy}{dx} - \frac{1}{x}y = 2x$$

Here, $P = -\dfrac{1}{x}$, $Q = 2x$

$$\text{I.F.} = e^{\int P\, dx} = e^{-\int \frac{1}{x}dx}$$
$$= e^{-\log x} = e^{\log x^{-1}} = x^{-1}$$

Multiple equation (i) by I.F.

$$x^{-1}\frac{dy}{dx} - \frac{1}{x^2}y = 2$$

$$\frac{d}{dx}\left(\frac{y}{x}\right) = 2$$

Integrating both sides:

$$\frac{y}{x} = \int 2\, dx + C$$

$$\frac{y}{x} = 2x + C$$

$$y = 2x^2 + Cx$$

which is required solution.

98. Solve the following differential equation :*

$$(y + 3x^2)\frac{dx}{dy} = x.$$

Sol. Given differential equation is

$$(y + 3x^2)\frac{dx}{dy} = x$$

$$\Rightarrow \qquad \frac{dx}{dy} = \frac{x}{y + 3x^2}$$

$$\Rightarrow \qquad \frac{x \times dy}{dx} = y + 3x^2$$

$$\Rightarrow \qquad \frac{dy}{dx} - \frac{y}{x} = 3x \qquad \text{...(i)}$$

Here $P = -\dfrac{1}{x}$, $Q = 3x$

$$\text{I.F.} = e^{\int P\, dx} = e^{-\int \frac{1}{x}dx} = e^{-\log x}$$
$$= e^{\log x^{-1}} = x^{-1} = \frac{1}{x}$$

Multiply equation (i) by I.F.

$$\frac{1}{x}\frac{dy}{dx} - \frac{1}{x^2}y = 3$$

$$\frac{d}{dx}\left(y \cdot \frac{1}{x}\right) = 3$$

Integrating both sides

$$\frac{y}{x} = 3x + C$$

which is required solution.

---

99. Find the particular solution of

$$\frac{dy}{dx} + 2y \tan x = \sin x$$

satisfying condition $x = \dfrac{\pi}{3}$ when $y = 0$. **[NCERT]**

Sol. Given differential equation is,

$$\frac{dy}{dx} + 2y \tan x = \sin x \qquad \text{...(i)}$$

Here $P = 2 \tan x$, $Q = \sin x$

$$\text{I.F.} = e^{\int P\, dx} = e^{2 \int \tan x\, dx}$$
$$= e^{2(-\log \cos x)}$$
$$= e^{\log (\cos x)^{-2}} = \frac{1}{\cos^2 x}$$

Multiplying equation (i) by I.F.

$$\frac{1}{\cos^2 x}\frac{dy}{dx} + 2y\frac{\tan x}{\cos^2 x} = \frac{\sin x}{\cos^2 x}$$

$$\frac{d}{dx}(y \sec^2 x) = \sec x \tan x$$

Integrating both sides

$$y \sec^2 x = \int \sec x \tan x\, dx + C$$
$$y \sec^2 x = \sec x + C \qquad \text{...(ii)}$$

When $\qquad x = \dfrac{\pi}{3}, y = 0$

$$0 = \sec \frac{\pi}{3} + C$$

$\therefore \qquad\qquad C = -2$

Put in equation (ii),

$$y \sec^2 x = \sec x - 2$$

which is the required solution.

100. Find the general solution of the differential equation $\dfrac{dy}{dx} - y = \sin x.$*

Sol. We have,

$$\frac{dy}{dx} - y = \sin x$$

Which is a liner differential equation of the form

$$\frac{dy}{dx} + Py = Q$$

Where, $\qquad P = -1$ and $Q = \sin x$

Now, $\qquad$ I.F. $e^{\int P\, dx} = e^{\int -1\, dx} = e^{-x}$

So, the required solution is

$$ye^{-x} = \int e^{-x} \sin x\, dx + C_1 \qquad \text{...(i)}$$

Let $\qquad\qquad I = \int e^{-x} \sin x\, dx \qquad \text{...(ii)}$

$$\Rightarrow I = \sin x \int e^{-x}\, dx - \int\left(\frac{d}{dx}(\sin x)\int e^{-x} dx\right) dx + C_2$$

$$\Rightarrow I = -\sin x\, e^{-x} + \int \cos x\, e^{-x}\, dx + C_2$$

$$\Rightarrow I = -\sin x\, e^{-x}$$
$$+ \cos x \int e^{-x}\, dx - \int\left(\frac{d}{dx}(\cos x)\int e^{-x} dx\right) dx$$

$$\Rightarrow I = -\sin x\, e^{-x} - \cos x \cdot e^{-x} - \int \sin x \cdot e^{-x}\, dx + C_2$$

$$\Rightarrow I = -\sin x \cdot e^{-x} - \cos x \cdot e^{-x} - I + C_2 \quad [\text{using (ii)}]$$

$$\Rightarrow \quad 2I = -e^{-x}(\sin x + \cos x) + C_2$$

$$I = \frac{-1}{2}\, e^{-x}(\sin x + \cos x) + C_2$$

By equation (i),

$$ye^{-x} = \frac{-1}{2}\, e^{-x}(\sin x + \cos x) + C_1 + C_2$$

$$\Rightarrow 2y = -(\sin x + \cos x) + 2Ce^{x} \qquad [\because C_1 + C_2 = C]$$

$\therefore 2y = 2Ce^{x} - \sin x - \cos x$ is the requied solution.

Long Answer Type Questions

101. Solve the differential equation :* $\qquad$ **[NCERT]**

$$\left(x\cos\frac{y}{x} + y\sin\frac{y}{x}\right) y - \left(y\sin\frac{y}{x} - x\cos\frac{y}{x}\right) x\frac{dy}{dx} = 0$$

Sol. Given differential equation is

$$\left(x\cos\frac{y}{x} + y\sin\frac{y}{x}\right) y - \left(y\sin\frac{y}{x} - x\cos\frac{y}{x}\right) x\frac{dy}{dx} = 0$$

$$\Rightarrow \left(x\cos\frac{y}{x} + y\sin\frac{y}{x}\right) y = \left(y\sin\frac{y}{x} - x\cos\frac{y}{x}\right) x\frac{dy}{dx}$$

$$\Rightarrow \quad \frac{dy}{dx} = \frac{\left(x\cos\dfrac{y}{x} + y\sin\dfrac{y}{x}\right) y}{\left(y\sin\dfrac{y}{x} - x\cos\dfrac{y}{x}\right) x}$$

$$= \frac{x\left(\cos\dfrac{y}{x} + \dfrac{y}{x}\sin\dfrac{y}{x}\right) y}{x\left(\dfrac{y}{x}\sin\dfrac{y}{x} - \cos\dfrac{y}{x}\right) x}$$

$$\Rightarrow \quad \frac{dy}{dx} = \frac{\left(\cos\dfrac{y}{x} + \dfrac{y}{x}\sin\dfrac{y}{x}\right) \dfrac{y}{x}}{\dfrac{y}{x}\sin\dfrac{y}{x} - \cos\dfrac{y}{x}} \qquad \text{...(i)}$$

Put $\qquad \dfrac{y}{x} = t$

$$\Rightarrow \qquad\qquad y = xt$$

Differentiate w.r.t. x

$$\frac{dy}{dx} = x\frac{dt}{dx} + t$$

Put in equation (i),

$$x\frac{dt}{dx} + t = \frac{t(\cos t + t\sin t)}{t\sin t - \cos t}$$

$$\Rightarrow \quad x\frac{dt}{dx} = \frac{t\cos t + t^2\sin t}{t\sin t - \cos t} - t$$

$$= \frac{t\cos t + t^2\sin t - t^2\sin t + t\cos t}{t\sin t - \cos t}$$

$$\Rightarrow \quad x\frac{dt}{dx} = \frac{2t\cos t}{t\sin t - \cos t}$$

$$\Rightarrow \quad \frac{t\sin t - \cos t}{2t\cos t}\, dt = \frac{dx}{x}$$

$$\left(\frac{t\sin t}{2t\cos t} - \frac{\cos t}{2t\cos t}\right) dt = \frac{dx}{x}$$

Integrating both sides

$$\int\left(\frac{1}{2}\tan t - \frac{1}{2t}\right) dt = \int\frac{dx}{x} + C$$

$$\Rightarrow \frac{1}{2}\left(-\log|\cos t| - \log|t|\right) = \log|x| + C$$

$$\Rightarrow \quad \log|\cos t| + \log|t| = -2\log|x| - 2C$$

$$\Rightarrow \qquad \log(t\cos t) = -\log x^2 - 2C$$

$$\Rightarrow \quad \log(t\cos t) + \log x^2 = -2C$$

$$\Rightarrow \quad \log(t\cos t \times x^2) = -2C$$

$$\Rightarrow \qquad x^2 t\cos t = e^{-2C}$$

$$\Rightarrow \qquad \frac{y}{x}\left(\cos\frac{y}{x}\right)x^2 = A \qquad \left[\because t = \frac{y}{x}\right]$$

$$\text{(where } A = e^{-2C})$$

$$\Rightarrow \qquad xy\cos\frac{y}{x} = A$$

which is required solution.

102. Find the particular solution of the following differential equation :

$$x\frac{dy}{dx} - y + x\sin\frac{y}{x} = 0,$$

given that when $x = 2$, $y = \pi$. **[NCERT]**

Sol. Given differential equation is,

$$x\frac{dy}{dx} - y + x\sin\frac{y}{x} = 0 \qquad ...(i)$$

Divide by x

$$\frac{dy}{dx} - \frac{y}{x} + \sin\frac{y}{x} = 0$$

$$\Rightarrow \qquad \frac{dy}{dx} = \frac{y}{x} - \sin\frac{y}{x} \qquad ...(ii)$$

Put $\dfrac{y}{x} = t \Rightarrow y = xt$

Differentiate w.r.t. x

$$\frac{dy}{dx} = x\frac{dt}{dx} + t$$

Put in equation (ii)

$$x\frac{dt}{dx} + t = t - \sin t$$

$$\Rightarrow \qquad x\frac{dt}{dx} = -\sin t$$

$$\Rightarrow \qquad \frac{dt}{\sin t} = -\frac{dx}{x}$$

$$\Rightarrow \qquad \operatorname{cosec} t\, dt = -\frac{dx}{x}$$

On integrating both sides, we have

$$\Rightarrow \qquad \int \operatorname{cosec} t\, dt = -\int\frac{dx}{x}$$

$$\Rightarrow \quad \log|\operatorname{cosec} t - \cot t| = -\log x + \log C$$

$$\Rightarrow \quad \log\left|\operatorname{cosec}\frac{y}{x} - \cot\frac{y}{x}\right| = -\log x + \log C$$

$$\Rightarrow \quad \log\left|\operatorname{cosec}\frac{y}{x} - \cot\frac{y}{x}\right| = \log\frac{C}{x}$$

$$\Rightarrow \qquad \operatorname{cosec}\frac{y}{x} - \cot\frac{y}{x} = \frac{C}{x} \qquad ...(iii)$$

Put $x = 2$, $y = \pi$

$$\Rightarrow \qquad \operatorname{cosec}\frac{\pi}{2} - \cot\frac{\pi}{2} = \frac{C}{2}$$

$$\Rightarrow \qquad 1 - 0 = \frac{C}{2}$$

$$\Rightarrow \qquad C = 2$$

Put in equation (iii)

$$\operatorname{cosec}\frac{y}{x} - \cot\frac{y}{x} = \frac{2}{x}$$

which is the required solution of given differential equation.

103. Show that the differential equation

$$x\frac{dy}{dx}\sin\frac{y}{x} + x - y\sin\frac{y}{x} = 0$$

is homogeneous and find the particular solution when $x = 1$ and $y = \dfrac{\pi}{2}$. **[NCERT]**

Sol. Given differential equation is,

$$x\frac{dy}{dx}\sin\frac{y}{x} + x - y\sin\frac{y}{x} = 0 \qquad ...(i)$$

$$\Rightarrow \qquad x\frac{dy}{dx}\sin\frac{y}{x} = y\sin\frac{y}{x} - x$$

$$\Rightarrow \quad \frac{dy}{dx} = \frac{y\sin\frac{y}{x} - x}{x\sin\frac{y}{x}}$$

$$\Rightarrow \quad \frac{dy}{dx} = \frac{\frac{y}{x}\sin\frac{y}{x} - 1}{\sin\frac{y}{x}} \qquad ...(ii)$$

which is homogeneous differential equation of the form $f\left(\frac{y}{x}\right)$

Put $\frac{y}{x} = t$, $\qquad y = xt$

Differentiate both sides w.r.t. x

$$\frac{dy}{dx} = x\frac{dt}{dx} + t$$

Put in equation (ii)

$$x\frac{dt}{dx} + t = \frac{t\sin t - 1}{\sin t}$$

$$\Rightarrow \quad x\frac{dt}{dx} = \frac{t\sin t - 1 - t\sin t}{\sin t}$$

$$\Rightarrow \quad x\frac{dt}{dx} = -\frac{1}{\sin t}$$

$$\Rightarrow \quad \sin t \, dt = -\frac{dx}{x}$$

Integrating both sides :

$$-\cos t = -\log x + C$$

$$\Rightarrow \quad -\cos\frac{y}{x} = -\log x + C \qquad ...(iii)$$

$$\left[\because t = \frac{y}{x}\right]$$

Put $x = 1$ and $y = \frac{\pi}{2}$

$$\Rightarrow \quad -\cos\frac{\pi}{2} = -\log 1 + C$$

$$\Rightarrow \quad C = 0$$

Equation (iii) becomes :

$$-\cos\frac{y}{x} = -\log x + 0$$

$$\Rightarrow \quad \cos\frac{y}{x} = \log x$$

which is the required particular solution.

104. Show that the given differential equation is homogeneous and solve each of them.

(i) $(x^2 + xy)\, dy = (x^2 + y^2)\, dx$ **[NCERT]**

Sol. The given differential equation is,

$$(x^2 + xy)\, dy = (x^2 + y^2)\, dx$$

$$\Rightarrow \quad \frac{dy}{dx} = \frac{x^2 + y^2}{x^2 + xy}$$

$$= \frac{x^2\left(1 + \dfrac{y^2}{x^2}\right)}{x^2\left(1 + \dfrac{y}{x}\right)}$$

$$\Rightarrow \quad \frac{dy}{dx} = \frac{1 + \left(\dfrac{y}{x}\right)^2}{1 + \dfrac{y}{x}} \qquad ...(i)$$

$\therefore$ It is homogeneous equation of the form $f\left(\dfrac{y}{x}\right)$

Put $\dfrac{y}{x} = t, \Rightarrow y = xt$

Differentiate w.r.t. x

$$\frac{dy}{dx} = x\frac{dt}{dx} + t$$

Put in equation (i),

$$x\frac{dt}{dx} + t = \frac{1 + t^2}{1 + t}$$

$$\Rightarrow \quad x\frac{dt}{dx} = \frac{1 + t^2}{1 + t} - t$$

$$\Rightarrow \quad x\frac{dt}{dx} = \frac{1 + t^2 - t - t^2}{1 + t}$$

$$\Rightarrow \quad x\frac{dt}{dx} = \frac{1 - t}{1 + t}$$

$$\Rightarrow \quad \frac{1 + t}{1 - t}\, dt = \frac{dx}{x}$$

Integrating both sides

$$\int\left(-1 + \frac{2}{-t + 1}\right) dt = \frac{dx}{x}$$

$$\Rightarrow \quad -t - 2\log |-t + 1| = \log x + C$$

$$\Rightarrow \quad -2\log |1 - t| = \log x + t + C$$

$$\Rightarrow \quad -2\log |1 - t| - \log x = t + C$$

$$\Rightarrow \quad -(2\log |1 - t| + \log x) = t + C$$

$$\Rightarrow \quad \log (1 - t)^2 + \log x = -t - C$$

$$\Rightarrow \quad \log [x\,(1 - t)^2] = -t - C$$

$$\Rightarrow \quad \log\left[x\left(1 - \frac{y}{x}\right)^2\right] = -\frac{y}{x} - C \quad \left(\because t = \frac{y}{x}\right)$$

$$\Rightarrow \quad x\left(1 - \frac{y}{x}\right)^2 = e^{-y/x - C}$$

$$\Rightarrow \quad x\left(1 - \frac{y}{x}\right)^2 = e^{-y/x} \cdot e^{-C}$$

$$\Rightarrow \quad \frac{x(x-y)^2}{x^2} = e^{-y/x} \cdot A,$$

$$\text{where } A = e^{-C}$$

$$\Rightarrow \quad (x-y)^2 = xe^{-y/x} A$$

which is the required solution.

(ii) $x^2 \dfrac{dy}{dx} = x^2 - 2y^2 + xy$ **[NCERT]**

Sol. Given differential equation is

$$x^2 \frac{dy}{dx} = x^2 - 2y^2 + xy$$

$$\Rightarrow \quad \frac{dy}{dx} = \frac{x^2}{x^2} - 2\frac{y^2}{x^2} + \frac{xy}{x^2}$$

$$\Rightarrow \quad \frac{dy}{dx} = 1 - 2\left(\frac{y}{x}\right)^2 + \frac{y}{x} \qquad \text{...(i)}$$

which is homogeneous equation of the form

$$f\left(\frac{y}{x}\right)$$

Put $\dfrac{y}{x} = t \Rightarrow \quad y = xt$

Differentiate w.r.t. x,

$$\frac{dy}{dx} = x\frac{dt}{dx} + t$$

Put in equation (i),

$$x\frac{dt}{dx} + t = 1 - 2t^2 + t$$

$$\Rightarrow \quad x\frac{dt}{dx} = 1 - 2t^2$$

$$\Rightarrow \quad \frac{dt}{1-2t^2} = \frac{dx}{x}$$

Integrating both sides

$$\frac{1}{2}\int \frac{dt}{\left(\frac{1}{\sqrt{2}}\right)^2 - t^2} = \int \frac{dx}{x} + C$$

$$\Rightarrow \quad \frac{1}{2}\cdot\frac{1}{2\times\frac{1}{\sqrt{2}}} \log\left|\frac{\frac{1}{\sqrt{2}} + t}{\frac{1}{\sqrt{2}} - t}\right| = \log x + C$$

$$\Rightarrow \quad \frac{1}{2\sqrt{2}} \log\left|\frac{1+\sqrt{2}t}{1-\sqrt{2}t}\right| = \log x + C$$

$$\Rightarrow \quad \frac{1}{2\sqrt{2}} \log\left|\frac{1+\sqrt{2}\,\frac{y}{x}}{1-\sqrt{2}\,\frac{y}{x}}\right| = \log x + C$$

$$\Rightarrow \quad \frac{1}{2\sqrt{2}} \log\left|\frac{x+\sqrt{2}\,y}{x-\sqrt{2}\,y}\right| = \log x + C$$

which is the required solution.

105. Find the particular solution of the differential equation $2xy + y^2 - 2x^2 \dfrac{dy}{dx} = 0,$ given $y = 2$ when $x = 1.$ **[NCERT]**

Sol. Given differential equation is,

$$2xy + y^2 - 2x^2 \frac{dy}{dx} = 0$$

$$\Rightarrow \quad 2x^2 \frac{dy}{dx} = 2xy + y^2$$

$$\Rightarrow \quad \frac{dy}{dx} = \frac{2xy}{2x^2} + \frac{y^2}{2x^2}$$

$$\Rightarrow \quad \frac{dy}{dx} = \frac{y}{x} + \frac{1}{2}\left(\frac{y}{x}\right)^2 \qquad \text{...(i)}$$

which is homogeneous equation of the form

$$f\left(\frac{y}{x}\right)$$

Put $\dfrac{y}{x} = t \quad \Rightarrow y = xt$

Differentiate w.r.t. x

$$\frac{dy}{dx} = x\frac{dt}{dx} + t$$

Put in equation (i),

$$x\frac{dt}{dx} + t = t + \frac{1}{2}t^2$$

$$\Rightarrow \quad x\frac{dt}{dx} = \frac{t^2}{2}$$

$$\Rightarrow \quad \frac{2dt}{t^2} = \frac{dx}{x}$$

$$\Rightarrow \quad 2t^{-2}\,dt = \frac{dx}{x}$$

Integrating both sides

$$\frac{2t^{-1}}{-1} = \log x + C$$

$$\Rightarrow \quad -\frac{2}{t} = \log x + C$$

$$\Rightarrow \quad \frac{-2x}{y} = \log x + C \quad \left[\because t = \frac{y}{x}\right] \text{...(ii)}$$

When $x = 1,\ y = 2$

$$-\frac{2}{2} = \log 1 + C$$

$$\therefore \quad C = -1$$

Put in equation (ii),

$$-\frac{2x}{y} = \log x - 1$$

$$\frac{2x}{y} = 1 - \log x$$

which is the required solution.

106. Find the particular solution of the differential equation $(x - y)\dfrac{dy}{dx} = (x + 2y)$, given that $y = 0$ when $x = 1.$* **[NCERT]**

Sol. We have,

$$(x - y)\frac{dy}{dx} = (x + 2y)$$

$$\frac{dy}{dx} = \frac{x + 2y}{x - y} \qquad \ldots(i)$$

Putting $y = Vx$ and

$$\frac{dy}{dx} = V + x\frac{dV}{dx}$$

$$V + x\frac{dV}{dx} = \frac{x + 2Vx}{x - Vx}$$

$$V + x\frac{dV}{dx} = \frac{1 + 2V}{1 - V}$$

$$x\frac{dV}{dx} = \frac{1 + 2V}{1 - V} - V$$

$$x\frac{dV}{dx} = \frac{1 + 2V - V + V^2}{1 - V}$$

$$\frac{1 - V}{1 + V + V^2} dV = \frac{dx}{x}$$

On integrating both sides, we get

$$\int \frac{1 - V}{1 + V + V^2} dV = \int \frac{dx}{x} \qquad \ldots(ii)$$

Let $\quad I = \displaystyle\int \frac{1 - V}{1 + V + V^2} dV$

$$= \frac{-1}{2}\int \frac{2(V - 1)}{1 + V + V^2} dV$$

$$= \frac{-1}{2}\int \frac{(2V + 1) - 3}{1 + V + V^2} dV$$

$$= \frac{3}{2}\int \frac{1}{1 + V + V^2} dV - \frac{1}{2}\int \frac{2V + 1}{1 + V + V^2} dV$$

Now put in (ii)

$$\frac{3}{2}\int \frac{1}{1 + V + V^2} dV - \frac{1}{2}\int \frac{1 + 2V}{1 + V + V^2} dV = \int \frac{dx}{x}$$

$$\frac{3}{2}\int \frac{dV}{\left(V + \frac{1}{2}\right)^2 + \left(\frac{\sqrt{3}}{2}\right)^2} - \frac{1}{2}\int \frac{1 + 2V}{1 + V + V^2} dV = \int \frac{dx}{x}$$

———

$$\sqrt{3}\,\tan^{-1}\left(\frac{2V + 1}{\sqrt{3}}\right) - \frac{1}{2}\log |1 + V + V^2|$$

$$= \log |x| + C$$

$$\sqrt{3}\,\tan^{-1}\left(\frac{2y + x}{\sqrt{3}x}\right) - \frac{1}{2}\log |x^2 + xy + y^2| = C \ \ldots(iii)$$

Now, given $y = 0$, when $x = 1$.

So, $\sqrt{3}\,\tan^{-1}\left(\dfrac{2(0) + 1}{\sqrt{3}}\right) - \dfrac{1}{2}\log |1 + 0 + 0| = C$

$$C = \sqrt{3}\,\tan^{-1}\left(\frac{1}{\sqrt{3}}\right)$$

$$= \frac{\sqrt{3}\pi}{6}$$

Putting the value of C in (iii), we get

$$\sqrt{3}\,\tan^{-1}\left(\frac{2y + x}{\sqrt{3}x}\right) - \frac{1}{2}\log |x^2 + xy + y^2|$$

$$= \frac{\sqrt{3}\pi}{6}$$

Which is the required solution.

107. Solve the following differential equation:

$$x\frac{dy}{dx} + y - x + xy\cot x = 0 \qquad \textbf{[NCERT]}$$

Sol. Given differential equation is

$$x\frac{dy}{dx} + y - x + xy\cot x = 0$$

$$\Rightarrow \quad x\frac{dy}{dx} + y(1 + x\cot x) = x$$

$$\Rightarrow \quad \frac{dy}{dx} + \frac{1 + x\cot x}{x}y = 1 \qquad \ldots(i)$$

Here $P = \dfrac{1 + x\cot x}{x}, Q = 1$

$$\text{I.F.} = e^{\int P\,dx} = e^{\int \left(\frac{1}{x} + \cot x\right)\,dx}$$

$$= e^{\log x + \log \sin x}$$

$$= e^{\log x \sin x}$$

$$\Rightarrow \quad \text{I.F.} = x \sin x$$

Multiply equation (i) by I.F.

$$x \sin x \frac{dy}{dx} + x \sin x \frac{1 + x\cot x}{x}y = x \sin x$$

$$\frac{d}{dx}(xy \sin x) = x \sin x$$

Integrating both sides :

$$xy \sin x = -x \cos x - \int (-\cos x)\,dx + C$$

$$xy \sin x = -x \cos x + \sin x + C$$

which is the required solution.

108. Solve the differential equation $x\dfrac{dy}{dx} + y = x\cos x$

$+ \sin x$, given that $y = 1$, when $x = \dfrac{\pi}{2}$.* **[NCERT]**

Sol. Given differential equation is :

$$x\frac{dy}{dx} + y = x\cos x + \sin x$$

$$\frac{dy}{dx} + \frac{y}{x} = \cos x + \frac{\sin x}{x}$$

which is of the form $\dfrac{dy}{dx} + Py = Q$

Where $P = \dfrac{1}{x}$, $Q = \cos x + \dfrac{\sin x}{x}$

$$\text{I. F.} = e^{\int P dx} = e^{\int \frac{1}{x} dx} = e^{\log x} = x$$

Required solution is

$$y . \text{I.F.} = \int Q . \text{I.F} + C$$

$$y . x = \int \left(\cos x + \frac{\sin x}{x} \right) x \, dx + C$$

$$= \int x\cos x \, dx + \int \sin x \, dx + C$$

$$= x . \int \cos x \, dx - \int \left[\frac{d}{dx}(x) . \int \cos x \, dx \right] dx$$

$$- \cos x + C$$

$$\Rightarrow \quad xy = x\sin x - \int \sin x \, dx - \cos x + C$$

$$\Rightarrow \quad xy = x\sin x + \cos x - \cos x + C$$

$$\Rightarrow \quad xy = x\sin x + C \qquad \ldots (i)$$

Given, $y = 1$ when $x = \dfrac{\pi}{2}$

From eq. (i),

$$1 \times \frac{\pi}{2} = \frac{\pi}{2}\sin\frac{\pi}{2} + C$$

$$\frac{\pi}{2} = \frac{\pi}{2} + C$$

$$\Rightarrow \qquad C = 0$$

Substitute the value of $c = 0$ in (i), we get

$$xy = x\sin x$$

$$y = \sin x, \text{ which is the required solution.}$$

109. Find the general solution of the differential equation

$$\frac{dy}{dx} + 3y = e^{-2x} \qquad \textbf{[NCERT]}$$

Sol. We have,

$$\frac{dy}{dx} + 3y = e^{-2x} \qquad \ldots (i)$$

It is linear equation of the form of

$$\frac{dy}{dx} + Py = Q$$

Here, $P = 3$, $Q = e^{-2x}$

$$\text{I.F.} = e^{\int P \, dx} = e^{\int 3 \, dx} = e^{3x}$$

Multiply equation (i) by I.F.

$$e^{3x}\frac{dy}{dx} + 3ye^{3x} = e^{3x} \cdot e^{-2x}$$

$$\frac{d}{dx}(ye^{3x}) = e^{x}$$

Integrating both sides

$$ye^{3x} = e^{x} + C$$

$$y = e^{-2x} + Ce^{-3x}$$

which is required solution.

Self - Assessment

110. Solve : $\sqrt{1+x^2}\, dy + \sqrt{1+y^2}\, dx = 0$

Sol. $(y + \sqrt{1+y^2})\,(x + \sqrt{1+x^2}) = A$

111. Solve : $3e^x \tan y \, dx + (1 - e^x)\sec^2 y \, dy = 0$

Sol. $\tan y = A(1 - e^x)^3$

112. Solve : $\dfrac{dy}{dx} = \sin^3 x \cos^2 x + xe^x$

Sol. $y = -\dfrac{1}{3}\cos^3 x + \dfrac{1}{5}\cos^5 x + (x-1)\,e^x + C$

113. Solve : $\dfrac{dy}{dx} = x\log x$

Sol. $y = \dfrac{x^2}{2}\left(\log x - \dfrac{1}{2}\right) + C$

114. Find the particular solution of differential equation $\log\dfrac{dy}{dx} = 3x + 4y$, given that $y = 0$ when $x = 0$.

Sol. $4e^{3x} + 3e^{-4y} = 7$

115. Solve : $\sec^2 x \tan y \, dx + \sec^2 y \tan x \, dy = 0$

Sol. $\tan x \tan y = A$

116. Solve : $(e^x + 1)\, y \, dy = (y + 1)\, e^x \, dx$

Sol. $y = \log | (y + 1)\,(e^x + 1)\, | + C$

117. Solve : $\dfrac{dy}{dx} + \dfrac{\cos x \sin y}{\cos y} = 0$

Sol. $\sin y = \pm\, e^c\, e^{-\sin x}$ or $\sin y = Ae^{-\sin x}$

118. Find the particular solution of the differential equation $e^{dy/dx} = x + 1$, given that $y = 3$ when $x = 0$.

Sol. $y = (x + 1) \log |x + 1| - x + 3$

119. Solve : $x\dfrac{dy}{dx} = y - x \tan \dfrac{y}{x}$

Sol. $x \sin \dfrac{y}{x} = A$

120. Solve : $x^2 \dfrac{dy}{dx} = x^2 - 2y^2 + xy$

Sol. $\log |x| = \dfrac{1}{2\sqrt{2}} \log \left| \dfrac{x + \sqrt{2}y}{x - \sqrt{2}y} \right| + C$

121. Solve : $(y^2 - x^2)\, dy - 3xy\, dx = 0$

Sol. $y^2(4x^2 - y^2)^3 = A$

122. Solve : $\left(x \sin \dfrac{y}{x} \right) dy = \left(y \sin \dfrac{y}{x} - x \right) dx$

Sol. $\cos \left(\dfrac{y}{x} \right) = \log |x| + C$

123. Solve : $x^2 \dfrac{dy}{dx} - xy = 1 + \cos \left(\dfrac{y}{x} \right),$

$x \neq 0$ and $y = \dfrac{\pi}{2}$ if $x = 1$

Sol. $\tan \left(\dfrac{y}{2x} \right) = -\dfrac{1}{2x^2} + \dfrac{3}{2}$

124. Solve : $\dfrac{dy}{dx} = \dfrac{x + y + 1}{2x + 2y + 1}$

Sol. $6y - 3x - \log |3x + 3y + 2| = A$

125. Solve : $\dfrac{dy}{dx} = (3x + y + 4)^2$

Sol. $3x + y + 4 = \sqrt{3} \tan [\sqrt{3}(x + A)]$

126. Solve : $\dfrac{dy}{dx} - 2y \cos x = -2 \sin 2x$

Sol. $y = 2 \sin x + 1 + ce^{2 \sin x}$

127. Solve : $(2x - 10y^3)\, dy + y\, dx = 0,\, y \neq 0$

Sol. $xy^2 = 2y^5 + C$

128. Solve : $y \sin 2x\, dx - (1 + y^2 + \cos^2 x)\, dy = 0$

Sol. $-\cos^2 x = 1 + \dfrac{1}{3}y^2 + \dfrac{A}{y}$

129. Solve : $\dfrac{dy}{dx} + ay = e^{mx}$

Sol. $y = \dfrac{e^{mx}}{m + a} + ce^{-ax}$

130. Solve : $\dfrac{dy}{dx} + \dfrac{y}{x} = \cos x + \dfrac{\sin x}{x},\, x > 0$

Sol. $y = \sin x + \dfrac{c}{x}$

131. Solve : $\dfrac{dy}{dx} + x \sin 2y = x^3 \cos^2 y$

Sol. $\tan y = \dfrac{1}{2}(x^2 - 1) + ce^{-x^2}$

132. Solve : $dy = \cos x\, (2 - y \cosec x)\, dx$

given that $y = 2$ when $x = \dfrac{\pi}{2}$

Sol. $y \sin x = -\dfrac{\cos 2x}{2} + \dfrac{3}{2}$

133. Solve : $\dfrac{dy}{dx} - 2y \tan x = y^2 \tan^2 x,\, 0 < x < \dfrac{\pi}{2}$

Sol. $y^{-1} \sec^2 x = c - \dfrac{1}{3} \tan^3 x$

134. Solve : $\dfrac{dy}{dx} + \dfrac{4x}{x^2 + 1}y = -\dfrac{1}{(x^2 + 1)^3}$

Sol. $y = \dfrac{c - \tan^{-1} x}{(x^2 + 1)^2}$

135. Solve : $\dfrac{dy}{dx} + 2y \tan x = \sin x,\, y = 0$ when $x = \dfrac{\pi}{3}$

Sol. $y = \cos x - 2 \cos^2 x$

Vectors

Chapter 10

Basic Concepts

1. **A scalar quantity** has only magnitude but no direction, *e.g.*, mass, volume, temperature and real number. By a scalar, we always mean a real number.

2. **A vector quantity** has magnitude as well as direction, e.g., force, velocity, displacement.

3. Given a line, there are two directions associated with it. Any line with one of these directions is called a **directed line**. Any segment of a directed line is called a **'directed line segment'**. Thus, a directed line segment has a magnitude and a direction and therefore is a vector.

4. The directed line, of which it is a part, is called its **support.**

5. Graphically, we represent vectors by directed line segments. A directed line segment $\overrightarrow{OP}$ has direction from O to P. P is called its **terminal point** (or terminus) and O is called its **initial point**.

Analytically, a vector is represented by a letter with an arrow on top of it, like : $\overrightarrow{a}, \overrightarrow{b}, \overrightarrow{c}$ etc.

Note: Any vector has (i) magnitude, (ii) direction and (iii) support. The magnitude of a vector is a scalar associated with it. More precisely, we have :

The modulus or magnitude of a vector is the positive number which is the measure of its length. For vector $\left|\overrightarrow{A}\right|$, its magnitude is denoted by $\left|\overrightarrow{A}\right|$.

6. Let P be any point in space having coordinates (x, y, z) with respect to origin O $(0, 0, 0)$. Then the vector $\overrightarrow{OP}$ with O as its initial and P as its terminal point is called the position vector of the point P with respect to O.

$$\left|\overrightarrow{OP}\right| = \sqrt{x^2 + y^2 + z^2}$$

7. A vector whose initial and terminal points coincide is called a **zero vector**. Clearly, the modulus or magnitude of the zero vector is the real number 0, but its direction is indeterminate. Zero vector is also called the **null vector**.

8. Vectors having the same initial point are called **coinitial vectors** (see figure).

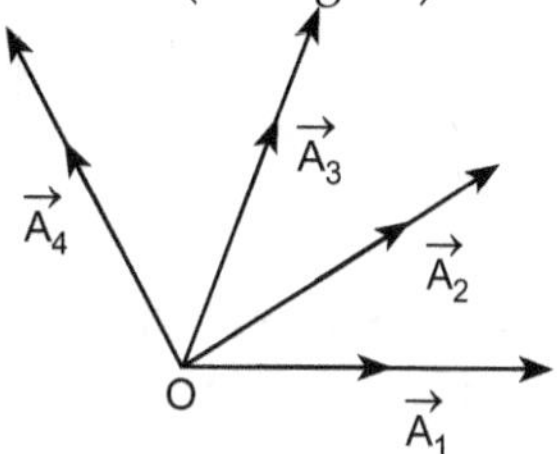

9. Vectors having the same terminal point are called coterminous vectors (see figure).

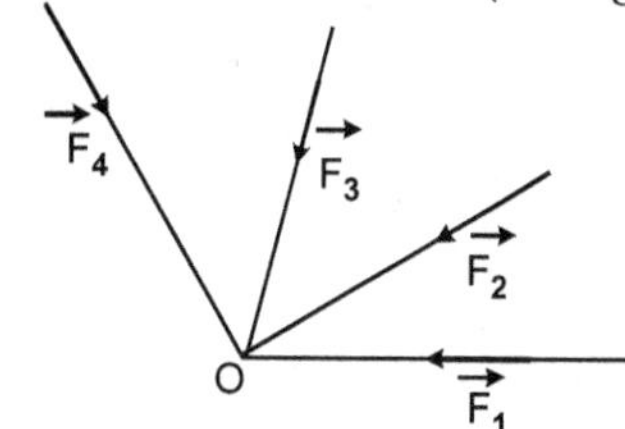

10. A vector whose magnitude is unity is called **unit vector**. The unit vector in the direction of given vector $\overrightarrow{a}$ is denoted by $\hat{a}$.

11. Two vectors $\overrightarrow{a}$ and $\overrightarrow{b}$ are called **equal vectors** if they have same magnitude and direction irrespective of positions of their initial points.

12. A vector whose magnitude is the same as that of a given vector but direction opposite to that of it, is called negative of the given vector.

13. We can consider vectors to lie in 2- or 3-dimensional space, as required by the application. For example, 2-dimensional vectors are considered to be free vectors but with an extra condition imposed - their initial and terminal points lie in the XY plane. Or, if the application is such, we may consider vectors to be lying in a 3-dimensional space. If the context does not make the dimension of the underlying space clear, you should assume that we are in 3-dimensional space.

14. Vector Addition: Vector addition is defined as follows.

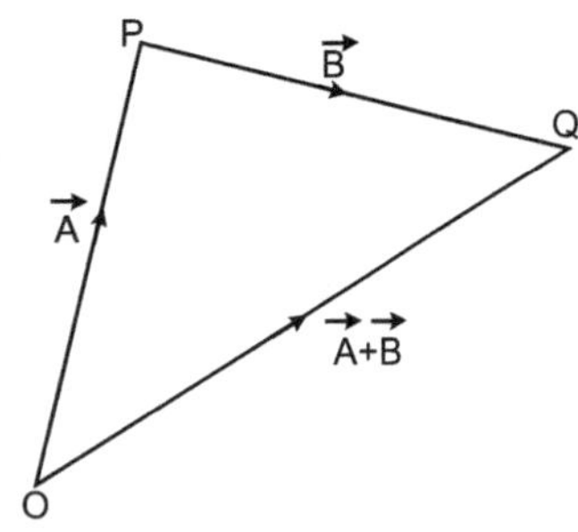

Let, $\vec{A}$, $\vec{B}$ be two given vectors.

Take any point O as the origin and let $\vec{OP} = \vec{A}$, $\vec{PQ} = \vec{B}$, so that the initial point of is the terminal point of $\vec{A}$.

Then, the vector $\vec{OQ}$ is called the sum of the vectors $\vec{A}$ and $\vec{B}$ and we write $\vec{OQ} = \vec{OP} + \vec{PQ} = \vec{A} + \vec{B}$.

Note:

(i) This law is called the **triangle law of addition** : If any two vectors are represented completely by two sides of a triangle taken in the same order, then the resultant of the two vectors is represented both in magnitude and direction by the third side of the triangle taken in the opposite order.

(ii) This sum does not depend upon the choice of O, the origin.

(iii) The triangle law of addition of two vectors is equivalent to the following parallelogram law of addition:

$$\vec{OC} = \vec{a} + \vec{b}$$

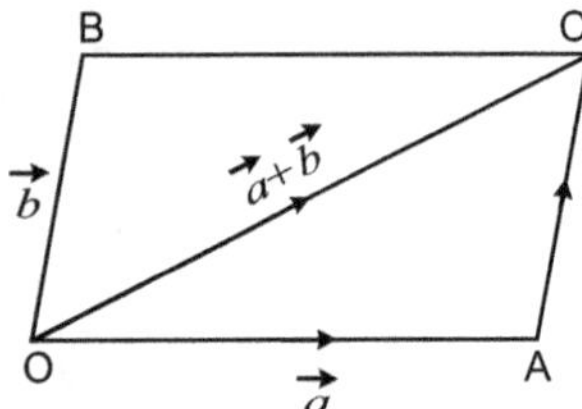

15. Laws of Vector Addition: The laws of addition of vectors are given by theorems 1 and 2 below.

Theorem 1: If $\vec{a}, \vec{b}, \vec{c}$ are any three vectors, then the following holds:

(i) $\vec{a} + \vec{b} = \vec{b} + \vec{a}$, i.e., vector addition is commutative.

(ii) $\vec{a} + \left(\vec{b} + \vec{c}\right) = \left(\vec{a} + \vec{b}\right) + \vec{c}$, i.e., vector addition is associative.

Theorem 2: For any vector $\vec{a}$,

(i) $\vec{a} + \vec{0} = \vec{0} + \vec{a} = \vec{a}$, where $\vec{0}$ denotes the zero vector and is called the **additive identity**.

(ii) $\vec{a} + \left(-\vec{a}\right) = \left(-\vec{a}\right) + \vec{a} = \vec{0}$ where $\left(\vec{a}\right)$ is called the **additive inverse**.

16. Vector Subtraction: The difference of vectors $\vec{a}$ and $\vec{b}$ denoted by $\vec{a} - \vec{b}$ is a vector, which when added to $\vec{b}$ gives the vector $\vec{a}$.

Graphically,

$$\vec{OP} = \vec{a}, \vec{PQ} = \vec{b}, \vec{PQ'} = -\vec{b}$$

$$\vec{OQ'} = \vec{OP} + \vec{PQ'} = \vec{a} - \vec{b}$$

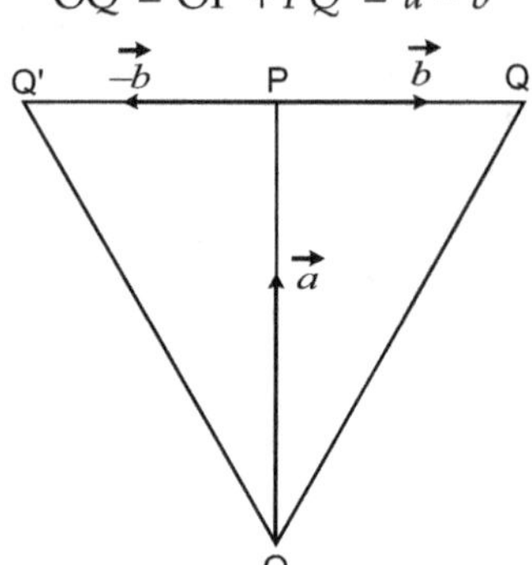

17. Scalar Multiplication of a Vector: The multiplication of a vector $\vec{a}$ by a scalar m is a vector $m\vec{a}$, whose

(i) Magnitude is $|m|$ times that of the magnitude of $\vec{a}$

(ii) Direction is the same as that of $\vec{a}$ if $m > 0$, and opposite to that of $\vec{a}$ if $m < 0$.

For example, $5\vec{a}$ is a vector whose magnitude is 5 times that of $\vec{a}$ and has the same direction as that of $\vec{a}$.

18. Laws of Scalar Multiplication:

Theorem: Let $\vec{a}$ be any vector and m, n, any scalars. Then, the following holds :

(i) $\vec{OA} = \vec{0}$ (ii) $(-1)\vec{a} = -\vec{a}$

(iii) $m(-\vec{a}) = (-m)\vec{a} = -(m\vec{a})$

(iv) $m(n)\vec{a} = (mn)\vec{a}$

(v) $(m + n)\vec{a} = m\vec{a} + n\vec{a}$

19. $\vec{a}$ is parallel to $\vec{b}$ if $\vec{a} = \lambda\vec{b}$ where λ is a scalar.

20. Components of a Vector in Three-Dimensions: Let OX, OY and OZ be three mutually perpendicular lines taken as the coordinate axes and let P(x, y, z) be any point.

Through P, draw planes parallel to the YZ-plane, ZX-plane and XY-plane to meet the X-axis, Y-axis and Z-axis in L, M and N respectively.

If $\hat{i}, \hat{j}, \hat{k}$ are the unit vectors along OX, OY and OZ respectively, then $\overrightarrow{OL} = x\hat{i}$, $\overrightarrow{OM} = y\hat{j}$ and $\overrightarrow{ON} = z\hat{k}$ are the components of $\overrightarrow{OP}$ along OX, OY and OZ respectively.

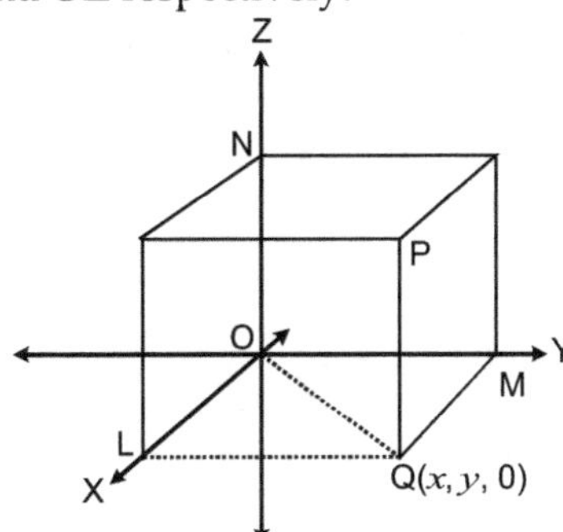

The magnitude of $\overrightarrow{OP}$ is

$$OP = \sqrt{x^2 + y^2 + z^2}$$

(using length of diagonal of cuboid)

Similarly, the components of $\overrightarrow{PQ}$, which is a join of $P(x_1, y_1, z_1)$ and $Q(x_2, y_2, z_2)$ are

$$(x_2 - x_1)\hat{i}, (y_2 - y_1)\hat{j}, (z_2 - z_1)\hat{k}$$

21. **Section Formula for Internal Division:** If P and Q be two points with position vectors $\overrightarrow{a}$ and $\overrightarrow{b}$ respectively and let R be a point dividing PQ internally in the ratio $m : n$. Then, $\overrightarrow{OR}$, the position vector of R, is given by $\overrightarrow{OR} = \dfrac{m\overrightarrow{b} + n\overrightarrow{a}}{m + n}$, where O is the origin.

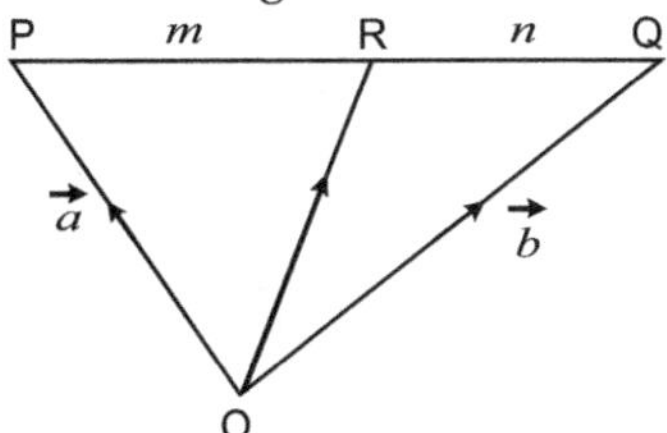

22. **Section Formula for External Division:** If $\overrightarrow{a}$, $\overrightarrow{b}$ be the position vectors of the points P and Q respectively and let R divide their join PQ in the ratio $m : n$ ($m \neq n$) externally. Then, the position vector of R is $\dfrac{m\overrightarrow{b} - n\overrightarrow{a}}{m - n}$

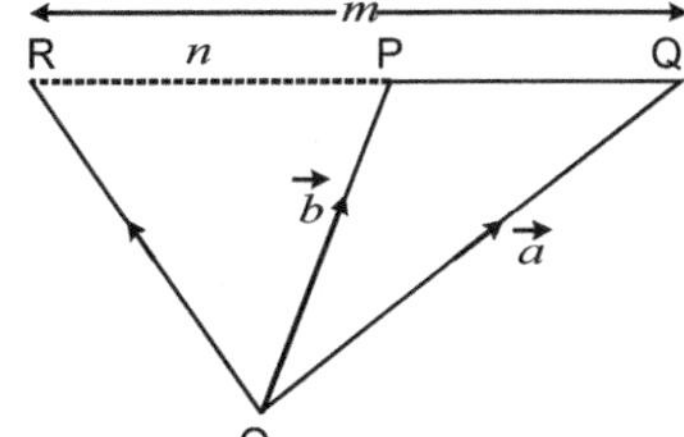

23. **Scalar Product:** For real numbers, multiplication is defined in a unique way, but for vectors, there are two ways to multiply — scalar (or dot) product and vector (or cross) product.

As is evident from the name, the former is a scalar quantity and the latter is a vector quantity. The scalar product is defined as follows:

Definition: The scalar product $\overrightarrow{a} \cdot \overrightarrow{b}$ of two vectors $\overrightarrow{a}$ and $\overrightarrow{b}$ is defined as $\overrightarrow{a} \cdot \overrightarrow{b} = ab \cos \theta$, where θ is the angle between $\overrightarrow{a}$ and $\overrightarrow{b}$.

This product is also called the dot product because of the notation involved in the multiplication process.

For example, if $\hat{i}$ and $\hat{j}$ are unit vectors along OX and OY in the Cartesian co-ordinate system, then,

$$\hat{i} \cdot \hat{j} = 1 \times 1 \times \cos 90° = 1 \times 0 = 0$$

similarly, $\quad \hat{j} \cdot \hat{k} = \hat{k} \cdot \hat{i} = 0$

Note: From the definition of a scalar product, we make a few observations:

(i) Two vectors $\overrightarrow{a}$ and $\overrightarrow{b}$ are perpendicular if the angle θ between them is 90°.

In this case, $\overrightarrow{a} \cdot \overrightarrow{b} = 0$

Thus, $\overrightarrow{a}$ and $\overrightarrow{b}$ are perpendicular, if $\overrightarrow{a} \cdot \overrightarrow{b} = 0$

(ii) For like vectors $\overrightarrow{a}$ and $\overrightarrow{b}$, $\overrightarrow{a} \cdot \overrightarrow{b} = \left|\overrightarrow{a}\right|\left|\overrightarrow{b}\right|$ For unlike vectors $\overrightarrow{a}$ and $\overrightarrow{b}$, $\overrightarrow{a} \cdot \overrightarrow{b} = -\left|\overrightarrow{a}\right|\left|\overrightarrow{b}\right|$ since the respective angles are 0° and π radians.

(iii) For any vector $\overrightarrow{a}$, $\overrightarrow{a} \cdot \overrightarrow{a} = \left|\overrightarrow{a}\right|^2$

(iv) If $\overrightarrow{a}$ and $\overrightarrow{b}$ are any vectors, then the angle θ between them is

$$\cos \theta = \frac{\overrightarrow{a} \cdot \overrightarrow{b}}{|\overrightarrow{a}||\overrightarrow{b}|} = \frac{\overrightarrow{a}}{|\overrightarrow{a}|} = \frac{\overrightarrow{b}}{|\overrightarrow{b}|} \hat{a} \cdot \hat{b}.$$

(v) If $\overrightarrow{a} = a_1\hat{i} + a_2\hat{j} + a_3\hat{k}$, $\overrightarrow{b} = b_1\hat{i} + b_2\hat{j} + b_3\hat{k}$, then $\overrightarrow{a} \cdot \overrightarrow{b} = a_1 b_1 + a_2 b_2 + a_3 b_3$

(vi) Scalar product of two vectors is a real number.

(vii) The scalar product of vectors has the following properties :

Theorem: If $\overrightarrow{a}$, $\overrightarrow{b}$ and $\overrightarrow{c}$ are three vectors and n is a scalar, then

(i) $\overrightarrow{a} \cdot \overrightarrow{b} = \overrightarrow{b} \cdot \overrightarrow{a}$ (scalar product of vectors is commutative)

(ii) $\overrightarrow{a} \cdot (n\overrightarrow{b}) = (n\overrightarrow{a}) \cdot \overrightarrow{b} = n(\overrightarrow{a} \cdot \overrightarrow{b})$

(iii) $\vec{a} \cdot \left(\vec{b} + \vec{c}\right) = \vec{a} \cdot \vec{b} + \vec{a} \cdot \vec{c}$

(scalar product distributes itself over the addition of vectors.)

24. Vector Product of Two Vectors: The vector product of two vectors is a vector, and it is defined as follows:

Definition: If $\vec{a}$ and $\vec{b}$ are two vectors, then their vector product (or cross product) $\vec{a} \times \vec{b}$ (taken in this order) is a vector $\vec{c}$ whose magnitude is $ab \sin \theta$, where θ is the angle between $\vec{a}$ and $\vec{b}$ and has a direction perpendicular to the plane of the vectors $\vec{a}$ and $\vec{b}$ such that $\vec{a}, \vec{b}$ and $\vec{c}$ form a right-handed system.

If $\hat{n}$ is the unit vector in the direction perpendicular to $\vec{a}$ and $\vec{b}$ so that $\vec{a}, \vec{b}, \hat{n}$ form a right-handed system, then,

$$\vec{c} = \vec{a} \times \vec{b} = |\vec{a}| |\vec{b}| \sin \theta \, \hat{n}, \, 0 < \theta < 2\pi.$$

If $\vec{a}$ and $\vec{b}$ are like vectors, then obviously, $\theta = 0°$ and if $\vec{a}, \vec{b}$ are unlike vectors, then $\theta = \pi$ in that case, $\vec{a} \times \vec{b} = 0$.

Same is the case, when $\vec{a}$ and $\vec{b}$ are collinear.

Therefore, if $\vec{a}, \vec{b}$ are collinear, then $\vec{a} \times \vec{b} = 0$

Note, that $\vec{a} \times \vec{b}$ can vanish in some other cases too.

Geometrically, $|\vec{a} \times \vec{b}|$ represents the area of a parallelogram with sides $\vec{a}$ and $\vec{b}$.

Let h be the height of the parallelogram with sides $\vec{a}$ and $\vec{b}$.

Then the area of the parallelogram = hA.

But $h = |\vec{b}| \sin \theta$ is the angle between $\vec{a}$ and $\vec{b}$

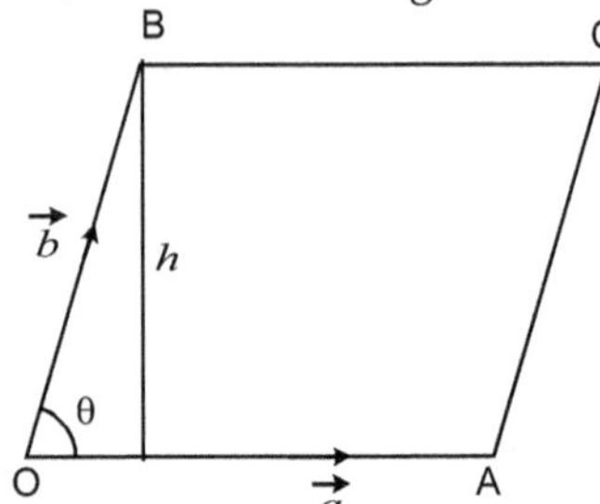

Therefore, the area of the parallelogram

$$= b(\sin \theta) \, a = ab \sin \theta = |\vec{a} \times \vec{b}|$$

25. We have the following relationship between scalar and vector for any two vectors and

$$|\vec{a} \times \vec{b}|^2 + (\vec{a} \cdot \vec{b})^2 = a^2 b^2$$

26. Properties of Vector Product

The properties are given by the following theorems :

Theorem 1: $\vec{a}$ and $\vec{b}$ are any two vectors and α is a scalar, then the following hold :

(i) $\vec{a} \times \vec{b} = -\vec{b} \times \vec{a}$, i.e., vector product is not commutative.

(ii) $\alpha(\vec{b} \times \vec{a}) = (\alpha\vec{a}) \times \vec{b} = \vec{a} \times (\alpha\vec{b})$

(iii) $\vec{a} \times \vec{b} = 0$

Theorem 2: Let $\vec{a}, \vec{b}, \vec{c}$ be any three vectors. Then $\vec{a} \times (\vec{b} + \vec{c}) = \vec{a} \times \vec{b} + \vec{a} \times \vec{c}$

Corollary: If $\vec{a} = a_1 \hat{i} + a_2 \hat{j} + a_3 \hat{k}$ and $\vec{b} = b_1 \hat{i} + b_2 \hat{j} + b_3 \hat{k}$, then,

$$\vec{a} \times \vec{b} = \begin{vmatrix} \hat{i} & \hat{j} & \hat{k} \\ a_1 & a_2 & a_3 \\ b_1 & b_2 & b_3 \end{vmatrix}$$

27. Two non-zero vectors $\vec{a}$ and $\vec{b}$ are parallel if $\vec{a} \times \vec{b} = 0$.

28. Area of triangle whose sides are $\vec{a}$ and $\vec{b}$ is

$$\frac{1}{2} |\vec{a} \times \vec{b}|$$

29. If $\hat{i}, \hat{j}, \hat{k}$ are vectors along X, Y and Z-axes then $\hat{i} \times \hat{i} = 0, \, \hat{j} \times \hat{j} = 0, \, \hat{k} \times \hat{k} = 0, \hat{i} \times \hat{j} = \hat{k}, \hat{j} \times \hat{k} = \hat{i}, \hat{k} \times \hat{i} = \hat{j}$

30. Unit vector $\hat{n}$ perpendicular to $\vec{a}$ and $\vec{b}$ is

$$\hat{n} = \frac{\vec{a} \times \vec{b}}{|\vec{a} \times \vec{b}|}$$

31. For vectors $\vec{a} \cdot \vec{b} = 0 \Leftrightarrow \vec{a} = 0, \vec{b} = 0$ or $\vec{a} \perp \vec{b}$.

32. Projection of $\vec{a}$ along $\vec{b}$ is $\dfrac{\vec{a} \cdot \vec{b}}{|\vec{b}|}$ and projection vector of $\vec{a}$ on $\vec{b}$ $(\neq \vec{0})$ (component of $\vec{a}$ along $\vec{b}$) is $\left(\dfrac{\vec{a} \cdot \vec{b}}{|\vec{b}|}\right) \vec{b}$

33. If $\hat{i}, \hat{j}, \hat{k}$ are unit vectors along X, Y and Z-axes then $\hat{i}^2 = \hat{j}^2 = \hat{k}^2 = 1, \, \hat{i} \cdot \hat{j} = 0, \hat{j} \cdot \hat{k} = 0, \, \hat{k} \cdot \hat{i} = 0$.

Multiple Choice Questions

1. The vector in the direction of the vector $\hat{i} - 2\hat{j} + 2\hat{k}$ that has magnitude 9 is:

[NCERT Exemplar]

(a) $\hat{i} - 2\hat{j} + 2\hat{k}$

(b) $\dfrac{\hat{i} - 2\hat{j} + 2\hat{k}}{3}$

(c) $3(\hat{i} - 2\hat{j} + 2\hat{k})$

(d) $9(\hat{i} - 2\hat{j} + 2\hat{k})$

Sol. (c) $3(\hat{i} - 2\hat{j} + 2\hat{k})$

Explanation :

Let $\vec{a} = \hat{i} - 2\hat{j} + 2\hat{k}$

Any vector in the direction of a vector $\vec{a}$ is given by $\dfrac{\vec{a}}{|\vec{a}|}$.

$$= \dfrac{\hat{i} - 2\hat{j} + 2\hat{k}}{\sqrt{1^2 + 2^2 + 2^2}} = \dfrac{\hat{i} - 2\hat{j} + 2\hat{k}}{3}$$

$\therefore$ Vector in the direction of with magnitude 9

$$= 9 \cdot \dfrac{\hat{i} - 2\hat{j} + 2\hat{k}}{3}$$

$$= 3(\hat{i} - 2\hat{j} + 2\hat{k}).$$

2. The vector having initial and terminal points as $(2, 5, 0)$ and $(-3, 7, 4)$, respectively is:

[NCERT Exemplar]

(a) $-\hat{i} + 12\hat{j} + 4\hat{k}$

(b) $5\hat{i} + 2\hat{j} - 4\hat{k}$

(c) $-5\hat{i} + 2\hat{j} + 4\hat{k}$

(d) $\hat{i} + \hat{j} + \hat{k}$

Sol. (c) $-5\hat{i} + 2\hat{j} + 4\hat{k}$

Explanation :

Required vector

$$= (-3 - 2)\hat{i} + (7 - 5)\hat{j} + (4 - 0)\hat{k}$$

$$= -5\hat{i} + 2\hat{j} + 4\hat{k}$$

3. The vectors $\lambda\hat{i} + \hat{j} + 2\hat{k}, \hat{i} + \lambda\hat{j} - \hat{k}$ and $2\hat{i} - \hat{j} + \lambda\hat{k}$ are coplanar, if:

[NCERT Exemplar]

(a) $\lambda = -2$

(b) $\lambda = 0$

(c) $\lambda = 1$

(d) $\lambda = -1$

Sol. (a) $\lambda = -2$

Explanation :

Let $\vec{a} = \lambda\hat{i} + \hat{j} + 2\hat{k}$, $\vec{b} = \hat{i} + \lambda\hat{j} - \hat{k}$ and $\vec{c} = 2\hat{i} - \hat{j} + \lambda\hat{k}$

For $\vec{a}$, $\vec{b}$ and $\vec{c}$ to be coplanar,

$$\begin{vmatrix} \lambda & 1 & 2 \\ 1 & \lambda & -1 \\ 2 & -1 & \lambda \end{vmatrix} = 0$$

$\Rightarrow \lambda(\lambda^2 - 1) - 1(\lambda + 2) + 2(-1 - 2\lambda) = 0$

$\Rightarrow \lambda^3 - \lambda - \lambda - 2 - 2 - 4\lambda = 0$

$\Rightarrow \lambda^3 - 6\lambda - 4 = 0$

$\Rightarrow (\lambda + 2)(\lambda^2 - 2\lambda - 2) = 0$

$\Rightarrow \lambda = -2$ or $\lambda = \dfrac{2 \pm \sqrt{12}}{2}$

$\Rightarrow \lambda = -2$ or $\lambda = \dfrac{2 + 2\sqrt{3}}{2} = 1 \pm \sqrt{3}$

4. If the vectors $\vec{a} = -2\hat{i} + 3\hat{j} + y\hat{k}$ and $\vec{b} = x\hat{i} - 6\hat{j} + 2\hat{k}$ are collinear, then the value of $x + y$ is:

(a) 4

(b) 5

(c) -3

(d) 3

Sol. (d) 3

Explanation :

Vectors $\vec{a}$ and $\vec{b}$ are collinear.

So $\dfrac{-2}{x} = \dfrac{3}{-6} = \dfrac{y}{2}$

$\Rightarrow x = 4$ and $y = -1$

so $x + y = 3$.

5. If $\vec{a} \cdot \vec{a} = 0$ then $\vec{a}$ is a:

(a) Proper vector

(b) Free vector

(c) Null vector

(d) None of these

Sol. (c) Null vector

Explanation :

By property of vectors, if $\vec{a} \cdot \vec{a} = 0$, then $\vec{a}$ is called null vector.

6. The value of p for which $p(\hat{i}+\hat{j}+\hat{k})$ is a unit vector is:

(a) 0   (b) $\pm\dfrac{1}{\sqrt{3}}$

(c) 1   (d) $\sqrt{3}$

Sol. (b) $\pm\dfrac{1}{\sqrt{3}}$

Explanation :

As $p(\hat{i}+\hat{j}+\hat{k})$ is a unit vector. So,

$$|p(\hat{i}+\hat{j}+\hat{k})| = 1$$

$$\Rightarrow \quad |p|\,|\hat{i}+\hat{j}+\hat{k}| = 1$$

$$\Rightarrow \quad |p|\sqrt{1^2+1^2+1^2} = 1$$

$$\Rightarrow \quad |p|\sqrt{3} = 1$$

$$\Rightarrow \quad |p| = \pm\dfrac{1}{\sqrt{3}}.$$

7. Find the magnitude of the vector $3\hat{i}+2\hat{j}+12\hat{k}$:

(a) $\sqrt{157}$ (b) $4\sqrt{11}$

(c) $\sqrt{213}$ (d) $9\sqrt{3}$

Sol. (a) $\sqrt{157}$

Explanation :

Magnitude of $3\hat{i}+2\hat{j}+12\hat{k}$

$$= \sqrt{3^2+2^2+12^2} = \sqrt{157}$$

8. Find the magnitudes of the vectors given below:

$$\vec{a} = 2\hat{i}+3\hat{j}+\hat{k},$$

$$\vec{b} = \hat{i}-2\hat{j}-3\hat{k},$$

$$\vec{c} = 5\hat{i}+2\hat{j}+4\hat{k}$$

(a) $\sqrt{3},\sqrt{15},1$ (b) $\sqrt{35},\sqrt{2},9$

(c) $1, 1, 1$ (d) $\sqrt{14},\sqrt{14},\sqrt{45}$

Sol. (d) $\sqrt{14},\sqrt{14},\sqrt{45}$

Explanation :

The given vectors are,

$$\vec{a} = 2\hat{i}+3\hat{j}+\hat{k}$$

$$\vec{b} = \hat{i}-2\hat{j}-3\hat{k}$$

$$\vec{c} = 5\hat{i}+2\hat{j}+4\hat{k}$$

Magnitude of $\vec{a}$,

$$|\vec{a}| = \sqrt{2^2+3^2+1^2}$$

$$= \sqrt{4+9+1}$$

$$= \sqrt{14}$$

Magnitude of $\vec{b}$,

$$|\vec{b}| = \sqrt{1^2+(-2)^2+(-3)^2}$$

$$= \sqrt{1+4+9}$$

$$= \sqrt{14}$$

Magnitude of $\vec{c}$,

$$|\vec{c}| = \sqrt{5^2+2^2+4^2}$$

$$= \sqrt{25+4+16}$$

$$= \sqrt{45}$$

Hence, the required magnitudes of the given vectors are $\sqrt{14},\sqrt{14}$ and $\sqrt{45}$.

So the correct option is (d).

9. Find the vector components of a vector having the initial point (6, 4) and the terminal point $(-2, 7)$:

(a) $2\hat{i},\hat{j}$ (b) $\hat{i},-7\hat{j}$

(c) $-8\hat{i},3\hat{j}$ (d) $-3\hat{i},8\hat{j}$

Sol. (c) $-8\hat{i},3\hat{j}$

Explanation :

Let, the initial point of the vector is A (6, 4) and the terminal point of the vector is B$(-2, 7)$.

∴ The required vector is,

$$\vec{AB} = (-2-6)\,\hat{i}+(7-4)\,\hat{j}$$

$$= -8\hat{i}+3\hat{j}$$

Hence, the required vector components of the vector are $-8\hat{i}$ and $3\hat{j}$.

So the correct option is (c).

10. The unit vector in the direction of the vector $\vec{a} = 2\hat{i}+\hat{j}+3\hat{k}$ is :

(a) $\dfrac{2}{\sqrt{7}}\hat{i}+\dfrac{1}{\sqrt{7}}\hat{j}+\dfrac{1}{\sqrt{7}}\hat{k}$

(b) $\dfrac{2}{\sqrt{14}}\hat{i}+\dfrac{1}{\sqrt{14}}\hat{j}+\dfrac{3}{\sqrt{14}}\hat{k}$

(c) $\dfrac{1}{\sqrt{14}}\hat{i}+\dfrac{1}{\sqrt{14}}\hat{j}+\dfrac{1}{\sqrt{14}}\hat{k}$

(d) $\dfrac{4}{\sqrt{14}}\hat{i}+\dfrac{1}{\sqrt{14}}\hat{j}+\dfrac{1}{\sqrt{14}}\hat{k}$

Sol. (b) $\dfrac{2}{\sqrt{14}}\hat{i}+\dfrac{1}{\sqrt{14}}\hat{j}+\dfrac{3}{\sqrt{14}}\hat{k}$

Explanation :

Let, the unit vector in the direction of the vector

$$\vec{a}=2\hat{j}+\hat{j}+3\hat{k} \text{ is } \hat{a}.$$

The unit vector $\hat{a}$ of the vector $\vec{a}$ is defined by

$$\hat{a}=\dfrac{\vec{a}}{|\vec{a}|}.$$

So, the magnitude of $\vec{a}$ is,

$$|\vec{a}|=\sqrt{2^2+1^2+3^2}$$

$$=\sqrt{4+1+9}$$

$$=\sqrt{14}$$

$\therefore$ The required unit vector is,

$$\hat{a}=\dfrac{\vec{a}}{|\vec{a}|}$$

$$=\dfrac{2\hat{i}+\hat{j}+3\hat{k}}{\sqrt{14}}$$

$$=\dfrac{2\hat{i}}{\sqrt{14}}+\dfrac{\hat{j}}{\sqrt{14}}+\dfrac{3\hat{k}}{\sqrt{14}}$$

$$=\dfrac{2}{\sqrt{14}}\hat{i}+\dfrac{1}{\sqrt{14}}\hat{j}+\dfrac{3}{\sqrt{14}}\hat{k}.$$

So the correct option is (b).

11. What is the unit vector in the direction of the vector $\overrightarrow{AB}$, where A and B are the points (2, 1, 2) and (1, 1, 1) respectively.

(a) $-\dfrac{1}{\sqrt{2}}\hat{i}-\dfrac{1}{\sqrt{2}}\hat{k}$

(b) $\dfrac{1}{\sqrt{2}}\hat{i}+\dfrac{1}{\sqrt{2}}\hat{k}$

(c) $\dfrac{1}{\sqrt{2}}\hat{i}-\dfrac{1}{\sqrt{2}}\hat{k}$

(d) $-\dfrac{1}{\sqrt{2}}\hat{i}+\dfrac{1}{\sqrt{2}}\hat{k}$

Sol. (a) $-\dfrac{1}{\sqrt{2}}\hat{i}-\dfrac{1}{\sqrt{2}}\hat{k}$

Explanation :

Given, A(2, 1, 2) and B(1, 1, 1) are the points of the vector $\overrightarrow{AB}$.

The unit vector in the direction of the vector $\overrightarrow{AB}$ is

$$\dfrac{\overrightarrow{AB}}{|\overrightarrow{AB}|}.$$

So, the vector $\overrightarrow{AB}$ is,

$$\overrightarrow{AB}=(1-2)\hat{i}+(1-1)\hat{j}+(1-2)\hat{k}$$

$$=-\hat{i}+0\cdot\hat{j}-\hat{k}$$

$$=-\hat{i}-\hat{k}$$

Magnitude of the vector $\overrightarrow{AB}$,

$$|\overrightarrow{AB}|=\sqrt{(-1)^2+(-1)^2}$$

$$=\sqrt{1+1}$$

$$=\sqrt{2}$$

Hence, the required unit vector is,

$$\dfrac{\overrightarrow{AB}}{|\overrightarrow{AB}|}=\dfrac{-\hat{i}-\hat{k}}{\sqrt{2}}$$

$$=\left(\dfrac{-\hat{i}}{\sqrt{2}}\right)+\left(\dfrac{-\hat{k}}{\sqrt{2}}\right)$$

$$=-\dfrac{1}{\sqrt{2}}\hat{i}-\dfrac{1}{\sqrt{2}}\hat{k}.$$

So the correct option is (a).

12. The direction cosines of the vector $\vec{a}=5\hat{i}+7\hat{j}+3\hat{k}$ are:

(a) $\dfrac{1}{\sqrt{83}},\dfrac{3}{\sqrt{83}},\dfrac{9}{\sqrt{83}}$

(b) $\dfrac{5}{\sqrt{83}},\dfrac{7}{\sqrt{83}},\dfrac{3}{\sqrt{83}}$

(c) $\dfrac{5}{\sqrt{83}},\dfrac{1}{\sqrt{83}},\dfrac{-3}{\sqrt{83}}$

(d) $\dfrac{5}{\sqrt{83}},\dfrac{-7}{\sqrt{83}},\dfrac{-3}{\sqrt{83}}$

Sol. (b) $\dfrac{5}{\sqrt{83}},\dfrac{7}{\sqrt{83}},\dfrac{3}{\sqrt{83}}$

Explanation :

The given vector is

$$\vec{a}=5\hat{i}+7\hat{j}+3\hat{k}$$

The magnitude of the vector $\vec{a}$

$$|\vec{a}|=\sqrt{5^2+7^2+3^2}$$

$$=\sqrt{25+49+9}$$

$$=\sqrt{83}$$

Hence, the direction cosines of the vector $\vec{a}$ are

$$\left(\frac{5}{\sqrt{83}}, \frac{7}{\sqrt{83}}, \frac{3}{\sqrt{83}}\right).$$

So the correct option is (b).

13. The direction cosines of the vector joining the points L(2, 2, 3) and M(– 3, 1, 1) directed from L and M are :

(a) $\left(-\dfrac{5}{\sqrt{30}}, -\dfrac{1}{\sqrt{30}}, -\dfrac{2}{\sqrt{30}}\right)$

(b) $\left(\dfrac{5}{\sqrt{30}}, \dfrac{1}{\sqrt{30}}, \dfrac{2}{\sqrt{30}}\right)$

(c) $\left(\dfrac{5}{\sqrt{30}}, -\dfrac{1}{\sqrt{30}}, -\dfrac{2}{\sqrt{30}}\right)$

(d) $\left(-\dfrac{5}{\sqrt{30}}, -\dfrac{1}{\sqrt{30}}, \dfrac{2}{\sqrt{30}}\right)$

Sol. (a) $\left(-\dfrac{5}{\sqrt{30}}, -\dfrac{1}{\sqrt{30}}, -\dfrac{2}{\sqrt{30}}\right)$

Explanation :

The given points are L(2, 2, 3) and M(– 3, 1, 1)

Therefore, the vector $\overrightarrow{LM}$ is,

$$\overrightarrow{LM} = (-3-2)\hat{i} + (1-2)\hat{j} + (1-3)\hat{k}$$

$$= -5\hat{i} - \hat{j} - 2\hat{k}$$

The magnitude of the vector $\overrightarrow{LM}$,

$$|\overrightarrow{LM}| = \sqrt{(-5)^2 + (-1)^2 + (-2)^2}$$

$$= \sqrt{25+1+4}$$

$$= \sqrt{30}$$

Hence, the direction cosines of the vector $\overrightarrow{LM}$ are, $\left(-\dfrac{5}{\sqrt{30}}, -\dfrac{1}{\sqrt{30}}, -\dfrac{2}{\sqrt{30}}\right).$

So the correct option is (a).

14. If $|\vec{a}| = 4$ and $-3 \le \lambda \le 2$, then the range of $|\lambda \vec{a}|$ is: **[NCERT Exemplar]**

(a) [0, 8] (b) [– 12, 8]
(c) [0, 12] (d) [8, 12]

Sol. (c) [0, 12]

Explanation :

We have, $|\vec{a}| = 4$ and $-3 \le \lambda \le 2$

$\therefore$ $\quad |\lambda \vec{a}| = |\lambda| |\vec{a}| = \lambda|4|$

$\Rightarrow \quad |\lambda \vec{a}| = |-3|4 = 12$, at $\lambda = -3$

$\quad |\lambda \vec{a}| = |0|4 = 0$, at $\lambda = 0$

and $\quad |\lambda \vec{a}| = |2|4 = 8$, at $\lambda = 2$

So, the range of $|\lambda \vec{a}|$ is [0, 12].

Alternative Method:

Since, $\quad -3 \le \lambda \le 2$

$\quad 0 \le |\lambda| \le 3$

$\Rightarrow \quad 0 \le 4|\lambda| \le 12$

$\quad |\lambda \vec{a}| \in [0, 12].$

15. The orthogonal projection of $\vec{a}$ on $\vec{b}$ is:

(a) $\dfrac{(\vec{a}\cdot\vec{b})\,\vec{a}}{|\vec{a}|^2}$ (b) $\dfrac{(\vec{a}\cdot\vec{b})\,\vec{b}}{|\vec{b}|^2}$

(c) $\dfrac{\vec{a}}{|\vec{a}|}$ (d) $\dfrac{\vec{b}}{|\vec{b}|}$

Sol. (b) $\dfrac{(\vec{a}\cdot\vec{b})\,\vec{b}}{|\vec{b}|^2}$

Explanation :

Projection of $\vec{a}$ on $\vec{b}$

$$= \frac{(\vec{a}\cdot\vec{b})}{\vec{b}} = \frac{(\vec{a}\cdot\vec{b})\,\vec{b}}{\vec{b}\cdot\vec{b}}$$

$$= \frac{(\vec{a}\cdot\vec{b})\,\vec{b}}{|\vec{b}|^2}$$

16. The position vector of the point which divides the join of points $2\vec{a} - 3\vec{b}$ and $\vec{a} + \vec{b}$ in the ratio 3 : 1, is: **[NCERT Exemplar]**

(a) $\dfrac{3\vec{a} - 2\vec{b}}{2}$ (b) $\dfrac{7\vec{a} - 8\vec{b}}{4}$

(c) $\dfrac{3\vec{a}}{4}$ (d) $\dfrac{5\vec{a}}{4}$

Sol. (d) $\dfrac{5\vec{a}}{4}$

Explanation :

Let the position vector of the point R divides the join of points $2\vec{a} - 3\vec{b}$ and $\vec{a} + \vec{b}$.

$\therefore$ Position vector R $= \dfrac{3(\vec{a}+\vec{b})+1(2\vec{a}-3\vec{b})}{3+1}$

Since, the position vector of a point R dividing the line segment joining the points P and Q, whose position vectors are $\vec{p}$ and $\vec{q}$ in the ratio $m : n$ internally, is given by $\dfrac{m\vec{q}+n\vec{p}}{m+n}$.

$\therefore \qquad\qquad R = \dfrac{5\vec{a}}{4}$.

17. Which of the following is true?

(a) $\vec{a}$ and $-\vec{a}$ are collinear

(b) Two collinear vectors are always equal in magnitude

(c) Two vectors having same magnitude are collinear

(d) Two collinear vectors having the same magnitude are equal

Sol. (a) $\vec{a}$ and $-\vec{a}$ are collinear

Explanation :

By properties of vector option (a) is correct.

18. Find the scalar components of a vector having the initial point $(5, 9)$ and $(-7, 4)$.

(a) $12, -5$ (b) $-12, 5$

(c) $-12, -5$ (d) $12, 5$

Sol. (c) $-12, -5$

Explanation :

Let, the initial point of the vector is A$(5, 9)$ and the terminal point of the vector is B$(-7, 4)$.

$\therefore$ The required vector is,

$$\vec{AB} = (-7-5)\,\hat{i}+(4-9)\,\hat{j} = -12\,\hat{i}-5\,\hat{j}$$

Hence, the required scalar components of the vector are -12 and -5.

So the correct option is (c).

19. The projection of the vector $\hat{i}+\hat{j}+\hat{k}$ along the vector $\hat{j}$ is:

(a) 1 (b) 0

(c) 2 (d) -1

Sol. (a) 1

Explanation :

Projection of the vector $\hat{i}+\hat{j}+\hat{k}$ along vector

$$\hat{j} = \dfrac{(\hat{i}+\hat{j}+\hat{k}).\,\hat{j}}{|\hat{j}|} = \dfrac{1}{1} = 1.$$

20. ABCD is a rhombus whose diagonals intersect at E. Then $\vec{EA} + \vec{EB} + \vec{EC} + \vec{ED}$ equals :

(a) $\vec{0}$ (b) $\vec{AD}$

(c) $2\vec{BC}$ (d) $2\vec{AD}$

Sol. (a) $\vec{0}$

Explanation :

The correct option is (a).

21. The angle between two vectors $\vec{a}$ and $\vec{b}$ with magnitudes $\sqrt{3}$ and 4, respectively and $\vec{a}\cdot\vec{b} = 2\sqrt{3}$ is: [NCERT Exemplar]

(a) $\dfrac{\pi}{6}$ (b) $\dfrac{\pi}{3}$

(c) $\dfrac{\pi}{2}$ (d) $\dfrac{5\pi}{2}$

Sol. (b) $\dfrac{\pi}{3}$

Explanation :

Here, $|\vec{a}| = \sqrt{3}, |\vec{b}| = 4$ and $\vec{a}\cdot\vec{b} = 2\sqrt{3}$ [given]

We know that,

$$\vec{a}\cdot\vec{b} = |\vec{a}||\vec{b}|\cos\theta$$

$$\Rightarrow \qquad 2\sqrt{3} = \sqrt{3}\cdot4\cdot\cos\theta$$

$$\Rightarrow \qquad \cos\theta = \dfrac{2\sqrt{3}}{4\sqrt{3}} = \dfrac{1}{2}$$

$$\therefore \qquad\qquad \theta = \dfrac{\pi}{3}.$$

22. Find the value of λ such that the vectors $\vec{a} = 2\hat{i}+\lambda\hat{j}+\hat{k}$ and $\vec{b} = \hat{i}+2\hat{j}+3\hat{k}$ are orthogonal: [NCERT Exemplar]

(a) 0 (b) 1

(c) $\dfrac{3}{2}$ (d) $\dfrac{-5}{2}$

Sol. (d) $\dfrac{-5}{2}$

Explanation :

Since, two non-zero vectors $\vec{a}$ and $\vec{b}$ are orthgonal *i.e.*, $\vec{a}\cdot\vec{b} = 0$.

$$\therefore \qquad (2\hat{i}+\lambda\hat{j}+\hat{k})\cdot(\hat{i}+2\hat{j}+3\hat{k}) = 0$$

$$\Rightarrow \qquad 2 + 2\lambda + 3 = 0$$

$$\therefore \qquad \lambda = \frac{-5}{2}.$$

23. The value of λ for which the vectors $3\hat{i} - 6\hat{j} + \hat{k}$ and $2\hat{i} - 4\hat{j} + \lambda\hat{k}$ are parallel, is:

[NCERT Exemplar]

(a) $\dfrac{2}{3}$ (b) $\dfrac{3}{2}$

(c) $\dfrac{5}{2}$ (d) $\dfrac{2}{5}$

Sol. (a) $\dfrac{2}{3}$

Explanation :

Since, two vectors are parallel *i.e.*, angle between them is zero.

$$\therefore \ (3\hat{i} - 6\hat{j} + \hat{k}) \cdot (2\hat{i} - 4\hat{j} + \lambda\hat{k})$$

$$= |3\hat{i} - 6\hat{j} + \hat{k}| \cdot |2\hat{i} - 4\hat{j} + \lambda\hat{k}|$$

$$[\because \vec{a} \cdot \vec{b} = |a||b|\cos 0° \Rightarrow \vec{a} \cdot \vec{b} = |\vec{a}||\vec{b}|]$$

$$\Rightarrow \quad 6 + 24 + \lambda = \sqrt{9 + 36 + 1}\,\sqrt{4 + 16 + \lambda^2}$$

$$\Rightarrow \quad 30 + \lambda = \sqrt{46}\,\sqrt{20 + \lambda^2}$$

$$\Rightarrow \quad 900 + \lambda^2 + 60\lambda = 46(20 + \lambda^2)$$

[on squaring both sides]

$$\Rightarrow \quad \lambda^2 + 60\lambda - 46\lambda^2 = 920 - 900$$

$$\Rightarrow \quad -45\lambda^2 + 60\lambda - 20 = 0$$

$$\Rightarrow \quad -45\lambda^2 + 30\lambda + 30\lambda - 20 = 0$$

$$\Rightarrow \quad -15\lambda(3\lambda - 2) + 10(3\lambda - 2) = 0$$

$$\Rightarrow \quad (10 - 15\lambda)(3\lambda - 2) = 0$$

$$\therefore \qquad \lambda = \frac{2}{3}, \frac{2}{3}$$

Alternate Method:

Let $\quad \vec{a} = 3\hat{i} - 6\hat{j} + \hat{k}$ and $\vec{b} = 2\hat{i} - 4\hat{j} + \lambda\hat{k}$

Since, $\qquad \vec{a} \parallel \vec{b}$

$$\Rightarrow \qquad \frac{3}{2} = \frac{-6}{-4} = \frac{1}{\lambda}$$

$$\Rightarrow \qquad \lambda = \frac{2}{3}.$$

24. If $\vec{a}, \vec{b}$ and $\vec{c}$ are unit vectors such that $\vec{a} + \vec{b} + \vec{c} = \vec{0}$, then the value of $\vec{a} \cdot \vec{b} + \vec{b} \cdot \vec{c} + \vec{c} \cdot \vec{a}$ is: **[NCERT Exemplar]**

(a) 1   (b) 3

(c) $-\dfrac{3}{2}$ (d) None of these

Sol. (c) $-\dfrac{3}{2}$

Explanation :

We have, $\vec{a} + \vec{b} + \vec{c} = 0$ and $\vec{a}^2 = 1,\ \vec{b}^2 = 1,\ \vec{c}^2 = 1$

$$\because \qquad (\vec{a} + \vec{b} + \vec{c}) \cdot (\vec{a} + \vec{b} + \vec{c}) = 0$$

$$\Rightarrow \vec{a}^2 + \vec{a} \cdot \vec{b} + \vec{a} \cdot \vec{c} + \vec{b} \cdot \vec{a} + \vec{b}^2$$

$$+ \vec{b} \cdot \vec{c} + \vec{c} \cdot \vec{a} + \vec{c} \cdot \vec{b} + \vec{c}^2 = 0$$

$$\Rightarrow \quad \vec{a}^2 + \vec{b}^2 + \vec{c}^2 + 2(\vec{a} \cdot \vec{b} + \vec{b} \cdot \vec{c} + \vec{c} \cdot \vec{a}) = 0$$

$$[\because \vec{a} \cdot \vec{b} = \vec{b} \cdot \vec{a},\ \vec{b} \cdot \vec{c} = \vec{c} \cdot \vec{b} \text{ and } \vec{c} \cdot \vec{a} = \vec{a} \cdot \vec{c}]$$

$$\Rightarrow \quad 1 + 1 + 1 + 2(\vec{a} \cdot \vec{b} + \vec{b} \cdot \vec{c} + \vec{c} \cdot \vec{a}) = 0$$

$$\Rightarrow \quad \vec{a} \cdot \vec{b} + \vec{b} \cdot \vec{c} + \vec{c} \cdot \vec{a} = -\frac{3}{2}.$$

25. If $\vec{a}, \vec{b}$ and $\vec{c}$ are the vectors such that $\vec{a} + \vec{b} + \vec{c} = \vec{0}$ and $|\vec{a}| = 2,\ |\vec{b}| = 3$ and $|\vec{c}| = 5$, then the value of $\vec{a} \cdot \vec{b} + \vec{b} \cdot \vec{c} + \vec{c} \cdot \vec{a}$ is:

[NCERT Exemplar]

(a) 0   (b) 1

(c) -19 (d) 38

Sol. (c) -19

Explanation :

Here, $\vec{a} + \vec{b} + \vec{c} = 0$ and $\vec{a}^2 = 4,\ \vec{b}^2 = 9,\ \vec{c}^2 = 25$

$$\therefore \qquad (\vec{a} + \vec{b} + \vec{c}) \cdot (\vec{a} + \vec{b} + \vec{c}) = \vec{0}$$

$$\Rightarrow \vec{a}^2 + \vec{a} \cdot \vec{b} + \vec{a} \cdot \vec{c} + \vec{b} \cdot \vec{a} + \vec{b}^2$$

$$+ \vec{b} \cdot \vec{c} + \vec{c} \cdot \vec{a} + \vec{c} \cdot \vec{b} + \vec{c}^2 = \vec{0}$$

$$\Rightarrow \quad \vec{a}^2 + \vec{b}^2 + \vec{c}^2 + 2(\vec{a} \cdot \vec{b} + \vec{b} \cdot \vec{c} + \vec{c} \cdot \vec{a}) = 0$$

$$[\because \vec{a} \cdot \vec{b} = \vec{b} \cdot \vec{a}]$$

$$\Rightarrow \quad 4 + 9 + 25 + 2(\vec{a} \cdot \vec{b} + \vec{b} \cdot \vec{c} + \vec{c} \cdot \vec{a}) = 0$$

$$\Rightarrow \quad \vec{a} \cdot \vec{b} + \vec{b} \cdot \vec{c} + \vec{c} \cdot \vec{a} = \frac{-38}{2} = -19.$$

26. If $\vec{a}$ and $\vec{b}$ are non-zero vectors such that $\vec{a} \cdot \vec{b} = 0$, then $\vec{a}$ and $\vec{b}$ are:

(a) Perpendicular   (b) Equal

(c) Parallel   (d) None of these

Sol. (a) Perpendicular

Explanation :

$$\vec{a} \cdot \vec{b} = ab \cos \theta = 0$$

$$\Rightarrow \quad \cos \theta = 0$$
$$\Rightarrow \quad \theta = 90°.$$

27. If θ be the angle between two vectors $\vec{a}$ and $\vec{b}$ then $\vec{a} \cdot \vec{b} \geq 0$ only when:

(a) $0 < \theta < \dfrac{\pi}{2}$ (b) $0 \leq \theta \leq \dfrac{\pi}{2}$

(c) $0 < \theta < \pi$ (d) $0 \leq \theta \leq \pi$

Sol. (b) $0 \leq \theta \leq \dfrac{\pi}{2}$

Explanation :

$$\vec{a} \cdot \vec{b} = ab \cos \theta$$

and $\quad ab \cos \theta \geq 0$

when $\quad \cos \theta \geq 0$

$\Rightarrow$ Hence, for $0 \leq \theta \leq \dfrac{\pi}{2}$.

28. If $|\vec{a}| = |\vec{b}| = 1$ and $|\vec{a} + \vec{b}| = \sqrt{3}$, then the value of $(3\vec{a} - 4\vec{b}) \cdot (2\vec{a} + 5\vec{b})$ is:

(a) -21 (b) $-21/2$

(c) 21 (d) $21/2$

Sol. (b) $-21/2$

Explanation :

$$(3\vec{a} - 4\vec{b}) \cdot (2\vec{a} + 5\vec{b})$$

$$= 6|\vec{a}|^2 - 20|\vec{b}|^2 + 7\vec{a} \cdot \vec{b}$$

$$= 6 - 20 + 7\vec{a} \cdot \vec{b} = 7\vec{a} \cdot \vec{b} - 14$$

Given, $\quad |\vec{a} + \vec{b}|^2 = (\sqrt{3})^2$

$$\Rightarrow \quad |\vec{a}|^2 + |\vec{b}|^2 + 2\vec{a} \cdot \vec{b} = 3$$

$$\Rightarrow \quad 1 + 1 + 2a.b = 3$$

$$\Rightarrow \quad 2\vec{a} \cdot \vec{b} = 1$$

$$\Rightarrow \quad \vec{a} \cdot \vec{b} = \dfrac{1}{2}$$

Therefore,

$$(3\vec{a} - 4\vec{b}).(2\vec{a} + 5\vec{b}) = 7 \times \dfrac{1}{2} - 14$$

$$= \dfrac{-21}{2}.$$

29. If $\vec{a}$, $\vec{b}$ and $\vec{c}$ are any vectors, then the true statement is:

(a) $\vec{a} \times (\vec{b} \times \vec{c}) = (\vec{a} \times \vec{b}) \times \vec{c}$

(b) $\vec{a} \times \vec{b} = \vec{b} \times \vec{a}$

(c) $\vec{a} \cdot (\vec{b} \times \vec{c}) = \vec{a} \cdot \vec{b} \times \vec{a} \cdot \vec{c}$

(d) $\vec{a} \cdot (\vec{b} - \vec{c}) = \vec{a} \cdot \vec{b} - \vec{a} \cdot \vec{c}$

Sol. (d) $\vec{a} \cdot (\vec{b} - \vec{c}) = \vec{a} \cdot \vec{b} - \vec{a} \cdot \vec{c}$

Explanation :

Using property of vector multiplication, the correct option is (d).

30. If $\vec{a} \cdot \vec{b} = \dfrac{1}{2} |\vec{a}| |\vec{b}|$, then the angle between $\vec{a}$ and $\vec{b}$ is:

(a) $0°$ (b) $30°$

(c) $60°$ (d) $90°$

Sol. (c) $60°$

Explanation :

We have, $\quad \vec{a} \cdot \vec{b} = \dfrac{1}{2} |\vec{a}| |\vec{b}|$

$$\Rightarrow \quad |\vec{a}| |\vec{b}| \cos \theta = \dfrac{1}{2} |\vec{a}| |\vec{b}|,$$

where θ is the required angle.

$$\Rightarrow \quad \cos \theta = \dfrac{1}{2}$$

$$\Rightarrow \quad \theta = 60°.$$

31. If $\vec{a} = \hat{i} - 2\hat{j} + 3\hat{k}$. If $\vec{b}$ is a vector such that $\vec{a} \cdot \vec{b} = |\vec{b}|^2$ and $|\vec{a} - \vec{b}| = \sqrt{7}$, then equals:

(a) 7 (b) 14

(c) $\sqrt{7}$ (d) 21

Sol. (c) $\sqrt{7}$

Explanation :

We have $\quad |\vec{a} - \vec{b}| = \sqrt{7}$

$$\Rightarrow \quad |\vec{a} - \vec{b}|^2 = 7$$

$\Rightarrow \quad (\vec{a} - \vec{b}).(\vec{a} - \vec{b}) = 7$

$\Rightarrow \quad |\vec{a}|^2 - 2\vec{a}.\vec{b} + |\vec{b}|^2 = 7$

$\Rightarrow \quad 14 - 2|\vec{b}|^2 + |\vec{b}|^2 = 7$

$$\begin{bmatrix} \because \vec{a}.\vec{b} = |\vec{b}|^2 \\ |\vec{a}| = \sqrt{1+4+9} = \sqrt{14} \end{bmatrix}$$

$\Rightarrow \quad |\vec{b}| = \sqrt{7}.$

32. If $\hat{i}, \hat{j}, \hat{k}$ are unit vectors along three mutually perpendicular directions, then:

(a) $\hat{i}.\hat{j} = 1$ (b) $\hat{i} \times \hat{j} = 1$

(c) $\hat{i}.\hat{k} = 0$ (d) $\hat{i} \times \hat{k} = 0$

Sol. (c) $\hat{i}.\hat{k} = 0$

Explanation :

As $\qquad \hat{i}.\hat{k} = |\hat{i}||\hat{k}| \cos \dfrac{\pi}{2}$

$\qquad\qquad = 1 \times 1 \times 0 = 0.$

33. If $\hat{a}, \hat{b}$ and $\hat{c}$ are mutually perpendicular unit vectors, then find the value of $|2\hat{a} + \hat{b} + \hat{c}|$.

(a) 6   (b) $\sqrt{6}$

(c) 7   (d) $\sqrt{7}$

Sol. (b) $\sqrt{6}$

Explanation :

Let $\quad y = |2\hat{a} + \hat{b} + \hat{c}|$

$\Rightarrow \quad y^2 = (2\hat{a} + \hat{b} + \hat{c}).(2\hat{a} + \hat{b} + \hat{c})$

$\Rightarrow \quad y^2 = 4|\hat{a}|^2 + 2\hat{a}.\hat{b} + 2\hat{a}.\hat{c} + 2\hat{b}.\hat{a} + |\hat{b}|^2$
$\qquad\qquad + \hat{b}.\hat{c} + 2\hat{c}.\hat{a} + \hat{c}.\hat{b} + |\hat{c}|^2$

Since $\hat{a}, \hat{b}$ and $\hat{c}$ are mutually perpendicular unit vectors.

Therefore, $y^2 = 4 \times 1 + 2 \times 0 + 2 \times 0 + 2 \times 0$
$\qquad\qquad\qquad + 1 + 0 + 2 \times 0 + 0 + 1$

$\therefore \qquad y = |2\hat{a} + \hat{b} + \hat{c}| = \sqrt{6}.$

34. The component of $\hat{i}$ in the direction of the vector $\hat{j} + \hat{j} + 2\hat{k}$ is:

(a) $\sqrt{6}$ (b) 6

(c) $6\sqrt{6}$ (d) $\dfrac{\sqrt{6}}{6}$

Sol. (d) $\dfrac{\sqrt{6}}{6}$

Explanation :

Unit vector along $\hat{i} + \hat{j} + 2\hat{k}$ is $\dfrac{\hat{i} + \hat{j} + 2\hat{k}}{\sqrt{6}}$

Hence, component of $\hat{i}$ along $\hat{i} + \hat{j} + 2\hat{k}$

$= $ Projection of $\hat{i}$ on $\dfrac{\hat{i} + \hat{j} + 2\hat{k}}{\sqrt{6}} = \hat{i}.\dfrac{\hat{i} + \hat{j} + 2\hat{k}}{\sqrt{6}}$

$= \dfrac{1}{\sqrt{6}} = \dfrac{\sqrt{6}}{6}.$

35. Find the angle between the vectors $\vec{a}$ and $\vec{b}$ whose magnitudes are $\sqrt{3}$ and $\sqrt{3}$, where $\vec{a}.\vec{b} = 3$.

(a) $0°$ (b) $\dfrac{\pi}{2}$

(c) $\dfrac{\pi}{4}$ (d) $\dfrac{\pi}{3}$

Sol. (a) $0°$

Explanation :

Given, the magnitude of $\vec{a}, |\vec{a}| = \sqrt{3}$ and the magnitude of $\vec{b}, |\vec{b}| = \sqrt{3}$

Also, $\qquad \vec{a}\cdot\vec{b} = 3$

We know that

$\qquad \vec{a}\cdot\vec{b} = |\vec{a}|\cdot|\vec{b}| \cos\theta$

$\qquad\qquad 3 = \sqrt{3} \times \sqrt{3} \times \cos\theta$

$\qquad\qquad \cos\theta = \dfrac{3}{\sqrt{3}\times\sqrt{3}}$

$\qquad\qquad \cos\theta = \dfrac{3}{3}$

$\qquad\qquad \cos\theta = 1$

$\qquad\qquad \theta = 0°$

Hence, the angle between the vectors $\vec{a}$ and $\vec{b}$ is $0°$.

So the correct option is (a).

36. Find the value of $(\vec{a} - 5\vec{b})\cdot(2\vec{a} + \vec{b})$.

(a) $2|\vec{a}|^2 - 9\vec{a}\cdot\vec{b} - 5|\vec{b}|^2$

(b) $|\vec{a}|^2 + 5\vec{a}\cdot\vec{b} - 9|\vec{b}|^2$

(c) $|\vec{a}|^2 + 5\vec{a}\cdot\vec{b} + |\vec{b}|^2$

(d) $|\vec{a}|^2 + \vec{a}\cdot\vec{b} + |\vec{b}|^2$

Sol. (a) $2|\vec{a}|^2 - 9\vec{a}\cdot\vec{b} - 5|\vec{b}|^2$

Explanation :

$(\vec{a} - 5\vec{b})\cdot(2\vec{a} + \vec{b})$

$$= \vec{a}\cdot 2\vec{a} + \vec{a}\cdot\vec{b} - 5\vec{b}\cdot 2\vec{a} - 5\vec{b}\cdot\vec{b}$$

$$= 2\vec{a}\cdot\vec{a} + \vec{a}\cdot\vec{b} - 10\vec{a}\cdot\vec{b} - 5\vec{b}\cdot\vec{b}$$

$$= 2|\vec{a}|^2 - 9\vec{a}\cdot\vec{b} - 5|\vec{b}|^2$$

So the correct option is (a).

37. The vectors from origin to the points A and B are $\vec{a} = 2\hat{i} - 3\hat{j} + 2\hat{k}$ and $\vec{b} = 2\hat{i} + 3\hat{j} + \hat{k}$ respectively, then the area of $\triangle OAB$ is equal to:

[NCERT Exemplar]

(a) 340

(b) $\sqrt{25}$

(c) $\sqrt{229}$

(d) $\dfrac{1}{2}\sqrt{229}$

Sol. (d) $\dfrac{1}{2}\sqrt{229}$

Explanation :

$\therefore$ Area of $\triangle OAB$

$$= \frac{1}{2}|\vec{OA} \times \vec{OB}|$$

$$= \frac{1}{2}|(2\hat{i} - 3\hat{i} + 2\hat{k}) \times (2\hat{i} + 3\hat{j} + \hat{k})|$$

$$= \frac{1}{2}\begin{vmatrix} \hat{i} & \hat{j} & \hat{k} \\ 2 & -3 & 2 \\ 2 & 3 & 1 \end{vmatrix}$$

$$= \frac{1}{2}|[\hat{i}(-3-6) - \hat{j}(2-4) + \hat{k}(6+6)]$$

$$= \frac{1}{2}|-9\hat{i} + 2\hat{j} + 12\hat{k}|$$

$\therefore$ Area of $\triangle OAB$

$$= \frac{1}{2}\sqrt{(81+4+144)} = \frac{1}{2}\sqrt{229}.$$

38. For any vectors $\vec{a}$, then the value of

$$(\vec{a} \times \hat{i})^2 + (\vec{a} \times \hat{j})^2 + (\vec{a} \times \hat{k})^2 \text{ is:}$$

[NCERT Exemplar]

(a) $\vec{a}^2$

(b) $3\vec{a}^2$

(c) $4\vec{a}^2$

(d) $2\vec{a}^2$

Sol. (d) $2\vec{a}^2$

Explanation :

Let $\qquad \vec{a} = x\hat{i} + y\hat{j} + z\hat{k}$

$\therefore \qquad \vec{a}^2 = x^2 + y^2 + z^2$

$$\therefore \quad \vec{a} \times \hat{i} = \begin{vmatrix} \hat{i} & \hat{j} & \hat{k} \\ x & y & z \\ 1 & 0 & 0 \end{vmatrix}$$

$$= \hat{i}[0] - \hat{j}[-z] + \hat{k}[-y]$$

$$= z\hat{j} - y\hat{k}$$

$$\therefore \quad (\vec{a} \times \hat{i})^2 = (z\hat{j} - y\hat{k})(z\hat{j} - y\hat{k})$$

$$= y^2 + z^2$$

Similarly, $\quad (\vec{a} \times \hat{j})^2 = x^2 + z^2$

and $\qquad (\vec{a} \times \hat{k})^2 = x^2 + y^2$

$$\therefore (\vec{a} \times \hat{i})^2 + (\vec{a} \times \hat{j})^2 + (\vec{a} \times \hat{k})^2$$

$$= y^2 + z^2 + x^2 + z^2 + x^2 + y^2$$
$$= 2(x^2 + y^2 + z^2)$$
$$= 2\vec{a}^2 .$$

39. If $|\vec{a}| = 10$, $|\vec{b}| = 2$ and $\vec{a}\cdot\vec{b} = 12$, then the value of $|\vec{a} \times \vec{b}|$ is: **[NCERT Exemplar]**

(a) 5

(b) 10

(c) 14

(d) 16

Sol. (d) 16

Explanation :

Here $|\vec{a}| = 10$, $|\vec{b}| = 2$ and $\vec{a}\cdot\vec{b} = 12$ [given]

$$\therefore \qquad \vec{a}\cdot\vec{b} = |\vec{a}||\vec{b}|\cos\theta$$

$$12 = 10 \times 2\cos\theta$$

$$\Rightarrow \qquad \cos\theta = \frac{12}{20} = \frac{3}{5}$$

$$\Rightarrow \quad \sin \theta = \sqrt{1 - \cos^2 \theta}$$

$$= \sqrt{1 - \frac{9}{25}}$$

$$\Rightarrow \quad \sin \theta = \pm \frac{4}{5}$$

$$\therefore \quad |\vec{a} \times \vec{b}| = |\vec{a}||\vec{b}||\sin \theta|$$

$$= 10 \times 2 \times \frac{4}{5}$$

$$= 16.$$

40. The number of vectors of unit length perpendicular to the vectors $\vec{a} = 2\hat{i} + \hat{j} + 2\hat{k}$ and $\vec{b} = \hat{j} + \hat{k}$ is: **[NCERT Exemplar]**

(a) one   (b) two

(c) three   (d) infinite

Sol. (b) two

Explanation :

The number of vectors of unit length perpendicular to the vectors $\vec{a}$ and $\vec{b}$ is $\vec{c}$ (say) i.e.,

$$\vec{c} = \pm(\vec{a} \times \vec{b})$$

So, there will be two vectors of unit length perpendicular to the vectors $\vec{a}$ and $\vec{b}$.

41. If θ be the angle between two vectors $\vec{a}$ and $\vec{b}$ such that $|\vec{a} \times \vec{b}| = |\vec{a} \cdot \vec{b}|$, then $\theta =$

(a) $0°$ (b) $45°$

(c) $120°$ (d) $180°$

Sol. (b) $45°$

Explanation :

We have $\quad |\vec{a} \times \vec{b}| = |\vec{a} \cdot \vec{b}|$

$$|\vec{a}||\vec{b}|\sin \theta = |\vec{a}||\vec{b}|\cos \theta$$

$$\sin \theta = \cos \theta$$

$$\Rightarrow \quad \tan \theta = 1$$

$$\Rightarrow \quad \theta = 45°.$$

42. For any vector $\vec{a}$, $\vec{a} \times \vec{a}$ is:

(a) $\vec{0}$ (b) 1

(c) $|\vec{a}|$ (d) None of these

Sol. (a) $\vec{0}$

Explanation :

$$\vec{a} \times \vec{a} = a^2 \sin \theta = a^2 \sin 0$$

$$= 0.$$

43. If $\vec{a}$ and $\vec{b}$ are unit vectors such that $\vec{a} \times \vec{b}$ is also a unit vector, then the angle between $\vec{a}$ and $\vec{b}$ is:

(a) 0 (b) $\dfrac{\pi}{3}$

(c) $\dfrac{\pi}{2}$ (d) π

Sol. (c) $\dfrac{\pi}{2}$

Explanation :

$$|\vec{a} \times \vec{b}| = 1$$

$$\Rightarrow \quad |\sin \theta| = 1 \Rightarrow \sin \theta = 1$$

$$\Rightarrow \quad \theta = \frac{\pi}{2}.$$

44. If $\vec{a} + \vec{b} + \vec{c} = 0$, then which relation is correct:

(a) $\vec{a} = \vec{b} = \vec{c} = 0$

(b) $\vec{a} \cdot \vec{b} = \vec{b} \cdot \vec{c} = \vec{c} \cdot \vec{a}$

(c) $\vec{a} \times \vec{b} = \vec{b} \times \vec{c} = \vec{c} \times \vec{a}$

(d) None of these

Sol. (c) $\vec{a} \times \vec{b} = \vec{b} \times \vec{c} = \vec{c} \times \vec{a}$

Explanation :

Since $\quad \vec{a} + \vec{b} + \vec{c} = 0,$

$$\Rightarrow \quad \vec{a} \times (\vec{a} + \vec{b} + \vec{c}) = 0$$

$$\Rightarrow \quad \vec{a} \times \vec{a} + \vec{a} \times \vec{b} + \vec{a} \times \vec{c} = 0$$

$$\Rightarrow \quad \vec{a} \times \vec{b} = -\vec{a} \times \vec{c} = \vec{c} \times \vec{a} \qquad ...(i)$$

Similarly, $\vec{b} \times (\vec{a} + \vec{b} + \vec{c}) = 0$

$$\Rightarrow \quad \vec{a} \times \vec{b} = \vec{b} \times \vec{c} \qquad ...(ii)$$

By (i) and (ii), we get

$$\vec{a} \times \vec{b} = \vec{b} \times \vec{c} = \vec{c} \times \vec{a}.$$

45. If $\vec{a}$ and $\vec{b}$ are two vectors such that $\vec{a} \cdot \vec{b} = 0$ and $\vec{a} \times \vec{b} = \vec{0}$ then:

(a) $\vec{a}$ is parallel to $\vec{b}$

(b) $\vec{a}$ is perpendicular to $\vec{b}$

(c) Either $\vec{a}$ or $\vec{b}$ is a null vector

(d) None of these

Sol. (c) Either $\vec{a}$ or $\vec{b}$ is a null vector

Explanation :

$$\vec{a} \cdot \vec{b} = ab \cos \theta$$

$$\Rightarrow \quad \cos \theta = 0, \theta = 90°$$

and $$\vec{a} \times \vec{b} = ab \sin \theta = 0$$

$$\Rightarrow \quad \sin \theta = 0$$

or $$ab = 0$$

i.e., either $a = 0$ or $b = 0$.

46. If $\vec{a} = 2\hat{j} + 3\hat{j} - 5\hat{k}$, $\vec{b} = m\hat{i} + n\hat{j} + 12\hat{k}$ and $\vec{a} \times \vec{b} = 0$ then $(m, n) =$

(a) $\left(-\dfrac{24}{5}, \dfrac{36}{5}\right)$

(b) $\left(\dfrac{24}{5}, \dfrac{-36}{5}\right)$

(c) $\left(-\dfrac{24}{5}, -\dfrac{36}{5}\right)$

(d) $\left(\dfrac{24}{5}, \dfrac{36}{5}\right)$

Sol. (c) $\left(-\dfrac{24}{5}, -\dfrac{36}{5}\right)$

Explanation :

$$\vec{a} \times \vec{b} = \begin{vmatrix} \hat{i} & \hat{j} & \hat{k} \\ 2 & 3 & -5 \\ m & n & 12 \end{vmatrix}$$

$$= (36 + 5n)\hat{i} - (24 + 5m)\hat{j} + (2n - 3m)\hat{k} = 0$$

$$\Rightarrow \quad m = \frac{-24}{5}, \ n = \frac{-36}{5}.$$

47. If θ is the angle between the vectors $\vec{a}$ and $\vec{b}$, then $\dfrac{|\vec{a} \times \vec{b}|}{|\vec{a} \cdot \vec{b}|}$ equal to:

(a) $\tan \theta$

(b) $-\tan \theta$

(c) $\cot \theta$

(d) $-\cot \theta$

Sol. (a) $\tan \theta$

Explanation :

$$\frac{|\vec{a} \times \vec{b}|}{|\vec{a} \cdot \vec{b}|} = \frac{ab \sin \theta}{ab \cos \theta} = \tan \theta.$$

48. The area of a triangle whose vertices are $A(1, -1, 2)$, $B(2, 1, -1)$ and $C(3, -1, 2)$ is:

(a) 13

(b) $\sqrt{13}$

(c) 6

(d) $\sqrt{6}$

Sol. (b) $\sqrt{13}$

Explanation :

Here, $$\vec{OA} = \hat{i} - \hat{j} + 2\hat{k}$$

and $$\vec{OB} = 2\hat{i} + \hat{j} - \hat{k}$$

and $$\vec{OC} = 3\hat{i} - \hat{j} + 2\hat{k}$$

These implies $\vec{AB} = \vec{OB} - \vec{OA}$

$$= \hat{i} + 2\hat{j} - 3\hat{k}$$

and $$\vec{AC} = \vec{OC} - \vec{OA} = 2\hat{i}$$

Hence, required area is given by

$$= \frac{1}{2}|\vec{AB} \times \vec{AC}|$$

$$\vec{AB} \times \vec{AC} = \begin{vmatrix} \hat{i} & \hat{j} & \hat{k} \\ 1 & 2 & -3 \\ 2 & 0 & 0 \end{vmatrix}$$

$$= -2(3\hat{j} + 2\hat{k})$$

$$\Rightarrow \text{Area of triangle} = \frac{1}{2} \times 2|3\hat{j} + 2\hat{k}|$$

$$= \sqrt{13}.$$

49. A unit vector perpendicular to both $\hat{i} + \hat{j}$ and $\hat{j} + \hat{k}$ is:

(a) $\hat{i} - \hat{j} + \hat{k}$

(b) $\hat{i} + \hat{j} + \hat{k}$

(c) $\dfrac{\hat{i} + \hat{j} - \hat{k}}{\sqrt{3}}$

(d) $\dfrac{\hat{i} - \hat{j} + \hat{k}}{\sqrt{3}}$

Sol. (d) $\dfrac{\hat{i} - \hat{j} + \hat{k}}{\sqrt{3}}$

Explanation :

Unit vector perpendicular to both

$$= \frac{(\hat{i} + \hat{j}) \times (\hat{j} + \hat{k})}{|(\hat{i} + \hat{j}) \times (\hat{j} + \hat{k})|}$$

$$= \frac{\hat{i} - \hat{j} + \hat{k}}{\sqrt{3}}.$$

50. If $(2\hat{i} + 6\hat{j} + 27\hat{k}) \times (\hat{i} + p\hat{j} + q\hat{k}) = \vec{0}$, then the value of p and q are:

(a) $p = 6, q = 27$

(b) $p = 3, q = \dfrac{27}{2}$

(c) $p = 6, q = \dfrac{27}{2}$

(d) $p = 3, q = 27$

Sol. (b) $p = 3, q = \dfrac{27}{2}$

Explanation :

As $(2\hat{i} + 6\hat{j} + 27\hat{k}) \times (\hat{i} + p\hat{j} + q\hat{k}) = \vec{0}$

so, $(2\hat{i} + 6\hat{j} + 27\hat{k}) \;\|\; (\hat{i} + p\hat{j} + q\hat{k})$

Therefore, $\dfrac{2}{1} = \dfrac{6}{p} = \dfrac{27}{q}$

($\because$ d.r.'s of parallel vectors are proportional)

Consider $\dfrac{2}{1} = \dfrac{6}{p}$ and $\dfrac{2}{1} = \dfrac{27}{q}$

$\therefore \qquad p = 3, q = \dfrac{27}{2}.$

51. Find the area of the parallelogram, whose diagonals are $\vec{d_1} = 5\hat{i}$ and $\vec{d_2} = 2\hat{j}$.

(a) 10 sq units

(b) 5 sq units

(c) 20 sq units

(d) 7.5 sq units

Sol. (b) 5 sq units

Explanation :

Area of the parallelogram

$$= \frac{1}{2}|\vec{d_1} \times \vec{d_2}|$$

$$= 5 \text{ sq units.}$$

52. If $(\vec{a} \times \vec{b})^2 + (\vec{a} \cdot \vec{b})^2 = 676$ and $|\vec{b}| = 2$, then $|\vec{a}|$ is equal to:

(a) 13

(b) 26

(c) 39

(d) None of these

Sol. (a) 13

Explanation :

We know,

$$(\vec{a} \times \vec{b})^2 + (\vec{a} \cdot \vec{b})^2 = |\vec{a}|^2|\vec{b}|^2$$

$$\Rightarrow \qquad 676 = |\vec{a}|^2 \times 4$$

$$\Rightarrow \qquad |\vec{a}|^2 = \frac{676}{4}$$

$$\Rightarrow \qquad \qquad = 169$$

$$\Rightarrow \qquad |\vec{a}| = 13.$$

53. If $\vec{a} + \vec{b} + \vec{c} = 0$, then $\vec{a} \times \vec{b} =$

(a) $\vec{c} \times \vec{a}$

(b) $\vec{b} \times \vec{c}$

(c) $\vec{0}$

(d) Both (a) and (b)

Sol. (d) Both (a) and (b)

Explanation :

Since $\qquad \vec{a} + \vec{b} + \vec{c} = 0$

$\Rightarrow \qquad \vec{a} \times (\vec{a} + \vec{b} + \vec{c}) = 0$

$\Rightarrow \qquad \vec{a} \times \vec{a} + \vec{a} \times \vec{b} + \vec{a} \times \vec{c} = 0$

$\Rightarrow \qquad \vec{a} \times \vec{b} = -\vec{a} \times \vec{c}$

$\qquad\qquad\qquad\quad = \vec{c} \times \vec{a} \qquad$ ...(i)

Similarly $\vec{b} \times (\vec{a} + \vec{b} + \vec{c}) = 0$

$\Rightarrow \qquad \vec{a} \times \vec{b} = \vec{b} \times \vec{c} \qquad$ ...(ii)

By (i) and (ii), we get

$$\vec{a} \times \vec{b} = \vec{b} \times \vec{c} = \vec{c} \times \vec{a}$$

54. Find the unit vector which is perpendicular to both the vectors $\vec{a} + \vec{b}$ and $\vec{a} - \vec{b}$, where

$$\vec{a} = \hat{i} + 2\hat{j} + \hat{k}$$

$$\vec{b} = 2\hat{i} - \hat{j} + \hat{k}.$$

(a) $\pm\dfrac{3}{\sqrt{35}}\hat{i} \pm \dfrac{1}{\sqrt{35}}\hat{j} \pm \dfrac{5}{\sqrt{35}}\hat{k}$

(b) $\pm\dfrac{3}{\sqrt{35}}\hat{i} \pm \dfrac{1}{\sqrt{35}}\hat{j} \pm \dfrac{2}{\sqrt{35}}\hat{k}$

(c) $\pm\dfrac{3}{\sqrt{35}}\hat{i} \pm \dfrac{4}{\sqrt{35}}\hat{j} \pm \dfrac{2}{\sqrt{35}}\hat{k}$

(d) $\pm\dfrac{3}{\sqrt{35}}\hat{i} \pm \dfrac{5}{\sqrt{35}}\hat{j} \pm \dfrac{2}{\sqrt{35}}\hat{k}$

Sol. (a) $\pm\dfrac{3}{\sqrt{35}}\hat{i} \pm \dfrac{1}{\sqrt{35}}\hat{j} \pm \dfrac{5}{\sqrt{35}}\hat{k}$

Explanation :

The given vectors are,

$$\vec{a} = \hat{i} + 2\hat{j} + \hat{k}$$

$$\vec{b} = 2\hat{i} - \hat{j} + \hat{k}$$

So, $\quad \vec{a} + \vec{b} = \hat{i} + 2\hat{j} + \hat{k} + 2\hat{i} - \hat{j} + \hat{k}$

$$= 3\hat{i} + \hat{j} + 2\hat{k}$$

Also, $\vec{a} - \vec{b} = (\hat{i} + 2\hat{j} + \hat{k}) - (2\hat{i} - \hat{j} + \hat{k})$

$$= \hat{i} + 2\hat{j} + \hat{k} - 2\hat{i} + \hat{j} - \hat{k}$$

$$= -\hat{i} + 3\hat{j}$$

$$\therefore (\vec{a} + \vec{b}) \times (\vec{a} - \vec{b}) = \begin{vmatrix} \hat{i} & \hat{j} & \hat{k} \\ 3 & 1 & 2 \\ -1 & 3 & 0 \end{vmatrix}$$

$$= \hat{i}(0-6) - \hat{j}(0+2) + \hat{k}(9+1)$$

$$= -6\hat{i} - 2\hat{j} + 10\hat{k}$$

$$\left| (\vec{a} + \vec{b}) \times (\vec{a} - \vec{b}) \right| = \sqrt{(-6)^2 + (2)^2 + (10)^2}$$

$$= \sqrt{36 + 4 + 100}$$

$$= \sqrt{140}$$

$$= 2\sqrt{35}.$$

Hence, the unit vector perpendicular to both the vectors $\vec{a} + \vec{b}$ and $\vec{a} - \vec{b}$ is,

$$\pm \frac{(\vec{a} + \vec{b}) \times (\vec{a} - \vec{b})}{\left| (\vec{a} + \vec{b}) \times (\vec{a} - \vec{b}) \right|} = \pm \frac{-6\hat{i} - 2\hat{j} + 10\hat{k}}{2\sqrt{35}}$$

$$= \pm \frac{6}{2\sqrt{35}}\hat{i} \pm \frac{2}{2\sqrt{35}}\hat{j} \pm \frac{10}{2\sqrt{35}}\hat{k}$$

$$= \pm \frac{3}{\sqrt{35}}\hat{i} \pm \frac{1}{\sqrt{35}}\hat{j} \pm \frac{5}{\sqrt{35}}\hat{k}$$

So the correct option is (a).

Assertion and Reason Based Questions

(a) Both (A) and (R) are individually true and (R) is the correct explanation of (A).

(b) Both (A) and (R) are individually true but (R) is not the correct explanation of (A).

(c) (A) is true but (R) is false.

(d) (A) is false but (R) is true.

55. Assertion (A): In a $\triangle ABC$, $\vec{AB} + \vec{BC} + \vec{CA} = 0$.

Reason (R): If $\vec{AB} = \vec{a}$, $\vec{BC} = \vec{b}$, then $\vec{AC} = \vec{a} + \vec{b}$ (Triangle law of addition).

Sol. (a) Both (A) and (R) are individually true and (R) is the correct explanation of (A).

Explanation :

$$\because \quad \vec{AB} + \vec{BC} + \vec{CA} = \vec{AC} + \vec{CA}$$

$$= \vec{AC} - \vec{AC}$$

$$= 0.$$

56. Assertion (A) : For $a = -\dfrac{1}{\sqrt{3}}$ the volume of the parallelopiped formed by vectors $\hat{i} + a\hat{j}$, $a\hat{i} + \hat{j} + \hat{k}$ and $\hat{j} + a\hat{k}$ is maximum.

Reason (R) : The V is the volume of the parallelopiped having three coterminous edges as $\vec{a}$, $\vec{b}$ and $\vec{c}$ then the volume of the parallelopiped having three coterminous edges as

$$\vec{\alpha} = (\vec{a} \cdot \vec{a})\vec{a} + (\vec{a} \cdot \vec{b})\vec{b} + (\vec{a} \cdot \vec{c})\vec{c},$$

$$\vec{\beta} = (\vec{a} \cdot \vec{b})\vec{a} + (\vec{b} \cdot \vec{b})\vec{b} + (\vec{b} \cdot \vec{c})\vec{c}$$

$$\vec{r} = (\vec{a} \cdot \vec{c})\vec{a} + (\vec{b} \cdot \vec{c}) + (\vec{c} \cdot \vec{c})\vec{c}$$

is V^3.

Sol. (d) (A) is false but (R) is true.

Explanation :

$$V = \begin{vmatrix} 1 & a & 0 \\ a & 1 & 1 \\ 0 & 1 & a \end{vmatrix} = a - 1 - a^3$$

$$\therefore \quad \frac{dV}{da} = 1 - 3a^2 = 0$$

$$\therefore \quad a = \pm \frac{1}{\sqrt{3}}$$

$$\Rightarrow \quad \frac{d^2V}{da^2} = -6a$$

$$\left. \frac{d^2V}{da^2} \right|_{a = \frac{1}{\sqrt{3}}} = -\frac{6}{\sqrt{3}} \ (-\text{ve})$$

$$\therefore \ V \text{ is maximum at } a = \frac{1}{\sqrt{3}}.$$

57. Assertion (A) : The scalar product of a force $\vec{F}$ and displacement $\vec{r}$ is equal to the work done.

Reason (R) : Work done is not a scalar.

Sol. (c) (A) is true but (R) is false.

Explanation :

$\because$ Work done, $W = \vec{F} \cdot \vec{r}$

$\therefore$ Work done is a Scalar quantity.

58. Assertion (A) : $|\vec{a}| = |\vec{b}|$ does not implies that $\vec{a} = \vec{b}$.

Reason (R) : If $\vec{a} = \vec{b}$, then $\vec{a} \cdot \vec{b} = |\vec{a}|^2 = |\vec{b}|^2$.

Sol. (b) Both (A) and (R) are individually true but (R) is not the correct explanation of (A).

Explanation :

If $\vec{a} = \vec{b}$, then $|\vec{a}| = |\vec{b}|$

$\therefore \qquad \vec{a} \cdot \vec{b} = \vec{a} \cdot \vec{a} = (\vec{a})^2 = |\vec{a}|^2$

and $\qquad \vec{a} \cdot \vec{b} = \vec{b} \cdot \vec{b} = (\vec{b})^2 = |\vec{b}|^2$

$\therefore \qquad \vec{a} \cdot \vec{b} = |\vec{a}|^2 = |\vec{b}|^2$

Suppose, if $\qquad \vec{a} = a_1 \hat{i} + a_2 \hat{j}$

Then, $\qquad |\vec{a}| = |a_1 \hat{i} + a_2 \hat{j}|$

$\qquad\qquad = |a_1 \hat{i} - a_2 \hat{j}|$

$\qquad\qquad = |-a_1 \hat{i} + a_2 \hat{j}|$

$\qquad\qquad = |-a_1 \hat{i} - a_2 \hat{j}|$

Hence, $\qquad |\vec{a}| = |\vec{b}|$

does not implies that $\vec{a} = \vec{b}$.

59. Assertion (A) : If $|\vec{a}| = 2, |\vec{b}| = 3, |2\vec{a} - \vec{b}| = 5$, then $2|2\vec{a} + \vec{b}| = 5$.

Reason (R) : $|\vec{p} - \vec{q}| = |\vec{p} + \vec{q}|$.

Sol. (c) (A) is true but (R) is false.

Explanation :

$\because \qquad |2\vec{a} - \vec{b}| = 5$

$\Rightarrow \qquad |2\vec{a} - \vec{b}|^2 = 5^2$

$\Rightarrow \qquad 4a^2 + b^2 - 4\vec{a} \cdot \vec{b} = 25$

$\Rightarrow \qquad 16 + 9 - 4\vec{a} \cdot \vec{b} = 25$

$\therefore \qquad \vec{a} \cdot \vec{b} = 0$

$\therefore \qquad |2\vec{a} + \vec{b}| = \sqrt{|2\vec{a} + \vec{b}|^2}$

$\qquad\qquad = \sqrt{[4a^2 + b^2 + 4(\vec{a} \cdot \vec{b})]}$

$\qquad\qquad = \sqrt{(16 + 9 + 0)}$

$\qquad\qquad = 5$

$\therefore \qquad |\vec{p} - \vec{q}| = |\vec{p} + \vec{q}|$

is possible only when $\vec{p} \perp \vec{q}$.

60. Assertion (A) : If $\vec{a}$ and $\vec{b}$ are reciprocal vectors, then $\vec{a} \cdot \vec{b} = 1$.

Reason (R) : If $\vec{a}$ and $\vec{b}$ are reciprocal, then $\vec{a} = \lambda \vec{b}, \lambda \in R^+$ and $|\vec{a}||\vec{b}| = 1$.

Sol. (a) Both (A) and (R) are individually true and (R) is the correct explanation of (A).

Explanation :

If $\vec{a}$ and $\vec{b}$ are reciprocal, then

$\vec{a} = \lambda \vec{b}, \lambda \in R^+$ and $|\vec{a}||\vec{b}| = 1$

$\Rightarrow \qquad |\vec{a}| = |\lambda||\vec{b}|$

$\therefore \qquad |\lambda| = \dfrac{|\vec{a}|}{|\vec{b}|} = \dfrac{1}{|\vec{b}|^2}$

$\because \qquad \lambda \in R^+$

$\therefore \qquad \lambda = \dfrac{1}{|\vec{b}|^2}$

$\therefore \qquad \vec{a} = \dfrac{\vec{b}}{|\vec{b}|^2}$

$\Rightarrow \qquad \vec{a} \cdot \vec{b} = \dfrac{\vec{b}}{|\vec{b}|^2} \cdot \vec{b} = \dfrac{|\vec{b}|^2}{|\vec{b}|^2} = 1$.

61. Assertion (A) : Three points with position vectors $\vec{a}, \vec{b}, \vec{c}$ are collinear if $\vec{a} \times \vec{b} + \vec{b} \times \vec{c} + \vec{c} \times \vec{a} = 0$.

Reason (R) : Three points A, B, C are collinear if $\overrightarrow{AB} = t\,\overrightarrow{BC}$, where t is scalar.

Sol. (a) Both (A) and (R) are individually true and (R) is the correct explanation of (A).

Explanation :

$$\because \ \overrightarrow{OA} = \vec{a}, \ \overrightarrow{OB} = \vec{b}, \ \overrightarrow{OC} = \vec{c}$$

$$\therefore \ \overrightarrow{AB} = \overrightarrow{OB} - \overrightarrow{OA} = (\vec{b} - \vec{a})$$

$$\text{and } \ \overrightarrow{BC} = \overrightarrow{OC} - \overrightarrow{OB} = (\vec{c} - \vec{b})$$

$\overrightarrow{AB}$ is parallel to $\overrightarrow{BC}$.

$$\therefore \qquad\qquad \overrightarrow{AB} \times \overrightarrow{BC} = 0$$

$$\Rightarrow \qquad\qquad (\vec{b} - \vec{a}) \times (\vec{c} - \vec{b}) = 0$$

$$\Rightarrow \ \vec{b} \times \vec{c} - \vec{b} \times \vec{b} - \vec{a} \times \vec{c} + \vec{a} \times \vec{b} = 0$$

$$\Rightarrow \qquad \vec{b} \times \vec{c} - 0 + \vec{c} \times \vec{a} + \vec{a} \times \vec{b} = 0$$

$$\text{Hence,} \qquad \vec{a} \times \vec{b} + \vec{b} \times \vec{c} + \vec{c} \times \vec{a} = 0$$

62. Assertion (A) : If a force $\vec{F}$ passes through Q, then moment of force $\vec{F}$ about $P(\vec{a})$ is $\vec{F} \times \vec{r}$ when $\vec{r} = \overrightarrow{PQ}$.

Reason (R): Moment is a vector.

Sol. (d) (A) is false but (R) is true.

Explanation :

Then, moment of force $\vec{F}$ about point P is $\vec{r} \times \vec{F}$ when $\vec{r} = \overrightarrow{PQ}$

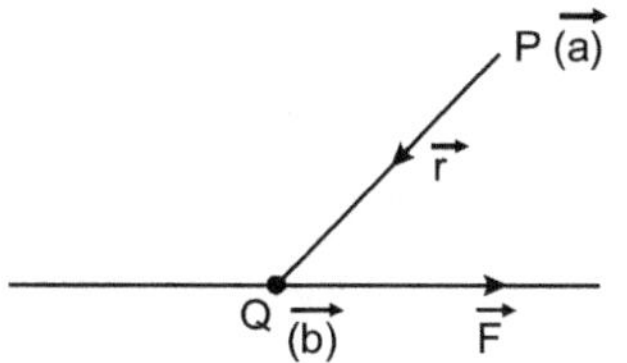

63. Assertion (A) : If $\vec{a} \times \vec{b} = \vec{c} \times \vec{d}$ and $\vec{a} \times \vec{c} = \vec{b} \times \vec{d}$, then $\vec{a} - \vec{d}$ is perpendicular to $\vec{b} - \vec{c}$.

Reason (R) : If $\vec{p}$ is perpendicular to $\vec{q}$, then $\vec{p} \cdot \vec{q} = 0$.

Sol. (c) (A) is true but (R) is false.

Explanation :

$$\text{We have,} \qquad \vec{a} \times \vec{b} = \vec{c} \times \vec{d} \qquad\qquad ...(i)$$

$$\text{and} \qquad \vec{a} \times \vec{c} = \vec{b} \times \vec{d} \qquad\qquad ...(ii)$$

$$\because \ (\vec{a} - \vec{d}) \times (\vec{b} - \vec{c})$$

$$= \vec{a} \times \vec{b} - \vec{a} \times \vec{c} - \vec{d} \times \vec{b} + \vec{d} \times \vec{c}$$

$$= \vec{c} \times \vec{d} - \vec{b} \times \vec{d} + \vec{b} \times \vec{d} - \vec{c} \times \vec{d}$$

$$= 0 \qquad\qquad \text{[From (i) and (ii)]}$$

$$\therefore \ \vec{a} - \vec{d} \ \text{and} \ \vec{b} - \vec{c} \ \text{are parallel.}$$

Case Based Questions

64. Raja was flying a kite from a point A in the direction of $\vec{a} = 5\hat{i} + \hat{j} + 4\hat{k}$. **His friend Sohan was watching him from the point B which is horizontal to A with the position vector** $\vec{b} = 2\hat{i} + 6\hat{j} + 3\hat{k}$. **The point B is just below the kite.**

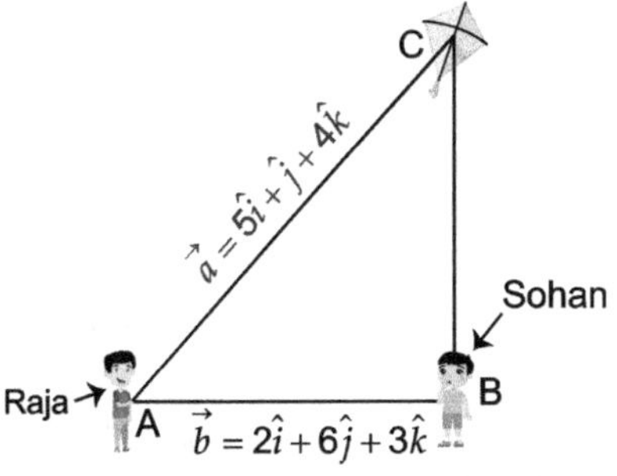

Answer the following questions :

(i) Find the distance between AB ?

   (a) 4   (b) 5

   (c) 6   (d) 7

Sol. (d) 7

Explanation :

Distance between

$$AB = |\overrightarrow{AB}|$$

$$= \sqrt{2^2 + 6^2 + 3^2} = \sqrt{4 + 36 + 9}$$

$$= 7 \text{ units.} \qquad\qquad \textbf{Ans.}$$

(ii) Find the length of the string ?

   (a) $\sqrt{77}$ units   (b) $\sqrt{42}$ units

   (c) $\sqrt{11}$ units   (d) 10 units

Sol. (b) $\sqrt{42}$ units

Explanation :

Length of string is

$$|\overrightarrow{AC}| = \sqrt{5^2 + 1^2 + 4^2} = \sqrt{25 + 1 + 16} = \sqrt{42} \text{ units.}$$

Ans.

(iii) Find the projection of $\overrightarrow{a}$ on $\overrightarrow{b}$?

(a) 1   (b) 2
(c) 4   (d) 3

Sol. (c) 4

Explanation :

$$\text{Projection of } \overrightarrow{a} \text{ on } \overrightarrow{b} = \frac{\overrightarrow{a} \cdot \overrightarrow{b}}{|\overrightarrow{b}|}$$

$$\overrightarrow{a} \cdot \overrightarrow{b} = (5\hat{i} + \hat{j} + 4\hat{k}).(2\hat{i} + 6\hat{j} + 3\hat{k})$$

$$= 10 + 6 + 12 = 28$$

$$\text{Projection} = \frac{28}{7} = 4$$

Ans.

(iv) Find a unit vector in the direction of $\overrightarrow{a}$ and $\overrightarrow{b}$?

(a) $\dfrac{\hat{i} + \hat{j} + \hat{k}}{3}$ (b) $\dfrac{\hat{i} + \hat{j} + \hat{k}}{\sqrt{3}}$

(c) $\hat{i} - \hat{j} + \hat{k}$ (d) $\dfrac{\hat{i} - \hat{j} + \hat{k}}{\sqrt{3}}$

Sol. (b) $\dfrac{\hat{i} + \hat{j} + \hat{k}}{\sqrt{3}}$

Explanation :

Unit vector in the direction of $\overrightarrow{a} + \overrightarrow{b}$ is

$$\frac{\overrightarrow{a} + \overrightarrow{b}}{|\overrightarrow{a} + \overrightarrow{b}|} = \frac{7\hat{i} + 7\hat{j} + 7\hat{k}}{\sqrt{7^2 + 7^2 + 7^2}} = \frac{7(\hat{i} + \hat{j} + \hat{k})}{\sqrt{147}}$$

$$= \frac{7(\hat{i} + \hat{j} + \hat{k})}{7\sqrt{3}} \cdot = \frac{\hat{i} + \hat{j} + \hat{k}}{\sqrt{3}}$$

Ans.

(v) Find the angle between $\overrightarrow{a}$ and $\overrightarrow{b}$:

(a) $\cos^{-1}\left(\dfrac{4}{\sqrt{42}}\right)$ (b) $\cos^{-1}\dfrac{4}{77}$

(c) $\cos^{-1}\dfrac{4}{11}$ (d) $\cos^{-1}\dfrac{4}{25}$

Sol. (a) $\cos^{-1}\left(\dfrac{4}{\sqrt{42}}\right)$

Explanation :

Angle between $\overrightarrow{a}$ and $\overrightarrow{b}$

$$\cos\theta = \frac{\overrightarrow{a} \cdot \overrightarrow{b}}{|\overrightarrow{a}||\overrightarrow{b}|} = \frac{28}{7 \times \sqrt{42}}$$

$$\theta = \cos^{-1}\left(\frac{4}{\sqrt{42}}\right)$$

Ans.

65. Two friends Raja and Rahul are standing on a point O from where they started to move in different directions with the position vector of $2\hat{i} - \hat{j} + \hat{k},\ \hat{i} - 3\hat{j} - 5\hat{k}$ respectively. Raja reaches to his office at point A and Rahul reaches his client office at point B which are opposite to each other. They decided to meet at a coffee shop situated on the way of AB coffee shop divided the road AB in the ratio of 2 : 1.

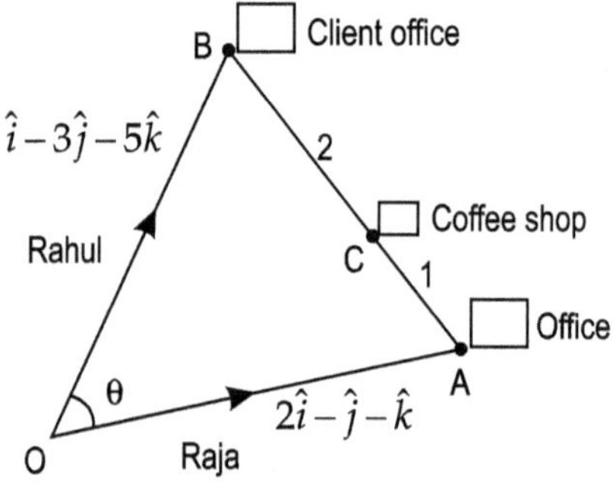

Give answers of the following questions (any 4) :

(i) How much distance is covered by Raja to reach his office 'A' ?

(a) 6 units   (b) $\sqrt{6}$ units
(c) $\sqrt{10}$ units   (d) $\sqrt{5}$ units

Sol. (b) $\sqrt{6}$ units

Explanation :

$$\overrightarrow{OA} = 2\hat{i} - \hat{j} + \hat{k}$$

$$|\overrightarrow{OA}| = \sqrt{2^2 + (-1)^2 + 1^2}$$

$$= \sqrt{4 + 1 + 1} = \sqrt{6} \text{ units}$$

Ans.

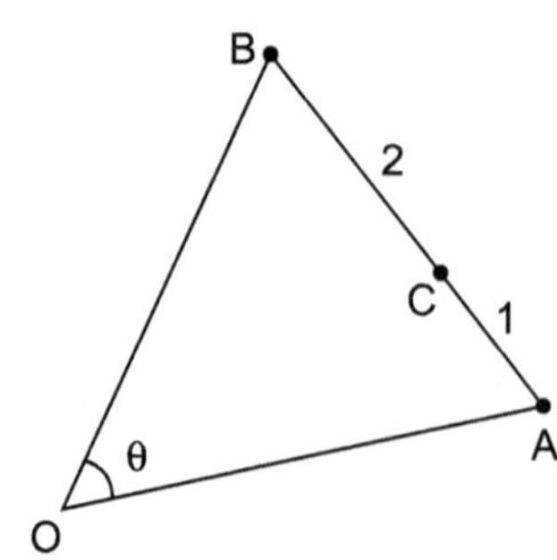

(ii) What is the distance between Rahul's starting point and terminating point ?

   (a) $\sqrt{35}$ units   (b) 6 units

   (c) $\sqrt{6}$ units   (d) $\sqrt{40}$ units

Sol. (a) $\sqrt{35}$ units

Explanation :

$$\overrightarrow{OB} = \hat{i} - 3\hat{j} - 5\hat{k}$$

Distance covered by Rahul is

$$|\overrightarrow{OB}| = \sqrt{1^2 + (-3)^2 + (-5)^2}$$
$$= \sqrt{1+9+25} = \sqrt{35} \text{ units.} \qquad \textbf{Ans.}$$

(iii) What is the distance between Raja's office and Rahul's client office ?

   (a) $\sqrt{6}$ units   (b) $\sqrt{35}$ units

   (c) 6 units   (d) $\sqrt{41}$ units

Sol. (d) $\sqrt{41}$ units

Explanation :

Distance between Raja office and Rahul's client office will be $|\overrightarrow{AB}|$.

$$\overrightarrow{AB} = \overrightarrow{OB} - \overrightarrow{OA}$$
$$= (\hat{i} - 3\hat{j} - 5\hat{k}) - (2\hat{i} - \hat{j} + \hat{k})$$
$$= -\hat{i} - 2\hat{j} - 6\hat{k}$$
$$|\overrightarrow{AB}| = \sqrt{(-1)^2 + (-2) + (-6)^2}$$
$$= \sqrt{1+4+36} = \sqrt{41} \text{ units.} \qquad \textbf{Ans.}$$

(iv) What are the coordinates of the point of coffee shop ?

   (a) $\left(\dfrac{5}{3}, \dfrac{-5}{3}, -1\right)$ (b) $\left(\dfrac{-5}{3}, \dfrac{5}{3}, -1\right)$

   (c) $\left(\dfrac{5}{3}, \dfrac{5}{3}, 1\right)$ (d) $\left(-1, \dfrac{5}{3}, \dfrac{-5}{3}\right)$

Sol. (a) $\left(\dfrac{5}{3}, \dfrac{-5}{3}, -1\right)$

Explanation :

2 | 1

B   C   A
$(\hat{i}-3\hat{j}-5\hat{k})$ $(2\hat{i}-\hat{j}+\hat{k})$

Let $\qquad \overrightarrow{OC} = x\hat{i} + y\hat{j} + z\hat{k}$

Which divides BA in the ratio 2 : 1. By section formula coordinates of C will be :

$$x = \frac{2(2)+1}{3}, \quad y = \frac{2(-1)+1(-3)}{2+1},$$
$$z = \frac{2(1)+1(-5)}{2+1}$$
$$x = \frac{4+1}{3} = \frac{5}{3}, \quad y = \frac{-2-3}{3} = \frac{-5}{3},$$
$$z = \frac{2-5}{3} = \frac{-3}{3} = -1$$

Coordinates of $C\left(\dfrac{5}{3}, \dfrac{-5}{3}, -1\right)$ **Ans.**

(v) If θ is the angle between $\overrightarrow{OA}$ and $\overrightarrow{OB}$, what is the value of θ ?

   (a) $0°$ (b) $60°$

   (c) $30°$ (d) $90°$

Sol. (d) $90°$

Explanation :

$$\cos\theta = \frac{a_1 a_2 + b_1 b_2 + c_1 c_2}{\sqrt{a_1^2 + b_1^2 + c_1^2}\sqrt{a_2^2 + b_2^2 + c_2^2}}$$
$$\cos\theta = \frac{2(1) + (-1)(-3) + (1)(-5)}{\sqrt{6}\sqrt{35}}$$
$$\cos\theta = \frac{2+3-5}{\sqrt{6}\sqrt{35}} = 0$$
$$\theta = 90° \qquad \textbf{Ans.}$$

Very Short Answer Type Questions

66. Find sum of vectors $\vec{a} = \hat{i} - 2\hat{j} + \hat{k}$ and $\vec{b} = 2\hat{i} - 4\hat{j} + 5\hat{k}$ and $\vec{c} = \hat{i} - 6\hat{j} - 7\hat{k}$.*

Sol. Sum of the vectors $\vec{a}, \vec{b}, \vec{c}$ is

$$\vec{a} + \vec{b} + \vec{c} = (\hat{i} - 2\hat{j} + \hat{k}) + (2\hat{i} - 4\hat{j} + 5\hat{k})$$
$$+ (\hat{i} - 6\hat{j} - 7\hat{k})$$
$$= 4\hat{i} - 12\hat{j} - \hat{k}$$

67. Find the scalar components of $\overrightarrow{AB}$ with initial point A(2, 1) and terminal point B(– 5, 7).*

Sol. Given, points A(2, 1) and B(– 5, 7). Scalar component of $\overrightarrow{AB}$ are $x_2 - x_1$ and $y_2 - y_1$ *i.e.*, $-5 - 2$ and $7 - 1$ *i.e.*, -7 and 6.

68. For what value of 'a', the vectors $2\hat{i} - 3\hat{j} + 4\hat{k}$ and $a\hat{i} + 6\hat{j} - 8\hat{k}$ are collinear ?*

Sol. Vectors $\vec{a}$ and $\vec{b}$ are said to be collinear, if

$$\vec{a} = k.\vec{b}, \text{ where } k = \text{scalar}$$

$$\therefore \quad 2\hat{i} - 3\hat{j} + 4\hat{k} = k(a\hat{i} + 6\hat{j} - 8\hat{k})$$

Above equation is satisfied when $a = -4$

$$\therefore \qquad a = -4$$

69. Write the direction cosines of vector

$$-2\hat{i} + \hat{j} - 5\hat{k}.*$$

Sol. Let $\qquad \vec{a} = -2\hat{i} + \hat{j} - 5\hat{k}$

$\therefore$ Direction cosines of $\vec{a}$ are

$$\frac{-2}{\sqrt{(-2)^2 + (1)^2 + (-5)^2}}, \frac{1}{\sqrt{(-2)^2 + (1)^2 + (-5)^2}},$$

$$\frac{-5}{\sqrt{(-2)^2 + (1)^2 + (-5)^2}} = \frac{-2}{\sqrt{30}}, \frac{1}{\sqrt{30}}, \frac{-5}{\sqrt{30}}$$

70. Write the position vector of mid-point of the vector joining points P(2, 3, 4) and Q(4, 1, – 2).*

Sol. Position vector of mid-point of a vector joining points P(2, 3, 4) and Q(4, 1, – 2) is

$$\frac{OP + OQ}{2} = \frac{(2\hat{i} + 3\hat{j} + 4\hat{k}) + (4\hat{i} + \hat{j} - 2\hat{k})}{2}$$

$$= \frac{6\hat{i} + 4\hat{j} + 2\hat{k}}{2} = 3\hat{i} + 2\hat{j} + \hat{k} = (3, 2, 1)$$

71. Write a unit vector in the direction of $\vec{a} = 2\hat{i} + \hat{j} + 2\hat{k}.*$

Sol. Unit vector in the direction of $\vec{a}$ is given as,

$$\hat{a} = \frac{\vec{a}}{|\vec{a}|}$$

$$= \frac{2\hat{i} + \hat{j} + 2\hat{k}}{\sqrt{(2)^2 + (1)^2 + (2)^2}}$$

$$= \frac{2\hat{i} + \hat{j} + 2\hat{k}}{\sqrt{9}}$$

$$= \frac{2}{3}\hat{i} + \frac{1}{3}\hat{j} + \frac{2}{3}\hat{k}$$

72. Find the magnitude of the vector

$$\vec{a} = 3\hat{i} - 2\hat{j} + 6\hat{k}.*$$

Sol. Magnitude of $\vec{a} = |\vec{a}|$

$$= \sqrt{(3)^2 + (-2) + (6)^2}$$

$$= \sqrt{9 + 4 + 36}$$

$$= \sqrt{49} = 7$$

73. Find a unit vector in the direction of vector

$$\vec{a} = 2\hat{i} + 3\hat{j} + 6\hat{k}.*$$

Sol. Unit vector in the direction of $\vec{a}$ is given as,

$$\hat{a} = \frac{\vec{a}}{|\vec{a}|}$$

$$= \frac{2\hat{i} + 3\hat{j} + 6\hat{k}}{\sqrt{(2)^2 + (3)^2 + (6)^2}}$$

$$= \frac{2\hat{i} + 3\hat{j} + 6\hat{k}}{\sqrt{49}}$$

$$= \frac{2}{7}\hat{i} + \frac{3}{7}\hat{j} + \frac{6}{7}\hat{k}$$

74. Find a vector in the direction of $\vec{a} = 2\hat{i} - \hat{j} + 2\hat{k}$ which has magnitude 6 units.*

Sol. First we find a unit vector in the direction of $\vec{a}$

$$\hat{a} = \frac{\vec{a}}{|\vec{a}|} = \frac{2\hat{i} - \hat{j} + 2\hat{k}}{\sqrt{(2)^2 + (-1)^2 + (2)^2}}$$

$$= \frac{2}{3}\hat{i} - \frac{1}{3}\hat{j} + \frac{2}{3}\hat{k}$$

Now, vector of magnitude 6 units

$$= 6\left[\frac{2}{3}\hat{i} - \frac{1}{3}\hat{j} + \frac{2}{3}\hat{k}\right]$$

$$= 4\hat{i} - 2\hat{j} + 4\hat{k}$$

75. Find a position vector of mid-point of line segment AB, where A is point (3, 4, – 2) and B is point (1, 2, 4).*

Sol. Position vector of mid-point of line segment AB, where A is (3, 4, –2) and B(1, 2, 4) is given as follows:

Let $\qquad \vec{OA} = 3\hat{i} + 4\hat{j} - 2\hat{k}$

and $\qquad \vec{OB} = \hat{i} + 2\hat{j} + 4\hat{k}$

$\therefore$ Position vector of mid-point of $\vec{AB}$

$$= \frac{\vec{OA} + \vec{OB}}{2}$$

$$= \frac{(3\hat{i} + 4\hat{j} - 2\hat{k}) + (\hat{i} + 2\hat{j} + 4\hat{k})}{2}$$

$$= \frac{4\hat{i}+6\hat{j}+2\hat{k}}{2}$$

$$= 2\hat{i}+3\hat{j}+\hat{k}$$

76. Write a vector of magnitude 15 units in the direction of vector $\hat{i}-2\hat{j}+2\hat{k}$.*

Sol. Let $\vec{a} = \hat{i}-2\hat{j}+2\hat{k}$

Unit vector in the direction of $\vec{a}$ is given as,

$$\hat{a} = \frac{\vec{a}}{|\vec{a}|} = \frac{\hat{i}-2\hat{j}+2\hat{k}}{\sqrt{(1)^2+(-2)^2+(2)^2}}$$

$$= \frac{\hat{i}-2\hat{j}+2\hat{k}}{\sqrt{9}}$$

$$= \frac{1}{3}\hat{i}-\frac{2}{3}\hat{j}+\frac{2}{3}\hat{k}$$

$\therefore$ Vector of magnitude 15 units

$$= 15\left(\frac{1}{3}\hat{i}-\frac{2}{3}\hat{j}+\frac{2}{3}\hat{k}\right)$$

$$= 5\hat{i}-10\hat{j}+10\hat{k}$$

77. What is the cosine of angle which the vector $\sqrt{2}\hat{i}+\hat{j}+\hat{k}$ makes with Y-axis?*

Sol. Let $\vec{a} = \sqrt{2}\hat{i}+\hat{j}+\hat{k}$

Now, unit vector in the direction of $\vec{a}$

$$= \frac{\vec{a}}{|\vec{a}|} = \frac{\sqrt{2}\hat{i}+\hat{j}+\hat{k}}{\sqrt{(\sqrt{2})^2+(1)^2+(1)^2}}$$

$$= \frac{\sqrt{2}\hat{i}+\hat{j}+\hat{k}}{2}$$

$$= \frac{\sqrt{2}}{2}\hat{i}+\frac{1}{2}\hat{j}+\frac{1}{2}\hat{k}$$

$\therefore$ Cosine of angle which the given vector makes with Y-axis is $\frac{1}{2}$.

78. If $\vec{a} = \hat{i}+2\hat{j}-\hat{k}$ and $\vec{b} = 3\hat{i}+\hat{j}-5\hat{k}$, find a unit vector in the direction of $\vec{a}-\vec{b}$*

Sol. Here,

$$\vec{a}-\vec{b} = (\hat{i}+2\hat{j}-\hat{k})-(3\hat{i}+\hat{j}-5\hat{k})$$

$$= -2\hat{i}+\hat{j}+4\hat{k}$$

Let, $\vec{a}-\vec{b} = \vec{c}$

Now, unit vector in the direction of $\vec{c}$

$$\frac{\vec{c}}{|\vec{c}|} = \frac{-2\hat{j}+\hat{j}+4\hat{k}}{\sqrt{(-2)^2+(1)^2+(4)^2}}$$

$$= \frac{-2\hat{i}+\hat{j}+4\hat{k}}{\sqrt{21}}$$

$$= -\frac{2}{\sqrt{21}}\hat{i}+\frac{1}{\sqrt{21}}\hat{j}+\frac{4}{\sqrt{21}}\hat{k}$$

79. A unit vector in the direction of the sum of the vectors $\vec{a} = 2\hat{i}+2\hat{j}-5\hat{k}$ and $\vec{b} = 2\hat{i}+\hat{j}-7\hat{k}$ is

....

Sol. $\frac{4}{13}\hat{i}+\frac{3}{13}\hat{j}-\frac{12}{13}\hat{k}$

Given, $\vec{a} = 2\hat{i}+2\hat{j}-5\hat{k}$

$$\vec{b} = 2\hat{i}+\hat{j}-7\hat{k}$$

$$\Rightarrow \vec{a}+\vec{b} = (2\hat{i}+2\hat{j}-5\hat{k})+(2\hat{i}+\hat{j}-7\hat{k})$$

$$= 4\hat{i}+3\hat{j}-12\hat{k}$$

and $|\vec{a}+\vec{b}| = \sqrt{4^2+3^2+(-12)^2}$

$$= \sqrt{16+9+144}$$

$$= \sqrt{169}$$

$$= 13$$

The unit vector in the direction of $\vec{a}+\vec{b}$ is

$$\frac{\vec{a}+\vec{b}}{|\vec{a}+\vec{b}|} = \frac{4\hat{i}+3\hat{j}-12\hat{k}}{13}$$

$$= \frac{4}{13}\hat{i}+\frac{3}{13}\hat{j}-\frac{12}{13}\hat{k}$$

80. The two vectors $\hat{j}+\hat{k}$ and $3\hat{i}-\hat{j}+4\hat{k}$ represent the two sides AB and AC, respectively of a $\triangle$ABC. Find the length of the median through A.*

Sol. In $\triangle$ABC

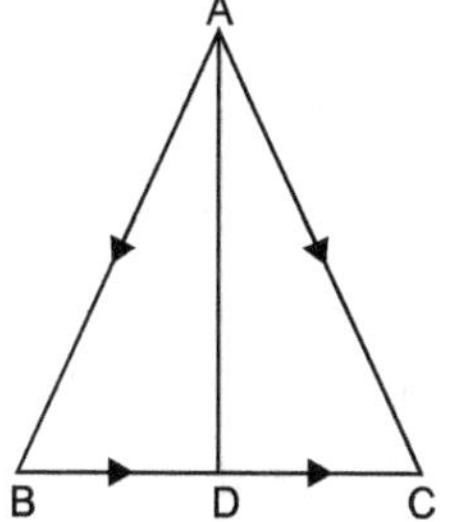

Using the triangle law of vector addition, we have

$$\vec{BC} = \vec{AC} - \vec{AB}$$

$$= (3\hat{i} - \hat{j} + 4\hat{k}) - (\hat{j} + \hat{k})$$

$$= 3\hat{i} - 2\hat{j} + 3\hat{k}$$

$$\therefore \qquad \vec{BD} = \frac{1}{2}\vec{BC} = \frac{3}{2}\hat{i} - \hat{j} + \frac{3}{2}\hat{k}$$

$$[\because \text{AD is the median}]$$

In $\triangle ABD$, using the triangle law of vector addition, we have

$$\vec{AD} = \vec{AB} + \vec{BD}$$

$$= (\hat{j} + \hat{k}) + \left(\frac{3}{2}\hat{i} - \hat{j} + \frac{3}{2}\hat{k}\right)$$

$$= \frac{3}{2}\hat{i} + 0\hat{j} + \frac{5}{2}\hat{k}$$

$$\therefore \qquad AD = \sqrt{\left(\frac{3}{2}\right)^2 + 0^2 + \left(\frac{5}{2}\right)^2} = \frac{1}{2}\sqrt{34}$$

Hence, the length of the median through A is $\frac{1}{2}\sqrt{34}$ units.

81. If $\vec{a} = 4\hat{i} + y\hat{j} - 3\hat{k}$ and $|\vec{a}| = 13$, then the value of y is ....

Sol. ± 2

Given, $\qquad\qquad |\vec{a}| = 13$

$$\Rightarrow \qquad |4\hat{i} + y\hat{j} - 3\hat{k}| = 13$$

$$\Rightarrow \qquad \sqrt{(16 + y^2 + 9)} = 13$$

$$\Rightarrow \qquad\qquad y^2 + 25 = 169$$

$$\Rightarrow \qquad\qquad y^2 = 144$$

$$\Rightarrow \qquad\qquad y = \pm 12.$$

82. If $\vec{a} = (-1, 2)$, $\vec{b} = (3, -2)$, $\vec{c} = (0, 5)$, then the value of $\vec{a} + \vec{b} - 2\vec{c}$ is ....

Sol. $(2, -10)$

$$\vec{a} + \vec{b} - 2\vec{c} = (-\hat{i} + 2\hat{j}) + (3\hat{i} - 2\hat{j}) - 2(0\hat{i} + 5\hat{j})$$

$$= 2\hat{i} - 10\hat{j}$$

$$= (2, -10).$$

83. If $\vec{a}$ and $\vec{b}$ are the position vectors of A and B respectively, then the position vector of a point C on the line AB, such that $\vec{AC} = 3\vec{AB}$ is ....

Sol. $3\vec{b} - 2\vec{a}$

Let $\vec{r}$ be the position vector of C.

Then $\qquad\qquad \vec{AC} = 3\vec{AB}$

$$\Rightarrow \qquad \vec{r} - \vec{a} = 3(\vec{b} - \vec{a})$$

$$\Rightarrow \qquad\qquad \vec{r} = 3\vec{b} - 2\vec{a}$$

84. If D, E, F are the mid-points of the sides BC, CA, AB respectively of the triangle ABC, then the value of $\vec{AD} + \vec{BE} + \vec{CF}$ is ....

Sol. 0

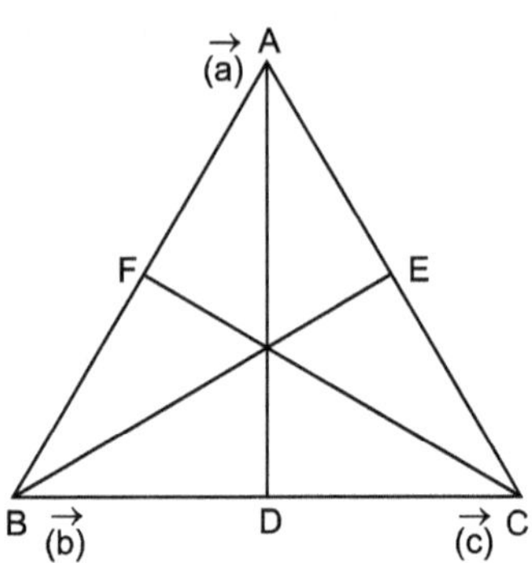

Let $\vec{a}, \vec{b}, \vec{c}$ be the position vectors of A, B, C of the triangle ABC.

Therefore, the position vector of

$$D = \frac{1}{2}(\vec{b} + \vec{c}),$$

the position vector of E $= \frac{1}{2}(\vec{c} + \vec{a})$

and the position vector of F $= \frac{1}{2}(\vec{a} + \vec{b})$

$$\Rightarrow \vec{AD} + \vec{BE} + \vec{CF}$$

$$= \left[\frac{\vec{b} + \vec{c}}{2} - \vec{a}\right] + \left[\frac{\vec{c} + \vec{a}}{2} - \vec{b}\right] + \left[\frac{\vec{a} + \vec{b}}{2} - \vec{c}\right]$$

$$= \frac{1}{2}[(\vec{b} + \vec{c} - 2\vec{a}) + (\vec{c} + \vec{a} - 2\vec{b}) + (\vec{a} + \vec{b} - 2\vec{c})]$$

$$= \vec{0}$$

85. The projection of the vector $\hat{i} - \hat{j}$ on the vector $\hat{i} + \hat{j}$ is ....

Sol. 0

Projection $\hat{i} - \hat{j}$ on $\hat{i} + \hat{j}$

$$= \frac{(\hat{i} - \hat{j}) \cdot (\hat{i} + \hat{j})}{|\hat{i} + \hat{j}|} = 0.$$

86. Find λ when projection of $\vec{a} = \lambda\hat{i} + \hat{j} + 4\hat{k}$ on $\vec{b} = 2\hat{i} + 6\hat{j} + 3\hat{k}$ is 4 units.*

Sol. Given that projection of $\vec{a}$ over $\vec{b}$ = 4

$$\Rightarrow \quad \frac{\vec{a}.\vec{b}}{|\vec{b}|} = 4$$

$$\left[\because \text{ projection of } \vec{a} \text{ over } \vec{b} = \frac{\vec{a}.\vec{b}}{|\vec{b}|}\right]$$

$$\Rightarrow \quad \frac{(\lambda\hat{i}+\hat{j}+4\hat{k}).(2\hat{i}+6\hat{j}+3\hat{k})}{\sqrt{(2)^2 + (6)^2 + (3)^2}} = 4$$

$$\Rightarrow \quad \frac{2\lambda+6+12}{\sqrt{49}} = 4$$

$$\Rightarrow \quad \frac{2\lambda+18}{7} = 4$$

$$\Rightarrow \quad 2\lambda + 18 = 28$$

$$\Rightarrow \quad 2\lambda = 10$$

$$\Rightarrow \quad \lambda = 5.$$

87. If $|\vec{a}| = 2$, $|\vec{b}| = 3$ and $\vec{a}.\vec{b} = 3$, find the projection of $\vec{b}$ on $\vec{a}$

Sol. Projection of $\vec{b}$ over $\vec{a}$

$$= \frac{\vec{b}.\vec{a}}{|\vec{a}|} = \frac{\vec{a}.\vec{b}}{|\vec{a}|} \quad [\because \vec{a}.\vec{b} = \vec{b}.\vec{a}]$$

$$= \frac{3}{2}$$

88. Find the projection of the vector $\hat{i} + 3\hat{j} + 7\hat{k}$ on the vector $2\hat{i} - 3\hat{j} + 6\hat{k}$.*

Sol. Let $\vec{a} = \hat{i} + 3\hat{j} + 7\hat{k}$ and $\vec{b} = 2\hat{i} - 3\hat{j} + 6\hat{k}$

$$\therefore \text{ Projection of } \vec{a} \text{ on } \vec{b} = \frac{\vec{a}.\vec{b}}{|\vec{b}|}$$

$$= \frac{(\hat{i}+3\hat{j}+7\hat{k}).(2\hat{i}-3\hat{j}+6\hat{k})}{\sqrt{2^2 + (-3)^2 + 6^2}}$$

$$= \frac{1\times 2 + 3\times(-3) + 7\times 6}{\sqrt{4+9+36}}$$

$$= \frac{2-9+42}{\sqrt{49}} = \frac{35}{7} = 5.$$

89. Write the position vector of the point which divides the join of points with position vectors $3\vec{a} - 2\vec{b}$ and $2\vec{a} + 3\vec{b}$ in the ratio 2 : 1.

Sol. Let A and B be the given points with position vectors $3\vec{a} - 2\vec{b}$ and $2\vec{a} + 3\vec{b}$ respectively.

Let P and Q be the points dividing AB in the ratio 2 : 1 internally and externally respectively. Then

$$\text{Position vector of P} = \frac{1(3\vec{a} - 2\vec{b}) + 2(2\vec{a} + 3\vec{b})}{1+2}$$

$$= \frac{7\vec{a}}{3} + \frac{4\vec{b}}{3}$$

$$\text{Position vector of Q} = \frac{1(3\vec{a} - 2\vec{b}) - 2(2\vec{a} + 3\vec{b})}{1-2}$$

$$= \vec{a} + 8\vec{b}$$

90. Find the projection of $\vec{a}$ on $\vec{b}$ if $\vec{a}.\vec{b}$ = 8 and $\vec{b} = 2\hat{i} + 6\hat{j} + 3\hat{k}$*

Sol. Projection of $\vec{a}$ on $\vec{b}$

$$= \frac{\vec{a}.\vec{b}}{|\vec{b}|}$$

$$= \frac{8}{\sqrt{(2)^2 + (6)^2 + (3)^2}}$$

$$= \frac{8}{\sqrt{49}} = \frac{8}{7}.$$

91. If $\vec{a}$ is a non-zero vector, then $(\vec{a}.\hat{i})\hat{i} + (\vec{a}.\hat{j})\hat{j} + (\vec{a}.\hat{k})\hat{k}$ equals ....

Sol. $\vec{a}$

Let $$\vec{a} = a_1\hat{i} + b_1\hat{j} + c_1\hat{k}$$

$$\therefore (\vec{a}.\hat{i})\hat{i} + (\vec{a}.\hat{j})\hat{j} + (\vec{a}.\hat{k})\hat{k}$$

$$= a_1\hat{i} + b_1\hat{j} + c_1\hat{k}$$

$$= \vec{a}$$

92. Write the angle between vectors $\vec{a}$ and $\vec{b}$ with magnitudes $\sqrt{3}$ and 2 respectively, having $\vec{a}.\vec{b} = \sqrt{6}$.*

Sol. Given $$|\vec{a}| = \sqrt{3}, |\vec{b}| = 2$$

---

and $\qquad \vec{a} . \vec{b} = \sqrt{6}$

Now, angle between $\vec{a}$ and $\vec{b}$ is given by

$$\cos \theta = \frac{\vec{a} . \vec{b}}{|\vec{a}| |\vec{b}|} = \frac{\sqrt{6}}{\sqrt{3} \times 2}$$

or $\qquad \cos \theta = \frac{1}{\sqrt{2}} = \cos \frac{\pi}{4}$

$\therefore \qquad \theta = \frac{\pi}{4} \qquad \left[\because \cos \frac{\pi}{4} = \frac{1}{\sqrt{2}} \right]$

93. For what value of λ are the vectors $\hat{i} + 2\lambda \hat{j} + \hat{k}$ and $2\hat{i} + \hat{j} - 3\hat{k}$ perpendicular ?*

Sol. Given that the vectors are perpendicular, so their dot product is zero.

$\therefore \quad (\hat{i} + 2\lambda \hat{j} + \hat{k}).(2\hat{i} + \hat{j} - 3\hat{k}) = 0$

$\Rightarrow \qquad 2 + 2\lambda - 3 = 0$

$\Rightarrow \qquad 2\lambda = 1$

or $\qquad \lambda = \frac{1}{2}$

94. If $|\vec{a}| = \sqrt{3}, |\vec{b}| = 2$ and angle between $\vec{a}$ and $\vec{b}$ is $60°$, find $\vec{a} . \vec{b}$ *

Sol. We know that

$$\cos \theta = \frac{\vec{a} . \vec{b}}{|\vec{a}| . |\vec{b}|}$$

Put $|\vec{a}| = \sqrt{3}$, $|\vec{b}| = \sqrt{2}$ and $\theta = 60°$, we get

$$\cos 60° = \frac{\vec{a} . \vec{b}}{\sqrt{3} \times 2}$$

or $\qquad \vec{a} . \vec{b} = \frac{1}{2} \times 2\sqrt{3} = \sqrt{3}$

$\therefore \qquad \vec{a} . \vec{b} = \sqrt{3}$

95. Find the value of λ, if the vectors $2\hat{i} + \lambda \hat{j} + 3\hat{k}$ and $3\hat{i} + 2\hat{j} - 4\hat{k}$ are perpendicular to each other.*

Sol. Given that the vectors are perpendicular, so their dot product is zero.

$\therefore \quad (2\hat{i} + \lambda \hat{j} + 3\hat{k}).(3\hat{i} + 2\hat{j} - 4\hat{k}) = 0$

$\Rightarrow \qquad 6 + 2\lambda - 12 = 0$

$\Rightarrow \qquad 2\lambda = 6$

$\Rightarrow \qquad \lambda = 3.$

96. Find $\vec{a} . \vec{b}$ if $\vec{a} = -\hat{i} + \hat{j} - 2\hat{k}$ and $\vec{b} = 2\hat{i} + 3\hat{j} - \hat{k}$ *

Sol. $\qquad \vec{a} . \vec{b} = (-\hat{i} + \hat{j} - 2\hat{k}) \cdot (2\hat{i} + 3\hat{j} - \hat{k})$

$\qquad = -2 + 3 + 2 = 3.$

97. If $\vec{a} . \vec{a} = 0$ and $\vec{a} . \vec{b} = 0$ then what can be concluded about the vector $\vec{b}$?*

Sol. $\qquad \vec{a} . \vec{a} = 0$

$\Rightarrow \qquad |a|^2 = 0$

$\Rightarrow \qquad |a| = 0 \qquad \qquad ...(i)$

and $\qquad \vec{a} . \vec{b} = 0$

$\Rightarrow \qquad |\vec{a}| |\vec{b}| \cos \theta = 0 \qquad ...(ii)$

From equations (i) and (ii), it can be concluded that $\vec{b}$ is either zero or non-zero or perpendicular vector to $\vec{a}$.

98. If $|\vec{a}| = \sqrt{3}, |\vec{b}| = 2$ and $\vec{a} . \vec{b} = 3$, find angle between $\vec{a}$ and $\vec{b}$.*

Sol. Angle between $\vec{a}$ and $\vec{b}$ is given by

$$\cos \theta = \frac{\vec{a} . \vec{b}}{|\vec{a}| |\vec{b}|}$$

$$= \frac{3}{\sqrt{3} \times 2}$$

$$= \frac{(\sqrt{3})^2}{\sqrt{3} \times 2}$$

$\therefore \qquad \cos \theta = \frac{\sqrt{3}}{2}$

$\Rightarrow \qquad \cos \theta = \cos \frac{\pi}{6}$

$\therefore \qquad \theta = \frac{\pi}{6}$

99. If $\vec{a}$ and $\vec{b}$ are two unit vectors such that $\vec{a} + \vec{b}$ is also a unit vector, then find the angle between $\vec{a}$ and $\vec{b}$.*

Sol. Given, $\qquad |\vec{a}| = 1, |\vec{b}| = 1$

and $\qquad |\vec{a} + \vec{b}| = 1$

$\Rightarrow \qquad |\vec{a} + \vec{b}|^2 = 1$

$\Rightarrow \qquad (\vec{a} + \vec{b}).(\vec{a} + \vec{b}) = 1$

*** are board exam questions from previous years**

$$\Rightarrow \quad \vec{a}.\vec{a} + \vec{a}.\vec{b} + \vec{b}.\vec{a} + \vec{b}.\vec{b} = 1$$

$$\Rightarrow \quad |\vec{a}|^2 + 2\vec{a}.\vec{b} + |\vec{b}|^2 = 1$$

$$\Rightarrow \quad 1 + 2\vec{a}.\vec{b} + 1 = 1$$

$$\Rightarrow \quad 2\vec{a}.\vec{b} = -1$$

$$\Rightarrow \quad 2|\vec{a}|.|\vec{b}|\cos\theta = -1$$

$$\Rightarrow \quad 2.1.1.\cos\theta = -1$$

$$\Rightarrow \quad \cos\theta = -\frac{1}{2}$$

$$\Rightarrow \quad \cos\theta = \cos 120°$$

$$\therefore \quad \theta = 120°.$$

100. If $\hat{a}, \hat{b}$ and $\hat{c}$ are mutually perpendicular unit vectors, then find the value of $|2\hat{a} + \hat{b} + \hat{c}|.$ *

Sol. Let $\quad x = |2\hat{a} + \hat{b} + \hat{c}|$

$$\therefore \quad x^2 = |2\hat{a} + \hat{b} + \hat{c}|^2$$

$$= 4|\hat{a}|^2 + |\hat{b}|^2 + |\hat{c}|^2$$

$$+ 2(2\hat{a}.\hat{b} + \hat{b}.\hat{c} + 2\hat{c}.\hat{a})$$

Since $\hat{a}, \hat{b}$ and $\hat{c}$ are mutually perpendicular unit vectors

$$\therefore \quad \hat{a}.\hat{b} = \hat{b}.\hat{c} = \hat{c}.\hat{a} = 0$$

So, $x^2 = 4 \times 1 + 1 + 1 + 2(2 \times 0 + 0 + 2 \times 0)$

$$x^2 = 6$$

$$\therefore \quad x = \sqrt{6}$$

Hence, $\quad |2\hat{a} + \hat{b} + \hat{c}| = \sqrt{6}$

101. If $\hat{P}$ is a unit vector and $(\vec{x} - \vec{P}).(\vec{x} + \vec{P}) = 80$, then the value of $|\vec{x}|$ is ....

Sol. ± 9

Given that $\hat{P}$ is a unit vector.

$$\therefore \quad |\vec{P}| = 1$$

Now, also given

$$(\vec{x} - \vec{P}).(\vec{x} + \vec{P}) = 80$$

$$\Rightarrow \quad |\vec{x}|^2 - |\vec{P}|^2 = 80$$

$$\Rightarrow \quad |x|^2 - 1 = 80$$

$$\therefore \quad |x|^2 = 81$$

$$\therefore \quad |x| = \pm 9.$$

102. Vectors $\vec{a}$ and $\vec{b}$ are such that $|\vec{a}| = \frac{2}{3}$, $|\vec{b}| = \sqrt{3}$ and $\vec{a} \times \vec{b}$ is a unit vector. Write the angle between $\vec{a}$ and $\vec{b}.$ *

Sol. Given $\vec{a} \times \vec{b}$ is a unit vector.

$$\therefore \quad |\vec{a} \times \vec{b}| = 1$$

$$\Rightarrow \quad |\vec{a}||\vec{b}|\sin\theta|\hat{n}| = 1$$

$$[\because \vec{a} \times \vec{b} = |\vec{a}||\vec{b}|\sin\theta\,\hat{n}]$$

$$\Rightarrow \quad \sqrt{3} \times \frac{2}{3} \times \sin\theta = 1 \qquad [\because |\hat{n}| = 1]$$

$$\Rightarrow \quad \sin\theta = \frac{3}{2\sqrt{3}}$$

$$\Rightarrow \quad \sin\theta = \frac{(\sqrt{3})^2}{2\sqrt{3}} = \frac{\sqrt{3}}{2}$$

$$\Rightarrow \quad \sin\theta = \sin\frac{\pi}{3}$$

$$\therefore \quad \theta = \frac{\pi}{3}$$

$\therefore$ Angle between $\vec{a}$ and $\vec{b} = \frac{\pi}{3}.$

103. If $\vec{a}$ and $\vec{b}$ are two vectors such that $|\vec{a}.\vec{b}| = |\vec{a} \times \vec{b}|$, then find angle between $\vec{a}$ and $\vec{b}.$ *

Sol. Given that $|\vec{a}.\vec{b}| = |\vec{a} \times \vec{b}|$

$$\Rightarrow \quad |\vec{a}||\vec{b}|\cos\theta = |\vec{a}||\vec{b}|\sin\theta \qquad [\because |\hat{n}| = 1]$$

$$\Rightarrow \quad \cos\theta = \sin\theta$$

Divide both sides by $\cos\theta$, we get

$$\tan\theta = 1$$

$$\therefore \quad \tan\theta = \tan\frac{\pi}{4} \qquad \left[\because 1 = \tan\frac{\pi}{4}\right]$$

$$\therefore \quad \theta = \frac{\pi}{4}$$

$\therefore$ Angle between $\vec{a}$ and $\vec{b} = \frac{\pi}{4}.$

104. Find λ, if

$$(2\hat{i} + 6\hat{j} + 14\hat{k}) \times (\hat{i} - \lambda\hat{j} + 7\hat{k}) = 0. *$$

Sol. Given that

$$(2\hat{i} + 6\hat{j} + 14\hat{k}) \times (\hat{i} - \lambda\hat{j} + 7\hat{k}) = 0$$

$$\Rightarrow \quad \begin{vmatrix} \hat{i} & \hat{j} & \hat{k} \\ 2 & 6 & 14 \\ 1 & -\lambda & 7 \end{vmatrix} = 0$$

$$\therefore \ \hat{i}(42+14\lambda)-\hat{j}(14-14)+\hat{k}(-2\lambda-6)=0$$

$$\Rightarrow \hat{i}(42+14\lambda)+\hat{k}(-2\lambda-6)=0\hat{i}+0\hat{j}+0\hat{k}$$

Comparing coefficients of $\hat{i}$ and $\hat{k}$ on both sides, we get

$$42+14\lambda=0$$
$$\Rightarrow \quad 14\lambda=-42$$
$$\Rightarrow \quad \lambda=-3$$
$$\text{and} \quad -2\lambda-6=0$$
$$\Rightarrow \quad -2\lambda=6$$
$$\therefore \quad \lambda=-3.$$

105. Find the angle between $\vec{a}$ and $\vec{b}$ with magnitude 1 and 2 respectively and when $|\vec{a}\times\vec{b}|=\sqrt{3}.$*

Sol. Given that $\quad |\vec{a}\times\vec{b}|=\sqrt{3}$

$$\Rightarrow \quad |\vec{a}||\vec{b}|\sin\theta=\sqrt{3}$$

$$[\because \vec{a}\times\vec{b}=|\vec{a}||\vec{b}|\sin\theta.\hat{n} \text{ and } |\hat{n}|=1]$$

$$\therefore \quad 1\times2\times\sin\theta=\sqrt{3}$$

$$\therefore \quad \sin\theta=\frac{\sqrt{3}}{2}=\sin\frac{\pi}{3}$$

$$\therefore \quad \theta=\frac{\pi}{3}$$

Angle between $\vec{a}$ and $\vec{b}$ $=\dfrac{\pi}{3}$.

106. Write the value of p for which $\vec{a}=3\hat{i}+2\hat{j}+9\hat{k}$ and $\vec{b}=\hat{i}+p\hat{j}+3\hat{k}$ are parallel vectors.*

Sol. Since, $\vec{a}$ and $\vec{b}$ are parallel,

$$\therefore \quad \vec{a}\times\vec{b}=0$$

$$\Rightarrow \quad \begin{vmatrix} \hat{i} & \hat{j} & \hat{k} \\ 3 & 2 & 9 \\ 1 & p & 3 \end{vmatrix}=0$$

$$\therefore \ \hat{i}(6-9p)-\hat{j}(9-9)+\hat{k}(3p-2)=0$$

$$\Rightarrow \quad \hat{i}(6-9p)+\hat{k}(3p-2)=0\hat{i}+0\hat{j}+0\hat{k}$$

Comparing coefficient of $\hat{i}$ and $\hat{k}$ on both sides, we get

$$6-9p=0$$
$$\Rightarrow \quad 9p=6$$
$$\therefore \quad p=\frac{6}{9}=\frac{2}{3}$$
$$\text{and} \quad 3p-2=0$$
$$\Rightarrow \quad 3p=2$$
$$\therefore \quad p=\frac{2}{3}.$$

107. Find $|\vec{a}\times\vec{b}|$ if $\vec{a}=\hat{i}-7\hat{j}+7\hat{k}$ and $\vec{b}=3\hat{i}-2\hat{j}+2\hat{k}.$*

Sol. Given, $\vec{a}=\hat{i}-7\hat{j}+7\hat{k},$

and $\vec{b}=3\hat{i}-2\hat{j}+2\hat{k}.$

$$\therefore \ \vec{a}\times\vec{b}=\begin{vmatrix} \hat{i} & \hat{j} & \hat{k} \\ 1 & -7 & 7 \\ 3 & -2 & 2 \end{vmatrix}$$

$$=\hat{i}(-14+14)-\hat{j}(2-21)+\hat{k}(-2+21)$$

$$=19\hat{j}+19\hat{k}$$

$$\therefore |\vec{a}\times\vec{b}|=\sqrt{(19)^2+(19)^2}$$

$$=\sqrt{2(19)^2}$$

$$=19\sqrt{2}$$

108. Write a unit vector perpendicular to both the vectors $\vec{a}=\hat{i}+\hat{j}+\hat{k}$ and $\vec{b}=\hat{i}+\hat{j}.$*

Sol. A vector perpendicular to both $\vec{a}$ and $\vec{b}$ is $\vec{a}\times\vec{b}.$

$\therefore$ Unit vector perpendicular to $\vec{a}$ and $\vec{b}$

$$=\frac{\vec{a}\times\vec{b}}{|\vec{a}\times\vec{b}|}$$

$$\text{Now,} \quad \vec{a}\times\vec{b}=\begin{vmatrix} \hat{i} & \hat{j} & \hat{k} \\ 1 & 1 & 1 \\ 1 & 1 & 0 \end{vmatrix}$$

$$=\hat{i}(0-1)-\hat{j}(0-1)+\hat{k}(1-1)$$

$$=-\hat{i}+\hat{j}$$

---

and $\quad |\vec{a} \times \vec{b}| = \sqrt{(-1)^2 + 1^2}$

$$= \sqrt{2}$$

$\therefore$ Required unit vector $= \dfrac{-\hat{i} + \hat{j}}{\sqrt{2}}$.

109. Write the number of vectors of unit length perpendicular to both the vectors $\vec{a} = 2\hat{i} + \hat{j} + 2\hat{k}$ and $\vec{b} = \hat{j} + \hat{k}$.*

Sol. We know that the unit vectors perpendicular to the plane $\vec{a}$ and $\vec{b}$ are $\pm \dfrac{\vec{a} \times \vec{b}}{|\vec{a} \times \vec{b}|}$

So, $\quad \vec{a} \times \vec{b} = \begin{vmatrix} \hat{i} & \hat{j} & \hat{k} \\ 2 & 1 & 2 \\ 0 & 1 & 1 \end{vmatrix}$

$$= (1-2)\hat{i} - (2-0)\hat{j} + (2-0)\hat{k}$$

$$= -\hat{i} - 2\hat{j} + 2\hat{k}$$

$\Rightarrow \quad |\vec{a} \times \vec{b}| = \sqrt{(-1)^2 + (-2)^2 + (2)^2}$

$$= \sqrt{9}$$

$$= 3$$

Hence, required vectors

$$= \pm \dfrac{1}{3}(-\hat{i} - 2\hat{j} + 2\hat{k}).$$

and number of vectors are 2.

110. Find the value of P, if

$$(2\hat{i} + 6\hat{j} + 27\hat{k}) \times (\hat{i} + 3\hat{j} + P\hat{k}) = 0.$$

Sol. Given that $(2\hat{i} + 6\hat{j} + 27\hat{k}) \times (\hat{i} + 3\hat{j} + P\hat{k}) = 0$

$\Rightarrow \quad \begin{vmatrix} \hat{i} & \hat{j} & \hat{k} \\ 2 & 6 & 27 \\ 1 & 3 & P \end{vmatrix} = 0$

$\therefore \ \hat{i}(6P - 81) - \hat{j}(2P - 27) + \hat{k}(6 - 6) = 0$

$\Rightarrow \ \hat{i}(6P - 81) - \hat{j}(2P - 27) = 0\hat{i} + 0\hat{j} + 0\hat{k}$

On comparing coefficients of $\hat{i}$ and $\hat{j}$, we get

$$6P - 81 = 0$$

$\Rightarrow \quad 6P = 81$

$\Rightarrow \quad P = \dfrac{81}{6} = \dfrac{27}{2}$

and $\quad 2P - 27 = 0 \Rightarrow 2P = 27$

$\therefore \quad P = \dfrac{27}{2}.$

Short Answer Type Questions

111. If a, b are the position vectors of A and B respectively, show that the position vectors of points C on the line AB is such that $\overrightarrow{AC} = 3\overrightarrow{AB}$ is $3\vec{b} - 2\vec{a}$.

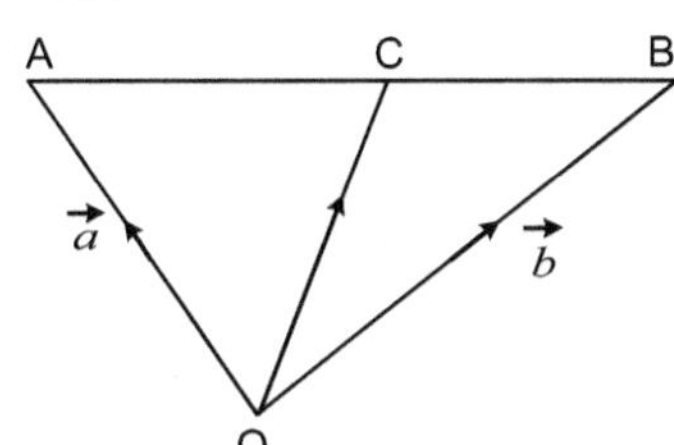

Sol. Let $\vec{v}$ be the position vector of the point C.

Now, $\quad \overrightarrow{AC} = 3\overrightarrow{AB}$ $\qquad$ (Given)

$\Rightarrow \quad (\vec{v} - \vec{a}) = 3(\vec{b} - \vec{a})$

$\Rightarrow \quad (\vec{v} - \vec{a}) = 3\vec{b} - 3\vec{a}$

$\Rightarrow \quad \vec{v} = 3\vec{b} - 3\vec{a} + \vec{a}$

$$= 3\vec{b} - 2\vec{a}$$

112. If $\vec{a} = 2\hat{i} + 4\hat{j} - 5\hat{k}$ and $\vec{b} = \hat{i} + 2\hat{j} + 3\hat{k}$, find the unit vector in the direction of $\vec{a} + \vec{b}$.

Sol. We have,

$$\vec{a} + \vec{b} = (2\hat{i} + 4\hat{j} - 5\hat{k}) + (\hat{i} + 2\hat{j} + 3\hat{k})$$

$$= 3\hat{i} + 6\hat{j} - 2\hat{k}$$

$\Rightarrow \quad |\vec{a} + \vec{b}| = \sqrt{(3)^2 + (6)^2 + (-2)^2}$

$$= \sqrt{(9 + 36 + 4)}$$

$$= \sqrt{49} = 7$$

Hence, the unit vector in the direction of $\vec{a} + \vec{b}$

$$= \dfrac{\vec{a} + \vec{b}}{|\vec{a} + \vec{b}|}$$

$$= \dfrac{1}{7}(3\hat{i} + 6\hat{j} - 2\hat{k})$$

$$= \dfrac{1}{7}\hat{i} + \dfrac{6}{7}\hat{j} - \dfrac{2}{7}\hat{k})$$

---

* are board exam questions from previous years

113. If ABCD is quadrilateral and E and F are the mid-points of AC and BD, prove that

$$\overrightarrow{AB} + \overrightarrow{AD} + \overrightarrow{CB} + \overrightarrow{CD} = 4\overrightarrow{EF}.$$

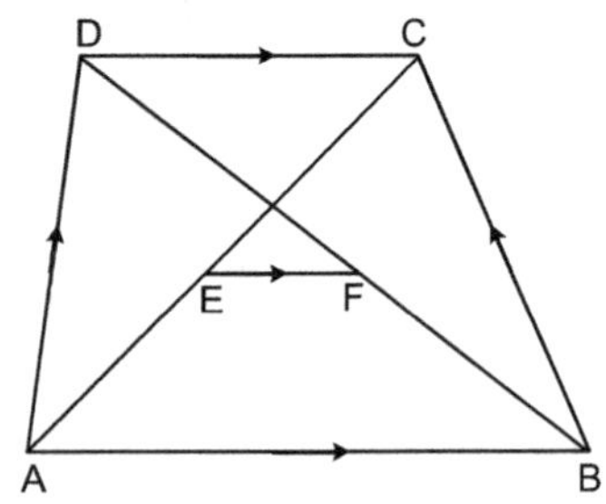

Sol. Let $\vec{a}, \vec{b}, \vec{c}$ and $\vec{d}$ be the position vectors of the vertices of the quadrilateral ABCD relative to some chosen point O as the origin.

Since, E and F are the mid-points of the sides AC and BD respectively, so the position vectors of E and F are

$$\frac{\vec{a} + \vec{c}}{2} \text{ and } \frac{\vec{b} + \vec{d}}{2}$$

We have, $\overrightarrow{AB} + \overrightarrow{AD} + \overrightarrow{CB} + \overrightarrow{CD}$

$$= (\vec{b} - \vec{a}) + (\vec{d} - \vec{a}) + (\vec{b} - \vec{c}) + (\vec{d} - \vec{c})$$

$$= 2(\vec{b} + \vec{d} - \vec{c} - \vec{a})$$

$$= 4\left(\frac{\vec{b} + \vec{d}}{2}\right) - 4\left(\frac{\vec{c} + \vec{a}}{2}\right)$$

$$= 4 \text{ [Position vectors of F-Position vector of E]}$$

$$= 4\overrightarrow{EF}$$

114. If P is the mid-point of the side BC of a triangle ABC, prove that $\overrightarrow{AB}^2 + \overrightarrow{AC}^2 = 2(\overrightarrow{AP}^2 + \overrightarrow{PB}^2)$

Sol. We have

$$\overrightarrow{AB}^2 + \overrightarrow{AC}^2 = |\overrightarrow{AB}|^2 + |\overrightarrow{AC}|^2$$

[The square of the vector is equal to the square of its modulus]

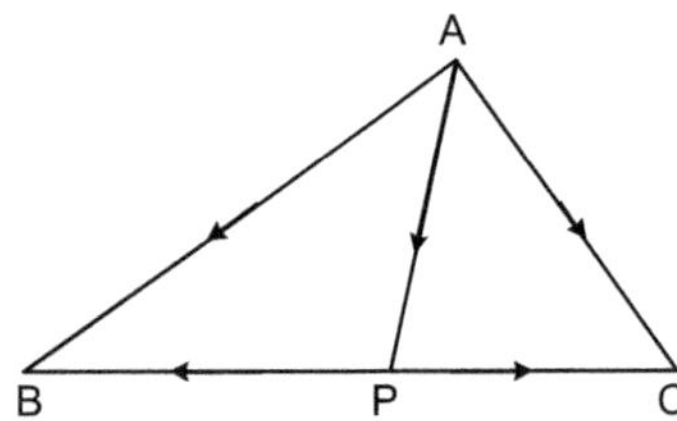

$\Rightarrow$ P is the mid-point of BC.

$\Rightarrow \qquad PB = PC$

$$AB^2 + AC^2 = (\overrightarrow{AP} + \overrightarrow{PB})^2 + (AP + PC)^2$$

$$= (\overrightarrow{AP} + \overrightarrow{PB})^2 + (\overrightarrow{AP} + \overrightarrow{PB})^2$$

$$= 2(\overrightarrow{AP}^2 + \overrightarrow{PB}^2).$$

115. Find the ratio in which the point $7\hat{i} - \hat{k}$ divides the join of $-2\hat{i} + 3\hat{j} + 5\hat{k}$ and $\hat{i} + 2\hat{j} + 3\hat{k}$.

Sol. Suppose the point $7\hat{i} - \hat{k}$ is C, $-2\hat{i} + 3\hat{j} + 5\hat{k}$ is A and $\hat{i} + 2\hat{j} + 3\hat{k}$ is B.

Let C divides AB in the ratio $1 : m$.
Then,

$$7\hat{i} - \hat{k} = \frac{(-2\hat{i} + 3\hat{j} + 5\hat{k})m + (\hat{i} + 2\hat{j} + 3\hat{k})}{1 + m}$$

Equating the coefficients of $\hat{i}, \hat{j}$ and $\hat{k}$ we get

$$m = -\frac{2}{3}$$

Thus, C is the point of external division and divides the join of A and B in the ratio $2 : 3$.

116. Find a vector of magnitude 5 units and parallel to the resultant of $\vec{a} = 2\hat{i} + 3\hat{j} - \hat{k}$ and $\vec{b} = \hat{i} - 2\hat{j} + \hat{k}$.

Sol. Given that $\qquad \vec{a} = 2\hat{i} + 3\hat{j} - \hat{k}$

and $\qquad \vec{b} = \hat{i} - 2\hat{j} + \hat{k}$

Now, resultant of above vectors

$$= \vec{a} + \vec{b}$$

$$= (2\hat{i} + 3\hat{j} - \hat{k}) + (\hat{i} + 2\hat{j} - \hat{k})$$

$$= 3\hat{i} + \hat{j}$$

Let $\qquad \vec{a} + \vec{b} = \vec{c}$

$\therefore \qquad \vec{c} = 3\hat{i} + \hat{j}$

Now, we find unit vector in the direction of $\vec{c}$

$$= \frac{\vec{c}}{|\vec{c}|}$$

$$= \frac{3\hat{i} + \hat{j}}{\sqrt{(3)^2 + (1)^2}} = \frac{3\hat{i} + \hat{j}}{\sqrt{10}}$$

$$= \frac{3}{\sqrt{10}}\hat{i} + \frac{1}{\sqrt{10}}\hat{j}.$$

Finally, vector of magnitude 5 units and parallel to resultant of $\vec{a}$ and $\vec{b}$ is given by

$$5\left(\frac{3}{\sqrt{10}}\hat{i}+\frac{1}{\sqrt{10}}\hat{j}\right) = \frac{15}{\sqrt{10}}\hat{i}+\frac{5}{\sqrt{10}}\hat{j}$$

117. Let $\vec{a} = \hat{i}+\hat{j}+\hat{k}, \vec{b} = 4\hat{i}-2\hat{j}+3\hat{k}$ and $\vec{c} = \hat{i}-2\hat{j}+\hat{k}$. find a vector of magnitude 6 units which is parallel to the vector $2\vec{a}-\vec{b}+3\vec{c}$.*

Sol. Given that $\vec{a} = \hat{i}+\hat{j}+\hat{k},$

$$\vec{b} = 4\hat{i}-2\hat{j}+3\hat{k}$$

and

$$\vec{c} = \hat{i}-2\hat{j}+\hat{k}$$

First we find the vector $2\vec{a}-\vec{b}+3\vec{c}$

$\therefore \quad 2\vec{a}-\vec{b}+3\vec{c} = 2(\hat{i}+\hat{j}+\hat{k}) - (4\hat{i}-2\hat{j}+3\hat{k})$

$$+ 3(\hat{i}-2\hat{j}+\hat{k})$$

$$= 2\hat{i}+2\hat{j}+2\hat{k} - 4\hat{i}+2\hat{j}-3\hat{k}$$

$$+ 3\hat{i}-6\hat{j}+3\hat{k}$$

$\therefore \quad 2\vec{a}-\vec{b}+3\vec{c} = \hat{i}-2\hat{j}+2\hat{k}$

Now, we find a unit vector in the direction of vector $2\vec{a}-\vec{b}+3\vec{c}$ which is equal to

$$\frac{\hat{i}-2\hat{j}+2\hat{k}}{\sqrt{(1)^2+(-2)^2+(2)^2}} = \frac{\hat{i}-2\hat{j}+2\hat{k}}{\sqrt{9}}$$

$$= \frac{\hat{i}-2\hat{j}+2\hat{k}}{3}$$

$\therefore$ Vector of magnitude 6 units parallel to the vector $2\vec{a}-\vec{b}+3\vec{c}$ is

$$= 6\left(\frac{1}{3}\hat{i}-\frac{2}{3}\hat{j}+\frac{2}{3}\hat{k}\right)$$

$$= 2\hat{i}-4\hat{j}+4\hat{k}$$

118. If $\hat{a}$ and $\hat{b}$ are unit vectors and θ is the angle between them, then show that

$$\sin\frac{\theta}{2} = \frac{|\hat{a}-\hat{b}|}{2}$$

Sol. $(\hat{a}-\hat{b})^2 = |\hat{a}|^2 + |\hat{b}|^2 - 2\hat{a}.\hat{b}\cos\theta$

$$= 1 + 1 - 2.1.1\cos\theta$$

$$= 2 - 2\cos\theta$$

$$= 2(1-\cos\theta)$$

$$= 2\left(2\sin^2\frac{\theta}{2}\right)$$

$$= 4\sin^2\frac{\theta}{2}$$

$\Rightarrow \quad |\hat{a}-\hat{b}|^2 = 4\sin^2\frac{\theta}{2}$

[since, square of a vector = square of its modulus]

$\Rightarrow \quad |\hat{a}-\hat{b}| = 2\sin\frac{\theta}{2}$

Hence, $\quad \sin\frac{\theta}{2} = \frac{|\hat{a}-\hat{b}|}{2}$

119. Find the position vector of a point R which divides the line joining two points P and Q whose position vectors are $(2\vec{a}+\vec{b})$ and $(\vec{a}-3\vec{b})$ respectively, externally in the ratio 1 : 2. Also show that P is the mid-point of line segment RQ.*

Sol. Given that $\overrightarrow{OP}$ = position vector of P = $2\vec{a}+\vec{b}$

$$\overrightarrow{OQ} = \text{position vector of Q} = \vec{a}-3\vec{b}$$

Let $\overrightarrow{OR}$ = position vector of point R, which divides PQ externally in the ratio 1 : 2.

We know that position vector of point R, which divides line PQ externally in the ratio 1 : 2 is given by

$$\overrightarrow{OR} = \frac{m(\overrightarrow{OQ})-n(\overrightarrow{OP})}{m-n} \qquad \text{...(i)}$$

Given, $m = 1, n = 2$

Putting above values in equation (i), we get

$$\overrightarrow{OR} = \frac{1(\vec{a}-3\vec{b})-2(2\vec{a}+\vec{b})}{1-2}$$

$$= \frac{\vec{a}-3\vec{b}-4\vec{a}-2\vec{b}}{-1}$$

$$= \frac{-3\vec{a}-5\vec{b}}{-1} = 3\vec{a}+5\vec{b}$$

Hence, $\quad \overrightarrow{OR} = 3\vec{a}+5\vec{b}$

Also, we have to show that P is the mid-point of RQ.

$\therefore$ We have to show that

$$\overrightarrow{OP} = \frac{\overrightarrow{OR} + \overrightarrow{OQ}}{2}$$

We have $\quad \overrightarrow{OR} = 3\vec{a} + 5\vec{b}$

$$\overrightarrow{OQ} = \vec{a} - 3\vec{b}$$

$$\frac{\overrightarrow{OR} + \overrightarrow{OQ}}{2} = \frac{(3\vec{a} + 5\vec{b}) + (\vec{a} - 3\vec{b})}{2}$$

$$= \frac{4\vec{a} + 2\vec{b}}{2}$$

$$= 2\vec{a} + \vec{b} = \overrightarrow{OP}$$

Hence,

$$\frac{\overrightarrow{OP} + \overrightarrow{OQ}}{2} = \overrightarrow{OP}$$

$\therefore$ P is mid-point of line segment RQ.

120. If $\vec{a}, \vec{b}, \vec{c}$ are three vectors such that $|\vec{a}| = 5$, $|\vec{b}| = 12, |\vec{c}| = 13$ and $\vec{a} + \vec{b} + \vec{c} = 0$, then find the value of $\vec{a} \cdot \vec{b} + \vec{b} \cdot \vec{c} + \vec{c} \cdot \vec{a}$.*

Sol. Given that $\vec{a} + \vec{b} + \vec{c} = 0$

Multiplying both sides by $(\vec{a} + \vec{b} + \vec{c})$, we get

$$(\vec{a} + \vec{b} + \vec{c}) \cdot (\vec{a} + \vec{b} + \vec{c}) = 0 \cdot (\vec{a} + \vec{b} + \vec{c})$$

$$\Rightarrow \vec{a} \cdot \vec{a} + \vec{a} \cdot \vec{b} + \vec{a} \cdot \vec{c} + \vec{b} \cdot \vec{a} + \vec{b} \cdot \vec{b} + \vec{b} \cdot \vec{c}$$
$$+ \vec{c} \cdot \vec{a} + \vec{c} \cdot \vec{b} + \vec{c} \cdot \vec{c} = 0$$

$$\Rightarrow |\vec{a}|^2 + |\vec{b}|^2 + |\vec{c}|^2 + 2(\vec{a} \cdot \vec{b} + \vec{b} \cdot \vec{c} + \vec{c} \cdot \vec{a}) = 0$$

$$\Rightarrow (5)^2 + (12)^2 + (13)^2 + 2(\vec{a} \cdot \vec{b} + \vec{b} \cdot \vec{c} + \vec{c} \cdot \vec{a}) = 0$$

$$\Rightarrow 25 + 144 + 169 + 2(\vec{a} \cdot \vec{b} + \vec{b} \cdot \vec{c} + \vec{c} \cdot \vec{a}) = 0$$

$$\Rightarrow 2(\vec{a} \cdot \vec{b} + \vec{b} \cdot \vec{c} + \vec{c} \cdot \vec{a}) = -338$$

Hence, $\quad \vec{a} \cdot \vec{b} + \vec{b} \cdot \vec{c} + \vec{c} \cdot \vec{a} = -169$.

121. If $\vec{a}, \vec{b}, \vec{c}$ are three vectors such that $|\vec{a}| = 3$, $|\vec{b}| = 4, |\vec{c}| = 5$ and each one of them being perpendicular to the sum of the other two, find $|\vec{a} + \vec{b} + \vec{c}|$.*

Sol. Given that $|\vec{a}| = 3, |\vec{b}| = 4, |\vec{c}| = 5$ ...(i)

Also, given that each of the vector $\vec{a}, \vec{b}, \vec{c}$ is perpendicular to sum of the other two vectors

i.e., $\qquad \vec{a} \perp (\vec{b} + \vec{c})$

$$\Rightarrow \vec{a} \cdot (\vec{b} + \vec{c}) = 0$$

[$\because$ when two vectors are perpendicular, their dot product is zero]

$$\Rightarrow \vec{a} \cdot \vec{b} + \vec{a} \cdot \vec{c} = 0 \qquad \text{...(ii)}$$

$$\vec{b} \perp (\vec{c} + \vec{a})$$

$$\Rightarrow \vec{b} \cdot (\vec{c} + \vec{a}) = 0$$

$$\Rightarrow \vec{b} \cdot \vec{c} + \vec{b} \cdot \vec{a} = 0 \qquad \text{...(iii)}$$

and $\qquad \vec{c} \perp (\vec{a} + \vec{b})$

$$\Rightarrow \vec{c} \cdot (\vec{a} + \vec{b}) = 0$$

$$\Rightarrow \vec{c} \cdot \vec{a} + \vec{c} \cdot \vec{b} = 0 \qquad \text{...(iv)}$$

Now, adding equations (ii), (iii) and (iv), we get

$$2(\vec{a} \cdot \vec{b} + \vec{b} \cdot \vec{c} + \vec{c} \cdot \vec{a}) = 0$$

$$\Rightarrow \vec{a} \cdot \vec{b} + \vec{b} \cdot \vec{c} + \vec{c} \cdot \vec{a} = 0 \qquad \text{...(v)}$$

Now, consider $(\vec{a} + \vec{b} + \vec{c}) \cdot (\vec{a} + \vec{b} + \vec{c})$

$$= \vec{a} \cdot \vec{a} + \vec{a} \cdot \vec{b}$$
$$+ \vec{a} \cdot \vec{c} + \vec{b} \cdot \vec{a} + \vec{b} \cdot \vec{b} + \vec{b} \cdot \vec{c}$$
$$+ \vec{c} \cdot \vec{a} + \vec{c} \cdot \vec{b} + \vec{c} \cdot \vec{c}$$

We know that

$$\vec{x} \cdot \vec{x} = |\vec{x}|^2,$$

$$\therefore |\vec{a} + \vec{b} + \vec{c}|^2 = |\vec{a}|^2 + |\vec{b}|^2 + |\vec{c}|^2$$
$$+ 2(\vec{a} \cdot \vec{b} + \vec{b} \cdot \vec{c} + \vec{c} \cdot \vec{a})$$

$$(\because \vec{a}^2 = |\vec{a}|^2)$$

From equations (i) and (v), we get

$$|\vec{a} + \vec{b} + \vec{c}|^2 = (3)^2 + (4)^2 + (5)^2 + 2(0)$$

$$\therefore |\vec{a} + \vec{b} + \vec{c}|^2 = 9 + 16 + 25 = 50$$

Hence, $|\vec{a} + \vec{b} + \vec{c}| = \sqrt{50}$

$$= \sqrt{25 \times 2} = 5\sqrt{2}$$

---

* are board exam questions from previous years

122. If $\vec{a}, \vec{b}$ and $\vec{c}$ are three mutually perpendicular vectors of equal magnitude, prove that $\vec{a} + \vec{b} + \vec{c}$ is equally inclined with vectors $\vec{a}, \vec{b}$ and $\vec{c}$. Also find the angle.*

Sol. Given that $\vec{a}, \vec{b}$ and $\vec{c}$ are three mutually perpendicular vectors of equal magnitude.

i.e.,
$$|\vec{a}| = |\vec{b}| = |\vec{c}| = x \text{ (say)} \quad ...(i)$$

and
$$\vec{a} . \vec{b} = 0 \quad ...(ii)$$

$$\vec{b} . \vec{c} = 0 \quad ...(iii)$$

and
$$\vec{c} . \vec{a} = 0 \quad ...(iv)$$

$$\Rightarrow \vec{a} \cdot \vec{b} = \vec{b} \cdot \vec{c} = \vec{c} \cdot \vec{a} = 0$$

To show $\vec{a} + \vec{b} + \vec{c}$ is equally inclined to $\vec{a}, \vec{b}$ and $\vec{c}$ i.e., $\vec{a} + \vec{b} + \vec{c}$ makes equal angle with $\vec{a}, \vec{b}$ and $\vec{c}$.

Now, we know that angle between two vector $\vec{x}$ and $\vec{y}$ is given by

$$\cos \theta = \frac{\vec{x} . \vec{y}}{|\vec{x}| |\vec{y}|}$$

Using above result, we find the angle between $\vec{a} + \vec{b} + \vec{c}$ and $\vec{a}, \vec{b}$ and $\vec{c}$. Let θ_1 be the angle between $\vec{a} + \vec{b} + \vec{c}$ and $\vec{a}$

$$\cos \theta_1 = \frac{(\vec{a} + \vec{b} + \vec{c}).\vec{a}}{|\vec{a} + \vec{b} + \vec{c}|.|\vec{a}|}$$

$$= \frac{\vec{a}.\vec{a} + \vec{b}.\vec{a} + \vec{c}.\vec{a}}{|\vec{a} + \vec{b} + \vec{c}|.|\vec{a}|}$$

$$= \frac{|\vec{a}|^2 + 0 + 0}{|\vec{a} + \vec{b} + \vec{c}|.|\vec{a}|}$$

[From equations (ii) and (iv)]

$$\therefore \quad \cos \theta_1 = \frac{|\vec{a}|}{|\vec{a} + \vec{b} + \vec{c}|}$$

$$= \frac{x}{|\vec{a} + \vec{b} + \vec{c}|} \quad ...(v)$$

Now, let θ_2 be the angle between $\vec{a} + \vec{b} + \vec{c}$ and $\vec{b}$

$$\therefore \quad \cos \theta_2 = \frac{(\vec{a} + \vec{b} + \vec{c}).\vec{b}}{|\vec{a} + \vec{b} + \vec{c}|.|\vec{b}|}$$

$$= \frac{\vec{a}.\vec{b} + \vec{b}.\vec{b} + \vec{c}.\vec{b}}{|\vec{a} + \vec{b} + \vec{c}|.|\vec{b}|}$$

$$= \frac{0 + |\vec{b}|^2 + 0}{|\vec{a} + \vec{b} + \vec{c}|.|\vec{b}|}$$

$$= \frac{|\vec{b}|}{|\vec{a} + \vec{b} + \vec{c}|}$$

[From equation (ii) and (iii)]

$$\therefore \quad \cos \theta_2 = \frac{x}{|\vec{a} + \vec{b} + \vec{c}|} \quad ...(vi)$$

Angle let θ_3 angle between $\vec{a} + \vec{b} + \vec{c}$ and $\vec{c}$

$$\therefore \quad \cos \theta_3 = \frac{(\vec{a} + \vec{b} + \vec{c}).\vec{c}}{|\vec{a} + \vec{b} + \vec{c}|.|\vec{c}|}$$

$$= \frac{\vec{a}.\vec{c} + \vec{b}.\vec{c} + \vec{c}.\vec{c}}{|\vec{a} + \vec{b} + \vec{c}|.|\vec{c}|}$$

$$= \frac{0 + 0 + |\vec{c}|^2}{|\vec{a} + \vec{b} + \vec{c}|.|\vec{c}|}$$

[From equation (iii) and (iv)]

$$= \frac{|\vec{c}|}{|\vec{a} + \vec{b} + \vec{c}|}$$

$$= \frac{x}{|\vec{a} + \vec{b} + \vec{c}|}$$

$$\therefore \quad \cos \theta_3 = \frac{x}{|\vec{a} + \vec{b} + \vec{c}|} \quad ...(vii)$$

Now, from equation (v), (vi) and (vii), we get

$$\cos \theta_1 = \cos \theta_2 = \cos \theta_3$$

$$\Rightarrow \quad \theta_1 = \theta_2 = \theta_3$$

Hence, $\vec{a}+\vec{b}+\vec{c}$ is equally inclined to $\vec{a},\vec{b}$ and $\vec{c}$

Also angle between the vectors is

$$\cos^{-1}\left(\frac{x}{|\vec{a}+\vec{b}+\vec{c}|}\right).$$

123. The scalar product of vector $\hat{i}+\hat{j}+\hat{k}$ with the unit vector along the sum of vectors $2\hat{i}+4\hat{j}-5\hat{k}$ and $\lambda\hat{i}+2\hat{j}+3\hat{k}$ is equal to one. Find the value of λ.*

Sol. Let

$$\vec{a} = \hat{i}+\hat{j}+\hat{k},$$

$$\vec{b} = 2\hat{i}+4\hat{j}-5\hat{k}$$

and

$$\vec{c} = \lambda\hat{i}+2\hat{j}+3\hat{k}$$

Now, given that dot product of $\vec{a}$ with unit vector along vector $\vec{b}+\vec{c}$ is one.

Now, $\vec{b}+\vec{c} = (2\hat{i}+4\hat{j}-5\hat{k})$

$$+ (\lambda\hat{i}+2\hat{j}+3\hat{k})$$

$$\vec{b}+\vec{c} = (2+\lambda)\hat{i}+6\hat{j}-2\hat{k}$$

Unit vector along $\vec{b}+\vec{c}$

$$= \frac{\vec{b}+\vec{c}}{|\vec{b}+\vec{c}|}$$

$$= \frac{(2+\lambda)\hat{i}+6\hat{j}-2\hat{k}}{\sqrt{(2+\lambda)^2+(6)^2+(-2)^2}}$$

$$= \frac{(2+\lambda)\hat{i}+6\hat{j}-2\hat{k}}{\sqrt{4+\lambda^2+4\lambda+36+4}}$$

$$= \frac{(2+\lambda)\hat{i}+6\hat{j}-2\hat{k}}{\sqrt{\lambda^2+4\lambda+44}}$$

Now, as per given condition, we get

$$(\hat{i}+\hat{j}+\hat{k})\cdot\frac{(2+\lambda)\hat{i}+6\hat{j}-2\hat{k}}{\sqrt{\lambda^2+4\lambda+44}} = 1$$

$$\Rightarrow \quad \frac{(2+\lambda)+6-2}{\sqrt{\lambda^2+4\lambda+44}} = 1$$

$$\Rightarrow \quad \lambda+6 = \sqrt{\lambda^2+4\lambda+44}$$

Squaring both side, we get

$$\lambda^2+4\lambda+44 = (\lambda+6)^2$$

$$\Rightarrow \quad \lambda^2+4\lambda+44 = \lambda^2+36+12\lambda$$

$$\Rightarrow \quad 4\lambda+44 = 36+12\lambda$$

$$\Rightarrow \quad 8\lambda = 8$$

$$\Rightarrow \quad \lambda = 1.$$

124. Three vectors $\vec{a},\vec{b},\vec{c}$ satisfy the condition $\vec{a}+\vec{b}+\vec{c}=0$.*

Find the value of $\mu = \vec{a}\cdot\vec{b}+\vec{b}\cdot\vec{c}+\vec{c}\cdot\vec{a}$, if $|\vec{a}|=1$, $|\vec{b}|=4$ and $|\vec{c}|=2$.

Sol. Given that for three vectors $\vec{a},\vec{b},\vec{c}$

$$\vec{a}+\vec{b}+\vec{c} = 0 \qquad \ldots(i)$$

Taking dot product with vector $\vec{a}+\vec{b}+\vec{c}$ on both sides of equation (i), we get

$$(\vec{a}+\vec{b}+\vec{c})\cdot(\vec{a}+\vec{b}+\vec{c})$$

$$= 0\cdot(\vec{a}+\vec{b}+\vec{c})$$

$$\Rightarrow \vec{a}\cdot\vec{a}+\vec{a}\cdot\vec{b}+\vec{a}\cdot\vec{c}+\vec{b}\cdot\vec{a}+\vec{b}\cdot\vec{b}+\vec{b}\cdot\vec{c}$$

$$+\,\vec{c}\cdot\vec{a}+\vec{c}\cdot\vec{b}+\vec{c}\cdot\vec{c} = 0$$

$$\Rightarrow |\vec{a}|^2+|\vec{b}|^2+|\vec{c}|^2+2(\vec{a}\cdot\vec{b}+\vec{b}\cdot\vec{c}+\vec{c}\cdot\vec{a}) = 0$$

$$\Rightarrow (1)^2+(4)^2+(2)^2+2(\vec{a}\cdot\vec{b}+\vec{b}\cdot\vec{c}+\vec{c}\cdot\vec{a}) = 0$$

$$[\because \text{given that } |\vec{a}|=1, |\vec{b}|=4, |\vec{c}|=2]$$

Put the value from eq. (i), (ii), (iii)

$$\Rightarrow \quad 1+16+4+2(\vec{a}\cdot\vec{b}+\vec{b}\cdot\vec{c}+\vec{c}\cdot\vec{a}) = 0$$

or $\quad 2(\vec{a}\cdot\vec{b}+\vec{b}\cdot\vec{c}+\vec{c}\cdot\vec{a}) = -21$

Hence, $\quad \vec{a}\cdot\vec{b}+\vec{b}\cdot\vec{c}+\vec{c}\cdot\vec{a} = -\dfrac{21}{2}$

125. If $\vec{a}=\hat{i}+\hat{j}+\hat{k}$ and $\vec{b}=\hat{j}-\hat{k}$, find a vector $\vec{c}$ such that $\vec{a}\times\vec{c}=\vec{b}$ and $\vec{a}\cdot\vec{c}=3$.*

Sol. Given that $\qquad \vec{a} = \hat{i}+\hat{j}+\hat{k}$

and $\qquad \vec{b} = \hat{j}-\hat{k}$

Let $\qquad \vec{c} = c_1\hat{i}+c_2\hat{j}+c_3\hat{k}$

Also, given that $\vec{a}\times\vec{c} = \vec{b}$

$$\Rightarrow \quad \begin{vmatrix} \hat{i} & \hat{j} & \hat{k} \\ 1 & 1 & 1 \\ c_1 & c_2 & c_3 \end{vmatrix} = \hat{j} - \hat{k}$$

$$\Rightarrow \hat{i}(c_3 - c_2) - \hat{j}(c_3 - c_1) + \hat{k}(c_2 - c_1) = \hat{j} - \hat{k}$$

Comparing coefficients of $\hat{i}, \hat{j}$ and $\hat{k}$ on both sides, we get

$$c_3 - c_2 = 0 \qquad \Rightarrow \qquad c_2 = c_3 \qquad \text{...(i)}$$
$$c_3 - c_1 = -1 \qquad \Rightarrow \quad c_1 - c_3 = 1 \qquad \text{...(ii)}$$
$$\text{and } c_2 - c_1 = -1 \quad \Rightarrow \quad c_1 - c_2 = 1 \qquad \text{...(iii)}$$

Again given that $\vec{a} \cdot \vec{c} = 3$

$$\therefore (\hat{i} + \hat{j} + \hat{k}) \cdot (c_1 \hat{i} + c_2 \hat{j} + c_3 \hat{k}) = 3$$

$$\Rightarrow \quad c_1 + c_2 + c_3 = 3 \qquad \text{...(iv)}$$

Putting $c_2 = c_3$ from equation (i) in equation (iv), we get

$$c_1 + 2c_3 = 3 \qquad \text{...(v)}$$

Subtracting equation (ii) from equation (v), we get

$$\begin{aligned} c_1 + 2c_3 &= 3 \\ c_1 - c_3 &= 1 \\ \underline{- \quad + \quad -} \\ 3c_3 &= 2 \end{aligned}$$

$$\Rightarrow \qquad c_3 = \frac{2}{3}$$

$$\because \qquad c_2 = c_3$$

$$\therefore \qquad c_3 = \frac{2}{3}$$

Putting $c_2 = c_3 = \dfrac{2}{3}$ in equation (iv), we get

$$c_1 + \frac{2}{3} + \frac{2}{3} = 3$$

$$\Rightarrow \qquad c_1 + \frac{4}{3} = 3$$

$$\Rightarrow \qquad c_1 = 3 - \frac{4}{3}$$

$$= \frac{9-4}{3} = \frac{5}{3}$$

$$\therefore \qquad c_1 = \frac{5}{3}$$

Hence, the requaired vector is

$$c = c_1 \hat{i} + c_2 \hat{j} + c_3 \hat{k}$$

$$= \frac{5}{3}\hat{i} + \frac{2}{3}\hat{j} + \frac{2}{3}\hat{k}.$$

126. A parallelogram, whose diagonals are equal, is a rectangle. Prove this using vectors.

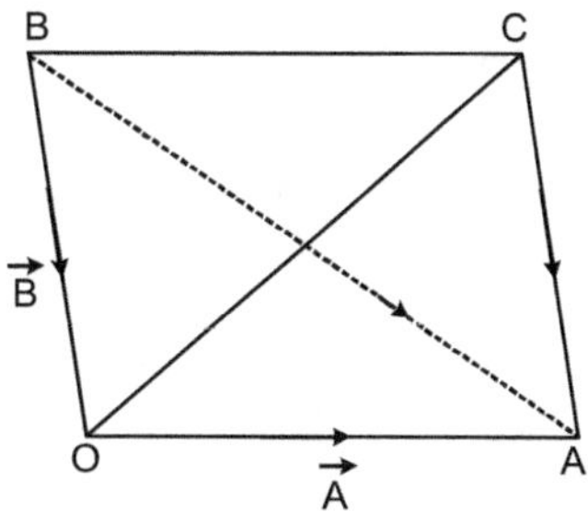

Sol. Let OACB be the parallelogram with $\overrightarrow{OA} = \vec{a}$, $\overrightarrow{OB} = \vec{b}$

Now, $\qquad \overrightarrow{OC} = \vec{a} + \vec{b}$

(Using triangle law of vector addition)

and $\qquad \overrightarrow{BA} = \vec{a} - \vec{b}$

$$\overrightarrow{OC} = \overrightarrow{BA}$$

(since the diagonal of a parallelogram are equal)

$$\Rightarrow \qquad OC^2 = BA^2$$

$$\Rightarrow \qquad \overrightarrow{OC} \cdot \overrightarrow{OC} = \overrightarrow{BA} \cdot \overrightarrow{BA}$$

$$\Rightarrow \qquad = (\vec{a} + \vec{b}) \cdot (\vec{a} + \vec{b}) = (\vec{a} - \vec{b}) \cdot (\vec{a} - \vec{b})$$

$$\Rightarrow \qquad = \vec{a} \cdot \vec{a} + \vec{b} \cdot \vec{a} + \vec{a} \cdot \vec{b} + \vec{b} \cdot \vec{b}$$

$$= \vec{a} \cdot \vec{a} - \vec{b} \cdot \vec{a} - \vec{a} \cdot \vec{b} + \vec{b} \cdot \vec{b}$$

But $\qquad \vec{a} \cdot \vec{b} = \vec{b} \cdot \vec{a}$

Therefore, $\quad 4\vec{a} \cdot \vec{b} = 0$

$$\Rightarrow \qquad \vec{a} \cdot \vec{b} = 0$$

$\Rightarrow$ OA is perpendicular to OB.
Therefore, the parallelogram is a rectangle.

127. If θ is the angle between two vectors $\hat{i} - 2\hat{j} + 3\hat{k}$ and $3\hat{i} - 2\hat{j} + \hat{k}$ find $\sin \theta$.*

Sol. Let

$$\vec{a} = \hat{i} - 2\hat{j} + 3\hat{k}$$

$$\vec{b} = 3\hat{i} - 2\hat{j} + \hat{k}$$

We know $\quad \vec{a} \cdot \vec{b} = |\vec{a}| |\vec{b}| \cos \theta$

$$\Rightarrow \qquad \cos \theta = \frac{\vec{a} \cdot \vec{b}}{|\vec{a}| |\vec{b}|}$$

$$[\because \vec{a} \cdot \vec{b} = |\vec{a}| |\vec{b}| \cos \theta]$$

$$= \frac{(\hat{i} - 2\hat{j} + 3\hat{k}) \cdot (3\hat{i} - 2\hat{j} + \hat{k})}{|\hat{i} - 2\hat{j} + 3\hat{k}| |3\hat{i} - 2\hat{j} + \hat{k}|}$$

$$= \frac{1(3)+(-2)(-2)+3(1)}{\sqrt{1+4+9}\sqrt{9+4+1}}$$

$$= \frac{3+4+3}{14} = \frac{10}{14} = \frac{5}{7}$$

$$\Rightarrow \qquad \cos\theta = \frac{5}{7}$$

Now, $\qquad \sin\theta = \sqrt{1-\cos^2\theta}$

$$= \sqrt{1-\left(\frac{5}{7}\right)^2} = \sqrt{1-\frac{25}{49}}$$

$$= \sqrt{\frac{49-25}{49}}$$

$$\Rightarrow \qquad \sin\theta = \sqrt{\frac{24}{49}}$$

$$= \frac{2\sqrt{6}}{7}.$$

128. Using vectors, find the area of triangle with vertices A(2, 3, 5), B(3, 5, 8) and C(2, 7, 8).*

Sol. Let $\qquad \vec{OA} = 2\hat{i}+3\hat{j}+5\hat{k}$

$$\vec{OB} = 3\hat{i}+5\hat{j}+8\hat{k}$$

and $\qquad \vec{OC} = 2\hat{i}+7\hat{j}+8\hat{k}$

A (2, 3, 5)

B (3, 5, 8)   C (2, 7, 8)

Now, $\quad \vec{AB} = \vec{OB}-\vec{OA} = (3\hat{i}+5\hat{j}+8\hat{k})$

$$- (2\hat{i}+3\hat{j}+5\hat{k})$$

$$\vec{AB} = \hat{i}+2\hat{j}+3\hat{k}$$

and $\qquad \vec{AC} = \vec{OC}-\vec{OA}$

$$= (2\hat{i}+7\hat{j}+8\hat{k})-(2\hat{i}+3\hat{j}+5\hat{k})$$

$$= 4\hat{j}+3\hat{k}$$

we know that area of triangle ABC

$$\Delta ABC = \frac{1}{2}|\vec{AB}\times\vec{AC}|$$

Now, $\quad \vec{AB}\times\vec{AC} = \begin{vmatrix} \hat{i} & \hat{j} & \hat{k} \\ 1 & 2 & 3 \\ 0 & 4 & 3 \end{vmatrix}$

$$= \hat{i}(6-12)-\hat{j}(3-0)+\hat{k}(4-0)$$

$$\vec{AB}\times\vec{AC} = 6\hat{i}+3\hat{j}+4\hat{k}$$

$$\therefore \qquad |\vec{AB}\times\vec{BC}| = \sqrt{(-6)^2+(-3)^2+(4)^2}$$

$$= \sqrt{36+9+16} = \sqrt{61}$$

$\therefore$ Area of triangle ABC

$$= \frac{1}{2}\sqrt{61} \text{ sq. units.}$$

129. Show that the points A, B, C with position vectors $2\hat{i}-\hat{j}+\hat{k}$, $\hat{i}-3\hat{j}-5\hat{k}$ and $3\hat{i}-4\hat{j}-4\hat{k}$ respectively, are the vertices of a right-angled triangle. Hence find the area of the triangle.*

Sol. Given the position vectors of the points A, B and C are $2\hat{i}-\hat{j}+\hat{k}$, $\hat{i}-3\hat{j}-5\hat{k}$ and $3\hat{i}-4\hat{j}-4\hat{k}$ respectively.

Then, $\qquad \vec{OA} = 2\hat{i}-\hat{j}+\hat{k},$

$$\vec{OB} = \hat{i}-3\hat{j}-5\hat{k}$$

and $\qquad \vec{OC} = 3\hat{i}-4\hat{j}-4\hat{k}$

Now, $\qquad \vec{AB} = \vec{OB}-\vec{OA}$

$$= \hat{i}-3\hat{j}-5\hat{k}-(2\hat{i}-\hat{j}+\hat{k})$$

$$= -\hat{i}-2\hat{j}-6\hat{k}$$

$$\vec{BC} = \vec{OC}-\vec{OB}$$

$$= 3\hat{i}-4\hat{j}-4\hat{k}-(\hat{i}-3\hat{j}-5\hat{k})$$

$$= 2\hat{i}-\hat{j}+\hat{k}$$

and $\qquad \vec{CA} = \vec{OA}-\vec{OC}$

$$= 2\hat{i}-\hat{j}+\hat{k}-(3\hat{i}-4\hat{j}-4\hat{k})$$

$$= -\hat{i}+3\hat{j}+5\hat{k}$$

$$\vec{AB}+\vec{BC}+\vec{CA} = (-\hat{i}-2\hat{j}-6\hat{k})+(2\hat{i}-\hat{j}+\hat{k})$$

$$+ (-\hat{i}+3\hat{j}+5\hat{k})$$

$$= 0$$

Thus, A, B and C forms a triangle.

Also, $\qquad \vec{BC}\cdot\vec{CA} = (2\hat{i}-\hat{j}+\hat{k})\cdot(-\hat{i}+3\hat{j}+5\hat{k})$

$$= -2-3+5 = 0$$

$$\therefore \qquad \vec{BC} \perp \vec{CA}$$

$\Rightarrow \qquad \angle C = 90°$

$\Rightarrow \qquad BC^2 + CA^2 = AB^2$

Hence A, B and C are the vertices of a right angled triangle.

Now, Area of $\triangle ABC = \dfrac{1}{2}|\overrightarrow{BC} \times \overrightarrow{CA}|$

$$\therefore \qquad \overrightarrow{BC} \times \overrightarrow{CA} = \begin{vmatrix} \hat{i} & \hat{j} & \hat{k} \\ 2 & -1 & 1 \\ -1 & 3 & 5 \end{vmatrix}$$

$$= -8\hat{i} - 11\hat{j} + 5\hat{k}$$

$$|\overrightarrow{BC} \times \overrightarrow{CA}| = \sqrt{(-8)^2 + (-11)^2 + (5)^2}$$

$$= \sqrt{64 + 121 + 25} = \sqrt{210}$$

Hence, Area of $\triangle ABC = \dfrac{1}{2}\sqrt{210}$ sq. units.

130. If $\vec{a} \times \vec{b} = \vec{c} \times \vec{d}$ and $\vec{a} \times \vec{c} = \vec{b} \times \vec{d}$, show that $\vec{a} - \vec{d}$ is parallel to $\vec{b} - \vec{c}$, where $\vec{a} \neq \vec{d}$ and $\vec{b} \neq \vec{c}$.*

Sol. Given that $\vec{a} \times \vec{b} = \vec{c} \times \vec{d}$ ...(i)

and $\qquad \vec{a} \times \vec{c} = \vec{b} \times \vec{d}$ ...(ii)

Subtracting equation (ii) from equation (i), we get

$$(\vec{a} \times \vec{b}) - (\vec{a} \times \vec{c}) = (\vec{c} \times \vec{d}) - (\vec{b} \times \vec{d})$$

$$\Rightarrow \quad (\vec{a} \times \vec{b}) - (\vec{a} \times \vec{c}) + (\vec{b} \times \vec{d}) - (\vec{c} \times \vec{d}) = 0$$

$$\Rightarrow \quad \vec{a} \times (\vec{b} - \vec{c}) + (\vec{b} - \vec{c}) \times \vec{d} = 0$$

$$\Rightarrow \quad \vec{a} \times (\vec{b} - \vec{c}) - \vec{d} \times (\vec{b} - \vec{c}) = 0$$

$$(\because \vec{a} \times \vec{b} = -\vec{b} \times \vec{a})$$

$$\Rightarrow (\vec{a} - \vec{d}) \times (\vec{b} - \vec{c}) = 0$$

$\therefore$ We have shown that cross product of vectors $\vec{a} - \vec{d}$ and $\vec{b} - \vec{c}$ is zero vector, so $\vec{a} - \vec{d}$ is parallel to $\vec{b} - \vec{c}$.

131. Find the angle between of any two diagonals of a cube.

Sol. The angle between the diagonal of a cube is the same for any size of the cube. Therefore, let us consider a unit cube, where its each edge is unit

length. Hence, let us represent its co-terminal edges OA, OB and OC by $\hat{i}, \hat{j}$ and $\hat{k}$, the usual unit vectors. Consider any two diagonals, say, OF and GC. Let the angle between OF and GC be θ. Now, the position of F is $\hat{i} + \hat{j} + \hat{k}$ and the position vector of G is $\hat{i} + \hat{j}$ and the position vectors of C is $\hat{k}$.

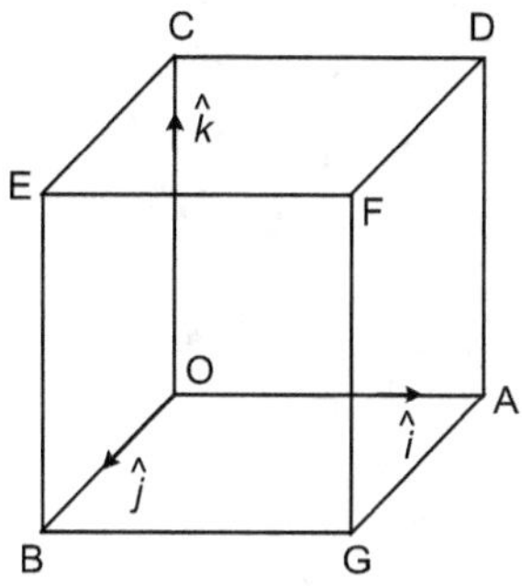

So, $\qquad \overrightarrow{OF} = \hat{i} + \hat{j} + \hat{k}$

and $\qquad \overrightarrow{GC} = \hat{k} - (\hat{i} + \hat{j})$

$$= -\hat{i} - \hat{j} + \hat{k}$$

Hence, $\quad \overrightarrow{OF} \cdot \overrightarrow{GC} = (\hat{i} + \hat{j} + \hat{k}) \cdot (-\hat{i} - \hat{j} + \hat{k})$

$$\therefore |\overrightarrow{OF}||\overrightarrow{GC}| \cos \theta = -1 - 1 + 1$$

$$\Rightarrow \left(\sqrt{1+1+1}\right)\left(\sqrt{(-1)^2 + (-1)^2 + 1^2}\right) \cos \theta = -1$$

$$\Rightarrow \left(\sqrt{3}\right)\left(\sqrt{3}\right) \cos \theta = -1$$

$$\Rightarrow \qquad \cos \theta = -\dfrac{1}{3}$$

$$\Rightarrow \qquad \theta = \cos^{-1}\left(-\dfrac{1}{3}\right)$$

132. Show that the points with position vectors $2\hat{i} + \hat{j} - \hat{k}, 3\hat{i} - 2\hat{j} + \hat{k}$ and $\hat{i} + 4\hat{j} - 3\hat{k}$ are collinear.

Sol. Let $\qquad \vec{a} = 2\hat{i} + \hat{j} - \hat{k}$

$$\vec{b} = 3\hat{i} - 2\hat{j} + \hat{k}$$

$$\vec{c} = \hat{i} + 4\hat{j} - 3\hat{k}$$

We know that if three point with position vectors $\vec{a}, \vec{b}$ and $\vec{c}$ are collinear, then

$$\vec{a} \times \vec{b} + \vec{b} \times \vec{c} + \vec{c} \times \vec{a} = 0$$

Now, $\quad \vec{a} \times \vec{b} = \begin{vmatrix} \hat{i} & \hat{j} & \hat{k} \\ 2 & 1 & -1 \\ 3 & -2 & 1 \end{vmatrix}$

$$= \hat{i}(1-2) - \hat{j}(2+3) + \hat{k}(-4-3)$$

$$= -\hat{i} - 5\hat{j} - 7\hat{k}$$

$$\vec{b} \times \vec{c} = \begin{vmatrix} \hat{i} & \hat{j} & \hat{k} \\ 3 & -2 & 1 \\ 1 & 4 & -3 \end{vmatrix}$$

$$= \hat{i}(6-4) - \hat{j}(-9-1) + \hat{k}(12+2)$$

$$= 2\hat{i} + 10\hat{j} + 14\hat{k}$$

$$\vec{c} \times \vec{a} = \begin{vmatrix} \hat{i} & \hat{j} & \hat{k} \\ 1 & 4 & -3 \\ 2 & 1 & -1 \end{vmatrix}$$

$$= \hat{i}(-4+3) - \hat{j}(-1+6) + \hat{k}(1-8)$$

$$= -\hat{i} - 5\hat{j} - 7\hat{k}$$

$\therefore \ \vec{a} \times \vec{b} + \vec{b} \times \vec{c} + \vec{c} \times \vec{a} = (-\hat{i} - 5\hat{j} - 7\hat{k})$

$$+ (2\hat{i} + 10\hat{j} + 14\hat{k}) + (-\hat{i} - 5\hat{j} - 7\hat{k}) = 0$$

Hence, the given points are collinear.

133. The two adjacent sides of a parallelogram are $2\hat{i} - 4\hat{j} - 5\hat{k}$ and $2\hat{i} + 2\hat{j} + 3\hat{k}$. Find the two unit vectors parallel to its diagonals. Using the diagonal vectors, find the area of the parallelogram.*

Sol. Let ABCD be a parallelogram such that

$$\vec{AB} = \vec{a} = 2\hat{i} - 4\hat{j} - 5\hat{k}$$

and $\quad \vec{BC} = \vec{b} = 2\hat{i} + 2\hat{j} + 3\hat{k}$

Then, $\quad \vec{AB} + \vec{BC} = \vec{AC}$

$$\vec{AC} = \vec{a} + \vec{b} = 4\hat{i} - 2\hat{j} - 2\hat{k}$$

and $\quad \vec{AB} + \vec{BD} = \vec{AD}$

$$\vec{BD} = \vec{AD} - \vec{AB}$$

$$\vec{BD} = \vec{b} - \vec{a} = 0\hat{i} + 6\hat{j} + 8\hat{k}$$

Now, $\quad \vec{AC} = 4\hat{i} - 2\hat{j} - 2\hat{k}$

$$|\vec{AC}| = \sqrt{(4)^2 + (-2)^2 + (-2)^2}$$

$$= \sqrt{24} = 2\sqrt{6}$$

and $\quad |\vec{BD}| = 0\hat{i} + 6\hat{j} + 8\hat{k}$

$$|\vec{BD}| = \sqrt{(0)^2 + (6)^2 + (8)^2}$$

$$= \sqrt{100} = 10$$

Unit vector along $\vec{AC}$

$$= \frac{\vec{AC}}{|\vec{AC}|} = \frac{1}{2\sqrt{6}}(4\hat{i} - 2\hat{j} - 2\hat{k})$$

$$= \frac{1}{\sqrt{6}}(2\hat{i} - \hat{j} - \hat{k})$$

Unit vector along $\vec{BD}$

$$= \frac{\vec{BD}}{|\vec{BD}|} = \frac{1}{10}(6\hat{j} + 8\hat{k})$$

$$= \frac{1}{5}(3\hat{j} + 4\hat{k})$$

Now, area of parallelogram

$$= \frac{1}{2}|\vec{AC} \times \vec{BD}| \qquad \ldots(i)$$

$\Rightarrow \quad \vec{AC} \times \vec{BD} = \begin{vmatrix} \hat{i} & \hat{j} & \hat{k} \\ 4 & -2 & -2 \\ 0 & 6 & 8 \end{vmatrix}$

$$= -4\hat{i} - 32\hat{j} + 24\hat{k}$$

and $\quad |\vec{AC} \times \vec{BD}| = \sqrt{(-4)^2 + (-32)^2 + (24)^2}$

$$= \sqrt{1616}$$

$$= 2\sqrt{404}$$

Area of parallelogram

$$= \frac{1}{2}|\vec{AC} \times \vec{BD}|$$

$$= \sqrt{404}$$

$$= 2\sqrt{101} \text{ sq. units.}$$

134. Find a unit vector perpendicular to each of the vector $\vec{a} + \vec{b}$ and $\vec{a} - \vec{b}$, where $\vec{a} = 3\hat{i} + 2\hat{j} + 2\hat{k}$ and $\vec{b} = \hat{i} + 2\hat{j} - 2\hat{k}$.*

Sol. Given that

$$\vec{a} = 3\hat{i} + 2\hat{j} + 2\hat{k}$$

and

$$\vec{b} = \hat{i} + 2\hat{j} - 2\hat{k}$$

Now,

$$\vec{a} - \vec{b} = (3\hat{i} + 2\hat{j} + 2\hat{k}) - (\hat{i} + 2\hat{j} - 2\hat{k})$$

$$= 2\hat{i} + 4\hat{k}$$

$$\vec{a} + \vec{b} = (3\hat{i} + 2\hat{j} + 2\hat{k}) + (\hat{i} + 2\hat{j} - 2\hat{k})$$

$$= 4\hat{i} + 4\hat{j}$$

Let

$$\vec{a} + \vec{b} = \vec{c}$$

and

$$\vec{a} - \vec{b} = \vec{d}$$

Therefore, we have

$$\vec{c} = 4\hat{i} + 4\hat{j}$$

and

$$\vec{d} = 2\hat{i} + 4\hat{j}$$

we know that a unit vector which is perpendicular to both vectors $\vec{c}$ and $\vec{d}$ is given by

$$\hat{n} = \frac{\vec{c} \times \vec{d}}{|\vec{c} \times \vec{d}|} \qquad \text{...(i)}$$

$$\therefore \quad |\vec{c} \times \vec{d}| = \begin{vmatrix} \hat{i} & \hat{j} & \hat{k} \\ 4 & 4 & 0 \\ 2 & 0 & 4 \end{vmatrix}$$

$$= \hat{i}(16 - 0) - \hat{j}(16 - 0) + \hat{k}(0 - 8)$$

$$\therefore \quad \vec{c} \times \vec{d} = 16\hat{i} - 16\hat{j} - 8\hat{k} \qquad \text{...(ii)}$$

and

$$|\vec{c} \times \vec{d}| = \sqrt{(16)^2 + (-16)^2 + (-8)^2}$$

$$= \sqrt{256 + 256 + 64}$$

$$= \sqrt{576}$$

$$= 24 \qquad \text{...(iii)}$$

Hence, the required unit vector

$$= \frac{16\hat{i} - 16\hat{j} - 8\hat{k}}{24}$$

[By using equations (i), (ii) and (iii)]

$$= \frac{8(2\hat{i} - 2\hat{j} - \hat{k})}{24}$$

$$= \frac{2}{3}\hat{i} - \frac{2}{3}\hat{j} - \frac{1}{3}\hat{k}$$

Long Answer Type Questions

135. Find a vector of magnitude $\sqrt{51}$ which makes equal angles with the unit vectors $\vec{a} = \frac{1}{3}(\hat{i} - 2\hat{j} + 2\hat{k})$, $\vec{b} = \frac{1}{5}(-4\hat{i} - 3\hat{k})$ and $\vec{c} = \hat{j}$.

Sol. Let the required vector be

$$\vec{r} = \alpha\hat{i} + \beta\hat{j} + \gamma\hat{k}$$

Where $\alpha^2 + \beta^2 + \gamma^2 = 51$ (given)

$$\Rightarrow |\vec{r}| = \sqrt{51} \qquad \text{...(i)}$$

Let θ be the angle which $\vec{a}, \vec{b}$ and $\vec{c}$ make with $\vec{r}$

Then, $\cos\theta = \dfrac{\vec{r} \cdot \vec{a}}{|\vec{r}||\vec{a}|} = \dfrac{\vec{r} \cdot \vec{b}}{|\vec{r}||\vec{b}|} = \dfrac{\vec{r} \cdot \vec{c}}{|\vec{r}||\vec{c}|}$

$$= \frac{\vec{r} \cdot \vec{a}}{\sqrt{51} \times 1} = \frac{\vec{r} \cdot \vec{b}}{\sqrt{51} \times 1} = \frac{\vec{r} \cdot \vec{c}}{\sqrt{51} \times 1}$$

[Since $|\vec{r}| = \sqrt{51}$ and $\vec{a}, \vec{b}$ and $\vec{c}$ are unit vectors]

$$\Rightarrow \quad \vec{r} \cdot \vec{a} = \vec{r} \cdot \vec{b} = \vec{r} \cdot \vec{c}$$

$$\Rightarrow (\alpha\hat{i} + \beta\hat{j} + \gamma\hat{k}) \cdot \left(\frac{\hat{i}}{3} - \frac{2\hat{j}}{3} + \frac{2\hat{k}}{3} \right)$$

$$= (\alpha\hat{i} + \beta\hat{j} + \gamma\hat{k}) \left(\frac{-4\hat{i}}{5} - \frac{3\hat{k}}{5} \right)$$

$$= (\alpha\hat{i} + \beta\hat{j} + \gamma\hat{k}) \cdot \hat{j}$$

$$\Rightarrow \frac{1}{3}(\alpha - 2\beta + 2\gamma) = \frac{1}{5}(-4\alpha - 3\gamma) = \beta$$

$$\Rightarrow 5\alpha - 10\beta + 10\gamma = -12\alpha - 9\gamma = 15\beta$$

$$\Rightarrow \quad 5\alpha - 25\beta + 10\gamma = 0$$

and $12\alpha + 15\beta + 9\gamma = 0$

$\Rightarrow \quad \alpha - 5\beta + 2\gamma = 0$ ...(i)

$\Rightarrow \quad 4\alpha + 5\beta + 3\gamma = 0$ ...(ii)

Hence, $\dfrac{\alpha}{-15-10} = \dfrac{\beta}{8-3} = \dfrac{\gamma}{5+20}$

$\Rightarrow \quad \dfrac{\alpha}{-25} = \dfrac{\beta}{5} = \dfrac{\gamma}{25} = \lambda$, (say)

$\Rightarrow \quad \dfrac{\alpha}{5} = \dfrac{\beta}{-1} = \dfrac{\gamma}{-5} = \lambda$

then $\qquad \alpha = 5\lambda, \beta = -\lambda, \gamma = -5\lambda$

Putting these values of α, β and γ in (i), we get,

$\quad 25\lambda^2 + \lambda^2 + 25\lambda^2 = 51$

$\Rightarrow \qquad 51\lambda^3 = 51$

$\Rightarrow \qquad \lambda^2 = 1$

$\Rightarrow \qquad \lambda = \pm 1$

Hence, the required vectors are

$$= \vec{r} \pm (5\hat{i} - \hat{j} - 5\hat{k})$$

136. Find the angles of a triangle ABC whose vertices are A(1, 2, 3), B(2, 4, 8) and C(3, 6, 7). **[NCERT]**

Sol. Let O be the origin.

Then, $\quad \vec{OA} = \hat{i} + 2\hat{j} + 3\hat{k},$

$\vec{OB} = 2\hat{i} + 4\hat{j} + 8\hat{k}$

and $\quad \vec{OC} = 3\hat{i} + 6\hat{j} + 7\hat{k}$

$\therefore \qquad \vec{AB} = \vec{OB} - \vec{OA}$

$= (2\hat{i} + 4\hat{j} + 8\hat{k}) - (\hat{i} + 2\hat{j} + 3\hat{k})$

$= \hat{i} + 2\hat{j} + 5\hat{k},$

$|\vec{AB}| = \sqrt{30},$

$\vec{BC} = \vec{OC} - \vec{OB}$

$= (3\hat{i} + 6\hat{j} + 7\hat{k}) - (2\hat{i} + 4\hat{j} + 8\hat{k})$

$= \hat{i} + 2\hat{j} - \hat{k},$

$|\vec{BC}| = \sqrt{6}$

$\vec{CA} = \vec{OA} - \vec{OC}$

$= (\hat{i} + 2\hat{j} + 3\hat{k}) - (3\hat{i} + 6\hat{j} + 7\hat{k})$

$= -2\hat{i} - 4\hat{j} - 4\hat{k},$

$|\vec{CA}| = \sqrt{36} = 6$

Now $\qquad \vec{AB} + \vec{BC} = 2\hat{i} + 4\hat{j} + 4\hat{k}$

Also, $\quad \vec{AB} + \vec{BC} + \vec{CA} = \vec{0}$

Which show that A, B and C are the vertices of a triangle.

Now, $\quad \vec{AB} \cdot \vec{BC} = (\hat{i} + 2\hat{j} + 5\hat{k}) \cdot (\hat{i} + 2\hat{j} - \hat{k})$

$= 1 + 4 - 5 = 0$

$\Rightarrow AB \perp BC$ and therefore, $\angle B = 90°$

Now, $\angle A$ is the angle between $\vec{AB}$ and $\vec{AC}$

and $\vec{AB} . \vec{AC} = (\hat{i} + 2\hat{j} + 5\hat{k}) \cdot (-2\hat{i} - 4\hat{j} - 4\hat{k})$

$= -2 - 8 - 20$

$= -30$

$\cos A = \dfrac{\vec{AB} \cdot \vec{AC}}{|\vec{AB}| \, |\vec{AC}|} = \dfrac{30}{\sqrt{30} \times 6} = \dfrac{\sqrt{30}}{6}$

But $\angle C$ is the angle between $\vec{CA}$ and $\vec{CB}$

Hence, $\cos C = \dfrac{\vec{CA} . \vec{CB}}{|\vec{CA}| \, |\vec{CB}|}$

$= \dfrac{(-2\hat{i} - 4\hat{j} - 4\hat{k}) \cdot (-\hat{i} - 2\hat{j} + \hat{k})}{6\sqrt{6}}$

$= \dfrac{2 + 8 - 4}{6\sqrt{6}} = \dfrac{6}{6\sqrt{6}}$

$= \dfrac{1}{\sqrt{6}} = \dfrac{\sqrt{6}}{6}$

Hence, *ABC* is a right-angled triangle, right-angled at *B*. The other two angles are

$$\cos^{-1} \dfrac{\sqrt{30}}{6} \text{ and } \cos^{-1} \dfrac{\sqrt{6}}{6}$$

137. If the diagonals of a parallelogram are determined by the vector $\vec{a}$ and $\vec{b}$, show that its area is $\dfrac{1}{2} |\vec{a} \times \vec{b}|$. **[NCERT]**

Sol. Let ABCD be a parallelogram. Its diagonals AC and BD intersect at O.

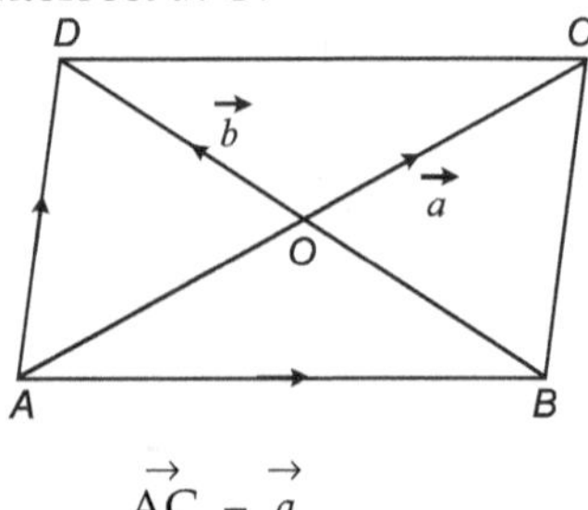

Let $\qquad \vec{AC} = \vec{a}$

and
$$\vec{BD} = \vec{b}$$

Since the diagonals of a parallelogram bisect each other, O is the mid-point of AC and BD.

$$\therefore \qquad \vec{OD} = \frac{1}{2}\vec{BD} = \frac{\vec{b}}{2},$$

$$\vec{OC} = \frac{1}{2}\vec{AC} = \frac{\vec{a}}{2},$$

$$\vec{OB} = -\frac{1}{2}\vec{BD} = -\frac{1}{2}\vec{b}$$

and
$$\vec{OA} = -\frac{1}{2}\vec{AC} = -\frac{1}{2}\vec{a}$$

$$\therefore \qquad \vec{AB} = \vec{OB} - \vec{OA}$$

$$= \left(-\frac{1}{2}\vec{b}\right) - \left(-\frac{1}{2}\vec{a}\right)$$

$$= \frac{1}{2}(\vec{a} - \vec{b})$$

and
$$\vec{AD} = \vec{OD} - \vec{OA} = \frac{\vec{b}}{2} - \left(-\frac{\vec{a}}{2}\right)$$

$$= \frac{1}{2}(\vec{a} + \vec{b})$$

Therefore, the area of parallelogram ABCD

$$= |\vec{AB} \times \vec{AD}|$$

$$= \left|\frac{1}{2}(\vec{a} - \vec{b}) \times \frac{1}{2}(\vec{a} + \vec{b})\right|$$

$$= \left|\frac{1}{4}(\vec{a} \times \vec{a} + \vec{a} \times \vec{b} - \vec{b} \times \vec{a} - \vec{b} \times \vec{b})\right|$$

$$= \frac{1}{4}|0 + \vec{a} \times \vec{b} + \vec{a} \times \vec{b} - 0|$$

$$= \frac{1}{4}|2(\vec{a} \times \vec{b})|$$

$$= \frac{1}{2}|\vec{a} \times \vec{b}|$$

Self - Assessment

138. Let $\vec{a}$ and $\vec{b}$ be the vectors determined by the adjacent sides of a regular hexagon as shown below in the figure.

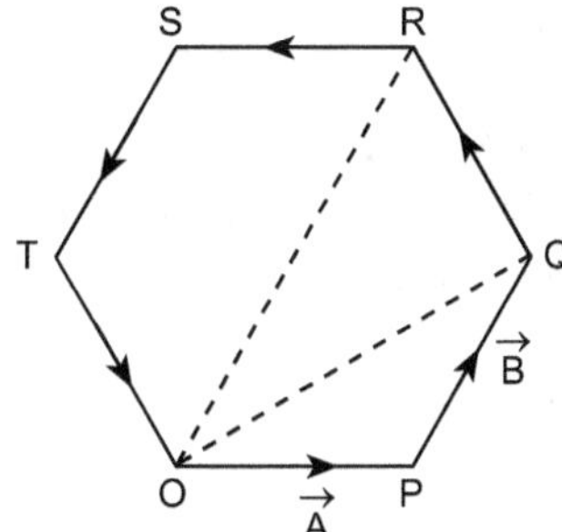

What are the vectors determined by the other sides taken in order ?

Sol. $\vec{QR} = \vec{b} - \vec{a}$

$\vec{RS} = \vec{a} - \vec{b}$

139. Let $\vec{a}$ be a vector in the north-east direction with magnitude 5 and $\vec{b}$ be another vector in the north-west direction with magnitude 5. What is the magnitude of $\vec{a} - \vec{b}$?

Sol. $5\sqrt{2}$ along QP

140. Interpret the equation $|\vec{a} + \vec{b}| = |\vec{a} - \vec{b}|$ geometrically.

Sol. rectangle.

141. If $\vec{a} + 3\vec{b} = \vec{c}$ and $\vec{b} - 3\vec{a} = 4\vec{c}$, then show that the directions of $\vec{a}$ and $\vec{b}$ are opposite to each other.

142. Find the component of $\vec{AB}$ with $A(1, 0)$ and $B(5, 0)$ along the line $y = x$.

Sol. $2\sqrt{2}$

143. Let $\vec{AB}$ be a vector in space whose magnitude is 10 units. It makes an angle of 60° with the X-axis. Find the component of $\vec{AB}$ along the coordinate axes.

Sol. 5 along the Z-axis and $5\sqrt{3}$ along the Y-axis.

144. Let $\vec{AB}$ be a vector in space whose magnitude is 20 units. It makes an angle of 60° each with the X-axis and the Y-axis. Find the acute angle it makes with Z-axis and also find its components along all the three coordinate axes.

Sol. $45°, 10, 10\sqrt{2}$

145. Let $\vec{A}, \vec{B}, \vec{C}$ be non-coplanar vectors. Show that $-2\vec{A} + 3\vec{B} + 5\vec{C}, \quad \vec{A} + 2\vec{B} + 3\vec{C}, \quad 7\vec{A} - \vec{C}$ are collinear.

146. Find the terminal point B of the vector $\overrightarrow{AB}$, whose initial point A is the point (4, 2) and the components along OX and OY are $5\hat{i}$ and $2\hat{j}$.

Sol. (9, 4)

147. If the components of a vector are 5, 0 and 3 along OX, OY and OZ respectively and its terminal point is (1, – 1, 1), find its initial point.

Sol. (– 4, – 1, – 2)

148. Find the magnitude of the vector $-4\hat{i}+\hat{j}+2\hat{k}$.

Sol. $\sqrt{21}$

149. Suppose A, B, C, D are vertices of a parallelogram and A is the point (2, 3), B is (1, 4) and C is (0, – 2). Find the coordinates of D.

Sol. (1, – 3)

150. Find the ratio in which the point $7\hat{i}-\hat{k}$ divides the join of $-2\hat{i}+3\hat{j}+5\hat{k}$ and $\hat{i}+2\hat{j}+3\hat{k}$.

Sol. Externally in the ratio 2 : 3.

151. Prove that the internal bisector of angle A of a triangle ABC divides the side BC in the ratio $AB : AC$.

152. Show that the sum of three vectors determined by the medians of a triangle directed from the vertices is zero.

153. Show that the vectors $-2\hat{i}-\hat{j}+\hat{k}$, $\hat{i}-3\hat{j}-5\hat{k}$ and $3\hat{i}-4\hat{j}-4\hat{k}$ are vertices of right angled triangle.

154. Find the component of $\overrightarrow{A}=\hat{i}-2\hat{j}+\hat{k}$ along $\overrightarrow{B}=4\hat{i}-4\hat{j}+7\hat{k}$.

Sol. $\dfrac{19}{81}(4\hat{i}-4\hat{j}+7\hat{k})$

155. Find the scalar product of $\hat{i}+\hat{j}+\hat{k}$ and $\hat{i}+\hat{j}-3\hat{k}$.

Sol. – 1

156. Show that $\overrightarrow{A}=2\hat{i}+\hat{j}+\hat{k}$, $\overrightarrow{B}=\hat{i}+\hat{j}-3\hat{k}$ and are $\overrightarrow{C}=-4\hat{i}+7\hat{j}+\hat{k}$ mutually perpendicular.

157. Prove that the vectors $5\hat{i}+2\hat{j}-\hat{k}$ and $\dfrac{7}{5}\hat{i}-\hat{j}+5\hat{k}$ are orthogonal.

158. Determine the unit vector perpendicular to the plane of $\overrightarrow{A}=2\hat{i}-6\hat{j}-3\hat{k}$ and $\overrightarrow{B}=4\hat{i}+3\hat{j}-\hat{k}$

Sol. $\dfrac{3}{7}\hat{i}-\dfrac{2}{7}\hat{j}+\dfrac{6}{7}\hat{k}$

159. Find the area of parallelogram determined by vectors $(\hat{i}+2\hat{j}+3\hat{k})$ and $(3\hat{i}-2\hat{j}+\hat{k})$.

Sol. $8\sqrt{3}$ square units.

160. Find the area of triangle with vertices (1, 1, 2), (2, 3, 5) and (1, 5, 5).

Sol. $\dfrac{\sqrt{61}}{2}$ square units

161. A cube has four diagonals, connecting opposite vertices. What is the angle between an adjacent pair of diagonals ?

Sol. $\cos^{-1}\left(\dfrac{1}{3}\right)$

○○

Three-Dimensional Geometry

Basic Concepts

1. The angles α, β and γ which a directed line OA makes with the positive direction of X-, Y- and Z-axes respectively are called the **direction angles** of the line OA.

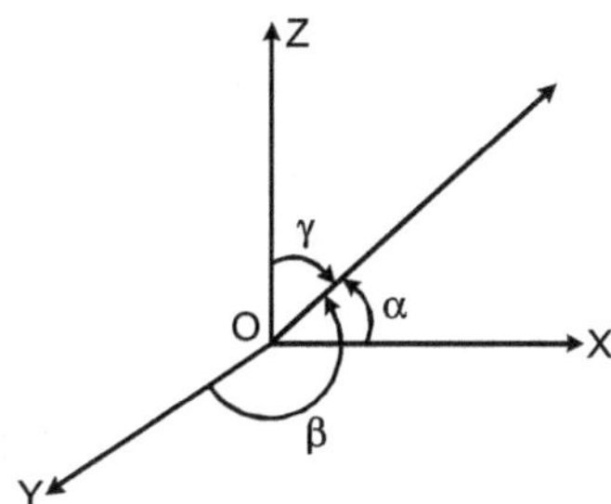

2. Cosines of the angles made by OA with the positive direction of the coordinates axes *i.e.*, cos α, cos β and cos γ are called the **direction cosines** of this line.

   The direction cosines of a line are usually denoted by the letters l, m, n.

3. Direction cosines of the X-axis are (1, 0, 0) that of the Y-axis are (0, 1, 0) and that of the Z-axis are (0, 0, 1).

4. **Relation between the Direction Cosines of a Line**
   $$l^2 + m^2 + n^2 = 1 \qquad \text{...(i)}$$
   Also $l = \cos \alpha$, $m = \cos \beta$ and $n = \cos \gamma$ ...(ii)
   From (i) and (ii), we can deduce:
   $$\cos^2 \alpha + \cos^2 \beta + \cos^2 \gamma = 1.$$

5. **The coordinates of a point A(x, y, z) in terms of the Direction Cosines**

   If l, m, n are the direction cosines of a line OA and $|OA| = r$.

   Then $\quad$ OA = $r \cos \alpha$ or $x = lr$ $\quad$ ($\because \cos \alpha = l$)

   Similarly $\quad y = mr$ and $z = nr$

   Therefore, the coordinates of the point A can be given as A(lr, mr, nr).

6. Direction cosines of a line joining two points P(x_1, y_1, z_1) and Q(x_2, y_2, z_2) are
   $$\frac{x_2 - x_1}{PQ}, \frac{y_2 - y_1}{PQ}, \frac{z_2 - z_1}{PQ}$$
   where PQ = $\sqrt{(x_2 - x_1)^2 + (y_2 - y_1)^2 + (z_2 - z_1)^2}$

7. A set of three numbers a, b, c which are proportional to the direction cosines of a line are called the **direction ratios** of the line.

   If l, m, n are the direction cosines and a, b, c are the direction ratios of a line, then

   (i) $\quad l : m : n = a : b : c$

   (ii) $\quad l = \dfrac{a}{\sqrt{a^2 + b^2 + c^2}} : m = \dfrac{b}{\sqrt{a^2 + b^2 + c^2}}$
   $$: n = \dfrac{c}{\sqrt{a^2 + b^2 + c^2}}$$

   (iii) The direction cosines of a line are unique as far as their magnitudes are concerned but a line may have an an infinite number of direction ratios.

   For example, the direction cosines of the X-axis are (1, 0, 0); those of the Y-axis are (0, 1, 0) and for the Z-axis are (0, 0, 1). These are unique, but $(- 3, 0, 0)$; (4, 0, 0) or in general $(k, 0, 0)$ (for any value of k) are direction ratios of the X-axis.

8. The vector equation of a line that passes through the given point whose position vector is $\vec{a}$ and is parallel to a given vector $\vec{b}$ is
   $$\vec{r} = \vec{a} + \lambda \vec{b}$$

9. Equation of a line through a point (x, y, z) and having direction cosines l, m, n is
   $$\frac{x - x_1}{l} = \frac{y - y_1}{m} = \frac{z - z_1}{n}$$

10. The vector equation of a line which passes throught two points whose position vectors are $\vec{a}$ and $\vec{b}$ is $\vec{a} + \lambda(\vec{b} - \vec{a})$.

11. Cartesian equation of a line that passes through two points (x_1, y_1, z_1) and (x_2, y_2, z_2) is
    $$\frac{x - x_1}{x_2 - x_1} = \frac{y - y_1}{y_2 - y_1} = \frac{z - z_1}{z_2 - z_1}$$

12. Two lines with direction ratios (a_1, b_1, c_1) and (a_2, b_2, c_2) are

    (i) $\quad$ perpendicular if $a_1 a_2 + b_1 b_2 + c_1 c_2 = 0$

(ii) parallel if

$$\frac{a_1}{a_2} = \frac{b_1}{b_2} = \frac{c_1}{c_2}$$

13. **Skew lines** are lines in space which are neither parallel nor intersecting each other. They lie in different planes.

14. **Shortest Distance between Two Skew Lines :** Shortage distance between two skew lines in the line segment perpendicular to both the lines.

   If $\vec{r} = \vec{a_1} + t\vec{b_1}$ and $\vec{r} = \vec{a_2} + t\vec{b_2}$ be two skew lines, then the shortest distance between them is given as

   $$d = \left| \frac{(\vec{b_1} \times \vec{b_2}) \cdot (\vec{a_2} - \vec{a_1})}{|\vec{b_1} \times \vec{b_2}|} \right|$$

   From here we deduce the following:

   (i) Two lines intersect if and only if $d = 0$ and only if $(\vec{b_1} \times \vec{b_2}) \cdot (\vec{a_2} - \vec{a_1}) = 0$.

   (ii) If two lines are parallel then their equations can be taken as

   $$\vec{r} = \vec{a_1} + t\vec{b_1} \text{ and } \vec{r} = \vec{a_2} + u\vec{b_2}.$$

15. **Shortest Distance between the Lines :**

   $$\frac{x - x_1}{a_1} = \frac{y - y_1}{b_1} = \frac{z - z_1}{c_1} \text{ and } \frac{x - x_2}{a_2} = \frac{y - y_2}{b_2} = \frac{z - z_2}{c_2} \text{ is}$$

   $$\frac{\begin{vmatrix} x_2 - x_1 & y_2 - y_1 & z_2 - z_1 \\ a_1 & b_1 & c_1 \\ a_2 & b_2 & c_2 \end{vmatrix}}{\sqrt{(b_1 c_2 - b_2 c_1)^2 + (c_1 a_2 - c_2 a_1)^2 + (a_1 b_2 - a_2 b_1)^2}}$$

16. Distance between parallel lines $a_1 + \alpha b$ and $a_2 + \beta b$ is $\left| \dfrac{\vec{b} \times (\vec{a_2} - \vec{a_1})}{|\vec{b}|} \right|$.

17. General equation of a plane in vector form is $\vec{r} \cdot \vec{n} = d$, where $\vec{n}$ is unit normal vector to the plane and d is the perpendicular distance of the plane from the origin. If

   $$\vec{r} = x\hat{i} + y\hat{j} + z\hat{k}, \quad \vec{n} = l\hat{i} + m\hat{j} + n\hat{k}$$

   and then $lx + my + nz = d$ is the general equation of plane in Cartesian form.

18. The equation of the plane passing through a point whose position vector is $\vec{a}$ and perpendicular to the vector $\vec{n}$ is $(\vec{r} - \vec{a}) \cdot \vec{n} = 0$.

19. **Cartesian form of equation of a plane passing through a point :** Let the given point A be (x_1, y_1, z_1) and P be (x, y, z) and direction ratios of $\vec{n}$ are a, b, c.

   So
   $$\vec{a} = x_1\hat{i} + y_1\hat{j} + z_1\hat{k}$$
   $$\vec{r} = x\hat{i} + y\hat{j} + z\hat{k}$$
   $$\vec{n} = a\hat{i} + b\hat{j} + c\hat{k}$$

   Substituting it in equation $(\vec{r} - \vec{a}) \cdot \vec{n} = 0$, we have

   $$((x - x_1)\hat{i} + (y - y_1)\hat{j} + (z - z_1)\hat{k}) \cdot (a\hat{i} + b\hat{j} + c\hat{k}) = 0$$
   $$(x - x_1)a + (y - y_1)b + (z - z_1)c = 0$$

   which is required equation in Cartesian form.

20. **Equation of a plane passing through a point A and parallel to two lines $\vec{r}, \vec{r}'$:**

   Let $\vec{a}$ be the position vector of point A.

   Let the plane be parallel to lines $\vec{r} = \vec{a} + \lambda \vec{b}$ and $\vec{r}' = \vec{a} + \mu \vec{b}'$.

   Let P be a point with position vector $\vec{r}$, then P lies in the plane iff $\overrightarrow{AP}, \vec{b}, \vec{b}'$ are coplanar.

   $$(\vec{r} - \vec{a}) \cdot (\vec{b} \times \vec{b}') = 0$$

   is the required vector equation of plane.

   Cartesian form : Let the plane passes through the point $A(x_1, y_1, z_1)$, parallel to lines whose direction ratios are b_1, b_2, b_3 and b_1', b_2', b_3'. Let $P(x, y, z)$ be any point on the plane with position vector $\vec{r}$. Then cartesian equation of plane is

   $$\begin{vmatrix} x - x_1 & y - y_1 & z - z_1 \\ b_1 & b_2 & b_3 \\ b_1' & b_2' & b_3' \end{vmatrix} = 0.$$

   Note : The above formula holds even if the two lines lie in the plane.

21. Equation of plane in normal form is $lx + my + nz = d$, where l, m, n are direction cosines of perpendicular from origin and $d (d \neq 0)$ is the distance of the plane from origin.

22. Equation of a plane passing through three non-collinear (but co-planar) points in vector form is given by

   $$(\vec{r} - \vec{a}) \cdot [(\vec{b} - \vec{a}) \times (\vec{c} - \vec{a})] = 0.$$

Where $\vec{a}, \vec{b}, \vec{c}$ are position vectors of non collinear points.

23. Equation of a plane passing through three non-collinear (but co-planar) points.

If $A(x_1, y_1, z_1)$, $B(x_2, y_2, z_2)$ and $C(x_3, y_3, z_3)$ are three collinear points and the coordinates of $\vec{r}$ are (x, y, z) then the equation of plane is given as,

$$\begin{vmatrix} x - x_1 & y - y_1 & z - z_1 \\ x_2 - x_1 & y_2 - y_1 & z_2 - z_1 \\ x_3 - x_1 & y_3 - y_1 & z_3 - z_1 \end{vmatrix} = 0.$$

24. Equation of a plane that cuts the coordinate axes at $(a, 0, 0)$, $(0, b, 0)$ and $(0, 0, c)$ is

$$\frac{x}{a} + \frac{y}{b} + \frac{z}{c} = 1.$$

25. Vector equation of a plane that passes through the intersection of planes $\vec{r} \cdot \vec{n_1} = d_1$ and $\vec{r} \cdot \vec{n_2} = d_2$ is

$$\vec{r} \cdot (\vec{n_1} + \lambda \vec{n_2}) = d_1 + \lambda d_2$$

In Cartesian form : Equation of a plane that passes through the intersection of two given planes

$A_1 x + B_1 y + C_1 z + D_1 = 0$ and $A_2 x + B_2 y + C_2 z + D_2 = 0$ is

$(A_1 x + B_1 y + C_1 z + D_1) + \lambda(A_2 x + B_2 y + C_2 z + D_2) = 0.$

26. Two lines are said to be **coplanar** if they lie in the same plane. Let the given lines be

$$\vec{r} = \vec{a_1} + \lambda \vec{b_1} \qquad \qquad ...(1)$$

and

$$\vec{r} = \vec{a_2} + \lambda \vec{b_2} \qquad \qquad ...(2)$$

The lines will be coplanar if

$$(\vec{a_2} - \vec{a_1}) \cdot (\vec{b_1} \times \vec{b_2}) = 0.$$

In Cartesian form : If the coordinates of points $A(x_1, y_1, z_1)$ and $B(x_2, y_2, z_2)$ and a_1, b_1, c_1 and a_2, b_2, c_2 are the direction ratios of vector $\vec{b_1}$ and $\vec{b_2}$ respectively the lines will be coplanar iff

$$\begin{vmatrix} x_2 - x_1 & y_2 - y_1 & z_2 - z_1 \\ a_1 & b_1 & c_1 \\ a_2 & b_2 & c_2 \end{vmatrix} = 0.$$

27. Distance of a Point from a Plane : Let $\vec{r} \cdot \vec{n} = d$ be the equation of a plane and A be the point with position vector $\vec{a}$ on the plane then distance of the plane from the point is given by

$$\left| \frac{\vec{a} \cdot \vec{n} - d}{|n|} \right|$$

In Cartesian form : The distance of a point (x_1, y_1, z_1) from the $Ax + By + Cz + D = 0$ is

$$\left| \frac{Ax_1 + By_1 + Cz_1 + D}{\sqrt{A^2 + B^2 + C^2}} \right|$$

Multiple Choice Questions

1. Distance of the point (α, β, γ) from Y-axis is:

[NCERT Exemplar]

(a) β

(b) $|\beta|$

(c) $|\beta| + |\gamma|$

(d) $\sqrt{\alpha^2 + \gamma^2}$

Sol. (d) $\sqrt{\alpha^2 + \gamma^2}$

Explanation :

Required distance

$$= \sqrt{(\alpha - 0)^2 + (\beta - \beta)^2 + (\gamma - 0)^2}$$

$$= \sqrt{\alpha^2 + \gamma^2}$$

2. If the direction cosines of a line are k, k and k, then: **[NCERT Exemplar]**

(a) $k > 0$

(b) $0 < k < 1$

(c) $k = 1$

(d) $k = \dfrac{1}{\sqrt{3}}$ or $-\dfrac{1}{\sqrt{3}}$

Sol. (d) $k = \dfrac{1}{\sqrt{3}}$ or $-\dfrac{1}{\sqrt{3}}$

Explanation :

Since, direction cosines of a line are k, k and k.

$\therefore \qquad l = k,\ m = k$ and $n = k$

We know that,

$$l^2 + m^2 + n^2 = 1$$

$$\Rightarrow \qquad k^2 + k^2 + k^2 = 1$$

$$\Rightarrow \qquad k^2 = \frac{1}{3}$$

$$\therefore \qquad k = \pm \frac{1}{\sqrt{3}}.$$

3. Under what condition do $\left\langle \dfrac{1}{\sqrt{2}}, \dfrac{1}{2}, k \right\rangle$ represent direction cosines of a line?

[NCERT Exemplar]

(a) $k = \dfrac{1}{2}$

(b) $k = \pm \dfrac{1}{2}$

(c) $k = -\dfrac{1}{2}$

(d) k can take any value

Sol. (b) $k = \pm \dfrac{1}{2}$

Explanation :

For $\left(\dfrac{1}{\sqrt{2}}, \dfrac{1}{2}, k \right)$ to represent direction cosines,

we should have

$$\left(\dfrac{1}{\sqrt{2}} \right)^2 + \left(\dfrac{1}{2} \right)^2 + k^2 = 1$$

or $\qquad\qquad \dfrac{1}{2} + \dfrac{1}{4} + k^2 = 1$

$\Rightarrow \qquad\qquad k = \pm \dfrac{1}{2}.$

4. Any three numbers which are proportional to the direction cosines of a line, are called:

[NCERT Exemplar]

(a) direction angles

(b) direction ratios

(c) another set of direction cosines

(d) None of the above

Sol. (b) direction ratios

Explanation :

Any three numbers which are proportional to the direction cosines of a line, are called the direction ratios of the line. If l, m and n are direction cosines and a, b and c are direction ratios of a line, then $a = \lambda l$, $b = \lambda m$ and $c = \lambda n$ for any non-zero $\lambda \in R$.

5. Direction ratios of two lines are a, b, c and $\dfrac{1}{bc}$, $\dfrac{1}{ca}$, $\dfrac{1}{ab}$, The lines are: **[NCERT Exemplar]**

(a) Mutually perpendicular

(b) Parallel

(c) Coincident

(d) None of these

Sol. (b) Parallel

Explanation :

As $\qquad \dfrac{a}{(1/bc)} = \dfrac{b}{(1/ca)} = \dfrac{c}{(1/ab)}$

Hence, lines are parallel.

6. Direction ratios of the line represented by the equation $x = ay + b$, $z = cy + d$ are:

(a) $(a, 1, c)$ (b) $(a, b - d, c)$

(c) $(a, 1, a)$ (d) (b, ac, d)

Sol. (a) $(a, 1, c)$

Explanation :

Given, $\qquad x = ay + b$, $z = cy + d$

$\therefore \qquad\qquad y = \dfrac{x - b}{a}, y = \dfrac{z - d}{c}$

$\therefore \qquad \dfrac{x - b}{a} = \dfrac{y}{1} = \dfrac{z - d}{c}$

Hence direction ratios are $(a, 1, c)$.

7. If α, β, γ are the angles that a line makes with the positive direction of x, y, z axis, respectively, then the direction cosines of the line are:

(a) $\sin \alpha$, $\sin \beta$, $\sin \gamma$

(b) $\cos \alpha$, $\cos \beta$, $\cos \gamma$

(c) $\tan \alpha$, $\tan \beta$, $\tan \gamma$

(d) $\cos^2 \alpha$, $\cos^2 \beta$, $\cos^3 \gamma$

Sol. (b) $\cos \alpha$, $\cos \beta$, $\cos \gamma$

8. The distance of a point $P(a, b, c)$ from x-axis is:

(a) $\sqrt{a^2 + c^2}$ (b) $\sqrt{a^2 + b^2}$

(c) $\sqrt{b^2 + c^2}$ (d) $b^2 + c^2$

Sol. (c) $\sqrt{b^2 + c^2}$

Explanation :

The required distance is the distance of $P(a, b, c)$

from $Q(a, 0, 0)$, which is $\sqrt{b^2 + c^2}$

So the correct option is (c).

9. A line makes equal angles with coordinate axis. Direction cosines of this line are:

(a) $\pm (1, 1, 1)$ (b) $\pm \left(\dfrac{1}{\sqrt{3}}, \dfrac{1}{\sqrt{3}}, \dfrac{1}{\sqrt{3}} \right)$

(c) $\pm \left(\dfrac{1}{3}, \dfrac{1}{3}, \dfrac{1}{3} \right)$ (d) $\pm \left(\dfrac{1}{\sqrt{3}}, \dfrac{-1}{\sqrt{3}}, \dfrac{-1}{\sqrt{3}} \right)$

Sol. (b) $\pm \left(\dfrac{1}{\sqrt{3}}, \dfrac{1}{\sqrt{3}}, \dfrac{1}{\sqrt{3}} \right)$

Explanation :

Let the line make angle α with each of the axis.

Then, its direction cosines are $\cos \alpha$, $\cos \alpha$, $\cos \alpha$.

Since $\cos^2 \alpha + \cos^2 \alpha + \cos^2 \alpha = 1$.

$\therefore \qquad\qquad \cos \alpha = \pm \dfrac{1}{\sqrt{3}}$

The correct option is (b).

10. The vector equation of the symmetrical form of equation of straight line $\dfrac{x-5}{3} = \dfrac{y+4}{7} = \dfrac{z-6}{2}$ is:

   [NCERT Exemplar]

   (a) $\vec{r} = (3\,\hat{i} + 7\,\hat{j} + 2\,\hat{k}) + \mu(5\,\hat{i} + 4\,\hat{j} - 6\,\hat{k})$

   (b) $\vec{r} = (5\,\hat{i} + 4\,\hat{j} - 6\,\hat{k}) + \mu(3\,\hat{i} + 7\,\hat{j} + 2\,\hat{k})$

   (c) $\vec{r} = (5\,\hat{i} - 4\,\hat{j} - 6\,\hat{k}) + \mu(3\,\hat{i} - 7\,\hat{j} - 2\,\hat{k})$

   (d) $\vec{r} = (5\,\hat{i} - 4\,\hat{j} + 6\,\hat{k}) + \mu(3\,\hat{i} + 7\,\hat{j} + 2\,\hat{k})$

Sol. (d) $\vec{r} = (5\,\hat{i} - 4\,\hat{j} + 6\,\hat{k}) + \mu(3\,\hat{i} + 7\,\hat{j} + 2\,\hat{k})$

Explanation :

$\dfrac{x-x_1}{a} = \dfrac{y-y_1}{b} = \dfrac{z-z_1}{c}$ have vector form

$$= (x_1\,\hat{i} + y_1\,\hat{j} + z_1\,\hat{k}) + \lambda(a\,\hat{i} + b\,\hat{j} + c\,\hat{k})$$

Required equation in vector form is

$$\vec{r} = (5\,\hat{i} - 4\,\hat{j} + 6\,\hat{k}) + \mu(3\,\hat{i} + 7\,\hat{j} + 2\,\hat{k})$$

11. The lines in a space which are neither intersecting nor parallel, are called: **[NCERT Exemplar]**

   (a) concurrent lines   (b) intersecting lines
   (c) skew lines   (d) parallel lines

Sol. (c) skew lines

Explanation :

In a space, there are lines which are neither intersecting nor parallel. Infact, such pair of lines are non-coplanar and are called skew-lines.

12. The two lines $x = ay + b$, $z = cy + d$ and $x = a'y + b'$, $z = c'y + d'$ will be perpendicular, if and only if: **[NCERT Exemplar]**

   (a) $aa' + cc' + 1 = 0$
   (b) $aa' + bb' + cc' + 1 = 0$
   (c) $aa' + bb' + cc' = 0$
   (d) $(a + a')(b + b') + (c + c') = 0$

Sol. (a) $aa' + cc' + 1 = 0$

Explanation :

$$x = ay + b$$
$$\Rightarrow \qquad y = \dfrac{x-b}{a}$$
$$z = cy + d$$
$$\Rightarrow \qquad y = \dfrac{z-d}{c}$$
$$\dfrac{x-b}{a} = \dfrac{y}{1} = \dfrac{z-d}{c} \qquad \ldots(i)$$
$$\text{Similarly} \quad \dfrac{x-b'}{a'} = \dfrac{y}{1} = \dfrac{z-d'}{c'} \qquad \ldots(ii)$$

Lines are perpendicular so the sum of corresponding product of their drs be zero. So For perpendicularity of lines $aa' + 1 + cc' = 0$.

13. A line makes angles of 45° and 60° with the positive axes of X and Y respectively. The angle made by the same line with the positive axis of Z, is: **[NCERT Exemplar]**

   (a) 30° or 60°   (b) 60° or 90°
   (c) 90° or 120°   (d) 60° or 120°

Sol. (d) 60° or 120°

Explanation :

Given $\alpha = 45°$, $\beta = 60°$, $\gamma = ?$

$\because \qquad \cos^2\alpha + \cos^2\beta + \cos^2\gamma = 1$

$\therefore \qquad \cos^2\gamma = 1 - \dfrac{1}{2} - \dfrac{1}{4} = \dfrac{1}{4}$

$\Rightarrow \qquad \gamma = 60°$ or $120°$.

14. If α, β, γ be the angles which a line makes with the co-ordinate axes, then: **[NCERT Exemplar]**

   (a) $\sin^2\alpha + \cos^2\beta + \sin^2\gamma = 1$
   (b) $\cos^2\alpha + \cos^2\beta + \cos^2\gamma = 1$
   (c) $\sin^2\alpha + \sin^2\beta + \sin^2\gamma = 1$
   (d) $\cos^2\alpha + \cos^2\beta + \sin^2\gamma = 1$

Sol. (b) $\cos^2\alpha + \cos^2\beta + \cos^2\gamma = 1$

Explanation :

It is obvious.

15. The equation of a line passing through the point $(-3, 2, -4)$ and equally inclined to the axes, are: **[NCERT Exemplar]**

   (a) $x - 3 = y + 2 = z - 4$

   (b) $\dfrac{x+3}{1} = \dfrac{y-2}{1} = \dfrac{z+4}{1}$

   (c) $\dfrac{x+3}{1} = \dfrac{y-2}{2} = \dfrac{z+4}{3}$

   (d) None of these

Sol. (b) $\dfrac{x+3}{1} = \dfrac{y-2}{1} = \dfrac{z+4}{1}$

Explanation :

Required equation of lines is

$$\dfrac{(x+3)}{1} = \dfrac{y-2}{1} = \dfrac{z+4}{1}$$

16. The equation of straight line passing through the point (a, b, c) and parallel to z-axis is: **[NCERT Exemplar]**

   (a) $\dfrac{x-a}{1} = \dfrac{y-b}{1} = \dfrac{z-c}{0}$

   (b) $\dfrac{x-a}{0} = \dfrac{y-b}{1} = \dfrac{z-c}{1}$

(c) $\dfrac{x-a}{1} = \dfrac{y-b}{0} = \dfrac{z-c}{0}$

(d) $\dfrac{x-a}{0} = \dfrac{y-b}{0} = \dfrac{z-c}{1}$

Sol. (d) $\dfrac{x-a}{0} = \dfrac{y-b}{0} = \dfrac{z-c}{1}$

Explanation :

The line through (a, b, c) is

$$\dfrac{x-a}{l} = \dfrac{y-b}{m} = \dfrac{z-c}{n} \qquad \text{...(i)}$$

Since the line is parallel to z-axis, therefore the direction cosines are $(0, 0, 1)$.

Hence the line will be $\dfrac{x-a}{0} = \dfrac{y-b}{0} = \dfrac{z-c}{1}$.

17. The length of the perpendicular from point $(1, 2, 3)$ to the line $\dfrac{x-6}{3} = \dfrac{y-7}{2} = \dfrac{z-7}{-2}$ is:

[NCERT Exemplar]

(a) 5 (b) 6

(c) 7 (d) 8

Sol. (c) 7

Explanation :

Let a point on a given line be A$(3\lambda + 6, 2\lambda + 7, -2\lambda + 7)$.

Let the point B be $(1, 2, 3)$.

$\therefore$ Direction ratios of AB

$= (3\lambda + 6 - 1, 2\lambda + 7 - 2, -2\lambda + 7 - 3)$

$= (3\lambda + 5, 2\lambda + 5, -2\lambda + 4)$

Given, direction ratios of the line are 3, 2, – 2.

$\because$ Lines are perpendicular.

$\therefore \quad 3(3\lambda + 5) + 2(2\lambda + 5) - 2(-2\lambda + 4) = 0$

$\Rightarrow \qquad 9\lambda + 15 + 4\lambda + 10 + 4\lambda - 8 = 0$

$\Rightarrow \qquad\qquad\qquad\qquad 17\lambda + 17 = 0$

$\Rightarrow \qquad\qquad\qquad\qquad\qquad \lambda = -1$

$\therefore$ Point A is $(3, 5, 9)$.

$\therefore$ The length of perpendicular

$= \sqrt{(3-1)^2 + (5-2)^2 + (9-3)^2}$

$= \sqrt{4 + 9 + 36}$

$= \sqrt{49}$

$= 7.$

18. Equation of x-axis is: **[NCERT Exemplar]**

(a) $\dfrac{x}{1} = \dfrac{y}{1} = \dfrac{z}{1}$ (b) $\dfrac{x}{0} = \dfrac{y}{1} = \dfrac{z}{1}$

(c) $\dfrac{x}{1} = \dfrac{y}{0} = \dfrac{z}{0}$ (d) $\dfrac{x}{0} = \dfrac{y}{0} = \dfrac{z}{1}$

Sol. (c) $\dfrac{x}{1} = \dfrac{y}{0} = \dfrac{z}{0}$

Explanation :

It is obvious.

19. The equations of x-axis in space are:

(a) $x = 0, y = 0$ (b) $x = 0, z = 0$

(c) $x = 0$ (d) $y = 0, z = 0$

Sol. (d) $y = 0, z = 0$

Explanation :

On x-axis the y-coordinate and z-coordinate are zero.

So the correct option is (d).

20. The lines $\dfrac{x-2}{1} = \dfrac{y-3}{1} = \dfrac{4-z}{k}$ and $\dfrac{x-1}{k} = \dfrac{y-4}{2} = \dfrac{z-5}{-2}$ are mutually perpendicular if the value of k is :*

(a) $-\dfrac{2}{3}$ (b) $\dfrac{2}{3}$

(c) -2 (d) 2

Sol. (a) $-\dfrac{2}{3}$

Explanation :

First line is,

$$\dfrac{x-2}{1} = \dfrac{y-3}{1} = \dfrac{z-4}{-k}$$

$\therefore$ Direction ratios of first line $= < 1, 1, -k >$

Second line is,

$$\dfrac{x-1}{k} = \dfrac{y-4}{2} = \dfrac{z-5}{-2}$$

$\therefore$ Direction ratios of second line $= < k, 2, -2 >$

We know, two lines are perpendicular to each other, if the dot product of their direction ratios is zero.

$i.e.,\ 1 \times k + 1 \times 2 + (-k) \times (-2) = 0$

$\Rightarrow \qquad\qquad k + 2 + 2k = 0$

$\Rightarrow \qquad\qquad\qquad 3k = -2$

$\Rightarrow \qquad\qquad\qquad k = -\dfrac{2}{3}$

So the correct option is (a).

21. The shortest distance between the lines $x = y + 2 = 6z - 6$ and $x + 1 = 2y = -12z$ is:

[NCERT Exemplar]

(a) $\dfrac{1}{2}$ (b) 2

(c) 1 (d) $\dfrac{3}{2}$

Sol. (b) 2

Explanation :

The lines are $\dfrac{x}{6} = \dfrac{y+2}{6} = \dfrac{z-1}{1}$

and $\dfrac{x+1}{12} = \dfrac{y}{6} = \dfrac{z}{-1}$

Here, $\vec{a_1} = -2\hat{j}+\hat{k},\ \vec{b_1} = 6\hat{i}+6\hat{j}+\hat{k},$

$\vec{a_2} = -\hat{i},$

$\vec{b_2} = 12\hat{i}+6\hat{j}-\hat{k}$

$$\vec{b_1} \times \vec{b_2} = \begin{vmatrix} \hat{i} & \hat{j} & \hat{k} \\ 6 & 6 & 1 \\ 12 & 6 & -1 \end{vmatrix}$$

$$= -12\hat{i}+18\hat{j}-36\hat{k}$$

$$\text{Shortest distance} = \frac{|(\vec{a_2}-\vec{a_1}).(\vec{b_1}\times\vec{b_2})|}{|\vec{b_1}\times\vec{b_2}|}$$

$$= \frac{|(-\hat{i}+2\hat{j}-\hat{k}).(-12\hat{i}+18\hat{j}-36\hat{k})|}{\sqrt{(-12)^2+(18)^2+(-36)^2}}$$

$$= \frac{|12+36+36|}{\sqrt{1764}} = \frac{84}{42} = 2.$$

22. The distance of the plane $\vec{r}.\left(\dfrac{2}{7}\hat{i}+\dfrac{3}{7}\hat{j}-\dfrac{6}{7}\hat{k}\right) = 1$

from the origin is: **[NCERT Exemplar]**

(a) 1 (b) 7

(c) $\dfrac{1}{7}$ (d) None of these

Sol. (a) 1

Explanation :

The distance of the plane $\vec{r}\cdot\left(\dfrac{2}{7}\hat{i}+\dfrac{3}{7}\hat{j}-\dfrac{6}{7}\hat{k}\right) = 1$

from the origin is 1.

[since, $\vec{r}\cdot\vec{n} = d$ is the form of above equation, where d represents the distance of plane from the origin *i.e.*, $d = 1$]

23. The locus represented by $xy + yz = 0$ is:

[NCERT Exemplar]

(a) a pair of perpendicular lines

(b) a pair of parallel lines

(c) a pair of parallel planes

(d) a pair of perpendicular planes

Sol. (d) a pair of perpendicular planes

Explanation :

We have, $xy + yz = 0$

$\Rightarrow \qquad xy = -yz$

So, a pair of perpendicular planes.

24. The vector equation of the plane which is at a distance of $\dfrac{6}{\sqrt{29}}$ from the origin and its normal vector from the origin is $2\hat{i}-3\hat{j}+4\hat{k}$ is:

[NCERT Exemplar]

(a) $\vec{r}.(2\hat{i}-3\hat{j}+4\hat{k})$

(b) $\vec{r}.\left(\dfrac{2}{\sqrt{29}}\hat{i}-\dfrac{3}{\sqrt{29}}\hat{j}+\dfrac{4}{\sqrt{29}}\hat{k}\right) = \dfrac{6}{\sqrt{29}}$

(c) Both (a) and (b)

(d) None of the above

Sol. (b) $\vec{r}.\left(\dfrac{2}{\sqrt{29}}\hat{i}-\dfrac{3}{\sqrt{29}}\hat{j}+\dfrac{4}{\sqrt{29}}\hat{k}\right) = \dfrac{6}{\sqrt{29}}$

Explanation :

Let $\vec{n} = 2\hat{i}-3\hat{j}+4\hat{k}$. Then,

$$\hat{n} = \frac{\vec{n}}{|\vec{n}|} = \frac{2\hat{i}-3\hat{j}+4\hat{k}}{\sqrt{4+9+16}} = \frac{2\hat{i}-3\hat{j}+4\hat{k}}{\sqrt{29}}$$

Hence, the required equation of the plane is

$$\vec{r}\cdot\left(\frac{2}{\sqrt{29}}\hat{i}+\frac{-3}{\sqrt{29}}\hat{j}+\frac{4}{\sqrt{29}}\hat{k}\right) = \frac{6}{\sqrt{29}}.$$

25. A plane meets the coordinate axes in points A, B, C and the centroid of the triangle ABC is (α, β, γ). The equation of the plane is:

[NCERT Exemplar]

(a) $\dfrac{x}{\alpha}+\dfrac{y}{\beta}+\dfrac{z}{\gamma} = 3$ (b) $\alpha x + \beta y + \gamma y = 3\alpha\beta\gamma$

(c) $\dfrac{x}{\alpha}+\dfrac{y}{\beta}+\dfrac{z}{\gamma} = \dfrac{1}{2}$ (d) None of these

Sol. (a) $\dfrac{x}{\alpha}+\dfrac{y}{\beta}+\dfrac{z}{\gamma} = 3$

Explanation :

Let the equation of the required plane be

$$\frac{x}{a}+\frac{y}{b}+\frac{z}{c} = 1 \qquad\qquad ...(i)$$

It meets co-ordinate axes in points.

$$A(a, 0, 0),\ B(0, b, 0),\ C(0, 0, c)$$

The centroid of $\triangle ABC$ is $\left(\dfrac{a}{3}, \dfrac{b}{3}, \dfrac{c}{3}\right)$

$\Rightarrow \qquad \dfrac{a}{3} = \alpha, \dfrac{b}{3} = \beta, \dfrac{c}{3} = \gamma$

$\Rightarrow \qquad a = 3\alpha, b = 3\beta, c = 3\gamma$

Hence the required plane is

$$\dfrac{x}{3\alpha} + \dfrac{y}{3\beta} + \dfrac{z}{3\gamma} = 1$$

i.e., $\qquad \dfrac{x}{\alpha} + \dfrac{y}{\beta} + \dfrac{z}{\gamma} = 3.$

26. If vector equation of the plane $\dfrac{x-2}{2} = \dfrac{2y-5}{-3}$

$= z + 1$, is $\vec{r} = \left(2\hat{i} + \dfrac{5}{2}\hat{j} - \hat{k}\right) + \lambda\left(2\hat{i} - \dfrac{3}{2}\hat{j} + p\hat{k}\right)$

then p is equal to: **[NCERT Exemplar]**

(a) 0   (b) 1

(c) 2   (d) 3

Sol. (a) 0

Explanation :

The given line is

$$\dfrac{x-2}{2} = \dfrac{2y-5}{-3} = z + 1,$$

$\Rightarrow \qquad \dfrac{x-2}{2} = \dfrac{y - \dfrac{5}{2}}{-\dfrac{3}{2}} = \dfrac{z+1}{0}$

This shows that the given line passes throught

he point $\left(2, \dfrac{5}{2}, -1\right)$ and has direction ratios

$\left(2, -\dfrac{3}{2}, 0\right)$. Thus, given line passes through

the point having position vector $\vec{a} = 2\hat{i} + \dfrac{5}{2}\hat{j} - \hat{k}$

and is parallel to the vector $\vec{b} = \left(2\hat{i} - \dfrac{3}{2}\hat{j} - 0\hat{k}\right)$.

So, its vector equation is

$$\vec{r} = \left(2\hat{i} + \dfrac{5}{2}\hat{j} - \hat{k}\right) + \lambda\left(2\hat{i} - \dfrac{3}{2}\hat{j} - 0\hat{k}\right)$$

Hence, $\qquad p = 0.$

27. The equation of the plane through $(1, 2, 3)$ and parallel to the plane $2x + 3y - 4z = 0$ is:

[NCERT Exemplar]

(a) $2x + 3y + 4z = 4$ (b) $2x + 3y + 4z + 4 = 0$

(c) $2x - 3y + 4z + 4 = 0$ (d) $2x + 3y - 4z + 4 = 0$

Sol. (d) $2x + 3y - 4z + 4 = 0$

Explanation :

Plane parallel to the plane $2x + 3y - 4z = 0$ is

$$2x + 3y - 4z + k = 0 \qquad \qquad \ldots(i)$$

also plane (i) is passing through $(1, 2, 3)$.

$\therefore \quad (2)(1) + (3)(2) - (4)(3) + k = 0$

$\Rightarrow \qquad\qquad k = 4$

$\therefore$ Required plane is $2x + 3y - 4z + 4 = 0$.

28. The equation of the plane passing thorugh the intersection of the planes $x + y + z = 6$ and $2x + 3y + 4z + 5 = 0$ the point $(1, 1, 1)$, is:

[NCERT Exemplar]

(a) $20x + 23y + 26z - 69 = 0$

(b) $20x + 23y + 26z + 69 = 0$

(c) $23x + 20y + 26z - 69 = 0$

(d) None of these

Sol. (a) $20x + 23y + 26z - 69 = 0$

Explanation :

$(x + y + z - 6) + \lambda(2x + 3y + 4z + 5) = 0$

$\Rightarrow \qquad\qquad \lambda = \dfrac{3}{14}$

$\Rightarrow \quad 20x + 23y + 26z - 69 = 0.$

29. If the given planes $ax + by + cz + d = 0$ and $a'x + b'y + c'z + d' = 0$ be mutually perpendicular , then:

[NCERT Exemplar]

(a) $\dfrac{a}{a'} = \dfrac{b}{b'} = \dfrac{c}{c'}$

(b) $\dfrac{a}{a'} + \dfrac{b}{b'} + \dfrac{c}{c'} = 0$

(c) $aa' + bb' + cc' + dd' = 0$

(d) $aa' + bb' + cc' = 0$

Sol. (d) $aa' + bb' + cc' = 0$

Explanation :

It is a fundamental concept.

30. If the planes $x + 2y + kz = 0$ and $2x + y - 2z = 0$ are at right angles, then the value of k is:

[NCERT Exemplar]

(a) $-\dfrac{1}{2}$ (b) $\dfrac{1}{2}$

(c) -2 (d) 2

Sol. (d) 2

Explanation :

Obviously, $2(1) + 1(2) - 2(k) = 0$

$\Rightarrow \qquad\qquad k = 2.$

31. The intercepts of the plane $5x - 3y + 6z = 60$ on the co-ordinate axes are:

(a) $(10, 20, -10)$ (b) $(10, -20, 12)$

(c) $(12, -20, 10)$ (d) $(12, 20, -10)$

Sol. (c) $(12, -20, 10)$

Explanation :

$$\frac{5x}{60} - \frac{3y}{60} + \frac{6z}{60} = 1$$

$$\Rightarrow \quad \frac{x}{12} - \frac{y}{20} + \frac{z}{10} = 1$$

Hence, the intercepts are $(12, -20, 10)$.

32. The two planes $x - 2y + 4z = 10$ and $18x + 17y + kz = 50$ are perpendicular, if k is equal to :*

(a) -4 (b) 4

(c) 2   (d) -2

Sol. (b) 4

Explanation :

$$18 - 34 + 4k = 0$$

$$\{\text{using } a_1a_2 + b_1b_2 + c_1c_2 = 0\}$$

$$\Rightarrow \quad 4k = 16 \Rightarrow k = 4$$

So the correct option is (b).

33. Let the points $(1, 1, p)$ and $(-3, 0, 1)$ be equidistant from the plane $\vec{r} \cdot (3\hat{i} + 4\hat{j} - 12\hat{k}) + 13 = 0$, then the value of p is: **[NCERT Exemplar]**

(a) $\dfrac{3}{7}$ (b) $\dfrac{7}{3}$

(c) $\dfrac{4}{3}$ (d) $\dfrac{3}{4}$

Sol. (b) $\dfrac{7}{3}$

Explanation :

The distance of point $(1, 1, p)$ from the plane

$$\vec{r} \cdot (3\hat{i} + 4\hat{j} - 12\hat{k}) + 13 = 0$$

or (in cartesian form) $3x + 4y - 12z + 13 = 0$ is

$$d_1 = \left| \frac{3 \times 1 + 4 \times 1 - 12 \times p + 13}{\sqrt{3^2 + 4^2 + (-12)^2}} \right|$$

$$= \left| \frac{3 + 4 - 12p + 13}{\sqrt{169}} \right| = \left| \frac{20 - 12p}{13} \right| \quad \dots(i)$$

The distance of the point $(-3, 0, 1)$ from the plane $3x + 4y - 12z + 13 = 0$ is

$$d_2 = \left| \frac{3 \times (-3) + 4 \times 0 - 12 \times 1 + 13}{\sqrt{3^2 + 4^2 + (-12)^2}} \right|$$

$$= \frac{8}{13}$$

According to the given condition,

$$d_1 = d_2$$

$$\Rightarrow \quad \left| \frac{20 - 12p}{13} \right| = \frac{8}{13}$$

$$\Rightarrow \quad \frac{20 - 12p}{13} = \pm \frac{8}{13}$$

Taking +ve sign, we get

$$\frac{20 - 12p}{13} = \frac{8}{13}$$

$$\Rightarrow \quad p = 1$$

Taking $-$ve sign, we get

$$\frac{20 - 12p}{13} = -\frac{8}{13}$$

$$\Rightarrow \quad p = \frac{28}{12} = \frac{7}{3}.$$

34. The distance of the plane $\vec{r} \cdot \left(\dfrac{2}{7}\hat{i} + \dfrac{3}{7}\hat{j} - \dfrac{6}{7}\hat{k} \right) = 1$ from the origin is: **[NCERT Exemplar]**

(a) 1   (b) 7

(c) $\dfrac{1}{7}$ (d) None of these

Sol. (a) 1

Explanation :

The distance of the plane $\vec{r} \cdot \left(\dfrac{2}{7}\hat{i} + \dfrac{3}{7}\hat{j} - \dfrac{6}{7}\hat{k} \right) = 1$ from the origin is equal to 1.

35. The length of the perpendicular from the origin to the plane $3x + 4y + 12z = 52$ is:

[NCERT Exemplar]

(a) 3   (b) -4

(c) 5   (d) None of these

Sol. (d) None of these

Explanation :

$$p = \left| \frac{-52}{\sqrt{9 + 16 + 144}} \right| = \left| \frac{-52}{13} \right| = |-4| = 4.$$

36. The equation of the plane which is parallel to the plane $x - 2y + 2z = 5$ and whose distance from the point $(1, 2, 3)$ is 1, is: **[NCERT Exemplar]**

(a) $x - 2y + 2z = 3$ (b) $x - 2y + 2z + 3 = 0$

(c) $x - 2y + 2z = 6$ (d) $x - 2y + 2z + 6 = 0$

Sol. (c) $x - 2y + 2z = 6$

Explanation :

Equation of plane parallel to $x - 2y + 2z = 5$ is

$$x - 2y + 2z + k = 0 \quad \dots(i)$$

Now, according to question,

$$\frac{1 - 4 + 6 + k}{\sqrt{9}} = \pm 1$$

or $k + 3 = \pm 3$

$\Rightarrow$ $k = 0$ or -6

$\therefore$ $x - 2y + 2z - 6 = 0$

or $x - 2y + 2z = 6.$

37. The distance of the plane $6x - 3y + 2z - 14 = 0$ from the origin is: **[NCERT Exemplar]**

(a) 2   (b) 1

(c) 14   (d) 8

Sol. (a) 2

Explanation :

Distance of plane from origin

$$= \frac{d}{\sqrt{a^2 + b^2 + c^2}} = \frac{14}{\sqrt{6^2 + 3^2 + 2^2}} = \frac{14}{\sqrt{49}} = \frac{14}{7} = 2.$$

38. The distance of the origin $(0, 0, 0)$ from the plane $-2x + 6y - 3z = -7$ is :*

(a) 1 unit   (b) $\sqrt{2}$ units

(c) $2\sqrt{2}$ units   (d) 3 units

Sol. (a) 1 unit

Explanation :

Given : Equation of plane is,

$$-2x + 6y - 3z = -7$$

$$\Rightarrow \quad -2x + 6y - 3z + 7 = 0$$

We know distance of point (x_1, y_1, z_1) from a plane $Ax + By + Cz + D = 0$ is given as

$$\text{Distance} = \left| \frac{Ax_1 + By_1 + Cz_1 + D}{\sqrt{A^2 + B^2 + C^2}} \right|$$

$$\therefore \quad \text{Distance} = \left| \frac{-2(0) + 6(0) + (-3)(0) + 7}{\sqrt{4 + 36 + 9}} \right|$$

$$= \left| \frac{7}{\sqrt{49}} \right| = \left| \frac{7}{7} \right| = 1 \text{ unit}$$

So the correct option is (a).

39. Let the line $\dfrac{x-2}{3} = \dfrac{y-1}{-5} = \dfrac{z+2}{2}$ lie in the plane $x + 3y - \alpha z + \beta = 0$, then (α, β) equals: **[NCERT Exemplar]**

(a) $(-6, 7)$ (b) $(-5, 5)$

(c) $(5, -15)$ (d) $(6, -17)$

Sol. (a) $(-6, 7)$

Explanation :

$\because$ The line $\dfrac{x-2}{3} = \dfrac{y-1}{-5} = \dfrac{z+2}{2}$ lie in the plane.

$$x + 3y - \alpha z + \beta = 0$$

$\therefore$ Point $(2, 1, -2)$ lies on the plane.

$i.e.,$ $2 + 3 + 2\alpha + \beta = 0$

or $2\alpha + \beta + 5 = 0$ …(i)

Also normal to plane will be perpendicular to line,

$\therefore$ $3 \times 1 - 5 \times 3 + 2 \times (-\alpha) = 0$

$\Rightarrow$ $\alpha = -6$

From equation (i) we have,

$$\beta = 7$$

$\therefore$ $(\alpha, \beta) = (-6, 7).$

40. The line $\dfrac{x-1}{1} = \dfrac{y-2}{-2} = \dfrac{z-1}{3}$ and the plane $x + 2y + z = 6$ meet at: **[NCERT Exemplar]**

(a) no point

(b) only one point

(c) infinitely many points

(d) none of these

Sol. (c) infinitely many points

Explanation :

Direction ratios, of given line are $1, -2, 3$ and the d.r. of normal to the given plane are $1, 2, 1$.

Since $1 \times 1 + (-2) \times 2 + 3 \times 1 = 0$, therefore, the line is parallel to the plane.

Also, the base point of the line $(1, 2, 1)$ lies in the given plane.

$(1 + 2 \times 2 + 1 = 6$ is true)

Hence, the given line lies in the given plane.

41. The lines $\dfrac{x-2}{1} = \dfrac{y-3}{1} = \dfrac{z-4}{-k}$ and $\dfrac{x-1}{k} = \dfrac{y-4}{2} = \dfrac{z-5}{1}$ are coplanar if: **[NCERT Exemplar]**

(a) $k = 3$ or -2 (b) $k = 0$

(c) $k = 1$ or -1 (d) $k = 0$ or -3

Sol. (d) $k = 0$ or -3

Explanation :

We know, if two lines are coplanar than

$$\begin{vmatrix} x_2 - x_1 & y_2 - y_1 & z_2 - z_1 \\ a_1 & b_1 & c_1 \\ a_2 & b_2 & c_2 \end{vmatrix} = 0$$

$$\therefore \quad \begin{vmatrix} 1-2 & 4-3 & 5-4 \\ 1 & 1 & -k \\ k & 2 & 1 \end{vmatrix} = 0$$

$$\Rightarrow \quad \begin{vmatrix} -1 & 1 & 1 \\ 1 & 1 & -k \\ k & 2 & 1 \end{vmatrix} = 0$$

Applying $C_1 \longrightarrow C_1 + C_2$ and $C_2 \longrightarrow C_2 - C_3$

$$\Rightarrow \quad \begin{vmatrix} 0 & 0 & 1 \\ 2 & 1+k & -k \\ k+2 & 1 & 1 \end{vmatrix} = 0$$

Expand along C_1

$$1\{2 - (1 + k)(2 + k)\} = 0$$

$$2 - (2 + 3k + k^2) = 0$$

$$k^2 + 3k = 0 \ i.e., \ k = 0, \ k = -3.$$

42. The line $\dfrac{x-2}{3} = \dfrac{y-3}{4} = \dfrac{z-4}{5}$ is parallel to the plane:*

(a) $2x + 3y + 4z = 0$ (b) $3x + 4y - 5z = 7$
(c) $2x + y - 2z = 0$ (d) $x - y + z = 2$

Sol. (c) $2x + y - 2z = 0$

Explanation :

D.R.: $\quad 3\hat{i} + 4\hat{j} + 5\hat{k} = \vec{a}$ (say)

$$\vec{a}.\vec{n} = 0$$

$$\therefore \quad (3\hat{i} + 4\hat{j} + 5\hat{k}).\vec{n} = 0$$

From option (c)

$$(3\hat{i} + 4\hat{j} + 5\hat{k}).(2\hat{i} + \hat{j} - 2\hat{k})$$

$$= 3(2) + 4(1) + 5(-2)$$

$$= 0.$$

Assertion and Reason Based Questions

(a) Both (A) and (R) are individually true and (R) is the correct explanation of (A).
(b) Both (A) and (R) are individually true but (R) is not the correct explanation of (A).
(c) (A) is true but (R) is false.
(d) (A) is false but (R) is true.

43. Assertion (A) : The direction ratios of the line joining origin and point (x, y, z) must be x, y, z.

Reason (R) : If P(x, y, z) is a point in space and OP $= r$, then direction cosines of OP are $\dfrac{x}{r}, \dfrac{y}{r}, \dfrac{z}{r}$.

Sol. (a) Both (A) and (R) are individually true and (R) is the correct explanation of (A).

Explanation :

$\because$ Direction ratios of OP are $x - 0, y - 0, z - 0$ i.e., x, y, z.

$\therefore$ Direction cosines of OP are $\dfrac{x}{r}, \dfrac{y}{r}, \dfrac{z}{r}$.

44. Assertion (A) : If centroid and circumcentre of a triangle are known its orthocentre can be found.

Reason (R) : Centroid, orthocentre and circumcentre of a triangle are collinear.

Sol. (b) Both (A) and (R) are individually true but (R) is the correct explanation of (A).

Explanation :

$\therefore$ Orthocentre, centroid and circumcentre are collinear and centroid divides orthocentre and circumcentre in the ratio 2 : 1 (internally).

$$\therefore \quad \alpha = \dfrac{x + 2\gamma}{2 + 1}$$

$$\Rightarrow \quad x = 3\alpha - 2\gamma$$

$$\text{and} \quad \beta = \dfrac{y + 2\delta}{2 + 1}$$

$$\Rightarrow \quad y = 3\beta - 2\delta$$

$\therefore$ Orthocentre is $(3\alpha - 2\gamma, 3\beta - 2\delta)$.

45. Assertion (A) : The shortest distance between the skew lines

$\dfrac{x+3}{-4} = \dfrac{y-6}{3} = \dfrac{z}{2}$ and $\dfrac{x+2}{-4} = \dfrac{y}{1} = \dfrac{z-7}{1}$ is 9.

Reason (R) : Two lines are skew lines if there exists no plane passing through them.

Sol. (b) Both (A) and (R) are individually true but (R) is not the correct explanation of (A).

Explanation :

Let l, m, n be the D.C.'s of the line of the common perpendicular (or SD) to the two given lines, Then, we have

$$-4l + 3m + 2n = 0$$

and $\quad -4l + 1m + 1n = 0$

Solving these, we get

$$\dfrac{l}{3-2} = \dfrac{m}{-8+4} = \dfrac{n}{-4+12}$$

or $\quad \dfrac{l}{1} = \dfrac{m}{-4} = \dfrac{n}{8} = \dfrac{\sqrt{(l^2 + m^2 + n^2)}}{\sqrt{(1)^2 + (-4)^2 + (8)^2}} = \dfrac{1}{9}$

$\therefore$ D.C.'s of SD are $\dfrac{1}{9}, \dfrac{4}{-9}, \dfrac{8}{9}$

Also, A$(-3, 6, 0)$ is a point on first line and B$(-2, 0, 7)$ is a point on second line, then

$$SD = \left| (-2+3)\dfrac{1}{9} + (0-6)\left(-\dfrac{4}{9}\right) + (7-0)\left(\dfrac{8}{9}\right) \right|$$

$$= 9$$

And two lines are said to be skew lines or non intersecting lines if they do not lie in the same plane.

46. Assertion (A) : The points $(2, 1, 5)$ and $(3, 4, 3)$ lie on opposite side of the plane $2x + 2y - 2z - 1 = 0$.

Reason (R) : The algebric perpendicular distance from the given points to the line have opposite sign.

Sol. (a) Both (A) and (R) are individually true and (R) is the correct explanation of (A).

Explanation :

Algebraic distance of (2, 1, 5) from the plane $2x + 2y - 2z - 1 = 0$ is

$$\frac{2(2) + 2(1) - 2(5) - 1}{\sqrt{(2)^2 + (2)^2 + (-2)^2}} = -\frac{5}{2\sqrt{3}} \qquad ...(i)$$

and algebric distance of (3, 4, 3) from the plane $2x + 2y - 2z - 1 = 0$ is

$$\frac{2(3) + 2(4) - 2(3) - 1}{\sqrt{(2)^2 + (2)^2 + (-2)^2}} = \frac{7}{2\sqrt{3}} \qquad ...(ii)$$

Since equations (i) and (ii) are of opposite sign. Hence, points (2, 1, 5) and (3, 4, 3) lie on opposite sides of the plane $2x + 2y - 2z - 1 = 0$.

47. Assertion (A) : The equation of the plane through the intersection of the planes $x + y + z = 6$ and $2x + 3y + 4z + 5 = 0$ and the point (4, 4, 4) is $29x + 23y + 17z = 276$

Reason (R) : Equation of the plane through the line of intersection of the planes $P_1 = 0$ and $P_2 = 0$ is $P_1 + \lambda P_2 = 0$, $\lambda \neq 0$.

Sol. (a) Both (A) and (R) are individually true and (R) is the correct explanation of (A).

Explanation :

$\because$ Equation of the plane through the line of intersection of the planes $x + y + z = 6$ and $2x + 3y + 4z + 5 = 0$ is

$$(x + y + z - 6) + \lambda\,(2x + 3y + 4z + 5) = 0 \qquad ...(i)$$

Since, it passes through (4, 4, 4), then

$$(4 + 4 + 4 - 6) + \lambda\,(8 + 12 + 16 + 5) = 0$$
$$\Rightarrow \qquad 6 + 41\,\lambda = 0$$
$$\therefore \qquad \lambda = -\frac{6}{41}$$

Then from equation (i),

$$41\,(x + y + z - 6) - 6(2x + 3y + 4z + 5) = 0$$
$$\Rightarrow \quad 29x + 23y + 17z = 276.$$

Case Based Questions

48. A Badminton Hall is to be constructed in the form of a cube in a sports complex in the 3-D as given below :

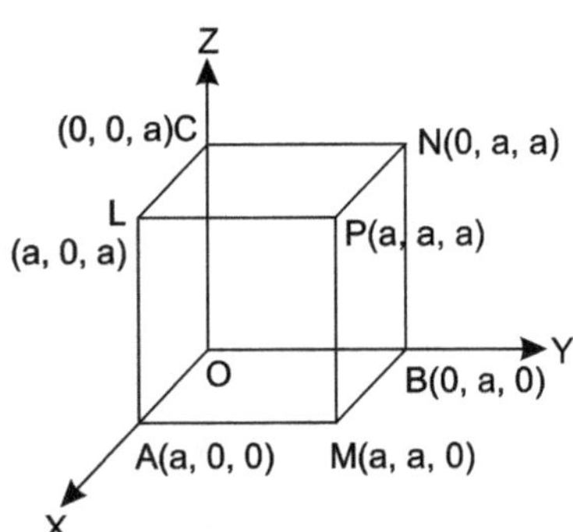

Length of side of cube be a units four diagonals are OP, MC, AN and BL.

From the above information given answer of the following questions :

(i) Find the direction cosines of diagonal AN :

(a) $\left(\dfrac{-1}{\sqrt{3}}, \dfrac{1}{\sqrt{3}}, \dfrac{1}{\sqrt{3}}\right)$ (b) $\left(\dfrac{1}{\sqrt{3}}, \dfrac{1}{\sqrt{3}}, \dfrac{1}{\sqrt{3}}\right)$

(c) $\left(\dfrac{-1}{\sqrt{3}}, \dfrac{-1}{\sqrt{3}}, \dfrac{-1}{\sqrt{3}}\right)$ (d) $\left(\dfrac{-1}{\sqrt{3}}, \dfrac{-1}{\sqrt{3}}, \dfrac{1}{\sqrt{3}}\right)$

Sol. (a) $\left(\dfrac{-1}{\sqrt{3}}, \dfrac{1}{\sqrt{3}}, \dfrac{1}{\sqrt{3}}\right)$

Explanation :

Directions ratios of diagonal AN

$$= \overrightarrow{ON} - \overrightarrow{OA}$$

$$\overrightarrow{ON} = 0\,\hat{i} + a\,\hat{j} + a\,\hat{k}$$

$$\overrightarrow{OA} = a\,\hat{i} + 0\,\hat{j} + 0\,\hat{k}$$

$$\overrightarrow{AN} = (x_2 - x_1)\,\hat{i} + (y_2 - y_1)\,\hat{j} + (z_2 - z_1)\,\hat{k}$$

$$= (0 - a)\,\hat{i} + (0 - a)\,\hat{j} + (a - 0)\,\hat{k}$$

$$= -a\,\hat{i} - a\,\hat{j} + a\,\hat{k}$$

d.r.'s $= \langle -a, a, a \rangle$

$$\text{d.c.'s} = \frac{-a}{\sqrt{a^2 + a^2 + a^2}}, \frac{a}{\sqrt{a^2 + a^2 + a^2}},$$
$$\frac{a}{\sqrt{a^2 + a^2 + a^2}}$$

$$= \left(\frac{-1}{\sqrt{3}}, \frac{1}{\sqrt{3}}, \frac{1}{\sqrt{3}}\right)$$

(ii) Write the direction cosines of diagonal MC :

(a) $\left(\dfrac{1}{\sqrt{3}}, \dfrac{1}{\sqrt{3}}, \dfrac{1}{\sqrt{3}}\right)$ (b) $\left(\dfrac{-1}{\sqrt{3}}, \dfrac{-1}{\sqrt{3}}, \dfrac{1}{\sqrt{3}}\right)$

(c) $\left(\dfrac{-1}{\sqrt{3}}, \dfrac{-1}{\sqrt{3}}, \dfrac{-1}{\sqrt{3}}\right)$ (d) $\left(\dfrac{1}{\sqrt{3}}, \dfrac{-1}{\sqrt{3}}, \dfrac{-1}{\sqrt{3}}\right)$

Sol. (b) $\left(\dfrac{-1}{\sqrt{3}}, \dfrac{-1}{\sqrt{3}}, \dfrac{1}{\sqrt{3}}\right)$

Explanation :

Coordinates of diagonal MC
$$M = (a, a, 0), \quad C = (0, 0, a)$$

d.r.'s of MC $= (0-a)\,\hat{i} + (0-a)\,\hat{j} + (a-0)\,\hat{k}$

$$= -a\,\hat{i} - a\,\hat{j} + a\,\hat{k}$$

d.c.'s of MC $= \dfrac{-a}{\sqrt{(-a)^2 + (-a)^2 + a^2}},$

$$\dfrac{-a}{\sqrt{(-a)^2 + (-a)^2 + a^2}},$$

$$\dfrac{a}{\sqrt{(-a)^2 + (-a)^2 + a^2}}$$

$$= \dfrac{-1}{\sqrt{3}}, \dfrac{-1}{\sqrt{3}}, \dfrac{1}{\sqrt{3}}.$$

(iii) Write the Cartesian equation of the side of the room BN :

(a) $\dfrac{x}{2} = \dfrac{y-a}{a} = \dfrac{z}{a}$
    (b) $x = y - a = z$

(c) $\dfrac{x}{0} = \dfrac{y-a}{0} = \dfrac{z}{a}$
    (d) $x = y - a = \dfrac{z}{a}$

Sol. (c) $\dfrac{x}{0} = \dfrac{y-a}{0} = \dfrac{z}{a}$

Explanation :

Cartesian equation of side BN where B(0, a, 0), N(0, a, a) is

$$\dfrac{x - x_1}{x_2 - x_1} = \dfrac{y - y_1}{y_2 - y_1} = \dfrac{z - z_1}{z_2 - z_1}$$

$$\dfrac{x - 0}{0 - 0} = \dfrac{y - a}{a - a} = \dfrac{z - 0}{a - 0}$$

$$\dfrac{x}{0} = \dfrac{y - a}{0} = \dfrac{z}{a}.$$

(iv) Write the direction ratios of the side of the room of Z-axis :

(a) $(0, a, 0)$
    (b) (a, a, a)

(c) $(a, 0, 0)$
    (d) $(0, 0, a)$

Sol. (d) $(0, 0, a)$

Explanation :

direction ratios of Z-axis $= |\,0, 0, a\,|$.

49. One light pole is inserted in the middle of the pond which is full of water. The pond is in the shape of plane whose equation is $\vec{r}\,.(2\,\hat{i} - \hat{j} + \hat{k}) + 3 = 0$ and pole is inserted in such a way that the length which is inside the water is exactly equal to the length outside the water. The light is fixed at the top of the pole whose position vector is $\hat{i} + 3\,\hat{j} + 4\,\hat{k}$.

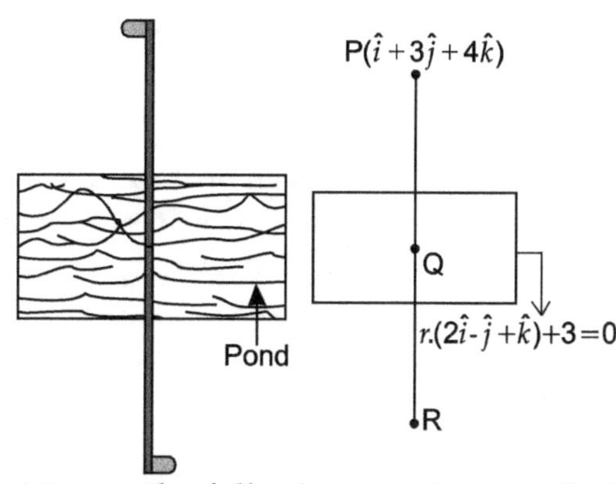

Attempt the following questions on the basis of above case study:

(i) What are the direction ratios of the light pole ?

(a) $(2, -1, -1)$
    (b) $(-2, 1, 1)$

(c) $(2, -1, 1)$
    (d) $(2, 1, 1)$

Sol. (c) $(2, -1, 1)$

Explanation :

Given equation of plane

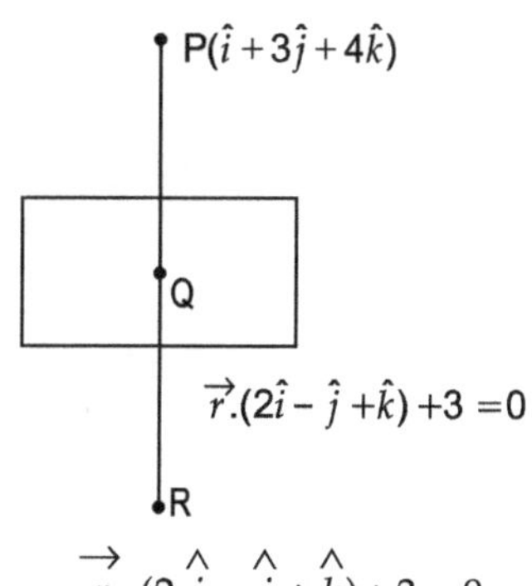

$$\vec{r}\,.(2\,\hat{i} - \hat{j} + \hat{k}) + 3 = 0$$

Cartesian form is $2x - y + z + 3 = 0$

d.r.'s of plane is equal to the line PQ.

dr's of line $= (2, -1, 1)$.

(ii) Find the foot of the pole on the water :

(a) $(1, 4, -3)$
    (b) $(1, -4, 3)$

(c) $(1, 4, 3)$
    (d) $(-1, 4, 3)$

Sol. (d) $(-1, 4, 3)$

Explanation :

Equation of line PQ passing through (1, 3, 4) with d.r.'s $(2, -1, 1)$ is

$$\dfrac{x - 1}{2} = \dfrac{y - 3}{-1} = \dfrac{z - 4}{1} = \lambda \text{ (say)}$$

$$x = 2\lambda + 1, \; y = -\lambda + 3, \; z = \lambda + 4$$

Let $Q(2\lambda + 1, -\lambda + 3, \lambda + 4)$ be the coordinates of foot of perpendicular for same value of λ.

Point Q lie on the plane.

$\therefore$ Satisfy its equation

$$2(2\lambda + 1) - (-\lambda + 3) + (\lambda + 4) + 3 = 0$$

$$4\lambda + 2 + \lambda - 3 + \lambda + 4 + 3 = 0$$
$$6\lambda + 6 = 0$$
$$\Rightarrow \qquad \lambda = -1$$
$$\text{Coordinates of } Q = (-1, 4, 3).$$

(iii) If R be the point of image which is end point of light pole, find the coordinates of R :

(a) $(-3, 5, 2)$ (b) $(3, 5, 2)$

(c) $(3, -5, 2)$ (d) $(3, 5, -2)$

Sol. (a) $(-3, 5, 2)$

Explanation :

R be the point of image.

$\therefore$ Q will be the mid-point of PR.

Let $R(x_1, y_1, z_1)$

$$\therefore \quad \frac{1+x_1}{2} = -1, \frac{3+y_1}{2} = 4, \frac{4+z_1}{2} = 3$$

$$1 + x_1 = -2, 3 + y_1 = 8, z_1 = 6 - 4$$

$$x_1 = -3, y_1 = 5, z_1 = 2$$

Point of image $(-3, 5, 2)$.

(iv) Find the total length of the pole PR :

(a) $2\sqrt{7}$ (b) $2\sqrt{6}$

(c) $3\sqrt{6}$ (d) $2\sqrt{8}$

Sol. (b) $2\sqrt{6}$

Explanation :

Length of pole is PR.

Coordinates of P and R : P(1, 3, 4), R(– 3, 5, 2)

$$PR = \sqrt{(-3-1)^2 + (5-3)^2 + (2-4)^2}$$
$$= \sqrt{16 + 4 + 4} = \sqrt{24} = 2\sqrt{6} \text{ units.}$$

(v) What is Cartesian equation of the pole PR ?

(a) $\dfrac{x-1}{2} = \dfrac{y-3}{-1} = \dfrac{z-4}{1}$

(b) $\dfrac{x+1}{-2} = \dfrac{y-3}{1} = \dfrac{z-4}{-1}$

(c) $\dfrac{x+1}{-2} = \dfrac{y-3}{-1} = \dfrac{z-4}{1}$

(d) $\dfrac{x+1}{3} = \dfrac{y+3}{2} = \dfrac{z+4}{1}$

Sol. (a) $\dfrac{x-1}{2} = \dfrac{y-3}{-1} = \dfrac{z-4}{1}$

Explanation :

Equation of PR passing through (1, 3, 4) with d.r.'s (2, – 1, 1) is

$$\frac{x-1}{2} = \frac{y-3}{-1} = \frac{z-4}{1}. \qquad \textbf{Ans.}$$

Very Short Answer Type Questions

50. The direction cosines of a line are proportional to 2, – 3, 6. Find the actual values of the direction cosines.*

Sol. If l, m, n are the direction cosines of the line then

$$l : m : n = 2 : -3 : 6$$

Hence $l = \dfrac{a}{\sqrt{a^2 + b^2 + c^2}}$, $m = \dfrac{b}{\sqrt{a^2 + b^2 + c^2}}$,

$$n = \frac{c}{\sqrt{a^2 + b^2 + c^2}}$$

$$l = \frac{2}{\sqrt{2^2 + (-3)^2 + 6^2}},$$

$$m = \frac{-3}{\sqrt{2^2 + (-3)^2 + 6^2}},$$

$$n = \frac{6}{\sqrt{2^2 + (-3)^2 + 6^2}}$$

$$i.e., \quad l = \frac{2}{7}, m = \frac{-3}{7}, n = \frac{6}{7}.$$

51. Find the distance between the points (2, 4, – 1) and (1, 3, 4) and then find the direction cosines of the line joining the points.

Sol. Let P(2, 4, – 1) and Q(1, 3, 4) be the given points.

$$\therefore \quad PQ = \sqrt{(2-1)^2 + (4-3)^2 + (-1-4)^2}$$
$$= \sqrt{1^2 + 1^2 + 5^2}$$
$$= \sqrt{27} = 3\sqrt{3}$$

$$\therefore \quad |\overrightarrow{QP}| = \sqrt{27}$$
$$= |\overrightarrow{PQ}|$$

The direction cosines of $\overrightarrow{PQ}$ are

$$\frac{1-2}{\sqrt{27}}, \frac{3-4}{\sqrt{27}}, \frac{4-(-1)}{\sqrt{27}}$$

$$i.e., \quad \frac{-1}{\sqrt{27}}, \frac{-1}{\sqrt{27}}, \frac{5}{\sqrt{27}}$$

52. If a line has direction ratios 2, – 1, – 2 then what are its direction cosines ?*

Sol. Given, direction ratios of line are 2, – 1, – 2.

$\therefore$ Direction cosines of above line are

$$\frac{2}{\sqrt{(2)^2 + (-1)^2 + (-2)^2}}, \frac{-1}{\sqrt{(2)^2 + (-1)^2 + (-2)^2}},$$

$$\frac{-2}{\sqrt{(2)^2 + (-1)^2 + (-2)^2}}$$

$$= \frac{2}{\sqrt{4+1+4}}, \frac{-1}{\sqrt{4+1+4}}, \frac{-2}{\sqrt{4+1+4}}$$

$$= \frac{2}{\sqrt{9}}, \frac{-1}{\sqrt{9}}, \frac{-2}{\sqrt{9}}$$

$$= \frac{2}{3}, \frac{-1}{3}, \frac{-2}{3}$$

53. Equation of line is $\dfrac{4-x}{2} = \dfrac{y+3}{2} = \dfrac{z+2}{1}$. Find the direction cosines of a line parallel to above line.*

Sol. Given equation of line can be written as

$$\frac{x-4}{-2} = \frac{y+3}{2} = \frac{z+2}{1}$$

∴ Direction cosines of line parallel to above line are given by

$$\frac{-2}{\sqrt{(-2)^2 + (2)^2 + (1)^2}}, \frac{2}{\sqrt{(-2)^2 + (2)^2 + (1)^2}},$$

$$\frac{1}{\sqrt{(-2)^2 + (2)^2 + (1)^2}}$$

$$= \frac{-2}{\sqrt{4+4+1}}, \frac{2}{\sqrt{4+4+1}}, \frac{1}{\sqrt{4+4+1}}$$

$$= \frac{-2}{\sqrt{9}}, \frac{2}{\sqrt{9}}, \frac{1}{\sqrt{9}} = -\frac{2}{3}, \frac{2}{3}, \frac{1}{3}.$$

Hence, required direction cosines of a line parallel to the given line is $\left(-\dfrac{2}{3}, \dfrac{2}{3}, \dfrac{1}{3}\right)$.

54. If the equation of line AB is $\dfrac{3-x}{1} = \dfrac{y+2}{2} = \dfrac{z-5}{4}$, write the direction ratios of line parallel to above line AB.*

Sol. Given equation of line can be written as

$$\frac{x-3}{-1} = \frac{y+2}{2} = \frac{z-5}{4}$$

∴ Direction ratios of line parallel to above line are $-1, 2, 4$ ($\because$ parallel lines have same direction ratios).

55. If P = (1, 5, 4) and Q = (4, 1, – 2), find the direction ratios of PQ.*

Sol. Given points are

$$P = (1, 5, 4) \text{ and } Q = (4, 1, -2)$$

∴ Direction ratios of PQ = 4 – 1, 1 – 5, – 2 – 4
= 3, – 4, – 6

[$\because$ Direction ratios of a line $P(x_1, y_1, z_1)$ and $Q(x_2, y_2, z_2)$ are $x_2 - x_1, y_2 - y_1, z_2 - z_1$]

56. If a line makes angles 90° and 60° respectively with the positive directions of X and Y axes, find the angle which it makes with the positive direction of Z-axis.*

Sol. We know,

$$l^2 + m^2 + n^2 = 1 \qquad \ldots(i)$$

and $\qquad l = \cos\alpha, \ m = \cos\beta, \ n = \cos\gamma$

Given $\qquad \alpha = 90°, \ \beta = 60°$

∴ $\qquad \cos\alpha = \cos 90° = 0$

and $\qquad \cos\beta = \cos 60° = \dfrac{1}{2}$

From equation (i),

$$0^2 + \left(\frac{1}{2}\right)^2 + n^2 = 1$$

$$n^2 = 1 - \frac{1}{4} = \frac{3}{4}$$

$$\Rightarrow \qquad \cos^2\gamma = \frac{3}{4}$$

or $\qquad \cos\gamma = \pm\dfrac{\sqrt{3}}{2}$

$$\Rightarrow \qquad \gamma = \cos^{-1}\left(\frac{\sqrt{3}}{2}\right) \text{ or } \cos^{-1}\left(\frac{-\sqrt{3}}{2}\right)$$

$$\Rightarrow \qquad \gamma = 30° \text{ or } 150°.$$

57. The equations of a line are $5x - 3 = 15y + 7 = 3 - 10z$. Write the direction cosines of the line.*

Sol. Given line is $5x - 3 = 15y + 7 = 3 - 10z$

Rewritting the equation in standard form :

$$5\left(x - \frac{3}{5}\right) = 15\left(y + \frac{7}{15}\right) = -10\left(z - \frac{3}{10}\right)$$

i.e.,
$$\frac{x - \dfrac{3}{5}}{\dfrac{1}{5}} = \frac{y + \dfrac{7}{15}}{\dfrac{1}{15}}$$

$$= \frac{z - \dfrac{3}{10}}{-\dfrac{1}{10}}$$

Thus, the direction ratios of the line are $\dfrac{1}{5}, \dfrac{1}{15}, \dfrac{-1}{10}$ *i.e.,* 6, 2, – 3.

Hence, its direction cosines are

$$\pm\frac{6}{\sqrt{6^2 + 2^2 + (-3)^2}}, \pm\frac{2}{\sqrt{6^2 + 2^2 + (-3)^2}}$$

$$\pm \frac{-3}{\sqrt{6^2 + 2^2 + (-3)^2}} \ \ i.e., \ \pm \frac{6}{7}, \pm \frac{2}{7}, \mp \frac{3}{7}$$

$$i.e., \ \frac{6}{7}, \frac{2}{7}, \frac{-3}{7} \ \text{or} \ \frac{-6}{7}, \frac{-2}{7}, \frac{3}{7}.$$

58. If O is the origin, OP = 3 with direction ratios – 1, 2, – 2 then the coordinates of P are ....

Sol. (– 1, 2, – 2)

Direction ratios of $\overrightarrow{OP}$ are – 1, 2, – 2.

Therefore, direction cosines of $\overrightarrow{OP}$ are

$$\frac{-1}{\sqrt{(-1)^2 + 2^2 + (-2)^2}}, \ \frac{2}{\sqrt{(-1)^2 + 2^2 + (-2)^2}},$$

$$\frac{-2}{\sqrt{(-1)^2 + 2^2 + (-2)^2}}$$

$$i.e., \ \frac{-1}{3}, \frac{2}{3}, \frac{-2}{3}$$

Hence

$$\overrightarrow{OP} = |\overrightarrow{OP}| (l\hat{i} + m\hat{j} + n\hat{k})$$

$$= 3\left(\frac{-1}{3}\hat{i} + \frac{2}{3}\hat{j} - \frac{2}{3}\hat{k}\right)$$

$$= -1\hat{i} + 2\hat{j} - 2\hat{k}$$

Therefore, coordinates of P are (– 1, 2, – 2).

59. If α, β, γ are the angles which a directed line makes with the positive directions of the coordinates axes, then the value of $\sin^2 \alpha + \sin^2 \beta + \sin^2 \gamma$ is ....

Sol. 2

Let l, m, n be the direction cosines of the line then

$$l = \cos \alpha, \ m = \cos \beta, \ n = \cos \gamma$$

Since $\qquad\qquad l^2 + m^2 + n^2 = 1$

$\Rightarrow \qquad \cos^2 \alpha + \cos^2 \beta + \cos^2 \gamma = 1$

$\Rightarrow \quad 1 - \sin^2 \alpha + 1 - \sin^2 \beta + 1 - \sin^2 \gamma = 1$

$\Rightarrow \qquad 3 - (\sin^2 \alpha + \sin^2 \beta + \sin^2 \gamma) = 1$

$\Rightarrow \qquad \sin^2 \alpha + \sin^2 \beta + \sin^2 \gamma = 3 - 1$

$\Rightarrow \qquad \sin^2 \alpha + \sin^2 \beta + \sin^2 \gamma = 2.$

60. If P is a point in the space such that OP = 12 and $\overrightarrow{OP}$ is inclined at angle of 45° and 60° with OX and OY respectively, then find the position vector of P.*

Sol. Let l, m, n be the direction cosines of $\overrightarrow{OP}$. Then, it is given that

$$l = \cos 45°, \ m = \cos 60°$$

$$\Rightarrow \qquad l = \frac{1}{\sqrt{2}}, \ m = \frac{1}{2}$$

Since $l^2 + m^2 + n^2 = 1$

$$\Rightarrow \qquad \frac{1}{2} + \frac{1}{4} + n^2 = 1$$

$$\Rightarrow \qquad \frac{3}{4} + n^2 = 1$$

$$\Rightarrow \qquad n^2 = \frac{1}{4}$$

$$\Rightarrow \qquad n = \pm \frac{1}{2}$$

Now $\qquad \vec{r} = |\vec{r}| (l\hat{i} + m\hat{j} + n\hat{k})$

$$\Rightarrow \qquad \vec{r} = 12\left(\frac{1}{\sqrt{2}}\hat{i} + \frac{1}{2}\hat{j} \pm \frac{1}{2}\hat{k}\right)$$

Therefore $\qquad \vec{r} = 6\sqrt{2}\,\hat{i} + 6\hat{j} \pm 6\hat{k}.$

61. Write the vector equation of the line given by
$$\frac{x-5}{3} = \frac{y+4}{7} = \frac{z-6}{2} \ *$$

Sol. Given equation of line in Cartesian form is
$$\frac{x-5}{3} = \frac{y+4}{7} = \frac{z-6}{2}$$

The point on line is (5, – 4, 6) and direction ratios are (3, 7, 2).

We know that vector equation of a line passing through $\vec{a}$ and parallel to $\vec{b}$ is

$$\vec{r} = \vec{a} + \lambda \vec{b}$$

Here, $\vec{a} = (5, -4, 6)$ and $\vec{b} = (3, 7, 2)$

Its equation in vector form is

$$\vec{r} = (5\hat{i} - 4\hat{j} + 6\hat{k}) + \lambda(3\hat{i} + 7\hat{j} + 2\hat{k})$$

62. Write the equation of line parallel to the line $\frac{x-2}{-3} = \frac{y+3}{2} = \frac{z+5}{6}$ and passing through point (1, 2, 3).*

Sol. Given equation of line is written as

$$\frac{x-2}{-3} = \frac{y+3}{2} = \frac{z+5}{6} \qquad ...(i)$$

Since, required line is parallel to given line, so direction ratios of required line will be proportional to – 3, 2 and 6.

$\therefore$ Equation of line passing through point (1, 2, 3) and parallel to equation (i) is

$$\frac{x-1}{-3} = \frac{y-2}{2} = \frac{z-3}{6}$$

$$\left[\text{using } \frac{x - x_1}{a} = \frac{y - y_1}{b} = \frac{z - z_1}{c}\right]$$

63. The equation of a line through the points $\hat{i}-2\hat{j}+\hat{k}$ and $3\hat{j}-2\hat{k}$ is ....

Sol. $(1-\lambda)\hat{i}+(5\lambda-2)\hat{j}+(1-3\lambda)\hat{k}$

Let $\quad \vec{a} = \hat{i}-2\hat{j}+\hat{k}$

$\qquad \vec{b} = 3\hat{j}-2\hat{k}$

Hence the equation of line is

$$\vec{r} = \vec{a}+\lambda(\vec{b}-\vec{a})$$

$$= (\hat{i}-2\hat{j}+\hat{k})+\lambda(-\hat{i}+5\hat{j}-3\hat{k})$$

$$= (1-\lambda)\hat{i}+(5\lambda-2)\hat{j}+(1-3\lambda)\hat{k}.$$

64. The vector equation of a line which passes through the points $(3, 4, -7)$ and $(1, -1, 6)$ is ....*

Sol. $(3\hat{i}+4\hat{j}-7\hat{k})+\lambda(-2\hat{i}-5\hat{j}+13\hat{k})$

$\because$ A = $(3, 4, -7)$ and B = $(1, -1, 6)$

$\therefore$ Direction ratios of AB = $<-2, -5, 13>$

$\therefore$ Equation of required line is,

$$\vec{r} = (3\hat{i}+4\hat{j}-7\hat{k})+\lambda(-2\hat{i}-5\hat{j}+13\hat{k})$$

65. The distance of point $(2, 3, 4)$ from X-axis is ....

Sol. 5 units

Let any point on X-axis be $P(x, 0, 0)$. Then distance of point $B(2, 3, 4)$ from P is given as

$$d = \sqrt{(x_2-x_1)^2+(y_2-y_1)^2+(z_2-z_1)^2}$$

Here $(x_1, y_1, z_1) = (2, 0, 0)$
and $(x_2, y_2, z_2) = (2, 3, 4)$

$$\Rightarrow \qquad d = \sqrt{(2-2)^2+(0-3)^2+(0-4)^2}$$

$$= \sqrt{9+16}$$

$$= \sqrt{25} = 5 \text{ units.}$$

66. The line of shortest distance between two skew lines is .... to both the lines.*

Sol. Perpendicular.

67. Find the Cartesian equation of the plane through the point with position vector $2\hat{i}-\hat{j}+\hat{k}$ and perpendicular to the vector $4\hat{i}+2\hat{j}-3\hat{k}$.

Sol. Plane is passing through the point A(say) having position vector

$$\vec{a} = 2\hat{i}-\hat{j}+\hat{k}$$

and is perpendicular to the vector

$$\vec{n} = 4\hat{i}+2\hat{j}-3\hat{k}$$

So, equation of plane is

$$(\vec{r}-\vec{a}).\vec{n} = 0 \text{ where}$$

$$\vec{r} = x\hat{i}+y\hat{j}+z\hat{k}$$

$$\Rightarrow [(x-2)\hat{i}+(y+1)\hat{j}+(z-1)\hat{k}].(4\hat{i}+2\hat{j}-3\hat{k})=0$$

$$\Rightarrow 4(x-2)+2(y+1)-3(z-1)=0$$

$$\Rightarrow 4x+2y-3z-3=0 \text{ is the required equation of plane.}$$

68. The position vector of two points P and Q are $3\hat{i}+\hat{j}+2\hat{k}$ and $\hat{i}-2\hat{j}-4\hat{k}$ respectively. Find the equation of the plane through Q and perpendicular to PQ.

Sol. $\quad \vec{PQ}$ = the position vector of Q

$\qquad\qquad$ – the position vector of P

$$= (\hat{i}-2\hat{j}-4\hat{k})-(3\hat{i}+\hat{j}+2\hat{k})$$

$$= -2\hat{i}-3\hat{j}-6\hat{k}$$

Therefore, the equation of the plane passing through the point Q and perpendicular to PQ is

$$[\vec{r}-(\hat{i}-2\hat{j}-4\hat{k})].(-2\hat{i}-3\hat{j}-6\hat{k}) = 0$$

$$[\text{Using } (\vec{r}-\vec{a}).\vec{n} = 0]$$

$$\Rightarrow \vec{r}.(-2\hat{i}-3\hat{j}-6\hat{k})$$

$$-(\hat{i}-2\hat{j}-4\hat{k}).(-2\hat{i}-3\hat{j}-6\hat{k}) = 0$$

$$\Rightarrow \vec{r}.(-2\hat{i}-3\hat{j}-6\hat{k})$$

$$-[1(-2)-2(-3)-4(-6)] = 0$$

$$\Rightarrow \vec{r}.(-2\hat{i}-3\hat{j}-6\hat{k})-[-2+6+24] = 0$$

$$\Rightarrow \vec{r}.(-2\hat{i}-3\hat{j}-6\hat{k})-28 = 0$$

$$\Rightarrow \vec{r}.(2\hat{i}+3\hat{j}+6\hat{k})+28 = 0$$

This is the equation of the required plane.

69. Find the vector equation of the plane through the point $2\hat{i}-\hat{j}-4\hat{k}$ and parallel to the plane $\vec{r}.(4\hat{i}-12\hat{j}-3\hat{k})-7 = 0.$

Sol. The equation of a plane parallel to the plane $\vec{r}.(4\hat{i}-12\hat{j}-3\hat{k})-7 = 0$ is

____

$$\vec{r} \cdot (4\hat{i} - 12\hat{j} - 3\hat{k}) + \lambda = 0 \qquad \ldots(i)$$

This plane passes through the point $2\hat{i} - \hat{j} - 4\hat{k}$

Therefore, $(2\hat{i} - \hat{j} - 4\hat{k}) \cdot (4\hat{i} - 12\hat{j} - 3\hat{k}) + \lambda = 0$

$\Rightarrow \qquad 2(4) - 1(-12) - 4(-3) + \lambda = 0$

$\Rightarrow \qquad 8 + 12 + 12 + \lambda = 0$

$\Rightarrow \qquad \lambda = -32$

Putting the value of λ in equation (i), we obtain the equation of the required plane as

$$\vec{r} \cdot (4\hat{i} - 12\hat{j} - 3\hat{k}) - 32 = 0$$

$$\Rightarrow \qquad \vec{r} \cdot (4\hat{i} - 12\hat{j} - 3\hat{k}) = 32.$$

70. Find the vector equation of the plane passing through the point (2, 1, – 1) and passing through the line of intersection of the planes

$$\vec{r} \cdot (\hat{i} + 3\hat{j} - \hat{k}) = 0 \text{ and } \vec{r} \cdot (\hat{j} + 2\hat{k}) = 0.$$

Sol. The vector equation of a plane passing through the line of intersection of the planes $\vec{r} \cdot (\hat{i} + 3\hat{j} - \hat{k}) = 0$ and $\vec{r} \cdot (\hat{j} + 2\hat{k}) = 0$ can be written as

$$[\vec{r} \cdot (\hat{i} + 3\hat{j} - \hat{k})] + \lambda[\vec{r} \cdot (\hat{j} + 2\hat{k})] = 0$$

This plane passes through $2\hat{i} + \hat{j} - \hat{k}$

Therefore, $[(2\hat{i} + \hat{j} - \hat{k}) \cdot (\hat{i} + 3\hat{j} - \hat{k})]$

$$+ \lambda[(2\hat{i} + \hat{j} - \hat{k}) \cdot (\hat{j} + 2\hat{k})] = 0$$

$\Rightarrow [2(1) + 1(3) - 1(-1)] + \lambda[2(0)$

$$+ 1(1) - 1(2)] = 0$$

$\Rightarrow \qquad 6 - \lambda = 0$

$\Rightarrow \qquad \lambda = 6$

Putting the value of λ in (i), we get the required equation of the plane as

$$[\vec{r} \cdot (\hat{i} + 3\hat{j} - \hat{k})] + 6[\vec{r} \cdot (\hat{j} + 2\hat{k})] = 0$$

$$\Rightarrow \qquad \vec{r} \cdot (\hat{i} + 9\hat{j} + 11\hat{k}) = 0.$$

71. Find the length of the perpendicular from the origin to the plane passing through the three non-collinear points $\vec{a}$, $\vec{b}$ and $\vec{c}$.

Sol. The vector equation of the plane passing through three non-collinear points $\vec{a}, \vec{b}, \vec{c}$ is

$$\vec{r} \cdot [\vec{a} \times \vec{b} + \vec{b} \times \vec{c} + \vec{c} \times \vec{a}] - [\vec{a}\ \vec{b}\ \vec{c}] = 0$$

Therefore, the length of the perpendicular from the origin to the plane is given by

$$\frac{|\vec{0} \cdot (\vec{a} \times \vec{b} + \vec{b} \times \vec{c} + \vec{c} \times \vec{a}) - [\vec{a}\ \vec{b}\ \vec{c}]|}{|\vec{a} \times \vec{b} + \vec{b} \times \vec{c} + \vec{c} \times \vec{a}|}$$

$$= \frac{[\vec{a}\ \vec{b}\ \vec{c}]}{|\vec{a} \times \vec{b} + \vec{b} \times \vec{c} + \vec{c} \times \vec{a}|}$$

72. Write the intercepts cut-off by plane

$$2x + y - z = 5 \text{ on X-axis.*}$$

Sol. Given equation of plane is

$$2x + y - z = 5$$

Divide both sides by 5, we get

$$\frac{2x}{5} + \frac{y}{5} - \frac{z}{5} = 1$$

or $\qquad \dfrac{x}{\left(\dfrac{5}{2}\right)} + \dfrac{y}{5} + \dfrac{z}{-5} = 1$

Comparing above equation of plane with the intercept form of equation of plane $\dfrac{x}{a} + \dfrac{y}{b} + \dfrac{z}{c}$

= 1, where a = x-intercept, b = y-intercept, c = z-intercept, we get

$$a = \frac{5}{2}$$

i.e., intercept cut-off on X-axis = $\dfrac{5}{2}$.

73. The direction cosines of the normal from the origin to the plane $\vec{r} \cdot (\hat{i} + \hat{j} - \hat{k}) = 2$ is ....

Sol. $\dfrac{1}{\sqrt{3}}, \dfrac{1}{\sqrt{3}}, \dfrac{1}{\sqrt{3}}$

Equation of plane is given as,

$$\vec{r} \cdot \vec{n} = d$$

So, $\qquad \vec{n} = \hat{i} + \hat{j} - \hat{k}$

and $\qquad d = 2$

Now, $\quad |\hat{i} + \hat{j} - \hat{k}| = \sqrt{1 + 1 + 1} = \sqrt{3}$

Therefore, we can rewrite the equation of the plane as

$$\vec{r} \cdot \frac{(\hat{i} + \hat{j} - \hat{k})}{\sqrt{3}} = \frac{2}{\sqrt{3}}$$

Thus $\hat{n} = \dfrac{\hat{i} + \hat{j} - \hat{k}}{\sqrt{3}}$ and has direction cosines

$$\frac{1}{\sqrt{3}}, \frac{1}{\sqrt{3}}, \frac{1}{\sqrt{3}}.$$

74. Find the distance between the planes $x + y - z = 3$ and $2x + 2y - 2z + 10 = 0$.

Sol. Let (x_1, y_1, z_1) lie on the plane $x + y - z - 3 = 0$

$\Rightarrow x_1 + y_1 - z_1 - 3 = 0$

Now distance of (x_1, y_1, z_1) from the plane $2x + 2y - 2z + 10 = 0$ is given by

$$d = \left| \frac{2x_1 + 2y_1 - 2z_1 + 10}{\sqrt{(2)^2 + (2)^2 + (-2)^2}} \right|$$

$$= \left| \frac{2(x_1 + y_1 - z_1) + 10}{\sqrt{4 + 4 + 4}} \right|$$

$\Rightarrow \quad d = \left| \dfrac{2(3) + 10}{\sqrt{12}} \right|$

$\Rightarrow \quad d = \left| \dfrac{16}{\sqrt{12}} \right|$

$\Rightarrow \quad d = \dfrac{16}{2\sqrt{3}}$

$\Rightarrow \quad d = \dfrac{8}{\sqrt{3}}$

$\Rightarrow \quad d = \dfrac{8\sqrt{3}}{3}$ units.

75. Find distance of the plane $3x - 4y + 12z = 3$ from the origin.*

Sol. Given equation of plane is $3x - 4y + 12z - 3 = 0$ and the point is $(0, 0, 0)$. We know that distance of the plane $Ax + By + Cz + D = 0$ to the point (x_1, y_1, z_1) is

$$d = \frac{|Ax_1 + By_1 + Cz_1 + D|}{\sqrt{A^2 + B^2 + C^2}}$$

Here, $x_1 = y_1 = z_1 = 0$ and $A = 3$, $B = -4$, $C = 12$, $D = -3$

$\therefore \quad d = \dfrac{|3(0) - 4(0) + 12(0) - 3|}{\sqrt{(3)^2 + (-4)^2 + (12)^2}}$

$d = \dfrac{|-3|}{\sqrt{9 + 16 + 144}}$

$= \dfrac{3}{\sqrt{169}}$

$= \dfrac{3}{13}$ unit.

76. The perpendicular distance from the origin to the plane through the point $(2, 3, -1)$ and perpendicular to the vector $3\hat{i} - 4\hat{j} + 7\hat{k}$ is

....

Sol. $\dfrac{13}{\sqrt{74}}$ units.

The equation of the plane through $(2, 3, -1)$ and perpendicular to $3\hat{i} - 4\hat{j} + 7\hat{k}$ is

$[\vec{r} - (2\hat{i} + 3\hat{j} - \hat{k})].(3\hat{i} - 4\hat{j} + 7\hat{k}) = 0$

$$[\text{using } (\vec{r} - \vec{a}).\vec{n} = 0]$$

$\Rightarrow \vec{r}.(3\hat{i} - 4\hat{j} + 7\hat{k})$

$\quad - (2\hat{i} + 3\hat{j} - \hat{k}).(3\hat{i} - 4\hat{j} + 7\hat{k}) = 0$

$\Rightarrow \quad \vec{r}.(3\hat{i} - 4\hat{j} + 7\hat{k}) - [6 - 12 - 7] = 0$

$\Rightarrow \quad \vec{r}.(3\hat{i} - 4\hat{j} + 7\hat{k}) + 13 = 0$

Now the length of the perpendicular from the origin to this plane is given by

$$\left| \frac{\vec{0}.(3\hat{i} - 4\hat{j} + 7\hat{k}) + 13}{\sqrt{(3)^2 + (-4)^2 + (7)^2}} \right| = \left| \frac{13}{\sqrt{9 + 16 + 49}} \right|$$

$$= \frac{13}{\sqrt{74}}$$

77. Find the value of λ such that the line $\dfrac{x - 2}{6} = \dfrac{y - 1}{\lambda} = \dfrac{z + 5}{-4}$ is perpendicular to the plane $3x - y - 2z = 7.*$

Sol. Given that line $\dfrac{x - 2}{6} = \dfrac{y - 1}{\lambda} = \dfrac{z + 5}{-4}$ is perpendicular to plane $3x - y - 2z = 7$

$$\frac{6}{3} = \frac{\lambda}{-1} = \frac{-4}{-2}$$

$[\because$ when a line is perpendicular to a plane, their direction ratios are proportional]

$\Rightarrow \qquad 2 = -\lambda = 2$

$\Rightarrow \qquad -\lambda = 2 \Rightarrow \lambda = -2.$

Short Answer Type Questions

78. Prove that if the direction cosines of a line PQ are l, m, n then the direction cosines of QP are

$$-l, -m, -n.$$

Sol. Let PQ make angles α, β, γ with the positive direction of the coordinate axes.

____

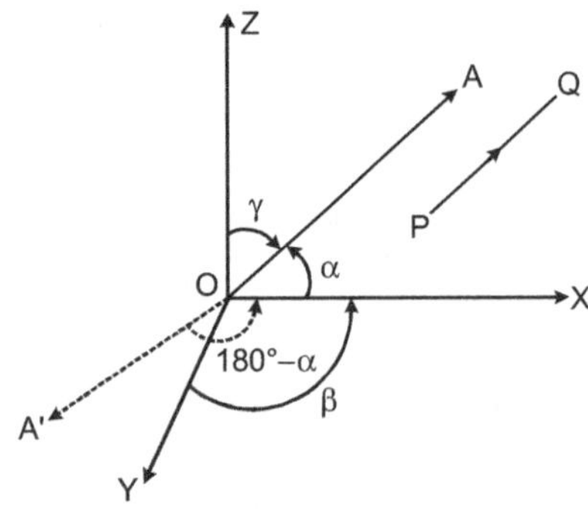

Then $\cos\alpha = l$, $\cos\beta = m$, $\cos\gamma = n$. Now through O, draw a line OA parallel to PQ and having the same sense as that of PQ. Then the angles which OA makes with the coordinate axes will be α, β, γ.

Now, the angles which QP makes with the coordinate axes will be the angles which AO produced (in the figure it is OA′) makes with the axes.

Therefore, the direction cosines of QP are $\cos(180° - \alpha)$, $\cos(180° - \beta)$, $\cos(180° - \gamma)$ or $-\cos\alpha$, $-\cos\beta$ and $-\cos\gamma$

i.e., $\quad -l, -m, -n$.

79. The direction cosines of a line are proportional to $2, -3, 6$. Find the actual values of the direction cosines.

Sol. If l, m, n are the direction cosines of the line then
$$l : m : n = 2 : -3 : 6$$

Hence $\quad l = \dfrac{a}{\sqrt{a^2 + b^2 + c^2}}$, $m = \dfrac{b}{\sqrt{a^2 + b^2 + c^2}}$,

$$n = \dfrac{c}{\sqrt{a^2 + b^2 + c^2}}$$

$$l = \dfrac{2}{\sqrt{2^2 + (-3)^2 + 6^2}}, \ m = \dfrac{-3}{\sqrt{2^2 + (-3)^2 + 6^2}},$$

$$n = \dfrac{6}{\sqrt{2^2 + (-3)^2 + 6^2}}$$

i.e., $\quad l = \dfrac{2}{7}$, $m = \dfrac{-3}{7}$, $n = \dfrac{6}{7}$.

80. If $P(1, 2, 3)$ and $Q(-1, 2, 1)$ are two points in space, find the direction cosines of PQ.

Sol. Let l, m, n be the direction cosines of the line PQ.

Then, $\quad l : m : n = (x_2 - x_1) : (y_2 - y_1) : (z_2 - z_1)$

$\qquad\qquad l : m : n = (-1 - 1) : (2 - 2) : (1 - 3)$

or $\qquad l : m : n = -2 : 0 : -2$

This shows that $-2, 0, -2$ are the direction ratios of the line PQ.

Hence $\quad l = \dfrac{a}{\sqrt{a^2 + b^2 + c^2}}$, $m = \dfrac{b}{\sqrt{a^2 + b^2 + c^2}}$,

$$n = \dfrac{c}{\sqrt{a^2 + b^2 + c^2}}$$

$$l = \dfrac{-2}{\sqrt{(-2)^2 + (-2)^2}}; \ m = \dfrac{0}{\sqrt{(-2)^2 + (-2)^2}};$$

$$n = \dfrac{-2}{\sqrt{(-2)^2 + (-2)^2}}$$

or $\qquad l = \dfrac{-1}{\sqrt{2}}$, $m = 0$, $n = \dfrac{-1}{\sqrt{2}}$.

81. Find the direction cosines of the line, which is perpendicular to the lines whose direction cosines are proportional to $1, -1, 2$ and $2, 1, -1$.

Sol. Let l, m, n be the direction cosines of the required line.

Then $\quad l(1) + m(-1) + n(2) = 0$

and $\quad l(2) + m(1) + n(-1) = 0$

$\Rightarrow \qquad\qquad l - m + 2n = 0 \qquad\qquad …(i)$

and $\qquad\qquad 2l + m - n = 0 \qquad\qquad …(ii)$

On solving (i) and (ii) by cross multiplication, we get

$$\dfrac{l}{1-2} = \dfrac{m}{4+1} = \dfrac{n}{1+2}$$

$$\Rightarrow \quad \dfrac{l}{-1} = \dfrac{m}{5} = \dfrac{n}{3} = \dfrac{\sqrt{l^2 + m^2 + n^2}}{\sqrt{(-1)^2 + (5)^2 + (3)^2}}$$

$$\Rightarrow \quad \dfrac{l}{-1} = \dfrac{m}{5} = \dfrac{n}{3} = \dfrac{1}{\sqrt{35}}$$

$$[\because l^2 + m^2 + n^2 = 1]$$

$\therefore \qquad l = \dfrac{-1}{\sqrt{35}}$, $m = \dfrac{5}{\sqrt{35}}$ and $n = \dfrac{3}{\sqrt{35}}$.

82. A line passes through the points $A(6, -7, -1)$ and $B(2, -3, 1)$. Find direction ratios and direction cosines of the line so directed that the angle α is acute.

Sol. The direction ratios of a vector passing through $P(x_1, y_1, z_1)$ and $Q(x_2, y_2, z_2)$ are
$$(x_2 - x_1), (y_2 - y_1) \text{ and } (z_2 - z_1)$$

Therefore, direction ratios of AB are
$$2 - 6, -3 + 7, 1 + 1$$

i.e., $-4, 4, 2$ or $-2, 2, 1$.

We know that if a, b, c are direction ratios of a vector then its direction cosines are

$$\pm \dfrac{a}{\sqrt{a^2 + b^2 + c^2}}, \pm \dfrac{b}{\sqrt{a^2 + b^2 + c^2}}, \pm \dfrac{c}{\sqrt{a^2 + b^2 + c^2}}$$

Therefore, direction cosines of AB are

$$\pm \dfrac{-2}{\sqrt{(-2)^2 + (2)^2 + (1)^2}}, \pm \dfrac{2}{\sqrt{(-2)^2 + (2)^2 + (1)^2}},$$

$$\pm \dfrac{1}{\sqrt{(-2)^2 + (2)^2 + (1)^2}}$$

i.e., $\pm \dfrac{-2}{3}$, $\pm \dfrac{2}{3}$, $\pm \dfrac{1}{3}$

Since α is acute, $\cos \alpha > 0$.

Therefore, the direction cosines of AB are $\dfrac{2}{3}, \dfrac{-2}{3}, \dfrac{-1}{3}.$ (Taking negative sign)

83. Find the vector equation of the line which is parallel to the vector $2\hat{i} - \hat{j} + 3\hat{k}$ and which passes through the point $(5, -2, 4)$. Also, find its Cartesian equation.

Sol. The vector equation of the line passing through the point $(5, -2, 4)$ and parallel to the vector $2\hat{i} - \hat{j} + 3\hat{k}$ is given by

$$\vec{r} = (5\hat{i} - 2\hat{j} + 4\hat{k}) + \lambda(2\hat{i} - \hat{j} + 3\hat{k}) \quad ...(i)$$

Let $\vec{r} = x\hat{i} + y\hat{j} + z\hat{k}$

Then,

$$(x\hat{i} + y\hat{j} + z\hat{k}) = (5\hat{i} - 2\hat{j} + 4\hat{k}) + \lambda(2\hat{i} - \hat{j} + 3\hat{k})$$

$$(x\hat{i} + y\hat{j} + z\hat{k}) = (5 + 2\lambda)\hat{i} + (-2 - \lambda)\hat{j} + (4 + 3\lambda)\hat{k}$$

$$\Rightarrow \qquad x = 5 + 2\lambda$$
$$y = -2 - \lambda$$
$$z = 4 + 3\lambda$$

$$\Rightarrow \qquad \frac{x-5}{2} = \frac{y+2}{-1} = \frac{z-4}{3} = \lambda$$

i.e., $\qquad \dfrac{x-5}{2} = \dfrac{y+2}{-1} = \dfrac{z-4}{3}$

is the Cartesian equation of the required line.

84. Find the vector equation of the line passing through the point $A(1, 2, -1)$ and parallel to the line $5x - 25 = 14 - 7y = 35z$.*

Sol. Given line is

$$5x - 25 = 14 - 7y = 35z$$
$$\Rightarrow \qquad 5(x - 5) = -7(y - 2) = 35z$$
$$\Rightarrow \qquad \frac{x-5}{1/5} = \frac{y-2}{-1/7} = \frac{z-0}{1/35}$$
$$\Rightarrow \qquad \frac{x-5}{7} = \frac{y-2}{-5} = \frac{z-0}{1}$$

Direction ratios of this line are $7, -5, 1$.

$\therefore$ Vector equation of the line which passes through the point $A(1, 2, -1)$ and whose direction ratios are proportional to $7, -5, 1$ is

$$\vec{r} = \hat{i} + 2\hat{j} - \hat{k} + \lambda(7\hat{i} - 5\hat{j} + \hat{k}).$$

85. Find the value of λ, so that following lines are perpendicular to each other.

$$\frac{x+5}{5\lambda + 2} = \frac{2-y}{5} = \frac{1-z}{-1} \text{ and } \frac{x}{1} = \frac{2y+1}{4\lambda} = \frac{1-z}{-3}.$$ *

* are board exam questions from previous years

Sol. Given equation of lines are

$$\frac{x+5}{5\lambda + 2} = \frac{2-y}{5} = \frac{1-z}{-1}$$

and $\qquad \dfrac{x}{1} = \dfrac{2y+1}{4\lambda} = \dfrac{1-z}{-3}$

Above equations can be written as

$$\frac{x+5}{5\lambda + 2} = \frac{y-2}{-5} = \frac{z-1}{1} \qquad ...(i)$$

and $\qquad \dfrac{x-0}{1} = \dfrac{2\left(y + \dfrac{1}{2}\right)}{4\lambda} = \dfrac{z-1}{3}$

or $\qquad \dfrac{x-0}{1} = \dfrac{y + \dfrac{1}{2}}{2\lambda} = \dfrac{z-1}{3} \qquad ...(ii)$

Comparing equations (i) and (ii) with one point form of line $\dfrac{x - x_1}{a} = \dfrac{y - y_1}{b} = \dfrac{z - z_1}{c}$, we get

$$a_1 = 5\lambda + 2, \ b_1 = -5, \ c_1 = 1$$

and $\qquad a_2 = 1, \ b_2 = 2\lambda, \ c_2 = 3$

Since, two lines are perpendicular,

$$\therefore \qquad a_1 a_2 + b_1 b_2 + c_1 c_2 = 0$$
$$\Rightarrow \qquad 1(5\lambda + 2) + 2\lambda(-5) + 3(1) = 0$$
$$\Rightarrow \qquad 5\lambda + 2 - 10\lambda + 3 = 0$$
$$\Rightarrow \qquad -5\lambda + 5 = 0$$
$$\Rightarrow \qquad 5\lambda = 5$$
$$\Rightarrow \qquad \lambda = 1.$$

86. Find the points on the line $\dfrac{x+2}{3} = \dfrac{y+1}{2} = \dfrac{z-3}{2}$ at a distance of 5 units from the point $P(1, 3, 3)$.*

Sol. Given equation of line is

$$\frac{x+2}{3} = \frac{y+1}{2} = \frac{z-3}{2}$$

We find any random point on the line as follows :

$$\frac{x+2}{3} = \frac{y+1}{2} = \frac{z-3}{2} = \lambda \text{ (say)}$$

$$\Rightarrow \qquad \frac{x+2}{3} = \lambda, \ \frac{y+1}{2} = \lambda, \ \frac{z-3}{2} = \lambda$$

$$\Rightarrow \qquad x = 3\lambda - 2, \ y = 2\lambda - 1, \ z = 2\lambda + 3$$

$\therefore$ We have the point $Q(3\lambda - 2, 2\lambda - 1, 2\lambda + 3)$ ...(i)

Now, given that distance between point $P(1, 3, 3)$ and $Q(3\lambda - 2, 2\lambda - 1, 2\lambda + 3)$ is 5 units.

i.e., $\qquad PQ = 5$

$$\Rightarrow \sqrt{(3\lambda - 2 - 1)^2 + (2\lambda - 1 - 3)^2 + (2\lambda + 3 - 3)^2} = 5$$

Squaring both sides, we get

$$(3\lambda - 3)^2 + (2\lambda - 4)^2 + (2\lambda)^2 = 25$$

$$\Rightarrow \quad 9\lambda^2 + 9 - 18\lambda + 4\lambda^2 + 16 - 16\lambda + 4\lambda^2 = 25$$

$\Rightarrow \qquad\qquad 17\lambda^2 - 34\lambda = 0$

$\Rightarrow \qquad\qquad 17\lambda(\lambda - 2) = 0$

$\Rightarrow$ Either $\quad 17\lambda = 0$ or $\lambda - 2 = 0$

$\Rightarrow \qquad\qquad \lambda = 0$ or 2

Putting $\lambda = 0$ and $\lambda = 2$ in equation (i), we get the required points as $(-2, -1, 3)$ and $(4, 3, 7)$.

87. Find the vector and Cartesian equation of line passing through point $(1, 2, -4)$ and perpendicular to two lines $\dfrac{x-8}{3} = \dfrac{y+19}{-16}$

$= \dfrac{z-10}{7}$ and $\dfrac{x-15}{3} = \dfrac{y-29}{8} = \dfrac{z-5}{-5}$.

Sol. Let the required equation of line passing through $(1, 2, -4)$ is

$$\frac{x-1}{a} = \frac{y-2}{b} = \frac{z+4}{c} \qquad \text{...(i)}$$

Given that line (i) is perpendicular to lines

$$\frac{x-8}{3} = \frac{y+19}{-16} = \frac{z-10}{7} \qquad \text{...(ii)}$$

and $\qquad \dfrac{x-15}{3} = \dfrac{y-29}{8} = \dfrac{z-5}{-5} \qquad \text{...(iii)}$

We know that when two lines are perpendicular then we have $a_1 a_2 + b_1 b_2 + c_1 c_2 = 0$, where a_1, b_1, c_1 and a_2, b_2, c_2 are the direction ratios of two lines. Using this property first in equations (i) and (ii) and then in equations (i) and (iii), we get

$$3a - 16b + 7c = 0 \qquad \text{...(iv)}$$
$$(\because a_1 a_2 + b_1 b_2 + c_1 c_2 = 0)$$

and $\quad 3a + 8b - 5c = 0 \qquad \text{...(v)}$

Subtracting equation (v) from equation (iv), we get

$$3a - 16b = -7c$$
$$3a + 8b = 5c$$
$$\overline{ - }$$
$$-24b = -12c$$

or $\qquad\qquad b = \dfrac{c}{2}$

Putting $b = \dfrac{c}{2}$ in equation (iv), we get

$$3a - 16\left(\frac{c}{2}\right) + 7c = 0$$

$\Rightarrow \qquad 3a - 8c + 7c = 0$

$\Rightarrow \qquad\qquad 3a - c = 0$

$\Rightarrow \qquad\qquad a = \dfrac{c}{3}$

Putting $a = \dfrac{c}{3}$ and $b = \dfrac{c}{2}$ in equation (i), we get

the required equation of line as

$$\frac{x-1}{\left(\dfrac{c}{3}\right)} = \frac{y-2}{\left(\dfrac{c}{2}\right)} = \frac{z+4}{c}$$

$\Rightarrow \qquad \dfrac{x-1}{2c} = \dfrac{y-2}{3c} = \dfrac{z+4}{6c}$

$\Rightarrow \qquad \dfrac{x-1}{2} = \dfrac{y-2}{3} = \dfrac{z+4}{6}$

Also, the vector equation of line is

$$r = (\hat{i} + 2\hat{j} - 4\hat{k}) + \lambda(2\hat{i} + 3\hat{j} + 6\hat{k})$$

88. Find the length and foot of perpendicular drawn from the point $(2, -1, 5)$ to line

$$\frac{x-11}{10} = \frac{y+2}{-4} = \frac{z+8}{-11}. *$$

Sol. Let AB be the line whose equation is

$$\frac{x-11}{10} = \frac{y+2}{-4} = \frac{z+8}{-11}$$

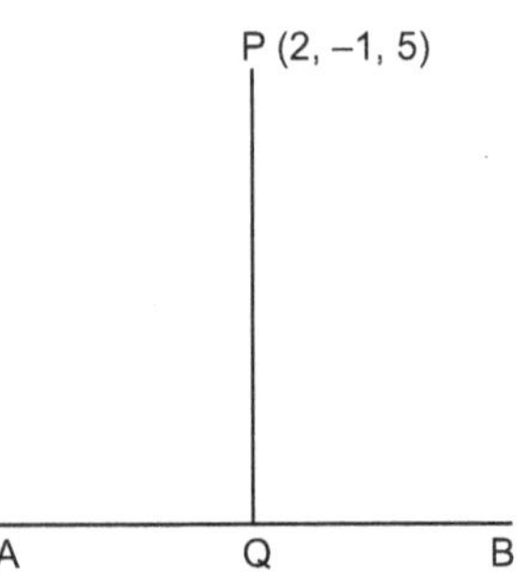

Let Q be the foot of perpendicular and PQ be the length of perpendicular.

Any point Q on the given line is given by

$$\frac{x-11}{10} = \frac{y+2}{-4} = \frac{z+8}{-11} = \lambda \text{ (say)}$$

$\Rightarrow \quad x = 10\lambda + 11, \; y = -4\lambda - 2, \; z = -11\lambda - 8$

$\therefore$ Coordinates of Q are $(10\lambda + 11, -4\lambda - 2, -11\lambda - 8)$

Now, direction ratios of the line PQ are

$$(10\lambda + 11 - 2, -4\lambda - 2 + 1, -11\lambda - 8 - 5)$$

$\therefore$ Direction ratios of PQ $= (10\lambda + 9, -4\lambda - 1, -11\lambda - 13)$

$\because \qquad\qquad PQ \perp AB$

$\therefore \qquad\quad a_1 a_2 + b_1 b_2 + c_1 c_2 = 0$

Where $a_1 = 10\lambda + 9, \; b_1 = -4\lambda - 1, \; c_1 = -11\lambda - 13$

(Direction ratios of PQ)

and $a_2 = 10, \; b_2 = -4, \; c_2 = -11$

(Direction ratios of AB)

$\therefore$ We get

$$10(10\lambda + 9) - 4(-4\lambda - 1) - 11(-11\lambda - 13) = 0$$

$\Rightarrow \quad 100\lambda + 90 + 16\lambda + 4 + 121\lambda + 143 = 0$

$\Rightarrow \qquad\qquad\qquad 237\lambda + 237 = 0$

$\Rightarrow \qquad\qquad\qquad\qquad \lambda = -1$

Putting $\lambda = -1$ in coordinates of point Q, we get

Foot of perpendicular

$$= Q(-10+11, 4-2, 11-8)$$
$$= Q(1, 2, 3)$$

Also, length of perpendicular PQ is given by

$$PQ = \sqrt{(2-1)^2 + (-1-2)^2 + (5-3)^2}$$
$$= \sqrt{1+9+4}$$
$$= \sqrt{14} \text{ units.}$$

89. Find the perpendicular distance of point $(1, 0, 0)$ from the line $\dfrac{x-1}{2} = \dfrac{y+1}{-3} = \dfrac{z+10}{8}$. Also, find the coordinates of foot of perpendicular and equation of perpendicular.*

Sol. Let AB be the line whose equation is given as

$$\frac{x-1}{2} = \frac{y+1}{-3} = \frac{z+10}{8}$$

Let P be the foot of perpendicular drawn from point $O(1, 0, 0)$ on line AB.

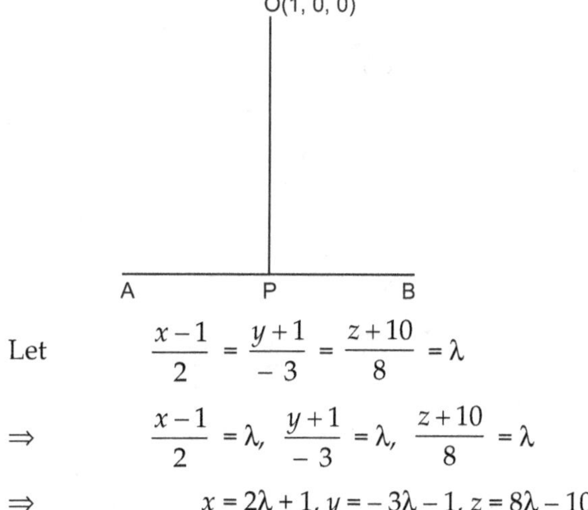

Let $\dfrac{x-1}{2} = \dfrac{y+1}{-3} = \dfrac{z+10}{8} = \lambda$

$\Rightarrow \quad \dfrac{x-1}{2} = \lambda, \ \dfrac{y+1}{-3} = \lambda, \ \dfrac{z+10}{8} = \lambda$

$\Rightarrow \quad x = 2\lambda+1, \ y = -3\lambda-1, \ z = 8\lambda-10$

$\therefore$ Coordinates of P are

$$(2\lambda+1, -3\lambda-1, 8\lambda-10)$$

$\Rightarrow$ Direction ratios of line OP

$$= (2\lambda+1-1, -3\lambda-1-0, 8\lambda-10-0)$$
$$= (2\lambda, -3\lambda-1, 8\lambda-10)$$

Since, $\quad OP \perp AB$

$\therefore a_1 a_2 + b_1 b_2 + c_1 c_2 = 0$

Where a_1, b_1, c_1 are direction ratios of line OP and a_2, b_2, c_2 are direction ratios of line AB.

$\therefore$ We get $\quad a_1 = 2\lambda, \ b_1 = -3\lambda-1, \ c_1 = 8\lambda-10$

and $\quad a_2 = 2, \ b_2 = -3, \ c_2 = 8$

$\therefore$ From equation (i)

$$2(2\lambda) - 3(-3\lambda-1) + 8(8\lambda-10) = 0$$
$$\Rightarrow \quad 4\lambda + 9\lambda + 3 + 64\lambda - 80 = 0$$
$$\Rightarrow \quad 77\lambda - 77 = 0$$
$$\Rightarrow \quad 77\lambda = 77$$
$$\Rightarrow \quad \lambda = 1$$

Coordinates of point P

$$= (2\lambda+1, -3\lambda-1, 8\lambda-10)$$
$$= (3, -4, -2)$$

Now, since P is the foot of perpendicular, so coordinates of foot of perpendicular $= (3, -4, -2)$.

Now, we find the perpendicular distance of the point $O(1, 0, 0)$ and the line which is equal to OP.

$\therefore$ Using distance formula,

$$OP = \sqrt{(3-1)^2 + (-4-0)^2 + (-2-0)^2}$$
$$= \sqrt{4+16+4} = \sqrt{24} = 2\sqrt{6} \text{ units}$$

$\therefore \qquad OP = 2\sqrt{6} \text{ units}.$

Finally, equation of perpendicular OP, where $O(1, 0, 0)$ and $P(3, -4, -2)$ is given by

$$\frac{x-1}{3-1} = \frac{y-0}{-4-0} = \frac{z-0}{-2-0}$$

$$\Rightarrow \quad \frac{x-1}{2} = \frac{y}{-4} = \frac{z}{-2}$$

which is the required equation of perpendicular.

90. By computing the shortest distance, determine whether the following lines intersects or not $\dfrac{x-1}{2} = \dfrac{y+1}{3} = z$ and $\dfrac{x+1}{5} = \dfrac{y-2}{1} = \dfrac{z-2}{0}$.

Sol. The given equations of the two lines are

$$\frac{x-1}{2} = \frac{y+1}{3} = \frac{z-0}{1} \qquad \text{...(i)}$$

and $\qquad \dfrac{x+1}{5} = \dfrac{y-2}{1} = \dfrac{z-2}{0} \qquad \text{...(ii)}$

The vector equations of the above two lines are

$$\vec{r} = (\hat{i} - \hat{j} + 0\hat{k}) + \lambda(2\hat{i} + 3\hat{j} + \hat{k})$$

$$\vec{r} = (-\hat{i} + 2\hat{j} + 2\hat{k}) + \mu(5\hat{i} + \hat{j})$$

Comparing these equations with $\vec{r} = \vec{a_1} + \lambda \vec{b_1}$ and $\vec{r} = \vec{a_2} + \mu \vec{b_2}$, we have

$$\vec{a_1} = \hat{i} - \hat{j}$$

$$\vec{a_2} = -\hat{i} + 2\hat{j} + 2\hat{k}$$

$$\vec{b_1} = 2\hat{i} + 3\hat{j} + \hat{k}$$

$$\vec{b_2} = 5\hat{i} + \hat{j}$$

Now, $(\vec{a_2} - \vec{a_1}) = -2\hat{i} + 3\hat{j} + 2\hat{k}$

and $\qquad \vec{b_1} \times \vec{b_2} = \begin{vmatrix} \hat{i} & \hat{j} & \hat{k} \\ 2 & 3 & 1 \\ 5 & 1 & 0 \end{vmatrix}$

$$= \hat{i}(0-1) - \hat{j}(0-5) + \hat{k}(2-15)$$

$$= -\hat{i} + 5\hat{j} - 13\hat{k}$$

Also, $|\vec{b_1} \times \vec{b_2}| = \sqrt{(-1)^2 + (5)^2 + (-13)^2}$

$$= \sqrt{1 + 25 + 169} = \sqrt{195}$$

$(\vec{a_2} - \vec{a_1}).(\vec{b_1} \times \vec{b_2})$

$$= (-2\hat{i} + 3\hat{j} + 2\hat{k}).(-\hat{i} + 5\hat{j} - 13\hat{k})$$

$$= 2 + 15 - 26 = -9$$

Therefore, the shortest distance between the lines

$$= \left| \frac{-9}{\sqrt{195}} \right| = \frac{9}{\sqrt{195}} \geq 0$$

Since, $\qquad d \neq 0$

Hence, the given lines do not intersect.

91. Check whether the lines

$$l_1 : \vec{r} = \hat{i} - \hat{j} + t(2\hat{i} + \hat{k})$$

and $\qquad l_2 : \vec{r} = 2\hat{i} - \hat{j} + u(\hat{i} + \hat{j} - \hat{k})$

are skew lines or not. Hence, find the shortest distance between them.

Sol. Clearly they are not parallel, since the l_1 is parallel

to $2\hat{i} + \hat{k}$ and line l_2 is parallel to $\hat{i} + \hat{j} - \hat{k}$.

If they intersect, then for some value of t and u.

$$2\hat{i} - \hat{j} + u(\hat{i} + \hat{j} - \hat{k}) = \hat{i} - \hat{j} + t(2\hat{i} + \hat{k})$$

Equating the coefficients, we get

$$2 + u = 1 + 2t, \qquad \qquad ...(i)$$

$$-1 + u = -1 \qquad \qquad ...(ii)$$

and $\qquad \qquad -u = t \qquad \qquad ...(iii)$

From (ii), we get

$$u = 0$$

From (iii), we get

$$t = 0$$

Putting these values in (i), we get $2 = 1$, which is not possible.

Thus, these are indeed skew lines.

The shortest distance between them is

$$\left| \frac{[(2\hat{i} + \hat{k}) \times (\hat{i} + \hat{j} - \hat{k})].(2\hat{i} - \hat{j} - \hat{i} + \hat{j})}{|(2\hat{i} + \hat{k}) \times (\hat{i} + \hat{j} - \hat{k})|} \right| = \frac{1}{\sqrt{14}} \text{ unit.}$$

92. Find the shortest distance between lines

$$\vec{r} = 6\hat{i} + 2\hat{j} + 2\hat{k} + \lambda(\hat{i} - 2\hat{j} + 2\hat{k})$$

and $\qquad \vec{r} = -4\hat{i} - \hat{k} + \mu(3\hat{i} - 2\hat{j} - 2\hat{k})*$

Sol. Given equations of lines are

$$\vec{r} = 6\hat{i} + 2\hat{j} + 2\hat{k} + \lambda(\hat{i} - 2\hat{j} + 2\hat{k}) \quad ...(i)$$

and $\qquad \vec{r} = -4\hat{i} - \hat{k} + \mu(3\hat{i} - 2\hat{j} - 2\hat{k}) \quad ...(ii)$

We know that vector form of equation of line is

$$\vec{r} = \vec{a} + \lambda \vec{b} \qquad \qquad ...(iii)$$

Comparing equations (i) and (ii) with equation (iii), we get

$$\vec{a_1} = 6\hat{i} + 2\hat{j} + 2\hat{k},\ \vec{b_1} = \hat{i} - 2\hat{j} + 2\hat{k}$$

$$\vec{a_2} = -4\hat{i} - \hat{k},\ \vec{b_2} = 3\hat{i} - 2\hat{j} - 2\hat{k}$$

We know that the shortest distance between two lines is given by

$$d = \left| \frac{(\vec{b_1} \times \vec{b_2}).(\vec{a_2} - \vec{a_1})}{|\vec{b_1} \times \vec{b_2}|} \right| \qquad ...(iv)$$

Now $\quad \vec{b_1} \times \vec{b_2} = \begin{vmatrix} \hat{i} & \hat{j} & \hat{k} \\ 1 & -2 & 2 \\ 3 & -2 & -2 \end{vmatrix}$

$$= \hat{i}(4+4) - \hat{j}(-2-6) + \hat{k}(-2+6)$$

$$\Rightarrow \quad \vec{b_1} \times \vec{b_2} = 8\hat{i} + 8\hat{j} + 4\hat{k} \qquad ...(v)$$

and $\quad |\vec{b_1} \times \vec{b_2}| = \sqrt{(8)^2 + (8)^2 + (4)^2}$

$$= \sqrt{64 + 64 + 16}$$

$$= \sqrt{144} = 12 \qquad \qquad ...(vi)$$

Also, $\quad \vec{a_2} - \vec{a_1} = (-4\hat{i} - \hat{k}) - (6\hat{i} + 2\hat{j} + 2\hat{k})$

$$\Rightarrow \quad \vec{a_2} - \vec{a_1} = -10\hat{i} - 2\hat{j} - 3\hat{k} \qquad ...(vii)$$

So from equations (iv), (v) and (vi) and (vii), we get

$$d = \left| \frac{(8\hat{i} + 8\hat{j} + 4\hat{k}).(-10\hat{i} - 2\hat{j} - 3\hat{k})}{12} \right|$$

$$\Rightarrow \qquad d = \left| \frac{-80 - 16 - 12}{12} \right|$$

$$= \left| \frac{-108}{12} \right| = \frac{108}{12} = 9$$

$\therefore$ Shortest distance = 9 units.

93. Find the shortest distance between the lines

$$l_1 : \frac{x-1}{1} = \frac{y-2}{-1} = \frac{z-1}{1} \text{ and } l_2 : \frac{x-2}{2} = \frac{y+1}{1}$$

$$= \frac{z+1}{2}.*$$

Sol. Given equation of lines are

$$\frac{x-1}{1} = \frac{y-2}{-1} = \frac{z-1}{1} \qquad \text{...(i)}$$

and

$$\frac{x-2}{2} = \frac{y+1}{1} = \frac{z+1}{2} \qquad \text{...(ii)}$$

Here, $\quad x_1 = 1, y_1 = 2, z_1 = 1$

$$a_1 = 1, b_1 = -1, c_1 = 1$$

and $\quad x_2 = 2, y_2 = -1, z_2 = -1$

$$a_2 = 2, b_2 = 1, c_2 = 2$$

Now, we know that the shortest distance between two lines is given by

$$d = \frac{\begin{vmatrix} x_2 - x_1 & y_2 - y_1 & z_2 - z_1 \\ a_1 & b_1 & c_1 \\ a_2 & b_2 & c_2 \end{vmatrix}}{\sqrt{(b_1 c_2 - b_2 c_1)^2 + (c_1 a_2 - c_2 a_1)^2 + (a_1 b_2 - a_2 b_1)^2}}$$

$$\therefore \quad d = \frac{\begin{vmatrix} 2-1 & -1-2 & -1-1 \\ 1 & -1 & 1 \\ 2 & 1 & 2 \end{vmatrix}}{\sqrt{(-2-1)^2 + (2-2)^2 + (1+2)^2}}$$

$$\Rightarrow \quad d = \frac{\begin{vmatrix} 1 & -3 & -2 \\ 1 & -1 & 1 \\ 2 & 1 & 2 \end{vmatrix}}{\sqrt{9+0+9}}$$

$$= \left| \frac{1(-2-1) + 3(2-2) - 2(1+2)}{\sqrt{18}} \right|$$

$$= \left| \frac{-3+0-6}{\sqrt{18}} \right| = \frac{9}{3\sqrt{2}} = \frac{3}{\sqrt{2}}$$

Hence, the required shortest distance is $\dfrac{3}{\sqrt{2}}$ units.

94. Find the shortest distance between lines

$$\vec{r} = (1+\lambda)\hat{i} + (2-\lambda)\hat{j} + (\lambda+1)\hat{k}$$

and $\quad \vec{r} = (2\hat{i} - \hat{j} - \hat{k}) + \mu(2\hat{i} + \hat{j} + 2\hat{k})$ *

Sol. Given equation of lines are

$$\vec{r} = (1+\lambda)\hat{i} + (2-\lambda)\hat{j} + (\lambda+1)\hat{k} \quad \text{...(i)}$$

and $\quad \vec{r} = (2\hat{i} - \hat{j} - \hat{k}) + \mu(2\hat{i} + \hat{j} + 2\hat{k}) \quad \text{...(ii)}$

Equation (i) can be written as

$$\vec{r} = \hat{i} + \lambda\hat{i} + 2\hat{j} - \lambda\hat{j} + \lambda\hat{k} + \hat{k}$$

or $\quad \vec{r} = (\hat{i} + 2\hat{j} + \hat{k}) + \lambda(\hat{i} - \hat{j} + \hat{k}) \quad \text{...(iii)}$

Comparing equations (ii) and (iii) with vector form of line $\vec{r} = \vec{a} + \lambda \vec{b}$, we get

$$\vec{a_1} = 2\hat{i} - \hat{j} - \hat{k}, \quad \vec{b_1} = 2\hat{i} + \hat{j} + 2\hat{k}$$

and $\quad \vec{a_2} = \hat{i} + 2\hat{j} + \hat{k}, \quad \vec{b_2} = \hat{i} - \hat{j} + \hat{k}$

Now, we know that shortest distance between two lines is given by

$$d = \left| \frac{(\vec{b_1} \times \vec{b_2}) \cdot (\vec{a_2} - \vec{a_1})}{|\vec{b_1} \times \vec{b_2}|} \right| \qquad \text{...(iv)}$$

Now, $\quad \vec{b_1} \times \vec{b_2} = \begin{vmatrix} \hat{i} & \hat{j} & \hat{k} \\ 2 & 1 & 2 \\ 1 & -1 & 1 \end{vmatrix}$

$$= \hat{i}(1+2) - \hat{j}(2-2) + \hat{k}(-2-1)$$

$$\Rightarrow \quad \vec{b_1} \times \vec{b_2} = 3\hat{i} - 3\hat{k} \qquad \text{...(v)}$$

and $\quad |\vec{b_1} \times \vec{b_2}| = \sqrt{(3)^2 + (-3)^2} = \sqrt{9+9}$

$$= 3\sqrt{2} \qquad \text{...(vi)}$$

Also, $\quad \vec{a_2} - \vec{a_1} = (\hat{i} + 2\hat{j} + \hat{k}) - (2\hat{i} - \hat{j} - \hat{k})$

$$= -\hat{i} + 3\hat{j} + 2\hat{k} \qquad \text{...(vii)}$$

From equations (iv), (v), (vi) and (vii), we get

$$d = \left| \frac{(3\hat{i} - 3\hat{k}) \cdot (-\hat{i} + 3\hat{j} + 2\hat{k})}{3\sqrt{2}} \right|$$

$$= \left| \frac{-3+0-6}{3\sqrt{2}} \right| = \left| \frac{-9}{3\sqrt{2}} \right|$$

$$= \frac{9}{3\sqrt{2}} = \frac{3}{\sqrt{2}}$$

$$\therefore \quad d = \frac{3\sqrt{2}}{2} \text{ units.}$$

95. Find the vector and Cartesian equation of the plane containing the two lines

$$\vec{r} = 2\hat{i} + \hat{j} - 3\hat{k} + \lambda(\hat{i} + 2\hat{j} + 5\hat{k})$$

and $\quad \vec{r} = 3\hat{i} + 3\hat{j} - 7\hat{k} + \mu(3\hat{i} - 2\hat{j} + 5\hat{k})$

Sol. Here $\quad \vec{a} = 2\hat{i} + \hat{j} - 3\hat{k}$

$$\vec{a'} = 3\hat{i} + 3\hat{j} - 7\hat{k}$$

$$\vec{b} = \hat{i} + 2\hat{j} + 5\hat{k}$$

$$\vec{b'} = 3\hat{i} - 2\hat{j} + 5\hat{k}$$

Vector equation of plane is

$$[\vec{r} - (2\hat{i} + \hat{j} - 3\hat{k})].[(\hat{i} + 2\hat{j} + 5\hat{k})$$

$$\times\,(3\hat{i} - 2\hat{j} + 5\hat{k})] = 0$$

$$\vec{b} \times \vec{b} = \begin{vmatrix} \hat{i} & \hat{j} & \hat{k} \\ 1 & 2 & 5 \\ 3 & -2 & 5 \end{vmatrix} = 20\hat{i} + 10\hat{j} - 8\hat{k}$$

$$[\vec{r} - (2\hat{i} + \hat{j} - 3\hat{k})].(20\hat{i} + 10\hat{j} - 8\hat{k}) = 0$$

$$\Rightarrow \quad \vec{r}.(20\hat{i} + 10\hat{j} - 8\hat{k}) - (40 + 10 + 24) = 0$$

$$\Rightarrow \quad \vec{r}.(20\hat{i} + 10\hat{j} - 8\hat{k}) = 74$$

or $\qquad \vec{r}.(10\hat{i} + 5\hat{j} - 4\hat{k}) = 37$ ...(i)

is the required vector equation.

Let $\qquad \vec{r} = x\hat{i} + y\hat{j} + z\hat{k}$

Using this in equation (i), we get

$10x + 5y - 4z = 37$ as the equation of plane in Cartesian form.

96. Find the ratio in which the join of A(2, 1, 5) and B(3, 4, 3) is divided by the plane $2x + 2y - 2z = 1$. Also, find the coordinates of the point of division.

Sol. Suppose the plane $2x + 2y - 2z = 1$ divides the line joining the points A(2, 1, 5) and B(3, 4, 3) at a point C in the ratio $\lambda : 1$.

Then, the coordinates of C are

$$\left(\frac{3\lambda + 2}{\lambda + 1}, \frac{4\lambda + 1}{\lambda + 1}, \frac{3\lambda + 5}{\lambda + 1} \right) \qquad \text{...(i)}$$

Since, the point C lies on the plane $2x + 2y - 2z = 1$, therefore, coordinates of C must satisfy the equation of the plane.

That is,

$$2\left(\frac{3\lambda + 2}{\lambda + 1} \right) + 2\left(\frac{4\lambda + 1}{\lambda + 1} \right) - 2\left(\frac{3\lambda + 5}{\lambda + 1} \right) = 1$$

$$\Rightarrow \qquad 6\lambda + 4 + 8\lambda + 2 - 6\lambda - 10 = \lambda + 1$$

$$\Rightarrow \qquad 8\lambda - 4 = \lambda + 1$$

$$\Rightarrow \qquad 8\lambda - \lambda = 1 + 4$$

$$\Rightarrow \qquad 7\lambda = 5$$

$$\Rightarrow \qquad \lambda = \frac{5}{7}$$

So, the required ratio is $\frac{5}{7} : 1$ or $5 : 7$.

Putting $\lambda = \dfrac{5}{7}$ in (i), the coordinates of the point

of division C are $\left(\dfrac{29}{12}, \dfrac{9}{4}, \dfrac{25}{6} \right)$.

97. Find the direction cosines of the perpendicular from the origin to the plane $\vec{r}.(6\hat{i} - 3\hat{j} - 2\hat{k}) + 1 = 0$.

Sol. The given equation of the plane is

$$\vec{r}.(6\hat{i} - 3\hat{j} - 2\hat{k}) + 1 = 0$$

$$\Rightarrow \qquad \vec{r}.(6\hat{i} - 3\hat{j} - 2\hat{k}) = -1$$

$$\Rightarrow \qquad \vec{r}.\vec{n} = -1 \qquad \text{...(i)}$$

where $\qquad \vec{n} = 6\hat{i} - 3\hat{j} - 2\hat{k}$

Now $\qquad |\vec{n}| = \sqrt{(6)^2 + (-3)^2 + (-2)^2}$

$$= \sqrt{36 + 9 + 4}$$

$$= \sqrt{49} = 7$$

Therefore, from (i), we have

$$\vec{r}.\vec{n} = -1$$

$$\Rightarrow \qquad \vec{r} \cdot \frac{\vec{n}}{|\vec{n}|} = \frac{-1}{|\vec{n}|}$$

$$\Rightarrow \qquad \vec{r}.\hat{n} = p$$

where $\qquad \hat{n} = \dfrac{\vec{n}}{|\vec{n}|}$

$$= \frac{6}{7}\hat{i} - \frac{3}{7}\hat{j} - \frac{2}{7}\hat{k}$$

and $\qquad p = \dfrac{-1}{7}.$

Therefore, direction cosines of $\hat{n}$ are $\dfrac{6}{7}, \dfrac{-3}{7}, \dfrac{-2}{7}.$

98. Find the vector equation of the plane passing through the intersection of the planes $\vec{r}.(2\hat{i} - 7\hat{j} + 4\hat{k}) = 3$ and $\vec{r}.(3\hat{i} - 5\hat{j} + 4\hat{k}) + 11 = 0$ and passing through the point $(-2, 1, 3)$.

Sol. The equations of the given planes are

$$\vec{r}.\vec{n}_1 = d_1 \text{ and } \vec{r}.\vec{n}_2 = d_2$$

where $\qquad \vec{r}.\vec{n}_1 = \vec{r}.(2\hat{i} - 7\hat{j} + 4\hat{k})$

$$\vec{r}.\vec{n}_2 = \vec{r}.(3\hat{i} - 5\hat{j} + 4\hat{k})$$

$$d_1 = 3 \text{ and } d_2 = -11$$

Therefore, the equation of the plane passing through the intersection of these two planes is

$$\vec{r}.(\vec{n}_1 + \lambda\,\vec{n}_2) = d_1 + \lambda d_2 \qquad \text{...(i)}$$

$$\Rightarrow \vec{r}.[\hat{i}(2 + 3\lambda) - \hat{j}(7 + 5\lambda) + \hat{k}(4 + 4\lambda)]$$

$$= 3 - 11\lambda \qquad \text{...(ii)}$$

If equation (ii) passes through $(-2, 1, 3)$, then the

vector $(-2\hat{i} + \hat{j} + 3\hat{k})$ should satisfy it.

$\therefore$ $(-2\hat{i}+\hat{j}+3\hat{k}).[\hat{i}(2+3\lambda)-\hat{j}(7+5\lambda)+\hat{k}(4+4\lambda)]$

$$= 3 - 11\lambda$$
$$\Rightarrow -2(2+3\lambda)+1(-7-5\lambda)+3(4+4\lambda) = 3-11\lambda$$
$$\Rightarrow -4-6\lambda-7-5\lambda+12+12\lambda = 3-11\lambda$$
$$\Rightarrow 1+\lambda = 3-11\lambda$$
$$\Rightarrow 12\lambda = 2$$
$$\Rightarrow \lambda = \frac{1}{6}$$

Substituting the value of λ in equation (ii), we get

$$\vec{r}.\left[\hat{i}\left(2+3.\frac{1}{6}\right)-\hat{j}\left(7+5.\frac{1}{6}\right)+\hat{k}\left(4+4.\frac{1}{6}\right)\right]$$

$$= 3-11\cdot\frac{1}{6}$$

$$\Rightarrow \vec{r}.\left[\frac{5}{2}\hat{i}-\frac{47}{6}\hat{j}+\frac{14}{3}\hat{k}\right] = \frac{7}{6}$$

$$\Rightarrow \vec{r}.[15\hat{i}-47\hat{j}+28\hat{k}] = 7$$

Hence $\vec{r}.[15\hat{i}-47\hat{j}+28\hat{k}] = 7$ is the required equation of the plane.

99. Write the equation of the plane whose intercepts on the coordinate axes are -4, 2 and 3.

Sol. We know that the equation of a plane whose intercepts on the coordinate axes are a, b and c respectively is

$$\frac{x}{a}+\frac{y}{b}+\frac{z}{c} = 1$$

Here, $a = -4, b = 2$ and $c = 3$

So, the equation of the required plane is

$$\frac{x}{-4}+\frac{y}{2}+\frac{z}{3} = 1$$

$$\Rightarrow \frac{-3x+6y+4z}{12} = 1$$

$$\Rightarrow -3x+6y+4z = 12$$

Therefore, $3x-6y-4z+12 = 0$.

This is the equation of the required plane.

100. Find the equation of plane (s) passing through the intersection of planes $x+3y+6 = 0$ and $3x-y-4z = 0$ whose perpendicular distance from origin is unity.*

Sol. Let the required equation of plane is

$$(x+3y+6)+\lambda(3x-y-4z) = 0 \quad …(i)$$

Above equation can be written as

$$x+3y+6+3\lambda x-\lambda y-4\lambda z = 0$$

$$\Rightarrow x(1+3\lambda)+y(3-\lambda)-4\lambda z+6 = 0 \quad …(ii)$$

Which is the general form of equation of plane.

Now, given that perpendicular distance of plane (i) from origin, *i.e.*, $(0, 0, 0)$ is unity, *i.e.*, one.

$\because$ Distance of point (x_1, y_1, z_1) from a plane $ax+by+cz+d = 0$ is given as

$$d = \left|\frac{ax_1+by_1+cz_1+d}{\sqrt{a^2+b^2+c^2}}\right|$$

Here $a = 1+3\lambda, b = 3-\lambda, c = -4\lambda$

$(x_1, y_1, z_1) = (0, 0, 0)$

$\therefore$ We have

$$\left|\frac{(1+3\lambda)(0)+(3-\lambda)(0)-(4\lambda)(0)+6}{\sqrt{(1+3\lambda)^2+(3-\lambda)^2+(-4\lambda)^2}}\right| = 1$$

$$\Rightarrow \left|\frac{6}{\sqrt{1+9\lambda^2+6\lambda+9+\lambda^2-6\lambda+16\lambda^2}}\right| = 1$$

$$\Rightarrow \frac{6}{\sqrt{26\lambda^2+10}} = 1$$

$$\Rightarrow 6 = \sqrt{26\lambda^2+10}$$

Squaring both sides, we get

$$36 = 26\lambda^2+10$$

$$\Rightarrow 26\lambda^2 = 26$$

$$\Rightarrow \lambda^2 = 1$$

$$\Rightarrow \lambda = \pm 1$$

Now putting $\lambda = 1$ in equation (i), we get

$$x+3y+6+3x-y-4z = 0$$

$$\Rightarrow 4x+2y-4z+6 = 0$$

$$\Rightarrow 2x+y-2z+3 = 0 \quad …(iii)$$

And putting $\lambda = -1$ in equation (i), we get

$$x+3y+6-3x+y+4z = 0$$

$$\Rightarrow -2x+4y+4z+6 = 0$$

$$\Rightarrow x-2y-2z-3 = 0 \quad …(iv)$$

Equations (iii) and (iv) are the required equations of the plane.

101. Find the equation of plane that contains the point $(1, -1, 2)$ and is perpendicular to each of planes $2x+3y-2z = 5$ and $x+2y-3z = 8$.*

Sol. Equation of plane passing through point $(1, -1, 2)$ is given by

$$a(x-1)+b(y+1)+c(z-2) = 0 \quad …(i)$$

Now, given that plane (i) is perpendicular to planes

$$2x+3y-2z = 5 \quad …(ii)$$

and $$x+2y-3z = 8 \quad …(iii)$$

We know that when two planes $a_1x+b_1y+c_1z = d_1$ and $a_2x+b_2y+c_2z = d_2$ are perpendicular then

$$a_1a_2+b_1b_2+c_1c_2 = 0$$

$\therefore$ we get

$$2a+3b-2c = 0 \quad \text{[from eq. (i) and (ii)]}$$

and $$a+2b-3c = 0 \quad \text{[from eq. (i) and (iii)]}$$

or we may write

$$2a+3b = 2c \quad …(iv)$$

$$a+2b = 3c \quad …(v)$$

Multiplying equation (v) by 2 and subtracting it from equation (iv), we get

$$2a + 3b = 2c$$
$$2a + 4b = 6c$$
$$\overline{}$$
$$-b = -4c$$
$$\Rightarrow \quad b = 4c$$

Putting $b = 4c$ in equation (v), we get

$$a + 8c = 3c$$
$$\Rightarrow \quad a = -5c$$

Now, putting $a = -5c$ and $b = 4c$ in equation (i), we get the required equation of plane as

$$-5c(x-1) + 4c(y+1) + c(z-2) = 0$$
$$\Rightarrow \quad -5(x-1) + 4(y+1) + (z-2) = 0$$

(divide both sides by 'c')

$$\Rightarrow \quad -5x + 5 + 4y + 4 + z - 2 = 0$$
$$\Rightarrow \quad 5x - 4y - z - 7 = 0.$$

102. Find the value of λ for which the points with position vector $\hat{i} - \hat{j} + 3\hat{k}$ and $3\hat{i} + \lambda\hat{j} + 3\hat{k}$ are equidistant from the plane $\vec{r} \cdot (5\hat{i} + 2\hat{j} - 7\hat{k}) + 9 = 0$.

Sol. Distance of point $\hat{i} - \hat{j} + 3\hat{k}$ and $\vec{r} \cdot (5\hat{i} + 2\hat{j} - 7\hat{k}) + 9 = 0$ is

$$d_1 = \left| \frac{(\hat{i} - \hat{j} + 3\hat{k}).(5\hat{i} + 2\hat{j} - 7\hat{k}) + 9}{\sqrt{5^2 + 2^2 + 7^2}} \right|$$

$$d_1 = \left| \frac{5 - 2 - 21 + 9}{\sqrt{78}} \right|$$

$$d_1 = \frac{9}{\sqrt{78}}$$

Distance of $\vec{b'} = 3\hat{i} + \lambda\hat{j} + 3\hat{k}$ from the plane, $\vec{r} \cdot (5\hat{i} + 2\hat{j} - 7\hat{k}) + 9 = 0$ is

$$d_2 = \left| \frac{(3\hat{i} + \lambda\hat{j} + 3\hat{k}).(5\hat{i} + 2\hat{j} - 7\hat{k}) + 9}{\sqrt{78}} \right|$$

$$= \left| \frac{15 + 2\lambda - 21 + 9}{\sqrt{78}} \right|$$

$$= \left| \frac{3 + 2\lambda}{\sqrt{78}} \right| = \frac{3 + 2\lambda}{\sqrt{78}}$$

$$\because \quad d_1 = d_2 \quad \text{(given)}$$

$$\therefore \quad \frac{9}{\sqrt{78}} = \frac{3 + 2\lambda}{\sqrt{78}}$$

$$\Rightarrow \quad 6 = 2\lambda$$
$$\Rightarrow \quad \lambda = 3.$$

103. Find the distance of the point $(-1, -5, -10)$ from the point of intersection of the line $\dfrac{x-2}{3} = \dfrac{y+1}{4} = \dfrac{z-2}{12}$ and the plane $x - y + z = 5$.

Sol. Equation of the given line is

$$\frac{x-2}{3} = \frac{y+1}{4} = \frac{z-2}{12} = k \text{ (say)}$$

$$\Rightarrow \quad x = 3k + 2$$
$$\Rightarrow \quad y = 4k - 1$$
$$\Rightarrow \quad z = 12k + 2$$

The coordinates of any point P on the line are

$$(3k + 2, 4k - 1, 12k + 2) \qquad \text{...(i)}$$

Now, P will be the point of intersection of the line and the plane only when P lies on the plane also.

The equation of the plane is

$$x - y + z = 5$$

As P lies on it therefore, we have

$$(3k + 2) - (4k - 1) + (12k + 2) = 5$$
$$\Rightarrow \quad 11k + 5 = 5$$
$$\Rightarrow \quad 11k = 0$$
$$\Rightarrow \quad k = 0$$

Putting the value of k in (i), we get the coordinates of the point of intersection of the line and plane as $(2, -1, 2)$.

Now, distance of the point $(-1, -5, -10)$ from the point P is given by

$$d = \sqrt{(2+1)^2 + (-1+5)^2 + (2+10)^2}$$
$$= \sqrt{(3)^2 + (4)^2 + (12)^2}$$
$$= \sqrt{9 + 16 + 144}$$
$$= \sqrt{169} = 13$$

Therefore, the required distance is 13 units.

104. Find the equation of the plane passing through the points $(-1, 2, 0)$, $(2, 2, -1)$ and parallel to the line·

$$\frac{x-1}{1} = \frac{2y+1}{2} = \frac{z+1}{-1}. \text{ *}$$

Sol. The equation of a plane passing through $(-1, 2, 0)$ is

$$a(x+1) + b(y-2) + c(z-0) = 0 \qquad \text{...(i)}$$

It also passes through $(2, 2, -1)$.

$$\therefore \quad a(2+1) + b(2-2) + c(-1-0) = 0$$
$$3a + 0b - c = 0 \qquad \text{...(ii)}$$

The given line is

$$\frac{x-1}{1} = \frac{2y+1}{2} = \frac{z+1}{-1}$$

$$\textit{i.e.,} \quad \frac{x-1}{1} = \frac{y+1/2}{1} = \frac{z+1}{-1}$$

$\therefore$ d.r.'s of line are 1, 1, – 1.

The plane (i) is parallel to the given line

$$a + b - c = 0 \qquad \ldots(iii)$$

Solving (ii) and (iii) by cross multiplication, we get

$$\frac{a}{1} = \frac{b}{2} = \frac{c}{3}$$

i.e., direction ratios of normal to the plane are 1, 2, 3.

$$\therefore \qquad 1(x + 1) + 2(y - 2) + 3(z - 0) = 0$$

i.e., $\qquad x + 2y + 3z = 3.$

which is the required equation of plane.

105. Find out that the following lines are coplanar or not

$$\vec{r} = 2\hat{i} + \hat{j} - 3\hat{k} + \lambda(\hat{i} + 2\hat{j} + 5\hat{k})$$

and $\qquad \vec{r}' = 3\hat{i} + 3\hat{j} - 7\hat{k} + \mu(3\hat{i} - 2\hat{j} + 5\hat{k})$

Sol. Here $\qquad \vec{a} = 2\hat{i} + \hat{j} - 3\hat{k},$

$$\vec{a}' = 3\hat{i} + 3\hat{j} - 7\hat{k},$$

$$\vec{b} = \hat{i} + 2\hat{j} + 5\hat{k}$$

$$\vec{b}' = 3\hat{i} - 2\hat{j} + 5\hat{k}$$

Lines are coplanar if

$$(\vec{a}' - \vec{a}) . (\vec{b} \times \vec{b}') = 0 \qquad \ldots(A)$$

Now, $\qquad \vec{a}' - \vec{a} = \hat{i} + 2\hat{j} - 4\hat{k} \qquad \ldots(i)$

and $\qquad \vec{b} \times \vec{b}' = \begin{vmatrix} \hat{i} & \hat{j} & \hat{k} \\ 1 & 2 & 5 \\ 3 & -2 & 5 \end{vmatrix} \qquad \ldots(ii)$

Using (i) and (ii) in (A), we get

$$(\hat{i} + 2\hat{j} - 4\hat{k}) . (20\hat{i} + 10\hat{j} - 8\hat{k})$$

$$= 20 + 20 - 32$$

$$= 8 \neq 0$$

So, the lines are not coplanar.

106. Find the equation of the plane passing through the point (– 1, 2, 1) and perpendicular to the line joining the points (– 3, 1, 2) and (2, 3, 4). Find also the perpendicular distance from origin to the plane.

Sol. The required plane passes through the point (– 1, 2, 1) having position vector $\vec{a} = -\hat{i} + 2\hat{j} + \hat{k}$ and is perpendicular to the line joining the points A(– 3, 1, 2) and B(2, 3, 4).

Therefore, a vector normal to the plane is given by

$$\vec{n} = \vec{AB}$$

= Position vector of B – Position vector of A

$$= (2\hat{i} + 3\hat{j} + 4\hat{k}) - (-3\hat{i} + \hat{j} + 2\hat{k})$$

$$= 5\hat{i} + 2\hat{j} + 2\hat{k}$$

We know that the vector equation of a plane passing through a point having position vector $\vec{a}$ and normal to vector $\vec{n}$ is given by

$$(\vec{r} - \vec{a}) . \vec{n} = 0$$

$$\Rightarrow \qquad \vec{r} . \vec{n} = \vec{a} . \vec{n}$$

Therefore, the equation of the required plane is

$$\vec{r} . (5\hat{i} + 2\hat{j} + 2\hat{k}) = (-\hat{i} + 2\hat{j} + \hat{k}) . (5\hat{i} + 2\hat{j} + 2\hat{k})$$

$$\Rightarrow \quad \vec{r} . (5\hat{i} + 2\hat{j} + 2\hat{k}) = (-1)(5) + (2)(2) + (1)(2)$$

$$= -5 + 4 + 2 = 1$$

$$\Rightarrow \quad \vec{r} . (5\hat{i} + 2\hat{j} + 2\hat{k}) = 1 \qquad \ldots(i)$$

To find the distance of this plane from the origin, we reduce its equation to normal form.

We have

$$\vec{n} = 5\hat{i} + 2\hat{j} + 2\hat{k}$$

$$\Rightarrow \qquad |\vec{n}| = \sqrt{(5)^2 + (2)^2 + (2)^2}$$

$$= \sqrt{25 + 4 + 4}$$

$$\Rightarrow \qquad |\vec{n}| = \sqrt{33}$$

Dividing (i) throughout by

$$|\vec{n}| = \sqrt{33}$$

$$\Rightarrow$$

We get $\quad \vec{r} . \left(\dfrac{5}{\sqrt{33}} \hat{i} + \dfrac{2}{\sqrt{33}} \hat{j} + \dfrac{2}{\sqrt{33}} \hat{k} \right) = \dfrac{1}{\sqrt{33}}$

So, the perpendicular distance from the origin to the plane is $\dfrac{1}{\sqrt{33}}$ units.

107. Find the Cartesian equation of the plane passing through points A(0, 0, 0) and B(3, – 1, 2), parallel to the line $\dfrac{x - 4}{1} = \dfrac{y + 3}{-4} = \dfrac{z + 1}{7}$.*

Sol. Equation of plane passing through the point A(0, 0, 0) is

$$a(x - 0) + b(y - 0) + c(z - 0) = 0$$

$$\Rightarrow \qquad ax + by + cz = 0 \qquad \ldots(i)$$

Since, the plane (i) passes through the point B(3, – 1, 2).

Put $x = 3, y = -1, z = 2$ in equation (i), we get

$$3a - b + 2c = 0 \qquad \ldots(ii)$$

Also, the plane (i) is parallel to the line

$$\frac{x - 4}{1} = \frac{y + 3}{-4} = \frac{z + 1}{7}$$

If the plane is parallel to the line, then normal to the plane is perpendicular to the line.

$$\therefore \qquad a_1a_2 + b_1b_2 + c_1c_2 = 0$$
$$\therefore \qquad a(1) + b(-4) + c(7) = 0$$
$$\Rightarrow \qquad a - 4b + 7c = 0 \qquad \text{...(iii)}$$

Now, multiplying equation (iii) by 3 and subtracting it from equation (ii), we get

$$3a - b + 2c = 0$$
$$3a - 12b + 21c = 0$$
$$\underline{\quad - \quad + \qquad - \qquad\qquad}$$
$$11b - 19c = 0$$

$$\Rightarrow \qquad b = \frac{19}{11}c$$

Putting $b = \dfrac{19}{11}c$ in equation (ii), we get

$$3a - \frac{19c}{11} + 2c = 0$$

$$\Rightarrow \qquad 3a + \frac{-19c + 22c}{11} = 0$$

$$\Rightarrow \qquad 3a + \frac{3c}{11} = 0$$

$$\Rightarrow \qquad 3a = -\frac{3c}{11} \Rightarrow a = -\frac{c}{11}$$

Now, putting $a = -\dfrac{c}{11}$ and $b = \dfrac{19}{11}c$ in equation (i), we get the required equation of plane as

$$-\frac{c}{11}x + \frac{19c}{11}y + cz = 0$$

$$\Rightarrow \qquad -\frac{x}{11} + \frac{19y}{11} + z = 0$$

$$\Rightarrow \qquad -x + 19y + 11z = 0$$

$$\Rightarrow \qquad x - 19y - 11z = 0.$$

Long Answer Type Questions

108. Find the direction cosines of the two lines which are connected by the relations.

$$l - 5m + 3n = 0 \text{ and } 7l^2 + 5m^2 - 3n^2 = 0.$$

Sol. Given lines are,

$$l - 5m + 3n = 0 \qquad \text{...(i)}$$
$$7l^2 + 5m^2 - 3n^2 = 0 \qquad \text{...(ii)}$$

Putting $l = (5m - 3n)$ from (i) into (ii), we get

$$7(5m - 3n)^2 + 5m^2 - 3n^2 = 0$$
$$\Rightarrow \quad 175m^2 + 63n^2 - 210mn + 5m^2 - 3n^2 = 0$$
$$\Rightarrow \quad 180m^2 + 60n^2 - 210\,mn = 0$$
$$\text{or} \qquad 6m^2 - 7mn + 2n^2 = 0$$

$$\text{or} \qquad 6\left(\frac{m}{n}\right)^2 - 7\left(\frac{m}{n}\right) + 2 = 0$$

$$\text{or} \qquad 6p^2 - 7p + 2 = 0$$

$$\text{where} \qquad p = \frac{m}{n}$$

$$\text{or} \qquad (3p - 2)(2p - 1) = 0$$

$$\therefore \qquad p = \frac{2}{3} \text{ or } p = \frac{1}{2}$$

So, $m/n = 2/3$ or $m/n = 1/2$ (since $p = m/n$)

Now
$$\frac{m}{n} = \frac{2}{3}$$

$$\Rightarrow \qquad \frac{m}{2} = \frac{n}{3}$$

$$\Rightarrow \qquad \frac{5m - 3n}{5 \times 2 - 3 \times 3} = \frac{l}{1} \qquad [\because\ 5m - 3n = l]$$

Thus, $\qquad \dfrac{l}{1} = \dfrac{m}{2} = \dfrac{n}{3}$

$$= \frac{\sqrt{l^2 + m^2 + n^2}}{1^2 + 2^2 + 3^2} = \frac{1}{\sqrt{14}}$$

$$\therefore \qquad l = \frac{1}{\sqrt{14}},\ m = \frac{2}{\sqrt{14}},\ n = \frac{3}{\sqrt{14}}$$

Again $\qquad \dfrac{m}{n} = \dfrac{1}{2} \Rightarrow \dfrac{m}{1} = \dfrac{n}{2}$

$$\Rightarrow \qquad \frac{5m - 3n}{5 \times 1 - 3 \times 2} = \frac{l}{-1}$$

Therefore $\qquad \dfrac{l}{-1} = \dfrac{m}{1} = \dfrac{n}{2}$

$$= \frac{\sqrt{l^2 + m^2 + n^2}}{\sqrt{(-1^2) + 1^2 + 2^2}} = \frac{1}{\sqrt{6}}$$

So $\qquad l = \dfrac{-1}{\sqrt{6}},\ m = \dfrac{1}{\sqrt{6}}$ and $n = \dfrac{2}{\sqrt{6}}$

Hence, the direction cosines of the lines are

$$\left(\frac{1}{\sqrt{14}}, \frac{2}{\sqrt{14}}, \frac{3}{\sqrt{14}}\right) \text{ and } \left(\frac{-1}{\sqrt{6}}, \frac{1}{\sqrt{6}}, \frac{2}{\sqrt{6}}\right)$$

109. Show that the straight lines whose direction cosines are given by the equations $al + bm + cn = 0$ and $ul^2 + vm^2 + wn^2 = 0$ are perpendicular. If $a^2(v + w) + b^2(u + w) + c^2(v + u) = 0$ are parallel, then show that

$$\frac{a^2}{u} + \frac{b^2}{v} + \frac{c^2}{w} = 0.$$

Sol. Given, $\qquad al + bm + cn = 0 \qquad \text{...(i)}$

and $\qquad ul^2 + vm^2 + wn^2 = 0 \qquad \text{...(ii)}$

Putting $l = -\dfrac{(bm + cn)}{a}$ from (i) into (ii), we get

$$\frac{u[-(bm+cn)]^2}{a^2} + vm^2 + wn^2 = 0$$

$$\Rightarrow \quad \frac{u(b^2m^2 + c^2n^2 + 2bcmn)}{a^2} + vm^2 + wn^2 = 0$$

$$\Rightarrow (ub^2 + va^2)\,m^2 + (uc^2 + wa^2)\,n^2 + 2u\,b\,c\,mn = 0$$

$$\text{or} \quad (b^2u + a^2v)\left(\frac{m}{n}\right)^2 + 2ubc\left(\frac{m}{n}\right)$$

$$+ (c^2u + a^2w) = 0$$

$$\text{[dividing throughout by } n^2 \text{]} \quad \text{...(iii)}$$

Let $\dfrac{m_1}{n_1}$ and $\dfrac{m_2}{n_2}$ be the roots of (iii).

Then, $\quad \dfrac{m_1}{n_1} \cdot \dfrac{m_2}{n_2} = \dfrac{c^2u + a^2w}{b^2u + a^2v}$

$$\therefore \quad \frac{m_1 m_2}{c^2u + a^2w} = \frac{n_1 n_2}{b^2u + a^2v} = \frac{l_1 l_2}{b^2w + c^2v} = k$$

$$\text{[by symmetry]}$$

So, $l_1 l_2 + m_1 m_2 + n_1 n_2$
$$= k(b^2w + c^2v + c^2u + a^2w + b^2u + a^2v)$$

For perpendicularity,

we have $\quad l_1 l_2 + m_1 m_2 + n_1 n_2 = 0$

i.e., $\quad a^2(v + w) + b^2(w + u) + c^2(u + v) = 0$

For the given lines to be parallel, the direction cosines must be equal and so the roots of (iii) must be equal.

Thus, we must have

$$4u^2b^2c^2 - 4(b^2u + a^2v) \times (c^2u + a^2w) = 0$$

$$\Rightarrow u^2b^2c^2 = b^2c^2u^2 + b^2c^2wu + a^2vuc^2 + a^4vw$$

or $\quad \dfrac{a^2}{u} + \dfrac{b^2}{v} + \dfrac{c^2}{w} = 0.$

$$\text{(Dividing throught by } a^2uvw\text{)}$$

110. Prove that the lines whose direction cosines are given by $al + bm + cn = 0$ and $fmn + gnl + hlm = 0$ are

(i) perpendicular if $\dfrac{f}{a} + \dfrac{g}{b} + \dfrac{h}{c} = 0$ and

(ii) parallel if $a^2f^2 + b^2g^2 + c^2h^2$
$$- 2(bcgh + cahf + abfg) = 0.$$

Sol. Given that

$$al + bm + cn = 0 \qquad \text{...(i)}$$

and $\quad fmn + gnl + hlm = 0 \qquad \text{...(ii)}$

From (i), $\quad al + bm = -cn$

$$\Rightarrow \quad n = -\left(\frac{al + bm}{c}\right) \qquad \text{...(iii)}$$

Substituting this value of n in (ii), we get

$$(fm + gl)\left(-\frac{al + bm}{c}\right) + hlm = 0$$

$$\Rightarrow \quad -(fm + gl)(al + bm) + hlmc = 0$$
$$\Rightarrow -aflm - agl^2 - bfm^2 - bglm + chlm = 0$$
$$\Rightarrow \quad agl^2 + (af + bg - ch)lm + bfm^2 = 0 \quad \text{...(iv)}$$

We note that both l and m cannot be zero.

For, if $\qquad\qquad l = m = 0$

Then from (iii), we get $n = 0$

which is wrong as $l^2 + m^2 + n^2 = 1$.

So, without any loss of generality we may take $m \neq 0$.

Dividing both sides of (iv) by m^2, we get

$$ag\left(\frac{l}{m}\right)^2 + (af + bg - ch)\left(\frac{l}{m}\right) + bf = 0 \quad \text{...(v)}$$

The above equation is quadratic in $\left(\dfrac{l}{m}\right)$ giving two values of $\left(\dfrac{l}{m}\right)$.

If (l_1, m_1, n_1) and (l_2, m_2, n_2) are the direction cosines of the two given line (i) and (ii), then

$\dfrac{l_1}{m_1}, \dfrac{l_2}{m_2}$ are roots of equation (v)

Therefore product of root $= \dfrac{bf}{ag}$

$$\Rightarrow \quad \left(\frac{l_1}{m_1}\right)\left(\frac{l_2}{m_2}\right) = \frac{bf}{ag}$$

$$\Rightarrow \quad \frac{l_1 l_2}{m_1 m_2} = \frac{f/a}{g/b}$$

$$\Rightarrow \quad \frac{l_1 l_2}{f/a} = \frac{m_1 m_2}{g/b}$$

$$\Rightarrow \quad \frac{l_1 l_2}{f/a} = \frac{m_1 m_2}{g/b} = \frac{n_1 n_2}{h/c}$$

$$\text{[By symmetry of result]}$$

Let $\quad \dfrac{l_1 l_2}{f/a} = \dfrac{m_1 m_2}{g/b} = \dfrac{n_1 n_2}{h/c} = \lambda$

where λ is a non-zero real number.

$$l_1 l_2 = \lambda \cdot \frac{f}{a},\ m_1 m_2 = \lambda \cdot \frac{g}{b},\ n_1 n_2 = \lambda \cdot \frac{h}{c}$$

Now, these lines whose direction cosines are given by (i) and (ii) are at right angles.

If $\qquad l_1 l_2 + m_1 m_2 + n_1 n_2 = 0$

i.e., if $\quad \lambda\dfrac{f}{a} + \lambda\dfrac{g}{b} + \lambda\dfrac{h}{c} = 0$

i.e., if $\quad \dfrac{f}{a} + \dfrac{g}{b} + \dfrac{h}{c} = 0$

Also, the two lines will be parallel if,
$$l_1 = l_2, \ m_1 = m_2, \ n_1 = n_2$$

i.e., if
$$\frac{l_1}{m_1} = \frac{l_2}{m_2}$$

i.e., if equation (v) has equal roots.

i.e., if discriminant of (v) is zero.

i.e., if $(af + bg - ch)^2 - 4agbf = 0$

i.e., if $a^2f^2 + b^2g^2 + c^2h^2 + 2abfg - 2bgch$
$$- 2afch - 4agbf = 0$$

i.e., if $a^2f^2 + b^2g^2 + c^2h^2 - 2(bcgh + cahf + abfg) = 0$.

111. Find the image of the point (1, 6, 3) on the line $\dfrac{x}{1} = \dfrac{y-1}{2} = \dfrac{z-2}{3}$. Also, write the equation of the line joining the given points and its image and find the length of segment joining given point and its image.*

Sol. Here, T is the image of point P(1, 6, 3). Q is the foot of perpendicular PQ on the line AB.

First, we find Q.

Equation of line *AB* is given by

$$\frac{x}{1} = \frac{y-1}{2} = \frac{z-2}{3} \qquad ...(i)$$

Let
$$\frac{x}{1} = \frac{y-1}{2} = \frac{z-2}{3} = \lambda \ (\text{say})$$

$$\Rightarrow \qquad x = \lambda, \ y - 1 = 2\lambda, \ z - 2 = 3\lambda$$
$$\Rightarrow \qquad x = \lambda, \ y = 2\lambda + 1, \ z = 3\lambda + 2$$

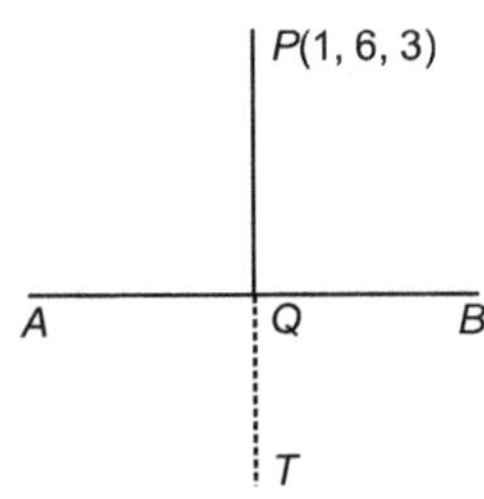

Let coordinates of
$$Q = (\lambda, 2\lambda + 1, 3\lambda + 2) \qquad ...(ii)$$

Now, direction ratios of line
$$PQ = (\lambda - 1, 2\lambda + 1 - 6, 3\lambda + 2 - 3)$$

$\therefore$ Direction ratios of PQ $= (\lambda - 1, 2\lambda - 5, 3\lambda - 1)$

Now, line $\qquad\qquad PQ \perp AB$

$\therefore \qquad\qquad a_1a_2 + b_1b_2 + c_1c_2 = 0$

Where $a_1 = \lambda - 1, \ b_1 = 2\lambda - 5, \ c_1 = 3\lambda - 1$

and $\qquad\qquad a_2 = 1, \ b_2 = 2, \ c_2 = 3$

$\therefore 1(\lambda - 1) + 2(2\lambda - 5) + 3(3\lambda - 1) = 0$

$\Rightarrow \qquad \lambda - 1 + 4\lambda - 10 + 9\lambda - 3 = 0$

$\Rightarrow \qquad\qquad\qquad 14\lambda - 14 = 0$

$\Rightarrow \qquad\qquad\qquad\qquad \lambda = 1$

Putting $\lambda = 1$ in equation (ii), we get
$$Q(1, 2 + 1, 3 + 2) = (1, 3, 5)$$

Now, as discussed earlier Q is the mid-point of PT.

Let coordinates of T $= (x, y, z)$

$\therefore$ Using by mid-point formula,
$$Q = \text{Mid-point of } P(1, 6, 3) \text{ and } T(x, y, z)$$
$$= \left(\frac{x+1}{2}, \frac{y+6}{2}, \frac{z+3}{2}\right)$$

But $\qquad\qquad Q = (1, 3, 5)$

$\therefore \left(\dfrac{x+1}{2}, \dfrac{y+6}{2}, \dfrac{z+3}{2}\right) = (1, 3, 5)$

$\Rightarrow \qquad \dfrac{x+1}{2} = 1, \ \dfrac{y+6}{2} = 3, \dfrac{z+3}{2} = 5$

$\Rightarrow \qquad x = 2 - 1, \ y = 6 - 6, \ z = 10 - 3$

$\Rightarrow \qquad\qquad x = 1, \ y = 0, \ z = 7$

$\therefore$ Coordinates of T $= (x, y, z) = (1, 0, 7)$

Hence, coordinates of image of point
$$P(1, 6, 3) = T(1, 0, 7).$$

112. The points A(4, 5, 10), B(2, 3, 4) and C(1, 2, – 1) are three vertices of parallelogram ABCD. Find the vector equations of sides AB and BC and also find coordinates of point D.*

Sol. First, we find vector equation of AB where A(4, 5, 10) and B(2, 3, 4).

We know that two points vector formula of line is given by

$$\vec{r} = \vec{a} + \lambda(\vec{b} - \vec{a}) \qquad ...(i)$$

Where a and b are the position vector of points through which the line is passing through.

Here $\quad \vec{a} = \overrightarrow{OA} = 4\hat{i} + 5\hat{j} + 10\hat{k}$

$$\vec{b} = \overrightarrow{OB} = 2\hat{i} + 3\hat{j} + 4\hat{k}$$

$\therefore$ Using equation (i), required equation of line AB is

$$\vec{r} = (4\hat{i} + 5\hat{j} + 10\hat{k}) + \lambda[(2\hat{i} + 3\hat{j} + 4\hat{k})$$
$$- (4\hat{i} + 5\hat{j} + 10\hat{k})]$$

$$\vec{r} = (4\hat{i} + 5\hat{j} + 10\hat{k}) + \lambda(-2\hat{i} - 2\hat{j} - 6\hat{k})$$

Similarly, vector equation of line BC where B(2, 3, 4) and C(1, 2, – 1) is

$$\vec{r} = (2\hat{i} + 3\hat{j} + 4\hat{k}) + \lambda[(\hat{i} + 2\hat{j} - \hat{k}) - (2\hat{i} + 3\hat{j} + 4\hat{k})]$$

$$\vec{r} = (2\hat{i} + 3\hat{j} + 4\hat{k}) + \lambda(-\hat{i} - \hat{j} - 5\hat{k})$$

Now let the coordinates of D be (x, y, z).

Mid-point of diagonal BD = Mid-point of diagonal AC.

$(\because$ diagonals of a parallelogram bisect each other)

$$\therefore \left(\frac{x+2}{2},\frac{y+3}{2},\frac{z+4}{2}\right) = \left(\frac{4+1}{2},\frac{5+2}{2},\frac{10-1}{2}\right)$$

Comparing corresponding coordinates

$$\Rightarrow \qquad \frac{x+2}{2} = \frac{5}{2}, \frac{y+3}{2} = \frac{7}{2}, \frac{z+4}{2} = \frac{9}{2}$$

$$\Rightarrow \qquad x = 3, y = 4, z = 5$$

$\therefore$ Coordinates of point $D(x, y, z) = (3, 4, 5)$.

113. Find the vector and cartesian equations of a line passing through $(1, 2, -4)$ and perpendicular to the two lines

$$\frac{x-8}{3} = \frac{y+19}{-16} = \frac{z-10}{7} \text{ and} \frac{x-15}{3} = \frac{y-29}{8} = \frac{z-5}{-5}.*$$

Sol. Cartesian equation of the line passing through $(1, 2 - 4)$ is

$$\frac{x-1}{a} = \frac{y-2}{b} = \frac{z+4}{c} \qquad \text{...(i)}$$

Given lines are

$$\frac{x-8}{3} = \frac{y+19}{-16} = \frac{z-10}{7} \qquad \text{...(ii)}$$

and

$$\frac{x-15}{3} = \frac{y-29}{8} = \frac{z-5}{-5} \qquad \text{...(iii)}$$

Let $\vec{b_1}, \vec{b_2}, \vec{b_3}$ are parallel vectors of (i), (ii) and (iii) respectively.

$\therefore$

$$\vec{b_1} = a\hat{i}+b\hat{j}+c\hat{k}$$

$$\vec{b_2} = 3\hat{i}-16\hat{j}+7\hat{k}$$

$$\vec{b_3} = 3\hat{i}+8\hat{j}-5\hat{k}$$

Given that (i) is perpendicular to both (ii) and (iii)

$\therefore$

$$\vec{b_1}.\vec{b_2} = 0$$

$$\Rightarrow \quad 3a - 16b + 7c = 0 \qquad \text{...(iv)}$$

and

$$\vec{b_1}.\vec{b_3} = 0$$

$$\Rightarrow \quad 3a + 8b - 5c = 0 \qquad \text{...(v)}$$

From equations (iv) and (v)

$$\frac{a}{80-56} = \frac{b}{21+15} = \frac{c}{24+48}$$

$$\frac{a}{24} = \frac{b}{36} = \frac{c}{72}$$

$$\frac{a}{2} = \frac{b}{3} = \frac{c}{6} = \lambda \text{ (say)}$$

$$\Rightarrow$$

$$\Rightarrow \qquad a = 2\lambda, b = 3\lambda, c = 6\lambda$$

Putting in equation (i)

$$\frac{x-1}{2\lambda} = \frac{y-2}{3\lambda} = \frac{z+4}{6\lambda}$$

$$\Rightarrow \qquad \frac{x-1}{2} = \frac{y-2}{3} = \frac{z+4}{6}$$

Which is the required cartesian equation of line and vector equation of this line is

$$\vec{r} = (\hat{i}+2\hat{j}-4\hat{k})+\lambda(2\hat{i}+3\hat{j}+6\hat{k})$$

114. Find the shortest distance and the vector equation of the line of shortest distance between the following pair of lines

$$\vec{r} = (1-\lambda)\hat{i}+(\lambda-2)\hat{j}+(3-2\lambda)\hat{k}$$

and $\qquad \vec{r} = (\mu+1)\hat{i}+(2\mu-1)\hat{j}-(2\mu+1)\hat{k}$

Sol. The vector equations of the two given lines are

$$l_1 : \vec{r} = (\hat{i}-2\hat{j}+3\hat{k})+\lambda(-\hat{i}+\hat{j}-2\hat{k}) \quad \text{...(i)}$$

and $\quad l_2 : \vec{r} = (\hat{i}-\hat{j}-\hat{k})+\mu(\hat{i}+2\hat{j}-2\hat{k}) \qquad \text{...(ii)}$

Let PQ be the shortest distance between the two lines l_1 and l_2. Then, the line of shortest distance is along PQ.

Let the position vector of P and Q be

$$(1-\lambda)\hat{i}+(\lambda-2)\hat{j}+(3-2\lambda)\hat{k} \qquad \text{...(iii)}$$

$$(\mu+1)\hat{i}+(2\mu-1)\hat{j}-(2\mu+1)\hat{k} \qquad \text{...(iv)}$$

respectively.

Then, $PQ = (\mu+\lambda)\hat{i}+(2\mu-\lambda+1)\hat{j}+(-2\mu+2\lambda-4)\hat{k}$

Since $\vec{PQ}$ is perpendicular to the line l_1.

Therefore, $\vec{PQ}$ is perpendicular to $(-\hat{i}+\hat{j}-2\hat{k})$

$$\Rightarrow \qquad \vec{PQ}(-\hat{i}+\hat{j}-2\hat{k}) = 0$$

$$\Rightarrow \quad -\mu-\lambda+2\mu-\lambda+1+4\mu-4\lambda+8 = 0$$

$$5\mu - 6\lambda + 9 = 0 \qquad \text{...(v)}$$

Next, since $\vec{PQ}$ is perpendicular to line l_2, therefore

$$(\mu+\lambda)+2(2\mu-\lambda+1)-2(-2\mu+2\lambda-4) = 0$$

$$\Rightarrow \quad \mu+\lambda+4\mu-2\lambda+2+4\mu-4\lambda+8 = 0$$

$$\Rightarrow \qquad 9\mu - 5\lambda + 10 = 0 \text{ ...(vi)}$$

Now solving (v) and (vi), we get

$$\lambda = \frac{31}{29} \text{ and } \mu = \frac{-15}{29}$$

As $\quad \vec{PQ} = \left(\frac{31}{29}-\frac{15}{29}\right)\hat{i}+\left(\frac{-30}{29}-\frac{31}{29}+1\right)\hat{j}$

$$+\left(\frac{30}{29}+\frac{62}{29}-4\right)\hat{k}$$

$$= \frac{16}{29}\hat{i}-\frac{32}{29}\hat{j}-\frac{24}{29}\hat{k}$$

$$= \frac{8}{29}(2\hat{i}-4\hat{j}-3\hat{k})$$

$$\Rightarrow \quad |\overrightarrow{PQ}| = \frac{8}{29}\sqrt{4+16+9} = \frac{8\sqrt{29}}{29}$$

Thus, the shortest distance between the two lines l_1 and l_2 is $\dfrac{8\sqrt{29}}{29}$ units.

Since, the line PQ passes through P and Q, the vector equation of PQ is

$$\overrightarrow{r} = \left(1-\frac{31}{29}\right)\hat{i}+\left(\frac{31}{29}-2\right)\hat{j}+\left(3-\frac{62}{29}\right)\hat{k}$$

$$+\lambda_1\frac{8}{29}(2\hat{i}-4\hat{j}-3\hat{k})$$

or $\overrightarrow{r} = \dfrac{-2}{29}\hat{i}-\dfrac{27}{29}\hat{j}+\dfrac{25}{29}\hat{k}+\dfrac{8}{29}\lambda_1(2\hat{i}-4\hat{j}-3\hat{k})$

115. Find the equation of the line of shortest distance between the lines $\dfrac{x-1}{2}=\dfrac{y+1}{-1}=\dfrac{z-3}{4}$ and $\dfrac{x-1}{3}=$

$\dfrac{y+6}{4}=\dfrac{z+1}{2}$. Also, find the shortest distance.

Sol. Let $\dfrac{x-1}{2} = \dfrac{y+1}{-1} = \dfrac{z-3}{4} = \lambda$ ...(i)

Therefore, a general point on the line (i) is

$$P(2\lambda + 1, -\lambda - 1, 4\lambda + 3)$$

Let $\dfrac{x-1}{3} = \dfrac{y+6}{4} = \dfrac{z+1}{2} = \mu$ ...(ii)

$\Rightarrow \quad x = 3\mu + 1, y = 4\mu - 6, z = 2\mu - 1$

Therefore, a general point on the line (ii) is

$$Q(3\mu + 1, 4\mu - 6, 2\mu - 1)$$

Let PQ be the shortest distance between the two given lines. Then, the line of shortest distance passes through P and Q.

Direction ratios of PQ are

$$(3\mu - 2\lambda, 4\mu + \lambda - 5, 2\mu - 4\lambda - 4)$$

Since, PQ is perpendicular to the line (i),

$$2(3\mu - 2\lambda) - 1(4\mu + \lambda - 5) + 4(2\mu - 4\lambda - 4) = 0$$

$\Rightarrow \quad 10\mu - 21\lambda - 11 = 0$ ...(iii)

Also, PQ is perpendicular to the line (ii).

$\therefore \ 3(3\mu - 2\lambda) + 4(4\mu + \lambda - 5) + 2(2\mu - 4\lambda - 4) = 0$

$\Rightarrow \quad 29\mu - 10\lambda - 28 = 0$ ...(iv)

Solving equations (iii) and (iv), we get

$$\frac{\lambda}{-280+319} = \frac{\mu}{110-588} = \frac{1}{-609+100}$$

$\Rightarrow \quad \dfrac{\lambda}{39} = \dfrac{\mu}{-478} = \dfrac{1}{-509}$

$\Rightarrow \quad \lambda = \dfrac{-39}{509}$

and $\quad \mu = \dfrac{478}{509}$

So, the required points, where the line of shortest distance meets the given lines are

$$P\left(\frac{431}{509}, \frac{-470}{509}, \frac{1371}{509}\right) \text{ and } Q\left(\frac{1943}{509}, \frac{-186}{509}, \frac{447}{509}\right)$$

Therefore, shortest distance = PQ

$$=\sqrt{\left(\frac{1943}{509}-\frac{431}{509}\right)^2+\left(\frac{-186}{509}+\frac{470}{509}\right)^2+\left(\frac{447}{509}-\frac{1371}{509}\right)^2}$$

$$=\sqrt{\left(\frac{1512}{509}\right)^2+\left(\frac{284}{509}\right)^2+\left(\frac{-924}{509}\right)^2}$$

$$=\frac{1}{509}\sqrt{2286144+80656+853776}$$

$$=\frac{1}{509}\sqrt{3220576}$$

$$=\frac{4}{509}\sqrt{201286} \text{ units}$$

Also, the line of shortest distance is

$$\frac{x-\dfrac{431}{509}}{\dfrac{1512}{509}} = \frac{y+\dfrac{470}{509}}{\dfrac{284}{509}} = \frac{z-\dfrac{1371}{509}}{\dfrac{-924}{509}}$$

i.e., $\dfrac{509x-431}{1512} = \dfrac{509y-470}{284} = \dfrac{509z-1371}{-924}$

116. Write the vector equations of the following lines and hence find the distance between them :*

$$\frac{x-1}{2}=\frac{y-2}{3}=\frac{z+4}{6}, \frac{x-3}{4}=\frac{y-3}{6}=\frac{z+5}{12}$$

Sol. Given equation of lines are

$$\frac{x-1}{2} = \frac{y-2}{3} = \frac{z+4}{6}$$

and $\quad \dfrac{x-3}{4} = \dfrac{y-3}{6} = \dfrac{z+5}{12}$

Now, the vector equation of lines are

$$\overrightarrow{r} = (\hat{i}+2\hat{j}-4\hat{k})+\lambda(2\hat{i}+3\hat{j}+6\hat{k}) \quad ...(i)$$

$[\because$ Vector form of equation of line is $\overrightarrow{r} = \overrightarrow{a}+\lambda\overrightarrow{b}\,]$

and $\quad \overrightarrow{r} = (3\hat{i}+3\hat{j}-5\hat{k})+\mu(4\hat{i}+6\hat{j}+12\hat{k}) \quad ...(ii)$

Here $\overrightarrow{a_1} = \hat{i}+2\hat{j}-4\hat{k}, \ \overrightarrow{b_1} = 2\hat{i}+3\hat{j}+6\hat{k}$

$\quad \overrightarrow{a_2} = 3\hat{i}+3\hat{j}-5\hat{k}, \ \overrightarrow{b_2} = 4\hat{i}+6\hat{j}+12\hat{k}$

Now, $\vec{b_1} \times \vec{b_2} = \begin{vmatrix} \hat{i} & \hat{j} & \hat{k} \\ 2 & 3 & 6 \\ 4 & 6 & 12 \end{vmatrix}$

$= \hat{i}(36-36) - \hat{j}(24-24) + \hat{k}(12-12)$

$= 0\hat{i} - 0\hat{j} + 0\hat{k} = 0$

$\because \ \vec{b_1} \times \vec{b_2} = 0$

$\Rightarrow$ Vector b_1 is parallel to b_2

$$[\because \ \vec{a} \times \vec{b} = 0, \text{then} \ \vec{a} \parallel \vec{b}]$$

Therefore the two lines are parallel.

$\therefore \quad \vec{b} = (2\hat{i} + 3\hat{j} + 6\hat{k})$ ...(iii)

[Since, direction ratios of given lines are proportional]

Since, the two lines are parallel, we use the formula for shortest distance between two parallel lines.

We know that

$$d = \left| \frac{\vec{b} \times (\vec{a_2} - \vec{a_1})}{|\vec{b}|} \right| \qquad ...(iv)$$

$\therefore$ From equations (iii) and (iv), we get

$$d = \left| \frac{(2\hat{i} + 3\hat{j} + 6\hat{k}) \times (2\hat{i} + \hat{j} - \hat{k})}{\sqrt{(2)^2 + (3)^2 + (6)^2}} \right| \qquad ...(v)$$

Now $(2\hat{i} + 3\hat{j} + 6\hat{k}) \times (2\hat{i} + \hat{j} - \hat{k})$

$$= \begin{vmatrix} \hat{i} & \hat{j} & \hat{k} \\ 2 & 3 & 6 \\ 2 & 1 & -1 \end{vmatrix}$$

$= \hat{i}(-3-6) - \hat{j}(-2-12) + \hat{k}(2-6)$

$= -9\hat{i} + 14\hat{j} - 4\hat{k}$

From equation (v), we get

$$d = \left| \frac{-9\hat{i} + 14\hat{j} - 4\hat{k}}{\sqrt{49}} \right|$$

$$= \frac{\sqrt{(-9)^2 + (14)^2 + (-4)^2}}{7}$$

$\therefore \quad d = \frac{\sqrt{81 + 196 + 16}}{7} = \frac{\sqrt{293}}{7}$ units

117. A variable plane which remains at a constant distance $3p$ from the origin cuts the coordinate axes at A, B, C. Show that the locus of the centroid of triangle ABC is $x^{-2} + y^{-2} + z^{-2} = p^{-2}$.*

Sol. Let the intercepts made by the plane with coordinate axes at A, B, C be a, b, c respectively.

Then, the equation of variable plane is

$$\frac{x}{a} + \frac{y}{b} + \frac{z}{a} = 1 \qquad ...(i)$$

Clearly, the coordinates of A, B, C are $(a, 0, 0)$, $(0, b, 0)$ and $(0, 0, c)$.

Since, the plane is at a distance of $3p$ from the origin,

$$\therefore \qquad 3p = \frac{1}{\sqrt{\frac{1}{a^2} + \frac{1}{b^2} + \frac{1}{c^2}}}$$

[$\because$ distance of a point (x_1, y_1, z_1) from a plane

$ax + by + cz + d = 0$ is $\dfrac{|ax_1 + by_1 + cz_1 + d|}{\sqrt{a^2 + b^2 + c^2}}$]

$$\Rightarrow \qquad \frac{1}{3p} = \sqrt{\frac{1}{a^2} + \frac{1}{b^2} + \frac{1}{c^2}}$$

$$\Rightarrow \qquad \frac{1}{9p^2} = \frac{1}{a^2} + \frac{1}{b^2} + \frac{1}{c^2} \qquad ...(ii)$$

Let (u, v, w) be the coordinates of the centroid of triangle ABC.

Then, $u = \dfrac{a}{3}, v = \dfrac{b}{3}$ and $w = \dfrac{c}{3}$

$\Rightarrow a = 3u, b = 3v, c = 3w$

Putting the values of a, b and c in equation (ii), we get

$$\Rightarrow \qquad \frac{1}{9p^2} = \frac{1}{9u^2} + \frac{1}{9v^2} + \frac{1}{9w^2}$$

$$\Rightarrow \qquad \frac{1}{p^2} = \frac{1}{u^2} + \frac{1}{v^2} + \frac{1}{w^2}$$

For locus, we replace u by x, v by y and w by z.

Therefore, the locus of the centroid of the triangle ABC is

$$\frac{1}{p^2} = \frac{1}{x^2} + \frac{1}{y^2} + \frac{1}{z^2}$$

i.e., $x^{-2} + y^{-2} + z^{-2} = p^{-2}$.

118. Find the image of the point $(3, -2, 1)$ in the plane $3x - y + 4z = 2$.

Sol.

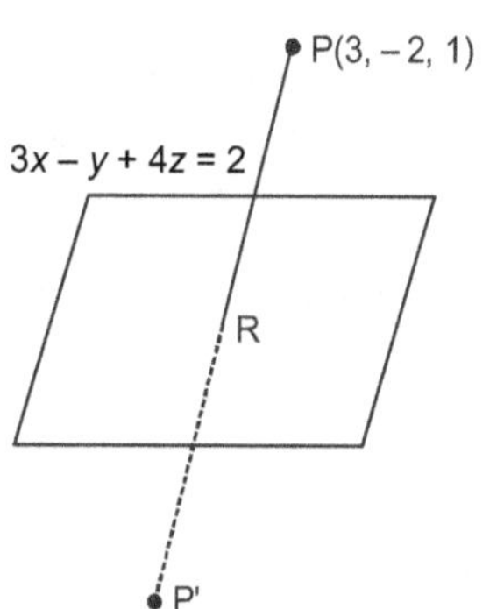

Let P′ be the image of the point P(3, – 2, 1) in the plane $3x - y + 4z = 2$.

Then, PP′ is normal to the plane.

Therefore, direction ratios of PP′ are 3, – 1, 4.

Since, PP′ passes through the point P(3, – 2, 1) and has direction ratios 3, – 1, 4.

Therefore, equation of PP′ is

$$\frac{x-3}{3} = \frac{y+2}{-1} = \frac{z-1}{4}$$

Let,

$$\frac{x-3}{3} = \frac{y+2}{-1} = \frac{z-1}{4} = k \text{ (say)}$$

$$\Rightarrow \qquad x = 3k + 3$$
$$y = -k - 2$$
$$z = 4k + 1$$

Let the coordinates of P′, for some values of k, be

$$P'(3k + 3, - k - 2, 4k + 1) \qquad \text{...(i)}$$

Let R be the mid-point of PP′

Therefore, coordinates of R are

$$\left(\frac{3k+3+3}{2}, \frac{-k-2-2}{2}, \frac{4k+1+1}{2} \right)$$

i.e., $\left(\dfrac{3k+6}{2}, \dfrac{-k-4}{2}, 2k+1 \right)$

Since, the point R lies on the plane $3x - y + 4z = 2$

$$\therefore \quad 3(3k + 6) + (k + 4) + 8(2k + 1) = 4$$
$$\Rightarrow \qquad 9k + 18 + k + 4 + 16k + 8 = 4$$
$$\Rightarrow \qquad\qquad 26k + 26 = 0$$
$$\Rightarrow \qquad\qquad 26k = -26$$
$$k = -1$$

Putting the value of k in (i), we get the coordinates of P′ as (0, – 1, – 3).

Thus, the image of the point (3, – 2, 1) in the plane $3x - y + 4z = 2$ is (0, – 1, – 3).

119. Find the equation of plane which contains the line of intersection of planes $\vec{r}.(\hat{i}+2\hat{j}+3\hat{k})-4=0$, $\vec{r}.(2\hat{i}+\hat{j}-\hat{k})+5=0$ and which is perpendicular to plane $(5\hat{i}+3\hat{j}-6\hat{k})+8=0.$ *

Sol. Given that the required plane contains the line of intersection of planes whose equations are

$$\vec{r}.(\hat{i}+2\hat{j}+3\hat{k})-4 = 0 \qquad \text{...(i)}$$

and $\qquad \vec{r}.(2\hat{i}+\hat{j}-\hat{k})+5 = 0 \qquad \text{...(ii)}$

Equations (i) and (ii) can be written in Cartesian form as

$$(x\hat{i}+y\hat{j}-z\hat{k}).(\hat{i}+2\hat{j}+3\hat{k})-4 = 0$$

and $\quad (x\hat{i}+y\hat{j}-z\hat{k}).(2\hat{i}+\hat{j}-\hat{k})+5 = 0$

$$\Rightarrow \qquad x + 2y + 3z - 4 = 0$$

and $\qquad\qquad 2x + y - z + 5 = 0$

So, let the required equation of plane is

$$(x + 2y + 3z - 4) + \lambda (2x + y - z + 5) = 0 \quad \text{...(iii)}$$
$$\Rightarrow \ x + 2y + 3z - 4 + 2\lambda x + \lambda y - \lambda z + 5\lambda = 0$$

$$\Rightarrow x(1 + 2\lambda) + y(2 + \lambda) + z(3 - \lambda) + (- 4 + 5\lambda) = 0$$
$$\text{...(iv)}$$

Now, given that plane (iv) is perpendicular to the plane $\vec{r}.(5\hat{i}+3\hat{j}-6\hat{k})+8=0$ which in Cartesian form can be written as

$$5x + 3y - 6z + 8 = 0$$

$\therefore$ We have $\qquad a_1a_2 + b_1b_2 + c_1c_2 = 0$

Where $\qquad a_1 = 1 + 2\lambda, b_1 = 2 + \lambda, c_1 = 3 - \lambda$

And $\qquad a_2 = 5, b_2 = 3, c_2 = - 6$

$\therefore \qquad 5(1 + 2\lambda) + 3(2 + \lambda) - 6(3 - \lambda) = 0$

$\Rightarrow \qquad 5 + 10\lambda + 6 + 3\lambda - 18 + 6\lambda = 0$

$\Rightarrow \qquad\qquad 19\lambda - 7 = 0$

$$\Rightarrow \qquad\qquad \lambda = \frac{7}{19}$$

Putting $\lambda = \dfrac{7}{19}$ in equation (iii) we get the required equation of plane as

$$(x + 2y + 3z - 4) + \frac{7}{19} (2x + y - z + 5) = 0$$

$\Rightarrow \ 19x + 38y + 57z - 76 + 14x + 7y - 7z + 35 = 0$

$\Rightarrow \qquad\qquad 33x + 45y + 50z - 41 = 0$

In vector form, the required equation is

$$\vec{r}.(33\hat{i}+45\hat{j}+50\hat{k}) = 41.$$

120. Find the equation of plane passing through the line of intersection of planes $\vec{r}.(\hat{i}+\hat{j}+\hat{k}) = 1$ and $\vec{r}.(2\hat{i}+3\hat{j}-\hat{k})+4 = 0$ and parallel to X-axis.*

Sol. Given equation of planes are

$$\vec{r}.(\hat{i}+\hat{j}+\hat{k}) = 1$$

and $\qquad \vec{r}.(2\hat{i}+3\hat{j}-\hat{k})+4 = 0$

Put $\vec{r}.(x\hat{i}+y\hat{j}+z\hat{k})$ then above equations can be written in Cartesian form as

$$x + y + z - 1 = 0 \qquad \text{...(i)}$$

and $\qquad 2x + 3y - z + 4 = 0 \qquad \text{...(ii)}$

Let the required equation of plane passing through the line of intersection of planes (i) and (ii) is

$$(x + y + z - 1) + \lambda(2x + 3y - z + 4) = 0$$
$$\Rightarrow \qquad x + y + z - 1 + 2\lambda x + 3\lambda y - \lambda z + 4\lambda = 0$$
$$\Rightarrow x(1 + 2\lambda) + y(1 + 3\lambda) + z(1 - \lambda) + (- 1 + 4\lambda) = 0$$
$$\text{...(iii)}$$

$\therefore$ Direction ratios of the above plane are $1 + 2\lambda$, $1 + 3\lambda$, $1 - \lambda$.

Also, direction ratios of the X-axis are (1, 0, 0).

Now, since given that above plane (iii) is parallel to the X-axis.

$\therefore$ We have $a_1a_2 + b_1b_2 + c_1c_2 = 0$

where $a_1 = 1 + 2\lambda$, $b_1 = 1 + 3\lambda$, $c_1 = 1 - \lambda$

and $a_2 = 1$, $b_2 = 0$, $c_2 = 0$

$\therefore \quad 1(1 + 2\lambda) + 0(1 + 3\lambda) + 0(1 - \lambda) = 0$

$\Rightarrow \qquad 1 + 2\lambda = 0$

$\Rightarrow \qquad 2\lambda = -1$

$\Rightarrow \qquad \lambda = -\dfrac{1}{2}$

Putting $\lambda = -\dfrac{1}{2}$ in equation (iii), we get the required equation of plane as

$$x\left(1 - \frac{2\times 1}{2}\right) + y\left(1 - \frac{3}{2}\right)$$

$$z\left(1 + \frac{1}{2}\right) + \left(-1 - \frac{4}{2}\right) = 0$$

$$-\frac{y}{2} + \frac{3z}{2} - \frac{6}{2} = 0$$

$\Rightarrow$

$\Rightarrow \qquad y - 3z + 6 = 0.$

121. Find the equation of plane passing through the point $(-1, 3, 2)$ and perpendicular to each of the planes $x + 2y + 3z = 5$ and $3x + 3y + z = 5$.★

Sol. Let the required equation of plane passing through $(-1, 3, 2)$ is

$$a(x + 1) + b(y - 3) + c(z - 2) = 0 \qquad \ldots(i)$$

Given that plane (i) is perpendicular to the planes whose equations are

$$x + 2y + 3z = 5 \qquad \ldots(ii)$$

and $\qquad 3x + 3y + z = 5 \qquad \ldots(iii)$

We have $\quad a_1a_2 + b_1b_2 + c_1c_2 = 0$

Using the above result first in equation (i), (ii) and then in eq. (i) and (iii), we get

$$a + 2b + 3c = 0 \qquad \ldots(iv)$$

and $\qquad 3a + 3b + c = 0 \qquad \ldots(v)$

Multiplying (iv) by '3' and subtracting it from equation (v), we get

$$3a + 3b + \ c = 0$$
$$3a + 6b + 9c = 0$$
$$\underline{\quad -\quad -\quad -\quad }$$
$$-3b - 8c = 0$$

$\Rightarrow \qquad\qquad -3b = 8c$

or $\qquad\qquad b = -\dfrac{8c}{3}$

Putting $b = -\dfrac{8c}{3}$ in equation (iv), we get

$$a + 2\left(-\frac{8c}{3}\right) + 3c = 0$$

$\Rightarrow \qquad a - \dfrac{16c}{3} + 3c = 0$

or $\qquad a = \dfrac{16c}{3} - 3c = \dfrac{16c - 9c}{3} = \dfrac{7c}{3}$

$\therefore \qquad a = \dfrac{7c}{3}$

Finally, putting $a = \dfrac{7c}{3}$ and $b = -\dfrac{8c}{3}$ in equation (i), we get the required equation of plane as

$$\frac{7c}{3}(x+1) - \frac{8c}{3}(y-3) + c(z-2) = 0$$

Divide both sides by 'c', we get

$$\frac{7}{3}(x+1) - \frac{8}{3}(y-3) + (z-2) = 0$$

$\Rightarrow \qquad 7x + 7 - 8y + 24 + 3z - 6 = 0$

or $\qquad\qquad 7x - 8y + 3z + 25 = 0.$

122. Find the vector equation of plane passing through the points A$(2, 2, -1)$, B$(3, 4, 2)$ and C$(7, 0, 6)$. Also find the Cartesian equation of plane.★

Sol. First we check whether the points are collinear or not.

Given points are A$(2, 2, -1)$, B$(3, 4, 2)$ and C$(7, 0, 6)$.

$\therefore \qquad$ AB $= \sqrt{(3-2)^2 + (4-2)^2 + (2+1)^2}$

$\qquad\qquad\quad = \sqrt{1+4+9}$

$\qquad\qquad\quad = \sqrt{14}$

$\qquad\qquad$ BC $= \sqrt{(7-3)^2 + (0-4)^2 + (6-2)^2}$

$\qquad\qquad\quad = \sqrt{16+16+16} = \sqrt{48} = 4\sqrt{3}$

$\therefore \qquad$ CA $= \sqrt{(2-7)^2 + (2-0)^2 + (-1-6)^2}$

$\qquad\qquad\quad = \sqrt{25+4+49}$

$\qquad\qquad\quad = \sqrt{78}$

$\because \qquad$ AB + BC $\neq$ CA

so points A, B, C are not collinear.

Now, the equation of plane passing through three non-collinear points (x_1, y_1, z_1), (x_2, y_2, z_2) and (x_3, y_3, z_3) is given by

$$\begin{vmatrix} x - x_1 & y - y_1 & z - z_1 \\ x_2 - x_1 & y_2 - y_1 & z_2 - z_1 \\ x_3 - x_1 & y_3 - y_1 & z_3 - z_1 \end{vmatrix} = 0$$

$\therefore$ We get $\quad \begin{vmatrix} x - 2 & y - 2 & z + 1 \\ 3 - 2 & 4 - 2 & 2 + 1 \\ 7 - 2 & 0 - 2 & 6 + 1 \end{vmatrix} = 0$

where $(x_1, y_1, z_1) = (2, 2, -1)$, $(x_2, y_2, z_2) = (3, 4, 2)$

and $\qquad\qquad\qquad (x_3, y_3, z_3) = (7, 0, 6)$

$$\Rightarrow \quad \begin{vmatrix} x-2 & y-2 & z+1 \\ 1 & 2 & 3 \\ 5 & -2 & 7 \end{vmatrix} = 0$$

Expanding along R_1

$\Rightarrow (x-2)(14+6) - (y-2)(7-15)$
$$+ (z+1)(-2-10) = 0$$
$\Rightarrow (x-2)\,20 - (y-2)\,(-8) + (z+1)\,(-12) = 0$
$\Rightarrow \qquad 20x - 40 + 8y - 16 - 12z - 12 = 0$
$\Rightarrow \qquad 20x + 8y - 12z - 68 = 0$

Dividing both sides by '4', we get

$5x + 2y - 3z = 17$ is the required Cartesian equation of plane.

Also, we have to find the vector equation of plane.

We know that vector form of Cartesian equation $ax + by + cz = d$ of plane is given by

$$\vec{r}.(a\hat{i} + b\hat{j} + c\hat{k}) = d$$

$\therefore$ Required vector equation of plane is

$$\vec{r}.(5\hat{i} + 2\hat{j} - 3\hat{k}) = 17.$$

123. Find the equation of plane determined by the points A(3, – 1, 2), B(5, 2, 4) and C(– 1, – 1, 6). Also, find the distance of point (6, 5, 9) from plane.*

Sol. Given points are A(3, – 1, 2), B(5, 2, 4) and C(– 1, – 1, 6).

First we check whether the points are collinear or not. Using distance formula, we have

$$AB = \sqrt{(5-3)^2 + (2+1)^2 + (4-2)^2}$$
$$= \sqrt{4+9+4}$$
$$= \sqrt{17}$$

$$BC = \sqrt{(-1-5)^2 + (-1-2)^2 + (6-4)^2}$$
$$= \sqrt{36+9+4}$$
$$= \sqrt{49}$$

$$CA = \sqrt{(3+1)^2 + (-1+1)^2 + (2-6)^2}$$
$$= \sqrt{16+0+16}$$
$$= \sqrt{32}$$

$\because$ AB + BC $\neq$ CA

$\therefore$ Given points are non-collinear.

Now, we know that equation of plane passing through three non-collinear points (x_1, y_1, z_1), (x_2, y_2, z_2) and (x_3, y_3, z_3) is given by

$$\begin{vmatrix} x-x_1 & y-y_1 & z-z_1 \\ x_2-x_1 & y_2-y_1 & z_2-z_1 \\ x_3-x_1 & y_3-y_1 & z_3-z_1 \end{vmatrix} = 0 \qquad ...(i)$$

** are frequently asked board exam questions

We have

$(x_1, y_1, z_1) = $ A(3, – 1, 2), $(x_2, y_2, z_2) = $ B(5, 2, 4)
and $\qquad (x_3, y_3, z_3) = $ C(– 1, – 1, 6)

Putting above values in equation (i), we get the required equation as

$$\begin{vmatrix} x-3 & y+1 & z-2 \\ 5-3 & 2+1 & 4-2 \\ -1-3 & -1+1 & 6-2 \end{vmatrix} = 0$$

$$\Rightarrow \begin{vmatrix} x-3 & y+1 & z-2 \\ 2 & 3 & 2 \\ -4 & 0 & 4 \end{vmatrix} = 0$$

$\Rightarrow (x-3)\,(12-0) - (y+1)\,(8+8)$
$$+ (z-2)\,(0+12) = 0$$
$\Rightarrow \quad 12x - 36 - 16y - 16 + 12z - 24 = 0$
$\Rightarrow \qquad 12x - 16y + 12z - 76 = 0$
$\Rightarrow \qquad 3x - 4y + 3z - 19 = 0$

Next, we find distance of point $P(6, 5, 9)$ to the above plane (ii) by using the formula

$$d = \frac{|Ax_1 + By_1 + Cz_1 + D|}{\sqrt{A^2 + B^2 + C^2}}$$

Between plane $Ax + By + Cz + D = 0$ and point (x_1, y_1, z_1).

Here, A = 3, B = – 4, C = 3, D = – 19, $x_1 = 6$, $y_1 = 5$, $z_1 = 9$

$$\therefore \qquad d = \left| \frac{18 - 20 + 27 - 19}{\sqrt{9 + 16 + 9}} \right|$$

$$= \left| \frac{6}{\sqrt{34}} \right|$$

$$= \frac{6}{\sqrt{34}}$$

$$\therefore \quad \text{Distance} = \frac{6\sqrt{34}}{34} \text{ units} = \frac{3\sqrt{34}}{17} \text{ units.}$$

124. Find the equation of the plane through the line of intersection of $\vec{r}.(2\hat{i} - 3\hat{j} + 4\hat{k}) = 1$ and $\vec{r}.(\hat{i} - \hat{j}) + 4 = 0$ and perpendicular to the plane $\vec{r}.(2\hat{i} - \hat{j} + \hat{k}) + 8 = 0$. Hence find whether the plane thus obtained contains the line $x - 1 = 2y - 4 = 3z - 12$.*

Sol. The equation of the plane passing through the line of intersection of the planes is :

$$\vec{r}.\left[(2\hat{i} - 3\hat{j} + 4\hat{k}) + \lambda(\hat{i} - \hat{j})\right] + 4\lambda - 1 = 0$$

$$\vec{r}.\left[(2+\lambda)\hat{i} - (3+\lambda)\hat{j} + 4\hat{k}\right] = 1 - 4\lambda$$

Taking $\vec{r} = x\hat{i} + y\hat{j} + z\hat{k}$, we get

$$(2+\lambda)\,x - (3+\lambda)\,y + 4z = 1 - 4\lambda \qquad ...(i)$$

$$\vec{r}.(2\hat{i} - \hat{j} + \hat{k}) + 8 = 0$$

Cartesian equation of this plane is :
$$2x - y + z + 8 = 0 \qquad \text{...(ii)}$$
$\because$ Planes (i) and (ii) are perpendicular

$\therefore \qquad (2 + \lambda)\,2 + (3 + \lambda) + 4 = 0$

$\Rightarrow \qquad 4 + 2\lambda + 3 + \lambda + 4 = 0$

$\Rightarrow \qquad 11 + 3\lambda = 0$

or $\qquad \lambda = \dfrac{-11}{3}$

From equation (i)
$$\left(2 - \frac{11}{3}\right)x - \left(3 - \frac{11}{3}\right)y + 4z = 1 - 4 \times \left(\frac{-11}{3}\right)$$
$$\frac{-5x}{3} + \frac{2}{3}y + 4z = \frac{47}{3}$$
$$\Rightarrow \qquad -5x + 2y + 12z = 47$$

Required vector equation of this plane is :
$$\vec{r}.(-5\,\hat{i} + 2\,\hat{j} + 12\,\hat{k}) = 47 \qquad \text{...(iii)}$$

Now, equation of the given line is,
$$x - 1 = 2y - 4 = 3z - 12$$
$$\frac{x-1}{1} = 2(y - 2) = 3(z - 4)$$
$$\frac{x-1}{1} = \frac{y-2}{1/2} = \frac{z-4}{1/3}$$
$$\Rightarrow \qquad \frac{x-1}{6} = \frac{y-2}{3} = \frac{z-4}{2}$$

Vector equation of this line is :
$$\vec{r} = (\hat{i} + 2\,\hat{j} + 4\,\hat{k}) + \lambda(6\,\hat{i} + 3\,\hat{j} + 2\,\hat{k}) \quad \text{...(iv)}$$

Obviously plane (iii) contains the line (iv) since the point $\hat{i} + 2\,\hat{j} + 4\,\hat{k}$ satisfy the equation of plane (iii).

[as $(\hat{i} + 2\,\hat{j} + 4\,\hat{k}).(-5\,\hat{i} + 2\,\hat{j} + 12\,\hat{k}) = -5 + 4 + 48 = 47$]

and vector $-5\,\hat{i} + 2\,\hat{j} + 12\,\hat{k}$ is perpendicular to $6\,\hat{i} + 3\,\hat{j} + 2\,\hat{k}$ as $(6\,\hat{i} + 3\,\hat{j} + 2\,\hat{k}).(-5\,\hat{i} + 2\,\hat{j} + 12\,\hat{k}) = -30 + 6 + 24 = 0$]

$\therefore$ Plane (iii) contains the line (iv).

125. Find the distance of the point $(-1, -5, -10)$ from the point of intersection of the line $\vec{r} = (2\,\hat{i} - \hat{j} + 2\,\hat{k}) + \lambda(3\,\hat{i} + 4\,\hat{j} + 2\,\hat{k})$ and the plane $\vec{r}.(\hat{i} - \hat{j} + \hat{k}) = 5.*$

Sol. Given equation of line and plane are
$$\vec{r} = (2\,\hat{i} - \hat{j} + 2\,\hat{k}) + \lambda(3\,\hat{i} + 4\,\hat{j} + 2\,\hat{k})$$
and $\qquad \vec{r}.(\hat{i} - \hat{j} + \hat{k}) = 5$

$\Rightarrow \qquad (x\,\hat{i} - y\,\hat{j} + z\,\hat{k}) = (2 + 3\lambda)\,\hat{i} + (-1 + 4\lambda)\,\hat{j} + (2 + 2\lambda)\,\hat{k}$

and $(x\,\hat{i} + y\,\hat{j} + z\,\hat{k}).(\hat{i} - \hat{j} + \hat{k}) = 5$

$\qquad$ (put $\vec{r} = x\,\hat{i} + y\,\hat{j} + z\,\hat{k}$)

Above equations in Cartesian form can be written as
$$\frac{x-2}{3} = \frac{y+1}{4} = \frac{z-2}{2} \qquad \text{...(i)}$$
and $\qquad x - y + z = 5 \qquad \text{...(ii)}$

First, we solve equations (i) and (ii) and find their point of intersection. Let the point of intersection be Q.

Let $\qquad \dfrac{x-2}{3} = \dfrac{y+1}{4} = \dfrac{z-2}{2} = \lambda$ (say)

$\Rightarrow \qquad \dfrac{x-2}{3} = \lambda, \ \dfrac{y+1}{4} = \lambda, \ \dfrac{z-2}{2} = \lambda$

$\Rightarrow \qquad x = 3\lambda + 2, \ y = 4\lambda - 1, \ z = 2\lambda + 2$

$\therefore$ any point Q on the given line is
$$Q(3\lambda + 2, \ 4\lambda - 1, \ 2\lambda + 2)$$

$\because$ Plane also passes through Q, so coordinates of Q satisfies equation (ii).
$$(3\lambda + 2) - (4\lambda - 1) + (2\lambda + 2) = 5$$
$$\Rightarrow \qquad 3\lambda + 2 - 4\lambda + 1 + 2\lambda + 2 = 5$$
$$\Rightarrow \qquad \lambda = 0$$

Putting $\lambda = 0$ in $Q(3\lambda + 2, \ 4\lambda - 1, \ 2\lambda + 2)$ we get the point of intersection as $Q(2, -1, 2)$.

Now, using distance formula, the required distance
$$PQ = \sqrt{(2+1)^2 + (-1+5)^2 + (2+10)^2}$$
$$= \sqrt{9 + 16 + 144}$$
$$= \sqrt{144 + 25} = \sqrt{169} = 13.$$

Hence, the required distance = 13 units.

126. Find the equation of plane passing through the line of intersection of planes $2x + y - z = 3$ and $5x - 3y + 4z + 9 = 0$ and parallel to line
$$\frac{x-1}{2} = \frac{y-3}{4} = \frac{z-5}{5}.*$$

Sol. Given equation of planes are
$$2x + y - z - 3 = 0 \qquad \text{...(i)}$$
and $\quad 5x - 3y + 4z + 9 = 0 \qquad \text{...(ii)}$

Let the required equation of plane which passes through the line of intersection of planes (i) and (ii) is
$$(2x + y - z - 3) + \lambda(5x - 3y + 4z + 9) = 0 \ \text{...(iii)}$$
$$\Rightarrow x(2 + 5\lambda) + y(1 - 3\lambda) + z(-1 + 4\lambda) + (-3 + 9\lambda) = 0 \ \text{...(iv)}$$

Here, direction ratios of plane are $2 + 5\lambda$, $1 - 3\lambda$, $-1 + 4\lambda$. Given that the plane (i) is parallel to the line whose equation as

$$\frac{x-1}{2} = \frac{y-3}{4} = \frac{z-5}{5}$$

Direction ratios of the line are 2, 4, 5.

Since, the plane is parallel to the line.

$\therefore$ We have $\qquad a_1 a_2 + b_1 b_2 + c_1 c_2 = 0$

where $\qquad a_1 = 2 + 5\lambda, b_1 = 1 - 3\lambda, c_1 = -1 + 4\lambda$

and $\qquad a_2 = 2, b_2 = 4, c_2 = 5$

$\Rightarrow \quad 2(2 + 5\lambda) + 4(1 - 3\lambda) + 5(-1 + 4\lambda) = 0$

$\Rightarrow \qquad 4 + 10\lambda + 4 - 12\lambda - 5 + 20\lambda = 0$

$\Rightarrow \qquad\qquad\qquad 18\lambda + 3 = 0$

or $\qquad\qquad \lambda = -\frac{3}{18} = -\frac{1}{6}$

Putting $\lambda = -\dfrac{1}{6}$ in equation (iii), we get the required equation of plane is

$$(2x + y - z - 3) - \frac{1}{6}(5x - 3y + 4z + 9) = 0$$

$\Rightarrow \quad 12x + 6y - 6z - 18 - 5x + 3y - 4z - 9 = 0$

$\Rightarrow \qquad\qquad 7x + 9y - 10z - 27 = 0.$

127. Find the equation of plane passing through the point (1, 2, 1) and perpendicular to line joining points (1, 4, 2) and (2, 3, 5). Also, find the coordinates of foot of the perpendicular and the perpendicular distance of the point (4, 0, 3) from the above found plane.*

Sol. First we find equation of plane passing through point R(1, 2, 1) and is perpendicular to line PQ where P(1, 4, 2) and Q(2, 3, 5).

Direction ratios of the line PQ are

$$= (2 - 1, 3 - 4, 5 - 2) = (1, -1, 3)$$

Let the required equation of plane which passes through point R(1, 2, 1) is

$$a(x - 1) + b(y - 2) + c(z - 1) = 0 \qquad \ldots(i)$$

Plane (i) is perpendicular to line PQ.

Since, line is perpendicular to the plane, then direction ratios of normal to the plane is proportional to the direction ratios of a line.

$\therefore \quad 1(x - 1) - 1(y - 2) + 3(z - 1) = 0$

or $\qquad x - 1 - y + 2 + 3z - 3 = 0$

or $\qquad\qquad x - y + 3z - 2 = 0 \qquad \ldots(ii)$

This is the required equation of plane.

Next, we have to find the foot of perpendicular and perpendicular distance of the point (4, 0, 3) from above plane.

So, let $B(x_1, y_1, z_1)$ be the foot of perpendicular on above plane (ii). So it must satisfy equation (ii).

$\therefore \qquad\qquad x_1 - y_1 + 3z_1 - 2 = 0 \qquad \ldots(iii)$

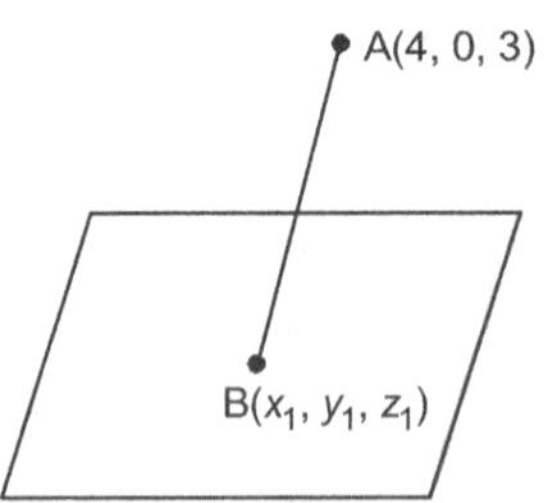

Also, direction ratios of line AB normal to above plane (i) are given by

$$x_1 - 4, y_1 - 0, z_1 - 3$$

$\because$ Direction ratios of line AB and plane (iii) are proportional.

$\therefore \qquad \dfrac{x_1 - 4}{1} = \dfrac{y_1 - 0}{-1} = \dfrac{z_1 - 3}{3}$

Let $\qquad \dfrac{x_1 - 4}{1} = \dfrac{y_1}{-1} = \dfrac{z_1 - 3}{3} = \lambda \qquad$ (say)

$\Rightarrow \qquad x_1 = \lambda + 4, y_1 = -\lambda, z_1 = 3\lambda + 3 \quad \ldots(iv)$

Putting above values of x_1, y_1 and z_1 in eq. (iii), we get

$$\lambda + 4 + \lambda + 9\lambda + 9 - 2 = 0$$

$\Rightarrow \qquad\qquad 11\lambda + 11 = 0$

$\Rightarrow \qquad\qquad 11\lambda = -11$

$\Rightarrow \qquad\qquad \lambda = -1$

Putting $\lambda = -1$ in equation (iv), we get the required foot of perpendicular as

$B(x_1, y_1, z_1) = B(\lambda + 4, -\lambda, 3\lambda + 3) = B(3, 1, 0)$

Also, perpendicular distance AB where A(4, 0, 3) and B(3, 1, 0) is given by using distance formula i.e.,

$$AB = \sqrt{(3-4)^2 + (1-0)^2 + (0-3)^2}$$

$$= \sqrt{1 + 1 + 9} = \sqrt{11} \text{ units.}$$

128. Find the distance of point $(-2, 3, -4)$ from the line $\dfrac{x+2}{3} = \dfrac{2y+3}{4} = \dfrac{3z+4}{5}$ measured parallel to the plane $4x + 12y - 3z + 1 = 0$.*

Sol. Let $P(-2, 3, -4)$ be the given point and the given line is

$$\frac{x+2}{3} = \frac{2y+3}{4} = \frac{3z+4}{5}$$

or $\qquad \dfrac{x+2}{3} = \dfrac{2\left(y+\dfrac{3}{2}\right)}{4} = \dfrac{3\left(z+\dfrac{4}{3}\right)}{5}$

or $\qquad \dfrac{x+2}{3} = \dfrac{y+\dfrac{3}{2}}{2} = \dfrac{z+\dfrac{4}{3}}{\left(\dfrac{5}{3}\right)} \qquad \ldots(i)$

Now, any random point T on the given line (i) is calculated as

$$\frac{x+2}{3} = \frac{y+\frac{3}{2}}{2} = \frac{z+\frac{4}{3}}{\left(\frac{5}{3}\right)} = \lambda \text{ (say)}$$

$$\Rightarrow \quad \frac{x+2}{3} = \lambda, \; \frac{y+\frac{3}{2}}{2} = \lambda, \; \frac{z+\frac{4}{3}}{\frac{5}{3}} = \lambda$$

$$\Rightarrow \quad x = 3\lambda - 2, \; y = \frac{4\lambda - 3}{2}, \; z = \frac{5\lambda - 4}{3}$$

∴ Coordinates of T are

$$\left(3\lambda - 2, \frac{4\lambda - 3}{2}, \frac{5\lambda - 4}{3}\right)$$

Now, direction ratios of line PT are

$$\left(3\lambda - 2 + 2, \frac{4\lambda - 3}{2} - 3, \frac{5\lambda - 4}{3} + 4\right)$$

$$= \left(3\lambda, \frac{4\lambda - 9}{2}, \frac{5\lambda + 8}{3}\right)$$

Since, the line PT is parallel to the plane $4x + 12 - 3z + 1 = 0$.

∴ We have $a_1 a_2 + b_1 b_2 + c_1 c_2 = 0$

where $a_1 = 3\lambda$, $b_1 = \dfrac{4\lambda - 9}{2}$, $c_1 = \dfrac{5\lambda + 8}{3}$ and $a_2 = 4$,

$b_2 = 12$, $c_2 = -3$

[Direction ratios of plane]

∴ We get $4(3\lambda) + 12\left(\dfrac{4\lambda - 9}{2}\right) - 3\left(\dfrac{5\lambda + 8}{3}\right) = 0$

$$\Rightarrow \quad 12\lambda + 24\lambda - 54 - 5\lambda - 8 = 0$$
$$\Rightarrow \quad 31\lambda - 62 = 0$$
$$\Rightarrow \quad 31\lambda = 62$$
$$\Rightarrow \quad \lambda = 2$$

∴ Coordinates of T are

$$\left(6 - 2, \frac{8 - 3}{2}, \frac{10 - 4}{3}\right) = \left(4, \frac{5}{2}, 2\right)$$

∴ The required distance = distance between the points P(−2, 3, −4) and $T\left(4, \dfrac{5}{2}, 2\right)$

∴ Using distance formula, we have

$$d = \sqrt{(4+2)^2 + \left(\frac{5}{2} - 3\right)^2 + (2+4)^2}$$

$$= \sqrt{36 + \frac{1}{4} + 36} = \sqrt{\frac{144 + 1 + 144}{4}}$$

$$= \sqrt{\frac{289}{4}} = \frac{17}{2} \text{ units}$$

---

129. From the point P(1, 2, 4), a perpendicular is drawn on the plane $2x + y - 2z + 3 = 0$. Find the equation, the length and the coordinates of foot of perpendicular.*

Sol. Let PT be the perpendicular drawn from the point P(1, 2, 4) to the plane whose equation is given by

$$2x + y - 2z + 3 = 0 \qquad \qquad ...(i)$$

We have to find equation, length and coordinates of foot of perpendicular.

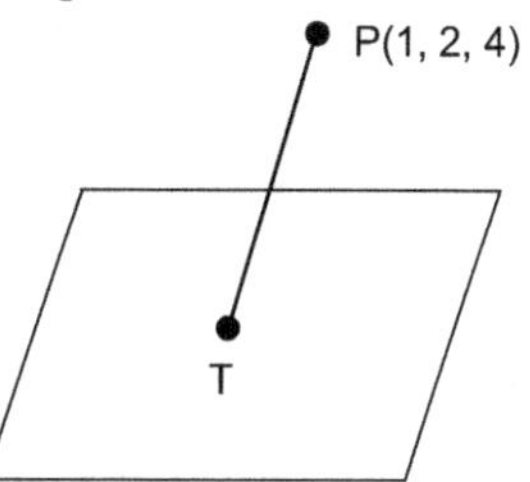

From eq. (i), direction ratios of plane are 2, 1, − 2. Since the line PT is normal to the plane, so direction ratios of line normal to plane are 2, 1, − 2.

∴ Equation of line PT from P(1, 2, 4) is given as

$$\frac{x-1}{2} = \frac{y-2}{1} = \frac{z-4}{-2} \qquad \qquad ...(ii)$$

Equation of line passing through one point is

Let $\quad \dfrac{x-1}{2} = \dfrac{y-2}{1} = \dfrac{z-4}{-2} = \lambda$ (say)

$$\Rightarrow \quad \frac{x-1}{2} = \lambda, \; \frac{y-2}{1} = \lambda, \; \frac{z-4}{-2} = \lambda$$

$$\Rightarrow \quad x = 2\lambda + 1, \; y = \lambda + 2, \; z = -2\lambda + 4$$

∴ Coordinates of any random point are

$$T(2\lambda + 1, \lambda + 2, -2\lambda + 4) \qquad ...(iii)$$

From the figure, we see that T lies on the given plane. So, we put $x = 2\lambda + 1$, $y = \lambda + 2$, $z = -2\lambda + 4$ in eq. (i),

$$2(2\lambda + 1) + (\lambda + 2) - 2(-2\lambda + 4) + 3 = 0$$
$$\Rightarrow \quad 4\lambda + 2 + \lambda + 2 + 4\lambda - 8 + 3 = 0$$
$$\Rightarrow \quad 9\lambda - 1 = 0$$
$$\Rightarrow \quad \lambda = \frac{1}{9}$$

Putting value of λ in equation (iii), we get the foot of perpendicular,

$$\left(\frac{2}{9} + 1, \frac{1}{9} + 2, -\frac{2}{9} + 4\right) = T\left(\frac{11}{9}, \frac{19}{9}, \frac{34}{9}\right)$$

Also, length of perpendicular PT = distance between points P and T

$$= \sqrt{\left(1 - \frac{11}{9}\right)^2 + \left(2 - \frac{19}{9}\right)^2 + \left(4 - \frac{34}{9}\right)^2}$$

$$\left[\because (x_1, y_1, z_1) = (1, 2, 4) \text{ and } (x_2, y_2, z_2) = \left(\frac{11}{9}, \frac{19}{9}, \frac{34}{9}\right)\right]$$

$$= \sqrt{\left(-\frac{2}{9}\right)^2 + \left(-\frac{1}{9}\right)^2 + \left(\frac{2}{9}\right)^2}$$

$$= \sqrt{\frac{4}{81} + \frac{1}{81} + \frac{4}{81}}$$

$$= \sqrt{\frac{9}{81}} = \sqrt{\frac{1}{9}} = \frac{1}{3}$$

Finally, the equation of perpendicular PT where $P(1, 2, 4)$ and $T\left(\frac{11}{9}, \frac{19}{9}, \frac{34}{9}\right)$ is given as

$$\frac{x-1}{\frac{11}{9}-1} = \frac{y-2}{\frac{19}{9}-2} = \frac{z-4}{\frac{34}{9}-4}$$

$$\Rightarrow \quad \frac{x-1}{\left(\frac{2}{9}\right)} = \frac{y-2}{\left(\frac{1}{9}\right)} = \frac{z-4}{\left(-\frac{2}{9}\right)}$$

$$\Rightarrow \quad \frac{x-1}{2} = \frac{y-2}{1} = \frac{z-4}{-2}$$

130. Find the equation of plane passing through points $(3, 4, 1)$ and $(0, 1, 0)$ and parallel to line $\frac{x+3}{2} = \frac{y-3}{7} = \frac{z-2}{5}$. *

Sol. Equation of plane passing through the point $(3, 4, 1)$ is given as

$$a(x-3) + b(y-4) + c(z-1) = 0 \qquad \text{...(i)}$$
$$\text{[using one point form]}$$

Since, given plane (i) is also passing through point $(0, 1, 0)$.

So, this point also satisfies equation of plane (i)

$\therefore \quad a(0-3) + b(1-4) + c(0-1) = 0$

or $\qquad\qquad -3a - 3b - c = 0$

or $\qquad\qquad 3a + 3b + c = 0 \qquad \text{...(ii)}$

Also, given that plane (i) is parallel to the line

$$\frac{x+3}{2} = \frac{y-3}{7} = \frac{z-2}{5}$$

$\therefore \qquad\qquad a_1a_2 + b_1b_2 + c_1c_2 = 0 \qquad \text{...(iii)}$

[$\because$ line is parallel to the plane, therefore, normal to the plane is perpendicular to the line]

where $\qquad\qquad a_1 = a, b_1 = b, c_1 = c$

and $\qquad\qquad a_2 = 2, b_2 = 7, c_2 = 5$

$\therefore$ We get

$$2a + 7b + 5c = 0 \qquad \text{...(iii)}$$

Multiplying equation (ii) by 2 and equation (iii) by 3 then subtracting, we get

$$\begin{array}{r} 6a + 6b + 2c = 0 \\ 6a + 21b + 15c = 0 \\ \hline -\ \ \ -\ \ \ -\ \ \ \\ \hline -15b - 13c = 0 \end{array}$$

$$\Rightarrow \quad -15b = 13c$$

or $\qquad\qquad b = \frac{-13}{15}c$

Putting $b = \frac{-13c}{15}$ in equation (ii), we get

$$3a + 3\left(-\frac{13c}{15}\right) + c = 0$$

$$\Rightarrow \quad 3a - \frac{13}{5}c + c = 0$$

$$\Rightarrow \quad 3a - \frac{8c}{5} = 0$$

$$\Rightarrow \quad 3a = \frac{8c}{5}$$

$$\Rightarrow \quad a = \frac{8c}{15}$$

Putting $a = \frac{8c}{15}$ and $b = -\frac{13c}{15}$ in eq. (i), we get the required equation of plane as

$$\frac{8c}{15}(x-3) - \frac{13c}{15}(y-4) + c(z-1) = 0$$

Divide both sides by 'c', we get

$$\frac{8}{15}(x-3) - \frac{13}{15}(y-4) + z - 1 = 0$$

$\Rightarrow \quad 8x - 24 - 13y + 52 + 15z - 15 = 0$

$\Rightarrow \qquad\qquad 8x - 13y + 15z + 13 = 0$

131. Find the distance of the point $P(3, 4, 4)$ from the point, where the line joining the points $A(3, -4, -5)$ and $B(2, -3, 1)$ intersects the plane $2x + y + z = 7$.★

Sol. Equation of the line joining the points $A(3, -4, -5)$ and $B(2, -3, 1)$ is

$$\Rightarrow \quad \frac{x-3}{2-3} = \frac{y+4}{-3+4} = \frac{z+5}{1+5}$$

$$\Rightarrow \quad \frac{x-3}{-1} = \frac{y+4}{1} = \frac{z+5}{6} = k \text{ (say)}$$

Coordinates of any point on the line are

$$Q(3-k, k-4, 6k-5)$$

The given line intersects the plane $2x + y + z = 7$

So, $\quad 2(3-k) + k - 4 + 6k - 5 = 7$

$\Rightarrow \qquad 6 - 2k + k - 4 + 6k - 5 = 7$

$\Rightarrow \qquad\qquad\qquad 5k = 10$

$\Rightarrow \qquad\qquad\qquad k = 2$

$\therefore$ Coordinates of a point where line intersect plane are

$(3-k, k-4, 6k-5) = (3-2, 2-4, 12-5) = (1, -2, 7)$

Now, the distance between the point $P(3, 4, 4)$ and $Q(1, -2, 7)$ is given by

$$PQ = \sqrt{(3-1)^2 + (4+2)^2 + (4-7)^2}$$

$$PQ = \sqrt{(2)^2 + (6)^2 + (-3)^2}$$

$$PQ = \sqrt{4 + 36 + 9} = \sqrt{49}$$

$$PQ = 7 \text{ units.}$$

132. Find the distance between the point $(-1, -5, -10)$ and the point of intersection of the line $\dfrac{x-2}{3} = \dfrac{y+1}{4} = \dfrac{z-2}{12}$ and the plane $x - y + z = 5$.*

Sol. Let

$$\frac{x-2}{3} = \frac{y+1}{4} = \frac{z-2}{12} = k$$

$$\Rightarrow \quad x = 3k + 2,$$
$$y = 4k - 1,$$
$$z = 12k + 2$$

Coordinates of any point on the line are
$$(3k + 2, 4k - 1, 12k + 2)$$

The point of intersection of the line $\dfrac{x-2}{3} = \dfrac{y+1}{4}$

$= \dfrac{z-2}{12}$ and the plane $x - y + z = 5$ will also be in the form $(3k + 2, 4k - 1, 12k + 2)$ and it will satisfy the equation of plane.

Now, putting, $x = 3k + 2,$
$$y = 4k - 1$$
and $\qquad z = 12k + 2$ in equation of plane

we get $3k + 2 - (4k - 1) + 12k + 2 = 5$

$\Rightarrow \qquad 11k + 5 = 5$

$\Rightarrow \qquad 11k = 0$

$\Rightarrow \qquad k = 0$

$\therefore \ x = 2, y = -1, z = 2.$

Hence, the point of intersection of $\dfrac{x-2}{3} = \dfrac{y+1}{4}$

$= \dfrac{z-2}{12}$ and the plane $x - y + z = 5$ is $(2, -1, 2)$.

$\therefore$ Distance between the points $(-1, -5, -10)$ and $(2, -1, 2)$.

Using distance formula

$$= \sqrt{(2+1)^2 + (-1+5)^2 + (2+10)^2}$$

$$= \sqrt{3^2 + 4^2 + 12^2}$$

$$= \sqrt{169}$$

$$= 13 \text{ units}$$

Hence, the distance between the point $(-1, -5, -10)$ and the point of intersection of the line $\dfrac{x-2}{3} = \dfrac{y+1}{4}$

$= \dfrac{z-2}{12}$ and the plane $x - y + z = 5$ is 13 units.

<hr>

133. If the lines $\dfrac{x-1}{2} = \dfrac{y+1}{3} = \dfrac{z-1}{4}$ and $\dfrac{x-3}{1} = \dfrac{y-k}{2}$

$= \dfrac{z}{1}$ intersect each other then find the value of k and hence find the equation of the plane containing these lines.*

Sol. The coordinates of any point on first line are

$$\frac{x-1}{2} = \frac{y+1}{3} = \frac{z-1}{4} = \lambda$$

$i.e.,$
$$x = 2\lambda + 1$$
$$y = 3\lambda - 1,$$
$$z = 4\lambda + 1$$

$i.e., (2\lambda + 1, 3\lambda - 1, 4\lambda + 1)$

and the coordinates of any point on second line are

$$\frac{x-3}{1} = \frac{y-k}{2} = \frac{z}{1} = \mu \ i.e., x = \mu + 3,$$
$$y = 2\mu + k,$$
$$z = \mu$$

$i.e., \ (\mu + 3, 2\mu + k, \mu)$

if these two lines intersect each other, then

$$2\lambda + 1 = \mu + 3, \ 3\lambda - 1 = 2\mu + k, \ 4\lambda + 1 = \mu$$

$i.e., \ 2\lambda - \mu = 2, \ 3\lambda - 2\mu = k + 1, \ 4\lambda - \mu = -1$

Solving, $2\lambda - \mu = 2$ and $4\lambda - \mu = -1$, we get

$$\lambda = \frac{-3}{2} \text{ and } \mu = -5$$

Now, substituting the values of λ and μ in $3\lambda - 2\mu = k + 1$, we get

$$k = \frac{9}{2}$$

Now, we have $\vec{b_1} = 2\hat{i} + 3\hat{j} + 4\hat{k}$ and $\vec{b_1} = \hat{i} + 2\hat{j} + \hat{k}$. So, the required plane contains both lines and it passes through a point $\vec{a}\,(1, -1, 1)$ and perpendicular vector $\vec{n}$, given by

$$\vec{n} = \vec{b_1} \times \vec{b_2}$$

$$\vec{n} = \begin{vmatrix} \hat{i} & \hat{j} & \hat{k} \\ 2 & 3 & 4 \\ 1 & 2 & 1 \end{vmatrix}$$

$$= \hat{i}(3-8) - \hat{j}(2-4) + \hat{k}(4-3)$$

$$= -5\hat{i} + 2\hat{j} + \hat{k}$$

$\therefore$ The equation of plane passing through $\vec{a}$ and perpendicular to $\vec{n}$ is given by

$$(\vec{r} - \vec{a}) \cdot \vec{n} = 0$$

$$[\vec{r}.(\hat{i}-\hat{j}+\hat{k})].(-5\hat{i}+2\hat{j}+\hat{k})=0$$

$$\Rightarrow \quad \vec{r}.(-5\hat{i}+2\hat{j}+\hat{k}) = (\hat{i}-\hat{j}+\hat{k}).(-5\hat{i}+2\hat{j}+\hat{k})$$

$$\Rightarrow \quad \vec{r}.(-5\hat{i}+2\hat{j}+\hat{k}) = -6$$

Writing $\vec{r} = (x\hat{i}+y\hat{j}+z\hat{k})$

or $5x - 2y - z - 6 = 0.$

134. Find the coordinates of the point P where the line through A(3, – 4, – 5) and B(2, – 3, 1) crosses the plane passing through three points L(2, 2, 1), M(3, 0, 1) and N(4, – 1, 0). Also, find the ratio in which P divides the line segment AB.*

Sol. The equation of the plane passing through three given points can be given by

$$\begin{vmatrix} x-2 & y-2 & z-1 \\ 3-2 & 0-2 & 1-1 \\ 4-2 & -1-2 & 0-1 \end{vmatrix} = 0$$

$$\Rightarrow \begin{vmatrix} x-2 & y-2 & z-1 \\ 1 & -2 & 0 \\ 2 & -3 & -1 \end{vmatrix} = 0$$

Solving the above determinant, we get

$$\Rightarrow (x-2)(2-0) - (y-2)(-1-0)$$
$$+ (z-1)(-3+4) = 0$$
$$\Rightarrow (2x-4) + (y-2) + (z-1) = 0$$
$$\Rightarrow 2x + y + z - 7 = 0$$

Therefore, the equation of the plane is

$$2x + y + z - 7 = 0.$$

Now, the equation of the line passing through two given points is

$$\frac{x-3}{2-3} = \frac{y+4}{-3+4} = \frac{z+5}{1+5} = \lambda$$

$$\Rightarrow \frac{x-3}{-1} = \frac{y+4}{1} = \frac{z+5}{6} = \lambda$$

$$\Rightarrow x = (-\lambda + 3), y = (\lambda - 4), z = (6\lambda - 5)$$

At the point of intersection, the above point satisfy the equation of the plane $2x + y + z - 7 = 0$. Putting the values of x, y and z in the equation of the plane, we get the value of λ as

$$2(-\lambda + 3) + (\lambda - 4) + (6\lambda - 5) - 7 = 0$$
$$\Rightarrow -2\lambda + 6 + \lambda - 4 + 6\lambda - 5 - 7 = 0$$
$$\Rightarrow 5\lambda = 10$$
$$\Rightarrow \lambda = 2$$

Thus, the point of intersection is P(1, – 2, 7).

Now, let P divide the line AB in the ratio $m : n$. By the section formula, we have

$$1 = \frac{2m + 3n}{m + n}$$

$$\Rightarrow m + 2n = 0$$
$$\Rightarrow m = -2n$$
$$\Rightarrow \frac{m}{n} = \frac{-2}{1}$$

Hence, P divides the line segment *AB* externally in the ratio 2 : 1.

Self - Assessment

135. Find the distance between the points (2, 4, – 1) and (1, 3, 4) and then find the direction cosines of the lines joining the points.

Sol. $\sqrt{27}; \dfrac{-1}{\sqrt{27}}, \dfrac{-1}{\sqrt{27}}, \dfrac{5}{\sqrt{27}}$

136. Find the cartesian equation of the line which is parallel to the vector $2\hat{i}-\hat{j}+3\hat{k}$ and which passes through the point (5, – 2, 4).

Sol. $\dfrac{x-5}{2} = \dfrac{y+2}{-1} = \dfrac{z-4}{-3}$

137. Find the equation of a line passing through (1, – 1, 0) and parallel to the line $\dfrac{x-2}{3} = \dfrac{2y+1}{2} = \dfrac{5-z}{1}.$

Sol. $\dfrac{x-3}{1} = \dfrac{y+1}{1} = \dfrac{z}{-1}$

138. Find the equation of the line that passes through the origin and is parallel to $\dfrac{x-5}{3} = \dfrac{y+1}{4} = \dfrac{z}{1}.$

Sol. $\dfrac{x}{3} = \dfrac{y}{4} = \dfrac{z}{1}$

139. Find the value of k such that the lines $\dfrac{x-1}{3} = \dfrac{14-7y}{2k} = \dfrac{3-z}{2}$ and $\dfrac{7x-7}{3k} = \dfrac{5-y}{1} = \dfrac{z-6}{5}$ are perpendicular to each other.

Sol. $\dfrac{70}{11}$

140. Find the value of k such that lines are perpendicular to each other.

$$\dfrac{x-2}{3} = \dfrac{-(y+1)}{3} = \dfrac{z-2}{0} \text{ and } \dfrac{x-1}{1} = \dfrac{2y-3}{3} = \dfrac{(z+5)}{k}$$

Sol. 2

141. A vector $\vec{r}$ is equally inclined to the coordinates axes and $|\vec{r}| = 15\sqrt{3}$. Find $\vec{r}$.

Sol. $15(\hat{i} + \hat{j} + \hat{k})$

142. Let the vector equation of two lines are

$$\vec{r} = \hat{i} + 2\hat{j} + \hat{k} + t(\hat{i} - \hat{j} + \hat{k}),$$

$$\vec{r} = 2\hat{i} - \hat{j} - \hat{k} + u(2\hat{i} + \hat{j} + 2\hat{k})$$

Find the shortest distance between them.

Sol. $\dfrac{3}{\sqrt{2}}$

143. Check whether the lines $l_1 : \vec{r} = \hat{i} - \hat{j} + t(2\hat{i} + \hat{k})$ and $l_2 : \vec{R} = 2\hat{i} - \hat{j} + u(2\hat{i} + \hat{j} - \hat{k})$ are skew lines or not. Hence, find the shortest distance between them.

Sol. Skew lines; $\dfrac{1}{\sqrt{14}}$

144. By computing the shortest distance, determine whether the following lines intersect or not. The lines are $\dfrac{x-1}{2} = \dfrac{y+1}{3} = z$ and $\dfrac{x+1}{5} = \dfrac{y-2}{1} = z - 2$.

Sol. The lines do not intersect.

145. Find out whether the pair of lines intersect or not :

$$\vec{r} = (1-t)\hat{i} + (t-2)\hat{j} + (3-2k)\hat{k}$$

and

$$\vec{r} = (s+1)\hat{i} + (2s-1)\hat{j} - (2s+1)\hat{k}$$

Sol. The lines do not intersect.

146. Find the Cartesian equation of the plane through the point with position vector $2\hat{i} - \hat{j} + \hat{k}$ and perpendi-cular to the vector $4\hat{i} + 2\hat{j} - 3\hat{k}$.

Sol. $4x + 2y - 3z - 3 = 0$

147. Find the vector and Cartesian equation of the plane containing the two lines

$$\vec{r} = 2\hat{i} + \hat{j} - 3\hat{k} + \lambda(\hat{i} + 2\hat{j} + 5\hat{k})$$

and

$$\vec{r} = 3\hat{i} + 3\hat{j} - 7\hat{k} + \mu(3\hat{i} - 2\hat{j} + 5\hat{k})$$

Sol. $\vec{r} \cdot (10\hat{i} + 5\hat{j} - 4\hat{k}) = 37,\ 10x + 5y - 4z = 37$

148. Find the equation of a plane passing through the points $A(1, 1, 1)$, $B(1, -1, 1)$ and $C(-7, -3, -5)$.

Sol. $3x - 4z + 1 = 0$

149. Obtain the equation of a plane passing through $(-2, -2, 2)$ and containing the line joining $(1, 1, 1)$ and $(1, -1, 2)$.

Sol. $x - 3y - 6z + 8 = 0$

150. Find the intercepts cut-off by the plane $x - 3y - 6z + 8 = 0$ with the coordinate axes.

Sol. $-8,\ \dfrac{8}{3},\ \dfrac{4}{3}$ on X, Y, Z axes respectively

151. Write the equation of the plane whose intercepts on the coordinate axes are $-4, 2$ and 3.

Sol. $3x - 6y - 4x + 12 = 0$

152. If the planes $\vec{r} \cdot (2\hat{i} + \hat{j} + \lambda\hat{k}) = 5$ and $\vec{r} \cdot (3\hat{i} + 2\hat{j} + 2\hat{k}) = 4$ are perpendicular. Find the value of λ.

Sol. $\lambda = -2$

153. Find the line represented by the intersection of the planes $x + y + z + 1 = 0$ and $4x + y - 2z + 2 = 0$.

Sol. $-\dfrac{1}{3}\hat{i} - \dfrac{2}{3}\hat{j} - \dfrac{t}{\sqrt{7}}(\hat{i} - 2\hat{j} + \hat{k})$

154. Find the distance of the point $\hat{i} + 2\hat{j} + 3\hat{k}$ from the plane $\vec{r}(\hat{i} + \hat{j} + \hat{k}) = 5$.

Sol. $-\dfrac{1}{\sqrt{3}}$

155. If the line $\vec{r} = (\hat{i} - 2\hat{j} + \hat{k}) + \lambda(2\hat{i} + \hat{j} + 2\hat{k})$ is parallel to the plane $\vec{r} \cdot (3\hat{i} - 2\hat{j} + m\hat{k})$ then find the value of m.

Sol. -2

◯◯

Probability

1. **Probability** is a measure of uncertainty of events in a random experiment.

2. In probability, a numerical value is assigned to the chance of happening of an event.

3. **Experiment** is an operation which can produce some well defined outcomes.

4. If all possible outcomes of an experiment are known but the exact output cannot be predicted in advance then the experiment is called a **random experiment.**

5. The set of all possible outcomes of an experiment is called the **sample space.**

6. Any subset of a sample space is called an **event**.

7. The probability of occurrence of an event E is defined as

$$P(E) = \frac{n(E)}{n(S)}$$

   where $n(E)$ = No. of elements in the event E

   $n(S)$ = No. of elements of the sample space S

8. Two or more events associated with a random experiment are **mutually exclusive** if no two or more of them can occur simultaneously in the same trial.

9. Two or more events associated with a random experiment are said to be **exhaustive** if their union is the sample space.

10. **(i)** The probability of a certain event *i.e.*, the event which is likely to happen is 1.

    (ii) The probability of any event E must be greater than or equal to 0 and less than or equal to 1 *i.e.*,

    $$0 \le P(E) \le 1.$$

    (iii) The probability of uncertain event *i.e.*, event which can not be possible is 0.

11. For any events A and B,

    $$P(A \cup B) = P(A) + P(B) - P(A \cap B).$$

12. If $\overline{A}$ or A' or A^c denotes (not A) then

    $$P(\overline{A}) = P(A') = P(A^c) = 1 - P(A).$$

13. If A and B are two independent events, then

    $$P(A \cap B) = P(A) \cdot P(B).$$

14. If A and B are two mutually exclusive events, then

    $$A \cap B = \phi \Rightarrow P(A \cap B) = 0.$$

15. Two events A and B are said to be **independent** if the occurrence of one does not depend upon the occurrence of the other.

16. If two events are not independent, they are said to be **dependent.**

17. **Addition theorem : (i)** When A and B are mutually exclusive events then probability of occurrence of either A or B is given by,

    $$P(A \cup B) = P(A) + P(B).$$

    (ii) When A and B are not mutually exclusive events then probability of occurrence either A or B is given by

    $$P(A \cup B) = P(A) + P(B) - P(A \cap B)$$

    For three mutually exclusive events A, B and C :

    $$P(A \cup B \cup C) = P(A) + P(B) + P(C) - P(A \cap B)$$
    $$- P(B \cap C) - P(C \cap A) + P(A \cap B \cap C)$$

18. If A and B are two events associated with the same sample space of a random experiment then the conditional probability of the event A given that B has already occurred *i.e.*, $P(A/B)$ is given by

    $$P(A/B) = \frac{P(A \cap B)}{P(B)} \text{ provided } P(B) \ne 0$$

    Similarly, $P(B/A) = \dfrac{P(A \cap B)}{P(A)}$ provided $P(A) \ne 0.$

19. Properties of conditional probability are as follows :

    (i) If A and B are the events of a sample space S of an experiment then

    $$P(A/A) = P(B/B) = 1$$

    (ii) If A and B are any two events of a sample space S and F is an event of S such that $P(F) \ne 0$, then

    $$P[(A \cup B)/F] = P(A/F) + P(B/F) - P[(A \cap B)/F]$$

    (iii) $P(A'/B) = 1 - P(A/B)$

20. Let A and B be two events associated with a sample space S.

Then $P(A \cap B) = P(A) \cdot P(B/A) = P(B) \cdot P(A/B)$

provided $P(A) \neq 0$ and $P(B) \neq 0$

This result is known as the **multiplication theorem of probability.**

21. **Multiplication theorem of probability for more than two events :** If A, B and C are three events of sample space S, then we have

$$P(A \cap B \cap C) = P(A) \cdot P(B/A) \cdot P(C/(A \cap B)]$$
$$= P(A) \cdot P(B/A) \cdot P(C/AB)$$

22. Two events A and B are said to be independent, if

$$P(B/A) = P(B), \text{ provided } P(A) \neq 0$$

and $P(A/B) = P(A)$, provided $P(B) \neq 0$

i.e., occurrence or non-occurrence of one event does not affect the probability of the occurrence or non-occurrence of other event.

23. Three events A, B and C are said to be mutually independent, if

$$P(A \cap B) = P(A) \cdot P(B)$$
$$P(A \cap C) = P(A) \cdot P(C)$$
$$P(B \cap C) = P(B) \cdot P(C)$$
$$P(A \cap B \cap C) = P(A) \cdot P(B) \cdot P(C)$$

24. If the events A and B are independent, then

(i) $\overline{A}$ and B are independent.

(ii) A and $\overline{B}$ are independent.

(iii) $\overline{A}$ and $\overline{B}$ are independent.

25. Let E_1, E_2, ..., E_n be a mutually exclusive and exhaustive events associated with a random experiment and S be the sample space.
Suppose that each of the events E_1, E_2, ..., E_n has non-zero probability of occurrence. Let A be any event associated with S, then

$$P(A) = P(E_1) \cdot P(A/E_1) + P(E_2) \cdot P(A/E_2)$$
$$+ P(E_3) \cdot P(A/E_3) + ... + P(E_n) P(A/E_n)$$

$$P(A) = \sum_{j=1}^{n} P(E_j) \cdot P(A/E_j)$$

This result is called the **law of total probability.**

26. **Bayes' Theorem :** Let S be the sample space and let E_1, E_2, ... E_n be n mutually exclusive and exhaustive events associated with a random experiment.

If A is any event of non-zero probability which occurs with E_1 or E_2 or ... or E_n, then

$$P(E_i/A) = \frac{P(E_i) \cdot P(A/E_i)}{\sum_{i=1}^{n} P(E_i) \cdot P(A/E_i)} \text{ for any } i = 1, 2, 3, ..., n$$

27. A random variable is a real valued function whose domain is the sample space of a random experiment.

28. A description giving the values of the random variable along with the corresponding probabilities is called the **probability distribution** of the random variable X.

29. The probability distribution of a random variable X is the system of numbers.

$$X: \quad x_1 \quad x_2 \quad ... \quad x_n$$
$$P(X): \quad p_1 \quad p_2 \quad ... \quad p_n$$

where $p_i > 0$, $\sum_{i=1}^{n} p_i = 1$, $i = 1, 2, 3, ..., n$

where x_i is the possible values of the random variable X.

p_i is the probability of random variable X taking the value x_i.

30. Trials of a random experiment are called **Bernoulli trials** if they satisfy the following conditions :

(i) There should be a finite no. of trials.

(ii) The trials should be independent of each other.

(iii) Each trial has exactly two outcomes : success or failure.

(iv) The probability of success remains the same in each trial.

31. In an experiment of n-Bernoulli's trials, the probabilities of 0, 1, 2, ..., n success can be obtained as 1st, 2nd, ... $(n + 1)^{th}$ terms in the expansion of $(q + p)^n$.

32. The probability of x success in n-Bernoulli trials is $^nC_x p^x q^{n-x}$, where $x = 0, 1, 2, ..., n$ and $q = 1 - p$.

Multiple Choice Questions

1. From the set $\{1, 2, 3, 4, 5\}$, two numbers a and $b(a \neq b)$ are chosen at random. The probability that $\dfrac{a}{b}$ is an integer is:*

(a) $\dfrac{1}{3}$ (b) $\dfrac{1}{4}$

(c) $\dfrac{1}{2}$ (d) $\dfrac{3}{5}$

Sol. (b) $\dfrac{1}{4}$

Explanation :

Total possible outcomes of (a, b) = {(1, 2), (1, 3), (1, 4), (1, 5), (2, 1), (2, 3), (2, 4), (2, 5), (3, 1), (3, 2), (3, 4), (3, 5), (4, 1), (4, 2), (4, 3), (4, 5), (5, 1), (5, 2), (5, 3), (5, 4)}

$\Rightarrow$ Number of possible outcomes = 20

Also, favourable outcomes of (a, b) = {(2, 1), (3, 1), (4, 1), (4, 2), (5, 1)}

$\Rightarrow$ Number of possible outcomes = 5

$\therefore \quad P\left(\dfrac{a}{b} \text{ is integer}\right) = \dfrac{5}{20} = \dfrac{1}{4}$

So the correct option is (b).

2. A bag contains 3 white, 4 black and 2 red balls. If 2 balls are drawn at random (without replacement), then the probability that both the balls are white is :*

(a) $\dfrac{1}{18}$ (b) $\dfrac{1}{36}$

(c) $\dfrac{1}{12}$ (d) $\dfrac{1}{24}$

Sol. (c) $\dfrac{1}{12}$

Explanation :

Required probability = $\dfrac{^3C_2}{^9C_2} = \dfrac{1}{12}$

So the correct option is (c).

3. A die is thrown once. Let A be the event that the number obtained is greater than 3. Let B be the event that the number obtained is less than 5. Then $P(A \cup B)$ is :*

(a) $\dfrac{2}{5}$ (b) $\dfrac{3}{5}$

(c) 0   (d) 1

Sol. (d) 1

Explanation :

$$S = \{1, 2, 3, 4, 5, 6\}$$
$$A = \{4, 5, 6\}$$
$$B = \{1, 2, 3, 4\}$$
$$P(A) = \dfrac{3}{6}$$
$$P(B) = \dfrac{4}{6}$$
$$A \cap B = \{4\}$$
and $\quad P(A \cap B) = \dfrac{1}{6}$

We know,
$$P(A \cup B) = P(A) + P(B) - P(A \cap B)$$
$$= \dfrac{3}{6} + \dfrac{4}{6} - \dfrac{1}{6}$$
$$= \dfrac{6}{6} = 1$$

So the correct option is (d).

** are board exam questions from previous years*

4. A number is chosen randomly from numbers 1 to 60. The prabability that the chosen number is multiple of 2 or 5 is:

(a) $\dfrac{2}{5}$ (b) $\dfrac{3}{5}$

(c) $\dfrac{7}{10}$ (d) $\dfrac{9}{10}$

Sol. (b) $\dfrac{3}{5}$

Explanation :

Let $\quad\quad\quad A$ = Numbers multiple of 2
$$(A) = 30$$
and $\quad\quad\quad B$ = Numbers multiple of 5
$$(B) = 12$$
$\therefore \quad P(A \cup B) = P(A) + P(B) - P(A \cap B)$
$$= \dfrac{30}{60} + \dfrac{12}{60} - \dfrac{6}{60}$$
$$= \dfrac{36}{60} = \dfrac{3}{5}$$

So the correct option is (b).

5. If $P(A) = \dfrac{4}{5}$ and $P(A \cap B) = \dfrac{7}{10}$, then $P(B|A)$ is equal to: **[NCERT Exemplar]**

(a) $\dfrac{1}{10}$ (b) $\dfrac{1}{8}$

(c) $\dfrac{7}{8}$ (d) $\dfrac{17}{20}$

Sol. (c) $\dfrac{7}{8}$

Explanation :

$\therefore \quad\quad P(A) = \dfrac{4}{5}, \ P(A \cap B) = \dfrac{7}{10}$

$\because \quad\quad P(B|A) = \dfrac{P(A \cap B)}{P(A)}$

$$= \dfrac{7/10}{4/5} = \dfrac{7}{8}.$$

6. If $P(A \cap B) = \dfrac{7}{10}$ and $P(B) = \dfrac{17}{20}$, then $P(A|B)$ is equal to: **[NCERT Exemplar]**

(a) $\dfrac{14}{17}$ (b) $\dfrac{17}{20}$

(c) $\dfrac{7}{8}$ (d) $\dfrac{1}{8}$

Sol. (a) $\dfrac{14}{17}$

Explanation :

Here, $P(A \cap B) = \dfrac{7}{10}$ and $P(B) = \dfrac{17}{20}$

$\therefore$ $P(A|B) = \dfrac{P(A \cap B)}{P(B)} = \dfrac{7/10}{17/20} = \dfrac{14}{17}.$

7. If $P(A) = \dfrac{3}{10}$, $P(B) = \dfrac{2}{5}$ and $P(A \cup B) = \dfrac{3}{5}$, then

$P(B|A) + P(A|B)$ is equal to:

[NCERT Exemplar]

(a) $\dfrac{1}{4}$ (b) $\dfrac{1}{3}$

(c) $\dfrac{5}{12}$ (d) $\dfrac{7}{12}$

Sol. (d) $\dfrac{7}{12}$

Explanation :

Here, $P(A) = \dfrac{3}{10}$, $P(B) = \dfrac{2}{5}$ and $P(A \cup B) = \dfrac{3}{5}$

$P(B|A) + P(A|B)$

$= \dfrac{P(B \cap A)}{P(A)} + \dfrac{P(A \cap B)}{P(B)}$

$= \dfrac{P(A)+P(B)-P(A \cup B)}{P(A)} + \dfrac{P(A)+P(B)-P(A \cup B)}{P(B)}$

$\left[\begin{array}{l} \because P(A \cup B) = P(A)+P(B)-P(A \cap B) \\ i.e., P(A \cap B) = P(A)+P(B)-P(A \cup B) \end{array} \right]$

$= \dfrac{\dfrac{3}{10}+\dfrac{2}{5}-\dfrac{3}{5}}{\dfrac{3}{10}} + \dfrac{\dfrac{3}{10}+\dfrac{2}{5}-\dfrac{3}{5}}{\dfrac{2}{5}}$

$= \dfrac{\dfrac{1}{10}}{\dfrac{3}{10}} + \dfrac{\dfrac{1}{10}}{\dfrac{2}{5}} = \dfrac{1}{3}+\dfrac{1}{4} = \dfrac{7}{12}.$

8. If $P(A) = \dfrac{2}{5}$, $P(B) = \dfrac{3}{10}$ and $P(A \cap B) = \dfrac{1}{5}$, then

$P(A'|B') \cdot P(B'|A')$ is equal to:

[NCERT Exemplar]

(a) $\dfrac{5}{6}$ (b) $\dfrac{5}{7}$

(c) $\dfrac{25}{42}$ (d) 1

Sol. (c) $\dfrac{25}{42}$

Explanation :

Here, $P(A) = \dfrac{2}{5}$, $P(B) = \dfrac{3}{10}$ and $P(A \cap B) = \dfrac{1}{5}$

$P(A'|B') = \dfrac{P(A' \cap B')}{P(B')} = \dfrac{1-P(A \cup B)}{1-P(B)}$

$= \dfrac{1-[P(A)+P(B)-P(A \cap B)]}{1-P(B)}$

$= \dfrac{1-\left(\dfrac{2}{5}+\dfrac{3}{10}-\dfrac{1}{5}\right)}{1-\dfrac{3}{10}}$

$= \dfrac{1-\left(\dfrac{4+3-2}{10}\right)}{\dfrac{7}{10}} = \dfrac{1-\dfrac{1}{2}}{\dfrac{7}{10}} = \dfrac{5}{7}$

and $P(B'|A') = \dfrac{P(B' \cap A')}{P(A')} = \dfrac{1-P(A \cup B)}{1-P(A)}$

$= \dfrac{1-\dfrac{1}{2}}{1-\dfrac{2}{5}} = \dfrac{1/2}{3/5} = \dfrac{5}{6}$

$\left[\because P(A \cup B) = \dfrac{1}{2} \right]$

$\therefore P(A'|B') \cdot P(B'|A') = \dfrac{5}{7} \cdot \dfrac{5}{6} = \dfrac{25}{42}.$

9. If A and B are two events such that $P(A) = \dfrac{1}{2}$,

$P(B) = \dfrac{1}{3}$ and $P(A/B) = \dfrac{1}{4}$, then $P(A' \cap B')$ is

equal to: **[NCERT Exemplar]**

(a) $\dfrac{1}{12}$ (b) $\dfrac{3}{4}$

(c) $\dfrac{1}{4}$ (d) $\dfrac{3}{16}$

Sol. (c) $\dfrac{1}{4}$

Explanation :

Here, $P(A) = \dfrac{1}{2}$, $P(B) = \dfrac{1}{3}$ and $P(A|B) = \dfrac{1}{4}$

$\because$ $P(A|B) = \dfrac{P(A \cap B)}{P(B)}$

$\Rightarrow$ $P(A \cap B) = P(A|B) \cdot P(B) = \dfrac{1}{4} \cdot \dfrac{1}{3} = \dfrac{1}{12}$

Now, $P(A' \cap B') = 1 - P(A \cup B)$

$= 1 - [P(A)+P(B)-P(A \cap B)]$

$= 1 - \left[\dfrac{1}{2}+\dfrac{1}{3}-\dfrac{1}{12}\right]$

$= 1 - \left[\dfrac{6+4-1}{12}\right]$

$= 1 - \dfrac{9}{12} = \dfrac{3}{12} = \dfrac{1}{4}.$

10. If $P(A) = 0.4$, $P(B) = 0.8$ and $P(B \mid A) = 0.6$, then $P(A \cup B)$ is equal to: **[NCERT Exemplar]**

(a) 0.24   (b) 0.3

(c) 0.48   (d) 0.96

Sol. (d) 0.96

Explanation :

Here, $P(A) = 0.4$, $P(B) = 0.8$ and $P(A \mid B) = 0.6$

$\because \quad P(B \mid A) = \dfrac{P(B \cap A)}{P(A)}$

$\Rightarrow \quad P(B \cap A) = P(B/A) \cdot P(A)$

$\qquad\qquad = 0.6 \times 0.4 = 0.24$

$\because \quad P(A \cup B) = P(A) + P(B) - P(A \cap B)$

$\qquad\qquad = 0.4 + 0.8 - 0.24$

$\qquad\qquad = -1.2 - 0.24 = 0.96.$

11. If A and B are two events and $A \neq \phi$, $B \neq \phi$, then:

[NCERT Exemplar]

(a) $P(A \mid B) = P(A) \cdot P(B)$

(b) $P(A \mid B) = \dfrac{P(A \cap B)}{P(B)}$

(c) $P(A \mid B) \cdot P(B/A) = 1$

(d) $P(A \mid B) = P(A)/P(B)$

Sol. (b) $P(A \mid B) = \dfrac{P(A \cap B)}{P(B)}$

Explanation :

If $A \neq \phi$ and $B \neq \phi$, then $P(A \mid B) = \dfrac{P(A \cap B)}{P(B)}.$

12. If A and B are two events such that $P(B) = \dfrac{3}{5}$, $P(A \mid B) = \dfrac{1}{2}$ and $P(A \cup B) = \dfrac{4}{5}$, then $P(A)$ is equal to: **[NCERT Exemplar]**

(a) $\dfrac{3}{10}$ (b) $\dfrac{1}{5}$

(c) $\dfrac{1}{2}$ (d) $\dfrac{3}{5}$

Sol. (c) $\dfrac{1}{2}$

Explanation :

Here, $P(B) = \dfrac{3}{5}$, $P(A \mid B) = \dfrac{1}{2}$ and $P(A \cup B) = \dfrac{4}{5}$

$\because \qquad P(A \mid B) = \dfrac{P(A \cap B)}{P(B)}$

$\Rightarrow \qquad \dfrac{1}{2} = \dfrac{P(A \cap B)}{3/5}$

$\Rightarrow \qquad P(A \cap B) = \dfrac{3}{5} \times \dfrac{1}{2} = \dfrac{3}{10}$

and $\qquad P(A \cup B) = P(A) + P(B) - P(A \cap B)$

$\Rightarrow \qquad \dfrac{4}{5} = P(A) + \dfrac{3}{5} - \dfrac{3}{10}$

$\therefore \qquad P(A) = \dfrac{4}{5} - \dfrac{3}{5} + \dfrac{3}{10} = \dfrac{8 - 6 + 3}{10} = \dfrac{1}{2}.$

13. If A and B are events such that $P(A) = 0.4$, $P(B) = 0.3$ and $P(A \cup B) = 0.5$, then $P(B' \cap A)$ is equal to: **[NCERT Exemplar]**

(a) $\dfrac{2}{3}$ (b) $\dfrac{1}{2}$

(c) $\dfrac{3}{10}$ (d) $\dfrac{1}{5}$

Sol. (d) $\dfrac{1}{5}$

Explanation :

Here, $P(A) = 0.4$, $P(B) = 0.3$ and $P(A \cup B) = 0.5$

$\because \qquad P(A \cup B) = P(A) + P(B) - P(A \cap B)$

$\Rightarrow \qquad P(A \cap B) = 0.4 + 0.3 - 0.5 = 0.2$

$\therefore \qquad P(B' \cap A) = P(A) - P(A \cap B)$

$\qquad\qquad = 0.4 - 0.2 = 0.2 = \dfrac{1}{5}.$

14. In question $P(B \mid A')$ is equal to:

[NCERT Exemplar]

(a) $\dfrac{1}{5}$ (b) $\dfrac{3}{10}$

(c) $\dfrac{1}{2}$ (d) $\dfrac{3}{5}$

Sol. (d) $\dfrac{3}{5}$

Explanation :

$P(B \mid A') = \dfrac{P(B \cap A')}{P(A')} = \dfrac{P(B) - P(B \cap A)}{1 - P(A)}$

$= \dfrac{\dfrac{3}{5} - \dfrac{3}{10}}{1 - \dfrac{1}{2}} = \dfrac{\dfrac{6-3}{10}}{\dfrac{1}{2}} = \dfrac{6}{10} = \dfrac{3}{5}.$

15. If $P(B) = \dfrac{3}{5}$, $P(A \mid B) = \dfrac{1}{2}$ and $P(A \cup B) = \dfrac{4}{5}$, then $P(A \cup B)' + P(A' \cup B)$ is equal to:

[NCERT Exemplar]

(a) $\dfrac{1}{5}$ (b) $\dfrac{4}{5}$

(c) $\dfrac{1}{2}$ (d) 1

Sol. (d) 1

Explanation :

Here, $\quad P(B) = \dfrac{3}{5},\ P(A\,|\,B) = \dfrac{1}{2}$

and $\quad P(A \cup B) = \dfrac{4}{5}$

Since, $\quad P(A\,|\,B) = \dfrac{P(A\cap B)}{P(B)}$

$\Rightarrow \quad P(A\cap B) = P(A\,|\,B)\cdot P(B)$

$$= \dfrac{1}{2}\times\dfrac{3}{5} = \dfrac{3}{10}$$

Also, $\quad P(A\cup B) = P(A) + P(B) - P(A\cap B)$

$\Rightarrow \quad P(A) = \dfrac{4}{5} - \dfrac{3}{5} + \dfrac{3}{10} = \dfrac{1}{2}$

$\therefore \quad P(A\cup B)' = 1 - P(A\cup B) = 1 - \dfrac{4}{5} = \dfrac{1}{5}$

and $\quad P(A'\cup B) = 1 - P(A - B)$

$$= 1 - P(A\cap B')$$

$$= 1 - P(A)\cdot P(B')$$

$$= 1 - \dfrac{1}{2}\cdot\dfrac{2}{5} = \dfrac{4}{5}$$

$\Rightarrow P(A\cup B)' + P(A'\cup B)$

$$= \dfrac{1}{5} + \dfrac{4}{5} = \dfrac{5}{5} = 1.$$

16. If $P(A) = \dfrac{7}{13}$, $P(B) = \dfrac{9}{13}$ and $P(A\cap B) = \dfrac{4}{13}$, then $P(A'\,|\,B)$ is equal to: **[NCERT Exemplar]**

(a) $\dfrac{6}{13}$ (b) $\dfrac{4}{13}$

(c) $\dfrac{4}{9}$ (d) $\dfrac{5}{9}$

Sol. (d) $\dfrac{5}{9}$

Explanation :

Here, $P(A) = \dfrac{7}{13}$, $P(B) = \dfrac{9}{13}$ and $P(A\cap B) = \dfrac{4}{13}$

$\therefore \quad P(A'\,|\,B) = \dfrac{P(A'\cap B)}{P(B)} = \dfrac{P(B) - P(A\cap B)}{P(B)}$

$$= \dfrac{\dfrac{9}{13} - \dfrac{4}{13}}{\dfrac{9}{13}} = \dfrac{\dfrac{5}{13}}{\dfrac{9}{13}} = \dfrac{5}{9}.$$

17. If A and B are such events that $P(A) > 0$ and $P(B) \neq 1$, then $P(A'/B')$ is equal to: **[NCERT Exemplar]**

(a) $1 - P(A\,|\,B)$ (b) $1 - P(A'\,|\,B)$

(c) $\dfrac{1 - P(A\cup B)}{P(B')}$ (d) $P(A')\,|\,P(B')$

Sol. (c) $\dfrac{1 - P(A\cup B)}{P(B')}$

Explanation :

$\because \quad P(A) > 0$ and $P(B) \neq 1$

$$P(A'\,|\,B') = \dfrac{P(A'\cap B')}{P(B')} = \dfrac{1 - P(A\cup B)}{P(B')}.$$

18. If A and B are two independent events with $P(A) = \dfrac{3}{5}$ and $P(B) = \dfrac{4}{9}$, then $P(A'\cap B')$ is equal to: **[NCERT Exemplar]**

(a) $\dfrac{4}{15}$ (b) $\dfrac{8}{45}$

(c) $\dfrac{1}{3}$ (d) $\dfrac{2}{9}$

Sol. (d) $\dfrac{2}{9}$

Explanation :

$P(A'\cap B') = 1 - P(A\cup B)$

$$= 1 - [P(A) + P(B) - P(A\cap B)]$$

$$= 1 - \left[\dfrac{3}{5} + \dfrac{4}{9} - \dfrac{3}{5}\times\dfrac{4}{9}\right]$$

$$[\because P(A\cap B) = P(A)\cdot P(B)]$$

$$= 1 - \left[\dfrac{27 + 20 - 12}{45}\right]$$

$$= 1 - \dfrac{35}{45}$$

$$= \dfrac{10}{45} = \dfrac{2}{9}.$$

19. If A and B be two events such that $P(A) = \dfrac{3}{8}$, $P(B) = \dfrac{5}{8}$ and $P(A\cup B) = \dfrac{3}{4}$, then $P(A\,|\,B)\cdot P(A'\,|\,B)$ is equal to: **[NCERT Exemplar]**

(a) $\dfrac{2}{5}$ (b) $\dfrac{3}{8}$

(c) $\dfrac{3}{20}$ (d) $\dfrac{6}{25}$

Sol. (d) $\dfrac{6}{25}$

Explanation :

Here, $P(A) = \dfrac{3}{8}$, $P(B) = \dfrac{5}{8}$ and $P(A\cup B) = \dfrac{6}{25}$

$\because \quad P(A\cup B) = P(A) + P(B) - P(A\cap B)$

$\Rightarrow \quad P(A\cap B) = \dfrac{3}{8} + \dfrac{5}{8} - \dfrac{3}{4} = \dfrac{3 + 5 - 6}{8} = \dfrac{2}{8} = \dfrac{1}{4}$

$$\because \quad P(A\,|\,B) = \frac{P(A\cap B)}{P(B)} = \frac{1/4}{5/8} = \frac{8}{20} = \frac{2}{5}$$

$$\text{and} \quad P(A'\,|\,B) = \frac{P(A'\cap B)}{P(B)} = \frac{P(B)-P(A\cap B)}{P(B)}$$

$$= \frac{\dfrac{5}{8}-\dfrac{1}{4}}{\dfrac{5}{8}} = \frac{\dfrac{5-2}{8}}{\dfrac{5}{8}} = \frac{3}{5}$$

$$\therefore \quad P(A\,|\,B) \cdot P(A'\,|\,B) = \frac{2}{5}\cdot\frac{3}{5} = \frac{6}{25}.$$

20. Assume that in a family, each child is equally likely to be a boy or a girl. A family with three children is chosen at random. The probability that the eldest child is a girl given that the family has atleast one girl is: **[NCERT Exemplar]**

(a) $\dfrac{1}{2}$ (b) $\dfrac{1}{3}$

(c) $\dfrac{2}{3}$ (d) $\dfrac{4}{7}$

Sol. (d) $\dfrac{4}{7}$

Explanation :

Here, $S = \{(B, B, B), (G, G, G), (B, G, G), (G, B, G),$ $(G, G, B), (G, B, B), (B, G, B), (B, B, G)\}$

E_1 = Event that a family has atleast one girl, then
$E_1 = \{(G, B, B), (B, G, B), (B, B, G), (G, G, B),$ $(B, G, G), (G, B, G), (G, G, G,)\}$

E_2 = Event that the eldest child is a girl, then
$$E_2 = \{(G, B, B), (G, G, B), (G, B, G),$$
$$(G, G, G)\}$$

$$\therefore \quad E_1 \cap E_2 = \{(G, B, B), (G, G, B), (G, B, G),$$
$$(G, G, G,)\}$$

$$\therefore \quad P(E_2\,|\,E_1) = \frac{P(E_1\cap E_2)}{P(E_1)} = \frac{4/8}{7/8} = \frac{4}{7}.$$

21. Two dice are thrown. If it is know that the sum of numbers on the dice was less than 6, the probability of getting a sum 3, is:
 [NCERT Exemplar]

(a) $\dfrac{1}{18}$ (b) $\dfrac{5}{18}$

(c) $\dfrac{1}{5}$ (d) $\dfrac{2}{5}$

Sol. (c) $\dfrac{1}{5}$

Explanation :

Let, E_1 = Event that the sum of numbers on the dice was less than 6

and E_2 = Event that the sum of numbers on the dice is 3

$\therefore \quad E_1 = \{(1, 4), (4, 1), (2, 3), (3, 2), (2, 2),$ $(1, 3), (3, 1), (1, 2), (2, 1), (1, 1)\}$

$\Rightarrow \quad n(E_1) = 10$

and $\quad E_2 = \{(1, 2), (2, 1)\}$

$\Rightarrow \quad n(E_2) = 2$

$\therefore$ Required probability $= \dfrac{2}{10} = \dfrac{1}{5}.$

22. In a college, 30% students fail in Physics, 25% fail in Mathematics and 10% fail in both. One student is chosen at random. The probability that she fails in Physics, if she has failed in Mathematics is: **[NCERT Exemplar]**

(a) $\dfrac{1}{10}$ (b) $\dfrac{2}{5}$

(c) $\dfrac{9}{20}$ (d) $\dfrac{1}{3}$

Sol. (b) $\dfrac{2}{5}$

Explanation :

Here, $\quad P_{(Ph)} = \dfrac{30}{100} = \dfrac{3}{10},\ P_{(M)} = \dfrac{25}{100} = \dfrac{1}{4}$

and $\quad P_{(M\cap Ph)} = \dfrac{10}{100} = \dfrac{1}{10}$

$$P(Ph\,|\,M) = \frac{P(Ph\cap M)}{P(M)} = \frac{1/10}{1/4} = \frac{2}{5}.$$

23. A and B are two students. Their chances of solving a problem correctly are $\dfrac{1}{3}$ and $\dfrac{1}{4}$, respectively. If the probability of their making a common error is, $\dfrac{1}{20}$ and they obtain the same answer, then the probability of their answer to be correct is: **[NCERT Exemplar]**

(a) $\dfrac{1}{12}$ (b) $\dfrac{1}{40}$

(c) $\dfrac{13}{120}$ (d) $\dfrac{10}{13}$

Sol. (d) $\dfrac{10}{13}$

Explanation :

Let E_1 = Event the both A and B solve the problem correctly.

$$\therefore \qquad P(E_1) = \frac{1}{3}\times\frac{1}{4} = \frac{1}{12}$$

Let E_2 = Event that both A and B got incorrect solution of the problem.

$$\therefore \qquad P(E_2) = \frac{2}{3} \times \frac{3}{4} = \frac{1}{2}$$

Let E = Event that they got same answer, correctly.

Here, $\qquad P(E | E_1) = 1, \ P(E | E_2) = \frac{1}{20}$

$$\therefore \quad P(E_1 | E) = \frac{P(E_1 \cap E)}{P(E)}$$

$$= \frac{P(E_1) \cdot P(E | E_1)}{P(E_1) \cdot P(E | E_1) + P(E_2) \, P(E | E_2)}$$

$$= \frac{\dfrac{1}{12} \times 1}{\dfrac{1}{12} \times 1 + \dfrac{1}{2} \times \dfrac{1}{20}} = \frac{1/12}{\dfrac{10+3}{120}}$$

$$= \frac{120}{12 \times 13}$$

$$= \frac{10}{13}.$$

24. Twelve cards numbered from 1 to 12 are placed in pack, mixed up throughly then one card is drawn randomly. If it is known the number on each drawn card is more than 6. What is the probability that it is an even number?

(a) $\dfrac{1}{2}$ (b) $\dfrac{3}{4}$

(c) $\dfrac{1}{6}$ (d) $\dfrac{3}{5}$

Sol. (a) $\dfrac{1}{2}$

Explanation :

$$A = \{2, 4, 6, 8, 10, 12\}$$

$$B = \{7, 8, 9, 10, 11, 12\}$$

$$P(A) = \frac{6}{12}, P(B) = \frac{6}{12}$$

$$A \cap B = \{8, 10, 12\}, P(A \cap B) = \frac{3}{12}$$

$$P(A / B) = \frac{P(A \cap B)}{P(B)}$$

$$= \frac{\dfrac{3}{12}}{\dfrac{6}{12}} = \frac{3}{6} = \frac{1}{2}$$

So the correct option is (a).

25. A dice is thrown twice and sum of the number appearing is observed to be 4. What is the conditional probability that number 2 atleast appear once?

(a) 0.22 (b) 0.54

(c) 0.33 (d) 0.66

Sol. (c) 0.33

Explanation :

$$F = \{(1, 3), (2, 2), (3, 1)\}$$

$$E = \{(2, 2)\}$$

$$(E \cap F) = \{(2, 2)\}$$

$$P(E \cap F) = \frac{1}{36}$$

$$P(E / F) = \frac{P(E \cap F)}{P(F)}$$

$$= \frac{\dfrac{1}{36}}{\dfrac{3}{36}} = \frac{1}{3} = 0.33$$

So the correct option is (c).

26. Given, $P(A) = \dfrac{5}{12}, P(B) = \dfrac{5}{12}, P(A / B) = \dfrac{2}{5}$, find $P(A \cup B)$.

(a) $\dfrac{4}{3}$ (b) $\dfrac{3}{4}$

(c) $\dfrac{1}{3}$ (d) $\dfrac{3}{5}$

Sol. (b) $\dfrac{3}{4}$

Explanation :

$$P(A \cap B) = P(A / B) \times P(B)$$

$$= \frac{2}{5} \times \frac{5}{12}$$

$$= \frac{2}{12} = \frac{1}{6}$$

$$\therefore \qquad P(A \cup B) = P(A) + P(B) - P(A \cap B)$$

$$= \frac{5}{12} + \frac{5}{12} - \frac{2}{12}$$

$$= \frac{10-2}{12}$$

$$= \frac{3}{4}$$

So the correct option is (b).

27. Three cards are drawn successively without replacements from a pack of 52 well suffled cards. What is the probability the first two cards are queen and third card drawn is a king?

(a) $\dfrac{5}{5525}$ (b) $\dfrac{3}{5525}$

(c) $\dfrac{2}{5525}$ (d) $\dfrac{1}{5525}$

Sol. (c) $\dfrac{2}{5525}$

Explanation :

Let Q denote the event that the cards drawn is queen and K is the event that the card drawn is an king, clearly we have to find $P(QQK)$.

Probability that the first card is queen, $P(Q) = \dfrac{4}{52}$

Also, $P(Q/Q)$ is the probability of second queen with the conditon that one queen has already been drawn. Now there will be three queens in 51 cards.

Probability that the second card is queen,

$$P(Q/Q) = \dfrac{3}{51}$$

Lastly, $P(K/QQ)$ is the probability of third drawn card to be a king, with the condition that two queens have already been drawn, now there are four kings left in 50 cards.

$$\text{Therefore, } P(K/QQ) = \dfrac{4}{50}$$

By multiplication law of probability, we have

$$P(QQK) = P(Q) \times P(Q/Q) \times P(K/QQ)$$

$$= \dfrac{4}{52} \times \dfrac{3}{51} \times \dfrac{4}{50}$$

$$= \dfrac{2}{5525}$$

So the correct option is (c).

28. Nine cards numbered from 1 to 9 are placed in pack, mixed up thoroughly then one card is drawn randomly. If it is known that the number on each drawn card is more than 6. What is the probability that it is an even number ?

(a) $\dfrac{1}{2}$ (b) $\dfrac{3}{4}$

(c) 1 (d) $\dfrac{3}{6}$

Sol. (c) 1

Explanation :

$$A = \{2, 4, 6, 8\}$$
$$B = \{8\}$$
$$P(A) = \dfrac{4}{9}, \ P(B) = \dfrac{1}{9}, \ A \cap B = \{8\}, \ P(A \cap B) = \dfrac{1}{9}$$

$$P(A/B) = \dfrac{P(A \cap B)}{P(B)}$$

$$= \dfrac{\dfrac{1}{9}}{\dfrac{1}{9}} = 1$$

So the correct option is (c).

29. A bag contains 5 red and 3 blue balls. If 3 balls are drawn at random without replacement, them the probability of getting exactly one red ball is:

[NCERT Exemplar]

(a) $\dfrac{45}{196}$ (b) $\dfrac{135}{392}$

(c) $\dfrac{15}{56}$ (d) $\dfrac{15}{29}$

Sol. (c) $\dfrac{15}{56}$

Explanation :

Probability of getting exactly one red (R) ball will be

$$= P(R).P(B).P(B) + P(B).P(R).P(B) + P(B).P(B).P(R)$$

$$= \dfrac{5}{8} \cdot \dfrac{3}{7} \cdot \dfrac{2}{6} + \dfrac{3}{8} \cdot \dfrac{5}{7} \cdot \dfrac{2}{6} + \dfrac{3}{8} \cdot \dfrac{2}{7} \cdot \dfrac{5}{6}$$

$$= \dfrac{15}{4 \cdot 7 \cdot 6} + \dfrac{15}{4 \cdot 7 \cdot 6} + \dfrac{15}{4 \cdot 7 \cdot 6}$$

$$= \dfrac{5}{56} + \dfrac{5}{56} + \dfrac{5}{56} = \dfrac{15}{56}.$$

30. Refer to above question, If the probability that exactly two of the three balls were red, then the first ball being red, is: **[NCERT Exemplar]**

(a) $\dfrac{1}{3}$ (b) $\dfrac{4}{7}$

(c) $\dfrac{15}{28}$ (d) $\dfrac{5}{28}$

Sol. (b) $\dfrac{4}{7}$

Explanation :

Let E_1 = Event that first ball being red
and E_2 = Event that exactly two of the three balls being red

$$\therefore \ P(E_1) = P_R \cdot P_R \cdot P_{\bar{R}} + P_R \cdot P_{\bar{R}} \cdot P_R$$

$$+ P_R \cdot P_{\bar{R}} \cdot P_R + P_R \cdot P_{\bar{R}} \cdot P_{\bar{R}}$$

$$= \dfrac{5}{8} \cdot \dfrac{4}{7} \cdot \dfrac{3}{6} + \dfrac{5}{8} \cdot \dfrac{4}{7} \cdot \dfrac{3}{6} + \dfrac{5}{8} \cdot \dfrac{3}{7} \cdot \dfrac{4}{6} + \dfrac{5}{8} \cdot \dfrac{3}{7} \cdot \dfrac{2}{6}$$

$$= \dfrac{60 + 60 + 60 + 30}{336} = \dfrac{210}{336}$$

$$P(E_1 \cap E_2) = P_R \cdot P_{\bar{R}} \cdot P_R + P_R \cdot P_R \cdot P_{\bar{R}}$$

$$= \dfrac{5}{8} \cdot \dfrac{3}{7} \cdot \dfrac{4}{6} + \dfrac{5}{8} \cdot \dfrac{4}{7} \cdot \dfrac{3}{6} = \dfrac{120}{336}$$

$$\therefore \ P(E_2 | E_1) = \dfrac{P(E_1 \cap E_2)}{P(E_1)} = \dfrac{120/336}{210/336} = \dfrac{4}{7}.$$

31. Three persons A, B and C, fire at a target in turn, starting with A. Their probability of hitting the target are 0.4, 0.3 and 0.2, respectively. The probability of two hits is: **[NCERT Exemplar]**
(a) 0.024 (b) 0.188
(c) 0.336 (d) 0.452

Sol. (b) 0.188

Explanation :

Here, $P(A) = 0.4$, $P(\overline{A}) = 0.6$, $P(B) = 0.3$, $P(\overline{B}) = 0.7$, $P(C) = 0.2$ and $P(\overline{C}) = 0.8$

$\therefore$ Probability of two hits

$= P_A \cdot P_B \cdot P_{\overline{C}} + P_A \cdot P_{\overline{B}} \cdot P_C + P_{\overline{A}} \cdot P_B \cdot P_C$

$= 0.4 \times 0.3 \times 0.8 + 0.4 \times 0.7 \times 0.2 + 0.6 \times 0.3 \times 0.2$

$= 0.096 + 0.056 + 0.036 = 0.188.$

32. A box contains 3 orange balls, 3 green balls and 2 blue balls. Three balls are drawn at random from the box without replacement. The probability of drawing 2 green balls and one blue ball is:

[NCERT Exemplar]

(a) $\dfrac{3}{28}$ (b) $\dfrac{2}{21}$

(c) $\dfrac{1}{28}$ (d) $\dfrac{167}{168}$

Sol. (a) $\dfrac{3}{28}$

Explanation :

Probability of drawing 2 green balls and one blue ball

$= P_G \cdot P_G \cdot P_B + P_B \cdot P_G \cdot P_G + P_G \cdot P_B \cdot P_G$

$= \dfrac{3}{8} \cdot \dfrac{2}{7} \cdot \dfrac{2}{6} + \dfrac{2}{8} \cdot \dfrac{3}{7} \cdot \dfrac{2}{6} + \dfrac{3}{8} \cdot \dfrac{2}{7} \cdot \dfrac{2}{6}$

$= \dfrac{1}{28} + \dfrac{1}{28} + \dfrac{1}{28} = \dfrac{3}{28}.$

33. A flashlight has 8 batteries out of which 3 are dead. If two batteries are selected without replacement and tested, then probability that both are dead is: **[NCERT Exemplar]**

(a) $\dfrac{33}{56}$ (b) $\dfrac{9}{64}$

(c) $\dfrac{1}{14}$ (d) $\dfrac{3}{28}$

Sol. (d) $\dfrac{3}{28}$

Explanation :

Required probability $= P_D \cdot P_D = \dfrac{3}{8} \cdot \dfrac{2}{7} = \dfrac{3}{28}.$

34. If two cards are drawn from a well shuffled deck of 52 playing cards with replacement, then the probability that both cards are queens, is:

[NCERT Exemplar]

(a) $\dfrac{1}{13} \cdot \dfrac{1}{13}$ (b) $\dfrac{1}{13} + \dfrac{1}{13}$

(c) $\dfrac{1}{13} \cdot \dfrac{1}{17}$ (d) $\dfrac{1}{13} \cdot \dfrac{4}{51}$

Sol. (a) $\dfrac{1}{13} \cdot \dfrac{1}{13}$

Explanation :

Required probability $= \dfrac{4}{52} \cdot \dfrac{4}{52}$

$= \dfrac{1}{13} \times \dfrac{1}{13}$

[with replacement]

35. A bag contains 8 black and 5 blue balls three balls are drawn at random without replacements. What is the probability that all drawn balls are black colours?
(a) 0.122 (b) 0.195
(c) 0.132 (d) 0.022

Sol. (b) 0.195

Explanation :

1st black ball drawn at random the probability

$= \dfrac{8}{13}$

2nd black ball drawn at random the probability

$= \dfrac{7}{12}$

3rd black ball drawn at random the probability

$= \dfrac{6}{11}$

$P = \dfrac{8}{13} \times \dfrac{7}{12} \times \dfrac{6}{11}$

So the total probability

$= \dfrac{28}{13 \times 11} = 0.195$

So the correct option is (b).

36. Three dice are thrown simultaneously. The probability of obtaining a total score of 5 is:*

(a) $\dfrac{5}{216}$ (b) $\dfrac{1}{6}$

(c) $\dfrac{1}{36}$ (d) $\dfrac{1}{49}$

Sol. (c) $\dfrac{1}{36}$

---

* are board exam questions from previous years

Explanation :

When three dice are thrown :
$$n(S) = 6 \times 6 \times 6 = 216$$
Let A be the event of getting total score 5.
Then $A = \{(1, 1, 3), (1, 3, 1), (3, 1, 1), (2, 2, 1),$
$$(2, 1, 2), (1, 2, 2)\}$$
$\therefore \qquad n(A) = 6$
$\therefore \qquad P(A) = \dfrac{n(A)}{n(S)} = \dfrac{6}{216} = \dfrac{1}{36}$

So the correct option is (c).

37. A card is picked at random from a pack of 52 playing cards. Given that the picked card is a queen, the probability of this card to be a card of spade is :*

(a) $\dfrac{1}{3}$ (b) $\dfrac{4}{13}$

(c) $\dfrac{1}{4}$ (d) $\dfrac{1}{2}$

Sol. (c) $\dfrac{1}{4}$

Explanation :

Let event A = Picked card is a queen. and event B = card of spade is picked.

$\therefore \qquad P(A) = \dfrac{4}{52}, \ P(B) = \dfrac{13}{52}$

and $\quad P(A \cap B) = \dfrac{1}{52} \ [\because A \cap B = \text{Queen of spade}]$

Now, required probability,

$$P(B/A) = \dfrac{P(A \cap B)}{P(A)} = \dfrac{1/52}{4/52} = \dfrac{1}{4}$$

So the correct option is (c).

38. If two events are independent, then:

[NCERT Exemplar]

(a) they must be mutually exclusive
(b) the sum of their probability must be equal to 1
(c) Both (a) and (b) are correct
(d) None of the above is correct

Sol. (d) None of the above is correct

Explanation :

If two events A and B are independent, then we know that
$$PA(\cap B) = P(A) \cdot P(B), P(A) \neq 0, P(B) \neq 0$$
Since, A and B have a common outcome.
Further, mutually exclusive events never have a common outcome.

In other words, two independent events having non-zero probabilities of occurrence cannot be mutually exclusive and conversely, *i.e.*, two mutually exclusive events having non-zero probabilities of outcome cannot be independent.

39. If the events A and B are independent, then P(A ∩ B) is equal to: **[NCERT Exemplar]**

(a) P(A) + P(B)   (b) P(A) – P(B)
(c) P(A) · P(B)   (d) P(A)|P(B)

Sol. (c) P(A) · P(B)

Explanation :

If A and B are independent, then
$$P(A \cap B) = P(A) \cdot P(B).$$

40. Two events E and F are indepenent. If $P(E_i) = 0.3$ and $P(E \cup F) = 0,5$ then $P(E|F) - P(F|E)$ is equal to: **[NCERT Exemplar]**

(a) $\dfrac{2}{7}$ (b) $\dfrac{3}{35}$

(c) $\dfrac{1}{70}$ (d) $\dfrac{1}{7}$

Sol. (c) $\dfrac{1}{70}$

Explanation :

Here, $P(E) = 0.3$ and $P(E \cup F) = 0.5$
Let $\qquad\qquad P(F) = x$
$\because \quad P(E \cup F) = P(E) + P(F) - P(E \cap F)$
$$= P(E) + P(F) - P(E) \cdot P(F)$$
$\Rightarrow \qquad 0.5 = 0.3 + x - 0.3x$
$\Rightarrow \qquad x = \dfrac{0.5 - 0.3}{0.7} = \dfrac{2}{7} = P(F)$

$\therefore \quad P(E|F) - P(F|E) = \dfrac{P(E \cap F)}{P(F)} - \dfrac{P(F \cap E)}{P(E)}$

$$= \dfrac{P(E \cap F) \cdot P(E) - P(F \cap E) \cdot P(F)}{P(E) \cdot P(F)}$$

$$= \dfrac{P(E \cap F)[P(E) - P(F)]}{P(E \cap F)}$$

$$= P(E) - P(F)$$

$$= \dfrac{3}{10} - \dfrac{2}{7} = \dfrac{21 - 20}{70} = \dfrac{1}{70}.$$

41. If a die is thrown and a card is selected at random from a deck of 52 playnig cards, then the probability of getting an even number of the die and a spade card is: **[NCERT Exemplar]**

(a) $\dfrac{1}{2}$ (b) $\dfrac{1}{4}$

(c) $\dfrac{1}{8}$ (d) $\dfrac{3}{4}$

Sol. (c) $\dfrac{1}{8}$

Explanation :

Let E_1 = Event for getting an even number on the die

and E_2 = Event that a spade card is selected

$\therefore \quad P(E_1) = \dfrac{3}{6} = \dfrac{1}{2}$ and $P(E_2) = \dfrac{13}{52} = \dfrac{1}{4}$

Then, $P(E_1 \cap E_2) = P(E_1) \cdot P(E_2) = \dfrac{1}{2} \cdot \dfrac{1}{4} = \dfrac{1}{8}.$

42. If $P(A) = \dfrac{2}{3}$ and $P(B) = \dfrac{2}{5}$, find $P(A \cap B)$ if A and B are independent events :

(a) $\dfrac{4}{15}$ (b) $\dfrac{3}{7}$

(c) $\dfrac{2}{15}$ (d) $\dfrac{1}{14}$

Sol. (a) $\dfrac{4}{15}$

Explanation :

$$P(A \cap B) = P(A) \times P(B)$$
$$= \dfrac{2}{3} \times \dfrac{2}{5}$$
$$= \dfrac{4}{15}$$

So the correct option is (a).

43. Probability of obtaining an odd prime number on each dice, when two dices are rolled :

(a) $\dfrac{2}{5}$ (b) $\dfrac{1}{2}$

(c) $\dfrac{1}{3}$ (d) $\dfrac{1}{9}$

Sol. (d) $\dfrac{1}{9}$

Explanation :

$E = \{(3, 3), (5, 5), (3, 5), (5, 3)\}$

Total number of events = 6×6
$$= 36$$
Number of events occurs = 4
$$P = \dfrac{4}{36}$$
$$= \dfrac{1}{9}$$

So, the probability is

So the correct option is (d).

44. The probability distribution of a discrete random variable X is given below:

X	2	3	4	5
P(X)	$\dfrac{5}{k}$	$\dfrac{7}{k}$	$\dfrac{9}{k}$	$\dfrac{11}{k}$

The value of k is: **[NCERT Exemplar]**

(a) 8   (b) 16

(c) 32   (d) 48

Sol. (c) 32

Explanation :

We know that,
$$\Sigma P(X) = 1$$
$$\Rightarrow \quad \dfrac{5}{k} + \dfrac{7}{k} + \dfrac{9}{k} + \dfrac{11}{k} = 1$$
$$\Rightarrow \quad \dfrac{32}{k} = 1$$
$$\therefore \quad k = 32.$$

Assertion and Reason Based Questions

(a) Both (A) and (R) are individually true and (R) is the correct explanation of (A).

(b) Both (A) and (R) are individually true but (R) is not the corect explanation of (A).

(c) (A) is true but (R) is false.

(d) (A) is false but (R) is true.

45. Assertion (A) : If A is any event and $P(B) = 1$, then A and B are independent.

Reason (R) : If $P(A \cap B) = P(A) \cdot P(B)$, then A and B are independent.

Sol. (a) Both (A) and (R) are individually true and (R) is the correct explanation of (A).

Explanation :

If A and B are independent, then
$$P(A \cap B) = P(A) \cdot P(B)$$
$$= P(A) \text{ here } A \subset B$$
$$[\because P(B) = 1]$$
and $\quad P(A \cup B) = P(A) + P(B) - P(A \cap B)$
$$= P(A) + P(B) - P(A)$$
$$= P(B)$$
$$= 1 \text{ which is true.}$$

46. Assertion (A) : If A, B, C are three events such that $P(A) = \dfrac{2}{3}$, $P(B) = \dfrac{1}{4}$ and $P(C) = \dfrac{1}{6}$, then A, B, C are mutually exclusive events.

Reason (R) : If $P(A \cup B \cup C) = P(A) + P(B) + P(C)$, then A, B, C are mutually exclusive events.

Sol. (d)   (A) is false but (R) is true.

Explanation :

For mutually exclusive events
$$P(A \cup B \cup C) = P(A) + P(B) + P(C)$$
$$= \frac{2}{3} + \frac{1}{4} + \frac{1}{6}$$
$$= \frac{13}{12} > 1$$

Which is not possible.

47. Assertion (A) : The probability that A and B can solve a problem is $\dfrac{1}{3}$ and $\dfrac{1}{4}$ respectively, then the probability that problem will be solved is $\dfrac{7}{12}$.

Reason (R) : Above mentioned events are independent events.

Sol. (d)   (A) is false but (R) is true.

Explanation :

Required probability
$= 1 -$ Probability that problem will not be solved
$$= 1 - P\,(\overline{A} \cap \overline{B})$$
$$= 1 - P\,(\overline{A})\,P(\overline{B})$$
$$= 1 - [1 - P(A)]\,[1 - P(B)]$$
$$= 1 - \left(1 - \frac{1}{3}\right)\left(1 - \frac{1}{4}\right)$$
$$= 1 - \frac{2}{3} \times \frac{3}{4} = 1 - \frac{1}{2} = \frac{1}{2}.$$

48. Assertion (A) : If A and B be mutually exclusive events in a sample space such that $P(A) = 0.3$ and $P(B) = 0.6$, then $P(\overline{A} \cap \overline{B}) = 0.28$.

Reason (R) : If A and B are mutually exclusive events, then $P(A \cap B) = 0$.

Sol. (d)   (A) is false but (R) is true.

Explanation :

$\because$ A and B are mutually exclusive
$$\therefore \quad P(A \cup B) = P(A) + P(B) - P(A \cap B)$$
$$= P(A) + P(B) - 0$$
$$= 0.3 + 0.6$$
$$= 0.9$$
$$\therefore \quad P(\overline{A} \cap \overline{B}) = P(\overline{A \cup B}) = 1 - P(A \cup B)$$
$$= 1 - 0.9 = 0.1$$

49. Assertion (A) : Out of 5 tickets consecutively numbered, three are drawn at random, the chance that the numbers on then are in AP is $\dfrac{2}{5}$.

Reason (R) : Out of $(2n + 1)$ tickets consecutively numbered three are drawn at random, the chance that the numbers on them are in AP is $\dfrac{(4n - 2)}{(4n^2 - 1)}$.

Sol. (c)   (A) is true but (R) is false.

Explanation :

$$\text{Total ways} = {}^{2n+1}C_3 = \frac{(2n+1)\,2n\,(2n-1)}{1 \cdot 2 \cdot 3}$$
$$= \frac{n\,(4n^2 - 1)}{3}$$

Let the three numbers a, b, c are drawn where $a < b < c$ and given a, b, c are in AP.

$$\therefore \qquad b = \frac{a+c}{2} \text{ or } 2b = a + c \qquad \text{...(i)}$$

It is clear that from equation (i) a and c are both odd or both even.

Out of $(2n + 1)$ tickets consecutively numbers either $(n + 1)$ of them will be odd and n of them will be even.

$$\therefore \quad \text{Favourable ways} = {}^{n+1}C_2 + {}^{n}C_2$$
$$= \frac{(n+1)n}{1 \cdot 2} + \frac{n(n-1)}{1 \cdot 2}$$
$$= \frac{n}{2}\,(n + 1 + n - 1)$$
$$= n^2$$

$$\therefore \text{ Required probability} = \frac{n^2}{\dfrac{n(4n^2 - 1)}{3}} = \frac{3n}{(4n^2 - 1)}$$

50. Assertion (A) : If A and B are two events such that $P(A) = \dfrac{1}{2}$ and $P(B) = \dfrac{2}{3}$, then $\dfrac{1}{6} \le P(A \cap B) \le \dfrac{1}{2}$.

Reason (R) : $P(A \cup B) \le \max\,\{P(A),\ P(B)\}$ and $P(A \cap B) \ge \min\,\{P(A),\ P(B)\}$

Sol. (c)   (A) is true but (R) is false.

Explanation :

We have
$$P(A \cup B) \ge \max\,\{P(A),\ P(B)\} = \frac{2}{3}$$
$$\text{or} \qquad P(A \cup B) \ge \frac{2}{3}$$

$$\Rightarrow P(A \cap B) = P(A) + P(B) - P(A \cup B) \geq P(A) + P(B) - 1$$

$$= \frac{1}{2} + \frac{2}{3} - 1 = \frac{1}{6}$$

or $\quad P(A \cap B) \geq \dfrac{1}{6} \qquad \qquad \text{...(i)}$

and $\quad P(A \cap B) \leq \min \{P(A), P(B)\} = \dfrac{1}{2}$

$\therefore \quad P(A \cap B) \leq \dfrac{1}{2} \qquad \qquad \text{...(ii)}$

From equations (i) and (ii), we get

$$\frac{1}{6} \leq P(A \cap B) \leq \frac{1}{2}.$$

51. Assertion (A) : If the probability of an event A is 0.4 and that of B is 0.3, then the probability of neither A nor B occuring depends upon the fact that A and B, are mutually exclusive or not.

Reason (R) : Two events are mutually exclusive, if they do not occur simultaneously.

Sol. (b) Both (A) and (R) are individually true but (R) is not the corect explanation of (A).

Explanation :

Two or more events, associated with the same space are called mutually exclusive events if they cannot occur simultaneously.

If events A and B are mutually exclusive, then
$$A \cap B = \phi \; i.e., \; P(A \cap B) = 0$$

Now, $P(\overline{A} \cap \overline{B}) = P(\overline{A \cup B}) = 1 - P(A \cup B)$
$$= 1 - \{P(A) + P(B) - P(A \cap B)\}$$
$$= 1 - P(A) - P(B) + P(A \cap B)$$
$$= 1 - 0.4 - 0.3 + 0 = 0.3$$

and if A and B are independent, then
$$P(A \cap B) = P(A) \, P(B)$$

$\therefore \quad P(\overline{A} \cap \overline{B}) = P(\overline{A}) \cdot P(\overline{B})$
$$= [1 - P(A)] \, [1 - P(B)]$$
$$= (1 - 0.4) \, (1 - 0.3)$$
$$= (0.6) \, (0.7)$$
$$= 0.42.$$

52. Assertion (A) : If A and B be two events in a sample space such that $P(A) = 0.3$, $P(B) = 0.3$, then $P(A \cap \overline{B})$ can not be found.

Reason (R) : $P(A \cap \overline{B}) = P(A) - P(A \cap B).$

Sol. (a) Both (A) and (R) are individually true and (R) is the correct explanation of (A).

Explanation :

$\because P(A \cap \overline{B}) = P(A) - P(A \cap B)$

$$\Rightarrow \quad P(A \cap \overline{B}) = 0.3 - P(A \cap B)$$

$\therefore \; P(A \cap \overline{B})$ cannot be found.

53. Assertion (A) : If a leap year is selected at random, the chance it will contain 53 Sundays is $\dfrac{2}{7}$.

Reason (R) : A leap year has 366 days.

Sol. (a) Both (A) and (R) are correct and R is the correct explanation.

Explanation :

A leap year has 365 days

i.e., 52 complete weeks and 1 days more.

The three days will be three consecutive days of a week.

The probability that 53 Sundays = $\dfrac{3}{7}$.

54. Assertion (A) : If $P(A/B) \geq P(A)$, then $P(B/A) \geq P(B)$

Reason (R) : $P(A/B) = \dfrac{P(A \cap B)}{P(B)}.$

Sol. (a) Both (A) and (R) are individually true and (R) is the correct explanation of (A).

Explanation :

$\because \qquad P(A/B) \geq P(A)$

$\Rightarrow \qquad \dfrac{P(A \cap B)}{P(B)} \geq P(A)$

or $\qquad \dfrac{P(A \cap B)}{P(A)} \geq P(B)$

or $\qquad \dfrac{P(B \cap A)}{P(A)} \geq P(B)$

$\therefore \qquad P(B/A) \geq P(B).$

55. A and B are two independent events.

$$P(A) = \frac{1}{2} \text{ and } P(B) = \frac{1}{5}$$

Assertion (A) : $P\left(\dfrac{A}{B}\right) = \dfrac{1}{2}$

Reason (R) : $P\left(\dfrac{A}{B}\right) = P(A)$

Sol. (a) Both (A) and (R) are individually true and (R) is the correct explanation of (A).

Explanation :

A and B are independent events.

$\therefore \qquad P(A \cap B) = P(A).P(B) = \dfrac{1}{2} \times \dfrac{1}{5} = \dfrac{1}{10}$

$$\therefore \quad P\left(\frac{A}{B}\right) = \frac{P(A \cap B)}{P(B)} = \frac{\dfrac{1}{10}}{\dfrac{1}{5}} = \frac{1}{2}$$

$\therefore$ Assertion A that $P\left(\dfrac{A}{B}\right)$ is equal to $\dfrac{1}{2}$ is correct.

$$\text{Reason (R)}: P\left(\frac{A}{B}\right) = \frac{1}{2} \ \& \ P(A) = \frac{1}{2} \qquad \text{(given)}$$

Clearly $P\left(\dfrac{A}{B}\right) = P(A)$ is also correct.

56. Assertion (A) : A number is chosen at random from the numbers 1, 2, 3, ..., $6n + 3$. Let A and B be defined as follows

$\qquad$ A : Number is divisible by 2

$\qquad$ B : Number is divisible by 3

Then, A and B are independent.

Reason (R) : If events A and B are independent, then $P(A \cap B) = P(A) \cdot P(B)$.

Sol. (d) (A) is false but (R) is true.

Explanation :

We have

$$A = \{2, 4, 6, 8, \dots, 6n, 6n + 2\}$$
$$B = \{3, 6, 9, 12, \dots, 6n, 6n + 3\}$$
and $\qquad A \cap B = \{6, 12, 18, \dots, 6n\}$

Here, $n(A) = 3n + 1$, $n(B) = 2n + 1$ and $n(A \cap B) = n$

$$\therefore P(A) = \frac{n(A)}{6n+3} = \frac{3n+1}{6n+3}, \ P(B) = \frac{n(B)}{6n+3} = \frac{1}{3}$$

and $\qquad P(A \cap B) = \dfrac{n(A \cap B)}{6n+3} = \dfrac{n}{(6n+3)}$

Since, $\quad P(A \cap B) \neq P(A) \, P(B)$

$\therefore$ A and B are not independent.

57. Assertion (A) : A and B are two candidates seeking admission in IIT. The probability that A is selected is 0.5 and the probability that both A and B are selected is at most 0.3. Then, the probability of B getting selected is 0.9.

Reason (R) : If E_1 and E_2 are the events of A and B selected respectively, then
$$P(E_1 \cap E_2) = P(E_1) \cdot P(E_2).$$

Sol. (d) (A) is false but (R) is true.

Explanation :

Given, $\quad P(E_1 \cap E_2) \leq 0.3$

$\Rightarrow \qquad P(E_1) \cdot P(E_2) \leq 0.3$

$\Rightarrow \qquad (0.5) \, P(E_2) \leq (0.3)$

$\therefore \qquad P(E_2) \leq \dfrac{(0.3)}{(0.5)}$

$\Rightarrow \qquad P(E_2) \leq 0.6$

$\qquad\quad P(E_2) \neq 0.9$

58. Assertion (A) : Ankit and Rahul are weak students in Mathematics and their chances of solving a problem correctly are $\dfrac{1}{8}$ and $\dfrac{1}{12}$ respectively. They are given a question and they obtain the same answer. If the probability of a common mistake is then $\dfrac{1}{1001}$, the probability that the answer was correct is $\dfrac{13}{14}$.

Reason (R) : If E_1 and E_2 are mutually exclusive and exhaustive events with non-zero probabilities of a random experiment and E is any other event of the same experiment, then

$$P\left(\frac{E_1}{E}\right) = \frac{P\left(\dfrac{E}{E_1}\right) \cdot P(E_1)}{P\left(\dfrac{E}{E_1}\right) \cdot P(E_1) + P\left(\dfrac{E}{E_2}\right) \cdot P(E_2)}$$

Sol. (a) Both (A) and (R) are individually true and (R) is the correct explanation of (A).

Explanation :

Let E_1 be the events of both getting the correct answer and E_2 the event of both getting wrong answers. Let E be the event of both obtaining the same answer.

$$\therefore \qquad P(E_1) = \frac{1}{8} \times \frac{1}{12} = \frac{1}{96}$$

and $\qquad P(E_2) = \left(1 - \dfrac{1}{8}\right)\left(1 - \dfrac{1}{12}\right)$

$$= \frac{7}{8} \times \frac{11}{12} = \frac{77}{96}$$

and $\quad P\left(\dfrac{E_1}{E_2}\right) = 1,$

$$P\left(\frac{E}{E_2}\right) = \frac{1}{1001}$$

$\therefore \qquad P\left(\dfrac{E_1}{E}\right) = \dfrac{P\left(\dfrac{E}{E_1}\right) \cdot P(E_1)}{P\left(\dfrac{E}{E_1}\right) \cdot P(E_1) + P\left(\dfrac{E}{E_2}\right) \cdot P(E_2)}$

$$= \frac{1 \times \dfrac{1}{96}}{1 \times \dfrac{1}{96} + \dfrac{1}{1001} \times \dfrac{77}{96}}$$

$$= \frac{13}{14}.$$

Case Based Questions

59. In an office three employees Vinay, Sonia and Iqbal process incoming copies of a certain form. Vinay process 50% of the forms. Sonia processes 20% and Iqbal the remaining 30% of the forms. Vinay has an error rate of 0.06, Sonia has an error rate of 0.04 and Iqbal has an error rate of 0.03.

$$P(V) = 50\% = \frac{1}{2},$$

$$P(S) = 20\% = \frac{1}{5},$$

$$P(I) = 30\% = \frac{3}{10}$$

Let E be the event that error occured.

$$P(E/V) = \frac{6}{100}$$

$$P(E/S) = \frac{4}{100}$$

$$P(E/I) = \frac{30}{100}$$

Based on the above information answer the following :

(i) The conditional probability that an error is committed in processing given that Sonia processed the form is :

(a) 0.0210   (b) 0.04

(c) 0.47   (d) 0.06

Sol. (b) 0.04

Explanation :

$$P(E/S) = \frac{4}{100} = 0.04$$

Hence (b) is correct option.

(ii) The probability that Sonia processed the form and comitted and error is :

(a) 0.005   (b) 0.006

(c) 0.008   (d) 0.68

Sol. (c) 0.008

Explanation :

$$P(E \cap S) = P(E/S) \cdot P(S)$$

$$= \frac{4}{100} \times \frac{20}{100} = 0.008$$

Hence (c) is correct option.

(iii) The total probability of committing an error in processing the form is :

(a) 0   (b) 0.047

(c) 0.234   (d) 1

Sol. (b) 0.047

Explanation :

$$P(E) = P(V)\,P(E/V) + P(S)\,P(E/S) + P(I)\,P(E/I)$$

$$= \frac{50}{100} \times \frac{6}{100} + \frac{20}{100} \times \frac{4}{100} + \frac{30}{100} \times \frac{3}{100} = 0{\cdot}047.$$

Hence (b) is correct option.

(iv) The manager of the company wants to do a quality check. During inspection he selects a form at random from the days output of processed forms. If the form selected at random has an error, the probability that the form is not processed by Vinay is :

(a) 1   (b) 30/47

(c) 20/47   (d) 17/47

Sol. (d) 17/47

Explanation :

$$P(V/E) = \frac{P(V)\,P(E/V)}{P(E)}$$

$$= \frac{\dfrac{50}{100} \times \dfrac{6}{100}}{\dfrac{47}{1000}} = \frac{30}{47}$$

$\therefore$ P(Not processed by Vinay)

$$= 1 - \frac{30}{47}$$

$$= \frac{17}{47}$$

Hence (d) is correct option.

(v) Let A be the event of committing an error in processing the form and let E_1, E_2 and E_3 be the events that Vinay, Sonia and Iqbal processed the form. The value of $\sum\limits_{i=1}^{3} P(E_i / A)$ is :

(a) 0   (b) 0.03

(c) 0.06   (d) 1

Sol. (d) 1

Explanation :

$$\sum_{i=1}^{3} P(E_i/A) = 1$$

[∵ Sum probabilities of all the possible event is 1]

60. **Sanjay, Ajay and Vijay are three best friends. After completing their MBA from IIM Lucknow. They apply for the job in the same company for the post of manager in finance department. chances of selection of Sanjay, Ajay and Vijay are in the ratio of 1 : 2 : 4. The probabilities that Sanjay can increase the profits of the company by his efforts is 0.8 whereas probabilities for the same task of Ajay and Vijay are 0.5 and 0.3 respectively.**

    From the above information attempt the following questions :

(i) If E_1, E_2 and E_3 are the events of selecting Sanjay, Ajay and Vijay, then find $P(E_1)$, $P(E_2)$ and $P(E_3)$:

   (a) $\dfrac{1}{7}, \dfrac{2}{7}, \dfrac{4}{7}$ (b) $\dfrac{2}{7}, \dfrac{4}{7}, \dfrac{1}{7}$

   (c) $\dfrac{4}{7}, \dfrac{2}{7}, \dfrac{1}{7}$ (d) $\dfrac{4}{7}, \dfrac{1}{7}, \dfrac{2}{7}$

Sol. (a) $\dfrac{1}{7}, \dfrac{2}{7}, \dfrac{4}{7}$

Explanation :

E_1 be event of selecting Sanjay

E_2 be event of selecting Ajay

E_3 be event of selecting Vijay.

$$P(E_1) = \frac{1}{7}$$

$$P(E_2) = \frac{2}{7}$$

$$P(E_3) = \frac{4}{7}$$

(ii) A be event of increase the profit then find if it is due to Ajay :

   (a) $\dfrac{3}{5}$ (b) $\dfrac{2}{3}$

   (c) $\dfrac{1}{2}$ (d) $\dfrac{2}{5}$

Sol. (c) $\dfrac{1}{2}$

Explanation :

A be the event of increasing profits.

$$P(A/E_1) = 0.8$$

$$P(A/E_2) = 0.5$$

$$P(A/E_3) = 0.3$$

$P(E_2/A)$

$$= \frac{P(E_2)\,P(A/E_1)}{P(E_1)\,P(A/E_1) + P(E_2)\,P(A/E_2) + P(E_3)\,P(A/E_3)}$$

$$= \frac{\dfrac{2}{7} \times 0.5}{\dfrac{1}{7} \times 0.8 \times \dfrac{2}{7} \times 0.5 + \dfrac{4}{7} \times 0.3}$$

$$= \frac{\dfrac{1}{7}}{\dfrac{0.8}{7} + \dfrac{1}{7} + \dfrac{1.2}{7}} = \frac{1}{2}$$

(iii) Find $P(E_1/A)$:

   (a) 1   (b) $\dfrac{1}{5}$

   (c) $\dfrac{3}{5}$ (d) $\dfrac{2}{5}$

Sol. (d) $\dfrac{2}{5}$

Explanation :

$P(E_1/A)$

$$= \frac{P(E_1)\,P(A/E_1)}{P(E_1)\,P(A/E_1) + P(E_2)\,P(A/E_2) + P(E_3)\,P(A/E_3)}$$

$$= \frac{\dfrac{1}{7} \times 0.8}{\dfrac{1}{7} \times 0.8 + \dfrac{2}{7} \times 0.5 + \dfrac{4}{7} \times 0.3} = \frac{\dfrac{0.8}{7}}{\dfrac{0.8 + 1 + 1.2}{7}} = \frac{0.8}{20} = \frac{2}{5}.$$

(iv) If E_1, E_2 and E_3 be events of not increase the profits, then find the probability that it is due to the appointment of Vijay ?

   (a) $\dfrac{5}{10}$ (b) $\dfrac{7}{10}$

   (c) $\dfrac{6}{10}$ (d) $\dfrac{9}{10}$

Sol. (d) $\dfrac{9}{10}$

Explanation :

P be event of not increase in profits.

$$P(P/E_1) = 1 - 0.8 = 0.2 = \frac{2}{10}$$

$$P(P/E_2) = 1 - 0.5 = 0.5 = \frac{5}{10}$$

$$P(P/E_3) = 1 - 0.3 = 0.7 = \frac{7}{10}$$

$P(E_3/P)$

$$= \frac{P(E_3)\,P(P/E_3)}{P(E_1)\,P(P/E_1) + P(E_2)\,P(P/E_2) + P(E_3)\,P(P/E_3)}$$

$$= \frac{\dfrac{4}{7} \times \dfrac{7}{10}}{\dfrac{1}{7} \times \dfrac{2}{10} + \dfrac{2}{7} \times \dfrac{5}{10} + \dfrac{4}{7} \times \dfrac{7}{10}} = \frac{\dfrac{28}{70}}{\dfrac{2}{70} + \dfrac{10}{70} + \dfrac{28}{70}}$$

$$= \frac{28}{40} = \frac{7}{10}.$$

(v) Find the probability that profit does not increase due to the appointment of Sanjay ?

(a) $\dfrac{7}{20}$ (b) 1

(c) $\dfrac{3}{20}$ (d) $\dfrac{1}{20}$

Sol. (d) $\dfrac{1}{20}$

Explanation :

$P(E_1/P)$

$$= \frac{P(E_1)\,P(P/E_1)}{P(E_1)\,P(P/E_1) + P(E_2)\,P(P/E_2) + P(E_3)\,P(P/E_3)}$$

$$= \frac{\dfrac{1}{7} \times \dfrac{2}{10}}{\dfrac{1}{7} \times \dfrac{2}{10} + \dfrac{2}{7} \times \dfrac{5}{10} + \dfrac{4}{7} \times \dfrac{7}{10}} = \frac{\dfrac{2}{70}}{\dfrac{2}{70} + \dfrac{10}{70} + \dfrac{28}{70}}$$

$$= \frac{2}{40}$$

$$= \frac{1}{20}.$$

Very Short Answer Type Questions

61. An urn contains 5 red balls, 6 green balls and 4 black balls. A ball is drawn at random from the urn. What is the probability that the ball drawn is either red or black ?

Sol. Given,

No. of red balls = 5

No. of green balls = 6

No. of black balls = 4

$\therefore$ Total no. of balls = 15 = $n(S)$

Let A be the event of drawing a red ball

$\Rightarrow$ $P(A) = \dfrac{5}{15}$

and B be the event of drawing a black ball

$\Rightarrow$ $P(B) = \dfrac{4}{15}$

Then $A \cap B = \phi$

$\therefore$ $P(A \cup B) = P(A \text{ or } B) = P(A) + P(B)$

$$= \frac{5}{15} + \frac{4}{15}$$

$$= \frac{9}{15} = \frac{3}{5}$$

Hence, the probability that the ball drawn is either red or black is $\dfrac{3}{5}.$

62. A bag contains 4 blue balls and 6 red balls. Two balls are drawn at random. Find the probability that they are of same colour.

Sol. Let S be the sample space. Then

$n(S)$ = Total number of ways of drawing 2 balls out of 10 balls

$\therefore$ $n(S) = {}^{10}C_2 = \dfrac{10\,!}{2\,!\,(8\,!)} = \dfrac{10 \times 9 \times 8\,!}{1 \times 2 \times 8\,!}$

$$= \frac{10 \times 9}{1 \times 2} = 45$$

Let A be the event of getting both balls of same colour.

Then, $n(A)$ = Total number of ways of drawing (2 balls out of 4 blue balls) or (2 balls out of 6 red balls)

$i.e.,$ $n(A) = {}^{4}C_2 + {}^{6}C_2 = \dfrac{4\,!}{2\,!\,2\,!} + \dfrac{6\,!}{2\,!\,4\,!}$

$$= \frac{4 \times 3}{1 \times 2} + \frac{6 \times 5}{1 \times 2}$$

$$= 6 + 15 = 21$$

$\therefore$ $P(A) = \dfrac{n(A)}{n(S)} = \dfrac{21}{45} = \dfrac{7}{15}.$

63. If a coin is tossed and a die is thrown. The probability that the outcome will be a tail or a number greater than 3 or both is ....

Sol. $\dfrac{3}{4}$

Let A = event of getting tail in a single toss of coin.

B = event of getting a number greater than 3, in a throw of die.

Then $P(A) = \dfrac{1}{2}$ and $P(B) = \dfrac{3}{6} = \dfrac{1}{2}$

$\therefore$ Required probability

$$= P(A \cup B)$$

$$= 1 - P(\overline{A}).P(\overline{B})$$

$$[\because A \text{ and } B \text{ are independent}]$$

$$= 1 - \left(1 - \frac{1}{2}\right)\left(1 - \frac{1}{2}\right)$$

$$= 1 - \left(\frac{1}{2} \times \frac{1}{2}\right)$$

$$= 1 - \frac{1}{4} = \frac{3}{4}.$$

64. If $P(X) = \dfrac{9}{10}$, $P(Y) = \dfrac{3}{10}$ and $P(X \cap Y) = \dfrac{7}{10}$. Find

(i) $P(X/Y)$, (ii) $P(Y/X)$.

Sol. (i) We have

$$P(X/Y) = \frac{P(X \cap Y)}{P(Y)}$$

$$= \frac{7/10}{3/10} = \frac{7}{3}.$$

(ii) We have,

$$P(Y/X) = \frac{P(X \cap Y)}{P(X)}$$

$$= \frac{7/10}{9/10} = \frac{7}{9}.$$

65. Two cards are drawn. What is the probability that an ace comes up given that a black card came up ?

Sol. Let A be the event of getting an ace and B be the event of getting a black card. Then,

$$P(A) = \frac{4}{52} = \frac{1}{13} \text{ and } P(B) = \frac{26}{52} = \frac{1}{2}$$

$$\therefore \quad P(A \cap B) = \frac{2}{52} = \frac{1}{26}$$

$\therefore$ Required probability

$$= P(A/B)$$

$$= \frac{P(A \cap B)}{P(B)} = \frac{1/26}{1/2} = \frac{1}{13}.$$

66. Find the probability of getting a multiple of 2 if two dice are thrown and it is known that the second die always shows a prime number.

Sol. Let A be the event of getting a multiple of 2 on first die and B be the event of getting a prime number on second die. Then

$$A = \{2, 4, 6\} \text{ and } B = \{2, 3, 5\}$$

$\therefore$ Required probability $= P(A/B)$

$$= \frac{P(A \cap B)}{P(B)} = \frac{1/6}{3/6} = \frac{1}{3}.$$

67. If A and B are two events such that $P(A) \neq 0$ and $P(B/A) = 1$, then the relation between A and B is ....

Sol. $A \subset B$

Given, $\quad P(A) \neq 0$ and $P(B/A) = 1$

We know that,

$$P(B/A) = \frac{P(B \cap A)}{P(A)}$$

$$\Rightarrow \quad 1 = \frac{P(B \cap A)}{P(A)}$$

$$\Rightarrow \quad P(A) = P(A \cap B)$$

$$\Rightarrow \quad A \subset B.$$

68. If four cards are drawn at random from a pack of 52 cards, then the probability of getting all four cards of the same suit is ....

Sol. $\dfrac{44}{4165}$

Total no. of cards = 52

No. of ways of drawing 4 cards = $^{52}C_4$

Number of suits = 4

Number of cards in each suit = $\dfrac{52}{4} = 13$

Number of ways of getting all 4 cards of same suit

$$= {}^{13}C_4 + {}^{13}C_4 + {}^{13}C_4 + {}^{13}C_4$$

$\therefore$ Required probability $= \dfrac{4({}^{13}C_4)}{{}^{52}C_4}$

$$= \frac{44}{4165}.$$

69. Let A and B be two events such that $P(A) = 3/8$ and $P(B) = 2/5$. Find :

(i) $P(A \text{ or } B)$, if A and B are mutually exclusive events.

(ii) $P(A \text{ and } B)$, if A and B are independent events.

Sol. (i) Let A and B be mutually exclusive events.

Then $\quad A \cap B = \phi$

$\therefore \quad P(A \text{ or } B) = P(A \cup B) = P(A) + P(B)$

$$= \frac{3}{8} + \frac{2}{5} = \frac{15 + 16}{40}$$

$$= \frac{31}{40}.$$

(ii) Let A and B be two independent events. Then,

$$P(A \cap B) = P(A) \times P(B)$$

$$= \frac{3}{8} \times \frac{2}{5} = \frac{6}{40} = \frac{3}{20}.$$

70. Let A and B be two events such that $P(A) = 0.3$ and $P(A \cup B) = 0.5$. Find $P(B)$ if :

(i) A and B are mutually exclusive

(ii) A and B are independent.

Sol. (i) Let A and B be mutually exclusive events.

$\Rightarrow \qquad A \cap B = \phi$

$\therefore \qquad P(A \cup B) = P(A) + P(B)$

$\Rightarrow \qquad 0.5 = 0.3 + P(B)$

$\Rightarrow \qquad P(B) = 0.2$

(ii) Let A and B be independent events. Then

$$P(A \cap B) = P(A) \times P(B)$$

$\therefore \qquad P(A \cup B) = P(A) + P(B) - P(A) \times P(B)$

$$0.5 = 0.3 + P(B)(1 - P(A))$$

$$0.5 - 0.3 = P(B)(1 - 0.3)$$

$$0.2 = P(B)(0.7)$$

$\therefore \qquad P(B) = \dfrac{0.2}{0.7}$

$$= \dfrac{2}{7}.$$

71. If X and Y are events such that $P(X) = \dfrac{1}{3}$, $P(Y) = \dfrac{6}{5}$ and $P(X \cap Y) = \dfrac{2}{5}$. Are the events X and Y independent ?

Sol. We know that,

$$P(X \cap Y) = \dfrac{2}{5} = \dfrac{1}{3} \times \dfrac{6}{5}$$

$$= P(X)\, P(Y)$$

So, X and Y are independent events.

72. Find the value of k and if X is a random variable with probability distribution as given below :

X	0	1	2	3
$P(X = x)$	$2k$	$3k$	$2k$	k

Sol. We know that sum of all $P(X = x) = 1$

$\therefore \quad 2k + 3k + 2k + k = 1$

$$8k = 1 \Rightarrow k = \dfrac{1}{8}.$$

73. Five cards are drawn successively with replacement from the pack of 52 cards. What is the probability that all five cards are diamonds ?

Sol. Let $\qquad n = 5$

$$x = \text{no. of diamonds}$$

$p = $ probability of getting a diamond $= \dfrac{13}{52} = \dfrac{1}{4}$

$q = $ probability of not getting a diamond

$$= 1 - \dfrac{1}{4} = \dfrac{3}{4}$$

$$P(X = 5) = {}^{5}C_5 \left(\dfrac{1}{4}\right)^5 \left(\dfrac{3}{4}\right)^0 = \dfrac{1}{1024}.$$

Short Answer Type Questions

74. A bag contains 5 green and 12 blue marbles. A second bag contains 7 green and 9 blue marbles. One marble is picked at random from first bag and mixed up with the marbles in the second bag. Then, a marble is randomly picked from it. Find the probability that the picked marble is green.

Sol. Let us consider the events :

$\quad X = $ Marble picked from first bag is green

$\quad Y = $ Marble picked from first bag is blue

and $A = $ Marble picked from second bag is green

Now, $\qquad P(X) = \dfrac{5}{17},$

$$P(Y) = \dfrac{12}{17}$$

Also, probability of picking up a green marble from second bag if X has already occured

$$P\,(A/X) = \dfrac{8}{17}$$

Similarly, $P\,(A/Y) = \dfrac{7}{17}$

$\therefore$ By the law of total probability, we get

$$P(A) = P(X)\, P(A/X) + P(Y)\, P(A/Y)$$

$$= \dfrac{5}{17} \times \dfrac{8}{17} + \dfrac{12}{17} \times \dfrac{7}{17}$$

$$= \dfrac{40}{289} + \dfrac{84}{289} = \dfrac{124}{289}.$$

75. Evaluate $P(A \cup B)$, if $2P(A) = P(B) = \dfrac{5}{13}$ and $P(A/B) = \dfrac{2}{5}.$

[NCERT]

Sol. Given, $\quad 2P(A) = \dfrac{5}{13}$

$\Rightarrow \qquad P(A) = \dfrac{5}{26}$ and $P(B) = \dfrac{5}{13}$

Also, $\qquad P(A/B) = \dfrac{2}{5}$

We know that

$$P(A/B) = \dfrac{P(A \cap B)}{P(B)} = \dfrac{2}{5}$$

$\Rightarrow \qquad P(A \cap B) = \dfrac{2}{5} \times P(B) = \dfrac{2}{5} \times \dfrac{5}{13}$

$\Rightarrow \qquad P(A \cap B) = \dfrac{2}{13}$

Also we know that

$$P(A \cup B) = P(A) + P(B) - P(A \cap B)$$
$$= \frac{5}{26} + \frac{5}{13} - \frac{2}{13} = \frac{5}{26} + \frac{3}{13}$$
$$= \frac{11}{26}.$$

76. An instructor has a question bank consisting of 300 easy True/False questions, 200 difficult True/False questions, 500 easy MCQ's and 400 difficult MCQ's. If a question is selected at random from the question bank, what is the probability that it will be an easy question given that it is a MCQ ?
[NCERT]

Sol. The given data can be tabulated as :

	True/False	MCQ's	Total
Easy	300	500	800
Difficult	200	400	600
Total	500	900	1400

Let us denote $\quad E$ = easy questions
$$M = \text{MCQ's}$$
$$D = \text{Difficult questions}$$
$$T = \text{True/False questions}$$

Total number of questions = 1400
Total number of MCQ's = 900

$$\therefore \; P(\text{selecting a MCQ}) = P(M) = \frac{900}{1400} = \frac{9}{14}$$

$$P(\text{selecting easy MCQ's}) = \frac{500}{1400} = \frac{5}{14}$$

Now, $P(E/M)$ represents the probability that a randomly selected question will be an easy question, given that it is a MCQ.

$$\therefore \quad P(E/M) = \frac{P(E \cap M)}{P(M)} = \frac{5/14}{9/14} = \frac{5}{9}.$$

77. A black and a red die are rolled together. Find the conditional probability of obtaining the sum 8, given that the red die resulted in a number less than 4.*

Sol. Let A be event that the sum of observations is 8.
$$\therefore \quad A = \{(2, 6), (3, 5), (5, 3), (4, 4), (6, 2)\}$$
$$\Rightarrow \quad n(A) = 5$$
$$\Rightarrow \quad P(A) = \frac{5}{36}$$

Let B be event that the observation on red die is less than 4.
$$\therefore \; B = \{(1, 1), (2, 1), (3, 1), (4, 1), (5, 1), (6, 1), (1, 2),$$
$$(2, 2), (3, 2), (4, 2), (5, 2), (6, 2), (1, 3), (2, 3), (3, 3), (4, 3),$$
$$(5, 3), (6, 3)\}$$
$$\Rightarrow \quad n(B) = 18$$

$$\Rightarrow \quad P(B) = \frac{18}{36} = \frac{1}{2}$$

Clearly $\quad A \cap B = \{(5, 3), (6, 2)\}$
$$\therefore \quad n(A \cap B) = 2$$
$$\therefore \quad P(A \cap B) = \frac{2}{36} = \frac{1}{18}$$

$$P(A/B) = \frac{P(A \cap B)}{P(B)} = \frac{\dfrac{1}{18}}{\dfrac{1}{2}}$$
$$= \frac{2}{18} = \frac{1}{9}.$$

78. An electronic assembly consists of two sub-systems, say A and B. From previous testing procedures, the following probabilities are assumed to be known :
$$P(A \text{ fails}) = 0\cdot2$$
$$P(B \text{ fails alone}) = 0\cdot15$$
$$P(A \text{ and } B \text{ fail}) = 0\cdot15$$
Evaluate the following probabilities :
(i) $P(A)$ fails given that B has failed, (ii) $P(A)$ fails alone.
[NCERT]

Sol. Let the event in which A fails and B fails be denoted by E_A and E_B respectively.
Then, $\quad P(E_A) = 0\cdot2$
$$P(E_A \text{ and } E_B) = 0\cdot15$$
$$P(B \text{ fails alone}) = P(E_B) - P(E_A \text{ and } E_B)$$
$$\therefore \qquad 0\cdot15 = P(E_B) - 0\cdot15$$
$$\therefore \qquad P(E_B) = 0\cdot15 + 0\cdot15 = 0\cdot3.$$

(i) $\qquad P(E_A/E_B) = \dfrac{P(E_A \cap E_B)}{P(E_B)}$

$$= \frac{0\cdot15}{0\cdot3} = 0\cdot5.$$

(ii) $P(A \text{ fails alone}) = P(E_A) - P(E_A \text{ and } E_B)$
$$= 0\cdot2 - 0\cdot15$$
$$= 0\cdot05.$$

79. A box has 2 apples out of which one is red and other is green. What is the probability that both of them are bad, if it is known that (i) the red apple is bad, (ii) the green apple is bad.

Sol. Let B_i and G_i denote the apples to be bad and good respectively where $i \in \{R, G\}$. R stands for red apple and G for green apple.

Then sample space is $S = \{G_R G_G \; B_R G_G, \; B_R B_G, \; G_R B_G\}$

Let us consider the events
$$A = \text{both apples are bad}$$
$$B = \text{red apple is bad}$$
$$C = \text{green apple is bad}$$

Then, $A = \{B_R B_G\}$, $B = \{B_R G_G, B_R B_G\}$ and $C = \{B_R B_G, G_R B_G\}$

and $\quad A \cap B = \{B_R B_G\}$, $A \cap C = \{B_R B_G\}$

∴ (i) Required probability

$$= P(A/B)$$

$$= \frac{P(A \cap B)}{P(B)} = \frac{1/4}{2/4} = \frac{1}{2}$$

(ii) Required probability

$$= P(A/C)$$

$$= \frac{P(A \cap C)}{P(C)} = \frac{1/4}{2/4} = \frac{1}{2}.$$

80. A problem in mathematics is given to three students whose chances of solving it correctly are $\dfrac{1}{2}, \dfrac{1}{3}$ and $\dfrac{1}{4}$ respectively. What is the probability that only one of them solves it correctly ?

Sol. Let A, B, C be the given students and let E_1, E_2, E_3 be the events that the problem is solved by A, B, C respectively. Then, $\overline{E}_1$, $\overline{E}_2$, $\overline{E}_3$ are the events that the given problem is not solved by A, B, C respectively. Then,

$$P(E_1) = \frac{1}{2}, \ P(E_2) = \frac{1}{3} \text{ and } P(E_3) = \frac{1}{4}$$

$$P(\overline{E}_1) = \left(1 - \frac{1}{2}\right) = \frac{1}{2}; \ P(\overline{E}_2) = \left(1 - \frac{1}{3}\right) = \frac{2}{3}$$

and $\quad P(\overline{E}_3) = \left(1 - \frac{1}{4}\right) = \frac{3}{4}$

$P($ exactly one of them solves the problem$)$

$$= P[(E_1 \cap \overline{E}_2 \cap \overline{E}_3) \text{ or } (\overline{E}_1 \cap E_2 \cap \overline{E}_3)$$

$$\text{or } (\overline{E}_1 \cap \overline{E}_2 \cap E_3)]$$

$$= P(E_1 \cap \overline{E}_2 \cap \overline{E}_3) + P(\overline{E}_1 \cap E_2 \cap \overline{E}_3)$$

$$+ P(\overline{E}_1 \cap \overline{E}_2 \cap E_3)$$

Now since $(E_1, \overline{E}_2, \overline{E}_3)$; $(\overline{E}_1, E_2, \overline{E}_3)$; $(\overline{E}_1, \overline{E}_2, E_3)$ are independent events respectively.

∴ $P($only one of A, B, C solve the problem correctly$)$

$$= [P(E_1) \times P(\overline{E}_2) \times P(\overline{E}_3)]$$

$$+ [P(\overline{E}_1) \times P(E_2) \times P(\overline{E}_3)]$$

$$+ [P(\overline{E}_1) \times P(\overline{E}_2) \times P(E_3)]$$

$$= \left(\frac{1}{2} \times \frac{2}{3} \times \frac{3}{4}\right) + \left(\frac{1}{2} \times \frac{1}{3} \times \frac{3}{4}\right) + \left(\frac{1}{2} \times \frac{2}{3} \times \frac{1}{4}\right)$$

$$= \frac{6 + 3 + 2}{24} = \frac{11}{24}$$

Hence, the required probability is $\dfrac{11}{24}$.

81. Three groups of children contain 3 girls and 1 boy; 2 girls and 2 boy and 1 girl and 3 boys. One child is selected at random from each group. Find the chance that the three children selected comprise 1 girl and 2 boys.

Sol. Let G_1, G_2, G_3 be the events of selecting a girl from the first, second and third group respectively. Let B_1, B_2, B_3 be the events of selecting a boy from the first, second and third group respectively.

Then $\quad P(G_1) = \dfrac{3}{4}$; $P(G_2) = \dfrac{2}{4} = \dfrac{1}{2}$; $P(G_3) = \dfrac{1}{4}$

$$P(B_1) = \frac{1}{4}; \ P(B_2) = \frac{2}{4} = \frac{1}{2}; \ P(B_3) = \frac{3}{4}$$

Now, $P($selecting 1 girl and 2 boys$)$

$$= P[(G_1 B_2 B_3) \text{ or } (B_1 G_2 B_3) \text{ or } (B_1 B_2 G_3)]$$

$$= P(G_1 B_2 B_3) + P(B_1 G_2 B_3) + P(B_1 B_2 G_3)$$

$$= [P(G_1) \times P(B_2) \times P(B_3)] + [P(B_1) \times P(G_2) \times P(B_3)]$$

$$+ [P(B_1) \times P(B_2) \times P(G_3)]$$

$[∵ G_1, G_2, G_3$ and B_1, B_2, B_3 are independent events respectively$]$

$$= \left(\frac{3}{4} \times \frac{1}{2} \times \frac{3}{4}\right) + \left(\frac{1}{4} \times \frac{1}{2} \times \frac{3}{4}\right) + \left(\frac{1}{4} \times \frac{1}{2} \times \frac{1}{4}\right)$$

$$= \frac{9}{32} + \frac{3}{32} + \frac{1}{32} = \frac{13}{32}$$

Hence, the chances of selecting 1 girl and 2 boys are $\dfrac{13}{32}$.

82. Five gems are drawn from a pack which contains 7 blue gems and 4 black gems. What is the probability that :

(i) all will be blue ?

(ii) 3 will be blue and 2 black

Sol. Total number of gems in the pack $= 7 + 4 = 11$

Hence the number of elementary events $= {}^{11}C_5$ (or number of ways in which 5 gems can be drawn out of 11)

(i) Total number of blue gems $= 7$

5 gems can be drawn out of 7 in ${}^{7}C_5$ ways.

∴ Required probability $= \dfrac{{}^{7}C_5}{{}^{11}C_5}$

$$= \frac{7!}{2!\,5!} \times \frac{5!\,6!}{11!}$$

$$= \frac{6 \times 5 \times 4 \times 3}{11 \times 10 \times 9 \times 8} = \frac{1}{22}.$$

(ii) Three blue gems out of 7 blue and 2 black gems out of 4 black gems can be drawn in $^7C_3 \times {}^4C_2$ ways.

∴ Required probability

$$= \frac{^7C_3 \times {}^4C_2}{^{11}C_5}$$

$$= \frac{7!}{4!\,3!} \times \frac{4!}{2!\,2!} \times \frac{5!\,6!}{11!}$$

$$= \frac{5 \times 4 \times 6 \times 5 \times 4 \times 3}{11 \times 10 \times 9 \times 8 \times 2 \times 1} = \frac{5}{11}.$$

83. Ram can find a solution of 60% of the problems given in mathematics examination paper and Shyam can find out 80% of it. What is the probability that atleast one of them will solve the problem that is selected at random ?

Sol. Let us consider the events :

$$A = \text{Ram finds the solution}$$

$$B = \text{Shyam finds the solution}$$

Since, A and B are independent events.

So $P(A) = \dfrac{60}{100} = \dfrac{3}{5}$ and $P(B) = \dfrac{80}{100} = \dfrac{4}{5}$

∴ Required Probability

$$= P(A \cup B)$$
$$= P(A) + P(B) - P(A \cap B)$$
$$= P(A) + P(B) - P(A)\,P(B)$$
$$[\because P(A \cap B) = P(A)\,P(B)]$$
$$= \frac{3}{5} + \frac{4}{5} - \frac{3}{5} \times \frac{4}{5} = \frac{7}{5} - \frac{12}{25} = \frac{23}{25}.$$

84. Given that the events A and B are such that $P(A) = \dfrac{1}{2}$, $P(A \cup B) = \dfrac{3}{5}$ and $P(B) = p$. Find p if they are :

(i) mutually exclusive events, (ii) independent events. **[NCERT]**

Sol. Given, $P(A) = \dfrac{1}{2}$ and $P(B) = p$, $P(A \cup B) = \dfrac{3}{5}$

(i) When A & B are mutually exclusive,

Then, $\qquad A \cap B = \phi$

∴ $\qquad P(A \cap B) = 0$

It is know that

$$P(A \cup B) = P(A) + P(B) - P(A \cap B)$$

$$\frac{3}{5} = \frac{1}{2} + p - 0$$

$$\Rightarrow \qquad p = \frac{3}{5} - \frac{1}{2} = \frac{6-5}{10} = \frac{1}{10}$$

(ii) When A and B are independent,

Then, $\quad P(A \cap B) = P(A) \cdot P(B)$

$i.e.,\qquad P(A \cap B) = \dfrac{1}{2} \times p$

$$P(A \cup B) = P(A) + P(B) - P(A \cap B)$$

$$\frac{3}{5} = \frac{1}{2} + p - \frac{p}{2}$$

$$\Rightarrow \qquad \frac{p}{2} = \frac{1}{10}$$

$$\Rightarrow \qquad p = \frac{1}{5}.$$

85. Two students are trying to solve a problem and the probability of solving the problem independently by the first and second student are $\dfrac{1}{4}$ and $\dfrac{1}{5}$ respectively. If both try to solve the problem independently, find the probability that (i) the problem is solved, (ii) exactly one of them solves the problem.

Sol. Let A and B be the events that problem is solved by first and second student respectively.

Probability of solving the problem by A

$$P(A) = \frac{1}{4}$$

Probability of solving the problem by B

$$P(B) = \frac{1}{5}$$

Since the problem is being solved independently

∴ $\qquad P(A \cap B) = P(A) \cdot P(B) = \dfrac{1}{4} \times \dfrac{1}{5} = \dfrac{1}{20}$

$$P(\overline{A}) = 1 - P(A) = 1 - \frac{1}{4} = \frac{3}{4}$$

$$P(\overline{B}) = 1 - P(B) = 1 - \frac{1}{5} = \frac{4}{5}$$

(i) Probability that the problem is solved

$$= P(A \cup B)$$
$$= P(A) + P(B) - P(A \cap B)$$
$$= \frac{1}{4} + \frac{1}{5} - \frac{1}{20}$$
$$= \frac{5+4}{20} - \frac{1}{20}$$
$$= \frac{8}{20}.$$

(ii) Probability that exactly one of them solves the problem is given by

$$P(A).P(\overline{B}) + P(B).P(\overline{A})$$

$$= \frac{1}{4} \times \frac{4}{5} + \frac{1}{5} \times \frac{3}{4} = \frac{4+3}{20}$$

$$= \frac{7}{20}.$$

86. A coin is tossed thrice. Let the event E be 'the first throw result in a head' and the event F be 'the last throw results in a tail'. Find whether the events E & F are independent.

Sol. When a coin is tossed three times, the sample space is given by

$$S = \{HHH, HHT, HTH, THH, HTT, TTH, THT, TTT\}$$

Now, E = event that the first throw results in a head

$$\therefore \quad E = \{HHH, HHT, HTH, HTT\}$$

and F = event that the last throw results in a tail

$$\therefore \quad F = \{HHT, THT, HTT, TTT\}$$

So, $\quad E \cap F = \{HHT, HTT\}$

Clearly, $n(E) = 4$, $n(F) = 4$, $n(E \cap F) = 2$ and $n(S) = 8$

$$\therefore \quad P(E) = \frac{n(E)}{n(S)} = \frac{4}{8} = \frac{1}{2}$$

$$P(F) = \frac{n(F)}{n(S)} = \frac{4}{8} = \frac{1}{2}$$

and $\quad P(E \cap F) = \frac{n(E \cap F)}{n(S)} = \frac{2}{8} = \frac{1}{4}$

Now, $\quad P(E \cap F) = P(E) \times P(F) = \frac{1}{2} \times \frac{1}{2} = \frac{1}{4}$

Hence 'E' and 'F' are independent events.

87. Prove that if E and F are independent events, then the events E and F are also independent.*

Sol. Since E and F are independent events :

$$\therefore \quad P(E \cap F) = P(E) \cdot P(F) \qquad \ldots(i)$$

Now $\quad P(E \cap F') = P(E) - P(E \cap F)$

$$= P(E) - P(E)\,P(F) \quad \text{[From (i)]}$$

$$= P(E)\,[1 - P(F)]$$

$$= P(E)\,P(F')$$

$\therefore$ E and F' are also independent.

88. A die, whose faces are marked 1, 2, 3 in red and 4, 5, 6 in green is tossed. Let A be the event "number obtained is even" and B be the event "number obtained is red". Find if A and B are independent events.*

Sol. Since A is the event of number obtained is even.

$$\therefore \quad A = \{2, 4, 6\}$$

and B is the event of number obtained is red.

$$\therefore \quad B = \{1, 2, 3\}$$

$$\therefore \quad A \cap B = \{2\}$$

So, $\quad P(A) = \frac{3}{6} = \frac{1}{2};$

$$P(B) = \frac{3}{6} = \frac{1}{2};$$

$$P(A \cap B) = \frac{1}{6}$$

Now, $\quad P(A \cap B) \neq P(A) \cdot P(B)$

$$\frac{1}{6} \neq \frac{1}{4}$$

Hence, the events A and B are not independent events.

89. A bag contains 4 balls. Two balls are drawn at random (without replacement) and are found to be white. What is the probability that all balls in the bag are white ?*

Sol. There are three possible cases. Thy are :

A_1 : The bag has 2 white balls and 2 balls and 2 balls of other colour

A_2 : The bag has 3 white balls and 1 ball of other colour

A_3 : The bag has 4 white balls

Now, $\quad P(A_1) = P(A_2) = P(A_3) = \frac{1}{3}$

Let E be the event of selecting 2 white balls.

$$\therefore \quad P\left(\frac{E}{A_1}\right) = \frac{{}^2C_2}{{}^4C_2} = \frac{1}{6}$$

$$P\left(\frac{E}{A_2}\right) = \frac{{}^3C_2}{{}^4C_2} = \frac{1}{2}$$

$$P\left(\frac{E}{A_3}\right) = \frac{{}^4C_2}{{}^4C_2} = 1$$

Applying Bayes theorem,

$$\therefore \quad P\left(\frac{A_3}{E}\right) = \frac{P(A_3)P\left(\dfrac{P}{A_3}\right)}{P(A_1)\,P\left(\dfrac{E}{A_1}\right) + P(A_2)P\left(\dfrac{E}{A_2}\right) + P(A_3)P\left(\dfrac{E}{A_3}\right)}$$

$$= \frac{\dfrac{1}{3} \times 1}{\dfrac{1}{3}\left(\dfrac{1}{6} + \dfrac{1}{2} + 1\right)} = \frac{3}{5}.$$

90. In a multiple choice test with five possible answers, the probability of a student guessing the correct answer by actually knowing it is p and the probability of his guessing the correct answer without knowing it is $\frac{1}{5}$. If the student has answered the questions correctly, then what is the probability that he actually knew the answer ?

Sol. Let A denote the event that the student has answered the questions correctly.

Let B denote the event that the student actually knows the answer, and $\bar{B}$, the event that he does not know the answer.

We have to find $P(B/A)$

Now, $P(A/B) = 1,\ P(A/\bar{B}) = \dfrac{1}{5},$

$$P(B) = p,\ P(\bar{B}) = 1 - p$$

So Bayes' theorem

$$P\left(\frac{B}{A}\right) = \frac{P(A/B)\,P(B)}{P(A/B)\,P(B) + P(A/\bar{B})\,P(\bar{B})}$$

$$= \frac{1.p}{1.p + \dfrac{1}{5}(1-p)}$$

$$= \frac{p}{p + \dfrac{1-p}{5}} = \frac{5p}{4p+1}.$$

91. The contents of bags I, II and III are as follows :

Bag I : 1 white, 2 black and 3 red balls

Bag II : 2 white, 1 black and 1 red ball

Bag III : 4 white, 5 black and 3 red balls

One bag is chosen at random and three balls are drawn from it. Two happen to be the red and one white. What is the probability that they came from bag III ?

Sol. Let B_i : Bag i is chosen, $i = 1, 2, 3$.

Therefore, the probability of choosing bag B_i is $P(B_i)$

$$= \frac{1}{3},\ \forall_i = 1, 2, 3$$

Let A : Two of the balls drawn are red and one is white

Then clearly,

$$P(A/B_1) = \frac{{}^1C_1 \times {}^3C_2}{{}^6C_3}$$

$$= \frac{3\,(3 \times 2 \times 1)}{6 \times 5 \times 4} = \frac{3}{20}$$

$$P(A/B_2) = \frac{{}^2C_1 \times 0}{{}^4C_3}$$

[∵ Two red balls cannot be chosen from the one available]

$$= 0$$

$$P(A/B_3) = \frac{{}^4C_1 \times {}^3C_2}{{}^{12}C_3}$$

$$= \frac{4 \times 3\,(3 \times 2 \times 1)}{12 \times 11 \times 10}$$

$$= \frac{3}{55}$$

By Bayes' theorem,

$$P(B_3/A) = \frac{P(A/B_3)P(B_3)}{\sum\limits_{i=1}^{3} P(A/B_i)\,P(B_i)}$$

$$= \frac{\dfrac{3}{55} \times \dfrac{1}{3}}{\dfrac{3}{20} \times \dfrac{1}{3} + 0 + \dfrac{3}{55} \times \dfrac{1}{3}}$$

$$= \frac{\dfrac{3}{55}}{\dfrac{(33+12)}{220}} = \frac{12}{45} = \frac{4}{15}$$

Therefore, the required probability is $\dfrac{4}{15}$.

92. A man is known to speak the truth 3 out of 4 times. He throws a die and reports that it is a six. Find the probability that it is actually a six.

Sol. Let E be the event that the man reports that six occurs in the throwing of the die. Let S_1 be the event that six occurs and S_2 be the event that six does not occur.

Then, $P(S_1) =$ probability that six occurs $= \dfrac{1}{6}$

$P(S_2) =$ probability that six does not occur

$$= 1 - \frac{1}{6} = \frac{5}{6}$$

$P(E/S_1) =$ probability that the man reports that six occurs when six has actually occurred $=$ probability that the man speaks the truth $= \dfrac{3}{4}$

$P(E/S_2) =$ Probability that the man reports that six occurs when six has not actually occurred $=$ probability that the man does not speak the truth

$$= 1 - \frac{3}{4} = \frac{1}{4}$$

Hence, by Bayes' theorem,

$P(S_1/E) =$ probability that the report of the man that six has occurred is actually a six

$$= \frac{P(S_1)\,P(E/S_1)}{P(S_1)\,P(E/S_1) + P(S_2)\,P(E/S_2)}$$

$$= \frac{\dfrac{1}{6} \times \dfrac{3}{4}}{\dfrac{1}{6} \times \dfrac{3}{4} + \dfrac{5}{6} \times \dfrac{1}{4}} = \frac{\dfrac{1}{8}}{\dfrac{3+5}{24}}$$

$$= \frac{1}{8} \times \frac{24}{8} = \frac{3}{8}$$

Hence, the required probability is $\dfrac{3}{8}$.

93. In a competitive examination, an examinee either guesses or copies or knows the answer to a multiple choice question with four options.

The probability that he makes a guess is $\dfrac{1}{3}$ and the probability that he copies the answer is $\dfrac{1}{6}$.

The probability that the answer is correct, given that he copied it is $\dfrac{1}{8}$ and the guesses it is $\dfrac{1}{4}$ and when he knows the answer to it is 1.

Find the probability that he knows the answer to the question, given that he answered it correctly.

Sol. Let B_1, B_2 and B_3 be the events that the examinee guess, copies and knows the answer, respectively.

$\therefore \qquad P(B_1) = \dfrac{1}{3},\ P(B_2) = \dfrac{1}{6},$

$$P(B_3) = 1 - [P(B_1) + P(B_2)]$$
$$= 1 - \dfrac{1}{3} - \dfrac{1}{6} = \dfrac{1}{2}$$

Let A be the event that the answer is correct. Then,

$$P(A/B_1) = \dfrac{1}{4},\ P(A/B_2) = \dfrac{1}{8},\ P(A/B_3) = 1$$

Using Bayes' theorem

$$P(B_3/A) = \dfrac{P(B_3)P(A/B_3)}{P(B_1)P(A/B_1) + P(B_2)P(A/B_2) + P(B_3)P(A/B_3)}$$

$$= \dfrac{\dfrac{1}{2} \times 1}{\dfrac{1}{3} \times \dfrac{1}{4} + \dfrac{1}{6} \times \dfrac{1}{8} + \dfrac{1}{2} \times 1}$$

$$= \dfrac{\dfrac{1}{2}}{\dfrac{1}{12} + \dfrac{1}{48} + \dfrac{1}{2}} = \dfrac{\dfrac{1}{2}}{\dfrac{4 + 1 + 24}{48}} = \dfrac{24}{29}.$$

94. In a school, 8% of the boys and 2% of the girls have an I.Q. of more than 120. In the school, 60% of the students are boys. A student with an I.Q. more than 120 is selected. Find the probability that the student selected is a boy.

Sol. Let E = event that the student has an I.Q. of more than 120.

Let B and G denote the events of choosing a boy and a girl respectively.

Therefore, $P(B) = P(\text{choosing a boy}) = \dfrac{60}{100} = 0.6$

and $P(G) = P(\text{choosing a girl}) = \dfrac{40}{100} = 0.4$ ...(i)

We have to find P (student selected is a boy given that his I.Q. is more than 120)

i.e., we have to find $P(B/E)$.

Given : $P\left(\dfrac{E}{B}\right) = \dfrac{8}{100} = 0.08$

and $P(E/G) = \dfrac{2}{100} = 0.02$ ...(ii)

By Bayes' theorem,

$$P(B/E) = \dfrac{P(B).P(E/B)}{P(B).P(E/B) + P(G).P(E/G)}$$

$$= \dfrac{0.6 \times 0.08}{(0.6 \times 0.08) + (0.4 \times 0.02)}$$

$$\text{[using (i) and (ii)]}$$

$$= \dfrac{0.048}{0.048 + 0.008} = \dfrac{0.048}{0.056} = \dfrac{6}{7}.$$

95. If a machine is set correctly, it produces 10% of defective items. If it is set incorrectly, it produces 10% good items. Chances for setting to be correct and incorrect are in the ratio 7 : 3. After a setting is made, the first item produced is found to be good item. What is the chance that the machine was set correctly ?

Sol. Let E_1 and E_2 be the events that the set-up is correct and incorrect respectively.

Let E be the event that the items produces are good ones.

Given that

$$\dfrac{\text{Setting is correct}}{\text{Setting is incorrect}} = \dfrac{7}{3}$$

$\Rightarrow \qquad P(E_1) = \dfrac{7}{10},$

$$P(E_2) = \dfrac{3}{10} \qquad \text{...(i)}$$

10% defective items means 90% good items.

Therefore, $P(E/E_1) = \dfrac{90}{100} = \dfrac{9}{10}$

and $P(E/E_2) = \dfrac{10}{100} = \dfrac{1}{10}$ ...(ii)

Therefore by Bayes' theorem,

$$P(E_1/E) = \dfrac{P(E_1).P(E/E_1)}{P(E_1).P(E/E_1) + P(E_2).P(E/E_2)}$$

$$= \dfrac{\dfrac{7}{10} \times \dfrac{9}{10}}{\dfrac{7}{10} \times \dfrac{9}{10} + \dfrac{3}{10} \times \dfrac{1}{10}} \quad \text{[using (i) and (ii)]}$$

$$= \dfrac{\dfrac{63}{100}}{\dfrac{63 + 3}{100}} = \dfrac{63}{66} = \dfrac{21}{22}.$$

96. Three urns contain 6 red, 4 black; 4 red, 6 black; 5 red, 5 black balls respectively. One of the urns is selected at random and a ball is drawn from it. If the ball drawn is red, find the probability that it was drawn from the first urn.*

Sol. Let E_1, E_2, E_3 be the events of choosing the first, second and third urn respectively.

Let A be the event of drawing a red ball.

Since an urn is selected at random from 3 urns, therefore,

$$P(E_1) = P(E_2) = P(E_3) = \frac{1}{3}$$

P (drawing a red ball when 1st urn is choosen)

$$= P\,(A/E_1) = \frac{6}{10}$$

Similarly, $P\,(A/E_2) = \dfrac{4}{10}$ and $P\,(A/E_3) = \dfrac{5}{10}$

P(red ball is drawn from the first urn) $= P\,(E_1/A)$

$$= \frac{P(E_1){\cdot}P(A/E_1)}{P(E_1){\cdot}P(A/E_1) + P(E_2){\cdot}P(A/E_2)}$$
$$\qquad\qquad\qquad + P(E_3){\cdot}P(A/E_3)$$

$$= \frac{\dfrac{1}{3}\times\dfrac{6}{10}}{\dfrac{1}{3}\times\dfrac{6}{10} + \dfrac{1}{3}\times\dfrac{4}{10} + \dfrac{1}{3}\times\dfrac{5}{10}} = \frac{6}{15} = \frac{2}{5}.$$

97. A letter is known to have come either from TATANAGAR or CALCUTTA. On the envelope just two consecutive letters TA are visible. What is the probability that the letter has come from CALCUTTA?

Sol. Let E_1 be the event that the letter is from CALCUTTA and E_2 be the event that the letter is from TATANAGAR.

Let A denote the event that two consecutive letters visible on the envelope are TA.

Since, the letters have come either from CALCUTTA or TATANAGAR,

$$\therefore \qquad P(E_1) = \frac{1}{2} = P(E_2)$$

If E_1 has occurred, then it means that the letters is from CALCUTTA.

There are seven consecutive letters namely CA, $AL, LC,\ CU\ UT,\ TT,\ TA$ out of which one case is favourable.

$$\Rightarrow \qquad P(A\,/\,E_1) = \frac{1}{7}$$

If E_2 has occurred, then the letter came from TATANAGAR.

There are eight consecutive letters namely TA, $AT,\ TA,\ AN,\ NA,\ AG,\ GA,\ AR$ out of which two cases are favourable.

$$\therefore \qquad P(A\,/\,E_2) = \frac{2}{8}$$

Using Bayes' theorem

$$P(E_1\,/\,A) = \frac{P(E_1).\,P(A\,/\,E_1)}{P(E_1).\,P(A\,/\,E_1) + P(E_2).P(A\,/\,E_2)}$$

$$= \frac{\dfrac{1}{2}\times\dfrac{1}{7}}{\left(\dfrac{1}{2}\times\dfrac{1}{7}\right) + \left(\dfrac{1}{2}\times\dfrac{2}{8}\right)} = \frac{4}{11}.$$

98. Often it is taken that a truthful person commands more respect in the society. A man is known to speak the truth 4 out of 5 times. He throws a die and reports that it is a six. Find the probability that it is actually a six.*

Sol. Let E_1, E_2 and A be the events defined as follows :

E_1 = Six occurs

E_2 = Six does not occur

and A = the man reports that it is a six

We have, $\qquad P(E_1) = \dfrac{1}{6}$

$$P(E_2) = \frac{5}{6}$$

Now $P(A/E_1)$ = Probability that the man reports that there is a six on the die given that six has occured on the die = 4/5 (probability that the man speaks truth) and $P(A/E_2)$ = Probability that the man reports that there is a six on the die given that six has not occurred on the die (probability that the man does not speak truth).

$$= 1 - \frac{4}{5} = \frac{1}{5}$$

By Bayes' theorem, we have

$$P(E_1/A) = \frac{P(E_1)\,P(A\,/\,E_1)}{P(E_1)\,P(A\,/\,E_1) + P(E_2)\,P(A\,/\,E_2)}$$

$$= \frac{\dfrac{1}{6}\times\dfrac{4}{5}}{\dfrac{1}{6}\times\dfrac{4}{5} + \dfrac{5}{6}\times\dfrac{1}{5}} = \frac{4}{4+5} = \frac{4}{9}.$$

99. Suppose a girl throws a die. If she gets 1 and 2 she tosses a coin three times and notes the number of tails. If she gets 3, 4, 5 and 6, she tosses a coin once and notes whether a 'head' or 'tail', is obtained. If obtained exactly one 'tail'. What is the probability that she threw 3, 4, 5 and 6 with the die ?*

Sol. Let E_1 be the event that girl gets 1 or 2 on the roll and E_2 be the event that girls gets 3, 4, 5 or 6 on the roll of a die.

$\therefore$
$$P(E_1) = \frac{2}{6} = \frac{1}{3}$$

$$P(E_2) = \frac{4}{6} = \frac{2}{3}$$

Let A be event that she gets exactly one tail.

If she tossed coin 3 times and gets exactly one tail then possible outcomes are HTH, HHT, THH.

$\therefore$
$$P(A/E_1) = \frac{3}{8}$$

If she tossed coin only once and exactly one tail shows, then

$$P(A/E_2) = \frac{1}{2}$$

$\therefore$
$$P(E_2/A) = \frac{P(E_2).P(A/E_2)}{P(E_1)\cdot P(A/E_1) + P(E_2)\cdot P(A/E_2)}$$

$$= \frac{\dfrac{1}{2} \times \dfrac{2}{3}}{\dfrac{1}{2} \times \dfrac{2}{3} + \dfrac{3}{8} \times \dfrac{1}{3}} = \frac{\dfrac{1}{3}}{\dfrac{1}{8} + \dfrac{1}{3}} = \frac{1/3}{11/24}$$

$$= \frac{8}{11}.$$

100. A city's data shows 5 men out of 100 and 25 women out of 1000 are colour blind. If a colourblind person is chosen at random, then find the probability of this person being a male (assuming males and females are in equal proportion in the city).

Sol. Let

M = Event that a person chosen at random is a male

F = Event that a person chosen at random is a female

C = Event that a person chosen at random is colour blind

Therefore, required probability = $P(M / C)$ given that $P(M) = P(F) = \dfrac{1}{2}$ (equal proportion)

Now, $P(C / M) = \dfrac{5}{100}$ and $P(C / F) = \dfrac{25}{1000}$

Hence, by Bayes' theorem

$$P(M/C) = \frac{P(C / M)\, P(M)}{P(C / M)\, P(M) + P(C / F)\, P(F)}$$

$$= \frac{\dfrac{5}{100} \times \dfrac{1}{2}}{\dfrac{5}{100} \times \dfrac{1}{2} + \dfrac{25}{1000} \times \dfrac{1}{2}}$$

$$= \frac{\dfrac{5}{200}}{\dfrac{5}{200} + \dfrac{25}{2000}} = \frac{2}{3}.$$

Long Answer Type Questions

101. A box contains 10 batteries out of which just three are defective. If a random sample of 5 batteries is drawn, find the probabilities that the sample contains :

(i) Exactly one defective battery

(ii) Exactly two defective batteries.

(iii) No defective batteries.

Sol. Out of 10 batteries 5 can be chosen in $^{10}C_5$ ways. So, total number of elementary events $= {}^{10}C_5$.

(i) There are 3 defective and 7 non defective batteries. The number of ways of selecting one defective battery out of 3 and 4 non-defective batteries out of 7 is $^3C_1 \times {}^7C_4$.

$\therefore$ Favourable number of elementary events
$$= {}^3C_1 \times {}^7C_4$$

So, required probability
$$= \frac{{}^3C_1 \times {}^7C_4}{{}^{10}C_5} = \frac{5}{12}$$

(ii) The number of ways of selecting 2 defective batteries out of 3 and 3 non-defective batteries out of 7 is $^3C_2 \times {}^7C_3$.

$\therefore$ Favourable number of elementary events
$$= {}^3C_2 \times {}^7C_3$$

So, the required probability
$$= \frac{{}^3C_2 \times {}^7C_3}{{}^{10}C_5}$$

$$= \frac{5}{12}$$

(iii) No defective battery means all non-defective batteries. The number of way of selecting all 5 non-defective batteries out of 7 is $^7C_5$.

$\therefore$ Favourable number of elementary events
$$= {}^7C_5.$$

So, the required probability is
$$\frac{{}^7C_5}{{}^{10}C_5} = \frac{1}{12}.$$

102. A fair dice is rolled consider events $E = \{1, 3, 5\}$, $F = \{2, 3\}$ and $G = \{2, 3, 4, 5\}$ find

(i) $P(E/F)$ and $P(F/E)$

(ii) $P(E/G)$ and $P(G/E)$

(iii) $P[(E \cup F)/G]$ and $P[(E \cap F)/G]$ **[NCERT]**

Sol. When a fair dice is rolled, the sample spaces will be $S = \{1, 2, 3, 4, 5, 6\}$

It is given that $E = \{1, 3, 5\}$, $F = \{2, 3\}$ and $G = \{2, 3, 4, 5\}$.

$$\therefore \quad P(E) = \frac{3}{6} = \frac{1}{2}$$

$$P(F) = \frac{2}{6} = \frac{1}{3}$$

$$P(G) = \frac{4}{6} = \frac{2}{3}$$

(i) $(E \cap F) = \{3\}$

$$\therefore \quad P(E \cap F) = \frac{1}{6}$$

$$P(E/F) = \frac{P(E \cap F)}{P(F)} = \frac{\frac{1}{6}}{\frac{1}{3}} = \frac{1}{2}$$

$$P(F/E) = \frac{P(F \cap E)}{P(E)} = \frac{\frac{1}{6}}{\frac{1}{2}} = \frac{2}{6} = \frac{1}{3}$$

(ii) $E \cap G = \{3, 5\}$

$$P(E \cap G) = \frac{2}{6} = \frac{1}{3}$$

$$P(E/G) = \frac{P(E \cap G)}{P(G)} = \frac{\frac{1}{3}}{\frac{2}{3}} = \frac{1}{2}$$

$$P(G/E) = \frac{P(G \cap E)}{P(E)} = \frac{\frac{1}{3}}{\frac{1}{2}} = \frac{2}{3}$$

(iii) $E \cup F = \{1, 2, 3, 5\}$

$$(E \cup F) \cap G = \{1, 2, 3, 5\} \cap \{2, 3, 4, 5\}$$
$$= \{2, 3, 5\}$$
$$E \cap F = \{3\}$$
$$(E \cap F) \cap (G) = \{3\} \cap \{2, 3, 4, 5\} = \{3\}$$
$$P((E \cup F) \cap G) = \frac{3}{6} = \frac{1}{2}$$

$$\therefore \quad P((E \cup F)/G) = \frac{P[(E \cup F) \cap G]}{P(G)}$$

$$= \frac{\frac{1}{2}}{\frac{2}{3}} = \frac{1}{2} \times \frac{3}{2} = \frac{3}{4}$$

$$P(E \cap F) = \frac{1}{6}$$

$$P((E \cap F) \cap G) = \frac{1}{6}$$

$$P((E \cap F)/G) = \frac{P[(E \cap F) \cap G]}{P(G)}$$

$$= \frac{\frac{1}{6}}{\frac{2}{3}} = \frac{1}{6} \times \frac{3}{2}$$

$$= \frac{1}{4}$$

103. In a girls hostel, 60% of the student read Hindi newspaper, 40% read English newspaper and 20% read both Hindi and English newspaper. A student is selected at random.

(i)   Find the probability that she reads neither Hindi nor English newspaper.

(ii) If she reads Hindi newspaper, find the probability that she reads English newspaper.

(iii) If she reads English newspaper, find the probability that she reads Hindi newspaper.

Sol. Let H denote the event that students who read Hindi newspaper and E denote the students who read English newspaper

It is given that,

$$P(H) = 60\% = \frac{60}{100} = \frac{3}{5}$$

$$P(E) = 40\% = \frac{40}{100} = \frac{2}{5}$$

$$P(H \cap E) = 20\% = \frac{20}{100} = \frac{1}{5}$$

(i) Probability that a student reads neither Hindi nor English newspaper is

$$P(H \cup E)' = 1 - P(H \cup E)$$
$$= 1 - [P(H) + P(E) - P(H \cap E)]$$
$$= 1 - \left\{ \frac{3}{5} + \frac{2}{5} - \frac{1}{5} \right\}$$
$$= 1 - \frac{4}{5} = \frac{1}{5}$$

(ii) Probability that a randomly chosen student reads English newspaper if she reads a Hindi newspaper is

$$P(E/H) = \frac{P(E \cap H)}{P(H)} = \frac{\frac{1}{5}}{\frac{3}{5}} = \frac{1}{3}$$

(iii) Probability that a randomly chosen student reads Hindi newspaper if she reads a English newspaper is

$$P\,(H\,/\,E) = \frac{P(H \cap E)}{P(E)} = \frac{\dfrac{1}{5}}{\dfrac{2}{5}} = \frac{1}{2}.$$

104. Consider the experiment of tossing a coin. If the coin shows tail, toss it again but if it shows head, then throw a die. Find the conditional probability of the event that 'the die shows a number greater than 4' given that 'there is atleast one head'.

Sol. The outcomes of the experiment can be represented in the following diagrammatic manner called the 'tree diagram'.

The sample space of the experiment may be described as

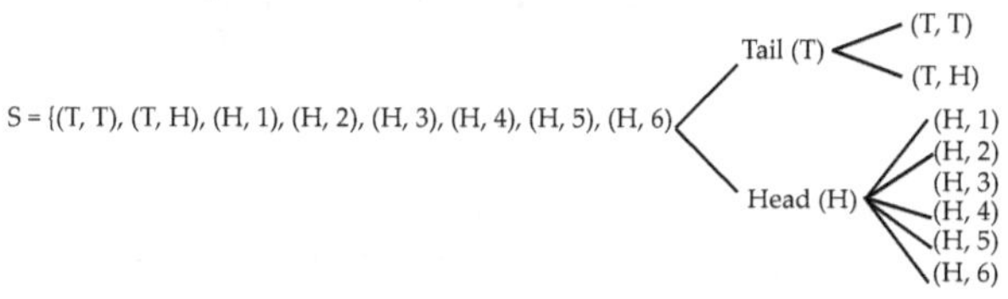

$S = \{(T, T), (T, H), (H, 1), (H, 2), (H, 3), (H, 4), (H, 5), (H, 6)\}$

where (T, T) denote that both the tosses result into tail and (H, i) denote the first toss result into a head and the number 'i' appeared on the die for

$$i = 1, 2, 3, 4, 5, 6$$

Thus, the probability assigned to the 8 elementary events $(T, T), (T, H), (H, 1), (H, 2), (H, 3), (H, 4), (H, 5),$

$(H, 6),$ are $\dfrac{1}{4}, \dfrac{1}{4}, \dfrac{1}{12}, \dfrac{1}{12}, \dfrac{1}{12}, \dfrac{1}{12}, \dfrac{1}{12}, \dfrac{1}{12}$ respectively

which is clear from the figure below.

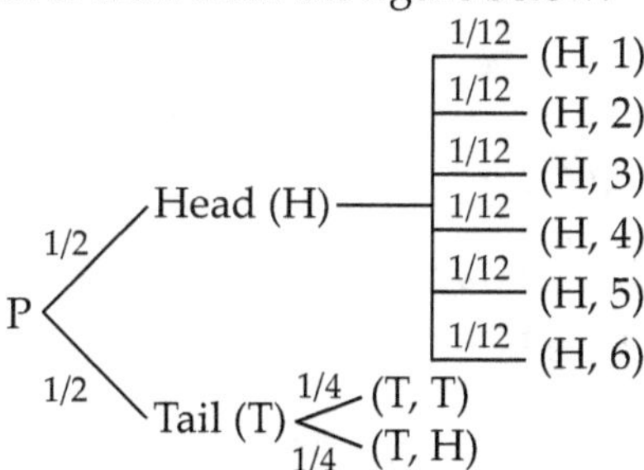

Let 'A' be the event that 'there is atleast one head' and 'B' be the event that 'the die shows a number greater than 4'.

Then

$$A = \{(T, H), (H, 1), (H, 2), (H, 3), (H, 4), (H, 5)$$
$$(H, 6)\}$$

$$B = \{(H, 5), (H, 6)\}$$

and $A \cap B = \{(H, 5), (H, 6)\}$

$$P\,(A) = P\,[(T, H)] + P\,[(H, 1)] + P\,[(H, 2)]$$
$$+ P\,[(H, 3)] + P\,[(H, 4)] + P\,[(H, 5)]$$
$$+ P\,[(H, 6)]$$

$$= \frac{1}{4} + \frac{1}{12} + \frac{1}{12} + \frac{1}{12} + \frac{1}{12} + \frac{1}{12} + \frac{1}{12}$$

$$= \frac{1}{4} + \frac{6}{12} = \frac{1}{4} + \frac{1}{2} = \frac{3}{4}$$

and $P\,(A \cap B) = P\,[\{(H, 5)\}] + P\,[\{(H, 6)\}]$

$$= \frac{1}{12} + \frac{1}{12} = \frac{1}{6}$$

Hence $P\,(B/A) = \dfrac{P(A \cap B)}{P(A)} = \dfrac{\dfrac{1}{6}}{\dfrac{3}{4}} = \dfrac{1}{6} \times \dfrac{4}{3} = \dfrac{2}{9}.$

105. Jagan, Magan and Gagan take part in a game. If Jagan wins the game 4 times out of 5; Magan wins the game 3 out of 4 times and Gagan wins it 2 out of 3 times, What is the probability that the game is won by at least 2 persons ?

Sol. Let A , B and C be the events that Jagan wins the game, Magan wins the game and Gagan wins the game respectively.

then $P\,(A) = \dfrac{4}{5};\ P(B) = \dfrac{3}{4}$ and $P\,(C) = \dfrac{2}{3}$

$$P(\overline{A}) = 1 - \frac{4}{5} = \frac{1}{5}$$

$$P(\overline{B}) = 1 - \frac{3}{4} = \frac{1}{4}$$

and $$P(\overline{C}) = 1 - \frac{2}{3} = \frac{1}{3}$$

Case I : Jagan, Magan and Gagan all win the game.

In this case , $P\,(A$ and B and $C\,)$
$$= P\,(A) \cdot P\,(B) \cdot P\,(C\,)$$
$[\because A, B$ and C are independent$]$
$$= \left[\frac{4}{5} \times \frac{3}{4} \times \frac{2}{3}\right]$$
$$= \frac{2}{5}$$

Case II : Jagan and Magan win but not Gagan.
In this case, $P\,(A$ and B but not $C)$
$$= P\,(A \cap B \cap C)$$
$$= P\,(A) \cdot P\,(B) \cdot P(\overline{C}\,)$$
$(\because A, B$ and $\overline{C}$ are independent$)$
$$= \left[\frac{4}{5} \times \frac{3}{4} \times \frac{1}{3}\right]$$
$$= \frac{1}{5}$$

Case III : Jagan and Gagan win but not Magan

In this case , P (A and C and not B)

$$= P(A \cap \bar{B} \cap C)$$

$$= P(A) \cdot P(\bar{B})_3 P(C)$$

$(\because A, \bar{B}$ and C are independent)

$$= \left[\frac{4}{5} \times \frac{2}{3} \times \frac{1}{4}\right] = \frac{2}{15}$$

Case IV : Magan and Gagan both win but not Jagan.

In this case, P (B & C and not A)

$$= P(B \cap C \cap \bar{A})$$

$$= P(B) \cdot P(C) \cdot P(\bar{A})$$

$(\because B, C$ and are $\bar{A}$ independent)

$$= \left[\frac{3}{4} \times \frac{2}{3} \times \frac{1}{5}\right] = \frac{1}{10}$$

Clearly, all these are mutually exclusive.

Hence, required probability

$$= \left(\frac{2}{5} + \frac{1}{5} + \frac{2}{15} + \frac{1}{10}\right) = \frac{5}{6}$$

106. Two balls are drawn at random with replacement from a box containing 10 black and 8 red balls. Find the probability that **[NCERT]**

(i) both are red

(ii) first ball is black and second is red

(iii) One of them is black and other is red.

Sol. Total number of balls = 10 black + 8 red

$$= 18$$

Number of black balls = 10

Number of red balls = 8

(i) Probability of getting a red ball in first draw

$$= \frac{8}{18} = \frac{4}{9}$$

The ball is replaced after the first draw.

$\therefore P$ (getting red ball in 2nd draw)

$$= \frac{8}{18} = \frac{4}{9}$$

Hence P (getting both red balls)

$$= \frac{4}{9} \times \frac{4}{9} = \frac{16}{81}$$

(ii) P (getting first ball black)

$$= \frac{10}{18} = \frac{5}{9}$$

The ball is replaced after first draw

P (getting second ball as red)

$$= \frac{8}{18} = \frac{4}{9}$$

Hence , P (getting first ball as black and second ball as red)

$$= \frac{5}{9} \times \frac{4}{9} = \frac{20}{81}$$

(iii) P {getting first ball as red}

$$= \frac{4}{9}$$

The ball is replaced after the first draw.

P (getting second ball as black)

$$= \frac{10}{18} = \frac{5}{9}$$

$\therefore P$ (getting first ball as black and second ball as red)

$$= \frac{4}{9} \times \frac{5}{9} = \frac{20}{81}$$

P (One of them is black and other is red)

= P (first ball black and second ball red)

$\qquad$ + P (first ball red and second ball black)

$$= \frac{20}{81} + \frac{20}{81} = \frac{40}{81} \cdot$$

107. One card is drawn at random from a well shuffled deck of 52 cards. In which of the following cards are the events E and F are independent ?

(i) E : 'the card drawn is a spade'

F : 'the card drawn is an ace'.

(ii) E : 'the card drawn is black'

F : 'the card drawn is a king'.

(iii) E : 'the card drawn is king or queen'

F : 'the card drawn is a queen or jack'. **[NCERT]**

Sol. (i) In a deck of 52 cards, 13 are spades and 4 cards are aces.

$$\therefore \ P(E) = \frac{13}{52} = \frac{1}{4} = P(\text{the card drawn is a spade})$$

$$P(F) = \frac{4}{52} = \frac{1}{13} = P(\text{the card drawn is an ace})$$

In a deck of cards, only 1 card is an ace of spades.

$\therefore P$(the card drawn is spade and ace)

$$= \frac{1}{52} = P(E \cap F)$$

$$P(E) \cdot P(F) = \frac{1}{4} \times \frac{1}{13} = \frac{1}{52}$$

Clearly, $\quad P(E \cap F) = P(E) \cdot P(F).$

Hence E and F are independent event.

(ii) In a deck of 52 cards, 26 cards are black and 4 cards are king.

$\therefore P$ (the card drawn is black)

$$= P(E)$$

$$= \frac{26}{52} = \frac{1}{2}$$

P (the card drawn is a king)

$$= P(F)$$

$$= \frac{4}{52} = \frac{1}{13}$$

In a deck of 52 cards 2 cards are black as well as kings

$\therefore \quad P(E \cap F) = P$ (the card drawn is a black king)

$$= \frac{2}{52} = \frac{1}{26}$$

$$P(E) \times P(F) = \frac{1}{2} \times \frac{1}{13} = \frac{1}{26}$$

Clearly, $\quad P(E \cap F) = P(E) \times P(F)$

Hence, E and F are independent events.

(iii) In a deck of 52 cards, 4 cards are kings, 4 cards are queens and 4 cards are jacks.

P (the card drawn is a king or queen)

$$= \frac{8}{52} = \frac{2}{13} = P(E)$$

P (the card drawn is a queen or jack)

$$= \frac{8}{52} = \frac{2}{13} = P(F)$$

There are 4 cards which are king or queen and queen or jack.

$\therefore P$ (the card drawn is a king / queen or queen / jack)

$$= \frac{4}{52} = \frac{1}{13}$$

i.e., $\qquad P(E \cap F) = \frac{1}{13}$

$$P(E) \times P(F) = \frac{2}{13} \times \frac{2}{13} = \frac{4}{169}$$

Clearly, $\quad P(E \cap F) \neq P(E) \cdot P(F)$

Hence, E and F are not independent events.

108. If A and B are two independent events such that $P(\overline{A} \cap B) = \frac{2}{15}$ and $P(A \cap \overline{B}) = \frac{1}{6}$, then find $P(A)$ and $P(B)$.*

Sol. Let $P(A) = x$ and $P(B) = y$

$$P(\overline{A}) = 1 - P(A) = 1 - x, \; P(\overline{B}) = 1 - y$$

We have,

$$P(\overline{A} \cap B) = \frac{2}{15} \text{ and } P(A \cap \overline{B}) = \frac{1}{6}$$

Now $\qquad P(\overline{A} \cap B) = \frac{2}{15}$

$$P(\overline{A})P(B) = \frac{2}{15}$$

$$(1 - x)y = \frac{2}{15} \qquad \ldots(i)$$

Since, A and B are independent events so are $\overline{A}$ and B as well as A and $\overline{B}$

Given, $\quad P(A \cap \overline{B}) = \frac{1}{6}$

$$P(A)P(\overline{B}) = \frac{1}{6}$$

$$x(1 - y) = \frac{1}{6}$$

$$x = \frac{1}{6 - 6y} \qquad \ldots(ii)$$

Putting the value of x in equation (i), we get

$$\left(1 - \frac{1}{6 - 6y}\right)y = \frac{2}{15}$$

$$-90y^2 + 87y = 12 \text{ or } 30y^2 - 29y + 4 = 0$$

Solving the quadratic equation, we get

$$y = \frac{4}{5}, \; y = \frac{1}{6}$$

For $\qquad y = \frac{4}{5}$; using (ii), we get

$$x = \frac{1}{6 - 6 \times \dfrac{4}{5}} = \frac{5}{30 - 24} = \frac{5}{6}$$

For $\qquad y = \frac{1}{6}$ using (ii), we get

$$x = \frac{1}{6 - 6 \times \dfrac{1}{6}} = \frac{1}{5}$$

$\therefore$ for $\qquad P(A) = \frac{5}{6}, \; P(B) = \frac{4}{5}$

or if $\qquad P(A) = \frac{1}{5},$ then $P(B) = \frac{1}{6}.$

109. An insurance company insured 2000 scooter drivers, 4000 car driver and 6000 truck drivers. The probability of accidents are 0.01, 0.03 and 0.15 respectively. One of the insured person meets with an accident. What is the probability that he is a scooter driver?

Sol. Let A, B and C be the respective events that the driver is a scooter driver, a car driver and a truck driver.

Let E be the event that the person meets with an accident.

$$\text{Number of scooter driver} = 2000$$

$$\text{Number of car driver} = 4000$$

and $\qquad \text{Number of truck driver} = 6000$

$\therefore \qquad \text{Total number of drivers} = 12000$

$P(A) = P$ (driver is a scooter driver)

$$= \frac{2000}{12000} = \frac{1}{6}$$

$P(B) = P$ (driver is a car driver)

$$= \frac{4000}{12000} = \frac{1}{3}$$

$P(C) = P$ (driver is a truck driver)

$$= \frac{6000}{12000} = \frac{1}{2}$$

Now, to find that the probability that a driver meets with an accident

P (scooter driver met with an accident)

$$= P(E/A) = 0.01 = \frac{1}{100}$$

P (car driver met with an accident)

$$= P(E/B) = 0.03 = \frac{3}{100}$$

P (truck driver met with an accident)

$$= P(E/C) = 0.15 = \frac{15}{100}$$

The probability that the driver is a scooter driver, who met with the accident is given by $P(A/E)$
By using Bayes' theorem, we obtain

$$P(A/E) = \frac{P(A)\cdot P(E/A)}{P(A)\cdot P(E/A) + P(B)\cdot P(E/B) + P(C)\cdot P(E/C)}$$

$$P(A/E) = \frac{\frac{1}{6}\cdot\frac{1}{100}}{\frac{1}{6}\cdot\frac{1}{100} + \frac{1}{3}\cdot\frac{3}{100} + \frac{1}{2}\cdot\frac{15}{100}}$$

$$= \frac{\frac{1}{6}\cdot\frac{1}{100}}{\frac{1}{100}\left[\frac{1}{6} + 1 + \frac{15}{2}\right]} = \frac{1}{6}\times\frac{6}{52} = \frac{1}{52}$$

Hence, the required probability is $\frac{1}{52}$.

110. Coloured gifts are placed in three shelves as shown in the following table :

Shelf	Colour of the Gift		
	Gold	Silver	Red
I	1	2	3
II	2	4	1
III	4	5	3

A shelf is selected at random and then two gifts are randomly taken from the selected shelf. They happen to be Gold and red. What is the probability that they are taken from shelf I ?

Sol. Let E_1, E_2, E_3 be the following events :

$$E_1 = \text{Shelf I is selected}$$
$$E_2 = \text{Shelf II is selected}$$
$$E_3 = \text{Shelf III is selected}$$

Let A be the event of getting a gold and red gift.

$$P(E_1) = P(E_2) = P(E_3) = \frac{1}{3}$$

$$P(A/E_1) = \frac{{}^1C_1 \times {}^3C_1}{{}^6C_2}$$

$$= \frac{1\times 3}{\frac{6\times 5}{2\times 1}} = \frac{3}{1}\times\frac{2}{30} = \frac{1}{5}$$

$$P(A/E_2) = \frac{{}^2C_1 \times {}^1C_1}{{}^7C_2}$$

$$= \frac{2\times 1}{\frac{7\times 6}{2\times 1}} = \frac{2}{1}\times\frac{2}{42} = \frac{2}{21}$$

$$P(A/E_3) = \frac{{}^4C_1 \times {}^3C_1}{{}^{12}C_2} = \frac{\frac{4\times 3}{12\times 11}}{\frac{2\times 1}{}}$$

$$= \frac{12}{1}\times\frac{2}{132} = \frac{2}{11}$$

Now using Bayes' theorem,

$$P(E_1/A) = \frac{P(E_1)\cdot P(A/E_1)}{P(E_1)\cdot P(A/E_1) + P(E_2)\cdot P(A/E_2) + P(E_3)\cdot P(A/E_3)}$$

$$= \frac{\frac{1}{3}\times\frac{1}{5}}{\left(\frac{1}{3}\times\frac{1}{5}\right) + \left(\frac{1}{3}\times\frac{2}{21}\right) + \left(\frac{1}{3}\times\frac{2}{11}\right)}$$

$$= \frac{\frac{1}{3\times 5}}{\frac{1}{3}\left[\frac{1}{5} + \frac{2}{21} + \frac{2}{11}\right]}$$

$$= \frac{1}{5}\times\frac{1}{\left[\frac{1}{5} + \frac{2}{21} + \frac{2}{11}\right]} = \frac{231}{551}.$$

111. A card from a pack of 52 cards is lost. From the remaining cards of the pack, two cards are drawn at random and are found to be both hearts. Find the probability of the lost card being a heart.*

Sol. Let A be the event that the lost card is a heart, B be the event that the card is not a heart.

$$P(A) = \frac{13}{52} = \frac{1}{4},$$

$$P(B) = \frac{39}{52} = \frac{3}{4}$$

Let 'C' be the event that two cards drawn from the remaining pack are hearts.

$$P (C / A) = \frac{^{12}C_2}{^{51}C_2}$$

(Since if one lost card is of diamond then we have 12 remaining diamonds out of 51 cards now.)

$$= \frac{\dfrac{12 \times 11}{2 \times 1}}{\dfrac{51 \times 50}{2 \times 1}} = \frac{12 \times 11}{51 \times 50} = \frac{132}{2550}$$

$$P (C / B) = \frac{^{13}C_2}{^{51}C_2} = \frac{\dfrac{13 \times 12}{2 \times 1}}{\dfrac{51 \times 50}{2 \times 1}} = \frac{13 \times 12}{51 \times 50}$$

$$= \frac{156}{2550}$$

By Bayes' theorem,

$\therefore$ P (that the lost card being a heart)

$$= P (A / C)$$

$$= \frac{P(A) \cdot P(C / A)}{P(A) \cdot P(C / A) + P(B) \cdot P(C / B)}$$

$$= \frac{\dfrac{1}{4} \times \dfrac{132}{2550}}{\left(\dfrac{1}{4} \times \dfrac{132}{2550}\right) + \left(\dfrac{3}{4} \times \dfrac{156}{2550}\right)}$$

$$= \frac{132}{132 + 468} = \frac{132}{600}$$

$$= \frac{11}{50}.$$

112. Given three identical bags contain 2 balls each. In bag I, both balls are red, in bag II, both are blue and in bag III, there is one red and one blue balls. A person chooses a bag at random and takes out a ball. If a ball is of red colour, what is the probability that the other ball in the bag is also of red colour?

Sol. Let A be the event that bag I is chosen,

B be the event that bag II is chosen,

C be the event that bag III is chosen,

Let 'E' be the event that ball chosen is of red colour.

We have,

$$P (A) = P (B) = P (C) = \frac{1}{3}$$

$P (E / A) =$ Probability of drawing a red ball from

$$\text{bag I} = \frac{2}{2} = 1$$

$P (E / B) =$ Probability of drawing a red ball from bag II $= 0$

$P (E / C) =$ Probability of drawing a red ball from

$$\text{bag III} = \frac{1}{2}$$

$\therefore$ Probability that the other ball in the bag is of red colour = Probability that red ball is drawn from the bag I

$$= P(A / E)$$

$$P (A / E) = \frac{P(A) \cdot P(E / A)}{P(A) \cdot P(E / A) + P(B) \cdot P(E / B) + P(C) \cdot P(E / C)}$$

$$= \frac{\dfrac{1}{3} \times 1}{\dfrac{1}{3} \times 1 + \dfrac{1}{3} \times 0 + \dfrac{1}{3} \times \dfrac{1}{2}} = \frac{1}{1 + \dfrac{1}{2}} = \frac{2}{3}$$

113. In a factory which manufactures bolts, machine A, B and C manufacture respectively 30%, 50% and 20% of the bolts. Of their outputs 3, 4 and 1 percent respectively are defective bolts. A bolt is drawn at random from the product and is found to be defective. Find the probability that this is not manufactured by machine B.*

Sol. Let E_1, E_2, E_3 and Q be the events defined as below :

E_1 = the bolt is manufactured by machine A

E_2 = the bolt is manufactured by machine B

E_3 = the bolt is manufactured by machine C

Q = the bolt is defective

then $P(E_1)$ = Probability that the bolt drawn is manufactured by machine $A = \dfrac{30}{100}$

$P(E_2)$ = Probability that the bolt drawn is manufactured by machine $B = \dfrac{50}{100}$

$P(E_3)$ = Probability that the bolt drawn is manufactured by machine $C = \dfrac{20}{100}$

$P(A/E_1)$ = Probability that the bolt drawn is defective given that it is manufactured by machine A.

$$P(Q/E_1) = \frac{3}{100}$$

Similarly, we have

$$P(Q/E_2) = \frac{4}{100} \text{ and } P(Q/E_3) = \frac{1}{100}$$

Now, using Bayes' theorem

$P(E_2/A)$ = Probability that the bolt is manufactured by machine B given that the bolt drawn is defective.

$$= \frac{P(E_2)P(Q/E_2)}{P(E_1)P(Q/E_1) + P(E_2)P(Q/E_2) + P(E_3)P(Q/E_3)}$$

$$= \frac{\dfrac{50}{100} \times \dfrac{4}{100}}{\dfrac{30}{100} \times \dfrac{3}{100} + \dfrac{50}{100} \times \dfrac{4}{100} + \dfrac{20}{100} \times \dfrac{1}{100}}$$

$$= \frac{200}{90 + 200 + 20} = \frac{200}{310} = \frac{20}{31}$$

Hence, the probability that this is not manufactured by Machine $B = 1 - P(E_2/A)$

$$= 1 - \frac{20}{31} = \frac{11}{31}.$$

114. Find the probability distribution of
  (i) Number of heads in two tosses of a coin.
  (ii) Number of tails in the simultaneous tosses of three coins.
  (iii) Number of heads in four tosses of a coin.

[NCERT]

Sol. (i) When one coin is tossed twice, the sample space is

$$S = \{HH, HT, TH, TT\}$$

Let X represent the number of heads

$\therefore X(HH) = 2; X(HT) = 1; X(TH) = 1; X(TT) = 0$

$\therefore X$ can take the value of 0, 1 or 2.

It is known that

$$P(HH) = P(HT) = P(TH) = P(TT) = \frac{1}{4}$$

$$\therefore \quad P(X = 0) = P(TT) = \frac{1}{4}$$

$$P(X = 1) = P(HT) + P(TH)$$

$$= \frac{1}{4} + \frac{1}{4} = \frac{2}{4} = \frac{1}{2}$$

$$P(X = 2) = P(HH) = \frac{1}{4}$$

Thus, the required probability distribution is as follows.

X	0	1	2
P(X)	$\dfrac{1}{4}$	$\dfrac{1}{2}$	$\dfrac{1}{4}$

(ii) When three coins are tossed simultaneously, the sample space is $\{HHH, HHT, HTH, HTT, THH, THT, TTH, TTT\}$.

Let X represent number of tails

Then X can take value of 0, 1, 2 or 3.

$$P(X = 0) = P(HHH) = \frac{1}{8}$$

$$P(X = 1) = P(HHT) + P(HTH) + P(THH)$$

$$= \frac{1}{8} + \frac{1}{8} + \frac{1}{8} = \frac{3}{8}$$

$$P(X = 2) = P(HTT) + P(THT) + P(TTH)$$

$$= \frac{1}{8} + \frac{1}{8} + \frac{1}{8} = \frac{3}{8}$$

$$P(X = 3) = P(TTT) = \frac{1}{8}$$

Thus, the probability distribution is as follows :

X	0	1	2	3
P(X)	$\dfrac{1}{8}$	$\dfrac{3}{8}$	$\dfrac{3}{8}$	$\dfrac{1}{8}$

(iii) When a coin is tossed four times, the sample space is

$S = \{$HHHH, HHHT, HHTH, HHTT, HTHT, HTHH, HTTH, HTTT, THHH, THHT, THTH, THTT, TTHH, TTHT, TTTH, TTT$\}$

Let X be the random variable, which represents the number of heads. It can be seen that X can take value of 0, 1, 2, 3, or 4.

$$P(X = 0) = P(TTTT) = \frac{1}{16}$$

$$P(X = 1) = P(TTTH) + P(TTHT) + P(THTT) + P(HTTT)$$

$$= \frac{1}{16} + \frac{1}{16} + \frac{1}{16} + \frac{1}{16} = \frac{4}{16} = \frac{1}{4}$$

$$P(X = 2) = P(TTHH) + P(HHTT) + P(THHT) + P(THTH) + P(HTHT) + P(HTTH)$$

$$= \frac{1}{16} + \frac{1}{16} + \frac{1}{16} + \frac{1}{16} + \frac{1}{16} + \frac{1}{16}$$

$$= \frac{6}{16} = \frac{3}{8}$$

$$P(X = 3) = P(HHHT) + P(HHTH) + P(HTHH) + P(THHH)$$

$$= \frac{1}{16} + \frac{1}{16} + \frac{1}{16} + \frac{1}{16} = \frac{4}{16} = \frac{1}{4}$$

$$P(X = 4) = P(HHHH) = \frac{1}{16}$$

Thus, the probability distribution is as follows :

X	0	1	2	3	4
P(X)	$\dfrac{1}{16}$	$\dfrac{1}{4}$	$\dfrac{3}{8}$	$\dfrac{1}{4}$	$\dfrac{1}{16}$

115. Three critics review a film. For the three critics, the odds in favour of the film are $(4 : 1)$, $(2 : 3)$ and $(3 : 2)$ respectively. Find the probability that the majority is in favour of the film.

Sol. Let A, B, C denote the events that the film be favoured by the first, second and third critic respectively. Then,

$$P(A) = \frac{4}{5};\ P(B) = \frac{2}{5};\ P(C) = \frac{3}{5}$$

$$P(\overline{A}) = 1 - P(A) = 1 - \frac{4}{5} = \frac{1}{5}$$

$$P(\overline{B}) = 1 - P(B) = 1 - \frac{2}{5} = \frac{3}{5}$$

$$P(\overline{C}) = 1 - P(C) = 1 - \frac{3}{5} = \frac{2}{5}$$

Required probability

= P (1 critic favours the film) or

P (2 critics favour the film)

= P [{A and B and not C} or {A and C and not B} or {B and C and not A}]

+ $P[A$ and B and $C]$.

= $P(A \cap B \cap \overline{C}) + P(A \cap \overline{B} \cap C)$

$$+ P(\overline{A} \cap B \cap C) + P(A \cap B \cap C)$$

$$= \{P(A) \times P(B) \times P(\overline{C})\} + \{P(A) + P(\overline{B})\}$$
$$\times P(C)\} + \{P(\overline{A}) \times P(B) \times P(C)\}$$
$$+ \{P(A) \times P(B) \times P(C)\}$$

$$= \left\{\frac{4}{5} \times \frac{2}{5} \times \frac{2}{5}\right\} + \left\{\frac{4}{5} \times \frac{3}{5} \times \frac{3}{5}\right\}$$

$$+ \left\{\frac{1}{5} \times \frac{2}{5} \times \frac{3}{5}\right\} + \left\{\frac{4}{5} \times \frac{2}{5} \times \frac{3}{5}\right\}$$

$$= \frac{16}{125} + \frac{36}{125} + \frac{6}{125} + \frac{24}{125}$$

$$= \frac{82}{125}$$

Hence, the required probability is $\dfrac{82}{125}$.

Self - Assessment

116. In a class, 40% of the students opted Spanish, 30% opted French and 20% opted both. If a student is selected at random, what is the probability that he has opted Spanish or French ?

Sol. $\dfrac{1}{2}$

117. In a simultaneous throw of a pair of dice, find the probability of getting a total more than 5.

Sol. $\dfrac{13}{18}$

118. Two dice are thrown together. What is the probability that the sum of the numbers on the two faces is divisible by 3 or 5 ?

Sol. $\dfrac{19}{36}$

119. If E_1 and E_2 are two independent events such that $P(E_1) = 0 \cdot 35$ and $P(E_1 \cup E_2) = 0 \cdot 60$, find $P(E_2)$.

Sol. $\dfrac{5}{13}$

120. What is the probability of getting two numbers whose product is odd when two dice are thrown simultaneously ?

Sol. $\dfrac{1}{4}$

121. An unbiased die is tossed. Find the probability of getting a multiple of 2.

Sol. $\dfrac{1}{2}$

122. In a lottery, there are 12 prizes and 28 blanks. A lottery is drawn at random. What is the probability of not getting a prize ?

Sol. $\dfrac{7}{10}$

123. Two dice are tossed. What is the probability that the total score is a prime number ?

Sol. $\dfrac{5}{12}$

124. A bag contains 5 green and 8 red balls. Two balls are drawn at random. Find the probability that they are of the same colour.

Sol. $\dfrac{19}{39}$

125. In a box, there are 8 white, 7 black and 6 violet balls. One ball is picked up randomly. What is the probability that it is neither white nor violet ?

Sol. $\dfrac{1}{3}$

126. Two dice are thrown simultaneously. What is the probability of getting two numbers whose product is even ?

Sol. $\dfrac{3}{4}$

127. Two cards are drawn at random one by one without replacement from a pack of 52 playing cards. Find the probability that both the cards are red.

Sol. $\dfrac{25}{102}$

128. A box of bulbs is inspected by examining three randomly selected bulbs drawn without replacement. If all the three bulbs are good, the box is approved for export, otherwise, it is rejected. Find the probability that a box containing 15 bulbs out of which 12 are good and 3 are bad will be approved for sale.

Sol. $\dfrac{44}{91}$

129. Bag A contains 2 white and 3 red balls and bag B contains 4 white and 5 red balls. One ball is drawn at random from one of the bags and it is found to be red. Find probability that it was drawn from bag B.

Sol. $\dfrac{25}{52}$

130. In a debate competition, the odds in favour of competitors A, B, C, D are 1 : 3, 1 : 4, 1 : 5 and 1 : 6 respectively. Find the probability that one of them wins the competition.

Sol. $\dfrac{114}{120}$

131. A group housing consists of 80 adults 25 of them are ladies and 55 gents; 10 of them are rich and the remaining poor; 20 of them are fair complexioned. What is the probability of selecting a fair complexioned rich lady ?

Sol. $\dfrac{5}{512}$

132. A coin is tossed 5 times. What is the probability of getting at least 3 tails ?

Sol. $\dfrac{1}{2}$

133. A die is thrown again and again until three sixes are obtained. Find the probability of obtaining the 3rd six in the 6th throw of the die.

Sol. $\dfrac{625}{23328}$

134. A person buys a lottery ticket in 50 lotteries. In each of the lottery, his chance of winning a prize is $\dfrac{1}{100}$. What is the probability that he will win a prize:
(i) at least once   (ii) exactly once
(iii) at least twice ?   **[NCERT]**

Sol. (i) $1-\left(\dfrac{99}{100}\right)^{50}$ (ii) $\dfrac{1}{2}\cdot\left(\dfrac{99}{100}\right)^{49}$

(iii) $1-\left(\dfrac{149}{100}\right)\left(\dfrac{99}{100}\right)^{49}$

135. Urn I contains 3 green and 4 blue balls and urn II contains 5 green and 6 blue balls. One ball is drawn at random from one of the urns and is found to be green. Find the probability that it was drawn from urn II.

Sol. $\dfrac{38}{68}$

136. Two cards are drawn from a pack of 52 cards. What is the probability that both are black or both are queen?

Sol. $\dfrac{55}{221}$

137. A card from a pack of 52 cards is lost. From the remaining cards of the pack, two cards are drawn and are found to be both hearts. Find the probability of the lost card being a heart.

Sol. $\dfrac{11}{50}$

138. On his vacation, Amar visited four cities A, B, C and D in a random order. What is the probability that he visits :
(i) A before B
(ii) A before B and B before C
(iii) A first and B last
(iv) A just before B

Sol. (i) $\dfrac{1}{2}$, (ii) $\dfrac{1}{6}$, (iii) $\dfrac{1}{12}$, (iv) $\dfrac{1}{4}$

139. Bag A contains 4 black and 6 red balls and bag B contains 7 black and 3 red balls. A die is thrown. If 1 or 2 appears on it, then bag A is chosen, otherwise bag B. If two balls are drawn at random (without replacement) from the selected bag, find the probability of one of them being red and another black.

Sol. $\dfrac{22}{45}$

140. Two dice are thrown. Find the probability that the numbers appeared have a sum 8 if it is known that the second die always exhibits 4.

Sol. $\dfrac{1}{6}$

141. Suppose that 5% of men and 0·25% of women have grey hair. A grey haired person is selected at random. What is the probability of this person being male ? Assume that there are equal number of males and females.

Sol. $\dfrac{20}{21}$

142. A committee of 4 students is selected at random from a group consisting of 8 boys and 4 girls. Given that there is at least one girl in the committee, calculate the probability that there are exactly 2 girls in the committee.

Sol. $\dfrac{168}{425}$

143. In a bulb factory, machines A, B and C manufactures 60%, 30% and 10% bulbs respectively. 1%, 2% and 3% of the bulbs produced respectively by A, B and C are found to be defective. A bulb is picked up at random from the product and is found to be defective. Find the probability that this bulb was produced by the machine A.

Sol. $\dfrac{2}{5}$